STAGECRAFT
Fundamentals

D0705715

Stagecraft Fundamentals, Fourth Edition, is an entry-level how-to guide and reference on backstage theatre, covering every aspect of basic theatre production.

The history of stagecraft, safety precautions, lighting, costumes, scenery, special effects, career planning tips, and more are discussed, illustrated by beautiful full-color images that display step-by-step procedures. This fourth edition improves upon the last, featuring a new chapter on Costume Crafts, which includes information on millinery, shoes, fabric dyeing, fabric modification, distressing, masks, armor, body padding, and accessories. Also included is an expanded discussion on sound, props, rigging, safety, production management, and projection design, new information on digital theatre, new end of chapter exercises, additional information on US/UK standards, and an emphasis on diversity and inclusion. Each chapter features exercises, discussion questions, and study words to help the teacher and student review the content before moving on to the next topic.

Stagecraft Fundamentals, Fourth Edition, is the must-have introductory theatre production book for Stagecraft, Technical Theatre, and Theatre Production courses.

A companion website (www.StagecraftFundamentals.com) features additional articles and information, downloadable images and paperwork, chapter quizzes, and an instructor's manual.

Rita Kogler Carver is an Emmy Award-winning lighting designer and a sought-after speaker, lecturer, and writer. She is the co-owner of BearFly Designs LLC and holds an MFA from New York University. Rita has worked on Broadway, off-Broadway, and in regional theatre, opera, and dance, and is affiliated with the International Association of Theatrical Stage Employees Local 829 and National Association of Broadcast Employees Local 16.

Praise for *Stagecraft Fundamentals*

"*Stagecraft Fundamentals* is beautifully illustrated throughout, and the profusion of color on every page gives this textbook the appearance of a coffee table book. The writing is clear and personal, which should be very appealing to students. Rita Carver covers all aspects of theatre production, from scenery, to lighting, to an actor's makeup. Her close ties to the New York theatre scene give this book a special insight into the professional world, one that goes well beyond what is found in most college textbooks."

John Holloway, *Professor in the Theatre Department at the University of Kentucky and President of the International Association of Theatrical Stage Employees (IATSE) Local 346*

"What a great idea! Thank heavens someone is doing this for students at that impressionable age. That has been one of my mantras—education of teachers and students on the use of scenic materials. The teachers don't have enough time in college to learn and do everything they have to teach. Most get thrown into the theatre area by default and struggle with designing/building/painting the scenery."

Jenny Knott, *Rosco*

"This text has tempted me to return to teaching with a textbook for the first time in seven years. The language is both accessible and informal yet the text goes a long way in debunking some of the typical jargon that may alienate students just getting into the field, or trying it out for the first time. The illustrations (the text is full of them) coupled with the stories reinforce the fundamental information being conveyed."

John Paul Devlin, *Associate Professor of Theatre at Saint Michael's College*

"Beautifully written! The author has succeeded in relaying technical theatre information without being too technical and putting the reader to sleep. I read three sentences and instantly knew this book was for me and the way I teach. When I think back on the insufferable intro to tech theatre books I had to read, I feel cheated I didn't have this one as a student. I will be using this text in my class!"

Rob Napoli, *Designer and Technical Director at Penn State University, Berks Campus*

"A few months ago a friend excitedly told me about a new book written by Rita Kogler Carver called *Stagecraft Fundamentals*. My first impression was, wow! it's big. My second impression was, wow! it's beautiful. This book makes an excellent classroom resource or a reference book for theatre professionals. I know I will keep mine close at hand and reference it often."

Richard Cadena, *author of* Electricity for Entertainment Electricians & Technicians *and* Automated Lighting: The Art and Science of Moving Light, *and freelance lighting designer*

"I can't thank you enough for *Stagecraft Fundamentals*. I have been teaching stagecraft since 1976 and you have saved me from the nightmare of writing a text to suit my class needs. After two semesters with your text, I have found that I had more time to develop the skills necessary within the classroom than before. The humor that you have infused in the book has enticed my students to read on. That alone makes this text invaluable."

Meta Lasch, *Assistant Professor, West Liberty University*

STAGECRAFT
Fundamentals

A GUIDE AND REFERENCE FOR THEATRICAL PRODUCTION

RITA KOGLER CARVER

FOURTH EDITION

Routledge
Taylor & Francis Group

NEW YORK AND LONDON

Designed cover image: © Shutterstock

Fourth edition published 2023
by Routledge
605 Third Avenue, New York, NY 10158

and by Routledge
4 Park Square, Milton Park, Abingdon, Oxon, OX14 4RN

Routledge is an imprint of the Taylor & Francis Group, an informa business

First edition published by Focal Press 2009
Third edition published by Routledge 2019

Library of Congress Cataloging-in-Publication Data
Names: Carver, Rita Kogler, author.
Title: Stagecraft fundamentals : a guide and reference for theatrical production / Rita Kogler Carver.
Description: Fourth Edition. | New York, NY : Routledge, 2023. | Includes index.
Identifiers: LCCN 2022043847 (print) | LCCN 2022043848 (ebook) | ISBN 9781032124513 (hbk) | ISBN 9781032124506 (pbk) | ISBN 9781003224600 (ebk)
Classification: LCC PN2053 .C32 2023 (print) | LCC PN2053 (ebook) | DDC 792.02--dc23
LC record available at https://lccn.loc.gov/2022043847
LC ebook record available at https://lccn.loc.gov/2022043848

ISBN: 978-1-032-12451-3 (hbk)
ISBN: 978-1-032-12450-6 (pbk)
ISBN: 978-1-003-22460-0 (ebk)

DOI: 10.4324/9781003224600

Typeset in Adobe Caslon Pro by Alex Lazarou

Access the companion website: www.StagecraftFundamentals.com

ACKNOWLEDGMENTS   xv
INTRODUCTION   xvii

PART ONE: HISTORY AND ART   1

1 **Where We've Been and Where We're Going**   3
A Brief History and Introduction

2 **It's All about Collaboration**   27
Design for Theatre

3 **Making It Visual**   45
Composition

4 **Black and White Are Colors Too!**   57
Color Theory

5 **Creating the Stage Picture**   73
Drawing, Rendering, and Drafting

PART TWO: SAFETY AND SCENERY   127

6 **Safety First!**   129
Safety

7 **Setting It All Up**   149
Scenic Tools and Materials

8 **How to Get It Done**   189
Scenery Techniques and Practices

9 **Deck the Halls**   217
Props

10 **A Little Dab Will Do Ya**   241
Paint

PART THREE: RIGGING, LIGHTING, AND SOUND   265

11 **Hanging by a Thread**   267
Rigging

12 **House to Half …**   293
Lighting

13 **Is This Thing On?**   329
Sound

PART FOUR: COSTUME AND MAKEUP — 347

14 All Dressed Up with Someplace to Go   349
Costumes

15 Accessories and Other Stuff   379
Costume Crafts by Denise Wallace-Spriggs

16 Put on a Happy Face   419
Hair and Makeup

PART FIVE: VIDEO AND SPECIAL EFFECTS — 441

17 Projections, LED, Screens, and Content—Oh My   443
Video

18 The Magic Behind the Curtain   479
Special Effects

PART SIX: MANAGEMENT, TOURING, AND CAREERS — 493

19 Warning, Standby, Go!   495
Stage Management

20 Taking the Show on the Road   517
Touring

21 What's Next?   531
Career Choices

APPENDIX A: GLOSSARY OF TERMS   545
APPENDIX B: STORY TIME—THEATRE TRADITIONS   573
APPENDIX C: PHOTO AND IMAGE CREDITS   577
INDEX   587

ACKNOWLEDGMENTS   xv
INTRODUCTION   xvii

PART ONE: HISTORY AND ART   1

1   Where We've Been and Where We're Going   3
A Brief History and Introduction
    Greek Theatre (700 BCE)   4
    Roman Theatre (1st Century BCE–4th Century CE)   6
    The Middle Ages (5th Century CE–14th Century CE)   8
    Noh (Japan, 14th Century CE until Present)   9
    Commedia dell'arte (Italy, 14th Century CE until Present)   10
    The Renaissance (15th Century CE–16th Century CE)   11
    Bunraku (Japan, 17th Century CE until Present)   13
    Kabuki (Japan, 17th Century CE)   14
    Chinese Theatre   17
    Modern Theatre (19th Century–20th Century)   17
        Proscenium Theatre   17
        Thrust Stage   19
        Arena Stage   20
        Traverse   21
    Theatre Venues   21

2   It's All About Collaboration   27
Design for Theatre
    Production Team Collaboration   28
    Design Process   29
        Reading the Script   30
        Meeting with the Director   31
        Script Breakdown   32
        Research   33
        Styles of Architecture   35
        Orders of Architecture   37
        Design Meeting   37
        Designers Draw, Render, and Draft   39

3   Making It Visual   45
Composition
    Rule of Thirds   46
    Putting the Composition Together   49
        Line and Direction   49

Shape   50

Texture   50

Line Weight   51

Balance and Proportion   51

Pattern   52

Scale   53

4   Black and White Are Colors Too!   **57**
Color Theory

Pigment and Light   58

Tints, Shades, and Tones   61

Interpreting Color   63

Black and White   64

Reference White   66

5   Creating the Stage Picture   **73**
Drawing, Rendering, and Drafting

What Are the Differences?   74

Sal's Test   76

Putting it in Proportion   78

Various Supplies and Tools   78

Dry Stuff   79

Wet Stuff   81

Fixing the Oops   82

Paper   83

Tools   84

Perspective Drawing   93

Rendering   99

Drafting   101

PART TWO: SAFETY AND SCENERY   **127**

6   Safety First!   **129**
Safety

Personal Safety   130

Fire Safety   138

Safety Data Sheets   142

Examples of Panic   144

7   Setting It All Up   **149**
Scenic Tools and Materials

Tools   149

Measuring and Marking   150

Cutting and Shaping   153

Cutting Tools and Saws   154

Assembly   161

Cleaning Up   172

Supplies		172
Wood		172
Metal		176
Fabric		177
Foams and Plastics		179
Hardware		180

8 How to Get It Done   **189**
Scenery Techniques and Practices

Scenic Techniques Develop through History	189
Scenic Design Process	192
Building Techniques	200

9 Deck the Halls   **217**
Props

Defining Props	218
Who Makes the List? Who Decides?	220
The List Is Made. What Next?	221
What about Special Props?	223
Shopped versus Built	224
Prop Supervisor/Manager (Formerly Prop Master)	228
Assistant Prop Manager and Artisans	228
Buyer	228
Properties Carpenter	228
Soft Goods Artisans and Graphic Arts Artisans	230
Step-by-Step Process	234

10 A Little Dab Will Do Ya   **241**
Paint

Overview	241
Safety	246
Tools and Supplies	246
Paints and Glazes	250
Paint Chemistry	251
Texturing	254
Step-by-Step Techniques	255
Schlepitchka (Feather Duster)	258
Wood	260

PART THREE: RIGGING, LIGHTING, AND SOUND   **265**

11 Hanging by a Thread   **267**
Rigging

Ropes	268
Knots	269
Rigging Systems	274
Hemp House	275

Single Purchase 278
Double Purchase 279
Winches 279
Truss 280

12 House to Half … **293**
Lighting
Electricity 299
Fixtures 303
Dimmers 313
Control 314
Expendables 315
Accessories 316
Paperwork 318

13 Is This Thing On? **329**
Sound
Sound Systems 330
World Clock 331
Microphones 331
Sound Basics 333
Recorded or Live? 334
Mixing Consoles 334
Signal Processing 336
Speakers 337
Connectors and Cables 340
Headsets 342
Assisted-Hearing Devices 342
Networks 343
IP Addresses 343

14 All Dressed Up with Someplace to Go **349**
Costumes
Fabrics 351
Tools and Accessories 354
Measurements 358
Sewing 364
Software 374

15 Accessories and Other Stuff **379**
Costume Crafts by Denise Wallace-Spriggs
Millinery—Making Hats 380
Equipment and Tools 381
Materials for Making Hats 383

Measurements	386
Pattern and Mock-Up	386
Cut and Sewn Hats	387
Covered Buckram Frame Hats	387
Shoes	389
Dyeing and Fabric Modification	392
Mask Making	393
Casting	394
The Comfort of the Model	395
Types of Casting	395
Sculpting or Manipulating the Shape of the Face	396
Fitting the Mask	396
Stage Armor	397
Fitting the Mock-Up	397
Altering the Mock-Up	398
Examples of Some Types of Stage Armor	398
Making the Armor	400
Surface Finishes	403
Body Modification Padding	404
Reticulated vs Polyurethane Foam	405
Polyester Batting: Quilt Type vs Upholstery Type	407
Smoothing Layers and Coverings	407
Paddings on a T-Shirt Base	409
Accessories/Jewelry	409
Prop or Costume?	409
Leather Work	411
The First Choice: Leather Types and Weights	411
Making the Pattern Pieces	412
Tools	412
Preparing the Goods	412
Surface Design and Tooling	412
Stitching Techniques	413
Hardware	413
Finishing Details	413
16 Put on a Happy Face	**419**
Hair and Makeup	
Design	420
Makeup Styles	421
Character Analysis	421
Facial Shapes	422
Process	422
Makeup and Tools	423
Hair	431
Makeup Application	434

PART FIVE: VIDEO AND SPECIAL EFFECTS — 441

17 Projections, LED, Screens, and Content—Oh My — 443
Video

Early Projections — 444
What's in a Title? — 451
    Video Designer/Projection Designer/Creative Director — 452
    Animator/Content Creator — 452
    Content/Media Manager — 452
    Video Programmer — 452
    Video Engineer/Video Crew Chief — 452
    Techs — 452
    Screens Producer — 452
Hardware — 466
    Projectors — 466
    LED — 466
    Bonus Concept: Screens — 466
    Media Server — 467
    Other Gack — 467
Software — 467
    Resolution, Codecs, and Frame Rates — 467
Video Content — 468

18 The Magic behind the Curtain — 479
Special Effects

Vintage Effects — 481
    Nature — 481
    Fire — 483
Modern Effects — 483
    Nature — 484
    Fire — 485
    Fog and Haze — 485
    Blood — 487
    Confetti — 488
    Projection Segue — 488

PART SIX: MANAGEMENT, TOURING, AND CAREERS — 493

19 Warning, Standby, Go! — 495
Stage Management

Stage Manager Kit — 496
Auditions — 497
Rehearsals — 497
Calling Script — 509
Technical Rehearsals — 510
Performances — 513

20 Taking the Show on the Road   **517**
Touring
    Types of Tours   517
    Design Modifications   519
        Dealing with Rental Shops   520
        Music   521

21 What's Next?   **531**
Career Choices
    Theatre Careers   532
        Pre-production   532
        Production   532
        Box Office Manager   533
        Company Manager   533
        Director   533
        House Manager   534
        Makeup Artist   534
        Producer   534
        Production Manager   534
        Rigger   535
        Scenic Artist   535
        Technical Director   535
        Wardrobe Supervisor   535
    Non-theatre Careers   535
    Interviews   536
        Prudence Jones Interview   537
        Kristi Ross-Clausen Interview   537
        Jennifer Newbold Interview   537
        Fernando Bermudez Interview   539
        Grace Brandt Interview   539
        Heather Carson Interview   539
        Anne Johnston Interview   540
        Michael Rizzo Interview   541

APPENDIX A: GLOSSARY OF TERMS   545
APPENDIX B: STORY TIME—THEATRE TRADITIONS   573
APPENDIX C: PHOTO AND IMAGE CREDITS   577
INDEX   587

20. Taking the Show on the Road

As always during acknowledgments, there are so many people to thank. And, like any good award acceptance speech, there are going to be people I forget to thank. So, first and foremost, I thank all of the people I am about to forget. I couldn't have done it without them, even though I can't remember their names at the moment. I'm sure their contributions helped me in more ways than I can remember.

I would like to thank Wonder Woman© of DC Comics. That's right, Wonder Woman. I grew up knowing that she was the one female superhero who didn't need a guy to swoop in and rescue her. She wasn't afraid to achieve her goals, to enlist help as needed, or to try new and different things no matter what public opinion said or thought. She is my hero!

I was privileged to study with an amazing man by the name of John Gleason while I was getting my MFA. John taught me that using your eyes is the best kind of research available, that you must learn to pick your fights, and that magenta doesn't actually occur anywhere in nature. My dad, who is still with me every day in spirit, believed that his daughters, as well as his sons, should know how to use tools—and gave me my first 10-inch Crescent© wrench when I started in the theatre.

Denise Wallace-Spriggs, my new collaborator, gets her own thank you. The new chapter on Costume Crafts is all hers and it is wonderful. I literally couldn't have done it without her. Many designers, and friends who happen to be designers, gave so generously of their time to share with me their insights. This truly has been a collaboration. They are Campbell Baird, Ken Billington, Laura Frank, Jackson Gallagher, Susan Goulet-Bennett, Paul Hadobas, Jeff Harris, Larry Heyman, Kyle Doughty Higgins, Don Holder, Prudence Jones, Jenny Knott, Jeremy Lechterman, Dan Slappy Mckenzie, Tom Morse, Jenn Newbold, Eric Nye, Bill Price, Patrick Rocheleau, Kristi Ross-Clausen, Bill Sapsis, Novella Smith, Sal Tagliarino, Justin Walsh, and many more. I'm sorry if I forgot to mention everyone. Companies such as Ben Nye, City Theatrical, Clair Brothers, FD Scene Changes, Flying by Foy, JR Clancy, Masque Sound, Period Corsets, and Thomas Engineering have been invaluable in sharing their wealth of knowledge as well. Beth Bergman openly searched her archives for opera images from the Metropolitan Opera among others.

My sister-in-law, Wendy Carroll, created many of the illustrations for this book. She is an awesome artist and a wonderful friend. My sister-by-choice, EA Kafkalas, has been beyond supportive and encouraging with her many visual and culinary talents. Last, and most importantly, as always there is my wonderful husband, John. It is simply this: Without him, there is nothing!

I have always been fascinated by the combination of history and the newest trends. For example, I love fountain pens *and* computers! I believe we must know what has come before, who first did something, and how they did it. In essence, we must know where we come from and honor that history. Otherwise, we spend a great deal of time reinventing, well, the wheel—literally. At the same time, we must continue to push, pull, and stretch ourselves as both designers and technicians, using the newest materials and technology currently available. This new technology allows us to do things that were previously unavailable to us. It also can make our lives easier on some of the more routine tasks. Technology is only as good as the use you have for it. It can be your best friend or your worst enemy, depending on how you choose to use it and, more importantly, why.

Theatre is a relatively small business. I have been fortunate to interview a great many working designers and technicians. I have quoted them throughout the book. I have also researched a great many of the superstitions or traditions we have all come to know in theatre, trying to find their origins. I also include this information, a little in each chapter, as a part of the industry's overall history. We always hear people saying "break a leg" or "the Scottish play." Now, we try to find out, as best we can, where these sayings started.

Stagecraft Fundamentals uses examples of past and current design ideas to make interesting comparisons. Not to say that one is right and the other is wrong—anything but that! A truly wonderful part of theatre is that we who work in it are constantly reinventing the design process. We do this not only through our concepts and ideas, but also through our implementation. Think of the classic musicals from the 1950s and 1960s such as *Hello, Dolly!*, *My Fair Lady*, or *Camelot*. Then, think more recently to musicals such as *Six*, *Dear Evan Hansen*, and *The Kite Runner*. What are the differences from a design point of view?

Don't immediately jump to the conclusion that the newer shows couldn't have been done 50 years ago. They absolutely could have, but they would have been very different. Not better, not worse. Different. We can look at the differences that may have been incorporated in the design and implementation process. This clearly shows how scripts have been able to expand their scope, at least in part, based on the expanded possibilities in design and implementation now available. The bigger we can dream, the more we can accomplish!

Theatre Traditions: Opening Night and Paying Customers

There is a superstition in theatre about the opening-night customers. As we all know, some tickets are given away through various connections with the production. These are called comps, or complimentary tickets. Supposedly, the first customer to be admitted into the auditorium must be a paying customer. This is said to ensure the financial success of the production. House managers have been known to refuse admittance to someone with a comp ticket prior to seating a paying customer.

My goal in writing this book is to bring the newest ideas and technologies available in professional theatre to the attention of anyone with an interest in backstage theatre. Each chapter goes into enough historical detail to give you a background and a perspective. Visual examples as well as explanations of current techniques not only bring you into the present but hopefully give a glimpse into the future.

Wow—sure does sound like an awful lot of information for one book! Well, it is. But I organized it in such a way that ideally it will make sense. We start slow and, with each new chapter, we build a little more on what has come before. Always keep in mind that this is a "fundamentals" book. There is more in-depth information out there once you've mastered the basics.

My goal is to get you excited about the theatre. Here is how we'll do it.

We start by honoring the history I talked about earlier. It all started with the Greeks, right? Our overall organization in the theatre as well as some of the basic conventions we still use all have their roots in Greece. If you've ever been backstage in a theater, it may seem like the technicians are speaking an entirely different language. Well, in some ways they are. In Chapter 1, we discuss many of the terms that form the foundation we build on in later chapters, as we continue to expand our new theatre vocabulary.

You want to be a technician, or you are at least interested in the topic, and you wonder why you should also be learning about design. The best way to be a good technician is to understand the designer's process. And, the best way to be a great designer is to understand what the technicians go through to realize your design. Then, as questions arise or perhaps problems need creative answers, you can be a part of the final solution. Chapter 2 discusses the design process. And, yes, it is a process. Designers don't sit down and just draw pretty pictures. They read scripts, do research, go to production meetings, and so forth.

The next logical step in the conversation is to discuss composition and color theory. Any visual artist needs to understand composition. Chapters 3 and 4 explore the basics of these topics. All the images that an audience sees and perceives are directly relayed to them through composition and color. Composition is the basis for all things visual. At its most basic, we can discuss whether a line is straight or curved. Does it have pattern or rhythm? This begins our discussion of composition. Color adds to the conversation about composition. It adds another element or layer. *Color* is usually defined and thought of in terms of primary and secondary colors. We discuss this and so much more. How we perceive the world around us is directly related to how we see color.

Chapter 5 starts the nitty gritty, so to speak. You have all these great ideas. How do you get these wonderful ideas out of your head and into the theatre? We jump right into our discussion of drafting, drawing, and rendering. You have to get the ideas out of your head and onto paper. That is the only way others can see *visually* what you've been describing *verbally*. The "old way" to do this is with a pencil and a piece of paper. And

many designers still work this way. The "new way," with technology, adds the use of computer drafting software and photo manipulation software as well as other programs written specifically for the theatre. The goal of creating drawings and drafting is still very simple. Get the ideas out of your head so they can be realized.

My students all know one of my favorite sayings: "I've never had to call 911 for a student, and you're not going to break my record." Chapter 6 talks about safety, both backstage in the theater and in the various shops related to implementation of the designs. There are standards for safety, and they are practiced for a reason. The theater can be a dangerous place. We are always trying to accomplish things that aren't supposed to be done inside a building, never mind in the dark! If you follow some basic safety rules, you will have better opportunities to stay safe. And, let's face it, most of us got into theatre because it looked like fun. Let's keep it that way.

Scenic tools and materials are discussed in detail in Chapter 7. You might need to do many different types of projects, and I give you the basic information you will need to walk into a scene shop and get the job done. This chapter has tons of information about the nuts and bolts—literally—of theatre. I also talk about how to choose the right tool or material for any job at hand.

Chapter 8 is all about scenery. Yes, we finally will get to talk about scenery. As we get into the "down and dirty" of implementing scenic ideas, you'll see how those first seven chapters have given you a background you didn't think you'd need, but is now coming in very handy! This chapter gives you a background in the traditional scenic elements: Flats, platforms, stairs, doors, and the like. As always, we honor the past before moving into the future. And keep in mind that, when the budget is tight, you may need this "historic" information to come up with a well-rounded solution to whatever problems might arise.

A new chapter in this edition is Chapter 9 and it covers props. Originally, props had been included, minimally, in Chapter 8. Now it has its very own chapter with lots of expanded information. Props is one area of theatre that can easily lead to jobs in film, advertising, and television as well. I'm very excited to add this new chapter.

The next logical topic is a discussion on paint. Chapter 10 addresses a range of painting tools and techniques. You might wonder how painting has changed or what new technologies there are. It's just a paintbrush and some paint, right? Wrong! There are many new developments in this area. Some changes are small, some are large, but all are important. There has been a resurgence of painted faux finishes both in the theatre and in homes. These techniques help to complete our picture of what is possible from a scenic point of view and they might even help you make your living room look better!

Chapter 11 follows with a discussion on rigging. Now that the scenery is built and painted, how do you get it into place? How do you get it into its storage position? Does it fly in and out, does it track on and off, or does it just sit there? Once you know the answers to these questions, the solution lies with the rigging department. Rigging at its most basic is all about knots. Where do these knots come from? Again, we look at the history of knots, which all come from sailors! Once we learn about the knots that make theatre rigging safe and easy, we move on to more complicated rigging, where new technology has really made a huge impact. Fifty years ago, if you wanted a platform to move across the stage, somebody had to push it. It sure is different today with the advent of hoists, motors, winches—and computers to control them.

From all things scenic to all things lighting: Chapter 12 discusses lighting. With the same concept as other chapters, we discuss the history of lighting through a variety of developments straight through to today's fixtures. Automation and light-emitting diodes (LEDs) are the biggest overall change. Conventional lighting (meaning nonmoving lights) and intelligent lighting (meaning the fixture automatically moves in some way) are both viable options in today's theaters. In some ways, this is one department where both old and new coexist on the stage seamlessly.

Chapter 13 explores sound. There are many aspects to what sound can do for a theatrical production. At the very least, sound can reinforce the spoken word. Sound can also create everything from simple enhancement to wild effects. With the advent of digital technology, the impact sound can have has drastically improved. Sound can now follow a performer around the stage, or around the entire theatre. Digital delays can ensure that audiences of 50–50,000 all hear the same thing at the same time.

Chapter 14 is all about costumes. Now, you may be thinking, "How can costumes use new technology?"

Well, of course, we look at history a bit, as many of those same techniques are still in use today! Many of the newer technologies that costume designers and shops use are not obvious in the actual costumes but in how they get built. Sewing machines have come a long way since the old treadle machines. Patterning software has undergone huge developments that dramatically change the way a costume shop functions.

Costume Crafts is the new Chapter 15. The duties of the craft artisan can include many of the processes for building a costume, except the actual draping or sewing of the garment. Those duties may include millinery, shoemaking or modification, fabric dyeing and painting, distressing, masks, armor, body padding, and accessories. Occasionally, the crafts artisan will make wigs or work closely with the wigmaker to achieve a design.

In Chapter 16, we start by exploring the basics of makeup beginning with evaluating the face. Makeup can show the era of the play, the age of the character, and so much more. We discuss street, or everyday, makeup, as well as aging and some special effects. Additional effects makeup can include everything from a broken nose to scarring, to injuries, to all sorts of fantasy characters. Hair styling and wigs are also discussed. There are pros and cons to using an actor's real hair, just as there are for using wigs.

Another new chapter is Chapter 17, where we will learn about projections. Projections had formerly been included in the special effects chapter. Since the third edition of this book was published, projections have become their own department with separate, dedicated designers. This chapter allows me to go into great depth about projections and the entire process surrounding them.

Special effects will be the focus of Chapter 18. We explore all varieties of effects, with the exception of projections as they now have their own chapter. Effects can fall into any of the departments we already discussed, or the production may add a special effects department if there is a need for many effects. A prop may need to explode into flames, rain or snow might be needed for a certain scene, one character might be portrayed as having some awful scar, and another character might need to fly through the air. All these effects can be handled in a variety of ways depending on the theatre space and the budget. Bringing in an expert in special effects is sometimes the only way to safely do these effects. Other times, if the effects are done simply enough, someone already on the production team can supervise them.

Now that we've done all the technical stuff, what next? The culmination of working in the theatre is always the actual performance. I don't think we'd ever get much of an audience if all we did was put the set and lighting on stage. Audiences have come to expect actors! Chapter 19 talks about production and stage management. This is an expansion from the former chapter on just stage management. Production managers oversee all aspects of a production, taking care of scheduling and budgeting in addition to many other details. The stage manager is responsible for organizing the initial rehearsals. The true test of a stage manager comes into play during the technical rehearsals and performances. Without the stage manager, we would never get as far as *house to half*. The stage management team—and, yes, it is a team—is responsible for everything that happens during the actual performances. Stage managers have to be organized, they have to love paperwork, and they need to work well with a variety of people.

Chapter 20: Touring. Another new chapter! Tours are more and more common. Not just theatre tours but also music tours, dance tours, and so on. Touring has become a big industry and as such employs a lot of theatre artisans. We will take a look at what it entails to get a show on the road while keeping a consistent look to the design of the show.

OK, great, you learned all this stuff. What is next? Chapter 21 discusses all the places you might find employment. There are many job opportunities out there, some of which are directly related to the theatre. Many of these possibilities are in related fields, and some are in what seem at first to be totally unrelated fields. We explore all of these options to make sure your training gets put to good use in an area where you will be happy.

Now, let's talk about the website! In addition to the printed book, there is a matching website full of additional information and resources. Check out the website at www.StagecraftFundamentals.com. There is so much information out there to reference that it could take an entire room full of bookshelves. Never mind the fact that the information is ever changing. The more information we can store digitally, the easier it is to search for the one exact thing you are looking for.

A new chapter called Costume Crafts has been added as mentioned above. Think of it as costume crafts relate to costumes as props relate to scenery. It is a chapter I've been wanting to add for a while and I am so glad it is finally here.

Also new to this fourth edition are some additions in each chapter. The first is called Exercises. Based on discussions with current teachers in each area of theatre, I've compiled a list of a few ideas for student exercises to be completed at the end of each chapter. The second new area isn't really new, just renamed. The "Discussion Questions" are now called "Check Your Knowledge" and are intended to help students and teachers recap the essence of each chapter.

Ideally I've given you enough of an idea of what fun theatre can be that you aren't running out of the classroom screaming. Theatre is fun. I wrote this book so you can learn some of the information you will need while having fun at the same time. Now, let's get started!

And remember, this book is a jumping-off point—don't stop here!

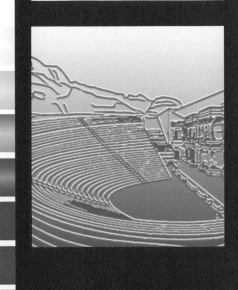

PART
ONE

History and Art

CHAPTER 1: Where We've
Been and Where We're
Going
*A Brief History and
Introduction*

CHAPTER 2: It's All about
Collaboration
Design for Theatre

CHAPTER 3: Making It Visual
Composition

CHAPTER 4: Black and White
Are Colors TOO!
Color Theory

CHAPTER 5: Creating the
Stage Picture
*Drawing, Rendering, and
Drafting*

Where We've Been and Where We're Going

A Brief History and Introduction

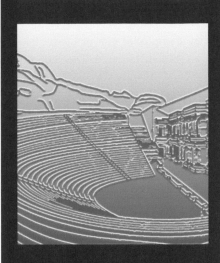

CHAPTER ONE

Student Learning Outcomes

Students will acquire:

- **An overview understanding of the major aspects, techniques, and directions in the area of the history of theatre.**

- **Fundamental, conceptual understanding of the expressive possibilities of theatre.**

- **A working knowledge of background, developments, and areas of growth applicable to the history of theatre.**

We start this chapter by honoring the history I talked about in the Introduction. I'm sure you either have or will be taking a full class on theatre history, so this first chapter is meant more as a refresher. Think of it as an abridged history, as the full history of theatre takes up a whole book the same size as this one and has its own class as well.

The pageantry that evolved into theatre is usually connected with the Greek theatre that we will discuss next. However, before this evolution there were many religious **passion plays**. These are the true predecessors and origin of today's theatrical performances as we know them. Many may have heard of Oberammergau, or perhaps you haven't. Let me explain. Oberammergau is a town in Bavaria, Germany. Its passion play came out of a vow in the year 1634, asking God to stop the bubonic plague that had been brought to the village by a traveler during the Christmas season. The villagers promised to perform a passion play, based on the last days of Christ from the Last Supper through to his Crucifixion, every ten years to thank God for saving their village. Their promise continues to this day.

Oberammergau was not the first time a passion play was ever performed. In this instance I use the phrase "passion play" a little loosely from its more modern meaning. The earliest known religious play dedicated to a culture's god is from about 2000 BCE in Egypt, based on a stone tablet in a German museum. The central figure in this play is the King-Divinity Osiris. Passion plays in his memory were performed annually. According to the accounts we have, these performances were quite realistic, and actor/warriors often died during battle scenes owing to the use of real weaponry.

Theatre history as we think of it actually started with the Greeks. Our overall organization of almost everything in the theatre as well as some of the basic conventions we still use have their roots in Greece. If you have ever been backstage in a theater, it may seem like the technicians are speaking an entirely different language. Well, in some ways, they are. In this chapter, we discuss the history of many of the terms that form a foundation on which we build in later chapters, as we continue to expand our new theatre vocabulary.

The word theatre comes from *theatrum* in Latin or *theatron* in Greek. It means a space designated for dramatic performances and spectacles. Only in more modern times have we come to use the same word for the actual buildings and for the performances.

> Question everything. Learn something. Answer nothing.
>
> —Euripides,
> Tragedian of Ancient Greece,
> 480–406 BCE

GREEK THEATRE (700 BCE)

Let's dive right into history and begin with the genre created by the Greeks. Since I said much of what we still do today is based on the Greek theatre, what does that actually mean? Well, keep in mind that what we actually know of the Greek theatre we gather from ruins of architecture as well as from artwork of that period. Most of today's scholars agree that the Greek theatre evolved from religious performances; in fact, most of theatre around the world did. The church has always contained an amount of pageantry that is easily transformed in

our thoughts into theatrical performances. In fact, many major religious festivals encouraged theatrical performances, and often prizes were awarded.

Very few texts from Ancient Greece survive today. But we do know that Thespis, Aeschylus, Aristophanes, Sophocles, and Euripides were the important playwrights. All these playwrights wrote with similar conventions and themes. The plays were written in what we would consider today to be four acts. The first three acts were concerned with everyday issues. The fourth act was often based more on mythology and usually had a lighter subject matter than the first three.

Theatre Traditions: The Origins of Thespians

In the 6th century BCE, a priest of Dionysus named Thespis first engaged in direct dialogue with the traditional chorus of actors. This is widely considered to be the birth of theatre, and subsequently Thespis is considered to the first true actor. Thus, actors ever since have been referred to as thespians.

These plays rarely had more than a few actors (all men, by the way), who played all the roles, using masks to change characters as needed. Have you heard of a Greek chorus? Well, the chorus was a group of people, sometimes as many as 50, onstage, who sang or chanted in unison to give the audience additional information that was usually moral in tone. Musicians often accompanied the chorus.

The Greek amphitheater was a huge, cavernous space. It was simple in its design, based on a circle. That circle often had a diameter of close to 80 feet. That is at least twice the size of most theaters we use today. The amphitheater was most often built into the slope of a hill, which allowed for seating a large number of people, often up to several thousand. Figure 1.1 shows all of these features.

Once the Greeks decided to perform a play and build the amphitheater, the next thing to worry about was sound. Would the audience be able to hear the

■ **Figure 1.1** The Epidaurus Theater during the 4th century BCE.

■ **Figure 1.2** Illustration of a Greek theater, showing the playing area, seating, and surrounding hillside.

actors? Remember all that math in high school you never thought you'd use again? Well, the Greeks used it and used it well. Mathematics played a huge role in the construction of these theaters and in the acoustics. In an audience that seats up to 15,000 people, how could anyone possibly hear the actors' voices? Many people today believe the Greeks were very advanced on the subject of acoustics, maybe even having a better understanding of it than we do today. However, how the Greeks were able to use acoustics is still not completely understood. Lost in the sands of time, so to speak. They needed to understand it as they couldn't simply turn to microphones and speakers for help. For a modern take on sound, see Chapter 13.

So, here is what they did. By building the theatre into the side of a hill, they used the natural acoustic properties of the hill to bounce sound up toward the audience (Figure 1.2).

Let's discuss the physical theater for a second. The first seats built for the audience were temporary wooden benches. Fairly quickly, these were changed to inlaid stone, which created permanent seating. Once the audience seating was set in stone, literally, the rest of the theater areas could be figured out. The next development came when the back wall was painted to help create the environment for the play. This backdrop served two purposes: It helped the audience better understand where the play was taking place, and it provided a space for the actors to change their costumes and masks out of the sight of the audience. This eventually developed into walls with doors and windows, becoming the type of sets we use today. Another addition of this time was to add columns on either side of the stage. This slowly transformed into what we call our proscenium arch.

If a proscenium arch exists, it is what formally separates the audience from the acting area. It creates a frame around the stage just like a picture frame for a painting, and some are very ornate. It lets viewers know where to look and, more important, where not to look. The proscenium is one of the most popular theater types today, and we discuss it more fully later in this chapter.

Theatre is all about the focus. The next logical step was to try to vary the audience's focus for effect. This meant the development of more complex scenery. Sets started to be two stories high. This gave many more possibilities for the actors in terms of entrances and exits. It also helped in the development of the new career path of set design.

ROMAN THEATRE
(1st Century BCE–4th Century CE)

Let's march onward to the Romans. They built the next viable genre of theatre. Roman theatre came directly on the heels of the Greeks and continued to build on the traditions already established. The initial plays were produced using Greek scripts and Greek staging. Two of the major playwrights from Rome were Seneca and Plautus. Although they primarily were doing translations

from Ancient Greek, they were still very important to this era of theatre.

There are a few basic differences between Greek and Roman theatre. The Greeks, as we discussed, dealt with earthly and mystical topics within the same performance. The Romans lived much more in the here and now. They didn't just talk about war in a play; they acted it out. This is definitely a reflection of the times. The audience in Rome started to participate more, cheering, booing, and applauding, as they deemed necessary. The audience was so loud at times that the plays would become more of a pantomime—actions without words.

The main Roman performance spaces were still circular, similar to the Greeks'. But, whereas the Greeks built their theaters into a natural amphitheater, the Romans tended to construct artificial walls to create their theaters. The acting stage was angled higher as it went away from the audience. This created a bowl-like effect where the sound would bounce around to all areas of the audience, and sight lines were increased as stages were raised. This type of angled stage is called a rake. The rake also established the basis for our modern stage directions.

The further away from the audience, the further "up" in the air the actor was physically. This is why we call the area of the stage furthest from the audience upstage (Figure 1.3). Obviously, that means that the area closest to the audience is considered downstage. The other terms we use all the time are stage left and stage right. These two terms are based on the actors' point of view. What does that mean? Well, picture an actor standing on

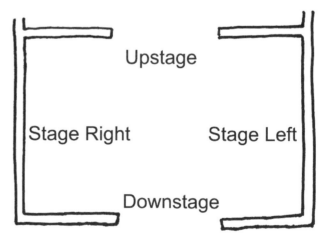

■ **Figure 1.3** Diagram of the key areas of today's stage as defined by the Greek's angled stage.

the stage facing the audience. To the actor's left is stage left, and to the actor's right is stage right.

The Colosseum (Figure 1.4), as the Romans called it, had a different configuration. It was circular in shape for one. The audience seating was raised, as if it had been built into the side of a hill. The playing area was flat—not raked—and at the lowest part of the Colosseum. At one end of the Colosseum was the stage with a scenic wall behind it.

He means "well" is useless unless he does well.

—Plautus,
Roman playwright, 254–184 BCE

Another major addition to the architecture of the Roman theater was the **vomitorium**, from the Latin *vomere*—to spew forth, disgorge. Most likely this is not what you are thinking! The vomitorium was, and still is, a hallway where the actors could enter unseen from the middle of the audience. This area usually led directly underneath the audience risers. The Roman theater had at least two vomitoria, one on each side. Not only did actors use these for entrances and exits, but also the audience was often ushered in and out of the theater using them.

Once the Greek plays had been seen repeatedly, original Roman scripts started to emerge. One big change at this time was in the structure of the Roman plays. They started to develop standard characters who would become very popular during commedia dell'arte. More on that later though—back to Rome. The actors

■ **Figure 1.4** The Roman Colosseum, as it exists today, in Rome, Italy.

■ **Figure 1.5** The Roman Odeum, as it exists today, in Pompeii, Italy.

used various costume pieces to let the audience know with just a glance which "character" they were playing. For example,

• Young men wore black wigs and purple robes
• Old men wore gray wigs and white robes
• Slaves wore red wigs
• Women wore yellow robes (keep in mind that men still played the women)

Now, this is really important: An actor playing a god wore a yellow tassel. I'm not sure why a tassel meant a god, but hey, it's one of those fun facts of theatre history.

THE MIDDLE AGES
(5th Century CE–14th Century CE)

The Middle Ages were an interesting time, to say the least. There was much upheaval of the political, economic, and religious life of the time. So, basically everything was

changing. What survived in the theatre was the base that had been established through the Greek and Roman genres. What emerged as new forms were the mimes, minstrels, and jugglers, who traveled from town to town to make their living. This makes perfect sense if you think about it. During any kind of upheaval, planning something to stay in one place can be problematic. Small shows that could easily move around would much better suit the situation of the time. Also, during a time of upheaval, the last thing you wanted to do was challenge the authorities through your art. Entertainment was the sole goal.

The next style of theatre was the liturgical drama. Based solely on religious stories from the Bible, this filled a need within the community. Quickly thereafter, the liturgical drama expanded to include dramas based on historical events and mysteries. These plays, teaching moral lessons, often used allegorical characters representing virtues and faults.

As this was the era of mobile theatre, the sets were often set up on wagon stages with wheels so that they could be moved more easily from one town to another.

England was the only Western country to continue the use of exclusive male casting. Other countries' casts were now integrating both men and women—finally.

Other styles of plays that became popular during this time were the passion plays and cycle plays. The passion plays were often performed annually during specific times in the religious calendar, as I mentioned at the beginning of this chapter. The cycle plays were massive extravaganzas that often involved hundreds of actors and multiple wagons in a processional. Keep in mind that both were religious in nature, as the church was often the only entity that had money to sponsor these types of events.

Speaking of sponsorship, it became a major part of this period. Much of the control of theatre began to shift during this time from the church to political control. Kings and queens were often patrons of the arts, commissioning plays to be written for special events and festivals. Not only did patronage in the form of sponsorship come to the forefront at this time, but so did licensing and censorship! It was an interesting time historically and, as so often happened, it was also an interesting time artistically.

NOH
(Japan, 14th Century CE until Present)

Noh theatre is the oldest style of Japanese theatre, originating in the 14th century. It evolved slowly from acrobatic techniques and became popular with both the common people and aristocrats (Figure 1.6). Noh uses masks—masks again—(Figures 1.7 and 1.8) and is known for its slow, graceful movements. Noh is also a chanted form of drama. Repetitive passages lacking melody are very reminiscent of a much newer form of poetry, haiku.

Noh has four basic categories or topics for the plays: Gods, warriors, women, and demons. Other topics occasionally were thrown in; however, these were the main four. Isn't it interesting to see how closely some of these conventions and topics fall in with what Western theatre was doing during a similar time frame?

■ **Figure 1.6** Illustration of a classical Noh performance.

■ **Figure 1.7** Noh facial mask of a woman.

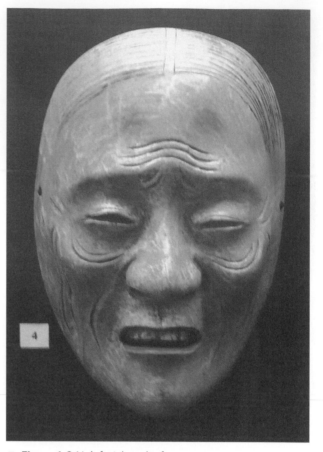

■ **Figure 1.8** Noh facial mask of a man.

COMMEDIA DELL'ARTE
(Italy, 14th Century CE until Present)

Commedia is a very interesting part of theatre history (Figure 1.9). Many of today's theatre characters are still based on the development of this era. Commedia was largely improvised around a base story with an established cast of characters. This gave the actors a great deal of freedom during each performance, as you can imagine. Based on this outline, it was easy for the players to make a performance timely and pertinent to the goings-on about the village or town.

There were four topics or basic stories: Adultery, jealousy, old age, and love. Sometimes, topics were combined within a story. Think about the last play or movie or TV show that you saw. Did the plot line fit into one of these topics? I bet it did. It's amazing how the themes of life haven't changed over time.

■ **Figure 1.9** A commedia troupe coming to town on their show wagon.

■ **Figure 1.10** The Pierrot commedia dell'arte character.

There are many characters within each type; it is really an almost endless list. This should at least give you an idea of how commedia was established and enable you to work with the various stories. Each troupe had specialties. What really survived from this era are the characters and the plots. They are eternally current because they address the basic parts of our lives.

THE RENAISSANCE
(15th Century CE–16th Century CE)

At the beginning of the Renaissance, there were still no formal theater buildings. Performances were mostly still outside at various celebrations. Commedia continued for a time until the masques came into being. Masques were elaborate spectacles, often performed in ballrooms. No expense was spared on these events. An entire ballroom might be transformed into heaven or some exotic location. There were often clouds on the ceiling, angels and cherubs flying about, and chariots racing into view. The story of the masque didn't matter; it was all about the spectacle. This may also sound eerily familiar in today's culture of arts and entertainment.

Scenery and props were minimal, although masks were still used to change actors from one character to another. (Remember that masks were also used during Greek plays. Masks are a recurring theme in theatre!) A commedia troupe often consisted of 12–15 actors, most of whom were (still) men. A major change is that the actors were paid by receiving a share in the profits from each performance—actual money, not just food. Commedia is the forerunner of today's style of improvisation.

The stock characters fell into four basic categories: Lovers, masters, servants, and clowns (Figure 1.10). Again, think about recent shows you've seen. If you break down the characters, you'll see categories at the base of each one. The characters were then divided into very specific types within each category. Each specific character had a very distinct costume and mask that easily identified him to the audience.

Our next step forward in the English-speaking world takes us to Shakespeare. Finally, something you've all heard of! You've heard of Shakespeare, right? Obviously, there were other literary figures from this era, and you might even have heard of some of them: Sir Francis Bacon, Ben Jonson, Christopher Marlowe, Sir Thomas More, and John Webster, to name the more famous. Anyway, during this time, two big developments occurred. One was to move the performances inside a building that had been specifically built for this purpose. Enter the theater—note the spelling. The other change was that people actually began to make a real living doing theatre. Yay! These two things combined to become a huge turning point for the future of the theatre.

Let's discuss the layout of this new theater building. There was, of course, a transition phase. Initially, the performances were held within the courtyards of inns. The theater managers would lay a platform down to cover watering troughs. Spectators (or audiences) would stand or sit at the opposite end. Properly planned theaters were built fairly quickly from this point. The most famous of these were the Curtain, the Rose, and, of course, the Globe (Figure 1.11).

The Globe is the theater where many of Shakespeare's plays were first produced. The architecture of the Globe became a reference for new theaters for years to come. The Globe was built as a hexagon that spanned 55 feet across. Now, think back to the Greeks. Their amphitheater was 80 feet across. The Globe was a much smaller space, but still larger than many today. Also, the audience area could hold only about 1500 people. How did this new space change or dictate the plays? Well, a smaller space allowed the shows to be much more intimate. Fifteen hundred in an audience today is considered large, but it's all about the perspective of what came before. They could now deal with quieter and more subtle plot lines within a show.

The Globe had a platform for the stage that was about half the size of the whole building. The stage had two levels for acting. The lower level contained a curtained area and usually two doors. The upper level had another curtained area and two windows. This is the beginning

■ **Figure 1.11** Illustration of the old Globe Theater, Shakespeare's "home" theater.

of the "inner above/inner below" idea, where good things happened on the upper level (closer to heaven) and bad things happened on the lower level (closer to hell).

The audience had two basic choices for viewing the show, which affected their proximity to the stage and their ticket cost. Class also played a factor, as the poorer people couldn't afford the more expensive tickets. If they wanted a less expensive ticket and were willing to stand, there was the open courtyard at the end of the stage, which was called the *pit*. The other option, if the audience wanted to sit and a pay a little more, was the galleries. In today's terms, these were basically semicircular balconies. By the way, speaking of "pits," have you ever heard of some other place near the edge of the stage being called a kind of pit? Always be thinking about today's words and where they come from. It is an interesting thing to study but, more importantly, it helps us figure out who we are by knowing where we come from.

BUNRAKU
(Japan, 17th Century CE until Present)

Bunraku-style theatre flourished after a period of wars that left the culture longing for some form of entertainment in about 1684. The more a culture is trying to divert itself from the reality or aftermath of war, the more stylized the art form chosen. This is true in every culture—Eastern and Western. There is one known playwright, Chikamatsu Monzaemon (1653–1725), who wrote thousands of plays during his lifetime, most of which are still used in Japan today. Plot topics included, as usual, conflicts between social obligations and human emotions. We've seen it before and we'll see it again: Bunraku is a highly stylized performance using puppets that are about one-third to one-half the size of a human. Bunraku is still one of the most elaborate and sophisticated uses for puppets in the world.

■ **Figure 1.12** In Bunraku, two out of three puppeteers are clad entirely in black.

> Do not seek to follow in the footsteps of the wise. Seek what they sought.
>
> —Matsuo Basho,
> Japanese poet, 1644–1694

Most of the puppets require three performers to manipulate them. Performers can train their entire lives to become master puppeteers. Only masters can operate the head and right arm of the puppet. Lesser puppeteers control the rest of the puppets' movements. One person will speak all the dialogue, changing his or her voice as needed for the various characters. Puppeteers perform in full view of the audience. To heighten the experience for the audience, performers wear black robes and hoods. Only the master puppeteer goes without a hood as a tribute to his or her training and talent.

KABUKI
(Japan, 17th Century CE)

Kabuki, as I said before, may be the one form of Japanese theatre with which you are familiar (Figure 1.13). When you hear the word *Kabuki*, what is the first thing that comes to mind? For me, it's kimonos and white face makeup. Kabuki actors were trained in many areas, including dancing, singing, pantomime, and even acrobatics. There are several periods of Kabuki, from its earliest beginnings to what we now recognize as this style.

From 1603 to 1629, Kabuki was initially considered a "drama-dance" and, in an interesting twist, was performed solely by *women* and become known historically as Female Kabuki! These performances were instantly popular, and troupes quickly formed to bring this new performance style to more audiences. Much of the allure was due to the suggestive plot themes—and the fact that most performers were often available after the performance as prostitutes. *Keep in mind that this*

■ **Figure 1.13** Illustration of an 1860s Kabuki theater and performance.

historic version of Kabuki is very different from what we see being performed today. Kabuki continued to develop, and it was the first time in Japanese history that a diverse group of people came together in one place to watch a performance of any kind. This was groundbreaking!

Kabuki theaters became "hot spots" of the current culture. It became about being seen at the theater, where everything, from current events to fashion to music to famous actors, was in attendance. Performances were often very long, even all-day, events. Local teahouses sponsored the events in the hopes of bringing in customers for food and drink. Around the teahouses sprang up souvenir shops of all things Kabuki. It is a fair assessment to say that this period in Kabuki history originated the first pop culture of Japan. And then—in 1629—female Kabuki was banned for being too erotic. It had run its course of what the government of the time would accept.

Kabuki did not disappear though. In fact, as resilient as theatre has been and continues to be, it reinvented itself. After a brief transition period where all actors were men, Kabuki transformed itself away from dance and into a drama-based art form. Kabuki came into its Golden Age, from 1673 to 1841—quite a long period. During this Golden Age, the structure and content of the plays developed into what we now recognize as Kabuki. Conventional character types and standard plots became commonplace. This was a long period, but, by the end of it, women were again allowed to perform—this time alongside the male counterparts.

The style of play had now developed into three main categories or plot topics: The historical play, the domestic play, and the dance. The sets for Kabuki plays are always similar (Figure 1.14). A walkway or ramp that extends into the audience is used for the actors' entrances and exits. This type of staging brought the actors much closer

■ **Figure 1.14** A modern Kabuki production showing actors, costumes, and scenery.

to the audience and made a more personal and intimate approach. Over time, the sets became more complicated as innovations, such as trapdoors and revolving stages, were invented.

There are a few traditional characteristics of Kabuki. I already mentioned the kimonos and makeup. The white makeup is made from a rice powder base and is used to exaggerate facial features to help create animal and more mystical characters. Another traditional part of Kabuki is posing (Figure 1.15). The actors pose, creating traditional silhouettes that are easily recognizable to the audience. This helps further the different plot lines. Have you ever seen posing used in a different art form, perhaps music?

■ **Figure 1.15** A modern Kabuki production showing an actor in a classic kabuki pose.

CHINESE THEATRE

Chinese theatre has a very long history, which has been complex at times. Let me explain. The first documented Chinese theatre took place in about 1500 BCE. That's right, BCE! These were simple performances, which often included music, clowning, and acrobatics. This led directly into shadow puppetry, with two styles of shadow puppets, Cantonese (from the south) and Pekingese (from the north).

Both genres generally performed the same style of plays. These plays were based heavily in adventure and fantasy. As opposed to other theaters we discussed, the Chinese had no interest in depicting the political struggles of the day on stage. Entertainment was a diversion from the struggles of real life.

The two genres differentiated themselves mainly in the making of the puppets. Cantonese puppets were larger and built using thick leather, which created strong shadows. Colors were used symbolically—a black face represented honesty, while a red one meant bravery. Pekingese puppets were smaller and more delicate. They were built using thin leather, which was almost translucent. Paint was used in vibrant colors that cast very colorful shadows. Keep in mind that this is the first extensive use of shadows.

> You should examine yourself daily. If you find faults, you should correct them. When you find none, you should try harder.
> —Wang Xizhi,
> **Chinese writer and calligrapher, 303–361** CE

One interesting story from this time is that the head of the puppet was removable. This allowed the heads to be removed when not in use, especially at night. There was a superstition at the time that, if the head was left on a puppet, the puppet might come to life. Imagine the nightmares children must have had when told of this legend. Some puppeteers went so far as to store the heads in a totally separate area from the body.

Puppet theatre was popular for many centuries. As centuries passed, more complex plots were developed.

The plays were also transformed into a four- or five-act structure. Shadow puppetry reached the height of its popularity in the 11th century. Eventually, the government began to use the theatre for its own needs, at which point the plots expanded to include more politically based stories.

OK, are you about ready to talk about the modern day and get to some information that may seem even more familiar? Well, we've finished with our brief history lesson, but keep it in mind, as we are not leaving it behind. We are taking it with us forward in time, as it is truly the basis for everything that we do today. That is why we had to look at the history before looking at the modern stuff. Let's begin—or continue.

MODERN THEATRE (19th Century–20th Century)

Modern theatre comes in many types and, to complicate our discussion even further, it has many venues, each with its own variations. Let's start with the types, then get into the actual venues. There are basically four types of performance space: Proscenium, thrust, arena, and traverse. We will break them down one by one. Sometimes, two styles are combined to form a hybrid. But, let us talk about the classical ideas behind these first before getting more complicated. Watch out for lots of new terms.

PROSCENIUM THEATRE

The proscenium theatre is possibly the most recognizable type of theatre today (Figure 1.16). This design was the most popular one during the 18th–20th centuries (Figure 1.17). *Proscenium*, as we learned earlier when discussing the Greeks, refers to an archway that separates the acting area from the audience. Usually, but not always, the proscenium arch is close to the downstage edge of the stage.

This type is called an *end stage* on occasion, which references the fact that the stage is at one end of the building, and the audience is at the other. The audience directly faces the stage but does not interact with the actors. As with the Greeks, the proscenium becomes a frame through which the audience views the play. In

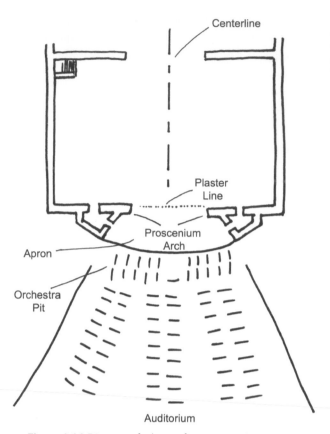

■ **Figure 1.16** Diagram of a layout for a proscenium-style theater.

Labels in diagram: Centerline, Plaster Line, Proscenium Arch, Apron, Orchestra Pit, Auditorium

■ **Figure 1.17** The side boxes in the 1869 Bardavon Opera House in Poughkeepsie, NY.

Russian, the opening of the proscenium is referred to as "the mirror of the stage," which possibly echoes back to Shakespeare. This frame is often referred to as the **fourth wall**. The actors treat the fourth wall as if it is a real wall and ignore the audience. Some plays call for the actors to look right at the audience and deliver their lines. This is called *breaking the fourth wall* for obvious reasons. It is a very powerful effect when used sparingly and with great textual purpose.

> Go on failing. Go on. Only next time, try to fail better.
>
> —Samuel Beckett,
> Irish novelist, playwright,
> theatre director, and poet, 1906–1989

Often, a curtain is placed directly upstage of the proscenium and acts as a **house curtain** (Figure 1.18). The house curtain is used to mask the stage from the audience's view prior to the performance. The house curtain is not always used in this manner today, as some less traditional productions choose to expose the stage (and the scenery) rather than hide it. Downstage of the house curtain usually hangs the **grand border**. A border is a short curtain that hangs up in the air and goes all the way across the stage from left to right. It helps to mask the workings of the theatre from the audience's view. In this case, the grand border is the one closest to the audience. It is often made of fabric to match the house curtain, rather than the plainer fabric traditionally used for other borders.

Let's talk about some of the architectural details of this type and what we call them. If the stage extends

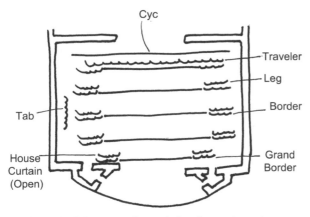

Figure 1.18 Diagram of sample borders and curtains for the theater.

downstage of the proscenium arch, that area of the stage is called the **apron**. The audience sits in seating located in the **auditorium**. This seating can be fixed or moveable. Most often, the seating area in the auditorium is raked, similar to the Greek and Roman theaters. It is good not only for natural acoustics but for seeing the stage unobstructed from anywhere in the audience.

While we're discussing seeing, let's introduce the term *sight lines*. If you draw an imaginary line between the audience's eye and the stage, that is called a *sight line* or *line of sight*. The common practice is to draw the line from a variety of places using the most extreme angles for both the audience and the stage. The goal for scenic designers is to make sure that the important parts of the set and action fall within this line and are therefore visible to as many audience members as possible. Sometimes, lower priced tickets for a show will be for what are called "obstructed view" seats. This means that some of the action will not be visible owing either to sight line issues or architectural elements within the auditorium.

There is often an area between the stage and the auditorium. It is called the **orchestra pit**. This is an obvious term to explain. The orchestra occupies this space if there is an orchestra. If there is no orchestra in the show, the pit may be covered to provide extra acting area. The name *pit* comes from the fact that most often this area is lower than the auditorium floor, creating a "pit," similar to the standing room area in Shakespeare's time.

There are many more terms to learn. Since these terms apply not only to the proscenium type but to the others as well, I will spread them out a bit as we go on to the next type.

THRUST STAGE

The **thrust stage** is usually considered to be a hybrid of the proscenium (Figure 1.19). There is most often a proscenium of some kind, but it is usually much less ornate. The big difference is with the apron. We talked about how the apron is the part of the stage that extends downstage between the proscenium and the auditorium. Well, in a thrust stage, the apron becomes much larger and "thrusts" into the auditorium. There is no rule about its shape or size, just that it extends substantially into the audience area *and* that the audience is seated on all three sides of the thrust.

The nice effect of a thrust stage is to bring the actors much closer to the audience while still keeping some backstage space for technical support. Since the audience ends up being located on three sides of the stage, it is a much more intimate setup for everyone. The audience members now feel like they are participating in the play, not just watching it, and the actors feel more connected to the audience. Another change with the thrust setup

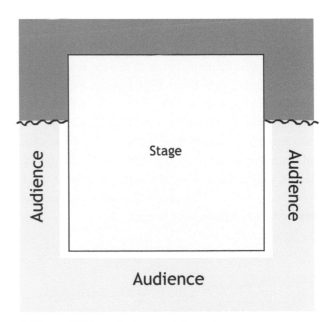

Figure 1.19 Layout of thrust-style theater.

is the addition of the vomitoria. Remember these from the Roman theatre? They also add to the intimacy of the experience. The audience can reach out and touch the actors. Not that I recommend this, but it's possible.

> Just say the lines and don't trip over the furniture.
>
> —Noel Coward,
> English playwright, composer, director, actor, and singer, 1899–1973

In terms of the scenic changes, both the proscenium and the thrust allow the possibility of a backdrop or cyclorama. A backdrop in today's theatre is a curtain placed upstage of all, or at least most of, the action. We see the actors against it, and, usually, it helps to inform us of where we are: The location or setting for the play. A cyclorama is slightly different. Traditionally, the cyclorama was a blank backdrop placed upstage; however, it was wide enough that the sides wrapped around and came downstage toward the audience. This was a more enveloping type of theatre. Eventually, the cyclorama starting getting called the cyc, and now *backdrop* and *cyc* are used almost interchangeably, even though a backdrop is often painted, and a cyc is unpainted.

Other scenic issues involve the fact that the audience is seated on three sides of the stage. It is great for the actors and audience, but very limiting for the set designer. This means that furniture needs to be kept low for sight lines. Remember sight lines? Well, imagine a tall-backed chair placed on the edge of the stage, right in front of an audience member. He or she would see nothing but the chair. Any actual scenery needs to be kept to a minimum and placed carefully, checking sight lines. Lighting also changes substantially when working on a thrust stage. Every angle that the audience will see the performance from needs to be taken into account.

ARENA STAGE

For the arena stage, think boxing ring and you've got the right idea (Figure 1.20). Arena stages are truly theatre-in-the-round, although not necessarily strictly round. The stage is in the center of the space, and the audience is seated on all sides. There are vomitoria in each diagonal corner, allowing the audience to be seated, as well as for the actors' entrances and exits. There are many more challenges for the actors, director, and designers with this type of stage. The actors' movements are almost always on a diagonal, allowing the maximum number of audience members to see their faces. Arena is reminiscent of some ancient Greek and Roman theaters. It wasn't until the mid-20th century that the arena type became truly popular. Plays of this period were written to be more confrontational, and the arena setup allows actors to directly address the audience as needed.

Think back to the discussion of the fourth wall. Arena basically has four fourth walls *or* none, depending on the production. Acting with four fourth walls is a very different experience for the actors as well! Scenery is a bigger challenge than in thrust, as there is no backstage area. Scenic design for an arena is about the furniture placement and the floor. Occasionally, the vomitoria have scenery in them as well. This can ease the transition of

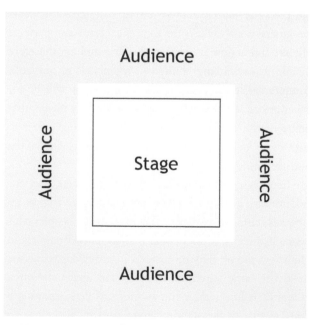

■ **Figure 1.20** Layout of an arena-style theater.

the scenery ending and auditorium beginning. Practicals go a long way in lighting arena stages and creating an environment. It is a particular challenge that some designers specialize in, while others avoid.

TRAVERSE

The traverse stage is sometimes called a corridor stage, an alley, or a catwalk. It is often used for period plays or fashion shows. The audience members sit on two opposing sides of the stage, looking at each other, with the stage between them. It makes for an intimate experience. But it has its challenges. Actors facing one side of the audience instantly have their backs to half the audience. Lighting is another challenge, as shadows can fall where you don't want them. Keep in mind that with challenges come opportunities for extreme creativity!

THEATRE VENUES

Theatre venues are our next topic. This is the fun part—a list of the various places you might get to work someday. Let me preface this list by saying that the best theatre in the world is not found in a specific venue. The best theatre in the world is found in the hearts of the performers and the audience. This is not a trite statement. I really mean that. Do not allow yourself to be swayed by what the reviewers say. If you go to a performance, no matter where it is, and you are really moved and touched by it, *it is good theatre*. Please keep in mind, as we begin to discuss venues, that the type of venue is in no way linked to the quality of the production.

Broadway (New York) and the West End (London) are considered the crème de la crème of theatre. These two classifications are for-profit, and the theaters involved are rented to the production companies on a show-by-show basis. Opera happens all around the world, from the Metropolitan Opera in New York to Covent Garden in London to the Staatsoper in Vienna. These all have huge shows with more special effects than almost anything except blockbuster films. Most of these venues have a traditional proscenium stage.

Off-Broadway in New York and the Fringe in London are the places for the smaller shows. The venues become a little less glamorous and vary from proscenium to thrust to arena. Off-off-Broadway is known for smaller, more remote, and less traditional spaces. These spaces can include gymnasiums, church basements, and black box theaters on the 10th floor of an office building, with smaller-budget, often new plays being tried out.

Next, let's talk about regional and repertory theaters. In my opinion, some of the best theatre happens here. Both types of venues are often not-for-profit and therefore depend on donations for their annual budget. Since they are not truly commercial, their goal is simply to create great theatre. Working for this type of venue is very freeing. The regional theaters are just what they sound like. They are located around the world in various geographic regions. The repertory theaters, by their name, are theatre companies that produce more than one show at a time and may have alternating performances within the schedule.

Summer stock is the next venue to discuss. Summer stock, as its name suggests, occurs during the summer. A "season" often consists of five separate productions being produced during a ten-week season. This is a major part of the training for young performers and technicians. The experience you get in such a short time is unrivaled anywhere else in the industry.

Community theaters often operate during the entire year, not just the summer. It is a similar experience to summer stock although at a slower pace, and amateur as opposed to summer stock being professional. Dinner theatre is a unique experience where your ticket price covers not only the show but also your meal. The room where you sit and eat your meal is the same room where the performance happens. Some people find this a little strange, but it can be a very enjoyable experience. You stay at your table, continuing to eat and enjoy the cuisine—and a show starts at the end of the room on a stage, or, better yet, the actors wander through the dining room, and it becomes more of environmental theatre. Often, your waiter is also an actor, so tip generously when the bill comes.

Fringe festivals, street theatre, and improvisational theatre all fall into a similar category. These are all examples of smaller, more experimental performances that are easily moved from one venue to another. Festivals are a great way to see a large number of performances in a short time. Street theatre is just plain fun but can also be quite moving. You simply walk down the street, and who knows what you will see or who will be performing.

The last venue I want to address is themed entertainment. Since the third edition of this book was published, themed entertainment has continued to strengthen its hold on its growing place in the industry. This is when theatre-type shows take place inside an amusement park, casino, cruise ship, or something similar. This is one of the fastest-growing venues in the industry. Think of it as theatre on vacation! The shows that take place in this type of venue are often more extensively designed and created than for other venues owing to budgets and audience expectations. This venue tends to also put on the show for the long term, even permanently. Permanence is not something we usually deal with in the theatre. It is unique. And themed entertainment has created many opportunities and many more jobs!

> I make theatre for myself, and if someone else can derive some value from it, fine.
> —Richard Foreman,
> American playwright
> and theater pioneer, 1937–

We finish our discussion by talking about the different styles of theatre. Different styles for a specific production are chosen by writers and directors based on the needs of the play and what they are trying to achieve. The following is a list of some, but certainly not all, of the styles prevalent in today's productions. This list is incomplete, as space is somewhat limited, and a complete list could become a book of its own. The glory of today's theatre is that parts of each style may be borrowed and combined to create new styles. This is an ever-changing and evolving list. I have tried to list, at the very least, the basics that we call on today.

- **Black comedy**: Using humor and satire, these plays make fun of serious or taboo subjects such as murder, suicide, or war in order to make the topic more accessible to the audience.
- **Comedy**: This style is not always full of humor, but usually focuses on a problem that has a happy outcome. Lighter themes are used, and often the comedy comes out of stressful situations.
- **Commedia dell'arte**: A stock group of characters improvised based on a standard group of plots. Masks were often used to become characters.
- **Docudrama**: A play based on an actual event or series of events. Characters are also based on real people or the combination of several people into one character.
- **Epic**: Social and political topics are presented in such a way as to ensure the audience is always aware it is watching a play. There is never an attempt at the traditional illusion of inclusion.
- **Fantasy**: These plays are often set in another realm. The interesting thing is that the characters are still dealing with the universal themes we've been discussing throughout.
- **Farce**: Farce is a more extreme form of comedy. The plot lines in farce tend to push the limits between physical and verbal stereotypes. Often, this includes a physical layout that does not follow conventional construction.
- **Feminist**: This style includes plays written by women, about women, and women-based topics. Topics include birth, motherhood, certain forms of cancer, and other women-specific health-related issues.
- **Melodrama**: This is a sentimental drama similar in themes to daytime soap operas. Melodramas feature

stock characters, such as the noble hero, the long-suffering heroine, and the cold-blooded villain.

- **Naturalism**: This attempts to create the illusion of reality on stage. It includes detailed non-exotic settings and three-dimensional characters. It can involve physical danger. No "theatre magic" is involved.
- **Realism**: This is similar to naturalism, but conflicts come from morals, ethical dilemmas, or inner conflict as opposed to physical danger.
- **Romantic comedy**: Romantic comedy is comedy in which the main characters are often romantically linked.
- **Theatre for Social Change**: Such theatre addresses social issues with the ideal of achieving societal change.
- **Theatre of the Absurd**: Experimental and surreal are the two words that define this style. Flat character **archetypes** are involved in plots that seem meaningless. Often the "meaning" is discernible after much thought once the experience is over.
- **Total theatre**: This is characterized by strong emotions, physicality that includes violence (real or perceived), vulgar language, and humiliation to name a few. Reactions are strong, landing clearly on love or hate, with little room for anything in the middle.
- **Tragedy**: This is a drama that deals in a serious and dignified way with sorrowful or terrible events.

So, you should now have a basic understanding of where we, as theatre geeks, come from. You should have enough knowledge in your head to take on the next chapter and begin moving forward to the glory we in the know call theatre!

EXERCISES

EXERCISE 1
GREECE VERSUS ROME

Design a simple set and place it onto the stage of the Greek theater. Then place it into the stage house of the Roman theater and notate what additional options this gives you.

EXERCISE 2
PERFORMANCE SPACES

Design a simple set and place it in the performance space of your choosing. Now, pick a different type of performance space and put your set in that. Adjust your set as needed to make it work in the new space. Discuss how your set must change from one space to another.

CHECK YOUR KNOWLEDGE

1. What does the word *theatre* mean, and where did we get it?
2. What is a chorus, in theatre terms? How is it used?
3. How did the Greeks solve the problem of hearing the actors given that they didn't have microphones? When else in history did this happen?
4. Make an argument for the use of a building specifically designed for theatrical performances and analyze the effect it may have had on playwriting.
5. Relate how the Greeks and Romans led us along the path to the Globe Theater.
6. Shakespeare and Kabuki were happening at almost the same time in different parts of the world. Contrast and compare these forms.
7. The vomitorium appeared in a variety of periods. Support its use and progression through time.
8. Make an argument for what you expect to be the next emerging trend in the history of theatre.
9. Choose a style, genre, and venue we discussed to illustrate a specific production you would like to work on. Support your answer by using an example from current cultural, political, or socio-economic trends.

- Apron
- Archetype
- Arena
- Auditorium
- Backdrop
- Black box
- Cyc
- Cyclorama
- Downstage
- Fourth wall
- Genre
- Grand border
- House curtain
- Orchestra pit
- Passion play
- Proscenium
- Rake
- Sight lines
- Stage
- Stage left
- Stage right
- Thrust
- Traverse
- Upstage
- Vomitorium

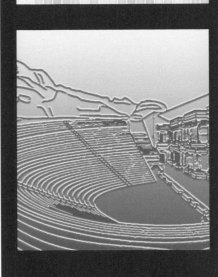

STUDY WORDS

Chapter 1

It's All about Collaboration

Design for Theatre

Student Learning Outcomes

Students will acquire:

- An overview understanding of the major aspects, techniques, and directions in the area of design.

- Fundamental, conceptual understanding of the expressive possibilities of theatre.

- A working knowledge of technologies, and concepts applicable to the area of design.

You want to be a technician (or think you might) and are wondering why you should be learning about design. The best way to be a good technician is to understand the designer's process. And the best way to be a designer is to be prepared and learn from others who have been doing it longer than you. Then, as questions arise or perhaps problems needing creative solutions, you can actually be part of the eventual solution. This is the point where we discuss the actual process of design. And, yes, it is a process. Designers don't sit down and just draw pretty pictures. They read scripts, do research, go to production meetings, and so forth.

> The director calls to ask if you're interested and you read the play to decide whether to say yes or no. Liking the play is most important! If you don't care about the play there's no point to doing it; you'll never come up with good ideas. After that, you and the director start to have conversations.
>
> —Derek McLane,
> American scenic designer

PRODUCTION TEAM COLLABORATION

There is a hierarchical order to the production staff. Each position reports to another. This order is what keeps the team organized and the production moving forward to opening night. Whatever position you might be interested in filling, it is very important to know how the team works. Take a look at Figure 2.1 to see how the whole production team is shown, from producer all the way to the running crew. We will get into job descriptions in Chapter 21. Where do you think you might want to fit in?

Let's move on to our discussion of designers. There are a number of reasons for taking a job. Maybe the director is someone you have always wanted to work with or someone you have worked with many times before. Maybe the script is new, exciting, or earth-shattering, or a revival of a play you always loved. Maybe the design team (the other designers) is composed of people you always wanted to work with or have worked with many times before. Maybe the director is assembling a team of people who know one another so well that the creative **collaboration** is already in place and you can communicate intuitively with one another's creative choices. Maybe the production is going to start out of town and move to Broadway. Or maybe, just maybe, the rent is due, and you have no other job.

To be perfectly honest, all these reasons can be the right reason to take a job. The hope is always that several

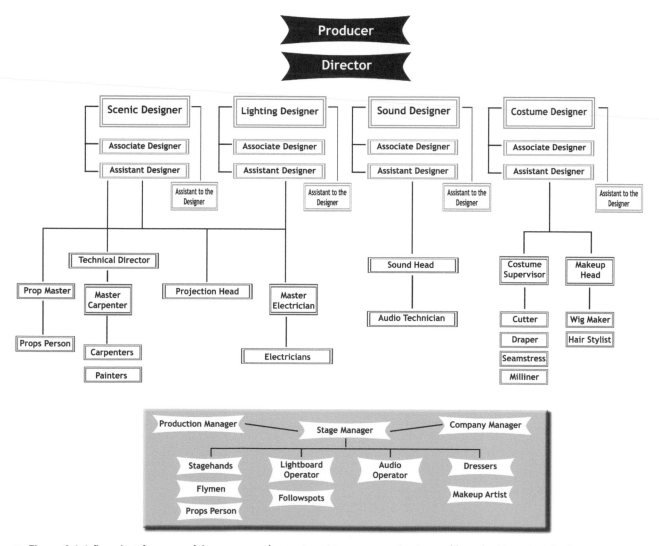

■ **Figure 2.1** A flow chart for some of the many employment positions on a production and how the hierarchy is laid out.

of these will be why you take the job. If you take the job just to cover the rent, be aware that this is what you are doing. If you have grander ideas about collaborating with your "dream team" of designers, be aware of that, too. Know why you are accepting a job and how that will influence your work. What do I mean by *influence*? Well, if you take a job because of the dream team, will you expect to work harder than if you take the job to pay the rent? Your answer should be *no*.

> I read a script until I understand that either I have something to contribute or I don't. If I don't, I don't take the job.
>
> **—Geoff Dunbar,**
> **designer**

You should be willing to work as hard as possible on every job you accept. There is no such thing as an inferior production, unless you make it one. There is also no such thing as a guaranteed career-making show. If you ask people how they got to where they are in their careers, you will hear a different story every time. This is important to know and remember, because there is not just one way to a successful career. Everyone must find his or her own path. And it always starts with the first step. Defining success is also different for everyone and may change as your career progresses. Be very aware of this!

So, what does that mean to you? Well, let's look at some possibilities. You accept a job even though the production is in a church basement, in some town that isn't even on the map yet. It turns out that a friend of a friend of someone connected to the show knows a "bigtime" director, and the director will be attending opening night. Wouldn't you be disappointed if you had done mediocre work because you thought of the production as a throw-away? The reverse can also be true. You have what you think will be the production to take your career to the next level, then no one "important" comes to see it. Are you disappointed? Does this make your work any less good? Absolutely not.

My goal has always been to do the best work I can, every single time. If I am happy with my work, then I can assume that someone will eventually see it and agree with me. This is how I started out my career, how I continued my career, and how my career has gotten to where it is today. Keep in mind that every production should be a learning experience as well. I do not say that because this is a textbook and you are a student. I say that because, when we stop learning, we stop growing. As artists, we should always be pushing ourselves to be better, to learn more, to strive for the next level. This is a mindset as much as anything else. If you stop striving, you stop creating. Let me repeat that: If you stop striving, you stop creating!

> It's not Show Fun … it's Show Business.
>
> **—ML Geiger,**
> **lighting designer**

OK, so, I got off on a tangent. Let's talk about *collaboration*. This is the single most important word to remember as a designer. Before you go off to work on your own part of the design and production, you must first begin the process of collaboration that will carry you all the way through to opening night. If we as theatre artists wanted to work by ourselves, we would be studio artists doing painting or sculpture alone in a studio somewhere. What makes us different, and unique, is that we actually enjoy the input other designers give us. Our goal must be to work as a team and collectively create a production where there once was none. We will continue to discuss collaboration throughout the chapter as it is the basis of every good design.

DESIGN PROCESS

Now, let's talk about the steps and stages of design. Each design discipline's process has some similarities and differences. We will discuss the similarities here. Later, during the individual chapters, we will delve into detail about differing design steps and theories during the implementation phase. That is where things will vary a bit.

So, the phone rings, and you are offered a design job or asked for an interview. It used to be that you had to sit at home waiting for that phone call. Obviously that isn't the case anymore. Today's technology means you may get a phone call on your cell phone, an email, instant message, tweet, or whatever. There are so many ways to keep in touch—who knows how the initial contact will happen. Any contact is a valid form of communication, and you have to be aware that they are now a necessary part of our world. Social media seem to be here to stay, at least for now.

READING THE SCRIPT

Contact has been made; what do you do next? Well, everybody has his or her own way of working. The design process varies slightly from one project to another. There is no one formula that works for everyone. With that said, certain things do have to happen in a certain order. The first thing most designers do is get a copy of the script and meet with the director. The script is really your road map (Figure 2.2). It should inform all your

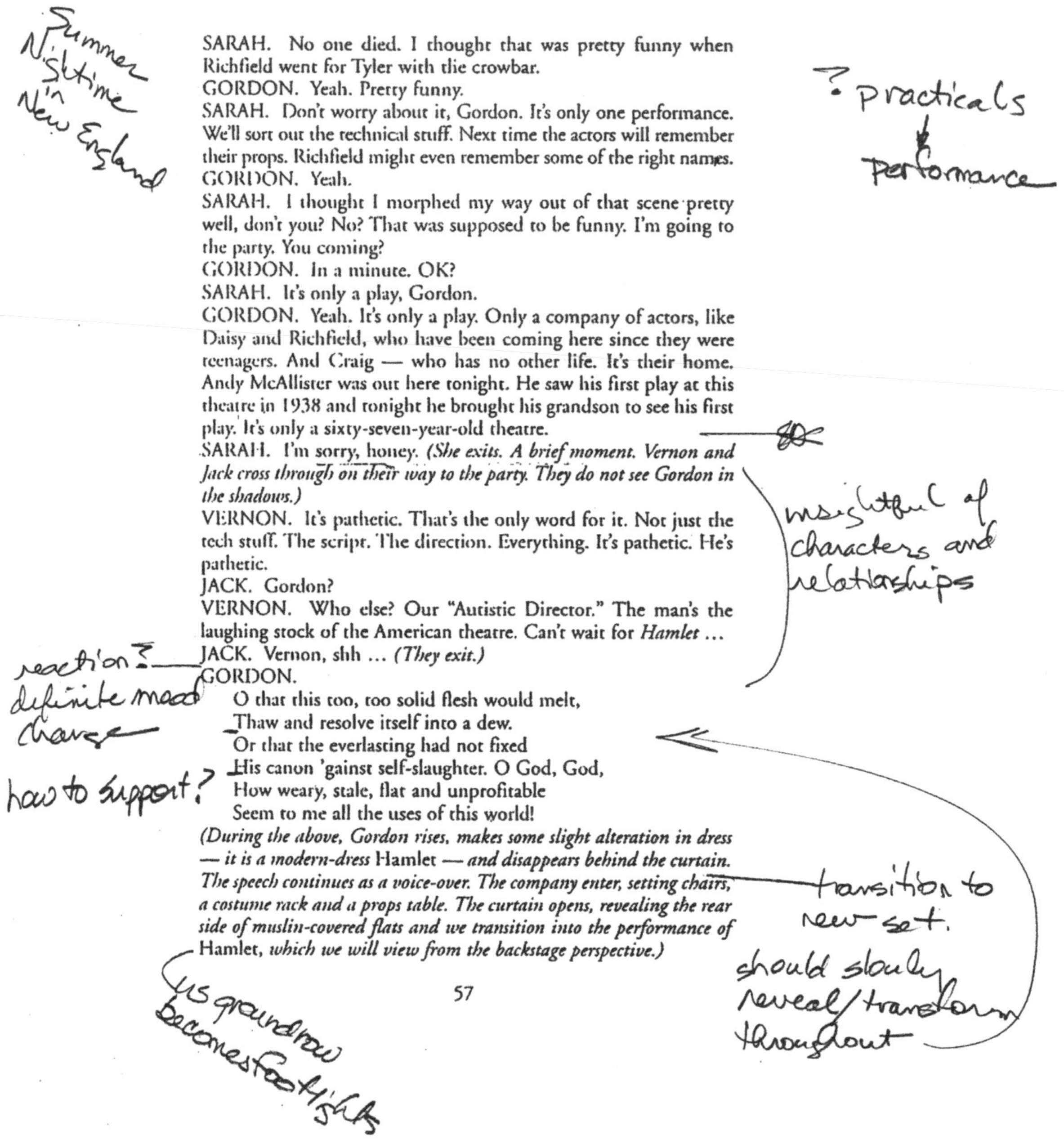

[Handwritten note:] Summer Nightime in New England

SARAH. No one died. I thought that was pretty funny when Richfield went for Tyler with the crowbar.
GORDON. Yeah. Pretty funny.
SARAH. Don't worry about it, Gordon. It's only one performance. We'll sort out the technical stuff. Next time the actors will remember their props. Richfield might even remember some of the right names.
GORDON. Yeah.
SARAH. I thought I morphed my way out of that scene pretty well, don't you? No? That was supposed to be funny. I'm going to the party. You coming?
GORDON. In a minute. OK?
SARAH. It's only a play, Gordon.
GORDON. Yeah. It's only a play. Only a company of actors, like Daisy and Richfield, who have been coming here since they were teenagers. And Craig — who has no other life. It's their home. Andy McAllister was out here tonight. He saw his first play at this theatre in 1938 and tonight he brought his grandson to see his first play. It's only a sixty-seven-year-old theatre.
SARAH. I'm sorry, honey. *(She exits. A brief moment. Vernon and Jack cross through on their way to the party. They do not see Gordon in the shadows.)*
VERNON. It's pathetic. That's the only word for it. Not just the tech stuff. The script. The direction. Everything. It's pathetic. He's pathetic.
JACK. Gordon?
VERNON. Who else? Our "Autistic Director." The man's the laughing stock of the American theatre. Can't wait for *Hamlet* …
JACK. Vernon, shh … *(They exit.)*
GORDON.
O that this too, too solid flesh would melt,
Thaw and resolve itself into a dew.
Or that the everlasting had not fixed
His canon 'gainst self-slaughter. O God, God,
How weary, stale, flat and unprofitable
Seem to me all the uses of this world!
(During the above, Gordon rises, makes some slight alteration in dress — it is a modern-dress Hamlet — and disappears behind the curtain. The speech continues as a voice-over. The company enter, setting chairs, a costume rack and a props table. The curtain opens, revealing the rear side of muslin-covered flats and we transition into the performance of Hamlet, which we will view from the backstage perspective.)

57

[Handwritten notes surrounding the script:]
? Practicals & Performance
insightful of characters and relationships
reaction? definite mood change
how to support?
transition to new set.
should slowly reveal/transform throughout
US groundrow becomes footlights

■ **Figure 2.2** A script page with designer notes from one of the first reads.

decisions and choices. Consider the director is the driver of the production. These are your first two points of contact—director and script—with any production and, possibly, job.

> The only reading that counts is the first; it determines if I will take the project. The script has to say something to me, and I have to see where my visions will best represent the author's vision.
>
> —Michael A. Fink, designer

Most designers admit to reading the script several times. The first time through the script is usually to read and enjoy the story, plot lines, and characters. Nothing more. If you read it through and you enjoy it, most likely you will accept the project. This first reading is like a first date. It should be a glance into the future. You will spend a good amount of time working on a production, and this is the critical moment when you have to decide whether you like the script enough to dedicate the next months or years of your life to it. Don't take this lightly.

MEETING WITH THE DIRECTOR

The next step is almost always the initial face-to-face meeting. This meeting is often between you and the director. Many designers prefer that the initial meeting is with the whole team: The director, set designer, costume designer, lighting designer, sound designer, and any specialty designers who may be needed. Specialty designers can include hair, makeup, projections, pyrotechnics, and any other specialty elements that will require a team of their own. It is important to have the whole team together for several reasons. In design, the most important word I can think of is *collaboration*. I know I said it before, but this is the major difference between theatre people and everyone else.

During this initial meeting, it is best to discuss what the play means in terms of the upcoming production. Why are we doing it? Why now? Why here? One main topic of conversation is usually about the **style** of the

Theatre Traditions: The Scottish Play

Perhaps the most prevalent superstition in all of theatre is about *Macbeth*. We are never supposed to mention aloud this name when we are in a theater building. It is said that, if you say the name, terrible things will happen. Apparently, this is based on the lustful greed for power that takes place in the plot of that play. Everyone calls it the *Scottish Play* instead, and we all know what they mean.

Theatre veterans can tell many tales about bad luck happening when this name is said aloud. It is often thought that supernatural forces of evil are behind this. But you're in luck, because there is a way to break the curse. If you say the name, you must spin around and spit on the floor. They say the spin turns back time, and the spit expels the poisonous word from your system.

production (Figure 2.3). You may ask, what is style? The terms *presentational* and *representational* are the most often-used styles of production. Let me explain the difference between the two. A **presentational** style offers a performance in which everyone is fully aware that the actors are at work on a stage, speaking and acting out a script, under lights, and in costumes. There is no attempt to disguise the fact that a theatrical performance is taking place to entertain the audience.

The **representational** style of production differs in that it shows truths about ordinary existence within specific situations. While we still know we are in a theater putting on a production, it is generally accepted that the actors won't acknowledge the audience's presence. This style can be broken into two sub-styles: Realism and naturalism. **Realism** is based in our own world, with recognizable characters having no supernatural powers. The characters do the sorts of things that ordinary people do every day. **Naturalism**, on the other hand, is much more specific, almost a heightened realism. The purpose of this very detailed world is to show how a person's character and

■ **Figure 2.3** A sketch for Verdi's *Macbeth*, designed by Salvatore Tagliarino.

life choices are determined in part by environmental or social forces. Production elements are as specific to the environment as the characters' descriptions. Often, "real" props, furniture, clothing, and lighting are assimilated into the production for that added feel of realism. Once a style is decided on, it becomes the reference for your entire range of choices.

Once the initial meeting is over, you sit down and start to think. You take in the information about style and how the director is approaching the script. You should now begin to come up with your **concept**, which is your unique way of looking at the show. Keep in mind that the director also has a concept, and that your concept *must* work with the director's. Again, collaboration. You may find an image, photograph, or painting that strikes you as the essence of the production. You can use this concept to guide your choices of color, shape, direction, and all the other choices you need to make.

SCRIPT BREAKDOWN

OK, so the first meeting is over, and you decided to stick with it and make this the best design you ever created. What is the next step, you wonder? Go back to the script. You should now read the script again, paying more attention to detail while keeping in mind all the information that came out of that initial meeting. How does the newly chosen directorial style help you to start visualizing the production? This reading is where you begin to break down the script.

Most designers have a very specific process for designing, regardless of the type of design they do. When I interviewed Michael Fink, he said his process is all about questions. I like this approach, so I will outline it here. And remember, don't stop asking questions until you get all the answers you need.

Who? How many characters, in what age range, or with what attitude? What is my vision of them from what is in the script and my own internal perceptions from life? Have I worked with the director before, and do we share a common language?

What? Is there a driving theme to the script or story or concept that it embodies? What is the vision—natural, farcical, strange, normal?

Where? Do the events in the script take place in an English drawing room, old fort, or bordello? What is the size of the theater, and what are its capabilities?

When? When does the play take place: Period play, time of day, season? Do we witness events as they unfold, as flashbacks, or as dreams?

Why? Why are the characters driven to do what they do? Why is there an interest in presenting this story?

How? How will each moment tell this story? If you can visualize your idea properly, it can come from the ethereal to the material.

The script breakdown will slightly vary depending on which design you will be creating. The basic idea is to identify the circumstances of the play. You need to determine whether the play takes place during the day or night. What season is it? Do the scenes take place inside or outside? Is there a specific geographic location? It doesn't matter what the style is; you have to determine these things before you can either follow them or abstract from them.

RESEARCH

The next step is to do your **research**. Now, what does that mean? You have to decide what the script requires and find out what equipment is available to achieve your ideas of that. Geoff Dunbar told me, "If a script needs a fire, I will research how fires are being done this year (in addition to already knowing how fires were done last year)."

Research also means that, if your production is set in 1818 London, you'd better find out what 1818 London looks, feels, sounds, and smells like. Do not guess, and certainly don't make it up—unless your production is about the fantasy of 1818 London! All designers should research the art, architecture, clothing, lighting, political events, atmosphere—everything you can think of concerning your locale. Your research should include shapes, lines, and colors that are appropriate. You are looking for pictures, images. They can be photos or drawings and paintings (Figure 2.4). Even sculpture can be research. Any visual reference that evokes your inner vision and helps inform

■ **Figure 2.4** Stained-glass art, *Long Beach*, by Isabella Rupp.

your choices is considered research. Once you have done your research and before you start making choices, you must consider how your research can be applied to the style decided on by the director.

The style, together with your research, helps you choose the right direction in which to move forward. You should be starting to form ideas now for your design. You might even be doing rough sketches, whether they be visual or auditory.

At this point, let's talk for a minute about audiences. After all, the audience is who actually pays to see our work. Andy Warfel has some interesting thoughts on audiences:

Disregarding the audience's expectations (or failing to research what those expectations might be) is basically disregarding the audience. This is a failure of the most basic reason for presenting a work: to make some sort of connection with an audience! Of course, one can (and should) trump/trash/exceed the expectations. But if one doesn't know what the expectations are to begin with, then it's less than a gamble … it's just arrogance! If you're not doing it for an audience, then it's just something that you should work out on paper at home, and save everyone else the hassle … and money!

—Andy Warfel,
production designer

Wow, I couldn't have said it better. So always, always keep the audience in mind while you research.

Part of the research process is to know about symbols. Huh? You might be thinking, why are symbols important? Well, first, let's define what a symbol is. A **symbol** is a picture, object, color, or other visual item that represents something else (Figure 2.5). As you start to get ideas of what you want the design to look like, you have to be aware of what things may mean when the audience sees them. Take some of the most common symbols. The eagle is used as a symbol of freedom; the skull and crossbones are a sign of danger (Figure 2.6);

■ **Figure 2.5** The yin-yang symbol refers to two opposing yet complementary aspects of a person or issue.

■ **Figure 2.6** The skull and crossbones are a symbol that can have many differing meanings, but they all refer to some kind of danger.

■ **Figure 2.7** A universal exit sign used in the European Union.

■ **Figure 2.8** The cross and crown are a traditional Christian symbol, appearing in many churches as well as in various versions of heraldry.

■ **Figure 2.9** Wearing variously colored ribbons is a symbolic action that shows support for certain causes.

the lightbulb is often used as a symbol for an idea. Have you got the idea? Every image has a meaning that comes along with it (Figure 2.7). The audience already knows these meanings, so you need to be aware of them before you use something that conjures a meaning other than what you intended. Of course, using symbols for crossed purposes can also be successful if done properly.

Let's take research in a slightly different direction. There are things about the history of architecture that you need to know. There are styles of architecture, periods of architecture, orders of architecture—you get the idea. Motifs within differing architectural orders can be used in all different areas of design, not just for scenery. Stay with me here. You need to understand the basic ideas of each, realizing you can always reference an actual history book when needed for more details. So, here we go!

STYLES OF ARCHITECTURE

The following examples relate to the stylistic feel of many elements pertaining to the visual part of a production. Think about art history as you read this section and start to make correlations between these periods and artistic trends. Bear with me; there are lots of new words, but they will come back again and again. Periods of architecture are usually named for the styles from which they came:

- **Classicism**: This style is based on idealistic models or established conservative standards. It embraces a high level of taste, sobriety, and proportion. Conventional formality is another way to think of classicism.
- **Romanticism**: This is an imaginative style emphasizing individualism in thought and expression in direct opposition to the restrictive formality of classicism. Other traits of this period are freedom of fancy in conception and treatment, picturesque strangeness, or suggestions of drama and adventure.
- **Realism**: This is a representation of nature without idealizing (as in classicism) or inclining to the emotional or extravagant (as in romanticism). There is an interest in the accurate and graphic that may degenerate into excessive detail and preoccupation with the trivial.
- **Impressionism**: This is a type of realism and romanticism combined that seeks to allow the

Figure 2.10 The different orders of architecture. The column capitals show the varieties possible, as well as how they grew and progressed throughout time.

artist to define the personality of the subject matter. Through the use of color and light, the subject matter's personality is revealed.

- **Expressionism**: This is a style in which the artist seeks to express an emotional experience placed onto the subject matter. This style allows the artist and the art to combine and form an altered reality.
- **Postmodernism**: This style rejects the preoccupation with purity of form and technique. Mixtures of style elements from the past are applied to sparse modern forms. The observer is asked to bring his or her opinions of this combined form, as there is no real standard or unity.
- **Deconstructivism**: This style followed on the heels of the postmodern movement. It was characterized primarily by the fragmentation of buildings and ideas within the whole. In addition, the overall surface of the form could be distorted and dislocated into non-rectilinear shapes.

ORDERS OF ARCHITECTURE

Again, keep in mind that this is key to understanding where things come from and how to use them today. Different column types fall into the five so-called classical orders, which are named *Doric, Ionic, Corinthian, Tuscan,* and *Composite*. Each order is made up of the column, its base, shaft, and capital. Each has its own distinctive proportions and character (Figure 2.10). The first three come from the early Greek design, while the last two come from Roman times. It is interesting to see how one order morphed into the next as each became more and more decorative within Greece and then seemed to start over with simplicity in Rome.

In Greece, the **Doric** was the earliest order to develop and it was used for the Parthenon and for most temples. It has no base and was developed in about the 5th century BCE. The **Ionic**, with scroll-like capitals, soon followed it. The **Corinthian** was rarely used until the Romans adapted it. This order includes leaves on the capitals in a more natural replica and dates from the end of the 5th century BCE. The Roman orders made greater use of ornaments than the Greek orders, and their column proportions were more slender. The Romans, in their temples and other public buildings, used all three of the Greek orders, together with two others of their own devising, the Tuscan and the Composite orders. The **Composite** first appeared on the arch of Titus in Rome in 82 CE. Although no **Tuscan** columns survive, this order was thought to originate in Etruscan times. There is obviously a lot more to the orders, but that is enough for now!

DESIGN MEETING

You did the research, right? Did you use all the available sources? Books vs internet vs magazines vs museums, etc. What is next? At about this point, there is usually another design meeting. This is the time to discuss with the design team any research you might have found and explain how you might use it.

A true collaboration continues during this step, as each designer brings his or her research and thoughts to the table. Thoughts exchanged freely at this meeting are the way to an exciting and successful production. Everyone's ideas are as valid and important as everyone else's. This meeting is to exchange those ideas. Each person brings his or her own perspective on what was discussed at the first meeting. This is the best way to collaborate and eventually produce a well-designed show.

After the meeting, you may want to do some additional research, based on new thoughts and ideas that came through the discussion. The next phase is to sketch. Scenic and costume designers will begin to sketch out their rough ideas. A working ground plan should be coordinated with the lighting designer and then further developed through collaboration of ideas (Figures 2.11 and 2.12). Sound designers will begin to collect short audio files. You get the idea. Working in a void makes for a disjointed production. Working together is definitively the way to go.

Design meetings continue to happen throughout the rehearsal process. In addition, designers often attend rehearsals. This gives them the opportunity to spend time with the director prior to the pressures of technical rehearsals and also to see how the director is using the stage. It allows the designers to see the development of the characters and blocking. It may seem that this is unrelated to design, but it is not. It's that collaboration thing again. The better informed you are about every aspect of the production, the better you can do your individual job.

■ **Figure 2.11** *Camelot Opening Scene*, watercolor rendering by Oliver Smith.

■ **Figure 2.12** *Camelot Outside Camelot*, watercolor rendering by Oliver Smith.

DESIGNERS DRAW, RENDER, AND DRAFT

We are now at the part of the process where designers do what we think they do: Draw, render, record, or draft. Some of this is discussed in detail in Chapter 5. But let me give you a brief look at what is in store. Drawing, rendering, and drafting are the best ways to get visual ideas across. Recording sounds or transitions for lighting and projections are also good means of communication. The first thing that needs to happen is for the director to experience what is in the designer's head. If the ideas stay inside your head, they do no good. You have to get the ideas out of your head so others can see and feel them, react to them, and help you implement them.

Another aspect of being a designer is keeping a morgue. No, not for dead bodies, for images. If you want to be a designer, you should start a morgue. A morgue is an organized collection of images or sounds.

There is no need to invent ideas when you have the whole World Wide Web at your fingertips. Different designers organize their morgues in different ways. Set designers may keep architectural research, landscaping research, furniture research, and the like. Costume designers may keep research of each period in history, organizing separately by men and women or hairstyles and accessories (Figure 2.13). Lighting designers may keep images that evoke different moods, different times of day, or different seasons. Sound designers may keep environmental sounds separate from sound effects. The goal is to have research at your disposal to help trigger ideas as you work on various productions.

We're now going to look at two plays, sharing four productions from the Shakespeare Theatre Company. Look at the differences between two different productions of *Coriolanus* that took place nine years apart (Figures 2.14 and 2.15) and two productions of

■ **Figure 2.13** *The Crucible* at the NYU Department of Graduate Acting/Department of Design for Stage and Film in April 2005. Director, Tazewell Thompson; scenic designer, Alexandre Corazzola; costume designer, Meg Zeder; and lighting designer, G. Benjamin Swope.

■ **Figure 2.14** *Coriolanus* at the Shakespeare Theatre Company in 2000. Director, Michael Kahn.

■ **Figure 2.15** *Coriolanus* at the Shakespeare Theatre Company in 1991. Director, William Gaskill.

■ **Figure 2.16** *Othello* at the Shakespeare Theatre Company in 2005. Director, Michael Kahn.
(Cast: Gregory Wood-dell, Avery Brooks, Colleen Delany, Patrick Page, and Lise Bruneau.)

■ **Figure 2.17** *Othello* at the Shakespeare Theatre Company in 1997. Director, Jude Kelly.
(Cast: George Causli and Lana Buss.)

Othello that took place eight years apart (Figures 2.16 and 2.17). Based on all our discussions in this chapter about the design process and the importance of the audience, look at the four photos and really start to "see" how the designs are different. Are the differences based on a change in the audience's expectations or changes due to the materials and techniques available, different designers, or all of these?

EXERCISES

EXERCISE 1
HIGH POINTS OF THE HUMAN CONDITION

Find visual research for each of the following that makes them personal to you:
- Birth
- Love
- Death
- Infinity

EXERCISE 2
STYLES OF ARCHITECTURE

Design a room on a stage containing a doorway with a door, a table, and a chair for three styles of architecture as shown on page 35.

EXERCISE 3
ESTABLISH A MORGUE

The set is the Throne Room in Shakespeare's *Macbeth*. Choose a time period (modern or period) and a style. Produce four or five pieces of photo research for the Throne Room that show your concept for the sets, lighting, or costumes.

CHECK YOUR KNOWLEDGE

1. Why is collaboration so important in theatre?
2. Describe the design process using the Who, What, Where, When, Why, and How process.
3. Name the periods of architecture and explain why they are important.
4. List the orders of architecture. How do they reflect the times they come from?
5. Explain a design process in simple terms that can be used as a basis for any project.
6. Support the need for knowledge of prior designs, either specific or simply stylistically, before beginning a new design project.

- Classicism
- Collaboration
- Composite
- Concept
- Corinthian
- Deconstructivism
- Doric
- Expressionism
- Impressionism
- Ionic
- Morgue
- Naturalism
- Postmodernism
- Presentational
- Realism
- Representational
- Research
- Romanticism
- Style
- Symbol
- Tuscan

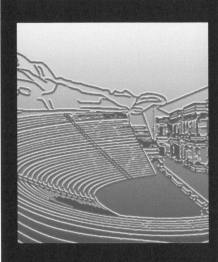

STUDY WORDS

Chapter 2

Making It Visual
Composition

Student Learning Outcomes

The next logical step in the conversation is to discuss composition. Theatre is a visual art form. To plan any production, the producers must hire visual people. These people are called *designers*. Designers are visual artists who need to understand composition. Let's explore the basics of this topic. All that the audience members see and perceive is directly related to them through composition and color. Composition is the basis for all things visual. At its most basic, we can discuss whether a line is straight or curved. Does it have pattern or rhythm? This begins our discussion of composition.

Students will acquire:

- An overview understanding of the major aspects, techniques, and directions in the area of composition.

- Fundamental, conceptual understanding of the expressive possibilities of theatre.

- A working knowledge of concepts applicable to the area of composition.

> Before you compose your picture it's a good idea to ask yourself why you're doing it.
>
> **—Anonymous**

We start by defining *composition*. As simply as I can say it, composition is the placement or arrangement of objects. Objects are placed in relation to other objects to form a grouping. This grouping is called a *composition*. The goal is to inform your viewers where you would like them to look within the composition. Composition is also used to inform the audience of what is important. The theatre stage is a dynamic composition. Scenery, lighting, and actors constantly move around the stage, reconfiguring the composition. In artwork, whether it be a painting on canvas or a sculpture, compositions are static. Another word for composition is *focus*.

RULE OF THIRDS

Many factors can affect a composition. Let's start with some basics. The basic rule of composition refers us directly to the **rule of thirds**. As you start to really look at images, analyze them (Figures 3.1–3.3). Draw lines through an image both horizontally and vertically, dividing the image into thirds in both directions. Important compositional elements should be placed along these lines and especially at the intersections.

People who follow this rule believe that following it creates more tension, energy, and interest than simply centering the image in the frame.

Notice how the "focus" in both photographs is not in the center of the image. Your eye is drawn in and around the photo. In Figure 3.1, the row of boats creates the reference horizon line. The water in the background, as well as the tree line on the left and right, comes to an apex above and to the left of the boats. The tree on the left side angles in toward the center. This has the effect of leading your eye around and through the image, then bringing your eye back into the photo to start again. Figure 3.2 has a much more obvious circular composition, continually leading your eye around and around.

The goal with any good composition is to have the audience's eyes continually moving around the image from focus point to focus point. Each area within the lines could be its own smaller composition. Our instinct is to look at the center of whatever we are looking at (Figure 3.4). Think about it for a second. When you look

■ **Figure 3.1** A photograph of rowboats lined up on the shore. Analyze the composition to see what we've been discussing.

■ **Figure 3.2** A different photograph of rowboats to analyze in different ways. On the left, white lines show the rule of thirds. On the right is the same image with white lines showing the true center as well as diagonal lines. Which do you think is more dynamic?

■ **Figure 3.3** A photograph of a stone wall and sidewalk. Follow the lines of the composition. Where does the composition lead your eye?

at a person, do you look at his or her whole body? No, you look at his or her face. And, within the face, you concentrate on the eyes. The eyes are the compositional center of the face.

By keeping the main subject of the composition outside of the center area and near the intersection of the lines, you assure the viewer will look at the whole image and not be drawn toward one detail to the exclusion of all others (Figure 3.5). If you want to simplify a composition that has only one focal point, obviously the best place to put the focal point is in the center of the image. Even with the central focus, you still need to help the composition and make sure that nothing competes with the focus. Blurring or darkening the background often

■ **Figure 3.4** Stained-glass art entitled *Sunday* by Isabella Rupp. The two circles are a focal point, and the swirling lines keep your eye moving.

helps to achieve this. Changes in color from dominant to recessive will work as well.

Now, let's translate the idea to the theatre (Figure 3.6). Think about a single actor on the stage, standing at the edge of the stage on the centerline. This is one of the few situations when simplifying the composition to this extreme will work in the theatre. If used too much though, it will get boring, and the audience will get either overwhelmed or bored. Compositional variety in theatre is key.

■ **Figure 3.5** Detail of the same stonewall and sidewalk photograph from Figure 3.3. Even in this composition, follow the lines of the stones.

■ **Figure 3.6** *42nd Street* tour, 2016. Lighting designer, Ken Billington; scenic designer, Kacie Hultgren (in combination with original set designer Beowulf Boritt); and costume designer, Roger Kirk. Notice the combined composition of staging, scenery, and lighting.

PUTTING THE COMPOSITION TOGETHER

OK, that is the background information. Now the question is, how do we do it? Well, creating a composition is like putting a puzzle together. You have a whole bunch of pieces that all have to be put together in the right order to make it all work. Next, we will discuss the elements that make up a composition and allow it to be varied for effect. Composition in the theatre is slightly different in its makeup than composition in art. The elements vary slightly. Keep in mind that color, although not mentioned in detail here, is a very important part of composition. It is so important that I dedicate an entire chapter solely to it!

Nothing goes by luck in composition. It allows for no tricks. The best you can write will be the best you are.

—Henry David Thoreau, American essayist, poet, and philosopher

LINE AND DIRECTION

The first element, or puzzle piece, to consider is the line (Figure 3.7). The mathematical definition of a **line** is the shortest distance between two points. Sounds easy, right? Well, a line also has **direction**. The designer or artist often infers what that direction is, as part of the composition. Direction gives you movement. This is critical to the composition, as I said before. The use of

■ **Figure 3.7** Draw two points and connect them to form a basic line, by Salvatore Tagliarino.

■ **Figure 3.8** Basic shapes from organic to geometric, by Salvatore Tagliarino.

movement in a composition helps the viewer to know where to look next.

SHAPE

Next, let's talk about shape. **Shape** is the definition of any two-dimensional (2D) or three-dimensional (3D) object that has created an enclosed space. Keep in mind that 3D drawing is simply an illusion. The line you draw holds the shape you see (Figure 3.8). Shapes can have light or line to help define them. You have to use shadow to turn a 2D image into a 3D image by giving it volume. The shape of the highlight, middle tone, and shadow are what add up to create the illusion. Shapes can be geometric or organic. Geometric shapes have very clear edges, while organic shapes are less well defined.

The arrangement of how the shapes go together creates the image. The visual images we see are all made up of shapes. These shapes are 2D images described by a line or series of lines. When put together in the right way and the right **proportion**, they create a compositional image. You can alter the image by distorting the shapes and their arrangement—or not. It's up to you, and this is what designers experiment with to create their designs.

> No matter what the illusion created, it is a flat canvas and it has to be organized into shape.
>
> **—David Hockney,**
> **English painter, printmaker,**
> **and stage designer**

TEXTURE

Texture is our next puzzle piece. Texture represents a 3D detail that we observe in a 2D drawing (Figure 3.9). It also represents the properties that differentiate objects of similar shapes from one another. Textures can be either

■ **Figure 3.9** Leonardo da Vinci's self-portrait. Notice the many lines and how they create shapes and textures without the use of an outline.

Figure 3.10 Basic textures showing repetition of pattern, by Salvatore Tagliarino.

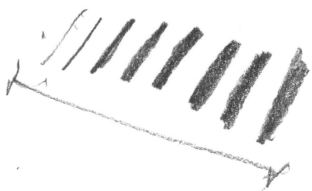

Figure 3.11 Basic line weights show thickness and darkness, by Salvatore Tagliarino.

tactile or non-tactile. Think of tactile texture as the surface detail you can feel when you touch something. It can be soft or hard, fuzzy or flat, wet or dry, and so forth.

Non-tactile textures can be patterns that can be seen but not touched. They are scaled up or down to differentiate objects when using line alone to describe the object (Figure 3.10). Keep in mind that, in two dimensions, you can only allude to real texture.

The drawings in Figure 3.10 might be grass, brick, concrete block, and stone. The difference between the brick and the block is the difference in proportion. Start keeping a mental log of everyday items and what they look like. For example, you probably have an idea in your head about the difference between traditional TV screens and high-definition (HD) sets. This is proportion, which we define in a minute. The difference between bricks versus blocks is that exact same thing. The more you keep in your mental log, the easier it will be for you to draw these things.

LINE WEIGHT

Next comes **line weight**. Any pencil, depending on its size and softness, has a thickness range it can create (Figure 3.11). **Contrast** in line weight is created by your choice of pencil and the pressure you apply as it relates to the color of the paper. This adds interest to your composition. It can also help focus the viewers' eyes. The better and more varied your line weight, the less you need other factors to define your shape. Keep in mind though, that it is just another piece to the overall puzzle. Take a look at some of the drawings by da Vinci and Raphael—look at the contrast in the line weight. It's important that they use line

weight, but it's more important *how* they use it! A single line does not have a single line weight. Each individual line can vary its weight within the distance of the line.

BALANCE AND PROPORTION

Balance is next. OK, picture an acrobat on a tightrope. That is **balance**, right? Right. It is similar in art. You have to get the composition balanced, and this usually means the contrast between all the different characteristics we already discussed. If the composition looks awkward, that means the contrast in the line, shape, texture, or line weight is out of whack.

Proportion is the most important thing and goes hand in hand with balance. **Proportion** is a mathematical thing, but you don't need a calculator to figure it out. It defines the relationship between two objects or two parts of the same object. You can measure proportion mechanically, and most people should, especially when they are first starting out. That is what a scale rule is about; that is what a tape measure is about. You might be one of those rare people who can look at something and know exactly how big it is. I can't do this, and neither can most people. So, if you can't "eyeball" the size and proportions of an object correctly, get a ruler and measure it. To relay graphical information clearly, that information, in scale or actual size, needs to be noted on the paper.

> Even in front of nature one must compose.
> —Edgar Degas,
> French painter and sculptor

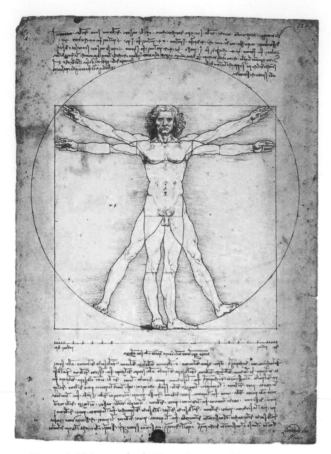

■ **Figure 3.12** Leonardo da Vinci's *Vitruvian Man*. Balance and proportion illustrated to perfection.

■ **Figure 3.13** A really cool tree showing many components of composition that we've discussed.

Let's talk for a minute about the best example of proportion known in the art world today. It is Leonardo da Vinci's *Vitruvian Man* (Figure 3.12). Vitruvius was a Roman writer, architect, and engineer born during the 1st century. He studied proportion in all things, culminating in understanding the proportions of the greatest work of art—the human body. This led Vitruvius to define verbally his concept for what has come to be known as the *Vitruvian man*. Leonardo da Vinci later illustrated this concept magnificently by showing the human body inscribed within a circle and a square.

Da Vinci's drawing is good because the line weight is good, the understanding of human anatomy is incredible, and the draftsmanship of the square and the circle is totally mathematical. Try to copy it! It may look simple, but, trust me, it's not. All the elements we've been discussing in the chapter are done to perfection in this figure. Don't be intimidated—look at the drawing. No, really look at it. Look at the line weight. See the differences in the lines that form the outside of the body versus the ones that are used for contour on the inside of the body. Look also at the lines around the body and notice how they help to set the body apart from the paper background.

OK, another way to look at proportion is to think of that gimmick when artists hold their arm out in front of themselves and look at their thumb—it is all about proportion. You can measure a tree with your thumb (Figure 3.13). It could be five thumbs tall versus three thumbs wide. This is a different way to measure the world, similar to using a tape measure or scale rule. All of these are just different techniques or tools. Each is valid and appropriate. You just have to determine which is right for which situation.

PATTERN

Our next puzzle piece is pattern. A **pattern** is a repeated element within a composition, such as a stripe or zigzag (Figure 3.14). Make any shape; if you repeat it, it becomes a pattern. Think about wallpaper or fabric for a second. They contain great examples of repeating patterns. Patterns can be horizontal, vertical, or diagonal. Plaids are complex patterns made up of various line weights and textures, assembled into a grid pattern. They can be symmetrical or not, according to choice.

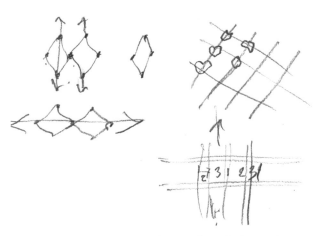

■ **Figure 3.14** Basic patterns that can form the basis of a composition, by Salvatore Tagliarino.

SCALE

Scale is the next piece to the puzzle. Scale is a term that relates to how big or small the object is, as well as the drawing of the object. In patterns, the scale is often determined by the spacing of the repeats that create the pattern. The world we live in has a set scale. In set design, the measure of the scale is the human being. In theatre, we generally use 6 feet as the height of a "standard" person. When we are determining relationships and the surrounding proportions, the 6-foot human height divides out easily in halves: 3 feet + 3 feet. A standard chair seat height is 16–18 inches. Tabletops are generally 30 inches high. The height and width of doors, windows, and other architectural elements are all based on this same scale. How the human body moves and bends determines how all of these details come together. A comedian once said, "Imagine what chairs would look like if our knees bent the other way." I rest my case—it's all about the scale of the human body. Pay attention to people who are above or below the average height. Notice how they appear to relate very differently to their environment just based on their size.

> **Man is the measure of all things.**
>
> **—Vitruvius,**
> **Roman author and architect**

It's all about the human ratio and how it translates onto the stage! Fashion designers aren't costume designers. Architects aren't set designers. Marc Chagall and David Hockney bridged the gap between the art world and the theatre world. They took visual style based on good line weight, proportion, and the like and, with help, translated the ideas into stage sets.

Now, let's put it all together: Line, direction, shape, texture, line weight, balance, proportion, pattern, and scale. These are the pieces of a composition. You can put them together in an infinite variety of ways to create the compositions that are in your head. The way to put the pieces together to form a good composition is by using contrast to create an emphasis or focus.

Theatre Traditions: Break a Leg

One possible explanation for this expression is its relation to "taking a knee," which itself has roots in chivalry. Meeting royalty, one would "take a knee"—in other words, bend down on one knee. That breaks the line of the leg, hence "break a leg," a wish that the performer will do so well that he or she will need to take bows.

Both kinds of balance also exist in costume design and in lighting design. A symmetrical scenic space can be lit asymmetrically to provide interest as the play or ballet or opera moves along—as a long room with windows at either end, perfectly balanced and symmetrical, will reshape according to the sunlight coming through the windows at different times of day.

Occult balance requires a discerning eye to discover how to balance the elements in a pleasing arrangement, one that keeps the eye in motion. On a costume, finding the perfect spot on the shoulder of an evening gown to attach a floral corsage demands an eye for occult balance. Where we place furniture in a box set to balance the doors and window openings and provide interesting places for the actors to sit and stand and move requires a pictorial eye for balance—both symmetrical and occult.

EXERCISES

EXERCISES 1–3: THRONE ROOM

Using Macbeth's Throne Room again, and in a style of your choosing, create the following:
1. Two drawings using two differing kinds of contrast.
2. Two drawings using two differing kinds of line weights.
3. Two drawings using two differing styles of proportion.

CHECK YOUR KNOWLEDGE

1. What is the purpose of composition as it relates to theatre?
2. What are the elements of composition? Define each with examples.
3. Which element of composition is not listed in this chapter? Why?
4. Illustrate a symmetrical and an occult composition using various elements of composition.
5. Discuss why da Vinci's *Vitruvian Man* is considered the best example of proportion.
6. Relate the human proportion to theatrical design citing instances of its importance.

- Balance
- Contrast
- Direction
- Emphasis
- Line
- Line weight
- Pattern
- Proportion
- Rule of thirds
- Scale
- Shape
- Texture

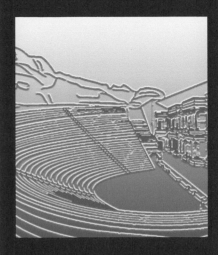

STUDY WORDS

Chapter 3

Black and White Are Colors Too!

Color Theory

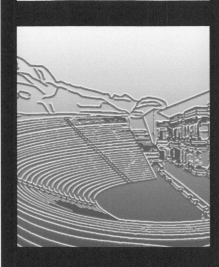

CHAPTER FOUR

Student Learning Outcomes

Students will acquire:

- An overview understanding of the major aspects, techniques, and directions in the area of color.

- Fundamental, conceptual understanding of the expressive possibilities of theatre.

- A working knowledge of concepts applicable to the area of color.

A whole chapter on color! Why, you may ask—you just want to learn how to build scenery. Well, if you want to work in any of the departments in a theatre, you need to know about color. The scene shop doesn't just build the scenery and props; it also paints them. The costume shop deals with color in the fabrics, threads, and accessories. The lighting department uses gel. And don't even get me started on the makeup department, where it is all about color! We think we know all about color from the moment we open our eyes and begin to see. Yeah, you know all about color—the grass is green, the sky is blue.

> Mere color, unspoiled by meaning, and unallied with definite form, can speak to the soul in a thousand different ways.
>
> —Oscar Wilde,
> Irish playwright, novelist, essayist, and poet

Color helps us perceive, distinguish, and recognize everything in the world around us. If you look at something in the distance,

Figure 4.1 A beautiful sunset overlooking the Hudson River.

Figure 4.2 The same sunset photo as Figure 4.1 *but* converted to black and white. A very different impact!

you may recognize it by its color long before you can actually "see" what it is. In fact, advertisers depend on this ability. Think of your favorite fast food restaurant or your favorite snack food.

The logo jumps into your head, doesn't it? These are all images that are recognizable while driving on the highway at 55 mph—or faster. Now try something a little different. Imagine the world without color for a while! It's a strange concept, I know. It's hard to picture the world in black and white.

Everybody loves a good sunset. Think about the most beautiful sunset you have ever seen. It can be a sunset at the beach, in the mountains, in the woods, or even a skyline of a big city (Figure 4.1). Any sunset will do. How does it make you feel? Is it pretty, or relaxing, or peaceful? Maybe it's even romantic. Now try to analyze the sunset you are imagining. Picture all the rich and vibrant colors: The reds, oranges, and yellows. Think about how those colors contrast with whatever small amount of blue is left in the sky.

What a nice sunset Figure 4.1 shows. Is it similar to what you were picturing in your head? If it is different, the differences are most likely in the subject matter, not the color. Now, let's put a twist on our image. What happens if we take away the color? Imagine if that image were in black and white. Take a look at Figure 4.2.

Pretty different image, no? Suddenly, the thoughts that come to mind are ominous, scary, and dark. What happened to pretty, relaxing, and peaceful? Those warm and fuzzy feelings disappear when the color does. This is why I say that color helps us perceive the world. We take

Figure 4.3 If you eliminate all the color, an orange and a grapefruit can look pretty similar. Can you tell which is which?

color for granted. We see it everywhere, and we know what an object is not just by its shape but also by its color.

And, that is only one example. Let's try it a different way. Think about the differences between an orange and a grapefruit. They can be about the same shape and have similar texture, but they are usually different sizes and different colors, right? What if you put a large orange and a small grapefruit side by side and photographed them in black and white (Figure 4.3)?

PIGMENT AND LIGHT

Color is often organized and displayed using something called a *color wheel*. The important thing to know right away is that there are actually two color wheels. Yes, that

■ **Figure 4.4** Primary color wheel for pigment.

■ **Figure 4.5** Secondary color wheel for pigment.

is right—there are two color wheels. There is the color wheel most of us are familiar with, the one for paint or pigment. The other color wheel is for light. It can be confusing when you are first learning it, but stay with me and I'll explain it.

The way you are most likely accustomed to using color is based on the pigment color wheel. The first three colors to know are the **primary** colors (Figure 4.4). Primaries are colors that cannot be created by mixing any other colors together. The primary colors in pigment are red, blue, and yellow.

> There is no blue without yellow and without orange.
>
> **—Vincent Van Gogh,
> Dutch Post-Impressionist painter**

The next three colors to learn are the **secondary** colors (Figure 4.5). Combining any two primary colors creates a secondary color. Secondary colors in pigment are purple, green, and orange. If you compare the two figures

showing primary and secondary colors, you will see how mixing any two primary colors creates a secondary color. If you take red and blue and mix them together, you get purple. Mix blue and yellow, you get green. Mix yellow and red, you get orange. It's that easy! At least, it's that easy at first.

So, basically, you mix two colors together, and their sum total becomes a new and unique third color. You can take two secondary colors and mix them together. The result is that you have now created what is called a **tertiary** color. In this way, you can continually divide the color wheel into smaller and smaller sections. Mixing color in this way is known as **subtractive** mixing. Simply explained, subtractive color mixing means that, when all three primary colors are mixed together in equal parts they "theoretically" make black. Thus, you are always mixing toward black, which equals subtractive color mixing.

OK, now that you have the basics, let us mix it up a little. The primary colors in light (instead of pigment) are red, blue, and green (Figure 4.6). That is right, green, not yellow. Secondary colors in light are magenta, cyan, and yellow (Figure 4.7). Of course, we need different color wheels now that we have different primary colors.

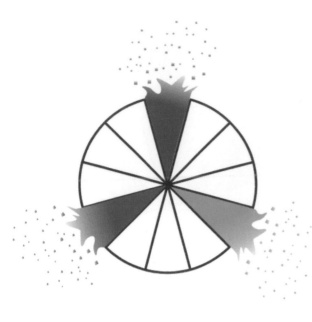

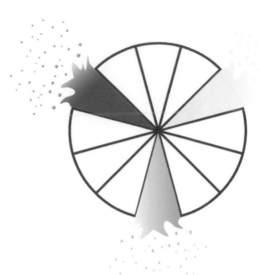

Figure 4.6 Primary color wheel for light.

Figure 4.7 Secondary color wheel for light.

Figure 4.8 Full color wheel for pigment. Notice how, when the colors overlap, they combine to form other colors using the subtractive method of mixing.

Figure 4.9 Full color wheel for light. Notice how, when the colors overlap, they combine to form other colors using the additive method of mixing.

■ **Figure 4.10** Primary green hue shown on backgrounds of black, white, blue, red, and yellow. Notice how different the green seems against differing hues, and the extreme contrast between the complementary colors of green and red.

Although the primary colors of light may be different, mixing the secondary colors happens the exact same way.

Another difference between pigment and light that continues the confusion is that color mixing in light is called **additive**, not subtractive. Additive color mixing means that, when all three primary colors of light are mixed together in equal parts, they theoretically make white light. The next step is where it can get very tricky. You can also do subtractive color mixing in light. Are you ready for this one? If you put one piece of color in front of a light, it is considered additive color mixing. If you put two pieces of color in front of the same light, you've now changed into subtractive color mixing for that one light. That means you change back to the pigment color wheel and all the rules that go along with it.

Making black paint or white light by mixing all the respective color wheel's primaries is theoretical at best. Making black or white in this manner really works properly only in a laboratory with the purest version of each color. It is interesting to try it, though, and see the results. If you try to do this in a theater or shop, you will most likely get a murky brown or a tinted version of white.

The full color wheel, meaning 12 colors, looks very similar to a rainbow. Look at Figures 4.8 and 4.9. Start at one color and work your way around to see how each color progresses from one to the next. Can you see how mixing two colors together can make the one in between? Is it starting to make sense?

Now that we have learned the basics of color theory, let's move on to the next principle. **Complementary** colors are those colors that are opposite each other on the full color wheel, as shown in Figures 4.8 and 4.9. For example, in pigment, red and green are complementary. Purple and yellow are as well. Complementary colors, when paired together, make each separate color appear more vibrant. They achieve this vibrancy because they have no colors in common. That is why they are opposite on the color wheel. Remember how they are made? Think of some typical color pairings for holidays, sports teams, or corporate logos. Often you will see complementary colors or a primary color combined with white or black. These combinations tend to "pop" and be more recognizable (Figure 4.10). That makes it more memorable, which is the kind of recognition a logo wants.

TINTS, SHADES, AND TONES

Let's explain some more definitions for various terms used to describe color. These terms work for either pigment or light. **Hue** is another word for color. *Color* and *hue* can be used interchangeably. Say, your favorite color is green, then your favorite hue is also green. A **tint** is a hue mixed with white. We often think of these as pastel colors. When any amount of white is added, the

■ **Figure 4.11** Paint samples of four different greens. From left to right: Primary green, green tint, green tone, and green shade.

hue is called a *tint*. The opposite of a tint is a **shade**. A shade is a hue mixed with black. Tones exist between tints and shades. A **tone** is a hue mixed with gray.

Saturation describes the amount of pure color a hue contains. **Chroma** is a word often used instead of *saturation*; they can be used interchangeably. It is a term that describes a hue in its purest form. Primary colors are very saturated; they have a high chroma level (Figure 4.11). Tints, shades, and tones are all less saturated because, by definition, they are a hue mixed with something else. Tones are the colors we see most often in everyday items such as clothing, cars, and houses. They are muted and tend to be less vibrant. The color makes less of a statement or impact. They, therefore, appeal more to our general sensibilities.

Two other color terms to be aware of are value and intensity. **Value** is the lightness or darkness of a color. **Intensity** is the brightness or dullness of a color. These two terms help describe our perception of a color. This perception dictates how we react to colors. For example, green is the color of money, the color of greed, and the color of envy. Green is also the color of grass, leaves, and much of nature. Each of these items contains different tints, tones, and shades of green, with differing values and intensities that give each item its individual characteristics.

When an entire composition is made up of tints, shades, and tones of the same hue, it is called a **monochromatic** composition. Each single color on the color wheel can have an infinite number of variations.

■ **Figure 4.12** *The Sorcerer*, by Michael A. Fink, is an example of an analogous composition with a one-color contrast.

The color violet, for example, can range from a shade of deep eggplant to a tint of light lavender. Using variations like this of a single color can create a monochromatic design.

> In a sense, light makes potential colors into actual colors.
>
> —Aristotle,
> **Ancient Greek philosopher and scientist**

Often, to create more interest, you will want to use a number of different hues, instead of just one, but still from within the same area of the color wheel. This is called an **analogous** color palette. To take your design to the next level of color contrast, and therefore add more interest, add one more step to the process. For this technique to work, design your background with analogous colors. Then, pick one item in the foreground, the focal point of your image, and make it an entirely different hue. This contrast helps to focus the eye on your chosen point. See an example of this in Figure 4.12.

Figure 4.12 uses a palette of almost exclusively cool colors. There is a range of blues and greens that make up almost 85 percent of the image. The central focus of the composition is all pinks and oranges. Notice how your eye keeps returning to the center. This is because it is the area of highest color contrast. The rest of the composition helps to focus your eye, as some of the lines point toward the center. Without the color contrast in the center, this would not be nearly as interesting an image. Color is really an amazing thing. It can focus your eye and it can sway your emotions. Color, just simple color, can do all that.

INTERPRETING COLOR

Interpreting color is the next step in our discussion. We start by dividing colors into cool and warm. It sounds easy, and it is, to a point. Warm colors are reds, oranges, and yellows. Cool colors are greens, blues, and purples. Now, here is the confusing part. Within the hue of red, for example, there are cool reds and warm reds. This goes

■ **Figure 4.13** Example of three different reds. The top center is primary red. The bottom left is a cool red created when primary red is mixed with a little blue. The bottom right is a warm red created when primary red is mixed with a little yellow. Can you start to see how purple and orange are made?

for every color! It's really all about contrast again. If you put a warm red next to a cool red, you will see them both in comparison to the other (Figure 4.13). It is an exercise for your eyes to play with. Look out at someone's front yard or into the woods behind your house. How many different greens do you see?

Theatre Traditions: Green Is a Bad Color

Don't wear green onstage. Actors used to perform outdoors on the green grass, so actors wearing green weren't seen very well. Also, a green light was often used to illuminate characters, and this limelight would make anyone wearing green appear practically invisible.

When working on a color composition, you should think about warm and cool colors. These two ideas can help you to choose the right color for a specific part of your design. Cool and warm colors also have emotional impact. A warm color palette can often benefit from a touch of coolness to create balance. Warm colors are more dominant and tend to appear as if they are coming toward you. That also means warm colors are more challenging, more energized, more vivid. Cool colors are more recessive and tend to appear as if they are receding into the background. This also means that cool colors are more calming, more soothing. Similarly, a cool palette can be livened up by a touch of warmth. Look again at the image of *The Sorcerer* in Figure 4.12. Try to imagine it without the warm colors in the middle. Very different, right?

All of these words have emotional counterparts that go along. This is how we react to color and, more important, why we react to color. Color choices you make, from what you wear to your car or the paint you choose for your room, all define who you are and how other people will react to you. Keep your eyes open for color all around you. Look at the clothing you are wearing. What color choices did you make this morning? What about your classmates or your teacher? Look at the color choices in your classroom. Why do you think the school chose those colors?

Colors can also have very specific meanings. Some meanings have a historical basis. Other meanings may be cultural and will vary from one country to another. For example, in the United States, the traditional color for a funeral is black, while in China the funeral color is white. Red can mean anger, danger, warning, or passion, depending on how it is used. Think for a second about a traditional traffic light: Red means stop, yellow means caution, green means go. Where else in your life do these colors have the same meanings?

BLACK AND WHITE

Now that we're beginning to get a handle on color, let's leave it behind for a second. Isn't this a chapter on color? To better understand color, we need to better understand black and white. Most people think black and white are not colors. Now, you know better, based on our color wheels. We know that, in pigment, black is the presence of all color. Even though it may seem strange, we also know that, in light, the presence of all color is white. We also talked about tints, shades, and tones, all of which have to do with the amount of black and white added to a color. So, let's spend a little time talking about the grayscale chart.

■ **Figure 4.14** A grayscale chart from black to white in 10 percent increments.

Figure 4.14 is a **grayscale** chart showing stepped gradations from black to white. Moving from left to right, each successive tint has 10 percent more white added to the black until we finally reach pure white. When different gray samples are organized like this, it is a called a *grayscale chart*. Often, these charts are used to calibrate computer monitors, printers, and much more. A very important thing to know is where a color falls on this grayscale chart (Figures 4.15 and 4.16). When you are combining colors to create interest, you will be far more successful if the colors are also in different areas of the grayscale chart. This is where tints, shades, and tones come into practice. From primary red to the palest pink, these colors are all based on the same hue. However, they create interest in different ways dependent on their value and intensity.

Did you think red and green would be so dark in black and white? Did you think they would be almost the same value? Did you think yellow would look almost white? These details are important to know and remember. Colors are tied not only to our designs but also to our emotions. All the qualities of a particular color—not just the actual hue but all its inherent qualities—inform how perception happens.

Perception is the key to it all. As you paint (whether it is with pigment or light), you may perceive a color as burgundy or dark red or a shade of red. Someone else may look at the same color and perceive it as a warm brown. All your intended emotions associated with using red are now thrown out the window. If you want your ideas to be clear, the implementation of your ideas must be clear as well. Your intentions need to be informed by how others may choose to perceive any individual part of your work. Simply put, know your audience. Their reaction to your choices is really what matters most.

How we perceive color is critical. Let's talk a little more about perception. **White balance** is a phrase often used when shooting video or film, but it is equally important to us in the theatre. You "teach" your camera (or in our

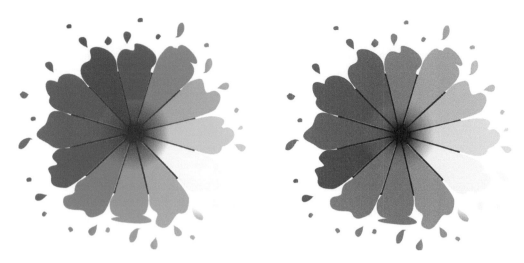

■ **Figure 4.15** Pigment color wheel in color, left, and converted to grayscale, right.

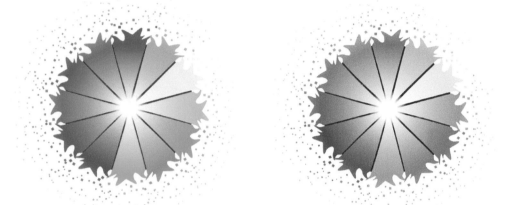

■ **Figure 4.16** Light color wheel in color, left, and converted to grayscale, right.

■ **Figure 4.17** The same photo, without white balancing the camera, taken under three different kinds of light. See how the entire image is changed. Which one is "right"? Answer: *None* and *all*.

case, our eyes) what white really looks like, then all other colors are seen in relation, or in perspective, to this newly defined "white." If you don't teach the camera what white looks like, it will mistake a different color for white, and your whole image will be altered (Figure 4.17).

REFERENCE WHITE

Reference white can be a bit confusing to wrap your head around, so let's take this slowly. There is no right or wrong, only what you intended. *White balance* and reference white are terms linked to each other as a baseline for all that we see and how we compare colors. Consider white balance to be the standard by which you judge all other colors. In actuality, "white" may not exist in your work. If so, then the reference you establish can be any color you want the audience to perceive as white.

■ **Figure 4.18** Eight steps from white to magenta are used to illustrate that reference white can really be any color you choose it to be.

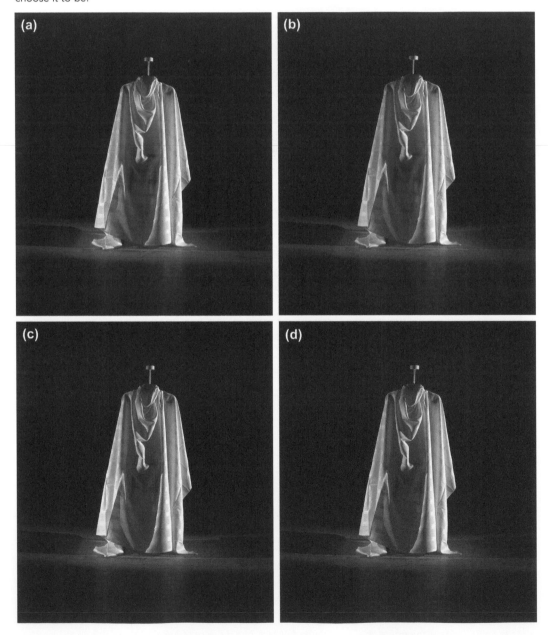

The white reference can change dramatically depending on what it is next to in a composition. Almost any color can be made to look white, simply by putting a color next to it that is more saturated.

In Figure 4.18, I demonstrate this concept in a series of steps to show how quickly your eye can get used to a certain color. As your eye adjusts, it tends to desaturate the color. This means it pulls the chroma out of a given color, making it appear paler to the eye. Look at the photos one at a time. Cover up all the photos, except the first, with your hand. Then, slowly move your eye

White is not a mere absence of color; it is a shining and affirmative thing, as fierce as red, as definite as black.

—Gilbert K Chesterton,
English writer, poet, dramatist,
and art critic

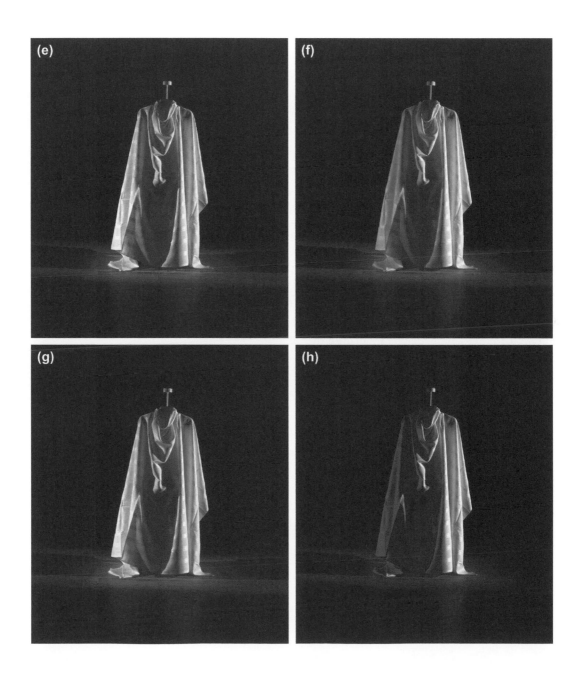

from one photo to the next as you uncover them. Isn't it amazing how white, pink, and magenta can all change their appearance from being saturated to being white? I go back and do this exercise all the time, and it never fails to amaze me how much the human eye wants to adjust everything it sees so that there is a reference white.

This demonstration is created in a very simple, methodical way. Let me explain how it works. You set up a mannequin at center stage with a white cloth draped around it. Then, you add a white light from one side. *White* in this instance means that there is no color in front of either light. The only color comes from the inherent qualities of the lightbulb. Now, you have the basic setup.

The next step is for you to add the palest pink you can find to the light on the other side. Notice what appears to happen to the color of the light. Find a pink that is slightly more saturated and put it on the first light. Look. Observe. The other side now looks white, even though you know it still has a pink color. Continue substituting more saturated pinks, alternating one side at a time, slowly progressing all the way to magenta. Look very closely at each step along the way. One color may look very pink. Then, you change the color on the opposite side, and suddenly the first color looks like white.

I have one last image for you on the topic of color. Keep in mind all that you learned in this chapter. Don't take color for granted. Remember for a second how you thought of color before reading this chapter. Now, look closely at Figure 4.19. Start immediately to analyze the color with your new knowledge and skills. What hues are used? How are they organized? What hues are next to what other hues? How does that affect your perception? What emotions do you feel as you look at it?

EXERCISES

EXERCISE 1
GRAYSCALE

Make a grayscale using black and white paint. Create a ten-step gradient from all black to all white. Then, create a 30-step gradient from all black to all white.

EXERCISE 2
TINT SCALE

Make a tint scale using a single color and white. Create a ten-step gradient from all color to all white. Then, create a 30-step gradient from all color to all white.

EXERCISE 3
SHADE SCALE

Make a shade scale using a single color and white. Create a ten-step gradient from all color to all black. Then, create a 30-step gradient from all color to all black.

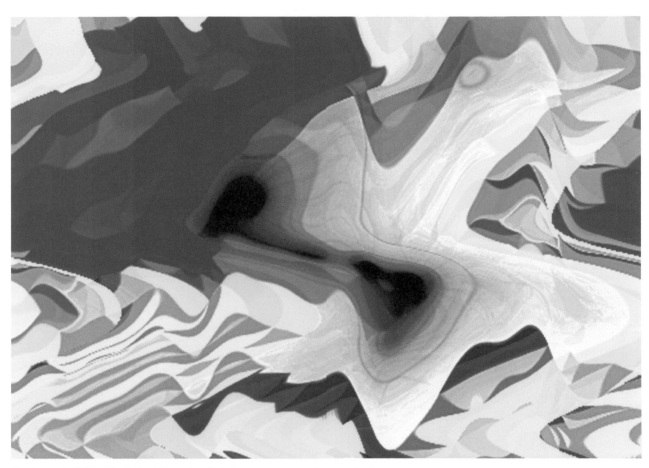

■ **Figure 4.19** *The Turtle*, by Michael A Fink, is a gorgeous explosion of color.

CHECK YOUR KNOWLEDGE

1. Evaluate how different colors represent and/or elicit differing emotions.
2. Summarize the differences between the pigment color wheel and the light color wheel.
3. Is there a way to redesign the color wheel and combine pigment and light into one wheel? Why or why not?
4. Discuss subtractive versus additive color mixing with real-life examples.
5. Justify how black and white are also colors. Why are they not on the color wheel?
6. Based on your current knowledge, explain how you could establish yellow as reference white. What ramifications would this have?

- Additive
- Analogous
- Chroma
- Complementary
- Grayscale
- Hue
- Intensity
- Monochromatic
- Primary
- Reference white
- Saturation
- Secondary
- Shade
- Subtractive
- Tertiary
- Tint
- Tone
- Value
- White balance

STUDY WORDS

Chapter 4

Creating the Stage Picture

Drawing, Rendering, and Drafting

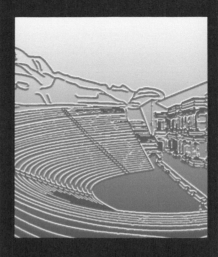

CHAPTER FIVE

Student Learning Outcomes

So, you have all these great ideas. How do you get these wonderful ideas out of your head and into the theatre? We jump right into our discussion of drafting, drawing, and rendering. This is the first tangible step for any designer. You have to get the ideas out of your head and onto paper or at least onto the computer screen. That is the only way others can see *visually* what you've been describing *verbally*. The traditional way to do this was with a pencil and a piece of paper. And many designers still work this way. A more updated way is to use computer-aided drawing and drafting (CAD) software, photo manipulation software, as well as other programs written specifically for the theatre. The goal of creating drawings and draftings, no matter how you do it, is still very simple. Get the ideas out of your head so they can be approved by the director and realized by the shop.

Students will acquire:

- An overview understanding of the major aspects, techniques, software, and directions in the area of drawing, rendering, and drafting.

- Fundamental, conceptual understanding of the expressive possibilities of theatre.

- A working knowledge of concepts and equipment applicable to the area of drawing, rendering, and drafting.

When I sit alone in a theater and gaze into the dark space of its empty stage, I'm frequently seized by fear that this time I won't manage to penetrate it, and I always hope that this fear will never desert me. Without an unending search for the key to the secret of creativity, there is no creation. It's necessary always to begin again. And that is beautiful.

—Josef Svoboda,
Czech artist and scenic designer

■ **Figure 5.1** Gustav Rehberger was my drawing instructor at the Art Students League in New York City. He drew this sketch in two minutes, without a model!

Semantics can be a nasty word. Picture this: You and the director are having your first conversation. He or she says his or her favorite color is green. They want the whole set to be green. Let us ignore their motivation for a second. If you are not careful, you'll walk away from this meeting thinking, OK, I can do that. Then, at the next meeting, when you show the director your sketch in glorious sage green, he or she screams in horror and says, "Not that green!" Theatre is a visual business—I said it before and I say it again. Theatre, film, and television all use the same visual disciplines. Drawing, drafting, and rendering are how you express yourself to the director. Keep in mind that, for some designers, visual imagery is the product!

Sometimes, words just don't cut it. Remember the saying "A picture is worth a thousand words"? Well, it sure is true. Your ideas will come across much clearer if they are presented in a visual way. That is what this chapter is all about. So, let's get on with it.

What is the big deal about drawing? You don't like to draw? You think you are no good at it? Well, here is the scoop. Drawing is simply combining writing and seeing. You can use drawing as an exercise to better look and see. The more closely you observe the world around you, the better you can describe it visually to others. Don't give up on drawing and sketching because you think you can't do it. It takes practice like everything else. But, it is some of the best training I ever received (Figure 5.1).

WHAT ARE THE DIFFERENCES?

Drawing, drafting, and rendering—let's break them down and discuss the basic ideas of each before moving on to the technical how-to. **Drawing** is often used interchangeably with sketching. I find it interesting that the dictionary tends to define *draw* as a pulling toward yourself. The artistic definition of to draw is much further down the list. Well, think about it for a second. Maybe we can use that part of the definition to indicate that we are pulling our ideas together and allowing them to form outside of our heads. Esoteric at best, but I think there is something interesting and important in this concept. **Sketch** has similar combinations of definitions. It is not only defined as a rough drawing but as a brief description. Here is another word we use—**render**. Today, we instantly think of a computer-generated image. From the dictionary, this time I find one meaning for render is to give back. I like that—giving back. I think, in a way, that is the key to design in a nutshell. Lastly, we get to drafting. In racing, *draft* means to stay close behind. Well, drafting—or technical drawing—is usually done shortly after the drawing and rendering are complete.

Now that we know how these terms are defined and why they are important to us, the next question is, how do we do them? In grammar school, you are taught how to write the alphabet and the numerals. These are the basic and most simplistic forms of communication. From those building blocks, you learn how to read and write. You still have to have some information (dog, cat, tree) to turn the information into a vocabulary. Drawing and painting are exactly the same. First of all, you need to have a graphic alphabet for it to work. The graphic alphabet is made up of all the things we discussed in Chapter 3 on composition and Chapter 4 on color.

Now you need the ideas for the information you want to write down. Drawing equals information. Take stock of your design and what details need to be conveyed. This is the information you need to have straight in your head. The better your information, the better the drawing. Masters of the art world such as Raphael, da Vinci, and Michelangelo were so good at this that the information they relayed to us was sublime. Once you reach sublime, you've got *art*. This level of drawing shows information that is so well organized, the transfer of information to the audience is perfectly clear. Keep in mind that sublime is very hard to achieve, but, as long as we keep striving for it, we might just make it.

Let's talk about insight for a moment. Insight is key to designing for the theatre as well as being a technician. Insight is observing the world around you and forming opinions. We do it every day. Most of the time, we don't realize we are doing it. Theater artists need to consciously observe every small detail of the world around them. We then need to take that information and form an opinion. One of the reasons Shakespeare's writing is so eternally viable is that it's poetry, good poetry. But also, and more important, he had an amazing insight into the human condition. He could observe and form opinions. Then, he translated these observations into amazing literary pieces. This is our hope. To observe, form opinions, and translate them onto the stage. Easy, right? Not exactly.

Drawing is like a puzzle, where you need all these characteristics, or pieces, to have a chance at making it good (Figure 5.2). All of these things coming together make a good design. You have to work your way to "good" using all these techniques and parts of the process we discussed earlier. The visual context we all grew up in (our family, neighborhood, time frame) is the one we memorize. What we call good art and bad art is a matter of taste based on context. Most people criticize art based on the information that is either clearly conveyed or not. Does it look like a rabbit or a chair? Any artist who starts a new style is often thought to be crazy. It seems to take about 40 years for the general public to accept something new and catch up. When you have time, look up the following artists: Pollock, Rothko, Warhol, and Seurat. They all started new movements in the art world, and it took quite some time for their work to be accepted.

Look! Look at everything! Remember things! Make your eye your strongest instrument, because it's through looking at what you see that you're able to absorb and use it. I'm never bored at airports—I spend my time looking at people and thinking, "Now what do they do?" and "Why did they choose to wear that?" and "Who are they?"

—Jane Greenwood,
British costume designer

■ **Figure 5.2** A lighting sketch for *Ancient Voice of Children*.

SAL'S TEST

Let's put all this information to work for us. Are you ready? Here is your first test, and the most enjoyable test you'll ever take. On a piece of paper, draw four things: A cube, a chair, a rabbit, and a human being. Now, I have to acknowledge that the test is not my own idea. Sal Tagliarino, one of my instructors from NYU, came up with this idea. I love it so much. I use it all the time and think it is an important idea to put into this book. Now, draw your four images. When you're done, keep reading.

OK, now, look at your drawing. This test is all about a way of learning to think and create. The outcome of those two things should be a relay of information. The test is used to explain information. Remember what I said earlier: Every day you should be observing and forming opinions. The test gives you several challenges

that are easily solved if you've been observing the world around you and forming opinions.

Let's take each of the drawings individually. The cube is all about mathematical information. You can't even draw a cube properly unless you have a basic understanding of plane geometry and have learned the rules of 3D constructs. Keep in mind that it also helps to observe items in the world around you, such as cardboard boxes, and notice how they are made as well. A cube, by definition, is the same exact length on all sides. A cube has a ratio of 1:1:1. This is very specific. If the cube you drew has a ratio closer to 1:1:2, then it's a rectangle box, not a cube. Understand?

The chair is structural information. This is the kind of information that architects use the most. There are all sorts of rules that govern this. Gravity, strength, and balance come to mind. Does your chair look like it will

■ **Figure 5.3** Albrecht Dürer's *Hare*, 1502.

float away? Does it look like someone could actually sit in it without it breaking? Does it look like all the feet touch the floor? Now, here is the hard question: Does it look like a "specific" chair?

The rabbit is organic. Most people tend to draw a cute rabbit because they have no good reference of stock information in their head about rabbits. How many of us were lucky enough to grow up seeing rabbits every day? I bet your drawing is good if you had a pet rabbit when you were younger. The more you are exposed to something, the more time you have to observe it and file that information away for a later time.

The artist Albrecht Dürer didn't make things up. He observed a rabbit to make his drawing, shown in Figure 5.3. If you observe what exists and you like it, methodically note it down with lines in the correct proportion you observe—your drawing should be as good as the thing you're copying if you copy the right proportion. If you do not copy the right proportion, you mess up. Now compare Dürer's very famous *Hare* with your little bunny rabbit. What are the differences? And don't fall into the trap of saying, "His is better than mine!" That is not the point of what we are doing. The point is not only to look but to *see* the differences. A major difference is most likely in the details. Dürer has drawn almost every hair. He has obviously studied this hare. Look further for ways to compare your drawing to his. What about the parts of the body? For example, did you draw a short-eared bunny or a long-eared one? Look at your line weight, shape, and value. Now look at Dürer's.

Now for the last drawing: The human being. We all know what they look like, right? I mean, honestly, we are human beings! But, have you ever taken the time to really look at the proportions of the human being? From a mathematical point of view it's pretty amazing. Symmetry is considered to equal beauty. You may not like an individual's specific symmetry, but we are all based on a symmetrical mold. Of course, everybody has variations here or there, so let's take a look for a second at the ideal person. No, it's not a supermodel!

PUTTING IT IN PROPORTION

Leonardo da Vinci read a paper by a Roman architect named Vitruvius. In his paper, Vitruvius described the basic proportions for the male human body and related them to mathematical calculations. For your reference, the box has an excerpt from Vitruvius's paper so you can see exactly what da Vinci read.

> The navel is naturally the exact centre of the body. For if a man lies on his back with hands and feet outspread, and the centre of a circle is placed on his navel, his fingers and toes will be touched by the circumference. Also a square will be found described within the figure, in the same way as a round figure is produced. For if we measure from the sole of the foot to the top of the head, and apply the measure to the outstretched hands, the breadth will be found equal to the height, just like sites which are squared by rule.
> **—Vitruvius Marcus Vitruvius Pollio, Roman author, architect, engineer**

Da Vinci chose to try to illustrate this theory and called it the *Vitruvian Man*. The basic information from the full text goes something like this:

- A palm is the width of four fingers
- A foot is the width of four palms
- A cubit (term for a measurement) is the width of six palms
- A man's height is 4 cubits or 24 palms
- A pace is 4 cubits
- The length of a man's outspread arms is equal to his height
- The distance from the hairline to the bottom of the chin is one-tenth of a man's height
- The distance from the top of the head to the bottom of the chin is one-eighth of a man's height
- The maximum width of the shoulders is one-quarter of a man's height
- The distance from the elbow to the tip of the hand is one-fifth of a man's height
- The distance from the elbow to the armpit is one-eighth of a man's height
- The length of the hand is one-tenth of a man's height
- The distance from the bottom of the chin to the nose is one-third of the length of the head
- The distance from the hairline to the eyebrows is one-third of the length of the face
- The length of the ear is one-third of the length of the face

Yikes! I bet you didn't realize drawing had anything to do with math. Drawing does have to do with observing. Any "tool" you use to help you observe is a valid tool. Math helps. So use it. Reread that list; take it slowly, and I bet it will all start to make sense. Go look at a photograph of yourself. Check the measurements—I bet they are pretty close. Now, here is the thing, no one is actually perfect. But, we are all based on the same mold.

The *Vitruvian Man* is the perfect blending of art and science. Mathematical precision and a keen interest in proportion are what drove da Vinci forward with this piece. This is clear observation. You need to use everything at your disposal to truly observe the world around you. Here is a fun idea: Wait until next year, then take Sal's test again. Don't wait for a teacher. Just do it. Keep the one you just finished. Put it away somewhere. Then, next year, do another test and compare them. I bet with every succeeding year your observations will be keener and more accurate. Notice I didn't say *better*. *Better* is relative.

VARIOUS SUPPLIES AND TOOLS

We start our next section by talking about what is involved in drawing, rendering, and drafting. It is important to have all the tools you need within reach so you need not hunt around for something at a critical moment of creative inspiration. This is the point where you have to start making choices. Many tools achieve similar results, but one is usually more appropriate for the job than another. If you have to go from New York City to Chicago, you could fly, drive, take a train, ride your bike, or walk. All these options get you to Chicago. Your choice depends greatly on the circumstances of your travel. Do you have to arrive by a certain time? Is your budget limited? Are you participating in a marathon fundraiser? Many things affect your choices. Got it?

Start with writing implements. You can use anything that leaves a mark. Of course, pens and pencils are much easier than grabbing a big hunk of burnt wood and trying to write with that. So, let us explore the options that are a little more realistic. I like to break them down into two categories: dry stuff and wet stuff.

DRY STUFF

Pencils

Let's start with pencils. You may be thinking, "Yeah, yeah, I know what a pencil is." I'm sure you do. But, do you know how many different kinds of pencils there are? The basic pencil that most people know has a graphite core surrounded by hexagonal-shaped wood with a pink eraser at the opposite end. If you've ever taken a standardized test in school and they required you to use a "#2 pencil," this is the kind of pencil you used. Did you ever wonder what that "2" stood for?

Pencil graphite is labeled by hardness (Figure 5.4). The harder the lead, the lighter the mark it makes. Conversely, the softer the lead, the darker the mark. Leads are divided into three groupings. The middle range we use mostly to write with consists of H (harder), F (fine), and HB and B (blacker). Pencils ranging from 2B to 9B are softer and are used primarily for sketching. The 2H to 9H pencils are harder than average and used mostly for drafting. So, your #2 pencil equals an HB on this scale. In order, the variety of leads available are (from hardest to softest) 9H, 8H, 7H, 6H, 5H, 4H, 3H, 2H, H, F, HB, B, 2B, 3B, 4B, 5B, 6B, 7B, 8B, 9B.

Let's dispel a quick misconception. The part of the pencil that does the writing is called the *lead*; however, it is not made of lead. Let me explain. Pencils originally had lead in them. It was sandwiched between two pieces of cedar wood. During the late 18th century, graphite became the substitute for lead. At this point, it was also discovered that, by mixing clay with the graphite, you could get different rates of hardness and softness. More clay makes the pencil harder; more graphite makes it softer. This is how pencils are still made today.

The next kind of pencil is a mechanical pencil (Figure 5.5). Most of you have already seen this type as well. Mechanical pencils use a variety of thicknesses of "lead"

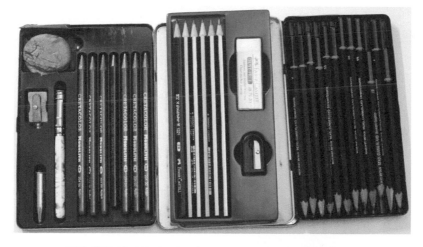

■ **Figure 5.4**
Various drawing and sketching pencils.

■ **Figure 5.5**
Hand drafting supplies: lead holder, leads, and mechanical pencil.

that comes in the same hardness/softness as regular pencils.

The diameter of the lead varies from 0.3 mm to 0.9 mm, and the mechanical pencil is specific to that size. There is no need to sharpen these leads since they are so thin. When the lead starts to get too short, you simply extend the lead, usually by pushing on the end cap. A larger-diameter lead, 2.0 mm, is used in a lead holder. This is a much thicker lead than the regular mechanical pencils and is usually used for drafting. This lead will not fit in a regular pencil sharpener. It needs what is called a lead pointer or sand paper to sharpen the tip.

Charcoal is our next drawing option. Charcoal comes either compressed in pencils or blocks or uncompressed in what is usually referred to as *willow* or *vine charcoal*. Willow and vine are much softer (and therefore darker) than compressed pencils and blocks.

Let's move onto color now. We are probably all familiar with color pencils (Figure 5.6). The biggest difference from regular pencils is that they come in a variety of colors instead of a variety of hardness and softness. Most colored pencils get darker simply by pressing harder. That is the only way to control the light and dark qualities. The oil color pencil is much creamier in texture than the traditional colored pencil. The creamier texture allows this pencil to make a denser, more solid mark on the page. Pastel pencils are able to draw sharp lines while still maintaining their ability to blend easily.

The last type of pencils we discuss are watercolor pencils. I saved these for last because these pencils are unique in that there are two very distinct ways of working with them. The first way to use them is like any other colored pencils—you draw. You can use them like this, and they never change. However, if you draw and then use a wet brush, the pencil lines turn into paint. If you are going to do this, make sure you are using watercolor paper so that it will hold up to being wet. We will talk about various paper choices soon.

Pastels and Crayons

Moving away from pencils, let us talk about pastels and crayons. Pastels come in three varieties, soft, hard, and oil. Pastels usually have a much more intense color than pencils (Figure 5.7). The color is very concentrated. Soft pastels are more powdery and therefore make more of a mess. But, if you can work with the powder dust, they are a great tool. Hard pastels are, well, harder. This means less dust, less powder, and unfortunately less vibrant color. Both hard and soft pastels are often described as "chalky." Oil pastels, on the other hand, are more "waxy." They can be less intense than regular pastels and also less messy. One nice attribute is that you can blend oil pastels using linseed oil as you would with oil paints.

Our last dry item is the crayon. I am talking about the "64 pack" you grew up with as well as many more new innovations. Crayons take on many different forms for the adult artist. Crayons traditionally used a binder of wax. This meant they were harder to blend, and the colors tended to be less intense. Newer versions of crayons have different binders. These forms include everything from products resembling hard pastels to water-soluble crayons that work similarly to the watercolor pencils. The key to remember is that there are options. Try as many as you can before you decide what you like and what you don't.

■ **Figure 5.6** Colored sketching pencils.

Figure 5.7 Pastels for sketching come in pencils and block shapes.

WET STUFF

Pens and Markers

We start off the wet stuff category with pens. Basic writing pens include everything from ballpoints to the newer gel ink pens. Just because they are meant for writing doesn't mean they can't be used for drawing as well! Fountain and calligraphy pens are different types of pen. They have replaceable nibs that determine the thickness of the line created. They also differ in terms of how they use ink. There are two ways they can get ink. First, there is the simple, basic dip pen. You have to sit with a bottle of ink and continually dip the nib into the ink bottle. The other style has a refillable bladder, cartridge holder, or other replaceable ink supply. Technical pens come in a variety of sizes, similar to mechanical pencils. Each size produces a different thickness of line. Again, there are many options to try before deciding what works best for your needs.

Let's talk about markers (Figure 5.8). Markers contain a hidden reservoir of ink that is pulled into the tip. Ink can be alcohol-based or water-based. Many different styles of markers are on the market today. Many are known by their brand name only. Let me try to explain the different styles.

Figure 5.8 Markers come in a variety of sizes, colors, and tips.

Permanent markers use ink that is alcohol-based or waterproof. This category includes the brand names Sharpie®, Copics, and Spectrum Noir, among many others, as well as most styles of highlighters. Alcohol-based markers can be used in conjunction with a blender tool for subtle variations. Water-based marker brand names to think of are Pantone® and Prismacolor®, among others.

The style of the marker is totally separate from the ink source. Artists of all kinds use layout and brush markers to do a variety of sketching techniques. Brush markers are just what they sound like. The tip is shaped like a paintbrush instead of like a pen. Layout markers often come with a writing tip at each end, usually in different sizes.

Paint markers are an aptly named hybrid. They are in the style of a regular marker; however, they actually dispense paint instead of ink. This can be useful for any number of reasons. A brand name to know is Pentel®.

Paint

Our next topic is paint. Let's start with watercolor. As the name suggests, in watercolor paints, the pigment, or color, is suspended in a water-soluble substance that allows it to be thinned with water. Transparency, or at least the potential for it, is a main artistic characteristic that sets watercolor apart from other paints. You can see the paper through the colors and layers of paint.

Watercolor paints come in both tubes and pans. Tubes of watercolor come in many quality levels. The biggest differences are the intensity of the pigment and range of colors. The paint-by-number kit you had when you were little most likely had pans of paint. Pans of paint still exist but are no longer the norm. Similar to tubes, they come in a range of qualities. They are also starting to make a bit of a comeback. Gouache is another type of watercolor paint. The difference between regular watercolor and gouache is that gouache is opaque. It is often used in conjunction with watercolor paint for the highlights.

Acrylic paint differs from watercolor in that the pigment is suspended in a polymer emulsion, similar to plastic. It can be thinned with water, but, once it is dry, it becomes water-resistant. Oil paint is rarely used in theatre, as it has a very slow drying time. As I bet you can guess, oil paint gets its name because the pigment is suspended in oil. Oil paint is generally opaque. Oils are often applied in fairly heavy layers. This gives them a deep color saturation that is often not possible in any other medium.

FIXING THE OOPS

Now, I prefer to think of it as a design change rather than a mistake. However, there will always be the inevitable "oops." A number of different eraser styles are available with which to make a change when using dry stuff such as pencils (Figure 5.9). The type of eraser you use depends entirely on what you are drawing with and how much of an "oops" you created. Let's go through each kind of eraser and look at the differences.

We start with the basics. A pink eraser is on the end of most of our pencils. The brand name for the bigger version of this is the Pink Pearl®. It has beveled ends for getting into those small areas. This is a longtime favorite, as it leaves no smudges on the paper. Gum erasers are another popular type of eraser. They are made of a soft, coarse rubber and work really well if you are trying to erase a large area. They leave a residue on the paper and are not extremely precise. Another form of the gum eraser is the dry cleaning pad. This is a mesh fabric pouch that is stuffed with powdered gum erasers and sewn closed. This is a much messier process. You are meant to tap the pad on your drawing before or after you finish.

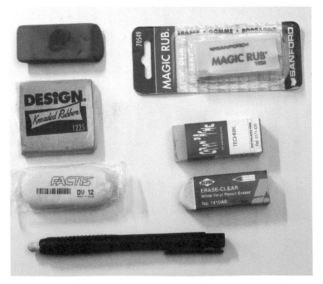

■ **Figure 5.9** Erasers can remove pencil, ink, even pastel.

It will remove smudge marks and oily deposits such as visible fingerprints.

Kneaded erasers are known for removing pencil, chalk, charcoal, and pastel. You can also use them to create a highlight in a drawing or to change part of the image. These erasers have wonderful powers of rejuvenation, for the drawing and for themselves! You can pull this eraser apart slightly, fold it into itself, and it is instantly clean of pencil residue. You can shape it to a point for getting into ultrafine detail. Another benefit is that kneaded erasers leave no residue on the paper.

Vinyl is another kind of eraser. This is a great eraser for use on drafting vellum, film, and tracing paper. It rarely smudges and leaves a minimum of residue. Brand names for this style include Sanford Magic Rub® and Alvin Erase Clear®. Vinyl erasers remove pencil and some pen.

There are electric erasers that can either plug into an outlet or run on batteries. They are great for doing large amounts of erasing, particularly on drafting. Refills for this type of eraser can include white vinyl, pink styles, or special ink erasers. The ink erasers are similar to compressed sand paper. You have to be very careful when using them or you can rip a hole in your paper.

I keep mentioning residue left behind. How do you fix that, you may ask? Well, the mighty and all-powerful drafting brush is the tool of choice. It has a long handle and very soft bristles. It whisks away eraser gunk without damaging or smudging your drawing. I usually have several of these handy, mostly because my cats like to play with them.

From the Pink Pearl, Gum, or Kneaded to Vinyl, there is an eraser for your need. Always choose the right tool for the job. When all else fails, there are always correction fluid and tape. They come in a variety of colors now. They are opaque and cover up just about anything. However, they do not blend into the rest of your drawing very well. So use this option only as a last resort.

PAPER

There are many different types of paper that come in a variety of sizes and shapes (Figure 5.10). They all have very specific purposes, and that is important to keep in mind. Newsprint paper is often used for quick sketches with pencil or charcoal. Newsprint is an inexpensive paper and doesn't hold up to repeated erasing or pressure with the drawing tool. It also is not archival and will fade over time. Drawing paper is sturdier than newsprint and is meant for a dry medium—pencil, charcoal, pastel, and crayon. Specific drawing papers are intended for use with pencil, charcoal, marker, or paint. The major differences are in the "tooth" or texture of the paper and its weight.

Illustration board is heavier and meant for a wet medium, such as pen and ink, marker, watercolor, or airbrush. Watercolor paper is just what it sounds like, paper for painting with watercolor paints. Watercolor paper is very specific and comes in a number of finishes that vary in texture. The texture changes how the paint adheres to the paper, giving very different effects.

For hand drafting, vellum was originally used when the drawings were inked. Now, a translucent paper, with or without a grid, is used so that you can trace an object from another drawing below. Speaking of tracing, there is actual tracing paper, which is a thicker version of the tissue paper you use when wrapping a gift. It is a more fragile paper, tearing easily and not being of archive quality. It is, however, great for quick sketches during research or meetings.

■ **Figure 5.10** Various pads of paper. Different papers are made for wet or dry media.

TOOLS

Let me start by talking about hand drawing and drafting and the tools you need for each, although many tools are similar, or identical when using a computer. This discussion applies to all areas of technical theatre! Whether you are drawing a ground plan, a light plot, a clothing pattern, or the beam spread of a projector's lens, you need the skills we are about to discuss. Later in this chapter, we discuss computer software and hardware. Keep in mind that, if you understand the basics of hand drafting, your computer drafting will go faster and be easier to understand.

The scale rule is possibly the most important tool of all (Figure 5.11). It is the basis for our shorthand way of drawing. I carry one with me at all times; you just never know. Here is how it works. If you wanted to draw the theater in its actual size, you would need a pretty big piece of paper. And that is just not practical. Scale allows you to draw things at a different size than they actually are. You have to keep the proportion right, and so you choose one of several ratios, larger or smaller, to have your object fit on the page. You need a scale rule not only for creating your drawings but also for reading other people's drawings.

In the USA, we use the scales of ¼, ½, 1, 1½, and 3 inches. There are lots of others using metric measurements, but let's limit ourselves to these for clarity of explanation at the moment since the principle is the same. A scale rule is normally a triangular-shaped ruler with six sides containing 11 scales. One of the six sides is a regular ruler, just like you are used to looking at.

The other sides have two scales on each side. One scale reads from right to left, the other from left to right. Let's pick one scale, and I'll explain how it works. Now, keep in mind that there are separate scale rules for imperial measures (used in the US) versus metric measures (used almost everywhere else). Look at Figure 5.12 for conversions back and forth between imperial and metric.

Drawing in ½-inch scale means that every 12 inches, or 1 foot, in reality will equal ½ inch on paper. It's that simple. Instead of making you figure out all the math in your head, someone came up with the brilliant idea to put the different conversions on a ruler. Trust me, it saves a lot of time! It may sound really confusing, but, after you

Conversion of US Linear Measure to Metric System	
1 inch	2.54 centimeters
1 foot	0.3048 meters
1 yard	0.9144 meters
1 mile	1.6093 kilometers
1 millimeter	0.03937 inches
1 centimeter	0.3937 inches
1 decimeter	3.937 inches
1 meter	39.37 inches
1 kilometer	0.62137 miles

■ **Figure 5.12** A conversion table for linear measurements from US to metric.

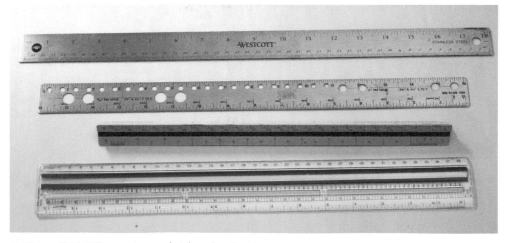

■ **Figure 5.11** Different sizes and styles of scale rulers.

■ **Figure 5.13** Ken Billington's studio with drafting table. Notice this modern studio has a very streamlined feeling.

make your first drawing this way, it will seem as easy as the proverbial riding of a bike.

The next thing you need is a surface on which to draw. Drafting tables are often used for sketching and layout as well as for drafting (Figure 5.13). This is because you can change the angle of the tabletop to whatever is comfortable for you. Sometimes, I sit while I draw and stand while I draft. I can adjust the table height and angle to whatever is the most comfortable. You need a good drafting chair or drafting stool, one that goes up and down to adjust to the height of your table. It should be comfortable and support your back. You will sit in this chair for long periods of time, so make sure it's comfy. Next, you need good light. Drafting table lights can clamp onto your table. This allows you to have consistent light whenever you change the angle of your desk. A good fluorescent lamp gives you a bright, even amount of light. The other nice thing about fluorescents is that they don't get hot. If you are working underneath the light for hours at a time, it is good to keep cool.

Most drafting tables come with the option of a parallel rule or offer an upgrade to a drafting machine. A parallel rule is a straight edge that travels up and down your table on two cables. The cables are on either side of your table. The rule typically has a brake to hold

it in place when you let go. The parallel rule allows you to draw horizontal lines that are consistently parallel to each other. It also provides a ledge to place a triangle for additional angle options. A drafting machine attaches on the top and lower edge of your table. It tracks left and right and up and down on one arm. The machine has two scale rulers, one vertical and one horizontal. The main advance in the drafting machine is that it can adjust to any angle you need. The oldest method you can choose, and the cheapest, is a T square. The T square is a tool shaped like a "T" (Figure 5.14). The short part of the T

■ **Figure 5.14** T square.

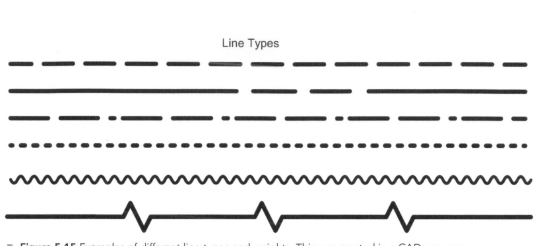

Line Weights

Line Types

leans against the side of your table. By sliding it up and down the length of your table, the long part of the T becomes an edge you can use to draw a horizontal line, similar to the parallel rule. The T square doesn't lock into place, it doesn't track easily, and it has no brake. However, it is more portable, meaning you can use it on any table where you sit down.

OK, great. You can draw horizontal, vertical, and angled lines. There are all sorts of lines types that represent different things on a drawing (Figure 5.15). Lines can show curtains, borders, centerlines, dimensions, and the like. Each has a different look. Line weights are also important. Heavier lines are generally more important on a drawing than lighter-weight lines.

What about vertical lines? Well, there is a great way to draw vertical and angled lines. The tool you need is called a **triangle**, if you don't have a drafting machine (Figure 5.16). There are many different types of triangles, and you will most likely need at least two or three. There are two ways to consider which triangle to purchase. The first and most important consideration is the angle of the triangle. Triangles come in two fixed configurations: 30/60 degrees and 45/90 degrees. You need both of these, and using them in combination gets you many more

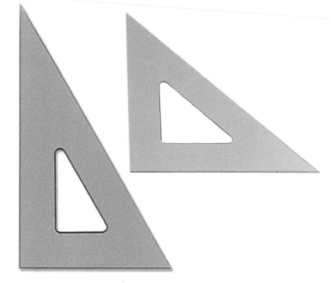

■ **Figure 5.16** Triangles.

angles. Another consideration is the adjustable triangle. These are usually able to adjust from 0 to 90 degrees.

I do not recommend using an adjustable triangle exclusively. I have found the best way for me is to use a combination of fixed and adjustable. Another consideration that affects all triangles is their overall size. They can come as small as 4 inches on the longest side all the way up to 18 inches and beyond. All triangles should be see-through, so that you can line up the edge of the triangle to your drawing underneath. Some triangles are clear and some, which I prefer, are orange. The orange makes them easier to find on the paper without being harder to see through. As with all the tools, try everything you can before deciding what works best for you.

Now that you can draw straight lines in many directions, what happens if you need a curve? Not a problem. Let me introduce you to the **French curve** (Figure 5.17). It is a template for drawing curves. It has curved edges and several scroll-shaped cutouts in the middle. The French curve is used by tracing one of its many edges. Then, you carefully move the template to the end of the curve you just drew and continue your curve tracing the template. You repeat this as many times as you need to create the proper curve for your design. You can now repeat this curve, using the template again, if it appears somewhere else in your design. This is a technique that needs practice to perfect, but it can produce great effects.

There are many other kinds of different templates that can come in handy (Figure 5.18). Scenic designers can find templates with furniture in different scales. Lighting designers can find a wide variety of lighting fixture

■ **Figure 5.17** French curves.

templates. Everybody can use shape templates that include circles, squares, triangles, arrows, or just about any shape you can think of. They come in handy whether you are drawing, drafting, or just doodling.

Another template of sorts is the **erasing shield**. In my opinion, this is one of the coolest things ever invented. It is a small, thin piece of polished steel with different shapes cut out of it. You lay the shield over your drawing, specifically the part you want to erase. Then, while holding it in place, you erase the offending line without the possibility of your eraser touching anything else on

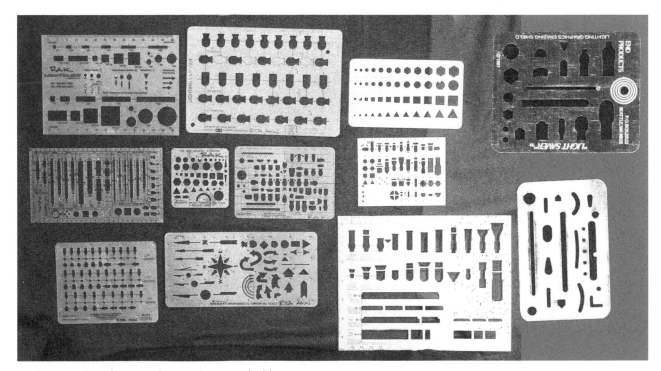

■ **Figure 5.18** Drafting templates and erasing shields.

Schoolhouse Printed

ABCDEFGHIJKLMNOPQRSTUVWXYZ

abcdefghijklmnopqrstuvwxzy

0123456789

Bradley Hand ITC

ABCDEFGHIJKLMNOPQRSTUVWXYZ

abcdefghijklmnopqrstuvwxzy

0123456789

Papyrus

ABCDEFGHIJKLMNOPQRSTUVWXYZ

abcdefghijklmnopqrstuvwxzy

0123456789

Tekton Pro

ABCDEFGHIJKLMNOPQRSTUVWXYZ

abcdefghijklmnopqrstuvwxzy

0123456789

■ **Figure 5.19** Samples of various computer fonts or lettering styles. All these can be replicated with hand lettering.

the paper. Practice with this as there is a little bit of a learning curve. Once you've figured it out, it's like magic, only better!

Let us talk about lettering for a minute (Figure 5.19). Sloppy lettering can make a good drawing look terrible. Even your notes, taken in the theater, should look good! If you want to look professional, practice your lettering. It is the quickest, easiest way to make your presentation jump up in quality a couple of notches. The Ames Lettering Guide (Figure 5.20) is going to be your best friend for learning lettering. It is yet another template. The left side is at a 90-degree angle to the bottom of the template; use this for making your vertical lines. The

■ **Figure 5.20** The Ames Lettering Guide is a favorite of mine, as it can be adjusted in many ways to suit differing sizes of text. I always keep one with me!

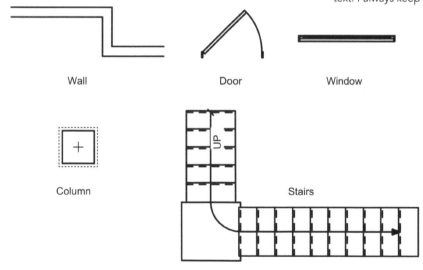

■ **Figure 5.21** There are conventions for drafting different parts of the scenery. See this figure for examples of a few.

right side is at a 60-degree angle; use it for angled letters such as *v* and *w*, for example.

Now for the really cool part of this guide! The center of this template is a circle that rotates. Inside the circle are a variety of little holes. You rotate the circle until you get the little holes to the right distance apart for the desired height of your letters based on the scale of your drawing. Put your pencil in any of the little holes and slide the guide along your parallel rule or T square to make faint guidelines.

The last tool to think about is tape. Should you be hand drafting, you will need this (Figure 5.21). Drafting tape and drafting dots are made by a variety of companies. This tape looks like regular masking tape, but it is less sticky. That means you can pull it up without leaving a residue or tearing your paper. This is important, as you will sometimes need to pull up the tape, reposition your paper, and put down new tape.

Computers

Some people use phones and tablets with apps; some use computers with software—OK, most of us use all of the above. Heck, I'm sitting at a computer right now writing this book. Apps and computers are the way of *today*! I still maintain that learning hand drafting and drawing is always helpful. The basis for creating a drawing of any kind, no matter how it will be generated. The conventions for one technique are the same as another. It's really only a matter of whether you have to go to someone with a blueprint machine or a plotter. So, let us talk hardware and software.

Hardware first. The big debate I always hear is, "Should I use a Windows computer or Apple computer?" Well, it's easy. It's the simplest choice of all. This is a true no-brainer. The answer is—it doesn't matter. Get whichever you are more comfortable with. You will always find programs made for your computer's operating system. All of the big software companies have finally figured out that both platforms are here to stay. You'll see what I mean when we talk about software.

When you are buying a new computer, my advice is simple. Get the fastest processor with the biggest hard drive and the most random access memory (RAM). Whatever you buy will be outdated within two years. You have a better chance of keeping your machine longer if you get the newest, best, and greatest now. Try out the

keyboard, mouse/trackpad, and monitor at the store. You must be comfortable with how these work. The same advice goes for peripherals: Digital cameras, scanners, printers, plotters—everything. We are not going to suddenly discover that we want to store everything at low resolution, right? So, use your student discount and get the best you can.

Now for the software. There are specific programs that everybody uses. Before I give you the list, I have to share something. Long before there were programs dedicated to theater needs, we all still got the paperwork done. So, keep in mind that, if you don't find exactly what you need, be creative! Find a work-around for whatever task you're trying to do. We are theater people, we're creative, it is what we do for a living! A knowledge of Microsoft Office, Google Office, or Apple office apps is a must. You need to be able to use a word processor and a spreadsheet at the bare minimum.

Let's discuss the specific software developed with our intended purposes in mind. Let me explain something first. The lighting department generates more paperwork, I think, than any other department. Various pieces of paperwork are updated on a daily basis, sometimes even hourly during tech. So, the first thought that comes to mind is John McKernon's Lightwright®. Lightwright began life officially as ALD® (Assistant Lighting Designer) in 1982 on a TRS-80 computer, before you were born! What humble beginnings, and now it is the industry standard for lighting paperwork. Lightwright is the new name for the program, and new versions come out regularly. Lightwright works on both the Mac and PC.

If you want to try one integrated software package that can generate all versions of the required lighting paperwork, try Stage Research's Light Shop®, Soft Plot®, and Soft Plot 3D®. The Soft Plot programs allow you to create and maintain all the necessary paperwork. Light Shop allows you to view the photometric data of more than 1500 fixtures. Don't worry, we will discuss photometric data in Chapter 10. Keep in mind that many people will use your paperwork. Everyone will need to use the same software you did to create it in order to make updates and changes.

Lighting and scenery require drafting many plans, sections, and other drawings for every show. Computer-aided drafting is now the standard (Figures 5.22 and 5.23). The granddaddy of all CAD programs is AutoCAD®

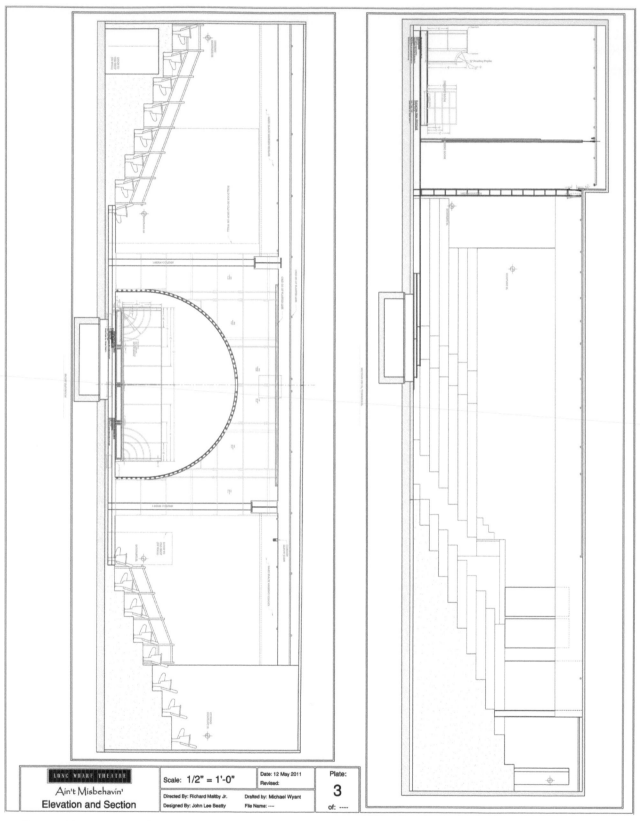

Figure 5.22 Computer-drafted elevation and section for *Ain't Misbehavin'* at Long Wharf Theatre, designed by John Lee Beatty.

■ **Figure 5.23** Computer-drafted elevation and rendering of portal for *Ain't Misbehavin'* at Long Wharf Theatre, designed by John Lee Beatty.

by Autodesk. It is a massive, expensive program used primarily by architects. If you have access to it, try it out. There are many plug-ins now to help us in theater work. For our needs in theater, you will use about 10 percent of the overall program! The most popular program for this purpose, however, is Vectorworks® by Nemetschek. It can handle 2D and 3D drafting. Vectorworks worked closely with the theater industry to create palettes for scenic objects, trusses, and assorted hardware. There is also a version called Spotlight® that allows for the insertion of lighting instruments. Lightwright interfaces seamlessly with it. This is truly one of the rare times when a commercial software package has actually catered to a small niche industry like ours.

Previsualization continues to be a hot topic today for many designers. Often referred to as *pre-vis*, it means just what you think. It's a way to "see" what the show will look like before you get to the theater. Almost everyone has very strong opinions about it, one way or the other. Some say it's a waste of time, while others say they wouldn't do a show without it. Pre-vis is a slow process. It is used mostly when time in the theater will be at a minimum. Software today has gotten to a point where you can actually cue lights in the computer, then load the disk into your light board and run cues. It's not a fast or easy process but can be time well spent in your studio that saves time onsite, which is always at a premium.

Costumers, don't feel left out. A few options are available for you as well. Dress Shop® and My Pattern Designer® were developed by the same team to cater to two different markets. Patternmaker® is another option created by people with a theatre background who understand our needs. Keep in mind that many more are being developed constantly, so there is always a new product hitting the market. Let's discuss the pros and cons of each I've mentioned.

> Clothing is architectural ... it's construction, just different construction methods.
> —William Ivey Long, American costume designer

Dress Shop has two versions, Standard and Pro, and is geared toward those of us who make clothing for others. Standard includes 150 patterns with a wide assortment of mix-and-match possibilities. You can also vary how many measurements you want to take or if you want to use standard sizes. Pro expands on all the options within Standard, adding more patterns and more flexibility.

My Pattern Designer is aimed at the person who is at home making clothing for him- or herself, although it will work just as well for the costumer. It is easier to use than Dress Shop. As it was designed with the home seamstress in mind, you can get started with as few as five key measurements. Combining different pieces from styles within a large library creates customized patterns.

Patternmaker has three versions that successively increase the patterning options you have. Patternmaker allows you to work from standard sizing or from your own measurements. The three versions are Home, Expert, and Marker. The Home version works with basic garments. Expert adds the capability to use a digitizer, and Marker helps with cost estimates.

Software is available that does very specific tasks to aid our jobs in the theatre. Other packages are available that are generic to our industry; these break down into four basic categories of graphics software: 2D graphic creation and manipulation, 3D graphic creation, video editing, and compositing. Many software packages are available in each of these categories. Before we get into the different options available, let's discuss a subject that influences the whole conversation. Intrigued? Read on.

Have you heard of the terms *raster* and *vector*? The software is divided between these types of processing for the images. Let me explain. Vector-based images are created using mathematical formulas to locate each point. Lines are then drawn to connect the dots. Raster, on the other hand, is a pixel-based technology. Now, here is the important part. If you need to scale the image you've created, vector can scale infinitely larger or smaller without losing resolution. Raster, on the other hand, becomes lower resolution instantly on changing the size. Keep this in mind when you are creating images. Choose your software depending on what you will eventually need to do with it. If you need to work in raster, work at the size you will need when you are done. Otherwise, you may be wasting a lot of time and have to recreate things.

So, let us talk about 2D graphic software. The king of the raster hill was, is, and continues to be Adobe's

■ **Figure 5.24** 2018 USA International Ballet Competition. Jackson, Mississippi. Lighting design by Jared A Sayeg.

Photoshop®. ProCreate for the iPad is close second to Photoshop now, and many scenic and costume designers are using it. Another option that performs slightly differently is Corel's Painter®. Both are awesome and powerful software programs that are raster-based. Adobe has a vector-based product named Illustrator®. It is also the king of the hill for what it does, as Adobe has kept up with the needs of the market. All these programs are available for both Windows and Mac platforms. So, check them out if you do not already know them.

Three-dimensional creation offers a wider range of programs. Cinema 4D® by Maxon and SoftImage® and Maya® (both by Autodesk) are a few that come to mind quickly. LightWave® by NewTek is another that focuses primarily on lighting but also does modeling. Vectorworks by Nemetschek is a 2D CAD program that also has a 3D component. It is nicely integrated. You can go back and forth between each module seamlessly. As with other software mentioned, there are so many new products hitting the market it is always good to talk to colleagues and look around before settling on any one program.

This is just the tip of the iceberg in terms of software. Many more options are available to you. I can't list them all here, as there isn't enough room, and the list is ever changing. The internet is truly your friend on this subject. Search around and see what you can find. Keep looking for newer versions and better options. The more we expect, the more the developers will give us.

PERSPECTIVE DRAWING

OK, now that we've gone through drawing and the potential tools, let's approach it from a slightly more technical side. Let's talk about perspective drawing and perspective projection. First, we define the terms. Perspective projection is a type of drawing that uses a 2D technique to approximate a 3D object. Let's look at how to do this from a very technical point of view. Many factors go into a good perspective drawing. Let's start to break it down.

The three main concepts to understand before we go much further are vanishing points, the horizon line,

■ **Figure 5.25** One-point perspective photo with a bit of a twist.

and foreshortening. We start with vanishing points. The most common forms of perspective are one-point, two-point, and three-point perspective (Figure 5.25). The name refers to the number of vanishing points used to construct the drawing. **Vanishing point** refers to the point in space where two parallel lines *seem* to converge. Think of railroad tracks. We know in reality they never touch, but they sure look like they do in photographs.

Every set of parallel lines can have its own vanishing point. Most often, however, sets of lines share a vanishing point. The most common scenarios for theater, as I said, are the one-, two-, and three-point drawings. Think for a second about an architect's sketch for a new building. How many parallel lines does it have? Lots! You can keep adding more vanishing points to a drawing, as long as it helps to further the clarity of the drawing. If it just makes it more confusing, you might want to consider limiting yourself. Now consider this: What if you are drawing a landscape with lots of nature, such as trees, flowers, and birds? If there are no parallel lines, there are no vanishing points. This is often referred to as *zero-point perspective*.

The **horizon line** is usually defined as the line that separates the earth from the sky (Figure 5.26). In our usage, it is the horizontal line that comes closest to the height of your eye. It divides the entire drawing into two

■ **Figure 5.26** The Mid-Hudson Bridge across the Hudson River in Poughkeepsie, NY, showing a clear horizon line.

■ **Figure 5.27** Foreshortening of a tree limb.

parts. Choosing where to put the horizon line determines a great deal about what your drawing looks and feels like. The horizon line tells us where we, the viewers, are standing to view the object that has been drawn. Are we below it or above it or right in the middle of it? This affects not only the outcome of the drawing but also our relation to it.

The last term I mentioned earlier is **foreshortening** (Figure 5.27). So far, we have been talking about placing the object to be drawn directly in front of us. It might possibly be above or below our line of sight, but it is centered on us. What happens if we move it off to the side? Instead of standing on the railroad tracks and looking straight down the rails, what happens if you stand off to the side and look down the rails? The rails appear shorter. This is obviously an optical illusion. The rails did not get shorter simply because we moved our position over. This is called foreshortening.

OK, now that we have some background to work from, let's dive into one-point perspective. This is the traditional railroad or street photo. The viewer is usually standing in the middle of the road or rail, looking straight ahead. There is one vanishing point in the distance, centered between two parallel lines. As the lines move toward the vanishing point, they are drawn closer together. Always keep in mind that this is an illusion, as the lines don't actually converge. The point (if you pardon the pun) is to draw something on paper and give it the illusion of three dimensions. It is that simple to create the impression of 3D on paper, making the illusion of distance where none actually exists.

Two-point perspective can be used to draw rails or roads as well as many other options. Think about a house for a second. If you stand at the corner of the house, there is a side on your left and a side on your right. Both sides go back to opposing vanishing points. Now, here is the cool part. The walls on the back side that we don't see are also drawn with the same vanishing points. Check it out in Figure 5.28.

■ **Figure 5.28** A perspective sketch, circa 1913.

Three-point perspective is next. It is the most complicated form that I address in this book. Keep in mind that there is much more to learn about perspective drawing. This is just a short introduction. Three-point usually has the effect of making the object appear over our heads or below our feet. Always keep in mind that the further the vanishing points are from your object, the gentler the angles of perspective will be.

There are several ways to create a perspective drawing. As we have already done, you can draw it completely freehand with no drawing tools other than paper and pencil. When drawing perspective by hand, I find it easiest to work on paper with a preprinted grid. The grid gives me an instant reference as I begin to draw. Add some grid paper and a straight edge, and you can become a little more mechanically accurate. Computers can also simulate this technique. Now, here is the funny part. Sometimes, and only sometimes, you can ignore the rules I just laid out and create a "different" version of perspective. The important thing to remember is that you have to know and understand the rules before

you can change them. Oliver Smith knew how to use the rules—then broke them for his purpose. We call it *Oliver perspective*. But, nobody can do this when new to perspective drawing. It took Oliver years and years.

For now, let's go back to the rules. We look at the development of a two-point perspective, step by step. Figure 5.29 shows a simplistic ground plan from a show. When you look at a ground plan, the next step is to figure out what it will look like standing up. This is the basis for a sketch. Let's get started. We first have to determine the floor line of the existing ground plan as well as the horizon line and base line for the sketch. The next thing to do is determine what vanishing points you want to use. For sketches like this, we often use a vanishing point close to what our eye line would be if we were standing in the drawing, the average person in the drawing being about 6 feet tall. Then, we have to draw leader lines to correspond with the different walls on the ground plan and where they intersect in the new sketch.

Now, you are ready to start drawing. All you need are paper, a pencil, and a straight edge. Start on the far left

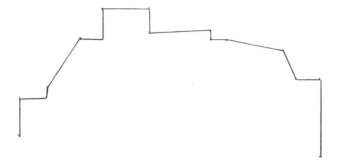

or right. Determine how tall your walls will be and mark that height on your paper (Figure 5.30). This is why grid paper comes in handy. I marked out 12 grid spaces to make my walls 12 feet tall. Once you have determined the height, draw your outside wall line. If the top or bottom of a wall is parallel to the top of your paper, draw the top and bottom of the first wall straight across to the next leader line. If the wall is angled or you moved on to the next wall, use the vanishing point on the far side of the drawing from your wall to connect the top and bottom of the next wall to the first.

The vertical lines on the walls stay vertical. The angled lines drawn from the vanishing point to the last wall determine their length (Figure 5.31). Continue drawing

each wall until you reach the middle of the sketch. Now, start again from the other side, using the opposite vanishing point. When you reach the middle again, your sketch should be almost done. The only thing left to do is to add any openings: Doors, windows, arches. If they are square, you follow the same rules. The vertical lines stay vertical, and the horizontal lines still reference the vanishing point on the opposite side of the stage.

Perspective drawing can be as simple or complicated as you choose or need it to be. I've gone over the basics. Feel free to experiment from here and play around with it. Keep in mind that the placement of the vanishing point(s) determines how distorted the final sketch is. Try making several sketches based on the same designs, with different vanishing points and horizon lines, to see how very different they look. Now, here is the important part. Which of your three sketches most "correctly" represents the scenery?

The answer is all or none. What? Well, the vanishing point changes make the perspective more extreme, which may or may not be accurate. Changing the horizon line means the audience is moving around the theater. One obvious note: If you moved the horizon line up into the ceiling, obviously, the audience won't be sitting there! Keep in mind a very important fact. Anything you can draw can be built exactly as it was drawn. It might take a

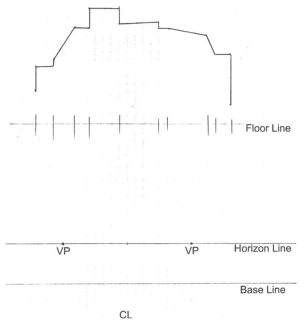

■ **Figure 5.30** Two-point perspective, step 2.

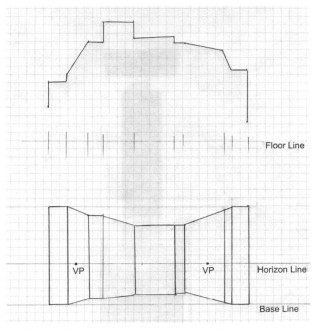

■ **Figure 5.31** Two-point perspective, step 3.

big budget or a very long schedule, but it can be done. So be careful what you draw and make sure it shows what has been bouncing around in your head. Otherwise, you mislead the director, and everyone is in for a big surprise when the load-in starts.

Your sketch looks great, except the stage is empty. Now, you have to add furniture, props, and people. Once your line drawing of a sketch is populated, it is time to add tone (light and shadow) to the sketch. This makes the black-and-white drawing come to life. Before you can begin, you have to think about how the set will be lit. Lighting becomes critical to making the scenery sketch look real and alive. More important, lighting is critical to make the scenery look at least similar to how it will appear in the theater.

■ **Figure 5.32** *My Fair Lady*, Higgins's study, watercolor rendering, by Oliver Smith.

RENDERING

Our next topic is rendering (Figure 5.32). This is the step where you definitely are showing your work to the director and other designers and potentially adding color as well. The initial perspective sketch may just be your way of working, which eventually turns into a rendering. It may never be for others to see. But, at some point, you, as the designer, have to show some representation of your design to the director. Otherwise, your budget will never get approved. So, on to the rendering step.

So, the sketches turn into the renderings. Is there a difference between a sketch and a rendering? It can be just semantics, but here is how I approach it. The color sketch is part of your process prior to the rendering (Figure 5.33). Sketching is traditionally known as being

■ **Figure 5.33** Sketch by George Allison for a Berkshire Opera production of *The Rape of Lucretia*.

a quicker, more relaxed process. Keep in mind that when you show the director and other designers your drawing, sketch, or rendering, one of the first things they react to is the "feel" of it.

When you are working on a sketch, sometimes, you have to back away from it for a little while. When you come back to it fresh, you may see something that you didn't see before. You may choose to keep this new "feature" or get rid of it. Just keep in mind that designing is not an accident waiting to happen. It should be considered. Then, if, as I call it, a "happy accident" occurs, you are ready to decide if you want to keep it or not. The nature of sketching is for it to be quick and not labored. Sometimes, the quickness of the sketch gives the image an energy that gets lost when you translate to a rendering. Be careful not to let this happen!

Let me interject here by saying that, at this stage of the design process, the computer may not be your best

friend. What I mean is that the passion, movement, and energy of a hand sketch is very difficult to create in computer rendering. Not impossible. Difficult. Even if you look at it as simply a homage to the past, take your time and learn how to draw with paper and pencil. The subtleties of what your hand can do with pressure on the tip of a pencil is not something to be taken for granted. And, now that tablets and styluses have gotten so sophisticated, they can do practically the same thing! That is why, throughout this book, I show hand drawings and draftings as well as computer-generated ones. Spend a moment or two comparing some of the illustrations in this book to see what I mean and why it is important to learn the "old school" ways as well as the modern ones.

The term *rendering* is frequently used for a full-color, finished sketch, finished being the key word. You should now have the furniture, props, and actors on the set. You should have chosen a specific moment in time from the play. The actors should be in place; the light cue should be evident. Your entire design team will look at this rendering for clues as to how you envision the final production.

Keep in mind, now you've finished your rendering, that there is another way to work. You can skip the perspective sketch and rendering completely. What? Why didn't I tell you that before? Well, if you skip these two very important steps, they are replaced most likely with a model. A model is a 3D representation of the scenery instead of a 2D sketch. A 3D model can be a long and laborious project. However, sometimes it is the only way to truly convey a production that is more sculptural. Again, as always, using the right tool for the right production is key.

DRAFTING

Let me start by saying that drafting is drafting. What do I mean? Well, drafting is meant to convey information, not an emotion. Certain things have to be in a pack of draftings to give all the information needed to build the set. Now, here is the key. Are you ready? It doesn't matter whether you are hand drafting or using a CAD program (Figure 5.34). How can that be? Well, it actually doesn't matter if you do your sketch by hand or in a program such as Photoshop either. What matters, and the only thing that matters, is that you convey the information needed in a way it can be used. The techniques, concepts, and ideas are all the same. Remember in Chapter 3 when we talked about focus? Well, it's the same thing here. You want the drafting to have a focus, so people know where to look first, where to look second, and so forth.

We begin by drafting an orthographic projection. **Orthographic projection** is a way of representing a 3D objection in two dimensions using multiple views. Have you ever taken a flat piece of cardboard and turned it into a box? Well, that is the idea (Figure 5.35). Say we are going to build a table. We first need to visualize the table inside a box. We then project each side of the table onto the surrounding box. Then we unfold the box, laying it flat. This creates two **plan views**, top and bottom, as well as four **side views**.

The carpenter or scene shop needs the information from each of these views to build the table. This is the basis for all the information you generate in your own drawings. If you are not the designer, it is the basis for all the information you need to create the design. We started this chapter by talking about using drawing to get the ideas out of your head and onto paper. Once the sketch is approved, you need to break down each part of the set into smaller pieces so the scene shop can build it and so the other designers know what to expect.

Let's talk about some of the standardized conventions. The first thing you are going to do, most likely, is draw a line. Well, what kind of line? A line is not just a line. Are you drawing the centerline of the theater, a leg, a border, or scenery? It makes a difference. Each of these types of lines has a convention for how it should be drawn. The United States Institute for Theatre Technology (USITT)'s Graphic Standards Board established all of the conventions we discuss next. If you don't follow the conventions, your drawings will be confusing to most people at best and unreadable at worst.

We discussed line weight in Chapter 3. It comes back now. You have to combine the correct line weight with the correct line style to follow the established conventions. Take a look at the examples that follow. These are a few of the many examples you need. A drafting class goes into much more detail, but this should give you a start. If you've ever seen a ground plan or section, I bet these examples will look pretty familiar.

- Border—a thick double line
- Plaster line—a thin dashed line
- Centerline—a thin line of long–short–long lines with note of *CL* near lower edge
- Section—uniform hatching on diagonal lines
- Leader line—a thin solid line with or without an arrow at the end
- Dimension/Extension lines—a thin line
- Break line—a thin line that extends beyond the edges of the break

Next, we talk about lettering and labeling. Drawing is one thing; writing is a whole other thing. This is one area where hand drafting and CAD drafting differ. I'll talk about each separately. There is one simple piece of advice to follow for lettering. Make it simple and legible. Remember, the goal is to convey information. If you try to get too fancy, no one will be able to read what you've

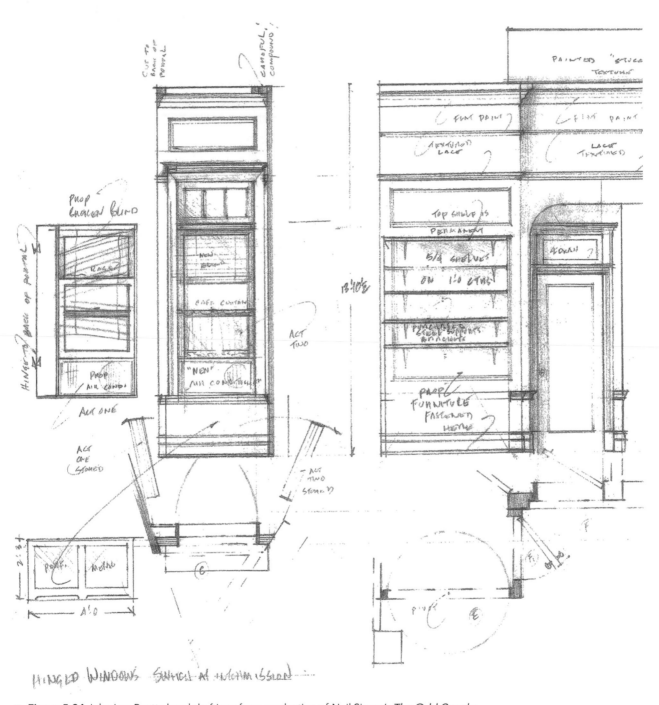

■ **Figure 5.34** John Lee Beatty hand draftings for a production of Neil Simon's *The Odd Couple*.

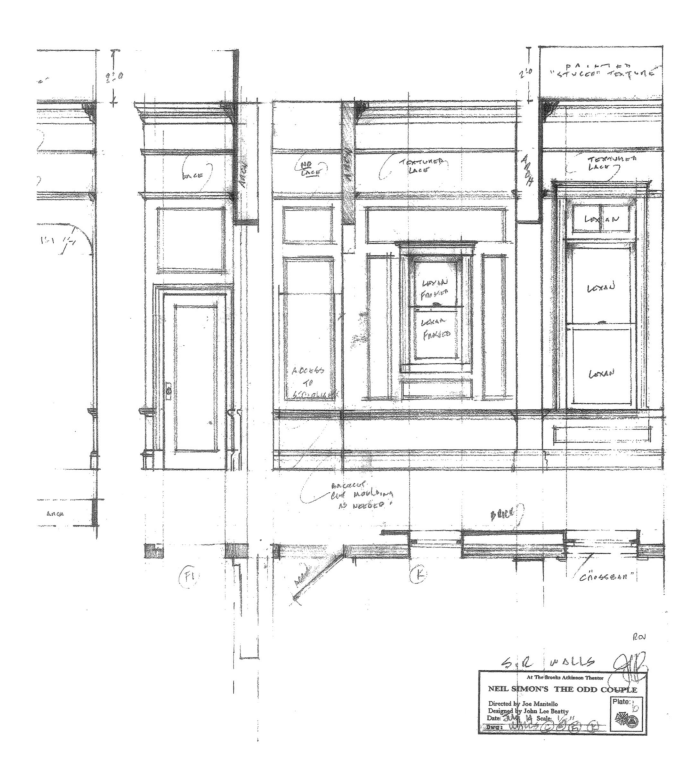

S R WALLS

At The Brooks Atkinson Theater

NEIL SIMON'S THE ODD COUPLE

Directed by Joe Mantello
Designed by John Lee Beatty
Date: JUN 14   Scale: ½"
Dwg: Plate:

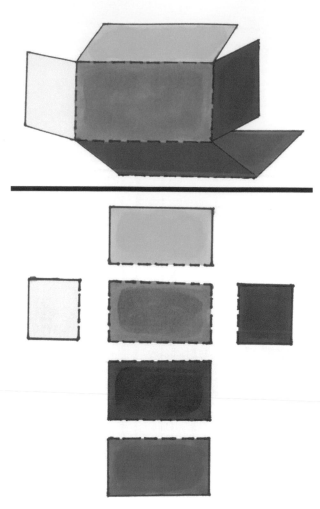

■ **Figure 5.35** To begin an orthographic projection, you must identify the different sides and begin to see how they are connected, as shown on the top. The final orthographic projection, on the bottom, shows each side lying flat to one another.

written. Most people feel that a straight, clean sans serif typeface is best. My feeling is to add a little style if you want, just don't let it get in the way of the main goal—conveying information.

When most people first start to hand draft, they are okay with the drawing but totally stress out when it comes to the lettering. Lettering takes practice, but a couple of hints will help you do a better job right away. First, remember, earlier in this chapter, I talked about the Ames Lettering Guide? Well, get one. The most important thing to know about lettering, and how to make it look good, is *consistency*. Use a triangle to keep the vertical part of the letters vertical. Use a parallel

or T square to keep the horizontal parts of the letters horizontal. This is a good start. Most drafting-style letters use true verticals while changing the horizontals into angles for a little extra flair.

CAD drafting and lettering are whole different things. They are easier for the most part, but you still have to pay attention to details. So, you're in your CAD program, you type in the text, and you think, "No problem, I'm done, what is so hard?" Well, you have to choose a font, a size, the attributes—there are many more choices. The good news is that a number of fonts are available now that actually look like hand-drafted lettering. Once you pick a font, you have to choose the size. Most important, you then have to stick with that font—remember, consistency. With hand drafting, we're usually lucky if we can get three sizes of lettering on the paper. You can choose 10 point or 11 point or whatever looks good. This is an option the hand drafter lacks. So, use your tools well. Vary the font options and the size to help give focus to what is most important.

Our next topic is dimensioning. Dimensions are used to confirm actual drawn sizes. Whoever reads your drafting will most likely have a scale rule at hand. A quick glance at your dimensioning lets that person know if the drawing is accurate. The scale rule confirms it. Dimensions are usually read when looking at the drafting from the bottom side. If you need to rotate a dimension based on the object or other spacing, make sure it reads from the right side. This is a convention that works well as long as you are consistent. If the drawn object's scaled size is different than the dimensions shown, the dimensions shown will take precedence. Always double check your dimensions!

There are three different styles of dimensions (Figure 5.36): Linear dimensions are used when you are measuring in a straight line; arc dimensions are used if you are measuring some kind of angle or radius; and the multiple dimension style is used when you are measuring several things in a row from the same starting point.

Certain conventions have already been established for drafting common objects. This makes your job easier. Somebody else already figured out how to draw a wall, floors, and curtains. You just need to use their symbols as a guide. This is like learning another language. But, after you've drawn them once, they will be second nature to

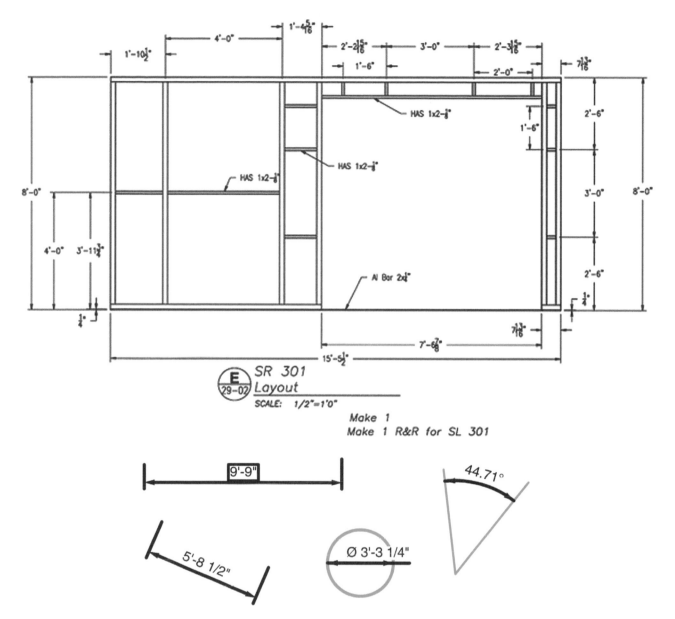

SR 301 Layout
SCALE: 1/2"=1'0"

Make 1
Make 1 R&R for SL 301

■ **Figure 5.36** Above, an elevation for a wall, fully dimensioned. Below, different styles of dimensioning for all situations.

you. In fact, when most designers doodle, they use these same conventions because it is a common language we all understand.

Walls on a set are divided into small, manageable parts called *flats*. When you are drawing a ground plan, you want to show the flats and where they are joined. There are two ways to do this. Solid walls are usually not the whole set. Usually, there are going to be openings in the walls for doors, arches, and windows, all of which have specific ways of being drawn. More on this in Chapter 7.

The scenic floor has become much more complicated in past years. It used to be that, unless there was a second level, like a balcony, the floor was just painted. Now full-stage decks are constructed to aid in automation of moving scenic units. Stairs and ramps are also used more frequently. So much information must be conveyed about the flooring that there is usually an entire drawing dedicated to the floor (Figure 5.37). In Chapter 7, we will go into more detail on this.

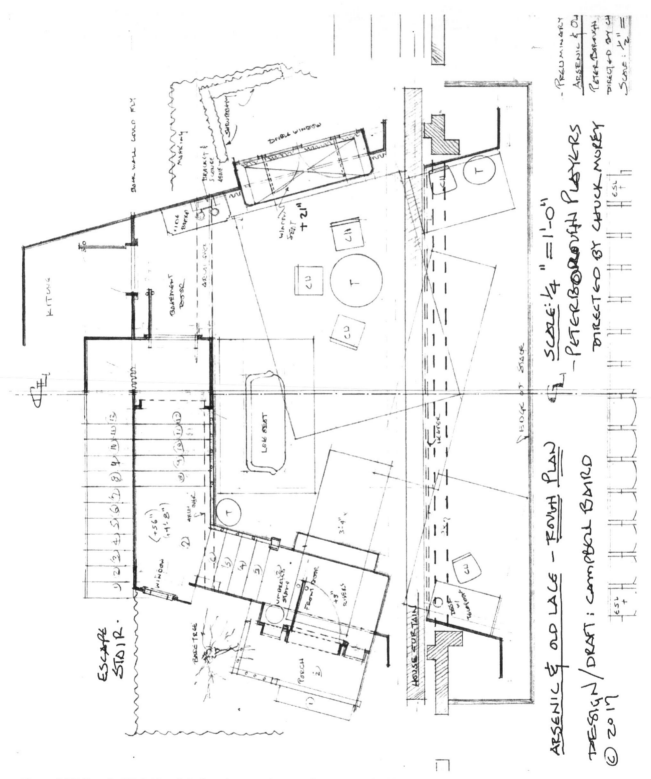

■ **Figure 5.37** Campbell Baird hand drafting for a production of *Arsenic and Old Lace*.

Draperies are the next topic. We are not talking about window curtains here. In the theater, all fabric items are called soft goods. All the fabric that hangs over and around the stage has different names depending on its function. Depending on what it does and how it hangs, each is also drawn differently. Some curtains are meant to touch the stage at all times, some are meant to never touch the stage, and some move around, sometimes touching and sometimes not. Curtains will be addressed in specific detail in Chapter 7.

Our next convention is one of the finishing touches to a drafting. It is the title block (Figure 5.38). A title block must be placed on every drafting. It also needs to be placed in the same place on each drawing—remember, consistency. The placement varies depending on the type of title block. If you use a floating title block, a small square or rectangle, it should be placed in the lower right corner of the drawing. If you use a docked title block, usually full height of the drawing but narrow, it is usually placed on the right edge or bottom edge of the drawing. The most important thing is to keep it consistent from one drawing to the next within a pack of draftings.

Regardless of the type of block you choose to use or its placement, it contains very important information (Figure 5.39). The following information should be included:

- Name of producing organization
- Name of production
- Drawing title
- Drawing number
- Predominant scale of the drawing
- Date the drawing was drafted
- Designer of the production
- Drafter, if different from the designer
- Drawing approval, if applicable
- Revisions, if applicable
- Union stamp, if applicable
- If it is a digital drafting, the file name can be put in the title block for reference

If there is a logo for the producer or production, feel free to put that in the title block instead of plain text. It helps make the drawing unique and easily recognizable. Any other information that you think is appropriate to all

■ **Figure 5.38** Scott Pask sample title block.

■ **Figure 5.39** Hudson Scenic sample title block.

drawings can be added at your discretion. The following is additional information you may want to include:

- Location of the venue
- Director of the production
- Other members of the production team
- Lighting assistant and/or master electrician
- Contact information (telephone and fax numbers, email addresses)
- Liability disclaimer

There are many ways to word a disclaimer. The important thing to realize is that we are designers and technicians, not engineers. On page 108 is a sample that you can customize as needed for your own use.

Visually tied into the title block is the border. The border should be a thick double line. It serves two purposes, one visual and one practical. The visual purpose is that the border acts like a frame and visually ends the

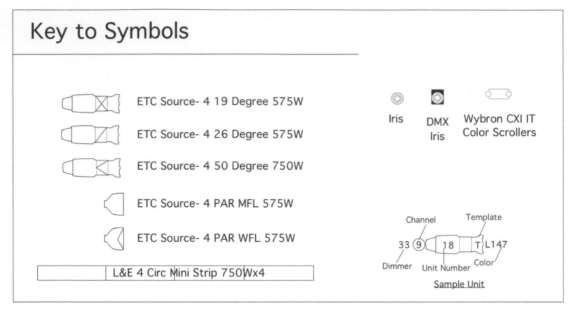

Key to Symbols

ETC Source- 4 19 Degree 575W

ETC Source- 4 26 Degree 575W

ETC Source- 4 50 Degree 750W

ETC Source- 4 PAR MFL 575W

ETC Source- 4 PAR WFL 575W

L&E 4 Circ Mini Strip 750Wx4

Iris   DMX Iris   Wybron CXI IT Color Scrollers

Channel   Template

33 ⑨ | 18 | T L147

Dimmer   Unit Number   Color

Sample Unit

■ **Figure 5.40** A sample key. Remember, the key can have as much or as little information as is needed to convey the information.

drawing. From a practical point of view, the border is very important. Anyone who looks at your drawing and sees a border on three sides will rightly assume they are missing part of the drawing. It alerts the viewers to the true edges of the drawing. That way, if something is missing, the next thing they do should be to call for another copy of the drawing.

The next item is the **key to symbols** (Figure 5.40). This is a common element specifically on a light plot, but let's discuss it now. Think of a street map for a second. There is always a legend on it. It's a little box with different symbols to help you figure out the difference between a town road and a state highway. Our key is the same thing. On a light plot, the key shows each of the lighting instruments used for the production and some of the accessories and attributes. Information may include:

- Graphical symbol as well as verbal description of the fixture
- Wattage of the lamp
- Color manufacturer designation (i.e., R = Roscolux®, L = Lee, G = GAM, A = Apollo, etc.)
- Template manufacturer designation, when applicable (R = Rosco, G = GAM, A = Apollo, S = SFX, etc.)
- Accessories such as templates, irises, color scrollers, top hats, barn doors, and so forth

Sample Liability Disclaimer

This drawing and the ideas, arrangement, design, and plans indicated hereon or represented hereby are owned by and remain the exclusive property of the designer. They have been created and developed for the use on and in connection with the specified project. Written dimensions on drawings shall have authority over scaled. Contractors and manufacturers shall verify and be responsible for all dimensions and the conditions on the job site. Any variations from the drawings are to be reported to the designer prior to performing work. These drawings represent visual concepts and construction and rigging suggestions only. The designer is unqualified to determine the structural appropriateness of this design and will not assume responsibility for improper engineering, construction, rigging, handling, or use of this lighting. All materials must comply with the most stringent applicable federal and local fire and safety codes.

USITT developed symbol guidelines for hand drafting. Vectorworks with Spotlight has its own set of symbols. Many of the manufacturers have developed CAD symbols for their fixtures. Independent programmers have symbols you can get as well. All this can be a little confusing. Here is the key (no pun intended). As long as the symbols on your light plot match the symbols in your key, everything will work out okay. Is it better to use something standardized? It helps others to understand what you want a little quicker. If they just finished working in a show with the USITT standard symbols, they are already used to them and know what they mean. If you use other symbols, they can still figure them out. It may just take a little longer initially.

Notes are an important part of every drafting. Scenic drawings tend to place the notes around the drawing as needed. Light plots tend to use a note box, where all the notes are located. Most lighting notes are applicable to the whole light plot, not just one light. Scenery notes are usually very specific to one piece of scenery. That is the difference in regards to placement.

When you began reading this book, you expected there to be a table of contents, individual chapters, and an index at the very least, right? You use these things to find what you want within the book. Well, drafting works the same way! A complete pack of scenic drafting should include:

- Sketch (scenery only)
- Ground plan or light plot
- Section
- Deck plan
- Elevations
- Detail drawings

Let's go through them briefly, one at a time. More detail will follow in the individual chapters and through illustrations. I think it is important to include the sketch as the first plate of drafting in a scenery pack (Figure 5.41). It gives everyone who will look at the drawings a context from which to compare all the individual pieces. Whenever I get a pack of drafting with the sketch attached, it always makes me relax knowing I have all the information in one place.

The ground plan and the light plot are similar drawings (Figure 5.42). Both are a plan view of the stage. Both show the theater architecture, which can include the proscenium arch, plaster line, smoke pocket, and other architectural details needed. The most important thing on either of these drawings is the **center line**. Let me say that again. The most important thing on either of these

■ **Figure 5.41** Complete packs of draftings must be stored and kept for reference.

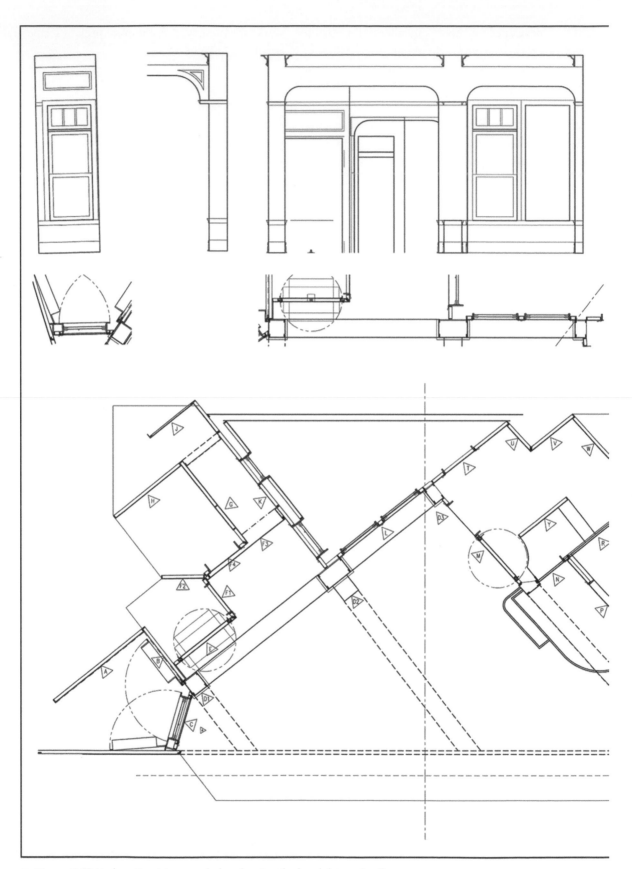

■ **Figure 5.42** Hudson Scenic's ground plan showing the breakdown of walls.

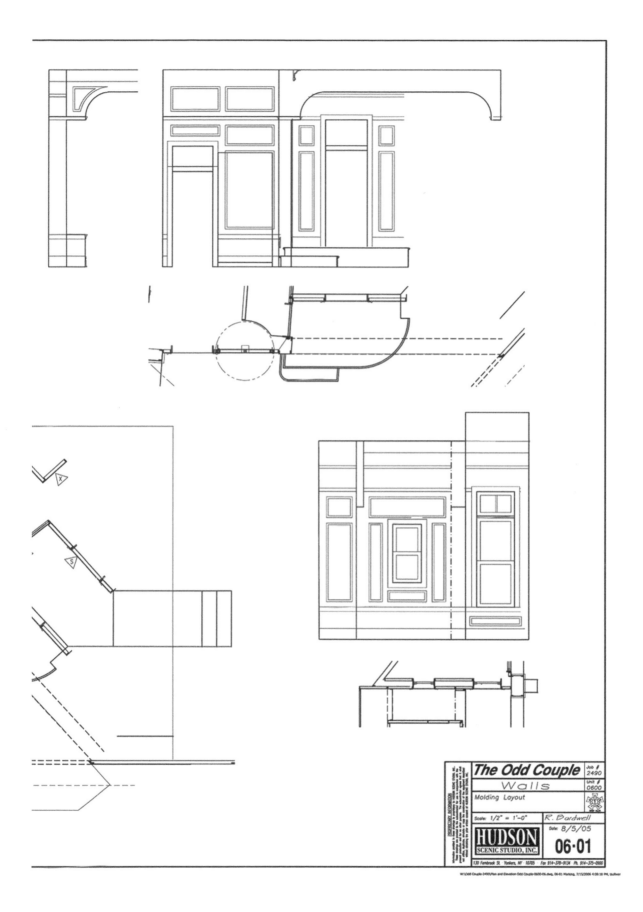

The Odd Couple

Job # 2490

Walls

Unit # 0600

Molding Layout

Scale: 1/2" = 1'-0"   R. Bardwell

HUDSON SCENIC STUDIO, INC.

Date: 8/5/05

06·01

130 Fernbrook St. Yonkers, NY 10705   Fax 914-376-9134 Ph. 914-375-0900

drawings is the centerline! Got it? Why, you might ask? Well, we know where the **plaster line** is, and that it is our reference for all upstage and downstage measurements. Our only reference for left and right measurements is the centerline. Here is the twist. Sometimes, the center of the stage is not the center of the auditorium. Sometimes, the set designer moves the center of the set to a different angle. So, how do you know which one to use? It's easy; the set designer selects the one that is the most critical to the set and therefore the production. The lighting designer then needs to use the same centerline. Otherwise, nothing will line up, things will have to be redone, and the schedule will go out the window. Let me just say one more thing. The most important thing on either of these drawings is the centerline!

The scenic ground plan should show all the scenic elements, assembled and in their positions, as this is the primary focus of the drawing. Major scenic elements should be identified through notes. Overhead items, whether static or moving, should be indicated with dotted lines. All curtains, backings, and masking should be shown in position relative to the sight lines.

Also on the ground plan is the line set inventory, also known as a line set schedule (Figure 5.43). This may

Line Set Schedule

Line Set	Position	Standard		Comment	Weight
	0	Plasterline		56' by 23'	
	5"	Fire Curtain		Not Used	
	11"	#1 Border/Legs		Arbor	
1	2' 8"	1st Elec.		42' Batten	350 lbs
	3' 4"	Water Pipe		Obstruction	
	3' 8"	Traveler		Dead Hung	a lot
2	4' 6"	Blackout			
3	5'	Border		55' by 8'	200 lbs
	6' - 7' 3"	Screen		56' by 23'	Winch
4	7' 9"			42' Batten	15 lbs
5	8' 4"	#2 Border		55' by 8'	150 lbs
	9' 6"	#2 Legs	2 - 2 Line	21' 3" Off Center	75 lbs
6	10'	Blackout		(2) 22' by 23'	200 lbs
7	11'	2nd Elec.		42' Batten	250 lbs
8	13'			2 - 21' Battens	50 lbs
9	14' 6"			42' Batten	100 lbs
10	16'	#3 Border		55' by 8'	150 lbs
	16' 6"	#3 Legs	2 - 2 Line	20' Off Center	75 lbs
11	17'			42' Batten	50 lbs
12	18' 6"			42' Batten	
13	19' 6"	3rd Elec.		42' Batten	300 lbs
14	21'			42' Batten	75lbs
15	22'	#4 Border		48' by 20'	200 lbs
16	23' 6"	Blackout		(2) 21' by 22'	200 lbs

■ **Figure 5.43** Sample line set inventory.

be one of the most important things to be referenced by everyone. The line set inventory is a list of pipes overhead, whether they be static or can be flown in and out. The inventory numbers the pipes, beginning at the plaster line and moving upstage as the numbers get higher. The distance upstage from the plaster line to the center of the pipe is shown. The set designer provides a description for what will be hung from this pipe. Last, the designer estimates how high the pipe will be in its playing and storage positions.

The light plot is similar to the ground plan and contains many of the same things (Figure 5.44). The light plot shows the scenic elements, although usually in less detail than on the ground plan. The focus of the light plot is to show the lighting equipment for the show, in relation to the scenery and masking. The light plot, by its nature, becomes a composite drawing. The scenic designer's ground plan is the base. Lighting is drawn over the top. The line set inventory is altered with the addition of the overhead electrics.

The section drawing, whether for scenery or lighting, is essential (Figure 5.45). Picture that the theater has been cut in half along the centerline and split wide open. If you stand between the two halves and look in the stage left wing, that is a "center section looking left." You can make the split anywhere that benefits showing the crucial information you need and you can look in either direction—or both. The key is to show a cut through the middle of important details, so that we can see how other parts of the show relate.

The deck plan is a drawing of the floor (Figure 5.46). That sounds simple. But it's really not in today's theater. Decks have often become the most complicated part of the design. The floor of the theater is often covered completely with platforms, called a show deck. The reason for this is that much more scenery moves now than ever before, and the deck can contain pieces of the automation package for doing this movement. There can also be multiple levels to create more interesting acting areas. That means stairs will be needed, both onstage to get the actors up and potentially offstage to get the actors back down. More on that entire idea later, but let's just say that a floor is not just a floor anymore.

Our next topic is the elevation. An elevation takes the ground plan and stands it up in three dimensions, one element at a time. This allows the scene shop and carpenters to see each individual piece as it is intended to be built. Measurements are critical at this stage, as building is about to begin. The elevation can go into much more detail than the ground plan because there is more room on the drawing for it. The ground plan is expanded so each piece stands by itself. The elevation is the main element, but for reference you will also see the plan and side view of each element near the elevation. Studying the elevations is one of the best ways to get to know the set and catch parts that may have been too crowded to see on the ground plan. Elevations are often drawn in the same scale as the ground plan.

Where the elevation leaves off, the detail drawings begin (Figure 5.47). Often, parts of the set require a much closer look. Let's say the scale of the ground plan was ¼ inch or ½ inch; the detail drawings could be 3 inches equal 1 foot or even full scale (Figure 5.49). Take a look at your scale rule and think about the difference between these scales. This allows for the detail to almost explode into view. It makes the dimensioning not only easier but doable. Detail drawings also include practicals. Practicals are scenic elements or props that plug into some form of electricity. These items must be planned out in great detail to make sure that they work properly and are safe. Practicals must also be coordinated with props, lighting, costumes, or whichever other department is involved.

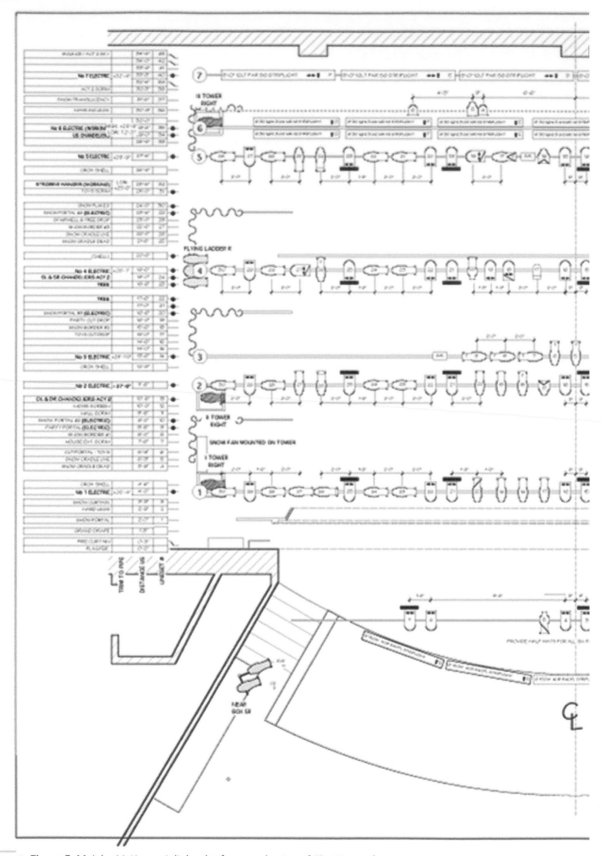

■ **Figure 5.44** John McKernon's light plot for a production of *The Nutcracker*.

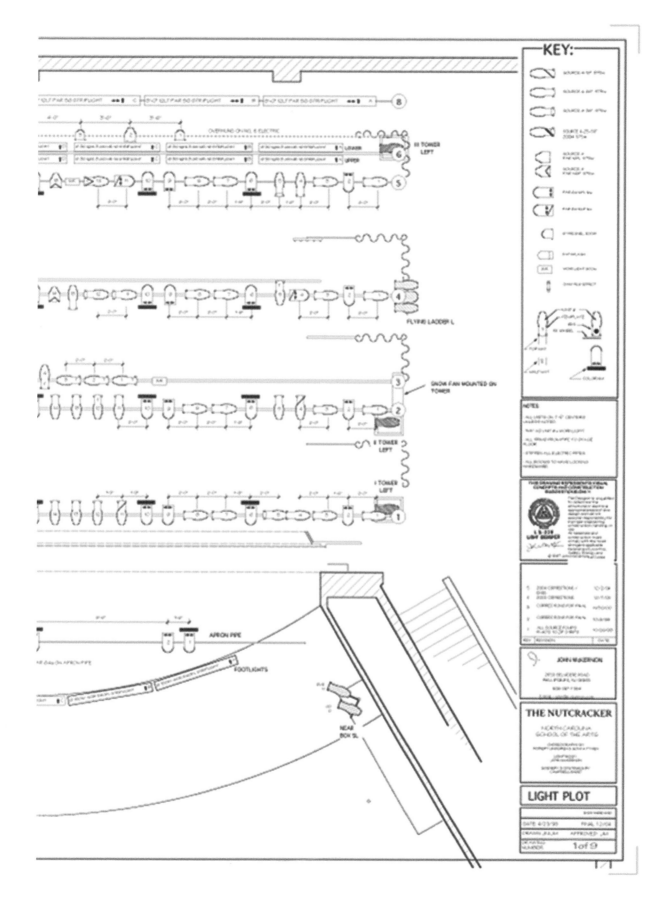

KEY:

THE NUTCRACKER

NORTH CAROLINA
SCHOOL OF THE ARTS

LIGHT PLOT

1 of 9

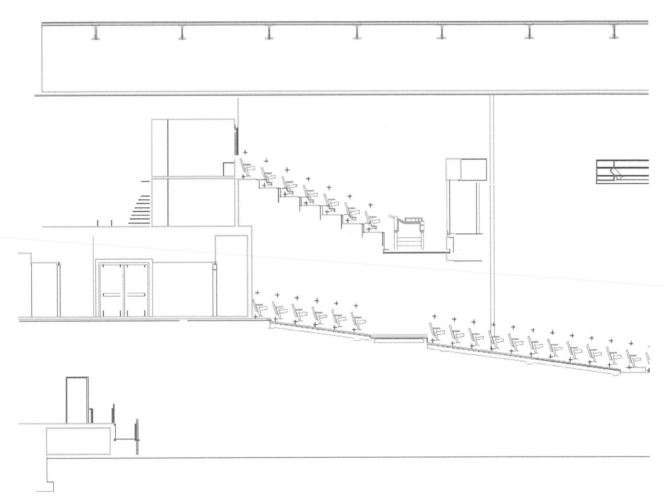

■ **Figure 5.45** Section for a high-school auditorium during new construction.

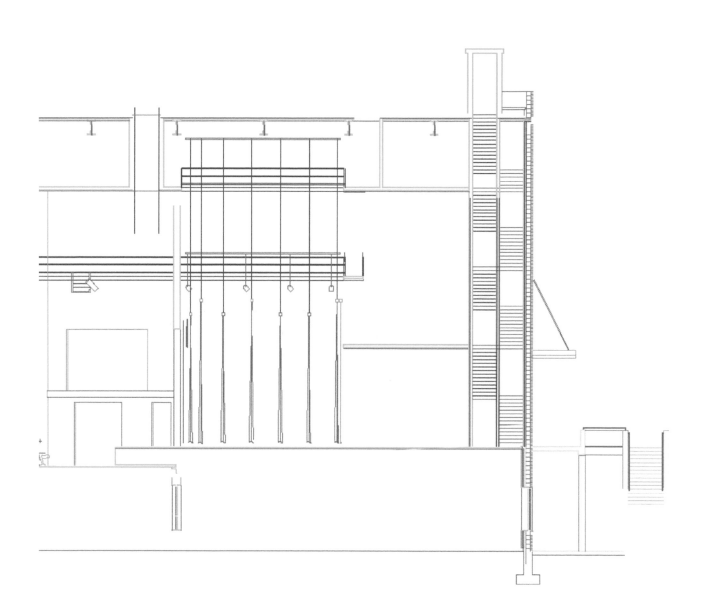

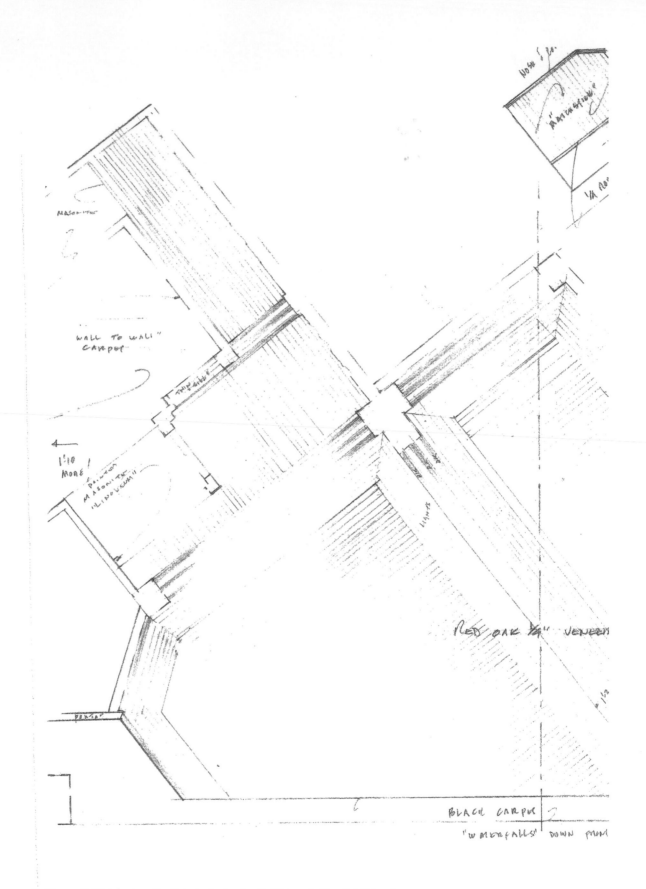

Figure 5.46 John Lee Beatty's deck plan for Neil Simon's *The Odd Couple*.

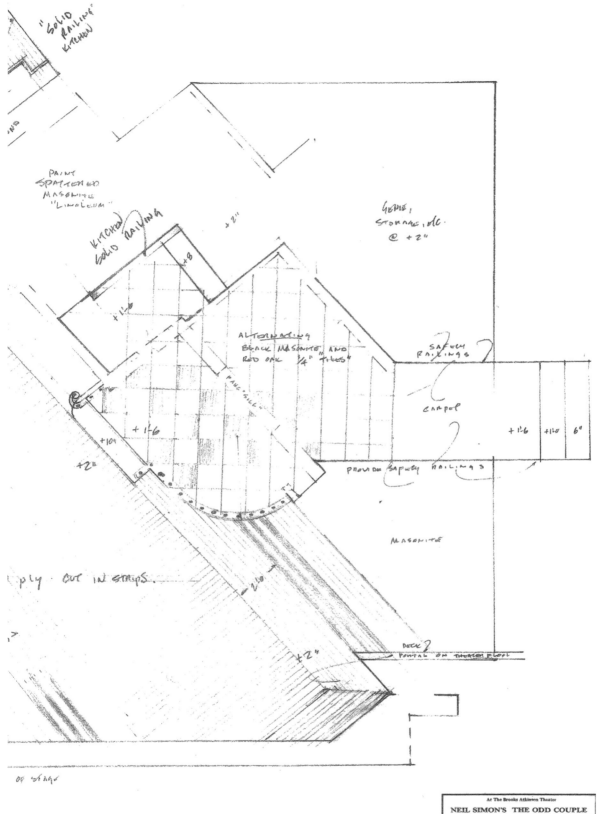

"SOLID RAILING" KITCHEN

PAINT SPATTERED MASONITE "LINOLEUM"

KITCHEN SOLID RAILING

GEDIE: STORAGE, etc. @ +2"

+2"

+8

+1'-0

ALTERNATING BLACK MASONITE AND RED OAK 1/4" TILES

FAUX SILL

SAFETY RAILINGS

CARPET

+1'-6

PROVIDE SAFETY RAILINGS

+1'-6 +1'-0 6"

+1'-6

+10"

+2"

MASONITE

ply · cut in strips.

2'-0

+2"

DECK? PORTAL ON THEATER FLOOR

OF STAGE

At The Brooks Atkinson Theater
NEIL SIMON'S THE ODD COUPLE
Directed by Joe Mantello
Designed by John Lee Beatty
Date: ___   Scale: 1/2"
DWG: DECK
Plate:

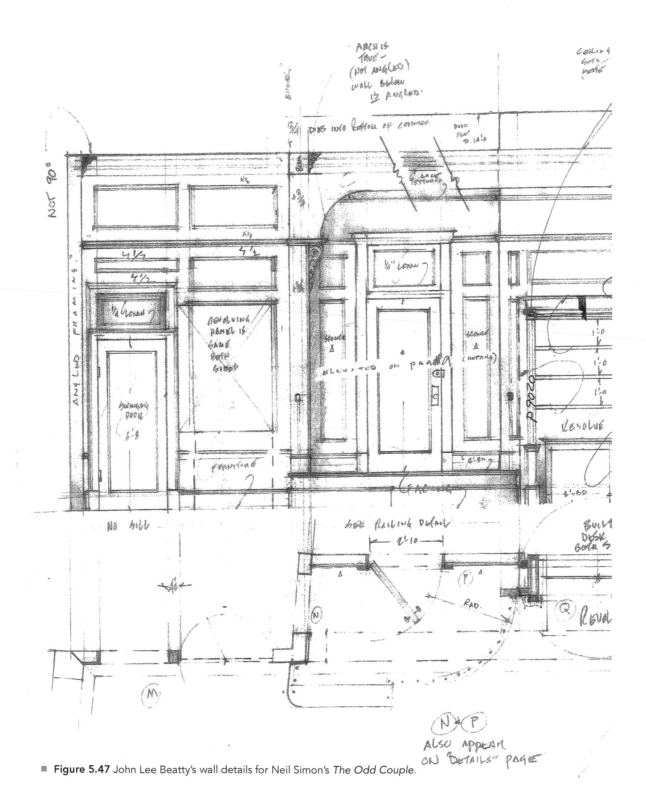

Figure 5.47 John Lee Beatty's wall details for Neil Simon's *The Odd Couple*.

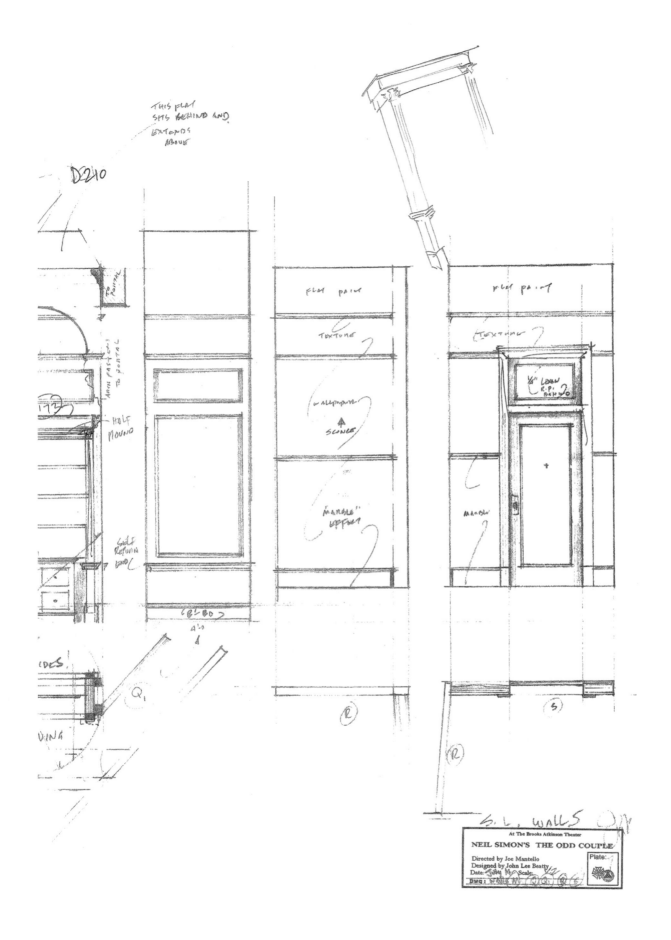

THIS FLAT
SITS BEHIND AND
EXTENDS ABOUT

D210

FLAT PAINT

FLAT PAINT

TEXTURE

(TEXTURE)

(WALLPAPER)

SCONCE

"MARBLE" EFFECT

MARBLE

HALF
ROUND

SELF
RETURN
END

(8'-0")

4'-0

At The Brooks Atkinson Theater

NEIL SIMON'S THE ODD COUPLE

Directed by Joe Mantello
Designed by John Lee Beatty
Date: July   Scale: ½

Dwg: Plate:

S.L. WALLS

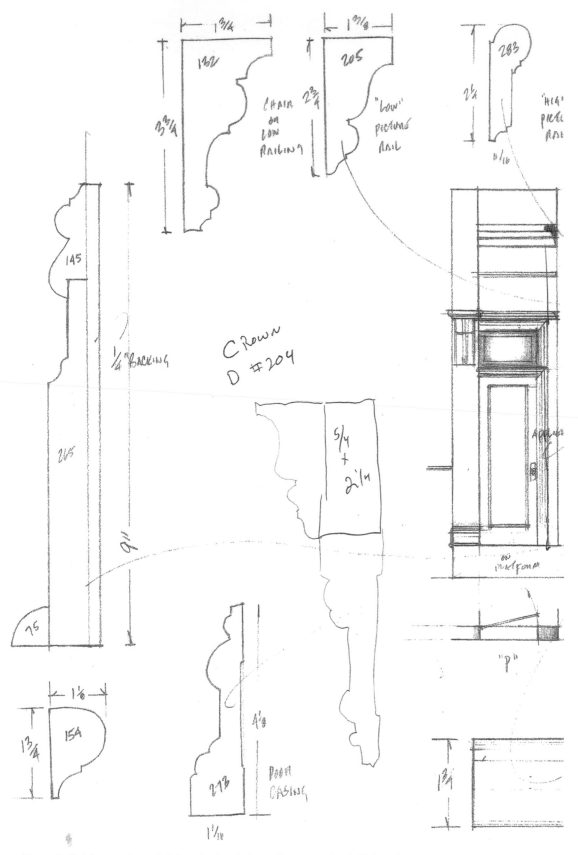

■ **Figure 5.48** John Lee Beatty's full-scale details for Neil Simon's *The Odd Couple*.

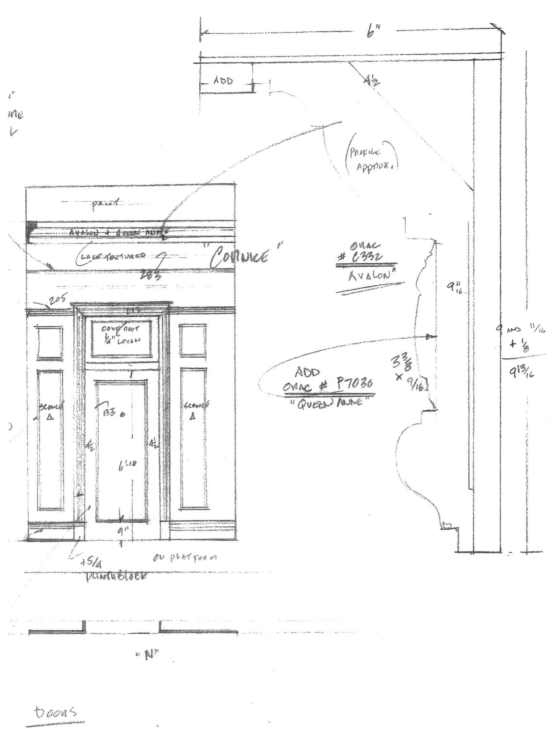

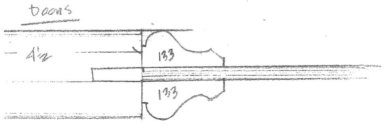

FULLSCALES-PLUS

At The Brooks Atkinson Theater

NEIL SIMON'S THE ODD COUPLE

Directed by Joe Mantello
Designed by John Lee Beatty
Date: July 14   Scale: Plate:
Dwg:

By the way, in case you were wondering, I once asked my professor to take his own drawing test (Figure 5.49). Remember the cube, chair, rabbit, and human?

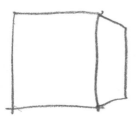

■ **Figure 5.49** Salvatore Tagliarino takes his own test!

EXERCISES

EXERCISE 1
SAL'S TEST

Draw a cube, chair, rabbit, and humanoid. Spend no more than three to four minutes on each drawing.

EXERCISE 2
TITLE BLOCK

Design and draw your own title block. Make sure to include all the critical information and leave placeholders as needed.

EXERCISE 3
DISCLAIMER

Write your own liability disclaimer to be used on your draftings.

CHECK YOUR KNOWLEDGE

1. Explain why drawing, drafting, and rendering are all vital to the theatre process.
2. Describe why insight is so important in a creative art such as theatre.
3. List the types of perspective we use in the theatre. Define each type and why it might be used in a specific situation.
4. Categorize the different types of lines used in drafting and what the symbolic representation is for each.
5. List the three types of dimensioning and when they are used.
6. Restate the information required for a title block. Determine which information should be the largest and explain why.
7. Define why a liability disclaimer is important.
8. Relate the standard drawings required in a pack of scenic drawings to those required in a pack of lighting drawings.
9. Explain why a line set inventory is so critical to the safety of a production.

- Arc dimensions
- CAD
- Center line
- Deck plan
- Detail drawing
- Drafting
- Drafting stool
- Drafting table
- Drafting tape
- Drawing
- Elevation
- Erasing shield
- Foreshortening
- French curve
- Ground plan
- Horizon line
- Insight
- Key to symbols
- Lettering guide
- Light plot
- Linear dimensions
- Line set inventory
- Multiple dimensions
- Orthographic projection
- Parallel rule
- Perspective
- Plan view
- Plaster line
- Practicals
- Previsualization
- Raster
- Rendering
- Scale rule
- Section
- Show deck
- Side view
- Sketch
- Soft goods
- Title block
- Triangle
- T square
- Vanishing point
- Vector

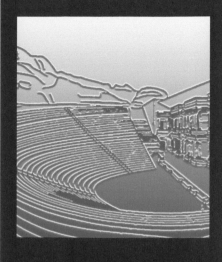

STUDY WORDS

Chapter 5

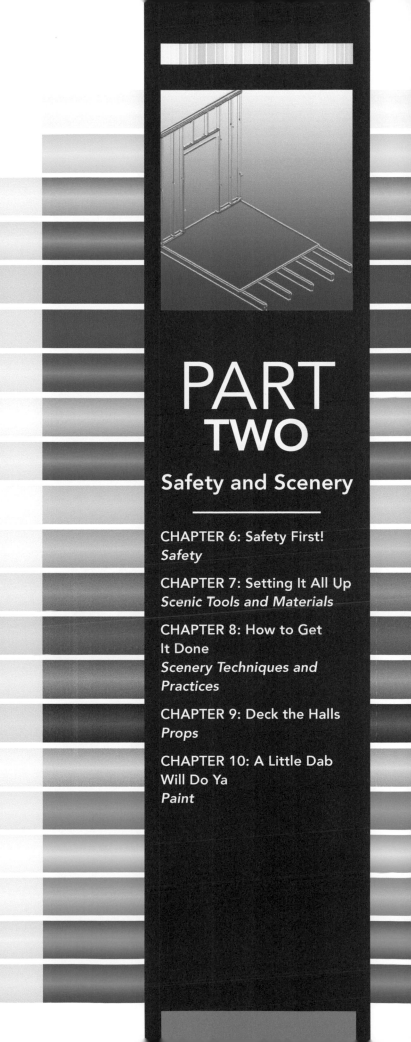

PART
TWO

Safety and Scenery

CHAPTER 6: Safety First!
Safety

CHAPTER 7: Setting It All Up
Scenic Tools and Materials

CHAPTER 8: How to Get
It Done
*Scenery Techniques and
Practices*

CHAPTER 9: Deck the Halls
Props

CHAPTER 10: A Little Dab
Will Do Ya
Paint

Safety First!

Safety

My students all know that my favorite saying is, "I've never had to call 911 for a student, and you're not going to break my record." That phrase doesn't mean there are bleeding students all over New England. It means I teach my students the correct procedures to keep them safe. This chapter talks about safety, both backstage in the theater and in the various shops related to the implementation of all the designs. Safety also is addressed in other chapters while we discuss specific techniques and tools.

There are established standards for safety, and they are' practiced for a reason. The theater can be a dangerous place. We are always trying to accomplish things that simply aren't supposed to be done inside a building, never mind in the dark! If you follow some basic safety rules, you will stay safe. But you've got to think. And, let's face it, most of us got into the theatre because it looked like fun. Let's keep it that way.

> Safety is just danger, out of place.
> —Harry Connick, Jr,
> American singer and actor

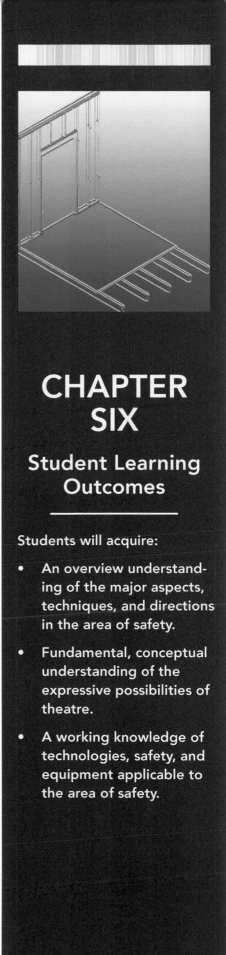

CHAPTER SIX

Student Learning Outcomes

Students will acquire:

- An overview understanding of the major aspects, techniques, and directions in the area of safety.

- Fundamental, conceptual understanding of the expressive possibilities of theatre.

- A working knowledge of technologies, safety, and equipment applicable to the area of safety.

Let me warn you. This chapter deals with a lot of information that doesn't seem like the "fun" theatre stuff I've been referring to. The only way to keep theatre fun is to keep it safe. I feel *very* strongly about this. Even with a hectic schedule, there is always time to slow down and do it the right way. If you do it the wrong way, because you are in a hurry, think about how much time you waste while you wait for the ambulance to come!

> Don't learn safety rules simply by accident.
> —Unknown

Many safety measures are often ignored for a few simple reasons. They are thought to be a bother, take too much time, or are "unnecessary." Well, let me tell you, none of these safety guidelines are created in a void just to frustrate you. Their basis began when someone was injured—then we realized there needed to be safety procedures to keep us safe. There is a reason why you should never scream "Fire!" in a crowded theater. More on that later. But let me tell you, it is downright dangerous. Theatre should be—and when done safely is—fun. Danger is a real possibility in many practices in the theatre. If you follow the guidelines in this chapter and any that get updated from here on out, you will find yourself in a much safer position.

PERSONAL SAFETY

I absolutely love the theatre and I have fun doing it. Safety should be a very personal thing for all of us, and it certainly is for me. You want to keep yourself safe. I have little tolerance for people being unsafe, because it puts everybody at risk. Keep in mind you are responsible for not just your safety, but the safety of those around you—and vice versa. There are very few things you do in the theater by yourself. You want to keep yourself and your coworkers safe—as well as the audience. So, let's get started, and I'll try not to use too many gory examples.

Let's start with the basics. You. Yes, you. You can be the most dangerous person in the theater if you don't keep safety in mind—let's hope you never get injured. That is

the point of this chapter—to give you the information so you can keep yourself safe. Any situation can turn from safe to dangerous quickly and unexpectedly. The best prevention against injury and danger is to be informed. Most people in theatre know that things go wrong in ways we'd least expect, and the last thing anyone wants is to cause someone harm through carelessness.

The two main categories of possible hazards fall into the areas of health and safety. They really go hand in hand, but we address each of these separately, using examples from OSHA and others for perspective. OSHA, the Occupational Safety and Health Administration, is an agency of the US government's Department of Labor. OSHA's mission, according to their website, is to "assure the safety and health of America's workers by setting and enforcing standards; providing training, outreach, and education; establishing partnerships; and encouraging continual improvement in workplace safety and health." No discussion of safety would be complete, or could even begin, without discussing OSHA. Its mission statement takes on a great deal, with extreme consequences for not complying. OSHA is discussed periodically throughout this chapter.

We continue by discussing some basic personal safety topics. Let's talk about your clothing first (Figure 6.1). Clothing that is too baggy can get caught in power tools. Clothes that are too tight restrict your movement, meaning you can't operate tools properly or move out of the way quickly in an emergency. Clothing that doesn't cover you properly won't protect you. Does this mean you can't dress in your own style? No, of course not. There is no stagehand uniform. Pants are better than shorts for protecting your legs. In the scene shop, wood splinters can go flying around. Pants protect your legs from getting splinters, for example. Now, you may say, What is the big deal with a splinter? Well, say you can't find the splinter and it gets infected, or you turn out to be allergic to something the splinter has in or on it. Well, that can stink—now you're off to the nurse or worse. Doesn't sound like fun, does it?

Shoes are next and a very important part of your wardrobe for technical work. One of my pet peeves is that flip-flops are for the beach, not the scene shop (Figure 6.1). But, you also don't need to buy steel-toe work boots. In fact, opinions are varied on whether steel-toe boots are good or bad in the theater. For minor incidents, they can help. But, if your foot starts to get crushed, the steel toe can actually do more damage rather than offering protection. What you want is a good sturdy-soled shoe. Take your shoe off and hold it sole down, with one hand near the toe and one hand near the heel. Try to bend the shoe in half. If it bends too easily, it won't protect your foot very well. The goal should be that, if you step on a nail, staple, or screw, it should not go straight through to your foot. The sole should slow it down enough that you notice something is wrong and stop to check.

OK, we've gotten to the last topic of personal safety, which is hair (Figure 6.2). Yes, hair. Long hair can be as dangerous as dangling jewelry or baggy clothes. Hair can obscure your vision, it can get caught in machines, and, yes, it can catch on fire. I've had all these things happen, because I thought it would take too long to pull my hair back. Now, I don't even walk into the shop without already having my hair pulled back or put up. You can also cover your hair with a bandana.

OK, let's move on to your jewelry. Chains, bracelets, earrings, or any body jewelry and rings—you all wear it, and that is fine to a point (Figure 6.4). Chains hanging loosely from your neck can get caught in a machine and pull you toward the blade or cutting edge. Bracelets can do the same thing. Dangling earrings can get caught in

■ **Figure 6.1** Take a look at the highlighted areas to see the good choices for clothing and shoes in the shop.

■ **Figure 6.2** Hair is one of the most overlooked safety concerns. Hair pulled back into a ponytail or braid will keep you safe.

■ **Figure 6.3** Taking proper safety measures cannot and should not be underrated. Safety glasses and work gloves give this stagehand the advantage against injury.

■ **Figure 6.4** No jewelry choices are good when working in the shop. They all pose a potential danger. See a stagehand with no jewelry, that's a safe stagehand.

more ways than I can list. And trust me when I say it's not too pleasant to have the earring pulled from your ear, never mind any other body jewelry. My father worked with machinery his whole life and never wore his wedding ring at work to be safe. He knew better. And that knowledge helped him keep all ten of his fingers! Say there is an accident, and your hand gets hurt. The first thing the doctors do is cut off your ring, so why wear it to begin with? Worst-case scenario is the ring can do more damage than the original accident.

Does all this mean that you have to take out all your jewelry, shave your head, and walk into the shop naked? No! In fact, please don't. Here is the right way to do it:

- Clothing should fit and cover your body
- Jewelry should be small, if not removed completely
- Shoes should be sturdy
- Hair should be pulled back or covered

It all sounds simple, and it is. It's better to be safe from the beginning than to try to fix the problem later. Keep these simple personal safety rules in your mind every time you know you are going to work in the theater. Take a look at the photos on the next few pages for good examples of these rules.

Think of it this way: When put under a lot of pressure, wood will usually break, and metal will crush whatever gets caught in the way. Flesh and bone, well, let's just say they are the weakest of all. We also deal with very sharp tools meant to cut or shape almost anything. Those same tools don't care if they are cutting wire or skin. So, we have to be careful. We have to be vigilant.

If my students show up for class wearing something inappropriate for the shop, I send them home, and they are considered absent from class that day! That is how strongly I feel about safety. My father taught me all these lessons, and one more: Don't fear tools; respect what they can do.

Take everything I say here as a guideline. Your teacher or the technical director knows more about the specific projects you are working on. Keep in mind that you should aim for at least the minimum amount of safety protection, but sometimes the maximum amount is better and more appropriate. Personal protective equipment, or PPE, is the things we can wear for safety. COVID-19

■ **Figure 6.5** A face shield and two styles of goggles, many of which fit easily over standard eyeglass frames, are the best line of defense to keep eyes safe and healthy.

PPE such as goggles or face shields, masks, and gloves are just the beginning of the list of safety measures you can and should take when working in the theater.

When you go out in the sun, you put on sunglasses, right? Well, when you work in the theater on certain jobs, you need to wear **goggles**. Even if you wear eyeglasses, you need to wear goggles over your eyeglasses. Regular glasses are not shatterproof and do not protect your eyes should an accident happen. The lenses in eyeglasses will break. This allows for the possibility of getting glass in your eye, causing more damage. Many people who work full-time in scene shops and wear glasses will often have a pair of googles made with prescription lenses. In fact, when you are working on certain tasks and with certain tools, you need a **face shield**, not just a pair of goggles (Figure 6.5). Wearing a face shield also helps when you need to be wearing a dust mask or a respirator, so it's a more versatile piece of PPE than goggles.

Protecting your eyesight is obviously very important. Wearing safety goggles or a face shield is the first line of defense for your eyes. Accidental exposure of your eyes to chemical substances can result in irritation (temporary or permanent), vision impairment, or blindness. This is not something to joke around about. Since we work with a variety of eye hazards in the theater, **eyecups** and **eyewash stations** are the next line of defense when something gets past the goggles or shield (Figures 6.6 and 6.7). We all know accidents can happen, and

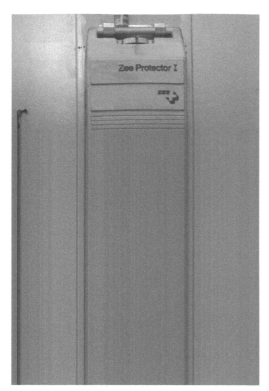

■ **Figure 6.6** An eyewash station, when closed and mounted to the wall, takes up very little room.

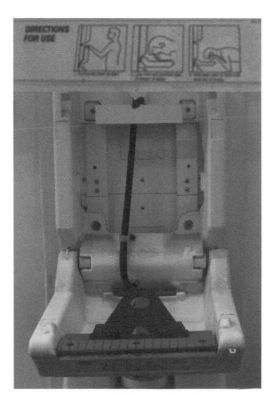

■ **Figure 6.7** An eyewash station, when opened for use showing its instructions, is ready for any emergency.

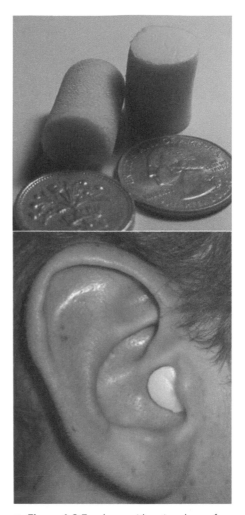

■ **Figure 6.8** Earplugs, with coins shown for scale, and how to wear them. The key is to be safe while still being aware of your surroundings.

eyewash stations provide an effective means of washing your eyes to minimize the time an irritant comes in contact with them. The first 15 seconds following exposure are the best time to properly cleanse your eyes to minimize further injury.

Let's talk about your hearing next. You will be working with many different types of power tools. All these make noise, to differing levels. Anybody exposed to excessive noise on a regular basis must use appropriate ear protection! Loss of hearing and possible deafness are nothing to play around with. Protection can include **earplugs** (Figure 6.8), **earmuffs**, or both.

It is often not possible to reduce the amount of noise we are exposed to in the theater. The best way to deal

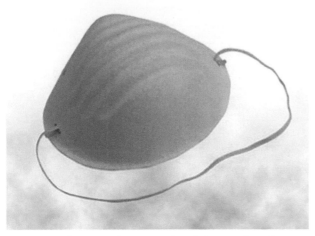

■ **Figure 6.9** Dust masks come in handy in a number of situations, everything from keeping particles away from you to keeping you from spreading germs.

■ **Figure 6.10** You need special training to select and use a respirator properly. These are used when a regular dust mask won't keep you safe from airborne chemicals.

with this is to use ear protection. Potential sources of noise hazards can include the following list, but keep in mind that any repetitive sound can ultimately affect you:

- Air compressors
- Power saws
- Power drills
- Grinders
- Welders

Now that we have dealt with your eyes and ears, let's deal with your nose. Or, a better way to say it is this: We are now going to talk about your entire respiratory system and how to keep it safe. If you breathe in the dust or spray from an irritant, it can quickly move from your nose to your throat and lungs. We start simple and easy. The **dust mask** is the first line of defense to keep you breathing normally (Figure 6.9). In the theater, we deal with many small particles: Dust and powdered dyes that are micro fine and prone to suspend in the air are just one example. Your basic dust mask can protect you from inhaling these.

Keep in mind that some of the most dangerous chemicals have no smell, so you may have little advance warning. Always follow the safety instructions for the product you are using (Figure 6.10). When moving on to things of greater potential risk, and therefore more needed protection, we will discuss **respirators**. There are two types of respirators, air-purifying and atmosphere-

supplying respirators. The names of these pretty much describe how they work. The air-purifying type has filters, cartridges, or canisters that remove irritants and contaminants from the air by passing the air through a filter before it reaches you. By the time the air gets to you, it has been "cleaned." Atmosphere-supplying respirators, on the other hand, supply clean air directly to you from an oxygen canister or other source rather than the air surrounding you.

The right respirator to use really depends on what environment you are in and what might be floating around in the air. A good guide to what type of protector you may need is found in the **safety data sheets**, referred to as *SDS*. These are discussed in detail later in the chapter. Just keep in mind you need not guess at safety. Guidelines and recommendations are in place because lots of people have studied the situations and figured out the best way to keep you safe. All you have to do is follow the established protocol.

Next, let's address your hands. You may be thinking, my hands—so what? Work gloves are an important part of every stagehand's tool kit (Figure 6.11). This is not about vanity and the perfect manicure. It's about keeping your hands intact and other people safe. First off, wearing gloves protects your hands from splinters, cuts, and worse. Second, gloves give you a better grip when holding or carrying heavy, slippery, or bulky objects. The better your grip, the less likely you are to drop something on either yourself or someone else.

■ **Figure 6.11** (1) Canvas and leather gloves, (2) cotton gloves with rubber nubs, (3) lined leather gloves, (4) leather gloves, (5) Setwear fingerless gloves, and (6) Setwear full-finger gloves. Find a pair that fits you well and is suited for your specific job.

Gloves come in a number of styles, fabrics, and of course costs. These combine to make a glove appropriate for one job and not another. Some jobs require a thinner glove, so that your sense of touch is still able to function. Some jobs require heavier gloves, insulated gloves, waterproof gloves, and so forth. You get the idea. It's all about using the proper tool for the job, and that is a theme we discuss throughout the book.

> He that's secure is not safe.
> —Benjamin Franklin,
> author, printer, politician, postmaster ...

Let's change our discussion now to reaching higher places. To do this we need to use one of a couple of devices. First, we talk about ladders (Figure 6.12). The four basic styles of ladders are (1) step, (2) straight or extension, (3) A-frame or trestle, and (4) articulated. The first two are self-supporting. That means they can stand up all by themselves. Extension ladders are considered non-self-supporting. I think you get it, but that means they have to lean against something. A hybrid of these is the Little Giant and Gorilla brand of ladders. They are articulated, meaning the same ladder can be used as either a step ladder or an extension ladder in varying configurations.

Figure 6.12 Ladders come in a range of styles and heights. Make sure you are comfortable going up and down a ladder before you try to do it on your own.

Figure 6.13 Motorized lifts come in a variety of types. These require special training before you try to use them.

OSHA developed strict rules for the proper and safe use of ladders. You should not use a ladder alone. There should always be someone with you to hold the ladder, sometimes more than one person, depending on the ladder and the situation. Even though we've all seen the little sticker that says the top rung is not a step, how many of us have used it as a step when something was just out of our reach and we needed the extra height? Well, this is actually not safe—there is a reason that sticker is there.

Stepladders must have a metal spreader or locking device to hold the front and back sections in an open position when the ladder is in use. Make sure this is engaged before beginning to climb. Dollies are often created for ladders so that the ladders can roll around. OSHA *does not* approve of this. Most theaters and

educational institutions have retired ladders on rolling bases in favor of personnel lifts so this is no longer a common practice.

So, the ladder won't get you high enough, especially since you can't stand on the top step anymore! Well, the next option is a bigger ladder if possible or a personnel lift. The personnel lift is a motorized lift with a bucket or platform (Figure 6.13). Common brand names are JLG®, Genie®, Condor®, and Snorkel®. Again, OSHA has strict guidelines for safe use of this equipment. Each piece of equipment has specific rules for safe use. One piece of safety equipment that is required for most non-drivable personnel lifts is outriggers. **Outriggers** are stabilizing legs that attach to the base of the lift. If the lift comes equipped with outriggers, the outriggers must be in place prior to raising or lowering the platform or basket. Many of today's lifts have a safety cutoff switch that will not allow the basket to rise without the proper placement of the outriggers. This may be frustrating, but, if you've ever been unfortunate enough to see a lift tip over, you understand the need!

Keep in mind the basket around the platform is there for your safety. Leaning over the basket takes your balance out of the center and makes for a more dangerous situation. There are exceptions to rules, but they usually have a counterpart. If you need to lean out of the basket, consider repositioning the lift, if at all possible. Otherwise, make sure to use a personal harness or lanyard as a safety precaution to keep you from falling. Also make sure to use a tool leash on all tools you take up in the air. A tool leash can be as simple as a piece of tie-line that connects you to your tool!

> Safety means first aid to the uninjured.
> —Unknown

No location should be without a first aid kit (Figure 6.14). This includes your home, your car, your school, and your workplace. Accidents can happen anywhere, at any time. Check the kit regularly. Make sure the flashlight batteries work. Check the expiration dates and replace any used or out-of-date contents. The contents of a first aid kit can be dangerous in the hands of young children, so store the kit safely and securely. Here are suggestions for the contents of a basic first aid kit. Your first aid kit may vary slightly depending on your actual needs.

- Hand sanitizer
- KN95 mask
- Disposable gloves
- Cold pack
- Disinfectant pads
- Antiseptic ointment
- Antihistamine cream, such as Benadryl
- Calamine lotion
- Aloe vera gel
- Band-aids (butterflies, knuckles, fingertips, assorted sizes)
- Eyecup

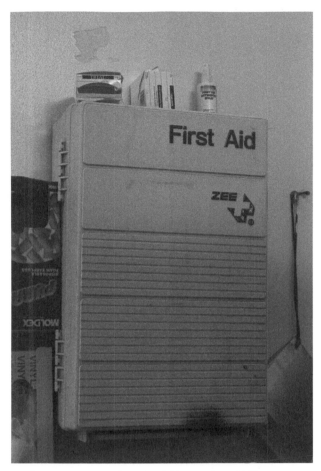

■ **Figure 6.14** Every shop should have a first aid kit. The person in charge determines the type of kit based on potential needs and where it is ultimately located.

- Saline
- Adhesive tape
- Gauze pads and roller gauze (assorted sizes)
- Triangular bandage
- Elastic bandages
- Plastic bags
- Scissors and tweezers
- Small flashlight and extra batteries

Safety can take another form. Allergies come in many forms, such as dust or glue. Another possibility is latex. I sometimes work with latex sponges or gloves. Before ever handing one to someone, I always ask if they have any known allergy to latex. Most often people say no. But I don't let it end there. I always keep an eye on the students who are using these products. At least once every year, I find a student with an allergy to latex who had never had a reaction before. Safety should never be taken lightly, never.

FIRE SAFETY

OK, now that we've gotten you safe, let's look at the work environment for other ways to stay safe. The first thing to do whenever you walk into a new theater or any place you've never been to before is to look around and find out where the exits are. Think about it! What is the first thing a flight attendant points out in the safety speech? The exits are over the wings, in the back, or in the front. Always look for the exit, it's that easy!

Our next topic is fire protection. There are several ways to prevent fires and several ways to put them out once they begin. We start with preventing them. This is really common sense. If you are going to use a candle on stage, the local fire department may require that a licensed person be in attendance whenever the candle is lit. This trained person may be a firefighter or someone else with similar training. Either way, having someone like this in attendance makes the show, the theater, and all the people in attendance safer as well. Make sure to check all local regulations before your production.

Other things that can get very hot and possibly cause fires are the lighting instruments. And lights are almost always near curtains and scenery. A piece of safety equipment that can be used in this situation is called **Zetex®**. Zetex is used in the theater as a **thermal barrier** to protect objects from heating up too much (Figure 6.15). Zetex is manufactured, among other things, into a fabric that can be hung on the pipes between the lights and other objects to protect them from the heat. Its use replaced asbestos when we finally figured out that asbestos was really bad for you. Zetex is also manufactured into gloves and other items that may come in handy when working in the theater. Zetex is further used in a number of products that are rated to protect for various degrees of heat.

Let's talk for a minute about the terms *fireproof* and *fire retardant*. These terms are sometimes used interchangeably and they shouldn't be. **Fireproof** implies that an item will not burn, smoke, or flame. **Fire retardant** implies that the item will burn, smoke, and

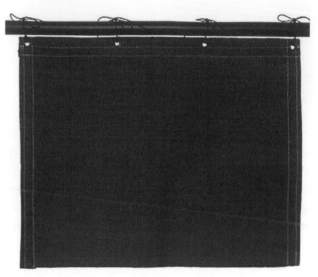

■ **Figure 6.15** Zetex can come in a natural canvas color or black and is the best thermal barrier we have today.

flame, although it will do all of these slower than other, untreated materials. Every state has its own specific rules governing fire retardancy. Make sure to check what is required in your area. All materials in the theater are susceptible to heat and fire damage when exposed to high temperatures for extended periods of time. With enough heat, even metal will melt. A fire-retardant material is one that is designed to resist burning and withstand heat for a certain amount of time. Most fabrics are treated with a flame-retardant chemical, either before or after painting (Figure 6.16). Keep in mind that any kind of laundering or dry cleaning means that costume or curtain has to be treated again. Scenery coming out of a scene shop is almost always treated in some manner.

One hundred percent of all scenery should be flame retardant. Scenic painters treat the curtains, and they need to be tested by someone who has a Supervision of Flame Retardancy certificate from the local fire department. All hard scenery is back painted with latex mixed with one of several different products to make it flame retardant. Certain materials, such as metal, provide resistance to high temperatures for limited periods of time.

Let's take our discussion from prevention to action in the event that prevention didn't work. There are several ways to put out fires once they start. Before the fire

■ **Figure 6.16** Hudson Scenic's shelves are full with various flameproofing products. Products vary depending on what you are treating.

actually starts, there are also ways to detect a problem that may be festering unseen.

A smoke detector or smoke alarm is an active fire protection device that detects airborne smoke or particles and issues an audible alarm, thereby alerting anyone nearby to the danger of fire (Figure 6.17). Most smoke detectors work either by optical detection or ionization,

> When you're safe at home you wish you were having an adventure; when you're having an adventure you wish you were safe at home.
>
> —Thornton Wilder,
> **American playwright and novelist**

■ **Figure 6.17** Smoke detectors are in our homes, as well as in our theaters. They are often the first line of defense should a fire start.

but some of them use both detection methods to increase sensitivity to smoke. If you are working on a production that uses any kind of smoke, fog, haze, or dry ice, make sure to ask the theater's technical director what type of smoke detector they use. If they use ionization detectors, your effects will set them off and call the fire department! There are ways to use these effects and still be safe. Check with the technical director to see if the detectors are wired in zones. You might be able to shut off one or two without disabling the whole system.

Smoke detectors may operate alone, be interconnected to cause all detectors in the premises to sound an alarm if one is triggered, or be integrated into a fire alarm or security system. Smoke detectors with flashing lights are available for the hearing impaired. A smoke detector cannot detect carbon monoxide to prevent carbon monoxide poisoning, unless it has an integrated carbon monoxide detector. There are also carbon monoxide detectors that operate separately.

In addition to possible carbon monoxide poisoning, we are all much more aware of allergies than we used to be. And there seem to be more things than ever before to be allergic to. Allergies and carbon monoxide poisoning can manifest in many different ways. There are several things to watch out for as you begin your career in the theatre:

■ **Figure 6.18** It is important to know how to use a fire extinguisher *before* the fire starts.

- Breathing difficulties that can range from shortness of breath to wheezing to coughing
- Swelling of your hands, arms, feet, or legs
- Discoloration of your skin
- Bumps or hives that may or may not itch

If you notice any of these symptoms, go *immediately* to your instructor. The last thing any of us want is to come across a student who has passed out. Our goal is always to keep you safe!

A fire extinguisher is an active fire protection device to put out fires, often in emergency situations (Figures 6.18 and 6.19). Fire extinguishers consist of pressurized containers of chemicals that, when discharged, can put out fires. It is important for everyone working in the theatre to be familiar with the different types and safe use of fire extinguishers.

In addition to handheld fire extinguishers that may be used for smaller fires, most theaters are equipped with one of three options:

1. Fire curtain.
2. Sprinkler system.
3. Deluge system.

Let's go into detail about each of these.

Choose The Right Fire Extinguisher

Class	Symbol	Type of Fire	Examples	ABC DRY CHEMICAL	BC DRY CHEMICAL	DRY POWDER	WATER	FOAM	WET CHEMICAL	HALOGENATED	CARBON DIOXIDE
A		Common Combustables	Wood, Paper, Fabric, etc.								
B		Flammable liquids & gases	Gasoline, propane, solvents								
C		Electrical	tools, lights, electronic equipment								

■ **Figure 6.19** There are different types of extinguishers; each is appropriate for different kinds of fires.

■ **Figure 6.20** In Europe, it is still the tradition to lower and raise the fire curtain before each performance to show the audience it is working. This photo is from the Vienna Opera House.

The **fire curtain** is the oldest of the three options listed, and its main purpose is to keep the audience safe from a fire on stage (Figure 6.20). It is used primarily in proscenium theaters. A fire curtain is a piece of fiberglass fabric or some other type of thermal barrier, such as Zetex. These curtains were originally made of asbestos, which is a naturally flame-resistant mineral, spun into fibers. Unfortunately, this was before we realized that breathing in asbestos dust causes lung cancer. They get hung between the audience and the stage, usually just upstage of the proscenium arch. Safety and health regulations say that the curtain must be able to "resist" fire and therefore prevent or at least slow fires starting on the stage from spreading into the auditorium and the rest of the theater.

The curtain travels up and down inside a guide called a **smoke pocket**. Traditionally, a piece of rope held the curtain up in the air. In the case of a fire, the rope is cut by a stage manager or stagehand, the curtain quickly

comes down to the stage and contains the fire, keeping the audience safe. Modern-day technology substituted a lever release for the rope and knife. Just turn or pull the lever and the curtain comes down! Much easier.

A **sprinkler system** is the next option (Figure 6.21). Most of you are used to seeing sprinkler heads in the ceiling of various rooms and buildings as you enter a classroom at school, a hotel, or an office building. Fire sprinklers are considered an active fire protection measure and are connected to a fire-suppression system that consists of overhead pipes fitted with sprinkler heads throughout the stage and auditorium. These pipes are continuously connected to a water source and can be used at a moment's notice.

Automatic fire sprinklers are individually heat activated and tied into a network of piping with water under pressure. When the heat of a fire raises the sprinkler temperature to its operating point (usually, 165°F), a solder link melts or a liquid-filled glass bulb

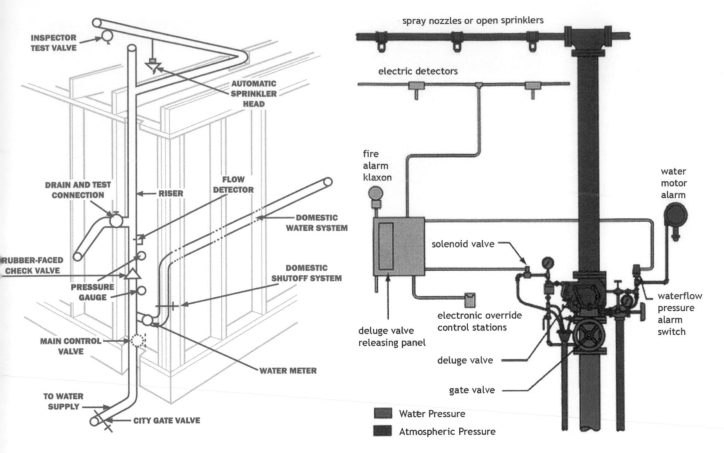

INSPECTOR TEST VALVE

AUTOMATIC SPRINKLER HEAD

DRAIN AND TEST CONNECTION

FLOW DETECTOR

RISER

DOMESTIC WATER SYSTEM

RUBBER-FACED CHECK VALVE

DOMESTIC SHUTOFF SYSTEM

PRESSURE GAUGE

MAIN CONTROL VALVE

WATER METER

TO WATER SUPPLY

CITY GATE VALVE

spray nozzles or open sprinklers

electric detectors

fire alarm klaxon

water motor alarm

solenoid valve

electronic override control stations

deluge valve releasing panel

waterflow pressure alarm switch

deluge valve

gate valve

■ Water Pressure

■ Atmospheric Pressure

■ **Figure 6.21** Sprinkler systems in the theater are critical to everyone's safety. Never try to disable the sensors for your convenience!

■ **Figure 6.22** A deluge system will flood the entire theatre. This is one of the least-used systems for fire protection today.

shatters to open that single sprinkler, releasing water directly over the source of the heat. Sprinklers operate automatically in the area of the fire's origin, preventing a fire from growing undetected to a dangerous size, while simultaneously sounding an alarm. Automatic fire sprinklers keep fires small. Only one or two sprinklers handle the majority of fires in buildings with sprinkler systems.

The last option we discuss is the deluge system. A **deluge** system is similar to a sprinkler system, except the sprinkler heads are all open and the pipe is not pressurized with air (Figure 6.22). Deluge systems are connected to a water supply through a deluge valve that is opened by the operation of a smoke- or heat-detection system. The detection system is installed in the same area as the sprinklers. When the detection system is activated, water discharges through all the sprinkler heads in the system simultaneously. Deluge systems are used in

places that are considered high-hazard areas, such as power plants, aircraft hangars, and chemical storage or processing facilities. Deluge systems are needed where high-velocity suppression is necessary to prevent fire spread. This type of system was once used in theaters, but the sprinkler system is now the norm.

SAFETY DATA SHEETS

You may have heard about **safety data sheets** or, as they often are referred to, SDS (Figure 6.23). I mentioned them before, but let me go into some detail now. These data sheets provide detailed hazard and precautionary information for hazardous materials. What the heck does that mean? Well, OK, *hazardous* you get, right? Anytime you are dealing with chemical compounds, such as paint, solvents, dyes, adhesives, or even fogger juice,

Rosco Laboratories Inc.
52 Harbor View Avenue
Stamford, CT, USA, 06902
Phone: (203) 708 8900

ROSCO F-1 FLUID

SDS No.: ROS003
Page 1 of 6

SDS Preparation Date: February 7, 2019

SAFETY DATA SHEET

SECTION 1 – PRODUCT AND COMPANY IDENTIFICATION

Product Name	**: ROSCO F-1 FLUID**
Product Use	: Fog fluid
Chemical Family	: Aqueous glycol solution
Supplier's name and address	**: Rosco Laboratories Inc.**
	52 Harbor View Avenue
	Stamford, CT, United States
	06902
24 Hr. Emergency Tel #	: (800) 424-9300 Chemtrec U.S.
	(703) 527-3887 Chemtrec Outside U.S.

HMIS Rating   : *- Chronic Hazard   0 – Minimal   1 – Slight   2 – Moderate 3 – Serious 4 – Severe

 Health: 1   Flammability: 0   Reactivity: 0

WHMIS Classes:

Unregulated

SECTION 2 – HAZARDS IDENTIFICATION

EMERGENCY OVERVIEW

Clear, colorless liquid. No odor. No special hazards exist with this product As with any chemical substance, caution and care will prevent unnecessary accidents and safety problems. Read instructions on label before use. HEALTH CAUTION: Fog from this fluid, like any other common material in an aerosolized state, may be irritating to or cause allergic symptoms in some persons with allergenic sensitivity. Persons with active asthma should limit their exposure to the fog.

***POTENTIAL HEALTH EFFECTS**

Target organs	: None reported by the manufacturer.
Routes of exposure	: *Inhalation:* YES *Skin Absorption:* NO *Skin & Eyes:* YES *Ingestion:* YES
Potential acute health effects	:
Eyes:	May cause mild transient irritation.
Skin:	Not a hazard under normal conditions of use.
Inhalation:	Inhalation problems are not anticipated. Prolonged exposure to high vapor or aerosol concentrations may cause:
	Possible transient irritation. Persons suffering from asthma or reactive airway disorders may experience asthma-like effects from exposure to this material.
Ingestion:	Not an expected route of entry. Ingestion of large amounts may cause nausea, vomiting, diarrhea, as well as depression of the central nervous system.
Potential chronic health effects	: None reported by the manufacturer.
Medical conditions aggravated by overexposure	
	: Pre-existing skin and respiratory disorders.
Addition health hazards	: None reported by the manufacturer.
Potential environmental effects	: None reported by the manufacturer.

■ **Figure 6.23** Data safety sheets are key to knowing how to safely use and clean up different materials.

there is no good way to know how these items (which are all chemically based by the way) might interact with other chemicals or, for that matter, with the human body. And this could cause a possibly dangerous situation. Based on all of this, OSHA originally established these data sheets. Now, the manufacturers are responsible for providing them as an informational document regarding the overall safety and safe handling procedures and precautions for materials used in the workplace.

EXAMPLES OF PANIC

I don't want to turn this chapter into a list of horror stories for all the things that can, and sometimes do, go wrong. However, I think it's good to get an idea of what can happen. The most dangerous times in a theater are during the load-in and load-out of a production. People are often rushing to get things done, and they may take a few shortcuts. Safety is often the thing that is compromised when we take shortcuts. Here are a couple of "horror stories" just to give you an idea of what can happen even with the best of all intentions.

It was the first day of stagecraft class, and we were walking around getting oriented in the theater and scene shop. Since it was the first day, I didn't know the students by name yet. I just kept taking a head count trying to make sure everyone was still there. Well, I always seemed to be missing at least one person, but I also saw people going in and out the door between the theater and shop. I found out after the class ended that one of my students had started to feel lightheaded. So she headed back to the theater to get her backpack and a piece of fruit. Good idea? Well, not really. She almost passed out in the theater, all by herself, because we were in the shop. Luckily she was found, had something to eat, and started to feel better. The moral of the story: If you are ill or injured, don't go off by yourself. Find someone to tell, so he or she can get you help or at least check in on you.

Better a thousand times careful than once dead.

—Proverb

Here is a story you may have already heard. It comes from the movies, specifically the making of the *Wizard of Oz* in 1939. An actor by the name of Buddy Ebsen was originally cast as the Tin Man. The makeup they were using to make him look like tin contained an aluminum powder. It was applied directly onto his skin. In 1939, there was no safety data sheet (SDS), and it turned out that applying tin to your skin is, well, toxic. It made him very ill, and he ended up in the hospital for two weeks. A different actor was cast as a replacement for the part so the filming could continue, using different makeup of course.

Another story comes from my days of assisting. I was working as the associate lighting designer on an opera. The designer and I ran up onto the stage from the house to do one last check before rehearsal started. While we were walking back toward the house, the electrician took the house lights out. I suddenly heard a thud. Now, let me tell you, this is not a sound you want to hear in a dark theater. I screamed for house lights. As the lights came on, I looked down into the orchestra pit in horror. The designer was lying where she had fallen, about 15 feet below the stage level. Luckily, she wasn't hurt seriously and recovered.

Two brief versions of stories involving fire follow to drive this point home. One from long ago, and one more recent. My point here is that safety can never be taken for granted. Be vigilant. You can never be too careful.

The Hartford Circus Fire happened in 1944 in Hartford, Connecticut. Ushers spotted the flames and threw buckets of water on it, but to no avail. Seconds later, the fire reached the roof. At the top of the center pole, the fire split in three directions. Because the big top had been coated with 1800 lb (816 kg) of paraffin and 6000 US gallons (23 m³) of gasoline, the flames spread rapidly. Why did they coat the tent in wax and gasoline? It was a common waterproofing method of the time that allowed the tent canvas to stand up to rain and dampness, extending its life—theoretically. Obviously we don't waterproof with flammable materials any longer!

Now, here is one that you may have heard about. In 2003, 100 people died and more than 200 were injured in a Rhode Island nightclub. The fire started just seconds into the headlining band's opening song, when pyrotechnics were set off. The special effects inadvertently lit soundproofing foam behind the stage that had not been flameproofed. The audience thought the flames were part of the act at first. Only as the fire reached the ceiling and smoke began to billow toward the audience did people realize it was unplanned. In less than a minute, the entire stage was engulfed in flames. An investigation of the fire, using computer simulations and a mockup of the stage area and dance floor, concluded that a sprinkler system could have successfully contained the fire and allowed everyone to get out safely.

One last word of caution. Being trained in the safe procedures for all of this doesn't necessarily make you safe. There are still variables. You might forget some of the rules. Or, you might be working with someone who doesn't know how to be safe. Do not allow yourself to settle into a false sense of security. Be aware not only of what you are doing, but also of your surroundings.

Theatre Traditions: "Stars and Stripes Forever"

In show business, particularly theatre and the circus, this hymn is called the "Disaster March." It is a traditional code signaling a life-threatening emergency. This helps theater personnel handle things and organize the audience's exit without panic. One example of its use was at the Hartford Circus Fire in July 1944.

EXERCISES

EXERCISE 1
SDS EXPLAINED

Choose an SDS for any material used in your theater. Read through it and explain what each of the sections mean and why they are important.

EXERCISE 2

Define the three main systems a theater can install to aid in the event of a fire.

EXERCISE 3

Summarize the four categories relating to personal safety. Describe the pros and cons of each.

CHECK YOUR KNOWLEDGE

1. Name two kinds of eye protection. Explain the first two ways to immediately treat an eye injury.
2. List what SDS stands for and explain why it is critical to the safe use of products in the shop.
3. Explain the difference between fireproof and fire retardant.
4. Illustrate why you should never yell "FIRE" in a theater.

- Deluge
- Dust mask
- Earmuffs
- Earplugs
- Eyecup
- Eyewash station
- Face shield
- Fire curtain
- Fireproof
- Fire retardant
- Goggles
- Safety data sheet
- OSHA
- Outrigger
- Respirator
- Smoke pocket
- Sprinkler system
- Thermal barrier
- Zetex

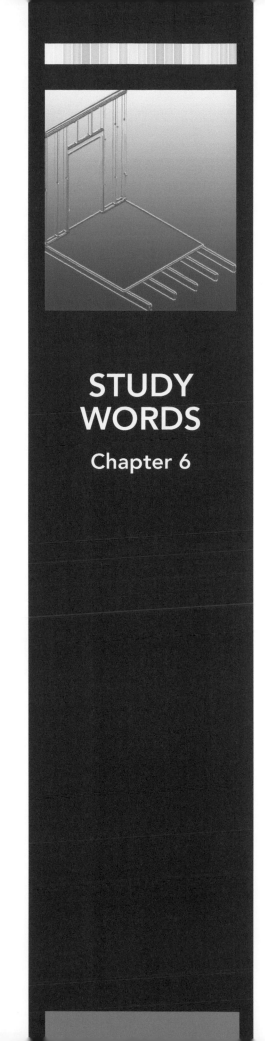

STUDY WORDS

Chapter 6

Setting It All Up

Scenic Tools and Materials

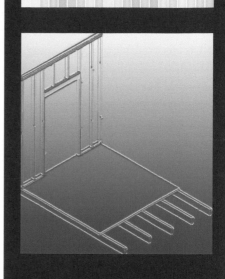

CHAPTER SEVEN

Student Learning Outcomes

___

Students will acquire:

- An overview understanding of the major aspects, techniques, and directions in the area of scenic techniques and tools.

- Fundamental, conceptual understanding of the expressive possibilities of theatre.

- A working knowledge of technologies, safety, and equipment applicable to the area of scenic techniques and tools.

OK, enough with all this theory stuff. Are you ready to dive in and learn about tools? And, yes, I know you may already know what some of them are. This book is all about theatre, so we look at tools from that specific perspective. There are many variations on the basic tools. We take a look at the most common ones you find in a scene shop, and, keep in mind, this is by no means a comprehensive list of every tool ever made. I put them into four main categories that follow the schedule for building. That means we explore tools that measure and mark first. Second, we look at tools that cut. And, third, we look at tools that assemble. Last, we look at pneumatic, or air-powered, tools. Are you ready? Let's get started.

TOOLS

The first and most important thing we need to talk about before we look at any individual tool is its safe use. The manufacturer of each tool issues some kind of a manual with operating instructions. This manual includes not only the safe and intended use for the specific tool, but also any safety precautions you need to take to operate the tool in the manner the manufacturer intended. Please continue to reference the safety chapter (Chapter 6) as well as any available manuals. Safety first!

Each of the three categories includes many tools. Every tool has an intended purpose. The key is to match up the right tool with the right job. As you go through this list, there will be tools that are appropriate for more than one job. Keep in mind that each job is specific; you have to know how to pick the right tool for the right job. This is the only way to get the job done safely. We look into this idea more within each category. As you go through the rest of this chapter, you'll see many photos of tools. Keep in mind that every style of tool can have many manufacturers. I can show only one version of each tool, so, if you see more than one tool in a certain brand, realize I am not showing a preference for that brand.

> Measure twice and cut once!
>
> —Al Kogler,
> my dad

So, you walk into the scene shop and are given a drawing of a flat (see Chapter 8) to build. On the side of the drawing is a list of the wood you will need to cut. You walk over to the lumber rack and pull out a piece of wood. What is the first tool you are going to reach for? Well, you have to measure the wood to know where to cut it, right? Measuring and marking tools come with a wide range of options. Let's look at them one at a time. We start with one more kind of pencil that we haven't discussed before.

MEASURING AND MARKING

In addition to the pencils we already discussed, there is such a thing as a **carpenter pencil**. This is different from a regular pencil in its shape and graphite. Its shape is a flattened octagon that prevents it from rolling. The graphite is thicker and stronger than a regular pencil, which comes in handy when writing on wood instead of paper. There are sharpeners (some used by hand and some that attach to your drill) for the carpenter pencils, but a pocketknife is so much easier and does a better job.

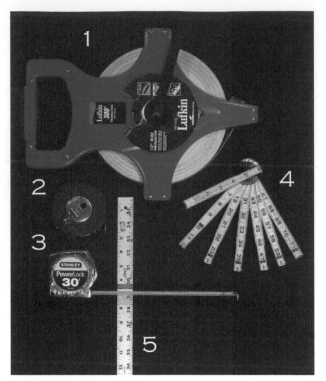

■ **Figure 7.1** (1) 300-foot tape measure, (2) 50-foot tape measure, (3) 30-foot tape measure, (4) folding ruler, and (5) metal ruler.

The **tape measure** we are most used to seeing these days is the self-retracting pocket tape measure (Figure 7.1). Its flexibility allows you to measure long lengths while still allowing it to be easily carried in your pocket. Now, you've probably all seen a tape measure, right? The tape measure is easy to read. A tape measure blade is usually marked both in inches and in feet. At the end of the blade is a metal edge called a tang. This tang is intentionally left loose to compensate for measuring outside dimensions versus inside dimensions of objects. Also, the case of the tape measure is usually labeled with its length, so that, if you are measuring an inside dimension, you will know how much to add for an accurate measurement.

Well, before we had today's version of a tape measure, there was the **folding rule**. The folding rule is sort of a combination of a regular ruler and a yardstick. It is made up of small sections in 6-inch increments connected by a pivot point. This allows for the whole length of the rule to compress and make it small enough to easily fit in your pocket or bag. The folding rule is the granddaddy of today's tape measure. You still see these occasionally in the shop, and every once in a while they are still the perfect tool!

The latest development in tape measuring is the **laser measure**. This is a totally amazing piece of equipment. Laser measuring can be more accurate than a traditional tape measure. Human error is all but eliminated. In most cases, you just press a button, the laser emits its beam until it hits a solid surface, and then a digital display shows the distance measured. You can usually measure indoors and outdoors. The key to a laser measure is that you can measure in those hard-to-reach places.

Sometimes, a tape measure won't quite do everything you need. Perhaps you are not doing a simple measurement, but more of a layout, drawing square shapes and so forth. The next line of tools that can help with this includes the framing square, combination square, speed square, and sliding bevel gauge. Let's take a look at these one at a time.

Framing squares are very versatile (Figure 7.2). They can vary in size, but the average looks like a big L, with the long side being 24 inches long and the shorter side being 16 inches long. They are made of metal. They are the most accurate of our squares because they have a fixed angle; you can make no adjustments. If you need to draw or measure a 90-degree angle, then this is your tool. A great deal of our initial layout in theatrical design is based on the 90-degree angle. This is the best tool to start with, and you can also re-square it if it gets out of square.

The **combination square** is the next tool to discuss. As the name implies, this differs from the framing square in that it is adjustable. Not only can the combination square handle 90-degree angles, it can also help you draw 45-degree angles. Another benefit is that you can loosen a knob and slide the square's head along the ruler, then tighten it down at a different location on the ruler. This allows you to transfer measurements from one place to another. The sliding head of the square contains a level. This can be very useful for certain types of measuring.

Next is the **speed square**. This is a metal triangle containing both 90-degree and 45-degree angles. There are measurement markings along the sides. The important difference between the speed square and other types of squares is that the speed square has a flange on one side that you can use to hold it square against the

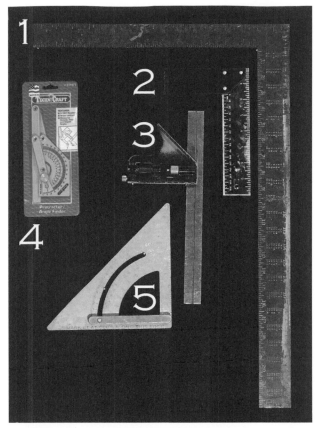

■ **Figure 7.2** (1) Framing square, (2) tri-square, (3) combination square, (4) speed square, and (5) protractor.

edge of your material. The flange (also called t-edge, lip, or lipped fence; there are probably other names for it as well) is on both sides of most speed squares.

When you are working with angles, you will need to measure an angle from a drawing or sample piece of research or scenery. The sliding **bevel gauge** is used to check or copy the angle of an existing unit or drawing. It consists of a handle or stock and a blade or tongue, connected by a wing nut. You place the handle against a straight edge and, by rotating the blade, you can match the angle of what you are trying to copy. A wing nut is loosened so that the blade can rotate to a variety of angles. This nut is then tightened to hold this new angle. It can then be used to copy an angle from one part of a unit to the next. Please note that this tool *does not* measure an angle. It simply copies the angle from something that already exists.

The compass is another tool for measuring (Figure 7.3). I think most of you have seen a compass. It consists

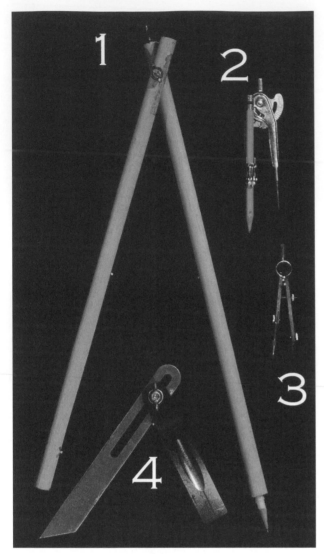

■ **Figure 7.3** (1) Large homemade compass, (2) compass with pencil, (3) compass with lead, and (4) bevel guide.

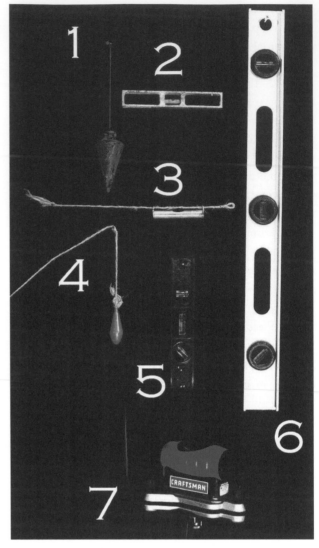

■ **Figure 7.4** (1) Plumb bob, (2) small spirit level, (3) string level, (4) plumb bob, (5) spirit level, (6) large spirit level, and (7) laser level.

of two pointed arms joined at the top by a pivot point. The end of each arm can contain a sharpened metal point. A pencil, or other writing device, can replace these points as needed. A compass can have two purposes. The primary purpose is to draw a circle. The secondary use is to measure a given distance and then copy that distance in equal-length segments. Trammel points are basically a compass but on a larger scale.

Levels are the next kind of tool. There are spirit or bubble levels, string levels, plumb bob, and laser levels (Figure 7.4). They all measure whether a surface is level or plumb, but they all do it in a slightly different way. The

spirit level is so named because the little vial containing liquid is actually partially filled with ethanol. There is enough room left in the vial to create a bubble, and this bubble is what we use to determine plumb. By placing the level on either a horizontal or vertical surface, the bubble will line up with one of the calibration marks on the vial.

A **string level** is fairly accurate for basic stuff. You use a string that is pulled fairly taut between two points in the area you are trying to measure. The string can't sag. This is the key. You hang the string level onto the string and watch to see where the bubble lands with the vial. It's the same basic idea as a regular spirit level.

A **plumb bob** can be used if you are trying to determine a level line from one point only. That means you can attach a string to the top of a wall. Let the string drop down with a plumb bob attached to the bottom. The plumb bob is a weight and will stop swinging at the point of making the string level. You then adjust the angle of the wall until everything lines up.

The **laser level** is similar to the laser tape measure in how it works. Some laser products are self-leveling, via a spinning sensor. Others are done manually, and you're responsible for getting it set up. Once the setup is complete, you push the button, and a laser emits its beam. The cool part is that the beam remains level as it goes into the distance. This is a great tool if you need to line up several items along the same line across a distance.

The **chalk line** is the last tool we will discuss in this category. A chalk line is an almost diamond-shaped container holding a very long string and powdered chalk (Figure 7.5). It is used to mark a straight line between two points. You must measure and mark where you want the line to be. Shake the chalk line to make sure the chalk inside has coated the string. Then, you stretch the string, holding it taut at both ends. Make sure you are lined up with your measurements. Snap the line once by pulling it up away from your surface about 5–6 inches and letting it go. When it snaps back down, it will hit the surface with enough force to transfer the powdered chalk along the string to your scenery. You now have a line of chalk that can be used as a guide for cutting, painting,

nailing, or pretty much anything. On a side note, because of the shape of the chalk line container, it can make a great plumb bob in a pinch!

CUTTING AND SHAPING

Now that you are all measured and marked, what is next? Cutting. We break cutting up into several smaller categories. There are hand tools, which you hold in your hand when there is no power source other than your own muscles. Then, we discuss power hand tools and power stationary tools as they relate to cutting. Keep in mind that many of the tools we discuss can cut wood or metal, depending on the blade you put into the tool. Our last topic is welding torches that specifically cut metal.

All these tools are meant to cut. Some are meant to cut wood, some metal. All cutting tools cut a variety of things indiscriminately. They aren't designed to cut one

Theatre Traditions: Monkey Wrench

The monkey wrench is an adjustable wrench that is rarely used today. Its use has generally been replaced by the adjustable-end wrench, which has a compact head and so is more easily used in confined places.

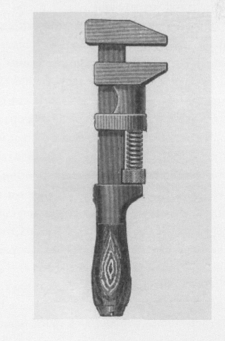

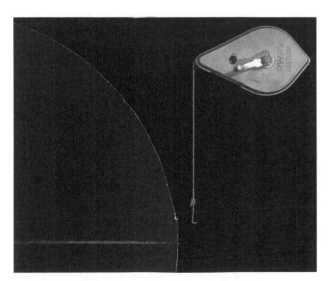

■ **Figure 7.5** A chalk line with evidence of its use!

thing and not another. Does that mean you can use a utility knife to cut a piece of wood? Yes, but it's not a smart choice, and I don't recommend it. Keep in mind that the tool can't tell what it is cutting. This means that, if skin, tendon, muscle, and bone get in the way, the tool will most likely keep cutting. So, choose the right tool for the job and use it safely. My father told me something a long time ago that I have always remembered. He said, "Don't fear tools, respect them." This basically means, know what the tool can do, but more important, know what the tool can't do. Choose the right tool for the right job!

CUTTING TOOLS AND SAWS

The most basic cutting tool we have is the pocketknife. You may have one of these in your pocket right now. They are simply designed. There is a blade that rotates out from inside the handle. When fully closed, you can't see the blade, and, more important, there is nothing sharp sticking out to hurt you.

The **utility knife** or mat knife is next (Figure 7.6). This type of knife comes in a metal or plastic handle. The blade is retractable, meaning it stores completely in the handle. It uses a two-sided blade. This means, when the blade gets dull, you can open the handle, pull out the blade, turn it around, and put it back in. Now you have a brand-new sharp edge to cut with.

Scissors or shears can be used for a lot of cutting. We all know about scissors. They are a tool with blades on two opposing sides, one facing up, the other facing down, joined at a pivot point somewhere between the blades and the handles. The scene shop often has to cut paper or fabric as a beginning preparatory step to other parts of the process. It's not all about wood. But, now that we've mentioned wood, none of the tools we talked about so far works very well on wood. So, let's start exploring.

Before we get into the individual saws, let's discuss the different kinds of saw blades. Blades for cutting wood come in one of two varieties of teeth: Crosscut and rip. The basic idea is that **rip blades** cut parallel to the grain, and **crosscut blades** cut across the grain (Figure 7.7). It sounds easy, but take a look at the visible difference between the blades. The crosscut blade has a much harder job to do. It should look much fiercer … and it does!

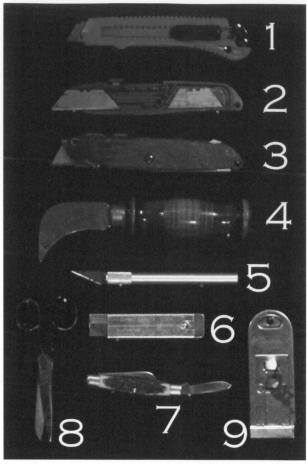

■ **Figure 7.6** (1) Snap-off utility knife, (2) open utility knife showing blades, (3) utility knife, (4) carpet or linoleum knife, (5) Xacto knife, (6) box cutter, (7) pocketknife, (8) scissors, and (9) razor scraper. Don't take these to the airport!

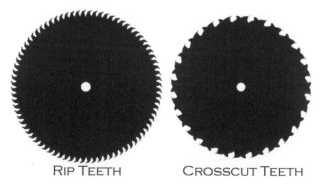

■ **Figure 7.7** Notice the difference in the teeth patterns between the rip and crosscut saw blade teeth.

The different materials the blade can be made out of also affect its use. High-speed steel blades are usually used for wood and the occasional light metal. Cobalt steel blades are harder and last longer, also holding the sharp edge better. Carbide blades are generally used for masonry board. Scrolling blades are typically the narrowest of this type and are appropriate for tight turns while cutting. Keep in mind, you should never plan to stop a saw blade in the middle of a piece of wood. Always finish the cut before turning off a saw. The various people-powered saws we discuss are hand saws, miter saws, coping saws, flush cut saws, and keyhole saws.

Hand saws first. There are two basic kinds. I bet you've guessed why. There is one style for crosscutting wood and another style for ripping wood. The handle and the metal blade can be identical. The difference between the two is the teeth on the blade. Always look at a hand saw when you first pick it up so that you know which saw you have and, more important, whether or not it is the right tool for the job you are about to do.

Mitering is making a joint, or corner, by combining two angled pieces of wood to make a third angle. It takes two separate pieces of wood with 45-degree angles that combine to make a 90-degree angle. A **miter saw** uses crosscut teeth (Figure 7.8). Miter saws are often used in conjunction with a **miter box**. A miter box has precut slots in it to guide the saw into a certain angle. This precision is critical or the miter won't turn into the correct angle needed for the project. With the use of power chop saws, many shops don't even have these any longer.

The next saw is the **coping saw**. The coping saw has a handle with a U-shaped steel frame. The very thin blade is held between the arms of the U. Turning the handle tightens or loosens the tension on the blade. Holders at either end of the blade can also be pivoted so that you can adjust the angle of the cut. Coping is similar to mitering. It is fitting two pieces of wood together when both pieces have an irregular surface. This usually refers to molding (also known as moulding or coving), whether on the wall or a picture frame. The coping saw allows you to make these kinds of cuts in very tight spaces, especially since they tend to be inside corner joints.

The **flush cut saw** has a handle with the blade coming straight out of one end. The blade is very flexible, cuts flush with the bottom surface, and has a very fine set of teeth that cut in one direction. That means the saw will

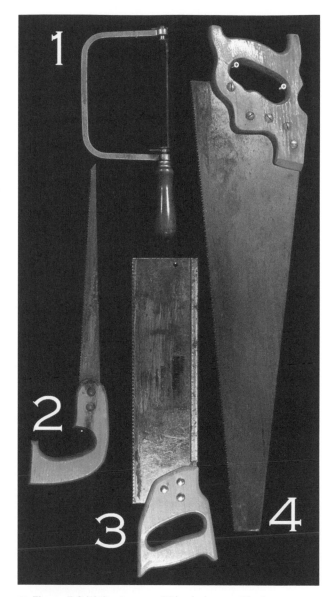

■ **Figure 7.8** (1) Coping saw, (2) keyhole saw, (3) miter saw, and (4) hand saw.

not cut on both the push and pull. It cuts only as you pull the saw toward you. This is used for detail finishing. Another benefit of the flush cut saw is that you rarely have to sand the wood afterwards owing to the fine teeth.

The **keyhole saw**, or drywall saw, is a long, narrow saw used for cutting small, awkward holes into a variety of building materials. The blade is secured into the handle by one or two screws. One recent modification to the keyhole saw is the addition of a sharpened point on the tip of the blade. This allows for jabbing the saw through soft materials such as dry wall to begin your cut.

Metal-Cutting Saws

We now change from saws that cut wood to saws that cut metal. Metal cuts very differently than wood. The blades on these saws have teeth much closer together and much sharper. Keep in mind, we are still talking about hand tools, with no power source other than you and me. OK, let's talk about hacksaws, tin snips, pipe cutters, tube cutters, pipe reamers, and pipe threaders. A quick safety note: Metal, especially the newly cut edges, can be very sharp. Be sure to wear goggles and work gloves when handling or cutting it.

Hacksaws are the one metal-cutting saw that most of you are already familiar with. They have a metal handle shaped in an arch with two places to attach the blade. The blade is both narrow and rigid. The teeth are angled, and the blade can be installed in the handle in either direction. This allows you to choose whether you will cut on the push or the pull motion. The replaceable blades come in a variety of types depending on your exact purpose.

Tin snips are used to cut thin sheets of metal (Figure 7.9). They work on the same premise as scissors, two opposing blades coming together. Tin snips come with different blade designs—straight cutting, left cutting,

and right cutting. Your individual project and material will inform your decision as to which is the correct tool. Use tin snips as you would use scissors on heavy cardboard. As you cut, open the jaws of the snips fully and make cuts as long as possible. Avoid snapping the jaws closed completely at the end of the cut, as this will nick the edges of the metal.

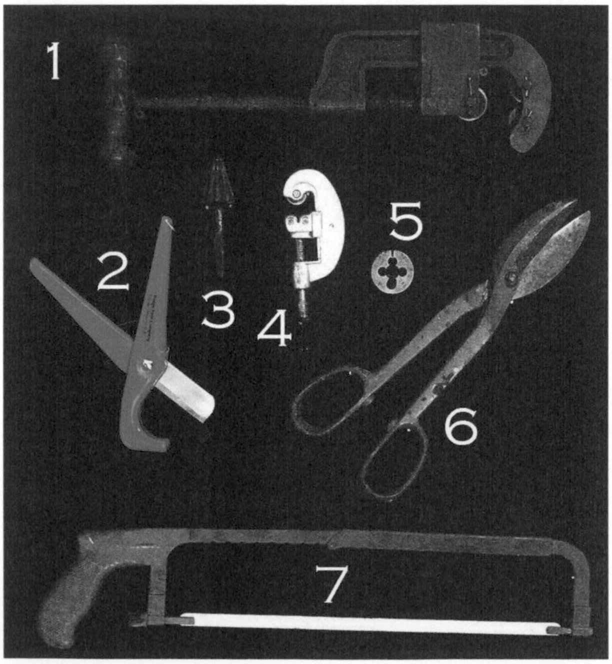

Pipe and tube cutters are very similar. Some look like a big pair of bolt cutters. You put the pipe or tube between the blades and squeeze the handles together. The other style is shaped like a C with a handle coming out of the bottom. You twist the handle, which tightens the pressure into the pipe. This forces the sharp blade into the pipe while wheels around the clamp continuously rotate the pipe. The pressure from the rotation is much stronger than you could possibly produce on your own! **Pipe cutters** are rated by the type and size of pipe they can cut.

Pipe reamers are used whenever a pipe is cut. Both the inside and outside of the cut edge may retain burrs, little pieces of sharp metal that can block the pipe from fitting to another piece of pipe. To remove the burrs from the inside of the pipe, use a reamer. Reamers are usually cone shaped with some sort of ratcheting handle. They have many cutting edges that remove the burrs on contact. Reamers are as sharp as the burrs, so be very careful! Now that your pipe is cut and free of burrs, you need a **pipe threader**. Your newly fabricated pipe may need to screw into a coupling or flange or some other type of mounting hardware. To do this, you need to create threads that screw into the other piece of hardware.

■ **Figure 7.9** (1) Pipe cutter, (2) PVC cutter, (3) reamer, (4) conduit cutter, (5) threader, (6) tin snips, and (7) hacksaw.

> Toys can turn into tools. The difference is usability.
>
> —Curt Ostermann
> American lighting designer

Powered Hand Tools

Next, we talk about hand tools for cutting that have an external power source, either a battery or a plug to go into an outlet. We discuss jigsaws, spiral saws, reciprocating saws, circular saws, routers, grinders, and **drills**. Before we go any further, remember that power tools require

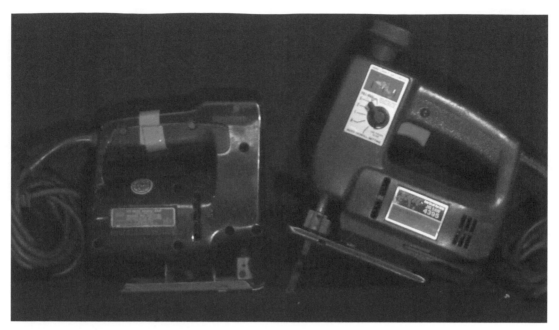

■ **Figure 7.10** On the left is a jigsaw, and on the right is a spiral saw.

steps taken to ensure safety. Always wear eye and ear protection when using these tools! Also, keep in mind that the blades can get bound up in the wood as the tools cut. If this happens, the saw will most likely want to kick back toward you. A good firm hold on the tool goes a long way to controlling this, should it happen. Being aware of this will keep you safe!

The **jigsaw**, also known as a *saber saw*, has a small straight blade that cuts with an up and down motion (Figure 7.10). Because of its small blade, it is great for cutting curves and not as good for cutting straight lines. Cutting a straight line requires some kind of guide. The guide is often called a **fence**. Different blades are available for cutting ceramic, leather, linoleum, plastic, wallboard, metal, and hardwood. Variable-speed blades and an adjustable foot for cutting at different angles are options that are important to have. You can think of the jigsaw as a powered version of the keyhole saw.

Reciprocating saws have a straight blade mounted at one end of the body (Figure 7.11). The blade moves back and forth (that is where they get their name), much like the action of a jigsaw. Reciprocating saws are much more powerful and versatile than jigsaws. A variety of blade options means they can cut through almost anything. The brand name Sawzall®, by Milwaukee Tool, has become synonymous with this type of saw. This saw is

■ **Figure 7.11** A variety of circular blades and straight blades for saws, also router bits.

perfect for big, rough cuts that might then be followed up with a jigsaw to refine the final look.

A **circular saw** is one of the more popular portable tools in the shop. It gets its name from the circular saw blade it uses. It is designed to make long, straight cuts.

This saw can crosscut or rip wood. The bottom foot can be angled to allow for a consistent angled cut. As with most of the tools in this category, circular tools can be corded or run from batteries. If your saw has a cord, please, please, make sure to always know where the cord is. Running over the cord is a very bad thing!

Routers are tools that typically cut grooves or decorative trims along the edge of a piece of wood. Think picture frame. Instead of a blade, like most of the saws we've been talking about, a router has a bit. This bit is shaped just like the shape you will be cutting out and is sharp on all edges. The shapes you can cut out are limited only by the number of router bits you have. To route a straight line, you use a straight fence. Routers typically rotate their bit in a clockwise motion. That means it is best, and safest, to cut from left to right. If you are left-handed, like me, this means you have to adjust your normal hold on the tool to operate it safely. Experiment with this idea before using the tool for the first time. Sometimes, you may want to mount the router in a table and use it as a stationary tool, especially if you have a lot of small cuts to make.

A **grinder** is a tool that drives an abrasive disc mounted on a geared head. The abrasive disc can be replaced when it becomes worn. Different discs can be used for a variety of tasks, such as cutting, sawing, and even buffing. These discs are intended primarily for metalworking. This particular tool requires different safety protocols. A face shield should always be worn, and gloves, respirators, earmuffs, long sleeves, and hard hats are highly recommended, depending on what you are grinding.

Powered Stationary Tools

Our next category is powered stationary tools. Stationary power tools differ from what we've been discussing by the fact that they are built into a table or stand of some sort. You bring your materials to the tool, not the other way around. The same safety precautions for eyes and ears that we already discussed are to be used here as well. We discuss table saws, radial-arm saws, panel saws, band saws, scroll saws, and the chop saw/compound miter saw.

The **table saw** is possibly the most-used tool in the whole scene shop. It works similarly to the circular saw in the last section. It is mounted in a table, which gives it more stability and allows for a more powerful engine.

(a)

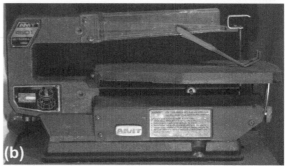
(b)

(c)

■ **Figure 7.12** (a) Panel saw, (b) scroll saw, (c) table saw, (d) radial-arm saw, (e) band saw, (f) compound miter, and (g) drill press.

(d)

(e)

(f)

(g)

A rip saw blade is usually installed. The tabletop gives stability to the wood you are cutting, allowing you to cut bigger pieces of wood more easily. A fence helps you line up your wood and keep it straight. A blade guard keeps you physically separated from the blade—a very good idea! The use of a SawStop is an even better idea. The SawStop works by using a small electrical signal that detects when skin contacts the blade and shuts down the saw in less than a second! The table saw has many other custom accessories that you can check out for helping with various types of cuts. This is a powerful and very useful tool.

Radial-arm saws work similarly to circular saws (Figure 7.12). A crosscut saw blade is usually installed. The blade head is suspended from a long arm, hence the name, in a yoke that allows for selectable degrees of rotation. There is a handle for moving the blade head forward and back while cutting the wood. If you need to cut many pieces of wood to the same length, you can set up a **jig**, or guide, at the correctly measured distance. The table saw and radial-arm saw complement each other perfectly.

Panel saws were originally used primarily by cabinetmakers. However, their use is also perfect for the scene shop. A panel saw is basically a circular saw with a big bracket on it to allow for movement across a large-scale predetermined grid. It can be either horizontal or vertical, although most scene shops prefer the vertical one to save space. Cutting sheets of plywood into smaller pieces is this tool's specialty. Today, there are even computer-controlled panel saws that can make multiple cuts and repeat them from one piece of wood to another with amazing accuracy. For repeated 90-degree cuts, this is the fastest way to do it.

Band saws are useful for cutting wood or metal into nonlinear shapes. A band saw is a unique tool in that the blade is one continuous loop, or band, stretched over two pulleys. The blade operates by moving in one direction continuously. It has teeth on only one side of the band. You move the material through the saw to create your design. Different bands are available for wood and metal, as well as with coarser and finer teeth. Keep in mind, there is no blade guard, and so safety is more of a concern here. However, the designs you can achieve are unique to the band saw.

Scroll saws are used for freehand cutting of intricate shapes in fairly thin wood. The scroll saw uses thin blades, similar to a jigsaw, to allow for the small radius needed to complete these designs. The band saw can do many of the same things, just not in as fine a degree of detail. This is the right tool if you need to create delicate inlaid designs. Scroll saws have size designations that are determined by the distance between the blade and the back arm. Like the band saw, there is no blade guard, so be careful! The band saw and the scroll saw complement each other very well.

The chop saw/compound miter saw is a very versatile tool. You can probably guess that just from its name. Chop saws/compound miter saws have a circular saw blade just like a circular saw. Originally, chop saws worked by having a pivoting arm containing the blade. The arm came down and cut, then went back up to its resting location, similar to a radial-arm saw but in the other direction. Newer chop saws still do this, and much more. They now also pivot around to become a miter saw. The newest addition to this tool is an arm that turns the saw into a radial-arm saw as well. Just remember that the more a tool can do, the more you have to be aware of its proper use to keep safe.

Next is the CNC (computer numerical control) router. This is a very expensive piece of machinery. Remember the hand router? Well, picture that on a huge horizontal table. Then, picture that it is computer-controlled. You can now upload a CAD file to the router's memory, and it will cut the exact design that has been drawn! This is not only amazing to watch, but also an unrivaled advancement in using technology in the scene shop.

> Just because you can, doesn't mean you should!
>
> —Curt Ostermann, American lighting designer

There is another type of cutting we haven't addressed at all yet. Oxyacetylene welding, commonly referred to as *gas welding*, is a process that relies on the proper combination of oxygen and acetylene. Welding metals is a specialized skill that requires training and a separate shop/shop area to work in, but I touch on it briefly. The equipment needed for oxyacetylene cutting and welding is very portable and easy to use once you have been thoroughly trained. Oxygen and acetylene gases are stored under pressure in steel cylinders. These cylinders are fitted with regulators and flexible hoses. The gases are then mixed together in the correct proportions to create a hot flame that can cut through metal. When welding, the operator must wear protective clothing and tinted colored goggles. This is not a thing to play around with, but can be a very useful tool in the right hands.

> When people describe rockets and wheels and a universe that is spinning through space, the mind spins.
>
> —Eugene Lee, American scenic designer

ASSEMBLY

We now segue from cutting and shaping tools to a category I call *assembly*. Once all your materials are cut out into the proper sizes and shapes, the next step is to put it all together into something that resembles the original drawing. We break these tools into the same basic categories as the cutting tools: Hand tools, power hand tools, and power stationary tools.

Hand Tools

Hand tools for assembly include the claw hammer, framing hammer, ball peen hammer, mallet, tack hammer, dead-blow hammer, nail set, center punch, stapler, and pry bar. Then, we move on to all kinds of wrenches. We're still talking about hand tools. Keep that in mind. Here is the list of wrenches: Adjustable wrench, open-ended wrench, box wrench, speed wrench, pipe wrench, nut driver, socket and ratchet, and Allen keys. For fastening, a couple of examples are Yankee screwdrivers and screwdrivers (flat versus Phillips).

Let's deal with all the hammers at once, since they all do a similar job. At their simplest, hammers are intended to push things together or take things apart. Keep in mind that the metal head of the hammer not only pushes a nail into wood, but it also can dent the wood. If you are concerned about damaging the wood, make sure to use some kind of buffer between the tool and the wood. Hammers can also be used for many jobs that were not intended for them. Be aware that the hammer's main job is pushing nails into wood and pulling them back out.

The **claw hammer** is most common and standard of all the hammers (Figure 7.13). This is the hammer you see the most in the scene shop. It has a metal head for striking a nail, or whatever else you need to hit, and a curved claw for ripping nails back out of the wood. The head usually weighs about 16 ounces but can vary quite a bit. **Framing hammers**, on the other hand, are much heavier and are meant for larger nails and harder woods. Carpenters putting up the framing of a house originally used them, so that is where they get their name. The claw is not as curved as on a claw hammer, and the head usually weighs about 22–28 ounces. A **tack hammer** is a much smaller hammer, usually used for the detail work on finishing projects. Small nails and tacks with very small heads are the perfect use for this tool. The head

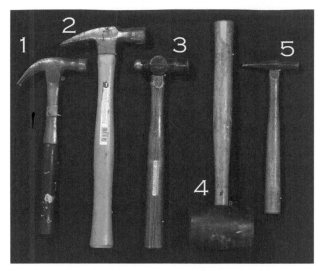

■ **Figure 7.13** (1) Claw hammer, (2) framing hammer, (3) ball peen hammer, (4) mallet, and (5) tack hammer.

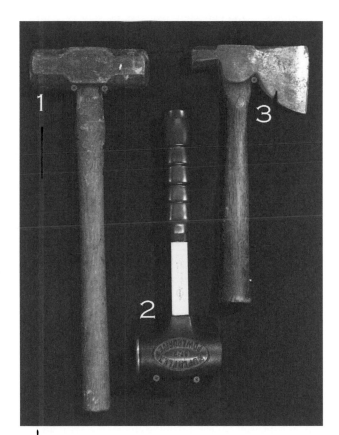

■ **Figure 7.14** (1) Sledge hammer, (2) dead-blow hammer, and (3) hatchet.

usually weighs 5–8 ounces, much smaller than what we've been discussing so far.

The **ball peen hammer** has a much harder head than other hammers. Because of this, it is used mainly on metal instead of wood. *Peen* in the dictionary definition talks about drawing, bending, or flattening. The ball end of the hammer is used for shaping. So, think about it. You have a hammer to bend, flatten, or shape metal. Sounds pretty handy, huh?

Dead-blow hammers may sound dangerous, but they are actually pretty cool (Figure 7.14). They are unique in that the head is filled with loose steel particles. This gives the hammer extra force on impact and very little recoil or bounce back. What does that really mean? Well, when you swing the hammer to hit something, the metal shot in the head sort of swings with your swing, adding momentum. It also means that, when the hammer hits something, the metal shot helps it to stay in contact with the object. All this adds up to a much more forceful strike with less effort! They also have a soft head that won't damage your project.

Mallets are another type of hammer with a soft head that helps avoid damaging delicate surfaces. The head of a mallet is also substantially larger than a regular hammer, and this helps to spread out the force of the hit. If you are hammering into a finished surface, a mallet may be the better choice than a claw hammer, as it is less marring to the surface.

A **nail set** is often used in conjunction with a tack hammer. It is made of metal with a flat surface on either end. The nail set is used for driving the head of a nail either flush or just below the finished surface. Line up the nail set with the nail head; use a hammer to hit the nail set, forcing the nail head into the wood. This gives you a smooth surface for painting or other finishes. The **center punch** is used in a similar way to the nail set. The difference is that it has a sharp, pointy end. It is used, primarily on metal, to mark a starting point for drilling into the material. Once you have used the center punch, it is much easier to begin drilling into metal without the drill slipping.

We all know what a stapler is, right? Well, this type is a little different than what you probably have sitting on your desk. A **stapler** binds things together by forcing thin metal staples into the material with pressure. But, you already knew that. What you may not know is that staples come in a variety of sizes, and you must make sure to choose the right size for your job. What you may also not know is that there are a variety of staplers. They vary in size, similar to the actual staples, but they also vary in how you load them, how you hold them, and what they look like. Always make sure the staples and stapler are meant to work together. Otherwise, the stapler will jam and cause you many headaches. We discuss this later in the chapter.

There are many kinds of **pry bars** (Figure 7.15). Pry bars are made of metal, and both ends are designed to be used for different purposes. Some pry bars have unique names, such as *wonderbar*, and are made only by certain manufacturers. They are used as leverage for separating objects. Some pry bars are meant to remove nails and do minor lifting. Some are bulky enough to be able to

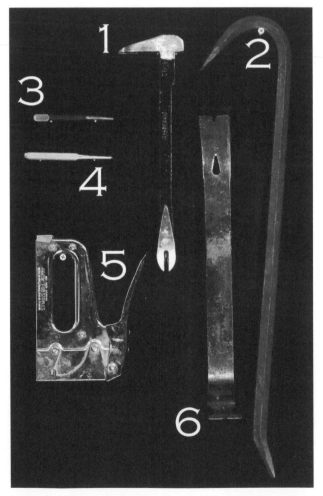

■ **Figure 7.15** (1) "Catspaw" pry bar, (2) large pry bar, (3) nail set, (4) center punch, (5) stapler, and (6) flat pry bar.

perform demolition. Your scene shop most likely has several types. Be aware of the capabilities of each to choose the right tool for the right job.

The **adjustable wrench** is often called a *crescent wrench* and with good cause (Figure 7.16). We are talking about an open-ended wrench with one fixed jaw and one adjustable jaw. The adjustment works by a screw positioned within the handle. This allows you to grasp any size nut or piece of hardware to loosen or tighten it. Although the wrench is shaped like a crescent, that is not where it gets its name. Its name actually comes from the original manufacturer, Crescent Tool Company, which began production in upstate New York in the early 1900s. Crescent® is a brand name, but it is used interchangeably for an adjustable wrench, as is the term C-wrench. Nowadays, adjustable wrenches are made by a wide variety of manufacturers and they are indispensable to the theatre technician!

The nonadjustable type of wrench is called an **open-ended wrench**. The open-ended wrench fits a specific size of hardware and has an open end, usually at a 30-degree angle away from the handle. This allows a greater range of motion when trying to tighten or loosen a nut. A **box wrench** has a closed end and fits only one size of hardware. The box often has from 6 to 12 points of contact to the hardware, which makes for a much more secure hold as you are trying to move the hardware.

A **speed wrench** is similar to a box wrench with one major exception. It contains a ratchet on both ends. This "speeds" up your usage and is how the wrench gets its name. A ratchet is a device used to restrict motion to one direction. This happens by the use of a gear inside the head of the wrench that engages in one direction to tighten or loosen hardware as required. On the backswing of the handle, the gear disengages, which allows it to reset with the moved hardware. Ratchets often have a lever that allows motion to be either clockwise or counterclockwise.

The **pipe wrench** is meant for gripping round objects such as, well, pipe, and so its design is a little different. Primarily, it is used for metal pipes, hence its name. It has an adjustable jaw similar to the adjustable wrench. It closes and opens by screwing itself tighter as the wrench clamps down on the pipe. When putting two pieces of pipe together, putting a pipe into a base, or separating pieces of pipe, the pipe wrench is the essential tool.

There is a range of tools for tightening and loosening small fasteners. Keep in mind, as always, that, although several tools may actually be able to do what you want, they are not all appropriate for the job. In this category, using the wrong tool can actually damage or destroy the fastener! Let's look at each of the tools in this small category.

Sockets and nut drivers work in similar ways. A **socket set** is a handle and a series of replaceable heads. Each head has an opening on one side; each opening is a different size to correspond to different sizes of bolt heads and nuts. Sockets work with a ratcheting technology that allows you to loosen or tighten the bolt or nut quickly (Figure 7.17). A **nut driver**, on the other hand, is a single tool, handle, and head in one that does not ratchet. These normally come in a set with various sizes.

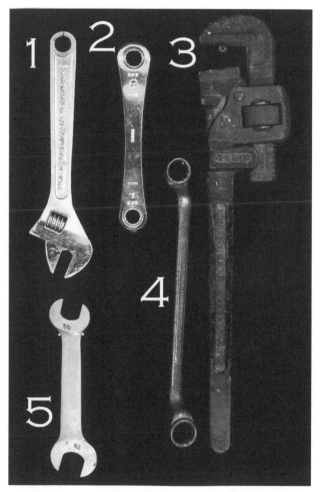

■ **Figure 7.16** (1) Adjustable wrench, (2) speed wrench, (3) pipe wrench, (4) box wrench, and (5) open-ended wrench.

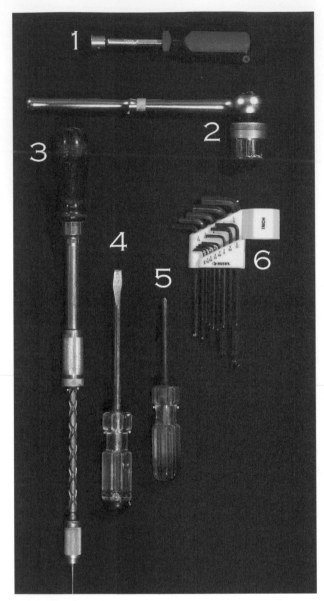

■ **Figure 7.17** (1) Nut driver, (2) socket wrench, (3) Yankee screwdriver, (4) slotted screwdriver, (5) Phillips screwdriver, and (6) Allen key set.

Allen key is a brand name for a tool having a hexagonal head for adjusting nuts with a recessed six-sided opening. You may have used one of these if you ever purchased self-assembly furniture. Allen keys can be bought as a single key, as a loose set, or as a full set packaged together within a shared handle. **Torx®** is also a brand name for a type of screw with a six-pointed star on the end. You may have heard of a star screwdriver—that is what this refers to. The Torx has better points of contact, and therefore you tend to damage the screw and your tool less than with an Allen key.

Now that we've gone through all of these "modern" tools, let's go back to the basics, the screwdriver. First, let's take a quick look at the **Yankee screwdriver**. It is also referred to as the *push screwdriver* and is an older style. This screwdriver has a spiral center so that, when you press down on the handle, the head turns the spiral center, and you can drive in or back out a screw by just pushing down on the handle. They have become less popular over time, but they are still out there.

Screwdrivers, as we know them today, have either a slotted or Phillips head. **Slotted screws** have a single straight indent in the top. **Phillips screws** have an X indented into the top. Slotted and Phillips screws come in different sizes, which we talk about later in this chapter. Just be aware that you must fit the driver to the screw. Stripped screw heads are the biggest problem to overcome, but most of the time it's the driver you choose and not the screw that creates the problem. Avoid the whole mess by choosing the right screwdriver for your projects. Using a driver that is too small or too large strips the screw head or damages the driver. Both are bad. Stripping a screw head means rounding out the slot or Phillips indentation. If this happens, you won't be able to easily tighten the screw or get the screw out again.

Let's continue with hand tools in a slightly different direction, by discussing ways to hold things during the assembly process. We will discuss linesman's pliers, slip-joint pliers, needle-nose pliers, vise grips, hand-screw clamps, bar clamps, spring clamps, carriage or carpenter clamps, and vises.

Linesman's pliers are your basic, average, all-around great pair of pliers (Figure 7.18). Linesman's pliers are very strong. They are great for holding, bending, and forming. Linesman's pliers' jaw surfaces are slightly toothed for better gripping. The jaws also have a built-in side-cutter tool. **Slip-joint pliers** are similar to linesman's pliers with one major difference. The joint that holds the two sides together is keyed so that the jaws can be opened wider as needed for certain jobs. **Needle-nose pliers** are good for smaller jobs. They are basic pliers, like the rest that we have talked about so far. The difference in their design is that the gripping end is not flat but comes to a small narrow point. This makes them great for holding much smaller items with more precision.

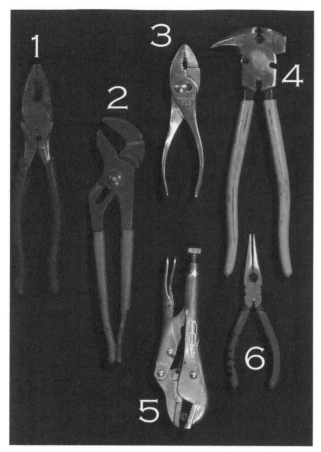

■ **Figure 7.18** (1) Linesman's pliers, (2) tongue and groove pliers, (3) slip-joint pliers, (4) fence pliers, (5) vise grips, and (6) needle-nose pliers.

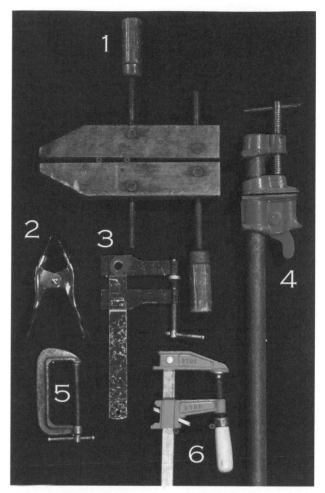

■ **Figure 7.19** (1) Hand-screw clamp, (2) squeeze clamp, (3) small flat bar clamp, (4) round bar clamp, (5) carpenter clamp, and (6) flat bar clamp.

Vise grips have an adjustable locking mechanism. If you are trying to loosen or tighten hardware where you will be using two tools, one to hold something in place and one to do the bulk of the work, vise grips lock their grip and hold it tightly for you, freeing up one of your hands to do the rest of the job. They come in a variety of sizes and shapes that make them applicable for many jobs.

The **hand-screw clamp** is an older style of clamp still used today (Figure 7.19). It is great when you need to be careful not to destroy your surface. This clamp is easy to recognize by its two heavy, broad wooden jaws. Passing through the jaws are screws with reverse threads at the ends so the jaws come together rapidly. Hand screws are available with jaw lengths from 4 to 16 inches. **Bar clamps** have a fixed jaw and a sliding jaw,

which makes them easily adjustable to different lengths. The determining factor of their usage is the bar they are attached to—the longer the bar, the bigger an object they can clamp!

Spring clamps are identified by the size their jaws can open. They are clamps that are strong and lightweight. They differ from the hand-screw and the bar clamps in that they tighten and loosen based on a spring's tension. These clamps usually feature soft, durable pads to protect fine finishes. They can be used on everything from wood to fabric. The last style of clamps is the **carpenter clamps**. They are the basic clamps you find in a scene shop. They are shaped like a C with a screw that tightens and loosens. They can leave marks on wood, so they are usually used when that is not a factor.

Vises are made from metal and are usually attached to a shop bench for stability. There are two jaws on the top that are usually fairly wide and smooth. By turning a screw, the jaws are brought together, thereby holding whatever has been caught inside. The screw can be loosened to reposition the object being held and retightened. The vise can be closed quite tightly so that your work can be held very firmly.

There are also various shaping tools to choose from during the assembly process for fitting and detailing. These are primarily chisels, planes, rasps, and files. Each has differences not only in how they are used but also in their shapes and way of working. Let's look at each group separately.

A **chisel** is a tool with a cutting edge on its end. It is used primarily for carving and cutting hard materials such as wood, stone, or metal. The sharp edge of the chisel is forced into the material, usually with a hammer or mallet. Chisels can have different shapes on their cutting edge. Some shapes are straight while others are more U-shaped and meant to gouge out pieces of the object.

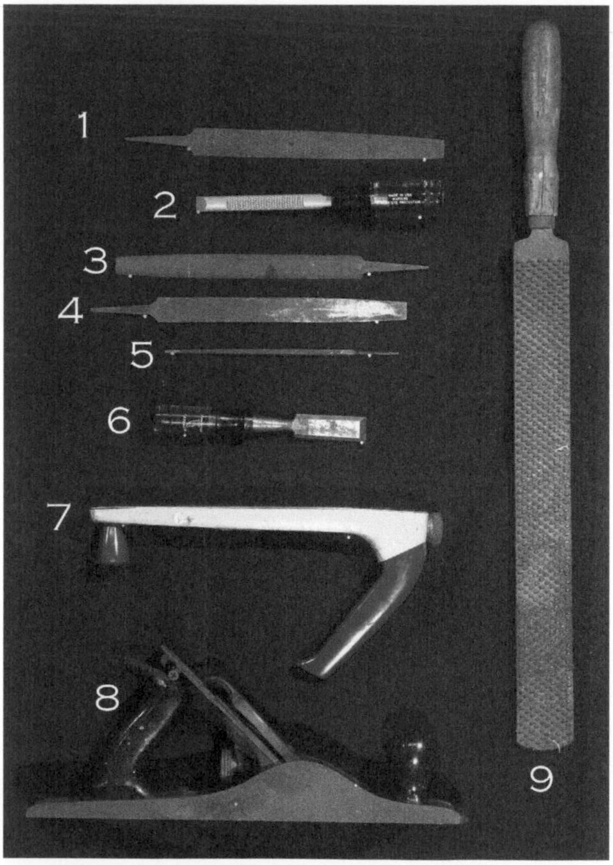

A **plane** is used to flatten, reduce the thickness of, and smooth the surface of a generally rough piece of lumber. Planes usually have a cutting edge on the bottom that is attached to the solid body of the plane. You move it back and forth over the wooden surface while the cutting edge removes uniform shavings a little at a time. This is a slow process, where all the pieces of the wood (usually at a joint) eventually become level.

A **rasp** is another woodworking tool for shaping the wood. It is made up of a long, narrow steel bar (Figure 7.20). There is a handle on one end, while the rest of the rasp has triangular teeth cut into it. When drawn across a piece of wood, it will shave away parts of the wood, very coarsely. A **file** is very similar to a rasp. The major difference is that a file has much finer teeth. The amount of wood removed is much smaller, and it is, overall, a gentler process.

■ **Figure 7.20** (1) Coarse rasp, (2) combination rasp/chisel, (3) half-round file, (4) flat file, (5) triangular needle file, (6) wood chisel, (7) hand rasp, (8) hand plane, and (9) ultra coarse rasp.

Powered Hand Tools

We move on to electric assembly tools with the same purposes as those hand tools we just discussed. We have the main tools and one big group of accessories: Drills, drill presses, hammer drills, and drill bits. Since this whole section is about drilling, let's talk about the basics of drilling for a second. A **drill** is a tool for making holes. The drill is a motor that can rotate the drill bit forward or in reverse. The size of the hole is determined by the size of the drill bit that does the cutting. The drill bit is held in place on the front of the drill by a chuck. The chuck is a hole in front of the motor. You insert the drill bit into the chuck and then tighten it, using a chuck key.

Electric drills have many different options and capabilities (Figure 7.21). The chuck size can vary for holding larger drill bits, they may have variable speed motors for both forward and reverse, and the newest addition is torque control. Drills operate on either battery or regular electricity. All of these options make this a versatile tool for the scene shop. Cordless, battery-powered drills are most popular, as they are more flexible and need not be tethered to an extension cord. They also

Figure 7.21 (1) Cordless drill, (2) corded drill, and (3) hammer drill.

Figure 7.22 (1) Belt sander, (2) palm sander, and (3) detail sander.

usually have keyless chucks for quick changing of your bits.

A **hammer drill** looks similar to the electric drills we discussed previously. It works in a similar way, with a drill bit that does the cutting. The added option in a hammer drill is that the chuck creates a short, rapid hammer-type action to break through hard or brittle material. This significantly speeds up the drilling process. Hammer drills are used mostly when working with masonry or stone.

The **drill press** is a stationary tool that does the same job as a regular drill. It has the added advantage of being mounted over a tabletop. There is usually a large handle on the side that moves the drill bit up and down into the material you are drilling. Since the drill is at a fixed angle and so is your material, you are guaranteed to drill exactly the same hole every time. This works out great for making multiple holes when working on a large project.

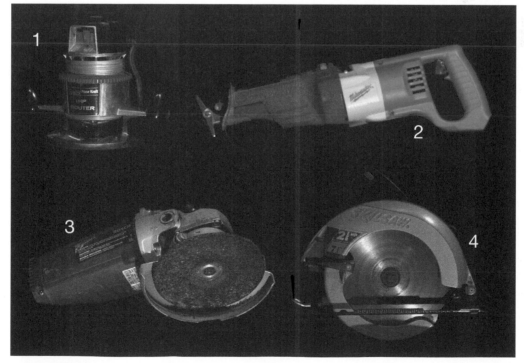

Figure 7.23 (1) Router, (2) reciprocating saw, (3) grinder, and (4) circular saw.

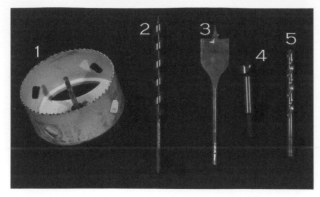

■ **Figure 7.24** (1) Hole saw, (2) auger bit, (3) spade bit, (4) Forstner bit, and (5) twist bit.

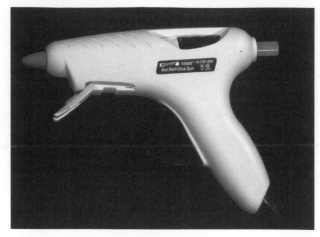

■ **Figure 7.25** Hot-glue gun.

OK, on to drill bits. Drill bits come in many sizes, as you can imagine, but they also come in different shapes (Figure 7.24). The bigger the hole you need to make, the stronger the drill bit needs to be! To choose the right bit, you need to know what material you will be drilling into as well as the size of the hole you need to make.

The basic drill bit you are most accustomed to seeing is the **twist bit**. This bit is a straight bit with spiral twists down its length. The front edge of each spiral is a cutting edge. The spiral design helps to remove the debris from the hole as you drill. These bits are usually made from high-speed steel, carbon steel, or tungsten carbide and can be used on wood, metal, or plastics. Titanium nitride is a coating sometimes used to increase the bit's hardness. But that is way too much chemistry stuff. All bits are marked in their packaging so just look for the info! Different manufacturers have different size ranges, but twist bits are usually available in a variety of sizes from $\frac{1}{64}$ inch to 1 inch. See Figure 7.24, numbers 2 and 5.

Spade bits, sometimes referred to as paddle bits, are the next category. See Figure 7.24, number 3. They come in larger diameters as well as longer lengths than regular twist bits, allowing for larger holes to be made. Spade bits are designed differently than twist bits. They have a straight shaft with a rectangular bottom that comes to a point. Think of a shovel (aka *spade*), and you get the visual. Spade bits are usually available in sizes ranging from ⅜ inch to 1 inch. **Forstner bits** are starting to be used as an alternative to spade bits. See Figure 7.24, number 4. They are sharper owing to their design. They

also have a rim instead of a center point, which makes for easier positioning. All of this combines to make a cleaner hole and makes the bits safer to use.

Need to make an even bigger hole? **Hole saws** make even larger holes. See Figure 7.24, number 1. These are no longer constructed in the same manner as a single drill bit. Think of a band saw blade, then make it smaller in diameter, and you'll be close to what a hole saw looks like. A piece of thin metal wrapped in a circle with teeth added on one side. These are awesome to work with. There is usually a small twist bit in the center of the hole saw. This allows you to get the hole started in the exact place you want it. Then the hole saw starts working! Sizes for hole saws usually range from ⅞ inch to 5¾ inches.

The last bit we talk about is not a drill bit but a **screw bit**. These are one of the most important items in the scene shop. Before their invention, all screwing was done by hand. I'm sure you've all used these. They come with slotted and Phillips heads and in different sizes. Sometimes, you can even find ones that are magnetic, which can be very helpful when you are working in tight spaces and the screw tends to drop off the screwdriver before you get it started! This is also really handy for keeping the screw on the end of the bit to begin with.

Our last tool fits into many categories and no categories all at the same time. It is the **hot-glue gun** (Figure 7.25). Hot glue is an amazing thing and has changed how we do many things in the theatre. You've probably seen these in craft stores, stationery stores, hardware stores, and maybe even grocery stores. They are very handy for a number of reasons. The basic idea is that you plug in the hot-glue gun, and it begins to get hot. Hot glue is a plastic material that is solid at room temperature but melts into a sticky fluid when heated. You insert a stick of solid hot glue into the gun. When you pull the trigger or push the glue in, the glue stick advances and begins to melt. Use it as you would any other adhesive, since all the glue has to do is cool down to produce a fast bond. Keep in mind that, if it gets heated up again, it will lose its holding power. Big safety note: Hot glue is really, really *hot!* You can burn yourself, so be careful.

Pneumatic Tools

So far we discussed hand tools and electrically powered tools. Now we move on to **pneumatic** tools, specifically nailers and staplers. However, a big disclaimer, almost all tools that are electric also come as pneumatic. Nailers and staplers are two used frequently in most shops. However, many, many pneumatic tools can be useful. Chisels, ratchets, grinders, and jigsaws are just a few of the options. Learn the technology first, and the tools will follow!

Pneumatic tools require a compressor to generate air pressure. Compressors have regulators on them that allow you to set the pressure your tool requires. The compressor then manufactures a high pressure, sending the air down the hose to the tool at the end. Think of holding a garden hose and putting your finger over part of the opening. Remember how the water pressure increases? It's not exactly the same, but it is similar.

This higher air pressure forces the nail or staple out of the gun and into whatever material you are working with. This is one of the fastest ways to work, once you are properly trained on the equipment. Keep in mind that there are different safety guidelines for this type of equipment. Make sure to follow the manufacturer's guidelines for safe use. Also make sure you are trained properly before beginning!

Pneumatic tools come in a wide variety of types with differing styles and features (Figure 7.26). Nailers are specifically designed to take certain lengths and weights

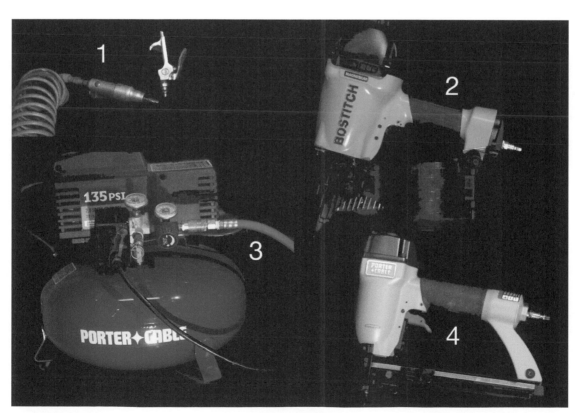

■ **Figure 7.26** Pneumatic tools: (1) pneumatic grinder on the left and pneumatic air nozzle on the right, (2) pneumatic coil nailer, (3) air compressor, and (4) pneumatic brad nailer.

of nails. Staplers are the same. You load a "clip" or a "cartridge," which contains varying amounts of nails or staples. Make sure that you have the right clip for the tool! This is really important. If you use the wrong nails or staples, it won't just jam; there is the possibility of the nails shooting out at the wrong angle and hurting you or someone else!

When working with metal, we need slightly different ways of joining pieces together. Please keep in mind that working with metals requires a completely different set of tools and skills than working with wood. Certain things about working with metal are much more dangerous than wood. If your shop has a metalworking area, make sure you are fully checked out on the equipment before even attempting to make a project.

Earlier, we discussed the use of oxyacetylene for cutting metal. Now, we look briefly at the variety of ways to join metals together. Welding is the most common way of permanently joining metal parts. A generic description of this process is heat being applied to metal pieces, melting and fusing them to form a permanent bond. There are many types of welding.

Welding Tools

Arc welding is the most common type. Standard arc welding involves two large metal alligator clips that carry a strong electrical current. One clip is attached to any part of the project being welded. The second clip is connected to a thin welding rod. When the rod touches the project, a powerful electrical circuit is created. The massive heat created by the electrical current causes both the project and the steel core of the rod to melt together, cooling quickly to form a solid bond.

Two common, but advanced, types of arc welding are tungsten inert gas (**TIG**) and metal inert gas (**MIG**) welding (Figure 7.27). TIG welding is used with stainless steel or aluminum. While TIG uses welding rods, MIG uses a spool of continuously fed wire, which allows the welder to join longer stretches of metal without stopping to replace the rod. In TIG welding, the welder holds the welding rod in one hand and an electric torch in the other hand. The torch is used to simultaneously melt the rod and a portion of the project's material. In MIG welding, the welder holds the wire feeder, which functions like the alligator clip in arc welding.

■ **Figure 7.27** Various gas tanks, gauges, and hoses for welding setups.

	Small Budget Tools	Medium Budget Tools
∘ Shop Vac	X	X
∘ Drill	X	X
∘ Jigsaw	X	X
∘ Circular Saw	X	X
∘ Hand sander	X	X
∘ Table Saw		X
∘ Chop Saw		X
∘ Band Saw		X
∘ Belt Sander		X
∘ Grinder		X
∘ Sawzall		X
∘ Router		X
∘ Radial Chop saw		
∘ Stationary Sander		
∘ Bench grinder		
∘ Router table		
∘ Impact drill		
∘ Hammer drill		
∘ Welder		
∘ Cold cutter		
∘ Panel Saw		
∘ Portable Compressor	X	X
∘ Narrow Crown Stapler	X	X
∘ Wide Crown Stapler		X
∘ Brad Gun		X
∘ Impact Wrench		
∘ Nail gun		
∘ Hand Saw	X	X
∘ Hammer	X	X
∘ Flat bar	X	X
∘ Screwdriver (flat and phillips)	X	X
∘ Tack Claw	X	X
∘ End Nippers	X	X
∘ Vise Grip	X	X
∘ Sliding T-Bevel	X	X

■ **Figure 7.28** Not every theater can afford every tool listed in this chapter. The chart above gives you a place to start and a place to expand as budget allows.

Like arc welding, **soldering** and **brazing** use molten metal to join two pieces of metal. The main difference between them is that the metal added during the process has a melting point lower than that of the material, so that only the added metal is melted, not the material. Soldering uses metals with a melting point below 800°F; brazing uses metals with a higher melting point. Because soldering and brazing do not melt the material, these processes normally do not create the distortions or weaknesses in the project that can occur with welding. Soldering commonly is used to join electrical, electronic, and other small metal parts. Brazing produces a stronger joint than soldering and often is used to join metals other than steel, such as brass.

CLEANING UP

OK, so the set is finally built. You're ready to move on to the next project. What is the first thing you should think about at this very moment? Clean up! That's right. If you don't clean up, you will be making your next project in the middle of a mess. You'll also suddenly realize you can't find any of your tools. And, wait a minute—there is no room to lay anything out. This includes all your flat, horizontal working areas such as tables, benches, saw horses, and roller stands! Have I made my point? At the end of every scheduled shop time, there should be a cleanup period before people head home. If everyone works together, it should take only about 15 minutes.

There is one tool left to talk about. It's for cleanup. It is technically referred to as the **wet/dry vacuum**. I'm sure you've all seen one, but, just in case, let me describe it. It is a vacuum cleaner with a substantial tank for collecting whatever you're cleaning up. And when I say *whatever*, I mean it. They are called wet/dry for a reason. With the flick of a switch, depending on the brand, you can go from vacuuming sawdust to water! They are rated based on how much liquid the canister holds. Some models also change from vacuuming to blowing. This can be very handy in all sorts of circumstances. And never forget the importance of a good broom—both shop brooms and hand brooms. They are the work horses of cleanup.

We are now at the end of our tool discussion. Keep in mind what I said at the beginning of this chapter. This is only a small sampling of what is out there. Keep on the lookout for other tools that may make a certain job easier. Many tools may be able to do a similar job, but it depends on the individual situation as to which one is *right* for the job. Also, always keep in mind the safe way to use these tools. I stress this all the way through the book, which is the same thing I do when I'm teaching. It's amazing how quickly a situation can turn from being fun as soon as someone gets hurt.

> When I sit alone in a theatre and gaze into the dark space of its empty stage, I'm frequently seized by fear that this time I won't manage to penetrate it, and I always hope that this fear will never desert me. Without an unending search for the key to the secret of creativity, there is no creation. It's necessary always to begin again. And that is beautiful.
>
> —Josef Svoboda,
> Czech artist and scenic designer

SUPPLIES

We're going to leave the tools behind for a little bit and explore some of the supplies that are out there. Once you are familiar with all the different options for materials and hardware out there, we go on to the next chapter, where we put it all together and start talking about building techniques. So, let's begin with wood.

WOOD

Wood is probably the most commonly used building material in theatre. Even with the advent of new technologies, there is still a huge amount of building and fabrication out of wood. Let's deal with some basic information about wood. There are hardwoods and softwoods. Hardwoods come from deciduous trees or trees that lose their leaves in the fall. Hardwoods are from trees such as cherry and maple, as well as oak, ash, or poplar. Softwoods come from evergreen trees. The most popular of these is the pine, cedar, fir, and spruce. For theatre, we tend to stick mostly to softwoods for our projects. They are most often affordable and available.

Dimensional Lumber

We use two cuts of wood: Dimensional lumber and sheet lumber. Dimensional lumber refers to solid wood that has been milled into standardized sizes, which are then used primarily for framing (Figure 7.29). Examples of this are probably common to you. Ever heard of a 2 × 4? That is only one example of dimensional lumber (Figure

■ **Figure 7.29** A lumberyard showing outdoor storage.

■ **Figure 7.30** Dimensional lumber, clearly labeled and organized by size, in storage.

7.30). Sheet lumber, on the other hand, is a composite of wood and glue that dries under pressure, sometimes with a hardwood veneer, sometimes not. As the name suggests, sheet lumber comes in large sheets, usually 4 × 8 feet. There are also different thicknesses, anything from ⅛ to ¼ to ½ to ¾ inch.

Dimensional lumber uses grading categories to describe its attributes:

- *Clear* wood is free of structural defects (warps, knots, etc.), though it may have minor imperfections (grain variations)
- *Select* wood is almost "clear" but has some natural characteristics such as knots and color variations
- *Common* wood has many more natural characteristics showing than either clear or select

Each of these three categories can be broken down with ratings of first, second, or third grade:

- *First*-grade wood has the best appearance, with minimal color variations and limited marking
- *Second*-grade wood is more variegated in appearance, both in color and texture
- *Third*-grade wood is very rustic in appearance, allowing all the wood's qualities to come through

Dimensional lumber comes in a variety of sizes as well as grades (Figure 7.30). Let's talk about the different sizes now. Many sizes of milled lumber are available. As with the tools, I discuss only the most common sizes used in theatrical building. Now, here is the confusing part: What we call a 2 × 4 is not actually 2 inches × 4 inches. Also notice that I didn't use the inches on the first usage of 2 × 4. That is technically a name and doesn't refer to the actual dimensions. The chart compares the **nominal size** (what we call it) against the **actual size**.

NOMINAL SIZE	ACTUAL SIZE
1 × 3	¾″ × 2½″
1 × 4	¾″ × 3½″
1 × 6	¾″ × 5½″
1 × 8	¾″ × 7¼″
1 × 10	¾″ × 9¼″
1 × 12	¾″ × 11¼″
5/4 × 4	1″ × 3½″
5/4 × 6	1″ × 5½″
5/4 × 8	1″ × 7¼″
5/4 × 10	1″ × 9¼″
5/4 × 12	1″ × 11¼″
2 × 4	1½″ × 3½″
2 × 6	1½″ × 5½″
2 × 8	1½″ × 7¼″
2 × 10	1½″ × 9¼″
2 × 12	1½″ × 11¼″
4 × 4	3½″ × 3½″

■ **Figure 7.31** *Hello, Dolly!* at Muhlenberg Summer Music Festival. Direction: Charles Richter; choreography: Karen Dearborn; scenic design: Campbell Baird; costume design: Dustin Cross; lighting design: John McKernon.

Sheet Lumber

We've gotten to sheets of wood. We use several kinds in theatrical construction: Plywood, lauan, homasote, hardboard (brand name Masonite), and medium-density fiberboard (MDF). What is wrong with that last sentence? One of the examples is not actually wood—read on to find out more! Let's look at a brief explanation of each and a listing of in what thicknesses they are available (Figure 7.32).

Plywood is graded differently than dimensional lumber. With plywood, the front and back of the sheet are graded separately. The front is graded with letters A, B, C, or D. "A" grade is sanded smooth and paintable. Some neatly made manufacturer repairs are acceptable; you should have little trouble finding A-grades that are free of repairs and knots. "B" grade is a solid surface with some repairs, usually football-shaped patches and/or wood filler, and may have tight knots (no chunks of wood missing) up to 1 inch and some minor splits. In "C" grade, you can expect

■ **Figure 7.32** (1) 1/8-inch hardboard (brand name Masonite), (2) 1/4-inch plywood, (3) 3/8-inch plywood, and (4) 5/8-inch plywood.

■ **Figure 7.33** *Pelléas et Mélisande* at the Metropolitan Opera. Director, Jonathan Miller; scenic designer, John Conklin; costume designer, Clare Mitchell; and lighting designer, Duane Schuler.

tight knots that are 1½ inches and knotholes to 1 inch and some splits or discoloration. Lastly, "D" grade has knots and knotholes up to 2½ inches, some splits, generally no repairs. In some ways, this is similar but somewhat poorer quality than the common grade for dimensional lumber.

The back of plywood is rated using a slightly different system. Numbers 1–4 are used. Numbers 1 and 2 provide for surfaces with all openings and/or repairs to be smaller than ¹⁄₁₆ inch. Number 3 provides for some open defects, meaning not repaired. This could include knotholes or splits and joints. Number 4 allows for open defects up to 4 inches in diameter. Plywood is commonly available in 4´-0˝ × 8´-0˝ sheets. It is also occasionally available in 4´-0˝ × 9´-0˝ and 4´-0˝ × 10´-0˝. Common thicknesses are ¼, ⅜, ½, ⅝, ¾, and 1 inch. You get the idea. There is a lot of flexibility in ordering plywood.

Lauan is a tropical hardwood plywood product and is pronounced *loo-on*. The name *lauan* comes from trees found in the Philippines but has become a generic term in the United States for imported tropical plywood. As this is a tropical wood, it comes mostly from the destruction of rainforests. Whenever possible, try to substitute another wood! If you must use lauan, it comes in 4´ × 8´ sheets in thicknesses of ⅛, ¼, ½, and ¾ inch.

Homasote is a type of wallboard made from recycled paper that is compressed under high temperature and pressure and held together with glue. Its primary use in the theatre is as sound proofing, either on top of platforms or as part of walls. Homasote is commonly available in 4´-0˝ × 8´-0˝ sheets, and occasionally in 4´-0˝ × 10´-0˝. Common thicknesses are ½, ⅝, and ¾ inch.

Hardboard is a wood by-product formed by taking wooden chips, blasting them into long fibers using steam, and then forming them into boards (Figure 7.32). These boards are then pressed and heated to create the finished product. The long fibers give hardboard a very high strength and stability. All of this combines to make a great product, which is incredibly heavy. Hardboard is commonly available in 4′-0″ × 8′-0″ sheets, and occasionally in 4′-0″ × 9′-0″ and 4′-0″ × 12′-0″. Common thicknesses are ⅛ and 3⁄16 inch.

MDF, otherwise known as *medium-density fiberboard*, is made from wood fibers glued under heat and pressure, similar to hardboard. The main difference between the two is that hardboard is very dense, and MDF is medium dense. This affects the weight and the cost! There are a number of reasons why MDF may be used instead of plywood. It is dense, flat, stiff, has no knots, and is easily machined. Because it is made up of fine particles, it does not have an easily recognizable surface grain. MDF can be painted to produce a smooth quality surface. However, MDF can be dangerous to use if the correct safety precautions are not taken. MDF contains a substance called *urea formaldehyde*, which may be released from the material through cutting and sanding. This can cause irritation to the eyes and lungs. Proper ventilation is required when using it; masks and goggles should always be worn at all times. MDF is commonly available in 4′-0″ × 8′-0″ sheets, and occasionally in 4′-0″ × 9′-0″ and 4′-0″ × 12′-0″ sheets. Thicknesses range from 1 to 2.5 inches.

Molding

That pretty much wraps up the typical wood types. Let's talk about molding for a little while. Although molding is primarily made of wood, it is also made from other material, which is why I saved it until the end of this part of our discussion. Molding falls into five basic categories: Baseboard, paneling, chair rail, picture rail, casing, and crown or cornice. From ceiling to floor, there are a number of places for the use of molding on walls. Typical placement for molding on walls is the cornice, picture rail, chair rail, and baseboard.

Moldings can be made from any number of types of woods, as well as MDF and even a flexible resin. The really great thing about moldings is that separate pieces can be joined to form a totally unique piece of finished molding. You can also combine bought molding with other pieces you have made from dimensional lumber with the use of a router. Take a look at Figure 7.34, showing molding pieces sold by Dykes Lumber, and you will see the variety of what is available.

■ **Figure 7.34** Molding stored horizontally by style. All ends are labeled with the design number.

METAL

We move from wood to metal next. This is going to be somewhat short and to the point. Metal is much more dangerous to work with than wood. Most school shops don't have a metalworking area. Here is the basic idea from the professional shops. They have a whole separate area of the shop, and separate personnel, dedicated to metalworking. Steel and aluminum are most commonly used. Steel is less expensive. Aluminum is much lighter but also more difficult to work with.

As I said throughout this chapter, look at all the choices for materials that are available, then decide which is the most appropriate for your design! Metals

■ **Figure 7.35** *Les Troyens* at the Metropolitan Opera. Director, Francesco Zambello; scenic designer, Maria Bjornson; costume designer, Anita Yavich; and lighting designer, James Ingalls.

can be fabricated into any shape you need (Figure 7.35). The potential for "custom" needs is much higher with metal than wood. Always defer to metal fabricators for advice and consultation before beginning any project of this type.

There is one metal I will address, as it is not necessary to have advanced skills in metalworking to use it. It is a personal favorite of mine—chicken wire! Chicken wire is a wire mesh that is usually used for making fences to keep in, you guessed it, chickens. It is fairly thin wire, very flexible, and easy to cut with the proper tool. When you need to make organic shapes, such as trees, rocks, and mountains, chicken wire can be bent and twisted to form the basic shape. It can then be stuffed or covered and finally painted. It is an old-fashioned way of doing

this type of building—it is inexpensive, supplies are easily available, and almost any skill level can do it!

FABRIC

Enough of this wood and metal stuff, let's move on to the softer side of scenery (Figure 7.36). Although any kind of fabric you can imagine can be used in the theatre, there are a few "standard" fabrics used commonly in the scenic realm (Figure 7.37). They are, in no particular order, velour, duvetyn, muslin, and scrim. Let's discuss each one's characteristics and uses.

Figure 7.36 *42nd Street* Tour, 2015. Lighting designer, Ken Billington; scenic designer, Kacie Hultgren (in combination with original set designer Beowulf Boritt); and costume designer, Roger Kirk.

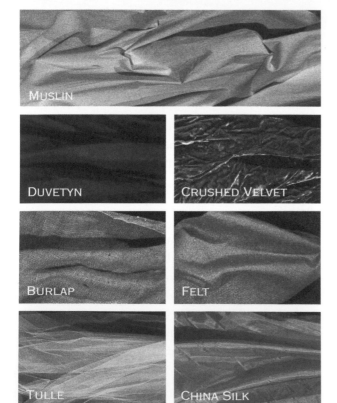

Velour

Velour is a very plush fabric with a feel similar to velvet. It comes in a variety of colors and thicknesses. The thickness of velour, or any fabric, is measured in ounces per linear yard. Velour is made in different ways. It can be 100 percent cotton to 100 percent polyester to anything in-between. The average width is 60 inches. The plushness is due to velour having a "nap." Think of nap in the same way as you think of wood grain. It doesn't really matter which way you use it, unless you are putting panels side by side. The nap has to all run the same way.

■ **Figure 7.37** Many different fabrics are used in the theatre. These are just a few of the samples.

Duvetyn

Duvetyn has a brushed matte finish and is therefore very different in feel than velour. It is 100 percent cotton, usually 54 inches wide, and comes in many colors. The most popular color is black. Duvetyn is much less expensive than velour and is used as a cheaper substitute for masking. Duvetyn is sometimes called *commando cloth*. Although they are similar, there is a difference. Duvetyn tends to be lighter weight, 8 ounces. Commando is heavier, starting at 10 ounces, and can be as heavy as 16 ounces.

Muslin

Muslin has many uses in the theatre. It is a 100 percent cotton plain-woven fabric and is used primarily as a base for other things. In costumes, muslin is used to make samples from patterns or as base layers that fancier fabrics are put on top of. In scenery, muslin is used to cover flats as well as for drops. More on flats and drops later. Muslin comes in widths from 44 inches to 39 feet. Yes, feet! It is an inexpensive fabric in regular widths, but can become quite expensive in the much wider widths. It is available in three general weights: Light, medium, and heavy. As opposed to other fabrics, it is not classified by ounces.

Scrim

Last, let's talk about scrim. Scrim is something of a specialty fabric, but it is so commonly used that I want to include it here. It is an open-weave netting, which means there is more open space than fabric. There are several styles of scrim. The most common is called *shark's tooth scrim*. There is also bobbinette, filled scrim, and netting. They vary by the openness of the weave as well as the

pattern of the weave. The really cool thing about scrim is that, depending on the lighting, you can either see through it or make it appear opaque. It is great for doing big reveals or for making things look like they are very far in the distance.

FOAMS AND PLASTICS

Styrofoam®—you know what it is. You've seen it. It comes in shipping boxes to keep fragile things safe. Then, you throw it away, right? Technically, Styrofoam is a trademark name. The actual name is extruded polystyrene—not nearly as fun, but accurate!

Foams

Well, the white Styrofoam you are used to seeing is actually called *bead foam*, because it is made up of tiny beads compressed together. It has great insulating properties and also resists moisture. Have you ever noticed that, if you break off a piece, you can see the little beads? The beads are always the drawback, as you couldn't easily get a smooth edge. It is also hard to paint! Well, this foam used to be used all the time for creating various 3D designs. Any design ideas that require organic shapes have to be fabricated using a number of materials that allow for that kind of freedom.

Enter the wonders of pink and blue foam (Figure 7.38). Both are denser than bead foam. The different colors have different densities and different insulation factors. Neither of those means anything to those of us in the theatre. We can pretty much use them interchangeably. These foams can be cut, joined, and carved to create almost any shape. However, a word of caution: If these foams are heated or even sanded vigorously, they can give off toxic and noxious fumes. Even breathing in the powder after sanding is a hazard. Make sure to use a respirator as needed when working with this material.

Ethafoam rods are another form of foam that we use. Ethafoam is round and comes in a variety of diameters and lengths. It is bendable and easily cut and shaped. It is made through a different process than the other foams we discussed, making it much safer to work with and use.

> The first show where I noticed this is what I wanted to do with my life was a Broadway revival of *West Side Story* in the early 1980s. I'd never seen a scrim before; I thought it was remarkable. Mind-blowing, like a movie special effect.
>
> —David Gallo,
> American scenic designer

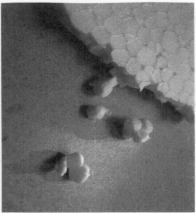

■ **Figure 7.38** Blue sheet foam on the left, with white bead Styrofoam on the top right, and ethafoam rods on the bottom right.

Plastics

A wide variety of plastics, silicones, and other materials are also used for scenic and prop fabrication. Most come in similar sizes and shapes similar to what we already discussed. The key differences to look for between similar materials are

- Sizes and shapes
- Weight
- Strength and weight bearing ability
- Tools and skills required
- Price
- Availability

HARDWARE

Let's move on to hardware, starting with fasteners. Once you've got the material, cut it to size, and shaped it, you are ready to put things together. One of the most important things to remember is that you want the fastener to penetrate at least three quarters of the way through your material. Halfway isn't strong enough to hold well, and all the way leaves the possibility of a sharp tip sticking out and hurting someone. Three parts can help to identify all nails, screws, and bolts: Head, shank, and tip. We discuss the differences next.

Nails

Nails—we all know what they are. We know what they look like. We all use them. But, are you aware of how many different kinds there are? *Nails*, *pins*, *tacks*, *brads*, and *spikes* are all names for nails. The head style of nails varies from round to nonexistent. Some nails have two heads so that, once you have hammered it into wood, another head is sticking out, which makes it easier to remove later. Shanks, for the most part, are smooth and round. Tips are pointed and sharp. Variations are all based on individual combinations of size, length (table follows), and diameter, as well as the head style (Figure 7.39).

■ **Figure 7.39** Nail styles vary to include length, diameter, head style, and so on. There is a nail for every job, so make sure to use the correct one for yours!

On a side note, nail sizes are designated by the word *penny*, which is indicated by the *d* after the size. This is based on a very old custom of selling nails in quantities of 100. The cost of the nails—6 penny, 10 penny, 20 penny—is how we now refer to that size of nail.

PENNY SIZE	LENGTH (IN.)	LENGTH (MM)
2d	1	25
3d	1¼	32
4d	1½	38
6d	2	51
7d	2¼	57
8d	2½	65
9d	2¾	70
10d	3	76
12d	3¼	83
16d	3½	89
20d	4	102
30d	4½	115
40d	5	127
50d	5½	140
60d	6	152

Screws and Bolts

Screws and bolts, we all know them as well (Figure 7.40). And we all use them. Head styles vary from pan, to round, to button, to truss, to flat. Another part of the head is the provision for turning the screw. There are various styles for this as well: Slotted, Phillips, Torx, Robertson, and hex. The shank has a thread formed on the surface that either partially or fully covers the shaft and also varies, depending on the individual screw and the material for which it is intended. Screws are identified using three numbers: The first is the diameter of the screw or bolt, the second number is the dimension between the threads, and the third is the overall length of the screw.

The tip can also vary. Tips that are pointed are tapping screws, and their shaft tends to be tapered. These types of screws include wood screws, lag screws, sheet metal screws, drywall screws (probably the most popular in the theatre), and screw eyes. Tips that are flat require predrilling and usually have shafts that are not tapered. These types include bolts, hex bolts, machine screws, eyebolts, carriage bolts, and thumb screws.

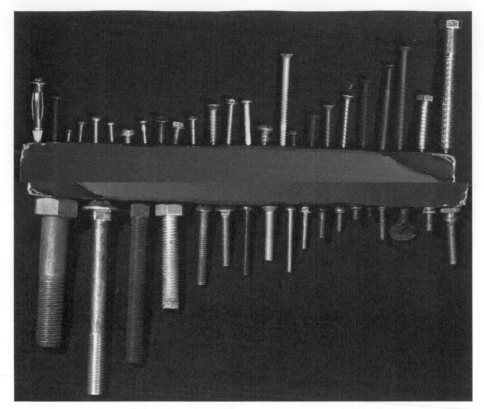

■ **Figure 7.40** There are so many types of bolts, it is amazing. They vary in length, width, screw thread, and head type.

Washers and Nuts

Screws work great by themselves. But bolts need a little extra help to stay put! A washer is a thin disk with a hole in the middle (think donut) used as a spacer between the bolt and the nut. Nuts come in various outside shapes, but the insides are round, threaded, and sized to match the bolt with which they are used. The bolt is put into the material from one side, washers can be used at either or both sides, and the nut is put on the other side from the bolt. As the nut is tightened, the material and hardware compress into a tight fit.

As with everything else, there are a variety of washers and nuts depending on the job you are doing (Figure 7.41). Washers can be plain, toothed, or cupped. Nut

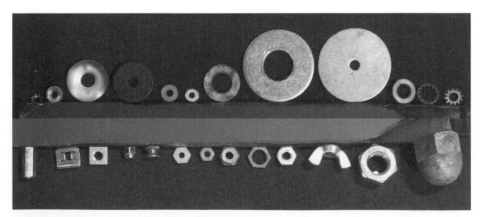

■ **Figure 7.41** There are as many types of washers and nuts as there are bolts, maybe even more. Here is a small sampling.

styles are hex nut, square nut, wing nut, cap nut, and T-nut. All work slightly differently, and it is important to know the different kinds. The actual use comes from learning from others and experience. Just keep your eyes and ears open, as it is easy information to pick up.

Staples

Staples—again we all use them to hold paper together. The same basic design works in the scene shop as well with some minor modifications. First, let's talk about the parts of the staple. We can break it down into the crown, the leg, and the teeth (Figure 7.42).

Staples come in a wide range of sizes and are much easier to produce than nails, screws, or bolts. Since they don't go into the material as far, they are not structural. But they are good for attaching thinner materials such as fabric. The sizes vary in both the crown and the leg dimensions (Figure 7.43).

Adhesives

Several kinds of adhesives are used in theatre. Drying adhesives are glues whereof, as they dry, the solvent they are made with evaporates. These are white glue, wood glue, Gorilla® glue, and Sobo®. Another adhesive group is contact adhesives. This group is applied to both pieces of material and allowed to dry a bit before joining the two items. It includes rubber cement and contact cement

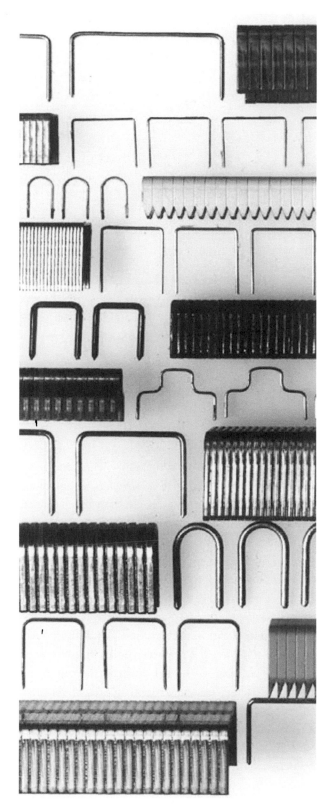

■ **Figure 7.43** Staples come in a variety of sizes and shapes depending on what type of stapler you will be using. Putting the wrong staples in the stapler will cause it to jam and cause a potentially dangerous situation.

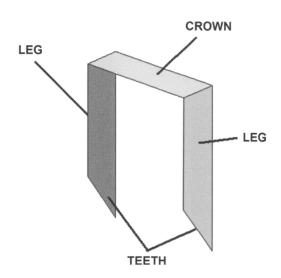

■ **Figure 7.42** Each part of the staple has a name. The different dimensions for these parts determine which staple to use for a job.

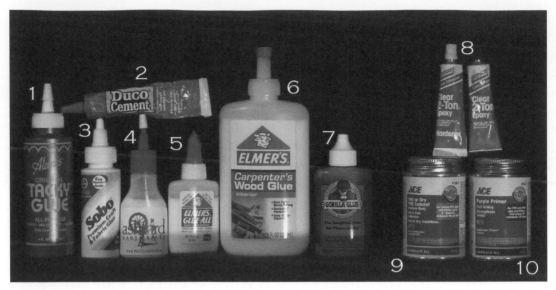

Figure 7.44 (1) All-purpose tacky glue, (2) Duco® cement, (3) Sobo craft glue, (4) wood adhesive, (5) Elmer's glue, (6) Elmer's wood glue, (7) Gorilla glue, (8) two-part clear epoxy, (9) PVC cement, and (10) PVC primer.

among others. Reactive adhesives are those where you mix two compounds together and they change each other to form an adhesive. Epoxy is an example of this. Let's talk about each one in a little detail.

White glue is your basic school glue (Figure 7.44). You have all used it. It works well, dries clear, and has a medium strength. Wood glue is very similar but much stronger. Sobo and Gorilla glues are both brand names. Sobo is white craft glue. It dries faster than regular white glue, can be frozen and thawed repeatedly, and is water soluble. Gorilla glues are strong like wood glue; they are 100 percent waterproof and easy to sand or paint.

Rubber cement—we all used it in elementary school. Remember, it was fun to play with once it dried. You could roll over it with your finger and play with it? Yeah, that is the stuff! Well, it is a very good adhesive even if you don't play with it. Use the brush in the cap of the can, spread rubber cement on both pieces of material, and wait for it to dry a bit, then put the items together. Contact cement works in a similar way.

Epoxy is the last adhesive we discuss. Epoxy is a two-part adhesive. By mixing together equal quantities of each part, you create a chemical reaction that forms epoxy. The two parts individually are fairly inert. When combined, they form a very strong adhesive.

Hinges

The next topic is hinges. The most common usage for a hinge that you have seen is most likely for a door. Hinges allow for something to pivot on a given point for a specific degree of rotation. Sound complicated? Not really. Let's talk about the different kinds of hinges, with examples, to make it easier to understand.

One of the most basic "options" with any hinge is the pin. Do you want the pin, or pivot point, to be fixed with the hinge or removable? There are reasons for each choice. Obviously, a fixed-pin hinge is very sturdy and strong as it is manufactured together. A loose-pin hinge does not make as rigid a pivot point. However, once each side of the hinge is attached to scenery, the loose pin can be removed, and the one big item can become two smaller items. This is very handy for shipping, storage, and the general running of the show. Keep this concept in mind as we go on to the specific kinds and shapes of hinges.

Strap hinges are an older style of hinge (Figure 7.45). They are most often used on large doors, like on a barn. When laid flat they look like two H triangles joined by a pivot. The design of these hinges makes them incredibly strong. T-hinges are similar to strap hinges. A T-hinge has one side shaped like a triangle while the other side is rectangular. Sort of makes it look like a T!

A back-flap hinge is one of the most commonly used hinges in theatre. Each side of the hinge is roughly

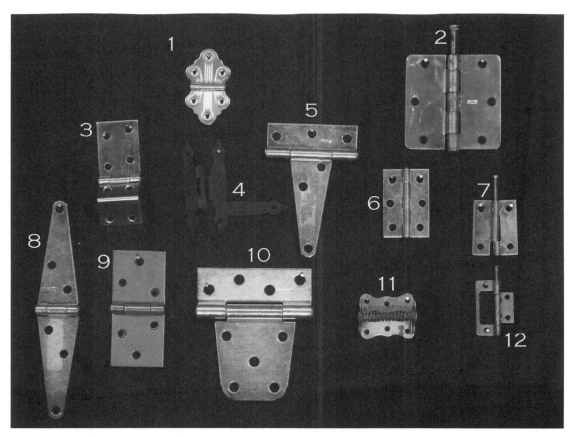

■ **Figure 7.45** (1) Cabinet hinge, (2) loose-pin broad butt hinge, (3) chest hinge, (4) decorative cabinet hinge, (5) T-hinge, (6) fixed-pin broad butt hinge, (7) small loose-pin broad butt hinge, (8) strap hinge, (9) back-flap hinge, (10) gate hinge, (11) spring hinge, and (12) nonmortised loose-pin hinge.

square, and there are usually three holes in each side for screwing into. A broad butt hinge is slightly smaller than a back flap. A broad butt hinge is rectangular in shape, about half the size of a back flap, and usually has two screw holes.

Piano hinges are named for—well—pianos. Think of the top lid on a piano. It has a long, skinny, thin hinge with lots and lots of tiny screws. Well, that is a piano hinge. It is the perfect tool when you need a long uninterrupted length of hinge, either for the aesthetic of it or for the stability. Double-acting hinges can swing their door both in and out, which makes them unique. Think of old Western movies. Remember the doors on the saloons? Now you have the image!

Casters

Our last topic in this chapter is casters. Yes, that is right, we've finally gotten to the end! A caster is a wheel within a mounting assembly and makes movement of heavy pieces of scenery much easier. So, you're going grocery shopping, and you always seem to get the shopping cart that won't steer properly? Blame it on the caster!

There are a wide variety of types and styles of casters (Figure 7.46). Let's address the two basic differences and the one thing you have to decide first when selecting a caster. Will your piece of scenery travel in a straight line? Or, does it need to turn a corner or move in different directions? If you need movement in only one direction, a fixed caster is for you. If you need multiple directions of movement, then choose the swivel caster. Swivel casters can rotate 360 degrees, but keep in mind, there is always a turning radius, or the amount of time and space the wheel needs to rotate.

The size of the mounting plate and the size of wheel are two of the determining factors when choosing a caster for a job. Another factor is the material the wheel is made from. Wheels can be made from metal, plastic, rubber, or wood.

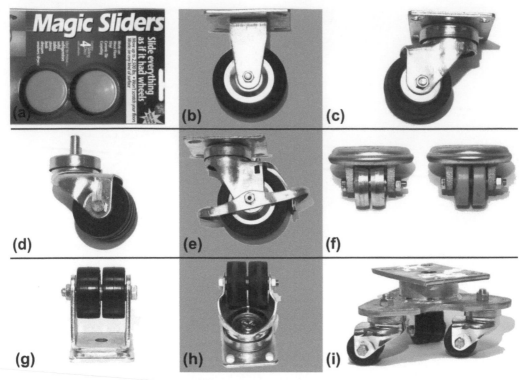

■ **Figure 7.46** (a) Furniture slides, (b) rigid caster, (c) swivel caster, (d) swivel caster with screw mount, (e) swivel caster with brake, (f) heavy-duty low-level casters, (g) low-profile double-fixed caster, (h) low-profile double-swivel caster, and (i) tri-way swivel turtle.

The last factor that should be considered when choosing a caster is whether or not you need it to lock. When you combine these four factors, you can roll almost anything, almost anywhere. Overall weight and sound are major factors with these choices. As with any hardware, know your application and choose what will work best, within your budget, of course.

EXERCISES

EXERCISE 1

Describe the correct situations for proper use of screws versus nails versus bolts.

EXERCISE 2

Analyze the design of a rip and a crosscut saw blade in order to explain the specific uses for each.

CHECK YOUR KNOWLEDGE

1. Summarize the three categories relating to scenic tools. Describe the intended uses of each.
2. Relate the framing, combination, and speed square tools to one another. Give examples of why each is appropriate in different situations.
3. Illustrate the differences between using a hand drill and using a drill press.
4. Contrast any hammer against a mallet in terms of functionality.

STUDY WORDS
Chapter 7

- Actual size
- Adjustable wrench
- Allen keys
- Arc welding
- Ball peen hammer
- Band saw
- Bar clamp
- Bevel gauge
- Box wrench
- Brazing
- Carpenter clamp
- Carpenter pencil
- Center punch
- Chalk line
- Chisel
- Chop saw/ Compound miter saw
- Circular saw
- Claw hammer
- Combination square
- Coping saw
- Crosscut blade
- Dead-blow hammer
- Drill
- Drill press
- Fence
- File
- Flush cut saw
- Folding rule
- Forstner bit
- Framing hammer
- Framing square
- Grinder
- Hacksaw
- Hammer drill
- Hand-screw clamp
- Hole saw
- Hot-glue gun
- Jig
- Jigsaw
- Keyhole saw
- Laser level
- Laser measure
- Linesman's pliers
- Mallet
- MIG
- Miter box
- Miter saw
- Nail set
- Needle-nose pliers
- Nominal size
- Nut driver
- Open-ended wrench
- Oxyacetylene
- Panel saw
- Phillips screws
- Pipe cutter
- Pipe reamer
- Pipe threader
- Pipe wrench
- Plane
- Plumb bob
- Pneumatic
- Pry bar
- Radial-arm saw
- Rasp
- Reciprocating saw
- Rip blade
- Router
- Scroll saw
- Slip-joint pliers
- Slotted screw
- Socket set
- Soldering
- Spade bit
- Speed square
- Speed wrench
- Spirit level
- Spring clamp
- Stapler
- String level
- Table saw
- Tack hammer
- Tape measure
- TIG
- Torx
- Twist bit
- Utility knife
- Vises
- Wet/Dry vacuum
- Yankee screwdriver

How to Get It Done

Scenery Techniques and Practices

CHAPTER SEVEN

Student Learning Outcomes

Students will acquire:

- An overview understanding of the major aspects, techniques, and directions in the area of scenery.

- Fundamental, conceptual understanding of the expressive possibilities of theatre.

- A working knowledge of technologies, safety, and equipment applicable to the area of scenery.

This chapter is all about scenery. Yes, finally we're going to talk about scenery. Did you think that scenery was going to be Chapter 1? Well, you have to lay the groundwork before jumping in. As we get into the "down and dirty" of implementing scenic ideas, you'll see how the first seven chapters have given you a background you didn't think you'd need but is now going to come in very handy. This chapter gives you a background in the traditional scenic techniques as well as how they developed over time. As always, we are honoring the theatre's past before moving into the future. And, keep in mind that, when the budget is tight, you will need this information to come up with a well-rounded solution to whatever "challenges" might arise. Once we get the basics in hand, we discuss some of the new technologies available today.

SCENIC TECHNIQUES DEVELOP THROUGH HISTORY

We continue our discussion from Chapter 1 (remember Chapter 1?) about history and catch up to when scenery started to really take off and come into its own. Playwrights and audiences always wanted more, and the theatre rose to the challenge. We discussed in Chapter 1 the use of the backdrop as it developed during the Greek genre. The Greeks also started to develop a back wall that contained doors for entrances and exits. The next set of scenic developments needed to wait until theatre was indoors or at least partially covered from changes in the weather.

This brings us to developments that happened primarily from the 16th to the 19th century. This time in theatre saw many developments to scenery. To create more of an illusion, the idea of the backdrop was expanded and continued further downstage. Each of the **wings** now had a **leg** on either side that was painted to continue the design of the backdrop. Overhead, to simulate the heavens, painted **borders** were added to complete the visual effect. The wings and borders also became known as **masking**, which had the added benefit that they blocked the backstage area from the audience's view. This style of scenery came to be known as the **wing and drop**, a term still used today.

Another element that had been used in the past but came into much popularity was the periaktoi. **Periaktoi** are triangular columns that revolve to reveal other sides and sets. Multiple periaktoi are usually used in each wing or across the upstage side of the stage, replacing the backdrop. Picture a backdrop cut vertically into five pieces. Each piece is then put onto one side of one periaktoi. A piece of another backdrop is put on the second side, and a piece of a third backdrop is put on the third side. The five periaktoi line up across the upstage wall and they create a backdrop. They all rotate so another side faces the audience, and, like magic, the backdrop has changed. This can be used for wings to create an extra sense of depth. It doesn't have to be used just for the backdrop. The rotation of the periaktoi was done originally with stagehands pulling on ropes. Later, it was automated with the use of the early winches.

Primitive flying effects had existed since the Greek genre came up with the idea of **deus ex machina**. They were only slightly more advanced here. Flying could indeed happen inside, which is an advance in and of itself. The designers were still concerned with masking the machinery and used 2D clouds to mask the machinery as it was raised and lowered. This technology often required a vertical track to be secured to a piece of scenery or the actual building. A horizontal beam or platform was then attached to the track. A scenic cloud was attached to the downstage side of the mechanism, so that it moved with the platform, as if to hide it. Of course, the track was in full view above and below the platform, and nobody seemed to mind that!

The next advance used was the predecessor to our current tracking decks. During the 17th century, banks of trolleys were installed under the stage to facilitate scenery moving within a predictable path. *Predictable* is the key here; the scenery had to go from point A to point B, moving along the same path, every time. These trolleys connected to scenery, usually the hard legs, through a series of ropes. Using a sandbag for a counterweight, a central shaft was rotated, pulling the ropes and moving the trolleys. Suddenly, the two legs had changed positions in the wing, and the scene change was complete.

These trolleys evolved into what we know today as a **traveler** track. Just like a curtain track in your house, only bigger and sturdier, the traveler can hold a very heavy curtain and allow it to move. This usually happens in full view of the audience, with the curtain splitting at center or moving from one side of the stage to the other.

Another addition to the scenic inventory at this point is the trap. A **trap** is a hole in the floor with a replaceable plug. When the plug is in place, the floor looks complete, and it is usually hard to detect where the plug may be. With the plug removed, you have direct access to below the stage floor. This idea can work great for surprise entrances or exits. Depending on the amount of room below the stage, ladders, scaffolding, and elevators were all used to convey actors and scenery up and down. The elevators were primitive, using traditional counterweighted sandbags. But, hey, it worked!

The 18th century brought with it a variety of ways to change the set. We are still dealing primarily with wing and drop changes. The wing change techniques advanced from the 17th-century device to eliminate the counterweight and add a winch—a primitive winch with a crank handle, but a winch! The borders and backdrops were now rolled around a tube that allowed them to be brought up and down. This combination of technologies allowed the whole set to be changed quickly, and apparently by magic.

The use of traps was also expanded during this time. Traps became much more popular, with many being built into an individual stage, instead of the original one, two, or three. There were now several ways to open a trap. The trap could be hinged, either up or down. There were

■ **Figure 8.1** *Wonder* by Steve Yockey. Directed by Rachel Chafkin; sets by Marta Ekhougen; costumes by Brenda Abbandandolo; lights by Bruce Steinberg. Tisch School of the Arts Graduate Acting in collaboration with Design for Stage and Film.

sliding traps that were not as obvious to the audience. The trap opened by sliding the cover to the side and basically was stored inside the stage floor.

Toward the end of the 19th century, the audience started to want more realism. This led to the elimination of the wing and drop sets. What developed is called the box set. A **box set** usually contained three walls and perhaps a ceiling. It was, and still is, used to represent interiors. Striving for realism led to other changes in scene design as well.

The raked stage was done away with in favor of a level stage floor. To ease the floor into the backdrop, a **scenic ground row** was added to the design. This ground row was two-dimensional and usually had a cutout design on the top to help the transition to the drop. Flying was curtailed, as this didn't fit in with the new "realism" mandate.

It was alright to put scenery on casters; this was not considered supernatural. So, rolling platforms (wagons) and revolving stages (turntables) became very popular. The revolving stage allowed for another kind of set change. You could set up three box sets on the stage, with their backs all touching, then revolve the stage from one to the next to the next—a complete set change in mere

seconds. This had never been seen before and became the newest kind of theatre magic!

The box set brought about an interesting development in the acting style of the day, which in turn influenced future design as well. As mentioned in Chapter 1, the **fourth wall** became a convention of acting within a box set, where you create an imaginary wall to complete the room. There is no recognition that the audience is in attendance. As a result, the act curtain began being used to close off the stage from the audience prior to the show. This created an atmosphere of catching the action in progress, making the audience a nonparticipating observer.

As theatre buildings became more technically able, variations in the normal way things are done started to pop up in standard use. One example of this is the tab curtain. Picture a normal masking leg in the wings. Now, take that leg and turn it 90 degrees so it hangs upstage to downstage. This, called a **tab**, is used to mask the wings from the audience. Many other variations are created as needed. Don't feel the need to be locked in by what you see in this book or any other!

SCENIC DESIGN PROCESS

Now that we have this perspective on a bit more of scenery history, let's talk about the scenic design process a little more in depth. We discussed, in Chapter 2, the phone call, meetings, research, and sketching. Part of this process is for the designer to complete color renderings or models. Keep in mind that, depending on the situation, time frame, and complexity of the design, parts of the process may be expanded or cut completely.

At some point, the director, producer, or someone who controls the aesthetics or money will approve the design. This is the point when the designer and however many assistants are hired to get to work on the pack of drawings. Let's break down the pack of drawings, as this will be essential to ultimately getting the show built. A pack of draftings consists of the following, as appropriate, since productions vary so much:

- Cover sheet with index of drawings
- Sketch or model photos
- Ground plan
- Section
- Deck plan
- Elevations
- Details

Each of these drawings, or groups of drawings, can be expanded as needed by the design. If there is a complicated deck with a lot of automation, there may be several drawings of the deck alone. It is for the designer to decide what drawings are needed to communicate with the scene shop. What we have been talking about are designer drawings. Let me explain.

Designer drawings are drawn, as you would expect, by the designer. They are meant to convey the artistic

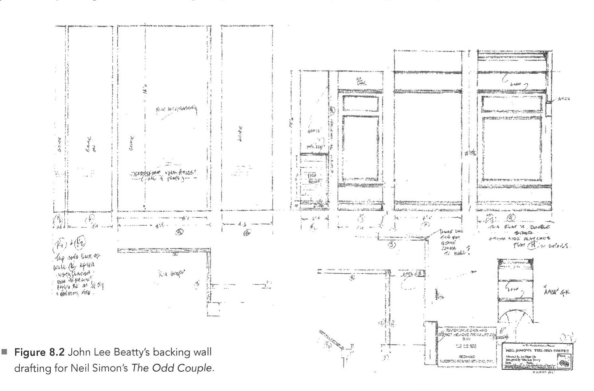

■ **Figure 8.2** John Lee Beatty's backing wall drafting for Neil Simon's *The Odd Couple*.

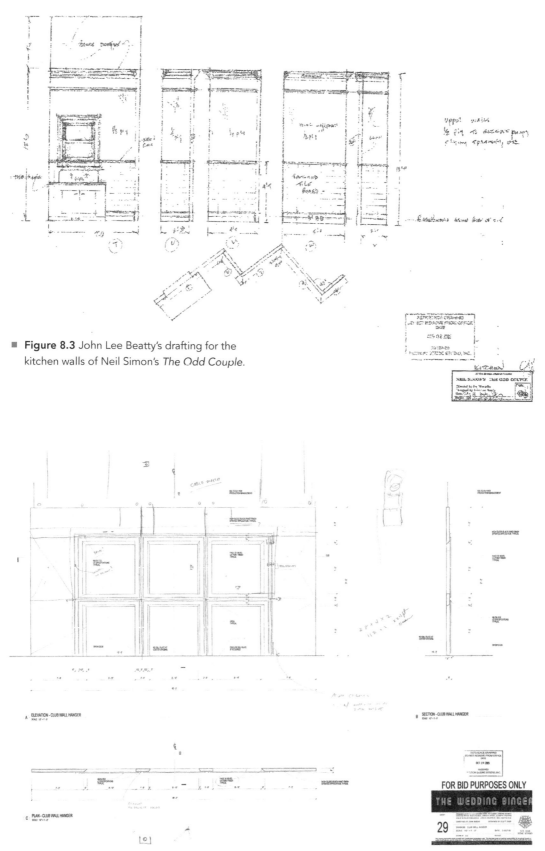

■ **Figure 8.3** John Lee Beatty's drafting for the kitchen walls of Neil Simon's *The Odd Couple*.

■ **Figure 8.4** Scott Pask's drawing for *The Wedding Singer*'s club wall hanger.

vision of the designer. They are critical to informing the shop what the designer's ideas and goals are. The shop must look at these drawings to determine a price and, more important, to begin building the set. Often, a scene shop will not get a full pack of drawings. Sometimes, they get a partial pack of draftings and a model (Figures 8.2–8.4). Obviously, the more information they have, the better chance they have to properly evaluate the design.

Let's talk about models for a second. A scenic model is a miniature 3D version of the completed set design. The model is in scale, usually ¼ or ½ inch, depending on the size of the theater. Making the model this small allows for easier portability to meetings. Some designers prefer to work in three dimensions instead of two. If the design is more sculptural than painterly, it can often give the director a better sense of the finished design. Remember, in Chapter 5, I talked about semantics and the need to put ideas into a visual form so that everyone could understand them better and more accurately? Well, the bottom line is that any tool at your disposal can be used to convey ideas. Quick pencil sketches on a napkin are as valid as

a drafting, rendering, or model. The only mandate is that visual ideas are conveyed in a nonverbal way.

> Just because you can, doesn't mean you should!
>
> **—Anonymous**

Before any building can be done, the shop must evaluate the designer drawings and determine the best way to interpret the drawings and translate them into wood, metal, paint, and whatever other materials are called for. Before the shop workers can begin to build the set, they must first create their own set of drawings. These are known as **construction drawings**, or working drawings (Figures 8.5–8.7). Construction drawings differ from designer drawings in that they are much more technical. For example, a designer drawing of a deck may show the outside shape and dimensions and materials

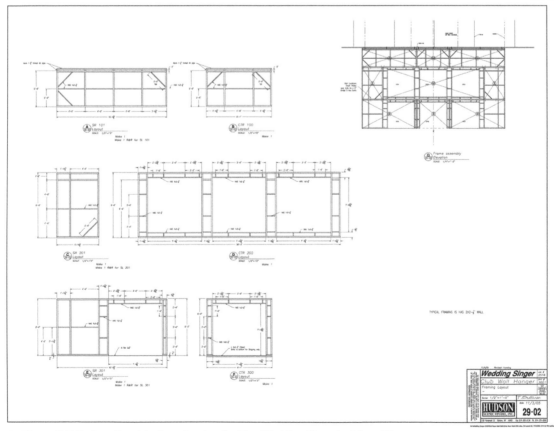

■ **Figure 8.5** Hudson Scenic's shop drawing for *The Wedding Singer*'s club wall hanger.

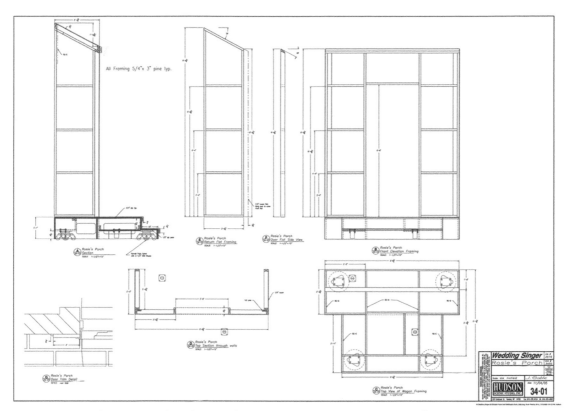

■ **Figure 8.6** Hudson Scenic's shop drawings for *The Wedding Singer*'s Rosie's porch framing.

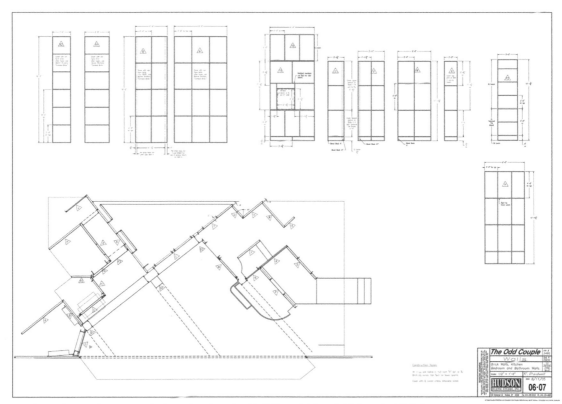

■ **Figure 8.7** Hudson Scenic's shop drawings for Neil Simon's *The Odd Couple*, Wall A.

choices. The construction drawing breaks the deck into manageable pieces to be built separately and put together during the load-in. This is a critical phase, as pieces of scenery need to fit out through the door of the shop, into a truck, and in the door at the theater. These doors are all different sizes. Materials then are identified and lists made of what is required for each piece.

A professional scene shop can vary greatly in its organization from a college scene shop. Professional shops usually have more people and are broken up into smaller departments. Let's look at Hudson Scenic Studio, Inc., for a moment, as they were kind enough to give me access to their shop during my research for this book. I am grateful to everyone there for their willingness to share their time, energy, and craft with me.

Hudson is a full-service production and scenic fabrication company. Its clients include producers of theatre, touring productions, television, casinos, themed environments, corporate presentations, live advertising, commercials, theme parks, industrial theatre, theme restaurants, and various special projects that involve many types of specialty construction.

Services that Hudson Scenic Studio, Inc., can provide include:

- Production design planning and budgeting
- Project management
- Technical supervision and installation
- Design engineering services
- Custom scenic fabrication: Carpentry and stagecraft
- Metal fabrication
- Scenic and backdrop painting
- Sculpting
- Automation, motion control, and mechanization
- CNC router design and fabrication
- Set electrics
- Soft goods and traveler track systems
- Rigging system design and installation

The process at Hudson can be broken up into very clear steps. The first step is, of course, to get the job. A designer presents documentation, as we discussed earlier. Hudson assigns a project manager, who will evaluate the design and begin assigning dollar amounts to the different parts of the scenery. A proposal is put together for the client, showing a total price to execute the design.

This may be approved right away or, more likely, there may be alterations or cuts to the design to fit within budget. Eventually, everyone will agree, and the proposal turns into an actual job!

The project manager then creates a job order; this is internal paperwork for use at the scene shop, so that all those working on the job have a frame of reference for the entire job, not just the piece they are working on. A kickoff meeting is scheduled. This is one of the most important parts of the process. From the production team, the designer and the technical supervisor are present at this meeting. The technical supervisor is responsible for everything technical on the production. This includes scenery, lighting, rigging, etc. This person is with the show from the first meetings through opening night.

Hudson will now assign an internal production manager to the project. This person will create a flowchart for all departments to use, which includes assignments of different units as well as a timeline from the very first day through trucking the scenery to the theater (Figure 8.8). These flowcharts are updated continuously, as schedules may need to shift within the shop. Details that go into the flowchart are which departments are needed for any given unit, when the department is available to work on the unit, and when materials are arriving. Also of importance are the scenic pieces that need more than one department's attention. If this is the case, scheduling may be even tighter. Materials have to be ordered, and the crew has to be hired. The goal, obviously, is to have the materials arrive before the crew!

Let's talk about the departments within a scene shop. Now, remember, in smaller shops, jobs can get combined. This doesn't mean that the task goes away; it just means that one person is doing lots more work! At its most spread out and organized, the departments of the scene shop are broken down into eight categories: Engineering, carpentry, iron, automation, electrics, rentals, scenic artists, and trucking. There are plenty of blurry lines between the different departments based on the fact that it is rare for a piece of scenery to be fully fabricated within one department. Let's go through the departments, one by one, to see what each does.

Engineering is the first department to begin work on a job. Let me interrupt by saying that there used to be a position called the *layout man*. This person would look at

The Drowsy Chaperone
10/5/05
Job #2502-Prepared by Mark O'Brien - Ver. 1

Unit #	Unit (Scenery)	Draft	Drafting Complete	Router Start	Router End	Metal Start	Metal End	Carpentry Start	Carpentry End	Automation Start	Automation End	Electrics Start	Electrics End	Paint Start	Paint End	Tech Start	Tech End	Load-out	Load-in	Notes
0300	Show Deck	RB	10/4			10/3	10/12	10/3	10/13					10/14	10/18			Wed 10/19	Sun 10/23	Sanding deck 10/13am
0400	Show Portal	JG	10/5					10/6	10/15									Fri 10/21		
0500	DS Plaster Arch	JG	10/5					10/6	10/15			10/14	1/2 day	10/17	10/20	10/14	10/15	Fri 10/21		
0600	US Plaster Arch	JG	10/6					10/6	10/15			10/14	1/2 day	10/17	10/20	10/14	10/15	Fri 10/21		
0700	Apartment Walls		10/3			10/4	10/7	10/4	10/12					10/14	10/18	10/12	10/12	Thu 10/20		Add jacks for door. Purchase drop box fabric and paint
0700	US Apartment Walls	JG	9/29			10/3	10/7	10/3	10/11					10/14	10/18	10/12	10/12	Thu 10/20		
0700	US Apartment Fiber Optics	DSR										10/19	10/20					Thu 10/20		
1000	SR and SL Windows	JG	10/7					10/12	10/17									Sat 10/22		
1200	Bridal Suite	CL	10/5	10/3	10/5			10/5	10/14			1 day		10/17	10/21			Sat 10/22		
1250	Flying Mirrors (2)	CL/JG	10/6	10/5	10/6			10/11	10/14			1/2 day		10/19	10/21			Sat 10/22		Flex Moulding due by 10/13
1600	French Doors	CL	10/3	10/3	10/5			10/3	10/12					10/17	10/20			Sat 10/22		
1700	Globe	AG																Fri 10/21		By Scenic Arts Studios and Costume Armour
1800	Swag Hanger with Chandelier																			
1900	Stairs (2)	RB	10/6			10/6	10/18	10/8	10/15					10/20	10/26			Wed 10/26		Need to make paint sample
2000	Murphy Bed Frame and Flats	DK	10/6															Wed 10/26		
2100	Beds (3)	DK	10/10															Wed 10/26		Beds go out to be upholstered
2200	Airplane	AG												10/17	10/25	10/22	10/24	Wed 10/26		
2300	Palace Portal Drop	TS				10/17	10/18							10/11				Thu 10/20		Need rendering
2400	Palace Backing Drop	TS				10/17	10/18							10/11				Thu 10/20		
2500	Vaudeville Drop	TS				10/17	10/18											Thu 10/20		
2600	Country Drop	TS																TBD		By Scenic Art Studios
2700	Fountain/Sunset Drop	TS				10/17	10/18							10/11				TBD		By Scenic Art Studios - Piece will drop ship from fiber optic vendor
2800	Cityscape Drop	TS				10/17	10/18											Thu 10/20		
2900	Palettes	RB	10/13															Fri 10/21		
3000	US Masking Portal					9/30												Fri 10/14		
3100	Black Serge Masking	TS																Fri 10/14		
3400	Ballet Drop	TS				10/17	10/18											Fri 10/14		
3500	Bounce Drop	TS				10/17	10/18											Fri 10/14		
3800	Serge Window Inserts w/fiber	AG						10/3	10/11									Fri 10/14		
1300	Garden units SR and SL	AG						10/3	10/12									Wed 10/26		By Scenic Art Studios
1400	Foliage Hanger	AG																Fri 10/21		By Scenic Art Studios
1500	Finale Trees	RB	10/11									1-1/2 days						Wed 10/26		Hudson builds the wagons and tree frame. Scenic Art studios provides the foliage
	Automation																			
	Rigging package	AG																Fri 10/14		
	Deck Track 1	AG																Wed 10/19		
	Deck Track 2	AG																Wed 10/19		
	Deck Track 3 - Tandem Split Ctr	AG																Wed 10/19		
	Deck Track 4 - Tandem Split Ctr	AG																Wed 10/19		
	Main Trap Sunroof	AG																Wed 10/19		
	Main Trap Lift	AG																Fri 10/14		
	DS Flying Walls	AG																Fri 10/14		
	US Flying Walls	AG																Fri 10/14		
	Airplane Fly Winch	AG								10/5	10/13							Wed 10/26		
	Airplane Propeller	AG																Wed 10/26		
	Fountain Sunset Fly Winch	AG																Fri 10/14		
	Murphy Bed Manual Rigging	AG																Fri 10/14		
	Automation control package	AG																Wed 10/19		

Figure 8.8 Hudson Scenic's production flowchart for *The Drowsy Chaperone*.

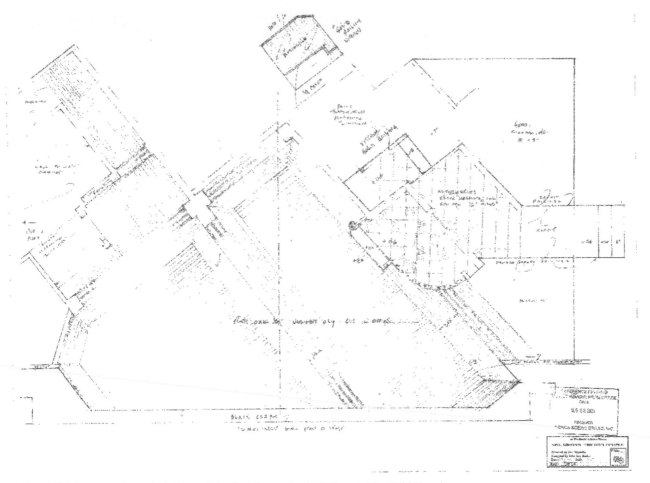

■ **Figure 8.9** John Lee Beatty's drafting of the floor layout for Neil Simon's *The Odd Couple*.

the drafting and sketch out the design in full scale on the actual wood to be used. Then, he or she would cut out the wood. It was that easy. This way of working has changed, and the position has evolved into that of an engineer. The engineer drafts the construction drawings and much, much more! The engineer drafts any automation and plans out the control for it. This often entails a custom control system, where software programming is required. The engineer also develops and plans the set electrics. Research of new products is another function of the engineering department.

The carpentry shop is filled with—carpenters. What a surprise! They deal with everything made of wood— measuring, layout, cutting, fabrication, everything. Another tool in the shop is a CNC router. This is a very cool piece of machinery. Basically, routers cut using different size and shape bits. Molding can be created with a router. Got the idea? Well, this router is huge and

computer-driven as opposed to manual. So, basically, the carpenters make a CAD file, load it into the router, and the cutting begins. The best part is that the level of accuracy is amazing.

The iron department is the same as the carpentry department, only instead of using wood it uses metal. Steel and aluminum are two metals used in the shop. Welding becomes an important skill, and there are major differences between welding these two metals. Measuring, layout, cutting, and fabrication are all dealt with. Today's designs seem to call for more metal and less wood. This has to do with the current aesthetic as well as the structural needs for these designs.

The automation department is next in line. Automation deals with anything that moves. That may sound simple, but, in today's theatre, it is anything but! The deck is not the only part of the set that may contain automation. There may very likely be flying elements.

■ **Figure 8.10** *Sweet Charity*, produced by James Madison University in February 2015. Scenery and projections are by Richard Finkelstein. Costumes are by Rebecca Lustig. Lighting is by Emily Becher-McKeever. Associate projection designer is David Willmore.

Any of these ideas may require automation. And, here is the key: All of the automation today is customized. There is no such thing as a standard deck with standardized automation. Often, pieces and parts need to be fabricated for a specific situation. A full machine shop can be a handy thing for just this reason. This is what the automation department specializes in.

Next is the electrical department. All set electrics are wired at the scene shop. That means anything that lights up and is built into the set is dealt with in the scene shop. This doesn't include the simple table lamp. The props department handles that, which often ends up as a sub-department. If a piece of scenery lights from within, then lighting fixtures are built into it, and the electrical department is responsible for all the wiring to make it work. If a unit requires dimmers or ballasts (more on both of those in Chapter 11) to travel with the scenery, this is also handled here. Now, here is something you might not have thought of: If the automation department needs to control a piece of scenery or put a control unit into a piece of scenery, it's going to need power. You guessed it! The electrical department handles that as well.

Here is the interesting twist—the rental department. It's a scene shop; why do they also have a rental inventory? Hudson rents out soft goods (legs, borders, curtains) as well as personnel lifts and some lighting equipment. In addition to straight rentals, the shop also rents some of the automation for the shows it is constructing. Productions basically have two options for automation: They can buy all the equipment for the automation design or they can rent certain portions of the equipment that may be more expensive to purchase. Shows can also rent the automation equipment whether or not their scenery is being built at Hudson.

Next, we move on to the scenic artists. Scenic artists paint, right? Well, they do paint and so much more. Scenic artists begin by sketching on paper what they will draw. It is then transferred to the actual scenic element before they begin to texture, sculpt, and paint. They create a sample for certain techniques to show the designer before completing the real piece.

The last department is trucking. You may think that this shouldn't be listed as a department. Well, without trucking, the audience would have to come to the scene shop! So, yes, trucking is important. The trucking department loads the trucks and drives them to the theater. This department is also utilized during the overnight shifts to help move large units into a position where they can be worked on.

BUILDING TECHNIQUES

This section is all about the building techniques currently in use today for the standard scenic elements. What do I mean by *standard*? Well, there are so many variations in today's designs that the best we can do is to learn the basic pieces. Once we have those established, you can combine them, or abstract from them, to create the specific design you need to accomplish. The three basic divisions are floors, walls, and ceilings. Sounds simple, right? Well, here goes!

The disclaimer: I am not an engineer; I am a designer. I draw pictures and then give those drawings to someone with specific training in rigging and engineering. The techniques I describe here are the "standard" practices in use today. Just remember, always, always consult a technical director to confirm all projects!

Scenic floors have a wide range in today's theatre productions. The simplest design is to use the actual floor of the theater as it exists. The next step up is to paint that floor with a design appropriate to the show. Another option is to use hardboard or MDF as a painted deck laid directly on top of your stage. You can also use ground cloths, Marley coverings, or specialties such as carpets, or tiles. For painting examples, check out Chapter 9. Anything beyond these examples requires building platforms, ramps, and stairs or possibly complete decks. Let's take a look at these one at a time.

> Sometimes it's hard to get back to building a basic platform out of wood. There is no need to always have a full deck made out of steel with automation.
>
> —Carrie Silverstein,
> production manager

Platforms are a mainstay in design. They've been around for a long time, and there always will be a use for them. **Platforms** are small sections of flooring that add height to the existing stage. A standard size for a platform is based on the sizes of sheet lumber. So, think of a 4′ × 8″ platform as a stock size. A stock size is one that can be used many times in different shows (Figure 8.11). It is good to build up an inventory of stock-size platforms to be available for quick build schedules. There are long-lasting platforms from Wenger or Steeldeck available commercially.

The framing lumber used for a platform is determined by the overall size of the platform as well as how it will be used. Common choices are 1 × 6 or 2 × 4 dimensional lumber. Always check with the technical director to confirm what type of lumber should be used. Once you have cut the lumber to the proper sizes, the frame is glued and either screwed or nailed together (Figure 8.11). The difference between screwing and nailing has to do with overall strength. Gluing can be eliminated if you have plans to take the platform apart and save the lumber after your show. Make sure to keep it square as you go, using a framing square! A plywood top, usually ¾ inch, is then glued and screwed or nailed to the frame. Ramps are framed out the same way; the difference is when you attach legs (Figure 8.12).

Legs for platforms and ramps have a couple of different styles. One style of leg is made from 2 × 4s. Another style uses 2 × 4 or 2 × 6 lumber, with two pieces making a right angle. This is a very strong configuration. Legs are either screwed, nailed, or bolted onto the platforms. They are usually not glued, since the legs can then be removed to make storage easier.

Stairs are more complicated (Figure 8.13). The first thing that has to be determined is the rise, tread, and overall length of the stairs (Figure 8.14). Then stringers (or carriage), or the side supports, must be cut out of wood. The easier solution is to buy a precut stringer from the hardware store. If that isn't an option for whatever reason, the usual stringer is cut from 2 × 12s. You need one stringer for each side. For wide stairs or heavy loads, a center stringer must be added.

The next step is to cut the treads and risers, if they are also a part of the design, to the correct length. Lumber for these is often 1 × whatever size is appropriate for the design. Assembly is relatively simple. The treads and

■ **Figure 8.11** A platform under construction at Hudson Scenic.

■ **Figure 8.12** A closeup of a platform leg under construction at Hudson Scenic.

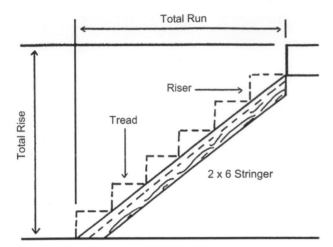

Figure 8.13 Stair diagram showing all the different parts' names.

risers are glued and screwed or nailed onto the stringers. The tricky part is that you can't lay the stairs flat until you are done, so extra hands are a must!

I mentioned a complete deck. Let's talk about that for a moment. Think of the **deck** as a complete replacement for the existing stage floor. The stage is completely covered by a series of platforms that interlock to form a new surface. Built within the deck is often machinery for moving large scenic elements, electrics as required, and any other elements that contribute to the overall design, which we want to hide from the audience's view (Figure 8.15).

Walls, doors, **arches**, and windows form our next discussion. As always, there are huge variables based on the style and design. Let's address the simple ideas with the knowledge that you can add things such as molding and decorative items as required.

Look around the room you are sitting in. Really look. What do you see? Start to break it down into smaller elements, as if you had to build a duplicate copy. Walls are vertical surfaces that usually start at the floor and go up to the ceiling, or at least the perceived ceiling. In the theatre, walls are divided up into manageable sizes. These wall pieces are called *flats*. The framing for flats is a bit different than for platforms (Figure 8.16). And, to complicate things further, there are two different kinds of flats: Soft flats and hard flats. We discuss the differences as we learn how to build them.

Soft flats (sometimes called Broadway flats), which are the traditional theatre type, have stiles and rails to form the outside frame (Figure 8.17). **Rails** are on the top and bottom, and **stiles** are on the sides. This frame is traditionally made from 1 × 3 lumber. The rails and

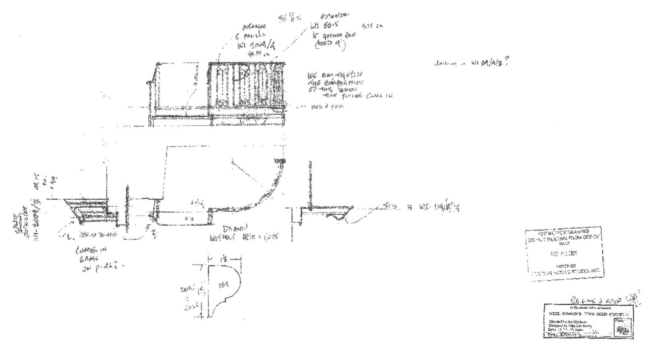

Figure 8.14 John Lee Beatty's drawing of stair and railing details for Neil Simon's *The Odd Couple.*

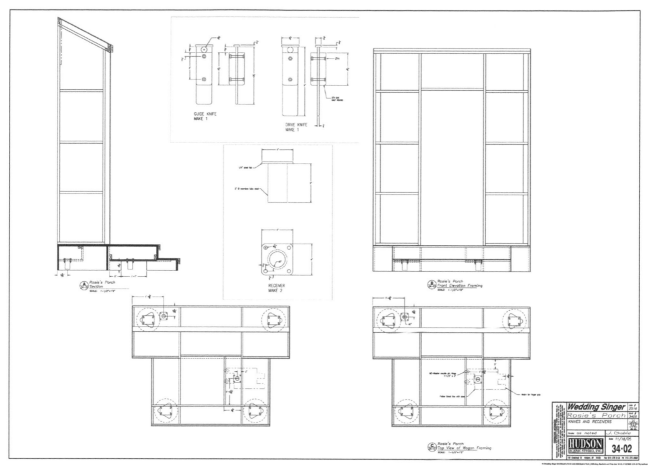

■ **Figure 8.15** Hudson Scenic's shop drawing of Rosie's porch receivers and trap door for *The Wedding Singer*.

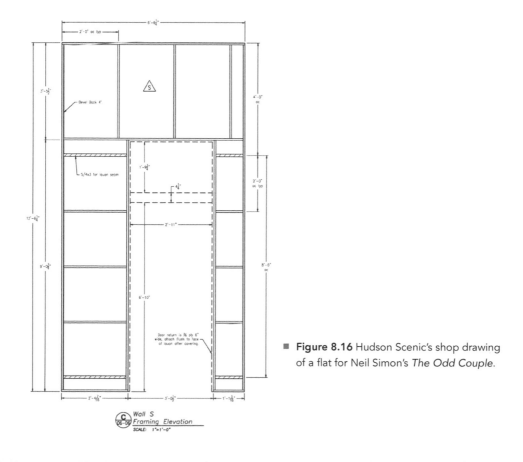

■ **Figure 8.16** Hudson Scenic's shop drawing of a flat for Neil Simon's *The Odd Couple*.

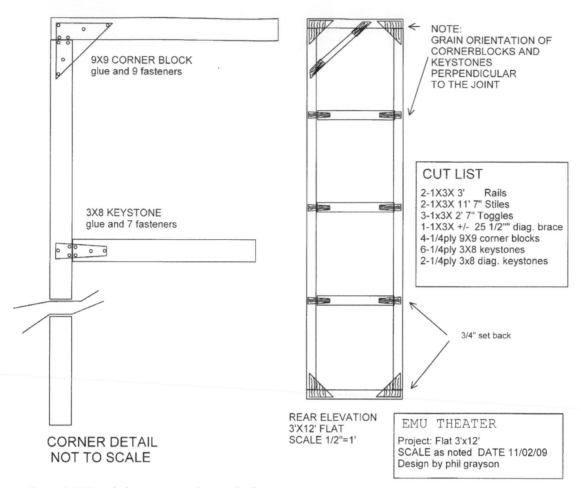

9X9 CORNER BLOCK
glue and 9 fasteners

3X8 KEYSTONE
glue and 7 fasteners

CORNER DETAIL
NOT TO SCALE

NOTE:
GRAIN ORIENTATION OF
CORNERBLOCKS AND
KEYSTONES
PERPENDICULAR
TO THE JOINT

CUT LIST

2-1X3X 3'   Rails
2-1X3X 11' 7" Stiles
3-1x3X 2' 7" Toggles
1-1X3X +/- 25 1/2"" diag. brace
4-1/4ply 9X9 corner blocks
6-1/4ply 3X8 keystones
2-1/4ply 3x8 diag. keystones

3/4" set back

REAR ELEVATION
3'X12' FLAT
SCALE 1/2"=1'

EMU THEATER

Project: Flat 3'x12'
SCALE as noted DATE 11/02/09
Design by phil grayson

■ **Figure 8.17** Detailed construction drawing for flats.

stiles are laid flat, edge to side. **Corner blocks**, which are triangular, and **keystones**, which are rectangular, are the next step. They are made of ¼″ sheet lumber. Traditionally, the wood has been lauan. This is a generic term for tropical wood that comes from Southeast Asia (see Chapter 7). These forests are now endangered, so more and more regular plywood is being used as a replacement; ¼″ plywood is stronger and a more structural option.

Corner blocks and keystones are used to connect the rails, stiles, and toggles. Use glue and screw or nail the frame together as shown in Figure 8.17. Make sure the wood grain of the corner block and keystones runs in the opposite direction of the joint between the rails and stiles. Also note the pattern for nailing, as it is very important to make a good tight bond while the glue dries.

The last step for a soft flat is to cover it. Use either lightweight or medium-weight muslin. Cut a piece

that is approximately 2 feet larger than the frame, both in height and width. Lay down a drop cloth. Then, put the frame on the drop cloth with the corner blocks and keystones facing down. From here on, have all your supplies ready, as the next steps need to be accomplished very quickly. Brush glue onto the frame's stiles and rails. Now, lay the muslin over the glued frame. Begin at the top or bottom and staple the muslin to the frame, starting in the center, while pulling gently to eliminate any fullness. Do the same on the other end. Then, work the two sides simultaneously.

You want the muslin to be tight, but not taut. Why? Because the next step will add even more tension to the fabric, and you don't want it to rip or pull your frame out of square. Next, mix a small bucket of glue with water in a ratio of 1:5. Brush the glue–water mixture everywhere on the muslin. Make sure to use a figure-eight stroke to get the glue into all parts of the fabric's weave. The flat

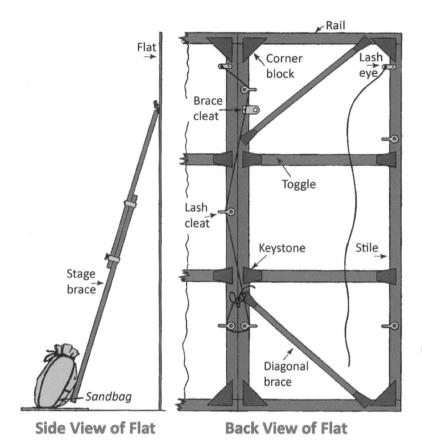

Side View of Flat   **Back View of Flat**

Labels in figure: Rail, Corner block, Lash eye, Brace cleat, Flat, Toggle, Lash cleat, Keystone, Stile, Stage brace, Diagonal brace, Sandbag

■ **Figure 8.18** Soft flat diagram showing all the parts and names you need to know to build and use a soft flat.

must now dry completely. And I mean completely! Once the flat is dry, use a utility knife to cut off the excess muslin, using the rails and stiles as guides.

Hard flats, sometimes called *Hollywood flats*, are traditional in television but becoming more standard in theatre and have stiles and rails just like a soft flat. This frame is traditionally made from 1 × 3 lumber, the difference being that the wood is laid on edge to assemble it. Corner blocks and keystones are not needed. Use glue and screw or nail the frame together as shown in Figure 8.19.

The last step for a hard flat is to cover it. Use ¼″ sheet lumber, trying to avoid the use of lauan, as we discussed before. Glue the top of the frame before proceeding. Lay the sheet of wood on top of the frame, squaring the wood and frame to each other. Nail or staple the sheet to the frame. That is it. Your hard flat is done!

There is a hybrid style of flat, where you frame as if you are making a soft flat but cover it as a hard flat (Figure 8.20). This style can be used when space is at a premium or if the design simply requires this style.

Doors, arches, and windows are the next possibility to consider. Obviously, all of this is guided by the design and drawings. Now, here is the scoop. It's easy to put in an opening, as long as you have a good frame to start with. You need to add crosspieces with the outside frame to create the opening as required by the design. Use the same type of lumber and attachment as we did in the outside frame. It's really that easy. Take a look at Figures 8.21 and 8.22.

One quick note about the arch. There are many different styles of arches: Roman, Tudor, and Gothic, just to name a few. Make sure to follow the designer's drawings to create the correct shape for the arch (Figures 8.23 and 8.24).

Let's talk briefly about ceilings. OK, so they are overhead and they connect the walls. Sometimes, in theatrical design, a ceiling or part of a ceiling is required. Depending on the design, often the ceiling is divided into smaller pieces and built as either soft or hard flats. The only difference is in how they are hung. That is discussed in Chapter 10.

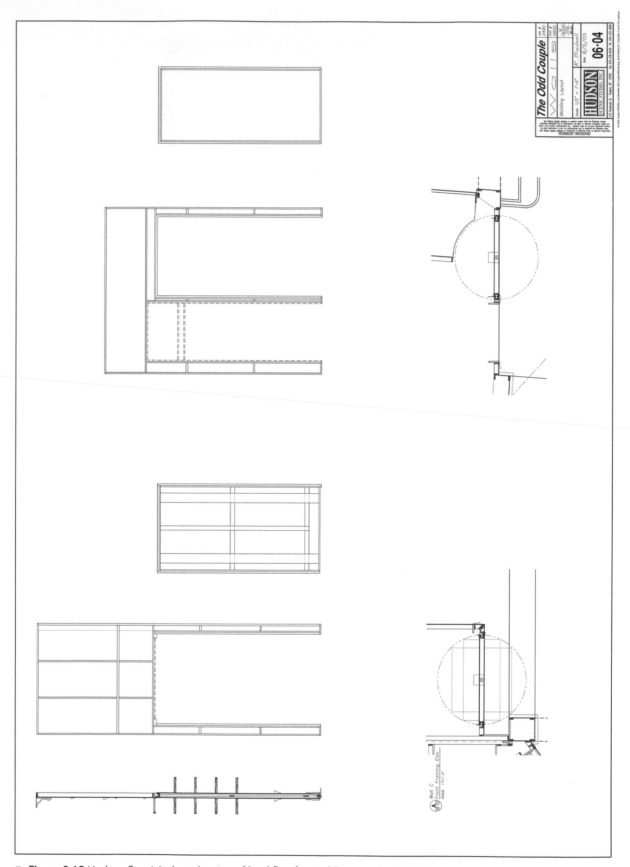

■ **Figure 8.19** Hudson Scenic's shop drawing of hard flats for Neil Simon's *The Odd Couple*.

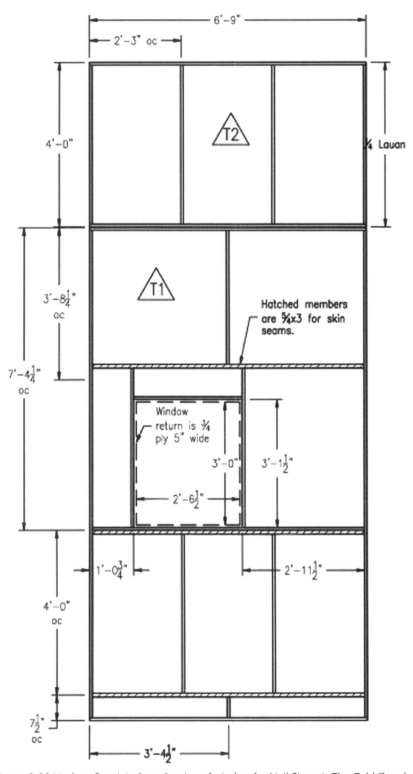

■ **Figure 8.20** Hudson Scenic's shop drawing of window for Neil Simon's *The Odd Couple*.

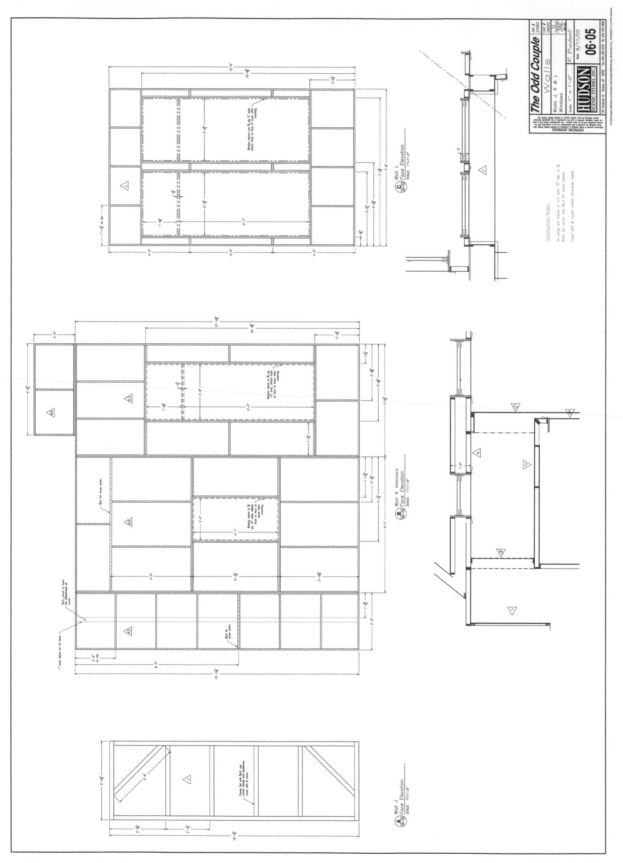

■ **Figure 8.21** Hudson Scenic's shop drawing of walls J, K, and L for Neil Simon's *The Odd Couple*.

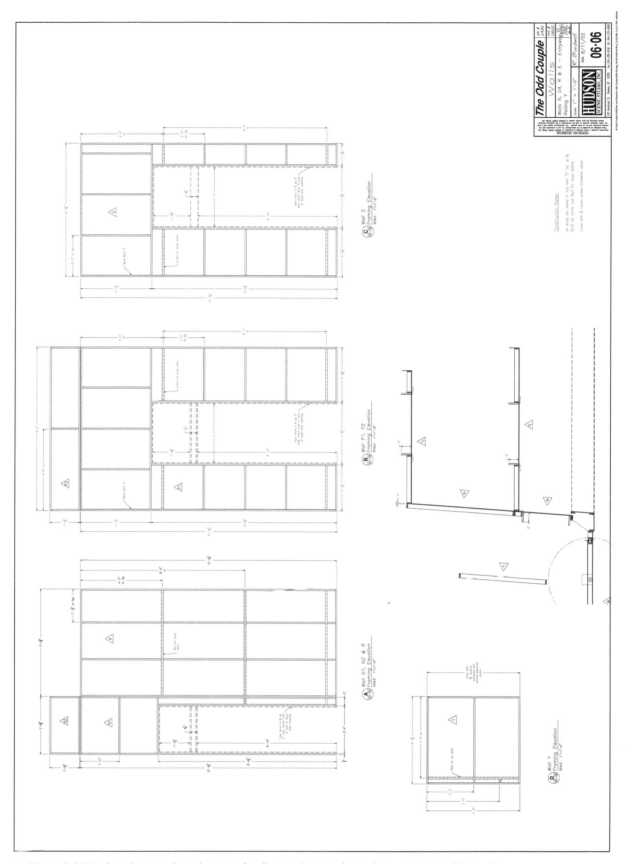

■ **Figure 8.22** Hudson Scenic's shop drawing of walls N, P, S, and Y for Neil Simon's *The Odd Couple*.

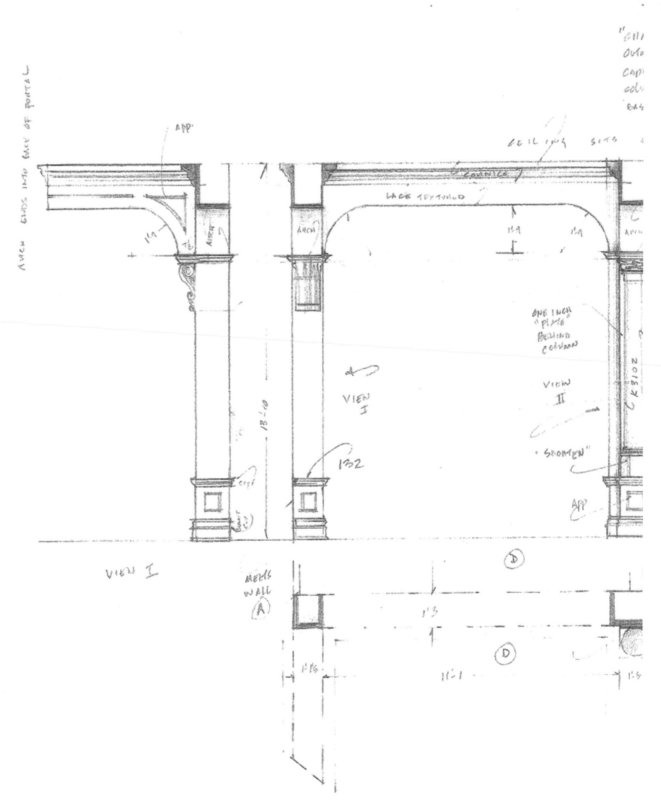

■ **Figure 8.23** John Lee Beatty's drafting of the wall arches for Neil Simon's *The Odd Couple*.

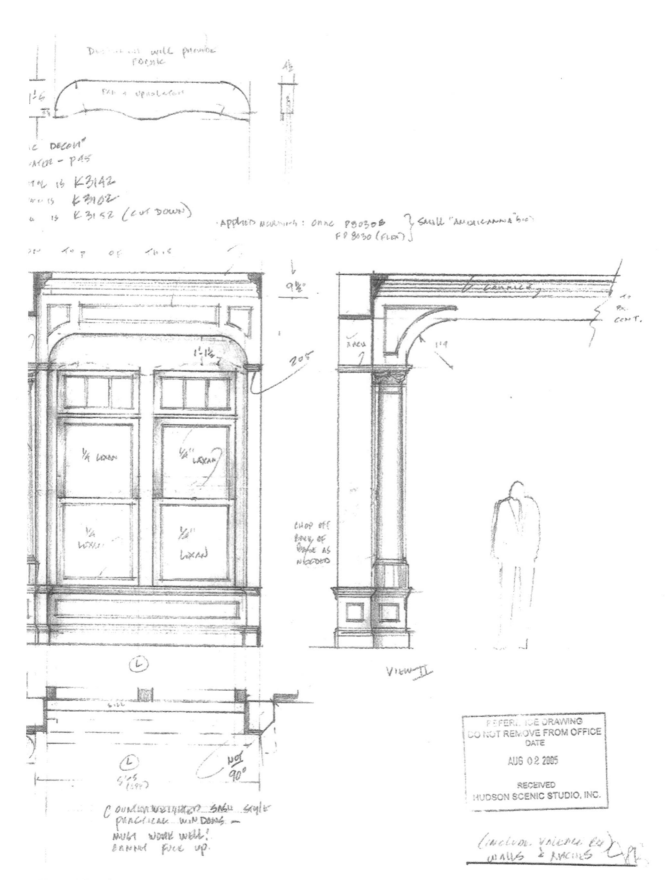

■ **Figure 8.24** John Lee Beatty's drafting of the wall arches for Neil Simon's *The Odd Couple*.

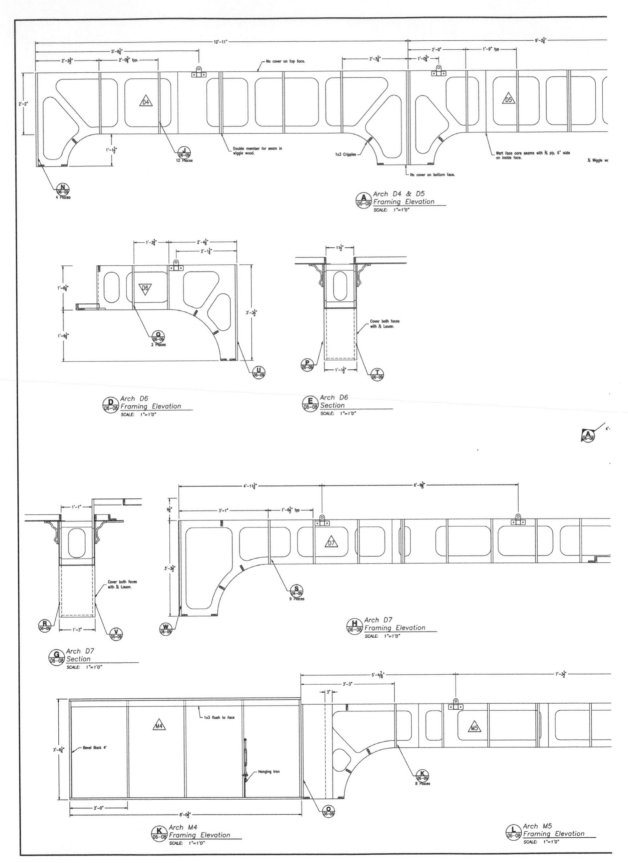

■ **Figure 8.25** More drawings from Hudson Scenic for Neil Simon's *The Odd Couple*.

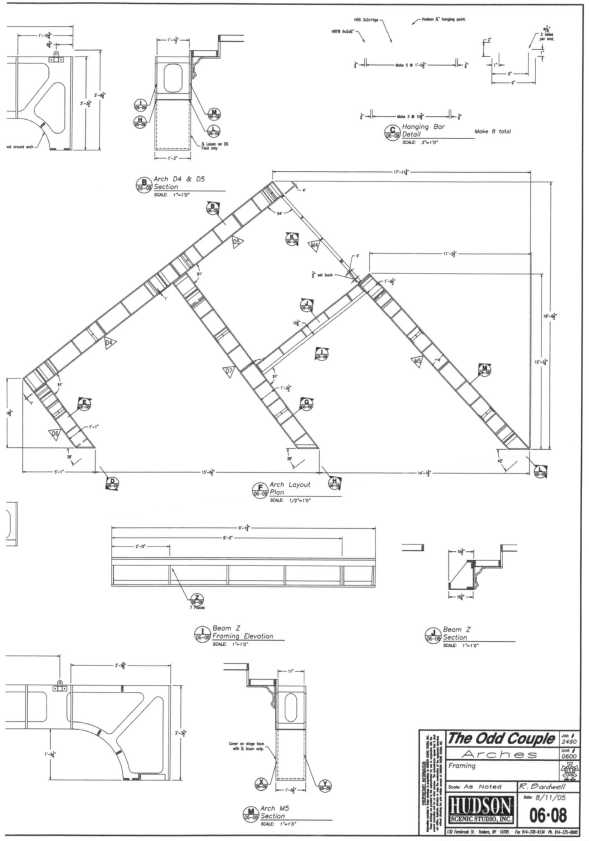

W:\Odd Couple-2490\Plan and Elevation Odd Couple-0600-06.dwg, 06-08 Arches, 7/15/2006 4:13:45 PM, tsullivan

EXERCISES

EXERCISE 1

Build a 2´ × 4´ soft covered flat with appropriate keystones.

EXERCISE 2

Build a 2´ × 4´ hard flat.

CHECK YOUR KNOWLEDGE

1. Define wing and drop scenery. Discuss why it is one of the most enduring design styles in all of theatre.
2. Explain the importance of traps in the stage as a theatrical device.
3. Outline the difference between a designer's and scene shop's pack of drawings.
4. Analyze the progression from a designer's deck plan to the construction deck plan.
5. List the different scene shop departments and describe their purposes.
6. Describe a situation where you would use both a soft and hard flat. Support the use of each.

- Arch
- Borders
- Box set
- Construction drawings
- Corner block
- Deck
- Designer drawings
- Deus ex machina
- Fourth wall
- Hard flat
- Keystone
- Kick-off meeting
- Leg
- Masking
- Periaktoi
- Platform
- Rail
- Scenic ground row
- Soft flat
- Stile
- Tab
- Trap
- Traveler
- Wing and drop
- Wings

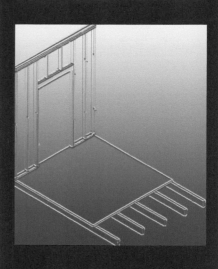

STUDY WORDS

Chapter 8

Deck the Halls

Props

CHAPTER NINE

Student Learning Outcomes

Students will acquire:

- An overview understanding of the major aspects, techniques, and directions in the area of props.

- Fundamental, conceptual understanding of the expressive possibilities of theatre.

- A working knowledge of technologies, safety, and equipment applicable to the area of props.

A chapter all about props. Props are often the elephant in the room at any production meeting, even if there is a designated prop supervisor! Why? Because often props or **properties** defy categorization. Props is a department that is often overlooked and underrated—until tech week. Then it often becomes one of the most discussed departments. This creates many logistical questions that need to be solved. Let's dive right in and see what this new chapter has to show us!

This chapter is about props or stage properties, the items that actors handle, use to cook, clean, places where they sit, objects of art that decorate their environs, and basically anything they handle while on stage that isn't a costume. What are props is a frequently asked question in theatre, but many of professional props people working today have agreed it's a good one. Imagine that the set of the play is a house, and the inhabitants are getting ready to move. When the movers arrive, everything they pack into the truck (except for the clothing) would fall into the category of props. More important, though, props are objects. They are objects that may be common or recognizable to the audience. In this, they are a way of connecting the audience to the characters and story in a deeply personal way. We all have objects and routines that involve everyday objects. This is something we have in common with the characters in a production. Props are the minutiae that we need but often take for granted in everyday life. Favorite pens, a water glass on a nightstand, and the mixing bowl used to make batches of cookies—are all items that a character in a play might use in some way.

Listening to the performers is important for both the director and designers. How heavy an object needs to be is often an issue. How much liquid is in the teapot? How large is a tray? The size and fragility of glassware and china are important. The size and fabric of napkins and tablecloths are not critical, but this information still helps the actor, as does the weight of drapery. All of these concerns should figure into specific choices.

DEFINING PROPS

So, how are props categorized? When making a list, how does the prop supervisor break down each item to get an idea of the scale, scope, and budgetary needs of a production? Asking the same group of working prop professionals to offer specific categories of props gave a consensus result. The general divisions are as follows:

- **Hand props: Anything that the actor touches, handles, or uses during the show. Often identified through subtext or stage directions.** For example, Lorraine Hansbury's 1955 play *A Raisin in the Sun* contains both text and subtext about the character

Lena preparing breakfast. Specifically, the text indicates that she's scrambling eggs. Therefore, when making the list of hand props, the prop supervisor can safely assume that she will need all the items necessary to complete the task; details are important. This section of the prop list may look like Table 8.1. Hand props are typically the smaller objects that are easily carried or moved around onstage.

- **Set props: Any item used by actors, including furniture, coat racks, appliances, and practical lighting such as lamps.** These objects are often placed on the prop list through collaboration with the director and set designer. For example, the opera *Little Women* indicates that part of the action takes place in an attic that specifically contains four blanket chests that are indicated in the libretto. The director and designer may ask for other attic type items—rocking chairs, dress forms, etc.—that will be handled, used, and sat on by performers. These objects, larger than hand props, are referred to as set props, a term that is more general than simply saying furniture, to encompass a large, but specific, category.

- **Set decoration props: Objects with which actors never interact but add to the narrative and storytelling about what's going on onstage.** I sometimes refer to the complete and final dressed set as the "world of the play." The opera *The Vaudevillian* is the story of American operatic soprano Rosa Ponselle, who begins her career as a performer in Vaudeville. One of the scenes takes place in her dressing room

■ **Table 9.1** Sample prop list layout

	SCRIPT LOCATION	ITEM	CHARACTER	USE/NOTES
001	Act I Scene1 Pg2	Bowl	Lena	For scrambling
002	Act I Scene1 Pg2	Eggs	Lena	Practical, 2 each perf.
003	Act I Scene1 Pg2	Fork	Lena	For scrambling
004	Act I Scene1 Pg2	Pan	Lena	Over heat source
005	Act I Scene1 Pg2	butter	Lena	For pan
006	Act I Scene1 Pg2	salt	Lena	A pinch for eggs
007	Act I Scene1 Pg2	milk	Lena	Added to bowl
008	Act I Scene1 Pg2	plate	Lena/Walter	For eggs
009	Act I Scene1 Pg2	fork	Walter	From drawer
010		napkin	Walter	Tabletop holder

■ **Figure 9.1** *The Vaudevillian* as produced at Oklahoma City University School of Theatre.

in an older, slightly dilapidated theater. Although the actress never handled much of what dressed the set, the photos on the wall over the mirror, makeup, costume jewelry, flowers in vases in various stages of dying, and costume pieces draped over furniture and a dressing screen all tell a story. The audience learns more about who she is, how long she's been performing, and how she has been lauded all through subtle details "painted" into the otherwise empty spaces on this set.

■ **Figure 9.2** *The Vaudevillian* as produced at Oklahoma City University School of Theatre.

Included in the above categories are a few subcategories that, while seemingly distinct, aren't generally used separately. These include:

- Practical or consumable food/beverages
- Weapons, firearms, arms, and armor
- Practical lighting
- Special problems or special effects

These classifications help the prop team better understand the demands of the show, but generally aren't stand-alone classifications unless the show has a large need for any one type of these. An example might be a Shakespeare Festival prop shop where one person is designated as the weapons handler or armorer, but even in those situations they may be asked to take on other tasks as well.

WHO MAKES THE LIST? WHO DECIDES?

Knowing the above classifications is helpful as the prop supervisor begins the task of making the prop list. The list should be developed like any of the other designs for a show. Rather than searching for existing lists for previous productions or copying the list that often comes printed in the back of the script, it's important for the prop supervisor to read and have a good understanding of the show. Stage directions and pre-printed lists are often simply notation from an earlier production—they don't necessarily dictate how your production will look. A prop supervisor should receive a copy of the script at the time that the play is selected and when scripts are sent to the rest of the production team. At that time, it's helpful to read through the script several times *before* attempting to make a prop list. Characters in a play may refer to what they're doing in the text, or the playwright may offer guidance such as that described in the scene from *A Raisin in the Sun* discussed earlier.

After making a preliminary list in which the following information is identified:

it will be helpful to schedule a meeting with the director to go through the list and discuss all the items needed, or in some cases not needed. A good example might be a production set that takes place in an unconventional location. Placing a work by Shakespeare in New York City set during the early 1980s will require props that are much different from a traditional production. It's helpful to create the document in a shareable format such as using Google Sheets. In this way, it is possible for the stage management team to access the document, answer questions from the cast or director, and make additions, cuts, and changes that are noted in rehearsal reports. The prop supervisor may also want to make separate tabs for maintaining budgets, creating work lists, and organizing a list for themselves that can be used to focus on workflow.

We know about different categories of props; let's add two more definitions: **Rehearsal props** and **performance props**. When rehearsals begin, there are certain objects that will be needed in order for the actors to begin work. Most often, these props are temporary place holders for the final version of the prop. One may be used as a trial to see how it works and how it looks. It may be something that is close but not exact to a prop that is being custom built. Performance props are the real deal. These are the objects the audience will see. Occasionally, performance props become available during rehearsals. If the props are fragile or custom made, they will most likely be kept away from rehearsal until the last minute.

PROP #	SCRIPT LOCATION	ITEM	PROP TYPE	CHARACTER	USE/NOTES/QUESTIONS

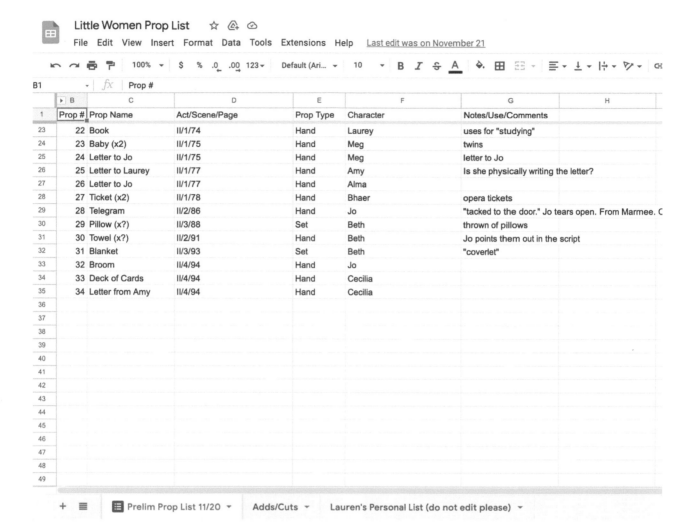

Figure 9.3 Google Sheets screen grab of *Little Women* prop list. Note the use of user customizable tabs at the bottom of the page.

THE LIST IS MADE. WHAT NEXT?

Once the list is complete, and the director has made their input, the prop supervisor then begins the task of making lists and deciding on specific projects with the input of the crew. Obviously, every show is different, but most theatre companies keep frequently used items in inventory. Depending on the size of the organization, many theaters keep a warehouse and use some sort of organizational system in which to keep items that have been purchased or donated such as furniture, light fixtures, and other items including set decoration.

Once the prop supervisor has created a comprehensive prop list for the show, the next step is to-do lists outlining the major tasks associated with the list. One of the systems, or ways of breaking down the list, that is commonly used is the "Pull, Build, Find, Buy" system. Depending on the complexity of the list, the period and style of the show, and the situations depicted, a list may contain everyday objects such as place settings, china, tea sets, coffee sets, trays, glasses as well as common furniture pieces. Those may be pulled from a well-stocked prop storage, purchased either online or from thrift stores or antique galleries, or assembled from common objects.

When a production does not have sufficient budget to purchase or rent all necessary objects, they may be found and altered by craftspeople in the shop. In a production of *Uncle Vanya*, the director, designer, and prop person

■ **Figure 9.4a–d** Prop storage must be organized and kept clean and inventoried. Breakable china and glassware must be kept safe!

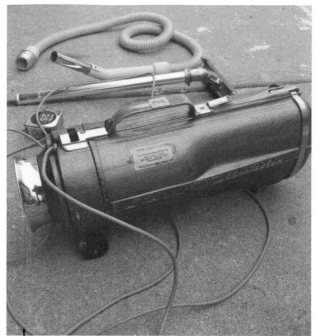

■ **Figure 9.5** Electrolux streamlined vacuum.

■ **Figure 9.4e** More prop storage as shown by Lawrence Heyman, Associate Professor of Properties Design and Fabrication at Oklahoma City University School of Theatre.

decided that the tea service should resemble something more obscure and historically accurate. The theatre had in its storage a period samovar, used in Eastern Europe to keep water hot and brew tea in the 18th and 19th centuries. Research revealed a set of small filigree tea glasses, objects that would not commonly be used or even found in common use. Instead of trying to find/buy rare expensive items, the prop artisans in the shop found glasses and built "holders" using a combination of lace, plastic, and common hardware fittings that were then "gilded" and treated with wax, paint, and glaze to create a false patina.

Sometimes, objects are neither elegant nor particularly artful, but necessary and hard to find not because they're so rare, but because nobody saved them or thought they'd be of much value. In a production of *Crazy for You* set in the 1930s, a character crosses the stage using a vacuum cleaner that is described in stage directions and dialogue. Vacuums weren't exactly rare in the 1930s, but finding them can be a challenge. It may require some creative thinking/searching to find one that will work for the show. Sometimes it's helpful when a product designed earlier goes unchanged for a while. Such is the case with the Electrolux canister vacuum shown in Figure 9.5. It may have been made in the 1940s, but the design dates to earlier.

WHAT ABOUT SPECIAL PROPS?

In Tony Kushner's play *A Bright Room Called Day*, there is a scene where the devil appears, takes a seat on a "throne" onstage, and has at his side a small "hell hound" with glowing red eyes. In this situation, the prop team found a small dog statue, replaced its eyes with red LEDs, and then had to wire it to an offstage battery pack so that it,

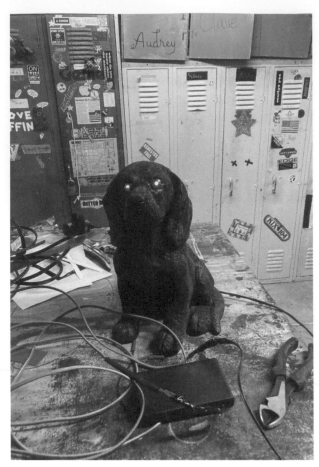

■ **Figure 9.6** *Bright Room Called Day* hell hound.

■ **Figure 9.7** Handmade theodolite after finishing work.

when it was struck, there was simply a cord with a small plug to detach. It was not a major undertaking, but it required some special skills and problem solving.

Similarly, in Tom Stoppard's play *Arcadia*, which takes place across two different time periods in the same room, there are multiple references to a surveyor's tool, a theodolite. While working at the Huntington Theatre in Boston, I visited a few stores specializing in antique equipment such as this. Not only was using a real one cost restrictive ($650 for the least expensive one I found), but the real objects are brass and quite heavy. The solution was to buy a combination of plumbing supplies, brass hardware, fittings, and knobs and use research images to construct an object that could "play" as the real thing. The process has been repeated now for a few subsequent productions of the same play.

SHOPPED VERSUS BUILT

When props are built to order, the time frame, budget, and skill set of the crew are of great importance. Many times specialty props can be rented for less than the time, money, and effort required to create them from scratch. (The various incarnations of Audrey Two in *Little Shop of Horrors* come to mind, and the blood release razors in *Sweeney Todd*.) Keep in mind, unless you are working on an original script, someone has already dealt with the challenges that are currently facing you. Don't be afraid to research and reach out to theatre companies that previously produced your show. You might get a wealth of information and help!

Let's discuss the pros and cons of shopping a prop versus building a prop. Of course, the decision is often very personal, although more than likely ruled by budget and availability. What do I mean by personal? Does the designer have a vested interest in creating a painting for the set wall because they have always wanted to do that? Does the sofa require a throw, and does the designer love to crochet? Strangely enough these kinds of preferences can lead the prop master to make certain choices.

Good. Fast. Cheap. The old adage is to pick two out of the three. You can have it good and fast, but not cheap. Or fast and cheap, but not good. You get the idea. It is always better to have more time when possible, especially if locating hard to find items that may eventually be designated as custom built because they can't be found. Keep in mind that, ultimately, the price tag is not necessarily higher solely because it's custom built. Conversely, the price tag is not lower simply because you found it in a store. It's about finding the balance of good, fast, and cheap as you try to find all the props needed for the show.

Each show presents different challenges, some common and others unique. There are times when a prop shop will hire additional help for a specific project, task, or problem. In the play *Pterodactyls*, by Nicky Silver, one of the characters builds a complete dinosaur skeleton onstage from bones he's found in the yard. (There's an absurdist metaphor here.) At the Huntington Theatre, for the production designed by Allen Moyer and directed by Mark Brokaw, we scaled down the size of the skeleton and built it in sections that could be assembled on stage. In addition to regular prop staff, we brought in a freelance puppet maker. The finished product was carved

from foam, built onto a conduit armature, coated with layers of scenic dope and cheese cloth, and then painted. The entire process took around three weeks.

From the description of the process so far, it is apparent that each show presents a unique and varied set of challenges to the prop team. One might assume from these descriptions that prop shops build more things than they do. In general, there are almost always a few built items, a majority of bought and found items, and then some items that are "altered." That can mean anything from sanding and refinishing a furniture piece to re-upholstering, to taking found objects and augmenting an existing item. So, based on all this, the question remains, who does all the work? The answer can be found by looking at regional theatre staffing positions. In most cases, larger theaters may employ seven to ten people in the prop shop. This equals one person in a college! A possible configuration follows:

- Prop manager or supervisor
- Assistant prop manager
- Buyer
- First prop artisan
- Second prop artisan (in larger shop)
- Prop carpenter
- Soft goods artisan
- Paper/Graphics/Artwork artisan (mostly in larger shops)

The configuration will vary depending on the skill set of the people working. For example, a single artisan may combine the general craft skills and soft goods and upholstery skills into one position. Another artisan my work part of the time on small prop crafts but possess the skills necessary to work as the prop carpenter as well. However the shop is configured, it's important for the supervisor or manager to have as many skill sets covered as possible. So, let's look at the various jobs listed and highlight what skills are helpful with each position.

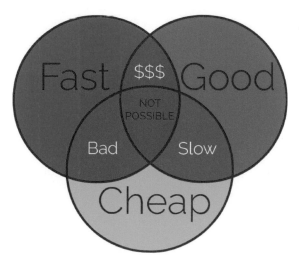

■ **Figure 9.8** Good, fast, cheap—you can only have two of the three!

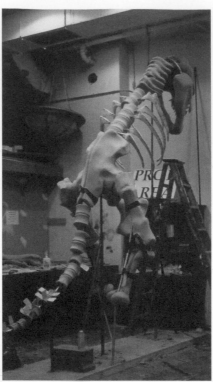

■ **Figure 9.9a–e** The T-Rex from *Pterodactyls* in various stages of completion.

■ **Figure 9.10** Rough designer elevation indicating set dressing. From a production of *Arsenic and Old Lace* designed by Campbell Baird.

■ **Figure 9.11** A production of *Arsenic and Old Lace* designed by Campbell Baird. Most of the set props in this photo were from the theater's own storage.

PROP SUPERVISOR/MANAGER
(Formerly Prop Master)

First, a lot of theater companies are abandoning the use of "master" in their terminology. To many, the word carries strong negative connotations. In order to create more inclusive workplaces, many theaters have chosen more neutral terminology. It will vary from place to place. Qualities of a good properties manager might include the following:

- Well organized
- Creative thinker
- Diplomatic in dealing with directors and other artists
- Ability to "see potential in objects"
- Drawing skills
- Memory for detail
- Sensitive to detail
- Understands period style and décor
- Understands period "technologies"
- Collaborates well with multiple designers
- Thinks outside the box
- Able to manage a budget
- Able to manage a crew
- Works well with department staff and over hire

ASSISTANT PROP MANAGER AND ARTISANS

These two positions are grouped together here because there may be some overlap in skill sets depending on the size of the shop. In general, these roles in the shop possess some of the following traits:

- Resourceful
- Good with people
- Understand common construction materials
- Understand common craft materials
- Understand common building and fabricating techniques
- Understand materials and processes—how to select the right material for a given project
- Innovative
- Inquisitive
- Able to step in and lead when needed
- Communicator
- Understand styles and décor

- Understand soft goods and upholstery techniques
- Drawing and painting skills
- Digital media skills
- Flexible
- Versatile
- Crafty
- Basic wiring skills
- Simple electronics and effects skills
- Knowledge of casting, mold making
- Knowledge of compounds such as plaster, plastics, rubbers, thermoplastics and more
- Understanding of surface treatments
- Knowledge and basic paint skills
- Three-dimensional printing skills
- Sculpting and casting skills
- Follow through

BUYER

In many theaters, this position is separate from the prop supervisor or assistant. In general, this person needs to be resourceful, able to work quickly, and good at something referred to as finding "off label" uses for things, being able to see items for how "they look" or how they "might" be used rather than simply buying catalog goods.

- Knowledgeable about resources
- Understands both wholesale and retail buying
- Able to think on their feet
- Works well with the prop supervisor
- Clever, creative, thinks outside the box
- Problem solver
- Excellent memory
- Excellent people skills
- Good with finances
- Safe driving record (always helps)

PROPERTIES CARPENTER

Some smaller shops may employ a supervisor, an artisan, and a carpenter. In these situations, the carpenter may do double duty and sometimes take on larger crafts. One such situation was a production of an absurdist play where one of the major props/scenic elements was a tree in a shopping cart. For this project, the prop carpenter became the lead person on the construction and crafting of the tree. In general, a prop carpenter will benefit from these skills:

- Complete working knowledge of all shop tools
- Versatility with woodworking, metalworking, and plastics
- An understanding of furniture construction techniques
- Working knowledge of adhesives, fasteners, coatings
- Ability to read and understand technical drawings
- Creative intelligence
- Ability to work well with others

- Innovative
- Self-motivating
- Understanding of planning and purchasing materials
- Excellent understanding of hardware
- Restoration skills
- Repair skills
- Wood finishing and refinishing
- Painting skills
- Understanding of surface treatments
- Attention to detail
- Meticulous

■ **Figure 9.12** An early process shot of the car from a production of *Crazy for You* designed by Campbell Baird.

■ **Figure 9.13** A photo of the finished car from a production of *Crazy for You* designed by Campbell Baird.

■ **Figure 9.14** A rough color scenic sketch from a production of *The Glass Menagerie* designed by Campbell Baird.

SOFT GOODS ARTISANS AND GRAPHIC ARTS ARTISANS

These positions are frequently held by third or ancillary prop artisans, working on overflow projects when needed. As one might imagine, soft goods artisans need to have a good understanding of the following:

- Fabric and textile construction
- Upholstery techniques
- Modern and period drapery
- Cutting, dyeing, and draping of fabric
- Fillers, foams, Dacron, and fiberfill
- Fabric attachment and fasteners
- Basic furniture construction
- The process of covering and recovering furniture
- Understanding of different sewing machines and their use

A graphic arts artisan, as mentioned, is a specialty position that may only be employed as over hire or in an ancillary role. It's therefore important to note that the skills listed below may be combined with skills found in any of the above positions. They are:

- An understanding of layout and print
- Knowledge of period and modern graphic design
- Knowledge of typefaces and fonts
- Knowledge of letterpress styles and printing
- Proficiency and expertise with graphic layout software, digital imaging software, and print manipulation
- Understanding of commercial and non-commercial printing
- Knowledge of offset and web fed offset processes
- Color theory
- Digital rendering
- Photography software for retouching and editing

■ **Figure 9.15** A close up of the father's portrait from a production of *The Glass Menagerie* designed by Campbell Baird.

One of the most infamous props I have ever come across is the portrait of the father in *The Glass Menagerie*. If you are unfamiliar with the play, the father is never seen onstage. His portrait hangs on the set, however. Many decisions obviously have to be made about what he looks like and the pose of the portrait. Figures 9.14–9.16 are several images that show how Campbell Baird dealt with this issue.

> When I used to do musical theatre, my dad refused to come backstage. He never wanted to see the props up close or the sets up close. He didn't want to see the magic.
> —**Nia Vardalos, Canadian actress**

As we will see, every designer has the potential of being involved in the production of props. Once the initial list is created, it will be constantly updated and refined during rehearsals by the stage manager. The director, designers, stage manager, actors, and of course

■ **Figure 9.16** A production photo from a production of *The Glass Menagerie* designed by Campbell Baird, showing the father's portrait.

the prop supervisor will all have a say in what the final item needs to be and also what it ultimately looks like. Of course, the director has final approval, but collaboration, as always, is key.

Sometimes you will be shopping for a modern item that is readily available. Then all you have to do is check availability and price. Simple! But what if it's a modern item that isn't easily findable? Technology can be your best friend with this. Easily findable is *almost* always an option today. Finding things on the internet via computer, phone, or tablet is not only easy, but you can shop at any time you want—not just when the store is open. And you are no longer limited by finding something in your home

> And finding the hat, I always like to find the hat. And then props just dress the set. It's all fabulous.
>
> —Morgan Freeman, American actor

■ **Figure 9.17** An early process shot of the candy box from a production of *Hello, Dolly!* designed by Campbell Baird.

■ **Figure 9.18** The final candy box from a production of *Hello, Dolly!* designed by Campbell Baird. Notice all the detail that has been added since the early process shot in Figure 9.17.

■ **Figure 9.19** *Equus*, James Madison University, September 2017. Directed by Ben Lambert. Scenic and projection design by Richard Finkelstein; costume design by Pam Johnson; lighting design by Kelly Rudolph.

country. Worldwide shopping and overnight shipping have become the norm.

What if the exact item you need is not available? You found something close but it is not exact. Now what? If all other options have been explored, then go for it. That means, buy the object that is close, but first come up with a plan to alter it into the correct object. Add fringe, change the buttons, tint the light bulb with color—whatever it takes. Sometimes, the combination of buying and then making additions or changes is the most exciting part of the process. It provides for a lot of creativity to be thrown into the process.

Theatre Traditions: Flowers

It is bad luck for an actor to receive flowers before the play begins, though flowers given after the play has ended is considered good luck.

I love theatrical props: a cup filled with solid fake tea, say, or a collection of fake food, including a rubber turkey, which, during the holidays, I wrap in tinfoil so it appears to have just come out of the oven.

**—Amy Sedaris,
American actor and comedian**

STEP-BY-STEP PROCESS

We are now going to take an in-depth look at one specialized prop from *The Glass Menagerie*: The glass unicorn. The following information is from a production that I directed and designed on a limited budget. After doing much research, I found that glass unicorns are available from a number of stores but can be quite expensive. The problem with this particular prop is that the unicorn may not be in the exact pose the director requires. It is also required to fall from an onstage table and break during every performance. It must be broken very specifically in that only the horn comes off. This creates a range of challenges.

I asked the technical director (TD) for advice on how to achieve this very important prop without using up the entire budget. When you are lucky enough to work with creative and talented people, you can throw out an open-ended question like that without too much concern. The TD, who also happens to be my husband, John, turned to me and said his now infamous line, "Give me a minute," and then he promptly disappeared into the shop.

Depending on the prop, several different people will have input into the final design. Once research has been done, sketches have been completed, and revisions have been made, you can begin the process of shopping or building the object. We are focusing on a built object. Let's take a look at some of the challenges that need to be solved with *The Glass Menagerie*'s unicorn:

Glass Menagerie

Unicorn research - Images

Task: Create a small statue of a glass unicorn that can hit the floor without shattering but the horn falls off.

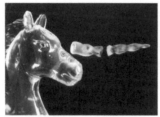

■ **Figure 9.20** Initial research for the glass unicorn to identify the exact shape and color.

■ **Figure 9.21** Completed custom fabricated unicorn for *Glass Menagerie*.

- Unicorn must not break in any other way when it falls
- Unicorn must fall from a table height of at least 30˝ during every performance
- Unicorn must appear to be glass and have the correct amount of "weight"
- Horn must separate from head every time it falls
- Horn must easily reattach and remain secure until unicorn falls

My TD showed up at my table about 2 hours later. When I looked up, he had a unicorn in his hand identical to the one pictured.

Let's take a look at his process. I can't really explain what goes on in his head. The best he has been able to tell me is that he thinks of practically everything as raw materials. That means anything he finds can become the building parts for whatever he needs to build. This is the epitome of thinking outside that old box! It is very liberating to think this way. As we go through his process, see if you can come up with a different way that is equally creative to achieve the unicorn.

First step is to gather the raw materials. In this instance, he used an old burned-out light bulb and a lot of hot glue. Yup. That's it, other than time, talent, and patience. The key to this kind of technique is that you must layer the hot glue slowly. In order for this illusion to work, you need to create one solid object as you go. If you layer the hot glue too quickly, without giving it time to solidify, you will end up with a gooey, dripping mess. Look at the step-by-step photos in Figures 9.23–9.36 to see how this idea works, and works really well. Ingenuity and creativity will always be the key!

■ **Figure 9.22** Raw materials are gathered prior to starting the unicorn.

■ **Figure 9.23** The light bulb is separated from its base.

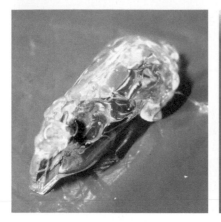

■ **Figure 9.24** Beginning to layer hot glue on the light bulb's glass envelope.

■ **Figure 9.25** Beginning to build up the legs with layers of hot glue.

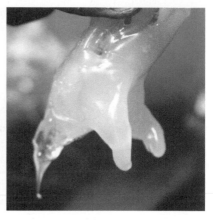

■ **Figure 9.26** A drip of hot glue becomes the basis for the tail.

■ **Figure 9.27** Adding feet …

■ **Figure 9.28** Finally able to stand the torso and legs up and attach it to its glass base.

■ **Figure 9.29** Beginning the front legs …

■ **Figure 9.30** Forming the hooves from tiny droplets.

■ **Figure 9.31** Starting to build up layers for the head.

■ **Figure 9.32** The beginning of the head is now visible.

■ **Figure 9.33** The head and mane are done. All that's left is the horn.

■ **Figure 9.34** Detail shot of the unicorn's head prior to adding horn.

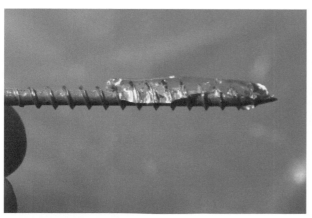

■ **Figure 9.35** Using a screw as the foundation for the horn, hot glue is applied and, once cooled, it is removed and twisted.

■ **Figure 9.36** Unicorn is completed.

EXERCISES

EXERCISE 1

Create a prop solely from recycled materials such as recycled paper or other random items that the student has in their dorm.

EXERCISE 2

Play "Stump the Teacher" by bringing in a random object and seeing if your teacher can name a play where the object would be an appropriate prop.

CHECK YOUR KNOWLEDGE

1. Define properties and illustrate the different classifications.
2. Explain how the director and designers may all need to work together on a specific prop and how that process may evolve.
3. Illustrate a good use of a shopped prop and a built prop. Explain your reasoning.

- Costume prop
- Food prop
- Furniture prop
- Hand prop
- Lighting prop
- Performance prop
- Properties
- Props
- Rehearsal prop
- Set prop
- Special effects prop

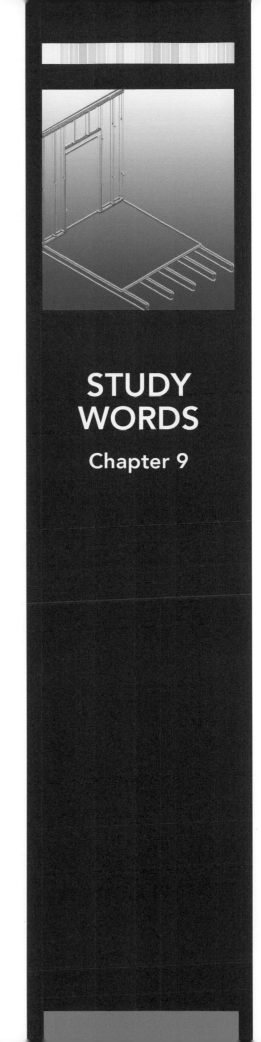

STUDY WORDS

Chapter 9

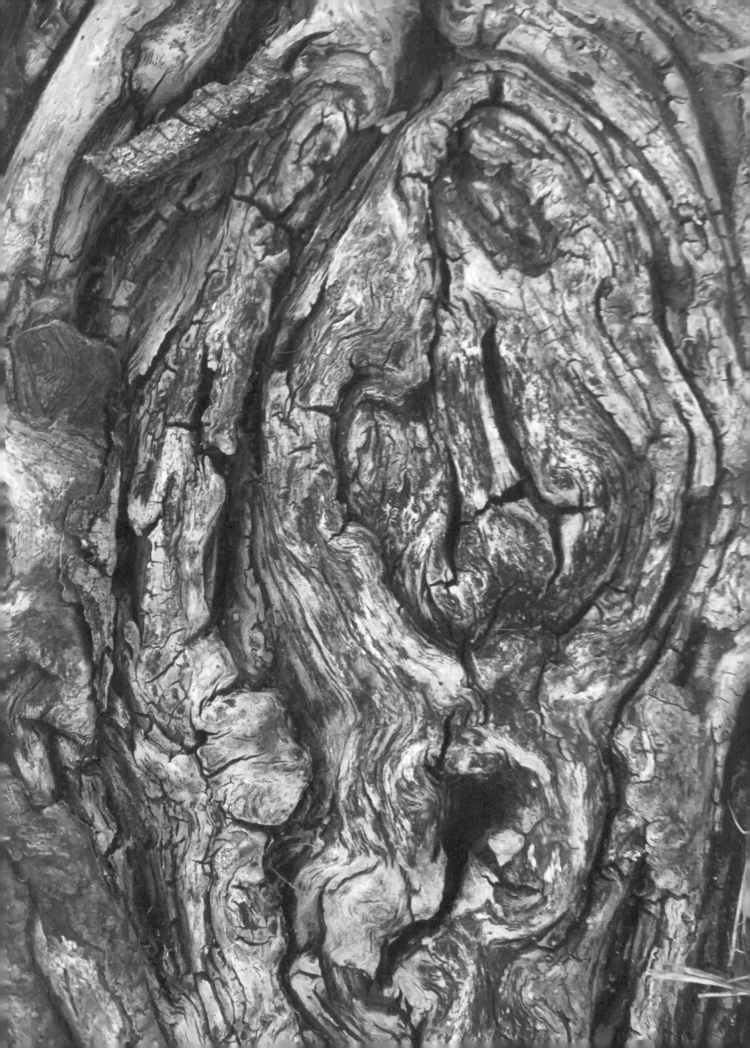

A Little Dab
Will Do Ya

Paint

The next topic is a discussion on paint. This chapter addresses the paint shop and its tools, as well as several paint techniques that have been in use for centuries. You might wonder how painting has changed or what new technologies are out there (or in use). It's just a paintbrush and some paint, right? Not quite. There are many new developments in this area. Some changes are small, some are large, but all are important. There has been a resurgence of painted faux finishes, both in the theatre and in homes. These techniques help complete our picture of what is possible from a scenic point of view as well as how to use these techniques in a nontheatrical way.

OVERVIEW

Let's start with a little background on getting a job as a scenic artist. What kind of training is needed to become a scenic artist? You need a good understanding of the periods of art history, architectural periods and styles, drawing, and perspective. Knowledge of basic techniques such as brick, wood, marble, and stone are expected. That kind of groundwork is the basis of many other techniques. Specialty techniques are a plus, but only if you

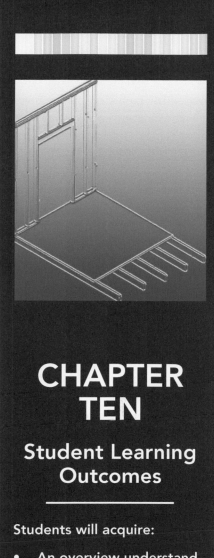

CHAPTER
TEN

Student Learning
Outcomes

Students will acquire:

- An overview understanding of the major aspects, techniques, and directions in the area of painting.

- Fundamental, conceptual understanding of the expressive possibilities of theatre.

- A working knowledge of technologies, safety, and equipment applicable to the area of painting.

also have a working knowledge of the list above. Perhaps most difficult, yet important, you need to be able to look at a rendering and understand what the designer intends.

> It is a huge help to have all scenic departments under one roof in the shop. Someone is always watching your back. The whole vision is evident. There is always camaraderie. You work better as a team.
> —Grace Brandt, American scenic painter

To paint something, it needs to be built first. Each scenic department collaborates to organize all the different schedules so that there is a smooth process following each element, from the first meeting all the way through to it being loaded on a truck. Most painted elements in the show will need a sample created by the paint department. The first week or two of production is usually for creating samples. There is no limit to the size of the samples (Figure 10.1). They can be large or small, whatever size is needed to show the color and texture properly. Samples have several functions. They may help to work out a process, they can be used to get designer or client approval, and they are helpful to the lighting and costume department for color and texture collaboration. This is the time when the final look for each technique is determined. The "recipe" for the paint color, texture, and technique is determined and documented, so that other scenic artists can share projects seamlessly (Figure 10.2). This is a crucial step, as everyone in a paint shop needs to be able to work on each piece and have it look like one person did everything. Communication is key here.

Backdrops are the one exception to this rule, as they can be started right away. Usually, the image for a backdrop design is first cartooned onto kraft paper with vine charcoal. **Cartooning** refers to drawing the design at full scale using a **grid** to enlarge it. After the drawing is complete, the next step is to **ink** it in using a permanent black marker to ensure the delicate

■ **Figure 10.1** Hudson Scenic's paint bay, empty and waiting for the next job.

charcoal image isn't accidentally removed. The **kraft paper**, also known as *brown butcher paper*, is then perforated (pounced). A **pounce** wheel is a small tool with sharp teeth around the wheel. Think of a small pizza cutter and you have the right idea. You roll the pounce wheel over the inked cartoon image, punching holes in the paper as you go. Lightly sand the back of the perforated drawing to "open up" the ripped paper holes so the charcoal powder will go through easily. To transfer the cartoon drawing from the kraft paper to the drop's fabric, lay the kraft paper on the fabric and use a pounce bag filled with powdered charcoal to transfer the design through the pounced/perforated holes. Do not use carpenters chalk as it contains a dye that will stain the fabric and may bleed through thinned paint layers. A faster technology is the Electronic Pounce Machine (Figure 10.3). It is much easier on your hand, taking less strength and doing the job much faster. It is also possible to use multiple sheets of paper to create more than one pounce of a specific image. Training and technique of the proper use with this tool is very important (Figures 10.4–10.8).

■ **Figure 10.3** Hudson Scenic painter Kyle Higgins using the Electronic Pounce Machine.

■ **Figure 10.2** Hudson Scenic's paint bay, in full swing with several projects and workers.

Figure 10.4 Painter's elevation by Scott Pask for *Nine*.

Figure 10.5 Full-color model by Scott Pask for *Nine*.

Figure 10.6 Backdrop in the process of being painted at Hudson Scenic for *Nine*.

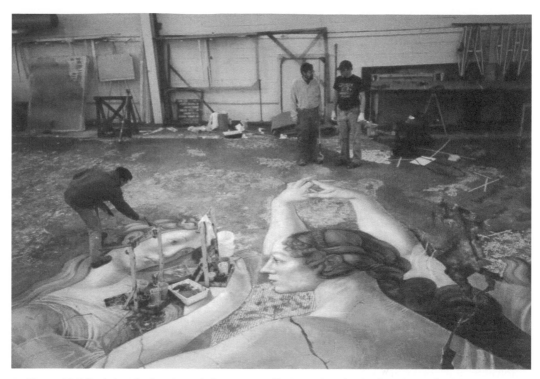

■ **Figure 10.7** Backdrop further through the process of being painted at Hudson Scenic for *Nine*.

■ **Figure 10.8** Finished painted backdrop for *Nine* at Hudson Scenic.

SAFETY

Next, let's address some safety concerns in the paint shop before moving on. First and most important, research all products before buying them to check for safe use practices. Safety data sheets (SDSs, which we discussed in the safety chapter) are available for almost all products, and you can download them to make sure your shop is properly set up to use the product. You should always keep a copy of the SDSs in the paint shop in case of an emergency. Employers must keep an SDS **for all hazardous chemicals used in the workplace**. While employers may keep electronic copies of an SDS, employees must have immediate access to an SDS in their work area even if the power or internet connection is lost.

Latex gloves used to be the standard in a paint shop, but they are now being replaced completely by nitrile gloves. The reason for this is that latex allergies are becoming a bigger and bigger concern.

Solvents and sprays must be stored in a certified flammables cabinet, as they are combustible. Theatre, as an industry, is getting away from the use of oil-based paints, bronzing powders, and metal flake for health and safety reasons. Ingredients in the metal flake and other types of these products have been shown to be fire accelerants. That is a bad thing, discussed more fully later in this chapter. There is really nothing you can do to change it. Just don't use them; find a safe substitute. There is an OSHA requirement that, when you are mixing different products together, you have to create a label for the container that states all the various elements you put into the mixture. Think about it for a second. You made a new chemical compound, whether you think of it that way or not. Labels are important to identify what types of paints went into the mixture, in case you need to make more of it, but also as a safety concern, since you might not be the only one to use it. Firefighters need to know what kinds of hazards are in a building to know how to fight them and how to protect themselves as well.

TOOLS AND SUPPLIES

Let's move onto tools for painting. A paintbrush isn't the only tool of the trade. And, there isn't just one kind of brush. Before we go into the different types and styles,

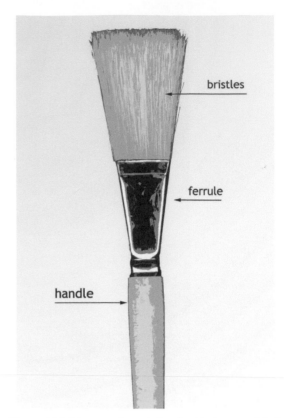

■ **Figure 10.9** Diagram of scenic brush with the parts labeled.

let's look at the anatomy of a brush. Every brush can be divided into three different parts: The bristles, ferrule, and handle (Figure 10.9). The bristles are what are dipped into the paint. They can be made from a variety of materials and have many shapes. The choice depends on what kind of paint you are going to use and how you will use the brush. The handle is what you hold and can come in a variety of different shapes and sizes.

The ferrule of a brush is usually a metal band that connects the bristles to the handle, and the crimp is the part of the ferrule that secures it to the handle.

Like bristles and handles, they can be made in a variety of ways to match the brush they are creating. This is the "weak" spot of the brush. What I mean by that is, if the brush is left sitting in liquid covering the ferrule before cleaning, the bristle adhesive can loosen its hold on the bristles and handle. Once the bristles are loose, they fall out. This is the main way that brushes are ruined!

The different styles and shapes of brushes have different names (Figure 10.10). A standard brush, used

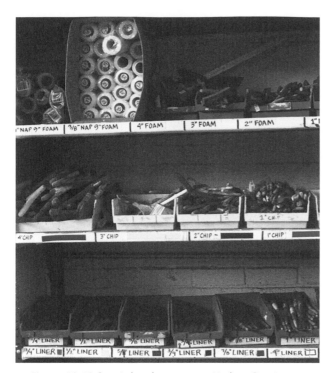

■ **Figure 10.10** Scenic brush storage at Hudson Scenic.

Lay-in brushes are specialty brushes used specifically for painting large areas, such as a drop or a large expanse of scenery. They are larger than most other brush types, with typical sizes of 5 and 6 inches. Owing to their large size and longer bristles, they can hold a lot more paint, so painting goes faster. That is good, but it also makes the brushes heavier, and properly cleaning them takes more time.

> Some painters transform the sun into a yellow spot; others transform a yellow spot into the sun.
>
> —**Pablo Picasso,**
> **artist**

most, is a flat cut brush like a natural bristle chip brush. It is a good rectangular utility paintbrush for many general uses. It comes in a variety of sizes and bristle thicknesses. Sizes include ¼, ½, ¾, 1, 1¼, 1½, 2, 3, and 4 inches. **Lining** brushes, also known as **fitch** brushes, have a much more defined shape. They are usually better made and much more expensive. The ferrule is seamless, which helps to keep its shape, and the bristles are natural not synthetic. They also come in a range of sizes, including ¼, ½, ¾, 1, 1¼, 1½, 2, and 3 inches.

Chip and **foam** brushes, as well as pads, are now popular as inexpensive alternatives to standard brushes. Chip brushes are a very inexpensive alternative to the standard paintbrush. They are less durable and considered to be disposable. They come in the same standard sizes as better-quality brushes. Foam brushes and pads come in a variety of sizes and are mostly rectangular or round. Instead of bristles, these brushes have a foam block that comes to a wedge at the tip. These are great for cutting in and keeping a straight line. Once the foam has been saturated for a while it tends to become limp. Although these brushes can be washed and, when completely dried, return to almost their original condition, they are considered to be disposable by some.

When you need to create a wood grain, **graining** brushes and tools come in a wide range of choices. Brushes typically look like a standard brush, with the bristle end varying in length and density to create the grain texture. These can be created and customized in the shop with more economical brushes such as chip brushes. Rubber rollers and rockers are another way to create wood grain. The rubber surface has the texture raised to grab the paint. As the tool is "rocked" or dragged along the painted surface, it can leave, or remove, paint to create a woodgrain likeness.

Brushes are cool, and now you have an understanding of the different kinds and their purposes. But how do you paint something that is farther than you can reach? With a piece of **bamboo**! Bamboo sticks come in a variety of lengths and diameters (Figure 10.11). Since bamboo is hollow, you can put your paintbrush handle into one end and secure it in place. Bamboo poles are an extension of the brush. They assist with being able to move quickly across the area of a backdrop while providing distance from your eyes to the surface, giving you a perspective of the overall project as it unfolds. It also helps to save your back from a lot of bending over or getting up and down. Another wonderful tool used to paint precise, straight lines is a **lining stick**. It is a beveled straight edge that allows you to run your brush along the side, using it as a guide for creating clean, straight lines. It usually has a handle to make holding it easier when working from a distance with a paintbrush in bamboo.

■ **Figure 10.11** Various lengths of bamboo at Hudson Scenic.

When you need to cover a large surface area, either with a single color or a mixture of colors, you can't rely on brushes alone. In come paint rollers and paint sprayers. Both the frames and the covers come in many sizes, textures, and widths. Most have an open-ended, grooved receiver at the end of the handle to accept a threaded extension pole. Paint roller covers come in different materials, from wool, to a synthetic version of wool, to microfiber/foam. Roller covers have different thicknesses. They range from ¼″ to 1½″. Each thickness has unique qualities. The lower the nap (thickness), the smoother the paint goes onto the surface (substrate).

Differing surface textures include smooth, semi-smooth, semi-rough, rough, and extra rough. Textures can be anything from a generalized texture to carpet stipple. Customized rollers can be created in many ways. Wrap a cotton rag around the roller body and secure it with rubber bands or put several rubber bands around a ⅜″ nap roller cover for a bark-like texture. Foam rollers can be cut into any design/pattern you need. You can also find "natural sponge" roller sleeves, usually available at "big box" tool stores. These may still require some "plucking" to enhance the desired pattern, but are a wonderful resource.

Another very handy tool is the **Hudson® sprayer**. The brand name Hudson has become synonymous with the metal canister type of compression sprayer. The **Floretta®** is a smaller, handheld version of the compression sprayer, plastic with a metal spray tip. These are the most recognized brands. Economical plastic compression sprayers can be found at local DIY or garden centers for a quarter the price. A sprayer allows you to put paint into a canister, put the top on, and then pressurize it for spraying by pumping air into the canister. An adjustable nozzle allows you to release the paint–air mixture in a fine-to-coarse mist or stream. You can also use the sprayers with water to help eliminate wrinkles in a backdrop This is a great tool for many, many uses.

You might also find available at home centers a spray tool called a Preval; this has a glass jar to filter your paint into and a pre-pressurized air canister to twist onto the glass bottle, essentially creating your own spray paint. The HVLP (high volume low pressure) sprayer is also a major tool in the scene shop. Hooked up to a pneumatic air hose, you can get a very fine or coarse spray. This tool may be more commonly used in automobile painting, but it is a useful tool to have for scenic art as well. Some new varieties of electric airless sprayers eliminate the need for straining the paint, as you do with pneumatic HVLP sprayers, while covering a large area quickly and without the need of an air compressor.

Sponges, plastic wrap, rags, and anything else that will hold paint and create a pattern are all viable choices for creating a texture in the paint. Most of these are messy techniques, so be aware and use gloves. All these "tools" are easy to use. Load them with paint by dunking, dipping, or whatever. The way you apply the paint to the wall controls the final look. Testing the different options and creating samples are important steps in the process, as so much variation can happen. Exploration, trial, and error are the keys to finding new tools and techniques for your project.

Flame retarding is an important step in the paint shop. You can use a variety of products, depending on the scenic element that needs to be treated. Any chemicals brought into the shop require proper handling and safety protocols. Following the manufacturer's instructions on the label and on a product tech sheet is vital. The fire department usually is the agency that will send in an AHJ (authority having jurisdiction) to properly test the scenery for flame retardant standards. If the scenery does not pass the flame test, the fire department will not let the show open.

There are a number of other general supplies that the paint shop needs (Figure 10.12). Among them are different colors, sizes, and grades of painter's tape and frisket liquids and papers. The painter's tape you may have seen and used at home. It is good for covering trim to give a clean edge when you are painting a wall. Frisket is a plastic or resistant sheet with an adhesive back or a removable liquid. It is used when you need to cover (mask) a specific part of a design (Figure

■ **Figure 10.12** More scenic tools in storage at Hudson Scenic.

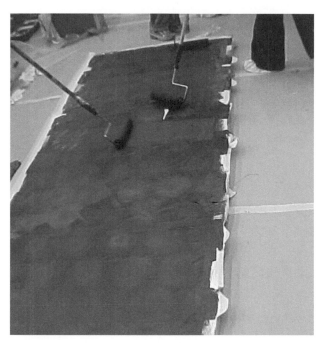

■ **Figure 10.13** Painting over a frisket at Hudson Scenic.

■ **Figure 10.14** Removing the frisket at Hudson Scenic.

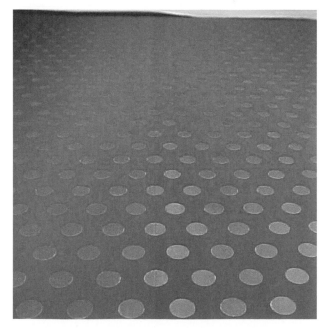

■ **Figure 10.15** Finished drop after frisket removal at Hudson Scenic.

■ **Figure 10.16** Alt-J at Glastonbury. Designers: FragmentNine.

10.13). You lay it down and cut a design out to reveal the portion you need to work on, leaving everything else masked and therefore safe from the new paint (Figures 10.13–10.15).

PAINTS AND GLAZES

Disclaimer alert for this whole chapter. Whenever I use the word *paint*, I mean anything you might apply to change the color of a surface. There are many different compounds that will do this, and I get into that shortly. It is easier to proceed if we all agree to a simple shorthand.

Historically, scenic paint was made from powdered colored pigment and some kind of binder. We used to start out by mixing different powdered pigments together until we achieved the color we needed. Then, we would need to make a binder and a medium that, when mixed together, became the sizing. Be happy you don't have to still do this! Here are the details. The binder was originally made from flake or ground glues. The protein colloid glue was made from parts of a horse or ox. The glue was dissolved in a double boiler, adding water and stirring constantly to create the strength of size for the project. Slowly mixing the sizing into the pigment, stirring constantly, created scenic paint. It had a unique odor. This process is generally used for historic restoration-type projects today and can be seen on stage in various productions of *Red* by John Logan, where the character of real-life painter Mark Rothko cooks paints from pigments.

PAINT CHEMISTRY

What makes paint paint? Basically, it is four things—colored pigments, binder, vehicle, and additives. All water-based paint is not created the same. There are hundreds of different types and combinations of binders. No two paints are alike unless they come from the same company and the same product line within that company. One company's water-based paint may not play well with a different company's water-based paint. Testing the products you would like to use for a project is the only way to know for sure they will work for your specific application. Things such as temperature during storage and application and humidity during application will affect the results. Paint in New Orleans during the winter will not behave like paint in Maine during the winter. Binders also determine other aspects such as the adhesion to specific substrates, overall performance, and sheen, to name a few.

Bottom line, test, test, test before jumping in and buying ten gallons of paint to repaint the deck. If in doubt of what kind of product is needed, call the manufacturer and explain the parameters to find out its recommendations.

There are a variety of manufacturers of theatrical paints out there. Rosco is a popular brand and is available globally. It offers a large variety of paint suited to the entertainment industry. Product choices include Off-Broadway®, Super Saturated®, Iddings Deep Colors®, and a variety of clear glazes. Special effects ultraviolet (UV) paints from Rosco include Fluorescent and Vivid FX®. All these Rosco listed products are water-based, which gives the ability to clean tools in water. It also means these paints can all be thinned with water for varying effects.

What is the difference between paint and glaze? Paint is usually opaque, straight out of the can. This means you can't see through it. I say *usually*. When you are painting, depending on the color you are using and the surface you are painting, it may take several coats of paint to cover. **Glazes** are used differently. Glazes are transparent or translucent instead of opaque. Glazes are used for a variety of effects that we will talk about shortly. The key with glazes is to make sure the first layer of paint is completely dry, not just dry to the touch. Apply them thinly, and let them dry completely before you disturb them. Otherwise you end up with an ugly mush of colors.

The concept of the economy of using scene paint is one subject that gets overlooked. The basis for this statement is that scenic paint has been formulated for use with various substrates and in scenic situations—i.e., flats made with wood or metal and luan that flex because they are handled and set up every night. Versus house type paint that goes on a flat, hard wall surface and never gets moved around. Scenic paint still has bright, concentrated, purer colors even though it may have been thinned out 2 to 1 or more with water or clear acrylic. Thinning out house paint is not a successful technique. The color and binder seem to disappear. Plus, with scenic paint diluted with water or water and a clear acrylic binder, you just made three gallons of paint that still have good coverage for the cost of one gallon. Compare that to the price of one gallon of house paint. Muslin drops can be painted more than one time with scenic paint and still remain fairly flexible. Not possible with house paint. House paint would add tons to the weight put on the fly rail and on the fibers of the fabric causing them to have stress tears. Or the paint is so thick it becomes crunchy and cracks.

—Jenny Knott, American USA829 freelance scenic artist

All of the paints listed can be mixed within their type to achieve the exact color you are trying for. Remember the color wheel from Chapter 4? Now is the time to use that knowledge. Easy to mix, easy to use, easy to clean up. Easy! Don't forget, you can experiment (aka play) and create your own techniques. Nothing is truly set in stone, except, of course, Excalibur.

Many other products are on the market for varying effects. What about metallics, you might ask? You want silver, gold, or copper? Well, some of the best metallic paints and powders on the market are from Europe via Benjamin Moore's Metallics series. Metallic paints are

■ **Figure 10.17** Paint storage at Hudson Scenic.

■ **Figure 10.18** Scenic tool storage at Hudson

used the same way as regular paints. If you get metallic powders, they need to be mixed into a binder of some sort to be used. Always read the label and SDS before using. Keep in mind that metallics, by their nature, have a higher possibility of being volatile. That means they can be unstable and must be used and stored according to the manufacturer's directions. Always read the SDS about a product before using it to make sure you follow health and safety protocols.

Here is a little trick that can be good to know. Whatever the color you are going for, if it is intense, it might be good to add a little ultraviolet (UV) paint. This makes the color pop out a bit. Of course, you can't do this if there will be UV lights used in the productions. If you add UV paint by accident to a mixture, there is no way to cover it up. So be careful, and be sure of yourself before you try this.

The last thing to discuss regarding paints and tools is their care (Figures 10.17–10.20). Paints must always be sealed tightly when you are done using them for the day. Otherwise, a skin will form across the top, and eventually the paint will completely dry out, or get rancid in the case of organic casein paints. Also, when scooping paint out of the "mother" container, be sure to use a clean, dry utensil. Dirty or damp tools can introduce bacteria into your lovely, concentrated scenic paint, causing the bacteria to feed and grow in the paint can. This creates

an interesting *objet d'art* if not opened very often. Good brushes and roller covers can cost a lot of money. While cheaper ones are meant to be disposable, not all are. Take care of your tools, and they will last a long, long time, even the so-called disposable ones.

Brushes and rollers require a good cleaning after each use. What you use to clean the brush depends on the type of paint you were using. Water-soluble and water-based compounds can be cleaned in good old-fashioned soap and water. Murphy's Oil Soap is a scenic artist's go-to soap for brushes. The key to cleaning is to make sure to remove all the paint that is possible. Tools have been specifically designed for cleaning brushes and roller covers. The brush cleaner looks like a metal hair comb. After wetting the bristles, insert it at the bottom of the ferrule/top of the bristle and gently pull down toward the end of the bristles. Be careful not to shred delicate, expensive specialty brush bristles. Roller covers can be cleaned using a five-in-one paint tool. This has been specifically designed for cleaning rollers and roller covers in a variety of ways to get the longest life from your tools.

Now that we know the tools and paints available, let's put them together (Figure 10.21). You can dip the brush in the paint to apply or you can dry brush, scumble, rag roll, spatter, sponge, wet blend, or stencil. Let's look at a few simple textures before we move on to some

Figure 10.19 More scenic tool storage at Hudson Scenic.

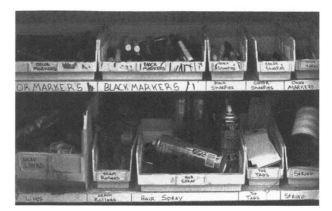

Figure 10.20 And yet more scenic tool storage at Hudson Scenic!

techniques that use them. Here is a yin and yang type idea. Any of the tools we discussed for applying paint can also be used to remove paint. Huh?! Well, think about it. You lay on a **base** color, then apply another color. While that color is wet, you can remove some of it to create the texture!

Figure 10.21 *Romeo et Juliette* at the Metropolitan Opera, November 2005. Director, Guy Joosten; scenic designer, Johannes Leiacker; costume designer, Jorge Jara; and lighting designer, Peter Cunningham.

TEXTURING

There are many methods for adding texture (Figure 10.22). **Dry brushing** is when the brush is kept as dry as possible, using only a minor amount of paint to move around. It can also be done using a brush with no paint to remove paint that has already been applied to the surface. **Scumbling** is putting a small amount of paint on your brush and lightly dragging it across a dry surface. This is often used as an overlay to a background image—for example, to create sunbeams coming out of clouds. Scumbling or skumbling is also a fairly dry application of opaque paint in a broken-up manner. The areas of color are easily discernible.

Wet blending is just what it sounds like. You apply one layer or color of paint and, while it is still wet, you apply a second color that blends partially or completely with the first.

Rag rolling can be done in two ways. You can use a roller and paint a surface, then take a cotton rag that has been bunched into a loose ball and roll the rag ball across the wet paint to remove paint while also making a texture. You can do the reverse by applying paint to the rag and rolling it onto the surface, adding paint and texture at the same time.

Spattering can be a messy texture, so be sure to use plenty of drop cloths. To spatter, you load a brush with a small amount of paint and then shake the brush at the surface without allowing them to touch. If you use too much paint all at once, it will just make big ugly blobs of paint. The paint for spattering is often thinned to avoid the thick blob issue. Another option for spattering large areas is to use a Hudson sprayer or garden sprayer to make it a little neater and get a finer mist of spatter dots along with more coverage, quickly.

Sponging is fun and can provide a great variety to the texture. Sea sponges are often used, as they are more natural in appearance than a kitchen sponge. However, any sponge can be used to apply paint. Just dip the sponge in paint, then dab it at the surface. You can vary

■ **Figure 10.22** Kyle Higgins, scenic painter, applies texture at Hudson Scenic.

the amount of texture and paint you use to create each part of a design. Another trick is to take a sponge and a pair of scissors and cut a design into the sponge. This will create a custom texture and design, which is a lot of fun.

> I found I could say things with color and shapes that I couldn't say any other way—things I had no words for.
>
> **—Georgia O'Keeffe,**
> **artist**

A texture I won't go into much detail on is distressing. **Distressing** is used in the theatre all the time. So, why don't I want to talk about it? Because there are so many different kinds and ways, it could fill a whole book. Let me just say, distressing is a way to make something new look like something old. The best way to distress anything is to get some research of the same item when it is old and copy that. Experience is great in this texturing idea, because everyone you talk to has different thoughts on how to do it. Keep a list of your favorites!

Three-dimensional texture can be created in any number of ways (Figure 10.23). I like to combine 2D and 3D techniques for the best result. If you want to add 3D texture, there are a variety of options. You can use joint compound, cheesecloth, sawdust, newspaper, chicken wire, or almost anything that adheres to the surface and is paintable in one fashion or another. The sky is really the limit here.

Before you do any of these techniques, one basic thing has to happen. You must use a good **primer** on your surface. Priming is a way to make a surface ready to accept paint. Raw wood or fabric soaks in a great deal of the first layer of paint. This is the basis for priming. It is better to use a neutral color and a less-expensive primer for this part of the process, since it won't be visible in the final product. Primer may look like paint but it has a specific job to do. A primer ensures better adhesion of paint to the surface/substrate. Sometimes, this step can be combined with the first step of a base coat by adding some color to the primer. Any techniques or process should be tested on a sample piece of the actual substrate. This allows for experimentation and confirmation of the compatibility of products and techniques.

> Creativity is allowing yourself to make mistakes. Art is knowing which ones to keep.
>
> **—Scott Adams,**
> **comic strip creator**

STEP-BY-STEP TECHNIQUES

The following are the basic scenic painting techniques that create a base for all other techniques. You should practice these and become familiar with each step. Then, and only then, you can begin to experiment with your own variations to create different images. Let me give you a couple of basic disclaimers before going into the step-by-step instructions. Most important, do not rush the drying time (Figure 10.25). If you start the next step before the paint is dry, you will not end up with a good, recognizable effect. You will, instead, end up with a murky mess. Don't skip the glazing either. Glazing is what helps to separate the differing layers of paint from one another, giving the visual effect of a 3D object.

Research becomes your last important phase before beginning to paint. You may have the designer's **paint**

■ **Figure 10.23** Hudson Scenic scenic artist working on a 3D texture project.

■ **Figure 10.24** *Pride and Prejudice* at the Guthrie Theatre in 2003.

■ **Figure 10.25** Floor fans at Hudson Scenic.

elevations (Figures 10.26 and 10.27). You may also have a sample that was created and approved. Or, you may have none of these, and it is all up to you. However the process goes, it is important to do your own research. How many different kinds of marble, brick, and wood do you think there are? How are they formed? You will be amazed. There are slight differences between each kind. The more specific you are when researching, the more realistic you will be when painting. Last, remember that each step is a part of the process and *not* the finished product. Have faith, keep your research nearby, and here we go!

It doesn't make sense to have painters searching through a pile to find the brush they want. Organization is key.

—Grace Brandt,
American scenic painter

■ **Figure 10.26** *"The Sound of Music" Outside the Trapp Villa,* watercolor rendering by Oliver Smith.

■ **Figure 10.27** *"Hello Dolly" Harmonia Gardens,* watercolor rendering by Oliver Smith.

SCHLEPITCHKA (FEATHER DUSTER)

Materials Used in the Example

- Tempered hardboard scrap
- Base coat lay-in brush
- Ostridge feather duster
- Paint tray
- Spatter brush
- Paint for base coat
- Paint for schlepitchka technique
- Clear acrylic glaze—gloss
- Bucket with water

Techniques Used

- Tinted primer coat
- Schlepitchka—feather duster texturing
- Spatter
- Glazing

Step 1: Tint white primer for double duty—priming and base coat. May need to thin a bit with water to get good flow off the brush or roller.

Step 2: Apply with roller or lay-in brush, depending on the size of the area to cover. A roller is faster than a brush. Let dry completely. May take longer than overnight if the temperature is cooler than 60ºF and the air is humid.

Step 3: Mix the schlepitchka (feather duster) transparent color, one part paint, two parts water, two parts clear acrylic glaze. The object is to add some "see-through" texture without completely covering up the base/prime coat color. Let dry.

Step 4: Mix the spatter color. Also, a transparent, not opaque, spatter color. Use a different color than the feather duster texture. Let dry completely.

Step 5: Mix the top translucent glaze color. This will unify the color to appear to be a solid color while giving the lighting designer interesting colors and textures to enhance for different moments of the production. Much more interesting than an actual solid color painted on a floor or wall. Use one part paint, four parts water, four or five parts clear acrylic glaze in flat, satin, or gloss. Apply with lay-in brush or paint pad. Let dry completely.

■ **Figure 10.28** Steps 2 and 3 are shown half and half on the sample. Note how distinct the feather texture is at this point.

■ **Figure 10.29** Spatter color being added creates another level of texture by using a different color.

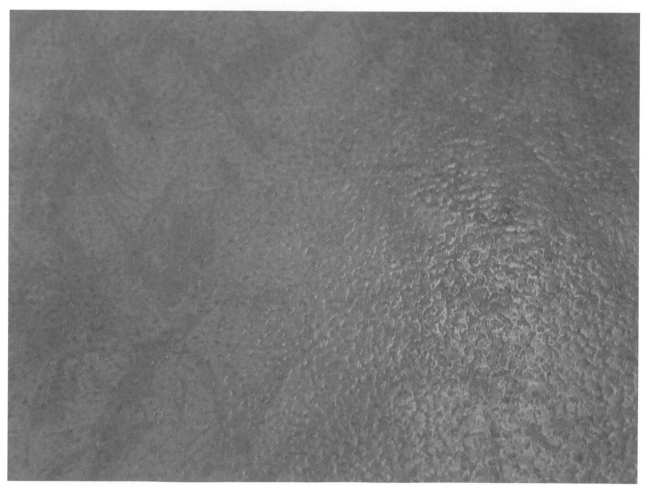

■ **Figure 10.30** The translucent glaze pulls everything into a single cohesive texture.

WOOD

Wood, like brick, comes in many types, including differences in color, texture, and grain. Factor in the age of a tree, and the possibilities are endless. The following technique gives you an idea for how to create thinned-out paint "stain" for an inlay floor. Keep in mind that research is still key, and you should keep it in front of you as you paint. As always: Follow the steps and, once you are comfortable with them, you can begin to put in your own variations.

Materials Used in the Example

- Chips brushes—as wide as the raw wood planks. In the example, the boards are 2″ strips of luan
- Paint for project:
  – Burnt sienna
  – Yellow ochre
  – Raw umber
  – Burnt umber
  – Van Dyke brown
  – Clear acrylic in gloss
- Foam brushes for painting edges— 1″ or 2″
- Bucket for water
- Water-based polyurethane—top sealer

Techniques Used

- Wet blend
- Glazing

Step 1: Mix yellow ochre one part paint to two parts water and two parts clear acrylic gloss.

Mix burnt sienna one part paint to three parts water and two parts clear acrylic gloss.

Mix raw umber one part paint to three parts water and two parts clear acrylic gloss.

Step 2: Randomly apply the thinned-out yellow ochre and burnt sienna to the raw luan boards. Make sure not to establish any patterns of application or even "strips" of the different colors. Use a separate brush for each color.

Step 3: While the board is still wet, softly blend the edges of the two colors using a clean, dry chip brush. If

■ **Figure 10.31** Diluting paint to get the correct color is the first and most important step.

■ **Figure 10.32** Step 3 shows the soft blend of two colors to begin the wood process.

■ **Figure 10.33** Use a foam brush to paint the edges of the planks.

the rendering requires the boards to be more muted, use the raw umber occasionally to soften the color. Let dry.

Step 4: Paint the edges of all the planks with thinned-out Van Dyke brown. Thin out two parts water to one part paint. This is to avoid any edge from being seen once the planks are randomly attached to a platform or the floor. It is difficult to touch up an edge after it has been attached and loaded in.

Step 5: Mix one part burnt umber to four parts water and four parts clear acrylic gloss.

Step 6: Apply the burnt umber top glaze coat on the planks. This will help to give the planks protection and to unify the floor color. If the burnt umber is too strong, thin it with more water and glaze. This should be a very thin, light, transparent glaze layer. Let it dry.

Step 7: Apply a clear top coat to protect the floor from heavy traffic. A water-based polyurethane is a good protective sealer. Sheen is your choice, based on the designer's rendering.

Step 8: Let dry and cure for at least 24 hours before walking on the surface.

■ **Figure 10.34** Steps 6 and 7 bring the wood together into a final product.

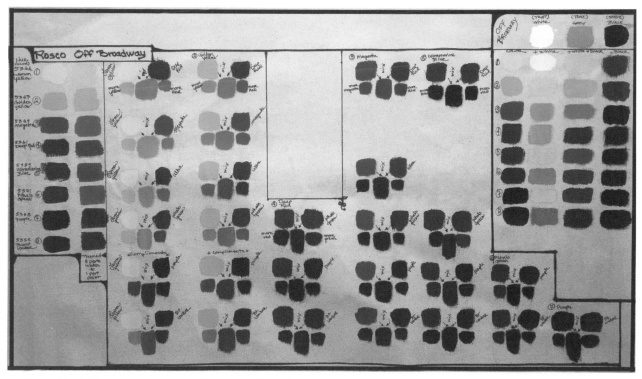

■ **Figure 10.35** Mixing chart for a few of Rosco's Off Broadway more common paints.

Green Practices

Combine all unused paint that isn't thinned out with a lot of water and use as "back paint" for hard scenery. It isn't flame retardant unless you add a flame-retardant additive to it. Water from the sink contains bacteria, and bacteria contamination may begin to produce mold or mildew the longer it sits and the warmer the air temperature is in the studio.

Clean and reuse paint containers.
When cleaning out buckets or brushes, having a three-step cleaning process will help to save water and save larger particles from going down the drain. The three-step system is: One bucket contains clean water, one bucket contains medium clean water, and one contains dirty water. Start cleaning in the dirty water, move to the medium dirty, then finish with the clean water. You may need to do a final rinse in the sink. Once the dirty water gets too dirty, turn the medium dirty bucket into the dirty bucket and move the clean bucket to the medium dirty bucket and then get a new clean bucket. The dirty bucket can sit for a few days undisturbed to allow the particles to settle in the bottom of the bucket. Then, carefully pour off the top several inches of the dirty bucket, leaving the sludge at the bottom to dry up and then scrape it out.

Always check with local disposal authorities to find out how your community handles paint waste. Some communities have paint care programs to recycle and reuse paint that has not been thinned out.

EXERCISES

EXERCISE 1
DILUTION

Use scenic paint. Using a measuring device such as a teaspoon, measure out one part paint and add one part water for a 1:1 ratio. Make sure to stir the paint well before brushing a 1″ area on watercolor paper or sized muslin on a frame.

Next, measure out four parts water to one part paint. Stir well, apply next to the 1:1 square. Continue with the dilution as far as you would like to go. Make sure to follow the same process, using the same tools, so it can be as precise as possible. Compare the strength of the pigment as you thin out the paint farther and farther.

EXERCISE 2
WRITE THE ALPHABET

Using thinned out scenic paint and a piece of bamboo with a fitch attached, write the alphabet on Kraft paper.

EXERCISE 3
CREATE A RAG ROLLER

Create a unique pattern using a roller cover, a rag, and rubber bands.

CHECK YOUR KNOWLEDGE

1. Describe the reasons behind reading a SDS before using the product it refers to.
2. Explain the main way that paint brushes are ruined and how to prevent it from happening.
3. List tools for applying paint other than a brush.
4. Restate why using household latex paint for theatrical applications is not a good idea.
5. Choose one of the three textures we discussed in detail and be prepared to explain each step of the process in detail.
6. Illustrate why glazing is an important technique to know.

- Bamboo
- Base coat
- Cartoon
- Chip
- Distressing
- Dry brushing
- Fitch
- Flogger
- Floretta
- Foam
- Frisket
- Glazes
- Gradient
- Graining
- Grid
- Hudson sprayer
- Kraft paper
- Lay-in
- Lining
- Lining stick
- Ombre
- Paint elevation
- Pounce
- Primer
- Rag rolling
- Scumble
- Spatter
- Sponging
- Tinted primer
- Wet blending

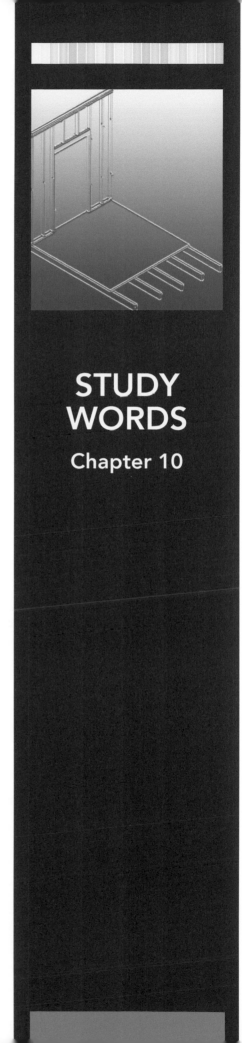

STUDY WORDS

Chapter 10

PART
THREE

Rigging, Lighting, and Sound

CHAPTER 11: Hanging by a Thread
Rigging

CHAPTER 12: House to Half ...
Lighting

CHAPTER 13: Is This Thing On?
Sound

Hanging by a Thread

Rigging

Now that the scenery is built, how do you get it into place? How do you get it into its storage position? Does it fly in and out, does it track on and off, or does it just sit there? Once you know the answer to these types of questions, the solution lies with the rigging department. Rigging is one of the most critically precise, and therefore dangerous, parts of theatre. We build scenery that is heavy, then we hang it over people's heads. We hang pipes with many lights and cables on them—over people's heads. If any of that weight is misjudged, it can be disastrous.

Theatre Traditions: Whistling

Whistling backstage can be taboo, because it supposedly brings dire results. This superstition may have its roots in the past, when managers hired sailors to run the fly loft, on the premise that the sailors' expertise with knots and raising and lowering sails made them ideal workers. A signal system of whistles cued the sailors. Someone whistling for personal enjoyment could sound like a cue, resulting in a dire event, like a heavy batten falling on actors' heads. Therefore, whistling can be considered bad luck.

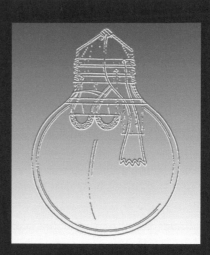

CHAPTER ELEVEN

Student Learning Outcomes

Students will acquire:

- An overview understanding of the major aspects, techniques, and directions in the area of rigging.

- Fundamental, conceptual understanding of the expressive possibilities of theatre.

- A working knowledge of technologies and equipment applicable to the area of rigging.

Rigging at its most basic is all about ropes and knots. What kind of ropes were first used? What kind are used now? Why? Where do we get these knots? Once we learn about the ropes and knots that make theater rigging safe and easy, we will move on to a discussion of more complicated rigging, where newer technology has really made a huge impact. Fifty years ago, if you wanted a platform to move across the stage, somebody had to push it! It sure is different today.

Some say the earliest stagehands in history were also sailors. Many of our knots, ways of rigging, and general traditions are shared with the standard uses on boats (Figure 11.1). More modern equipment and techniques come from mountain climbers. It is an interesting combination that gives the theatre the capability to fly things into the air (Figure 11.2).

ROPES

Let's start at the beginning and talk about rope. You can pretty much divide rope into two overall categories: Natural and synthetic. Natural ropes are made from a wood pulp fiber that is harvested from plants such as jute, hemp, and bamboo. The fibers are then twisted, braided, or both to add strength to the fibers. Watch out for splinters as the rope ages, especially if you might be allergic to hemp! There are no longer any real advantages to natural rope (Figure 11.3). It starts degrading the moment it is made, because it was once alive. It loses its moisture and elasticity; basically, it's biodegrading as you use it, becoming weaker all the time.

Synthetic fibers include nylon and polyester. Synthetic ropes are made through the twisting and braiding process as well (Figure 11.4). Abrasion, chemicals, heat, and UV (sunlight) all affect synthetic rope and cause it to degrade. Rope can also be made from wire, but we will discuss

■ **Figure 11.1** All of our rigging techniques and traditions come from sailing. Take a look at this fully rigged boat for comparison.

■ **Figure 11.2** Backstage at the 1869 Bardavon Opera House. Look at the rigging as it is both below and above the locking rail.

that later in the chapter. Originally, theatre used natural rope, because it was the only option. Natural fibers are subject to major changes from heat and humidity, which can make them stretch and weaken. Synthetic fibers don't have this problem and therefore can have a longer life. For example, the replacement schedule for natural rope is seven years, whether it has been used or not!

■ **Figure 11.3** Natural rope made from hemp.

■ **Figure 11.4** Synthetic rope made from nylon.

There is no replacement schedule for synthetic rope. It lasts practically forever with proper care. Both types of rope come in a variety of thicknesses and lengths. The material the rope is made from, the thickness, and the manufacturing process all combine to give the rope its strength rating. Always check a rope's rating for how much weight it will hold *before* you use it. The best advice about rigging I can give you is to be cautious and never attempt anything you are unsure of. Always ask for help if you need it. One last thing, wear gloves when working with rope. It will help you to keep a good hold on the rope and, should the rope slip, you will have a better chance of re-gripping the rope and not hurting your hands. Rope burns are a total drag, so avoid them at all cost!

KNOTS

Knots are the basis of rigging. There are many different knots, and a handful of those are critical to theatre. The overhand knot, square knot, bowline, clove hitch, belaying, and coiling are all essential to theatre rigging. The **overhand knot** is the simplest of them all (Figure 11.5). Hold the rope with both hands parallel to the ground; cross the left over the right to form a loop; wrap the right-hand end up through the loop; and pull! Congratulations, you've just learned a knot. Of course, you probably already knew this one—and be careful not to use it too much, since it is the one knot that can destroy rope faster than any other.

The **square knot** is the basis for so much (Figure 11.6). Almost everyone knows how to tie this knot, or at least has heard of it. Also known as a *reef knot*, the square knot is secure and fairly easy to untie. While holding both ends of the rope, cross the right side over left and wrap up and around the left, just like when starting to tie your shoes. Then, cross the left over the right and wrap the same way. Pull to make the knot tight. To untie, hold both ends and both sides of the loop. Then, push them toward each other, and the knot will loosen.

The **bowline** is my personal favorite (Figure 11.7). I learned it in Girl Scouts, where we were told to recite the following story while tying the knot: The little bunny comes out of the hole, walks around the tree, and goes back in the hole. OK, so you'll understand that better

■ **Figure 11.5** Tying an overhand knot illustrated step-by-step.

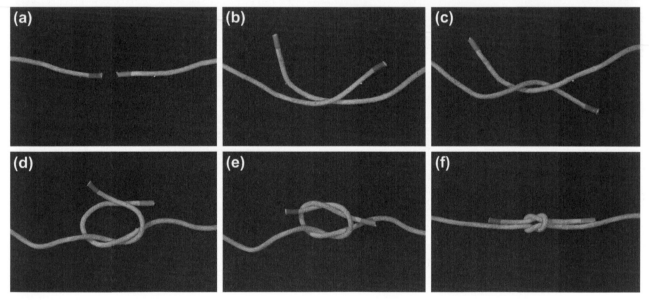

■ **Figure 11.6** Tying a square knot illustrated step-by-step.

after I describe it more fully. A bowline is one of the most important knots to know. If properly tied, it will not slip and can be used to secure and lift things or people. Hold one end of the rope in your left hand. With the portion of rope in your left hand, make a small loop in the rope above your hand with the part going away from you on the underside of the loop. With the piece of rope in your right hand, feed it through this small loop from the bottom. Take it around the piece of rope going

away from you. Bring the end back down through the small loop. Pull the end tight.

The clove hitch is very important to almost every rigging job in the theatre. Used as a traditional hitch that secures only one end of a rope, the clove hitch is liable to slip. It requires a load, or pressure, attached to each end of the rope in order to be effective. Since the clove hitch is almost always a load-bearing knot, it should not be tied with rope that is thin or very slippery as it can

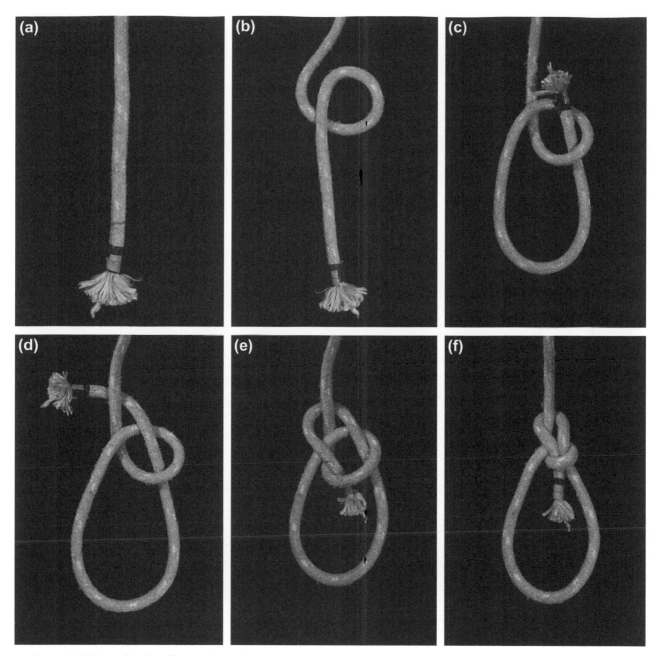

■ **Figure 11.7** Tying a bowline illustrated step-by-step.

work itself loose, especially under a swinging or rotating load. However, for this very reason, the knot is useful in situations where the length of the rope ends needs to be adjustable. For the most part, the clove hitch is easy to release but can occasionally jam and become difficult to untie, so be aware of this.

To tie a clove hitch, first place a loop around the pipe, with the working end (longer of the two ends) of the rope on top (Figure 11.8). Run the working end around

the pole once more until you meet the place where the ropes cross, then pass the working end under the cross. Pull to tighten. Sounds easy, right? Well, going correctly under the cross can be confusing, and it is the step that makes the clove hitch secure. Practice this repeatedly until you can do it almost without having to think about it. As a side note, according to Bill Sapsis, of Sapsis Rigging, this description of a clove hitch is technically accurate. However, in practice, in the backstage world, a

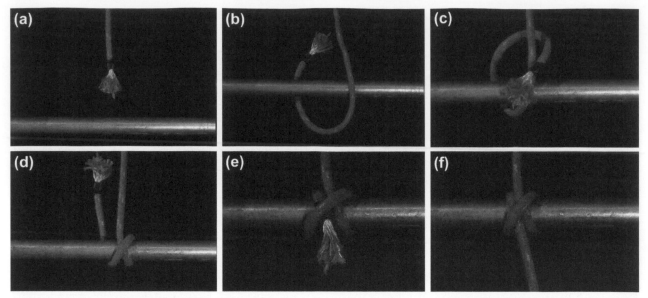

■ **Figure 11.8** Tying a clove hitch illustrated step-by-step.

clove hitch is *always* finished with a half hitch on top to prevent the knot from loosening. This means that the de facto clove hitch in the theatre includes a half hitch as an integral component.

You can use the clove hitch to join two pieces of pipe or wood together. You can also use it for pulling a straight length of pipe up into the air. To do this, you also need the half hitch. The half hitch is really a cornerstone knot that forms the basis for a multitude of other knots, and so you should take the time to truly master it. By itself, it is not particularly reliable. To tie a half hitch, loop your rope around the pipe. Cross the short end under the long length of the rope. Bring the short end over and down through the hole between where the rope crosses and the pole. Push the knot to the pole and pull to tighten!

Now you can raise straight pipes using a combination of the clove hitch and the half hitch: Grab the pipe, tie a clove hitch at the bottom, flick the rope around the top, and do a half hitch to pull the pipe up without it flailing around. Now, you've learned the basic knots used in the theatre. So what's next? *Practice.* Most other knots are based on these. Once these are mastered, all the other ones are easily learned.

Belaying is not technically a knot, but it does have to do with all of our rigging (Figure 11.9). To belay, you need a cleat or pin. The goal is to secure a rope by winding it in a figure-eight pattern around the cleat. To secure the belay, the final figure-eight wrap gets a 180-degree twist before being put on the cleat. Pull down on the working end of the rope to tighten.

A quick note about working with any kind of rope. Every time you tie a knot in it, you weaken the rope at the point of the knot. Keep this in mind and realize that rope does have a life span. Knowing all of this helps you to properly store rope in order to extend its life, as well as keeping your backstage area as clean and safe as possible. This brings us to the last knot I discuss, and again it is not actually a knot.

Coiling rope is one of the few ways you can safely store rope without putting any new bends, kinks, or knots in it and therefore continuing the weakening process. It doesn't take much time to learn or to do it on a regular basis. Once you are in the habit, you'll wonder how you continually stepped over piles of rope in the dark for so long. To coil a rope, take one end and make a big loop. The loop size will change depending on the diameter of the rope, but let's say it should be around 18 inches. Continue to loop more and more of the rope in this way until you have about 2 feet left. Hold the looped rope in your left hand and grab the remaining rope in your right. Begin to wrap the remaining rope around the top of the loop; it will probably take five to six wraps. Then, thread the loose end of the rope through the coils and pull tight.

The monkey's fist is an interesting knot to know about, based on its history (Figure 11.10). I won't explain how to tie it, as you will probably never need it.

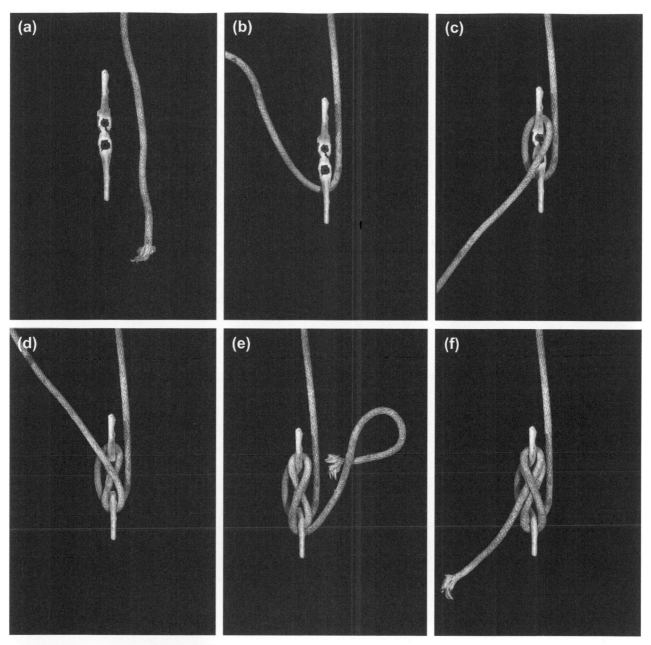

■ **Figure 11.9** Belaying illustrated step-by-step.

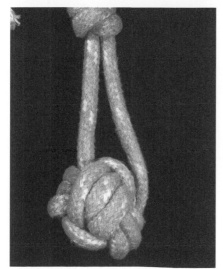

■ **Figure 11.10**
The monkey's
fist is a kind
of knot that is
more about
tightening than
tying. It's fun to
attempt once
you are more
advanced.

However, there are interesting stories about it, and it is a fun knot to know about. Sailors on boats are reported to have originally used the monkey's fist. Once the knot is tightened, it adds a substantial amount of weight to the end of the rope. This allowed the sailors to throw the rope up into the air, going over the top of the intended object, and have the rope come back down. The extra weight helped especially with that last part. Putting a stone or marble into the fist and tying the knot around it is another way to do it. This also added more weight to the end of the rope and made it easier to tighten the knot. The key with this knot is not tying it, but tightening it. I like to tie it without the stone or marble as more of a challenge.

RIGGING SYSTEMS

Before we go into the different kinds of rigging systems, let's discuss for a moment what happens if your theater is a black room with a 12′ ceiling. Well. Rigging is very different in this type of theater from everything that comes next in this chapter. A theater space without a tall ceiling or fly loft will use other conventions for moving lights and scenery around the stage. In most spaces like this, a fixed pipe grid will be hung from the low ceiling for lighting.

If scenery needs to move, pulleys and traveler tracks are often mounted to the underside of the pipe grid.

Let's continue on our story of rigging by looking at a basic rigging system within what we think of as a more traditional theater. Most theaters have some part of the following in common. Let's start by talking about line sets. Line sets are a combination of the individual rigging points, rope and pipe used together for hanging pipes and scenery in the air. It doesn't matter how they are hung; if they are in the air, they are line sets. The line set inventory, or line set schedule, tells everyone where the pipes are in relation to the plaster line (Figure 11.11). That way everyone has a physical line they can all reference. If everyone agrees to the same point of reference, then any information after that is coordinated.

Over time, while working in the theater, you may be exposed to four basic rigging systems: Hemp house, single purchase, double purchase, and winch or

■ **Figure 11.11** Sample line set inventory as it might appear on a ground plan.

■ **Figure 11.12** *Everybody* by Branden Jacobs-Jenkins. Produced in 2019 by James Madison University School of Theatre and Dance. Directed by Dennis Beck, scenic design by Brian Ruggaber, costume design by Katerina Moser, and lighting design by Daniel McGann-Bartleman.

automated. We will look at each system one at a time, explaining the varying reasons for each. All are still in use today at different theaters, and all are viable options for many of the techniques you'll learn, which carry over to other rigging topics we discuss. There is something to learn within each style and use elsewhere on other types of systems.

HEMP HOUSE

I spoke with Jason Adams at the 1869 Bardavon Opera House in Poughkeepsie, NY, while the stage house was being renovated. Jason said the theater had evaluated many options before deciding to keep the rigging system a hemp house. A **hemp house**, or rope house, is defined as such since the lift lines from the pipes are organic or synthetic rope, but not wire. A hemp system is counterweighted, with sandbags tied onto the individual lines as needed. Wow, hang on, what is a counterweight?

A **counterweight** is used to offset the objects you are trying to lift. Think of a seesaw (Figure 11.13): There is a pivot point in the middle, and a child sits on one end, which makes that side drop to the ground. If a child sits on the other end (providing a counterweight), then the first child can rise into the air. It's a similar concept in the theater.

■ **Figure 11.13** Playground seesaw with a center pivot point. How does this apply to the rigging techniques we've discussed?

The locking device to make sure nothing falls down unexpectedly is called a **pin rail**. Belaying, which we just learned, is done using the working end of the rope and the pin rail. When you do this, keep in mind you are holding all the weight of that pipe until you get it tied off properly and securely. The same is true when you are untying the line. Make sure you have a good hold on the rope above the pin rail. Once the belay is released, you will be holding all the weight, and it could be a lot. Remember earlier when I mentioned wearing gloves?

The next step in the rigging progression is to add weight to the working line before belaying to the pin rail. Huh? This is that seesaw idea that helps to balance the weight on the other side. **Sandbags** are just what they sound like—a bag filled with sand (Figure 11.14). They come in a variety of shapes and sizes. The difference in the sizes changes the amount of sand and therefore the weight of the filled bag. The goal is to add enough sandbags to the working end of the rope to equal the weight on the pipe connected to the other end of the rope.

For all of this to work properly, a number of pieces of hardware have to be in place. Let's discuss those now, so we can expand our view of the rigging system. We look at each type of system individually. Some of the hardware repeats for each system, so, as we go, it will get a little easier but right now we are starting with a blank slate. Let's continue with a hemp house as it is the simplest of the rigging systems to explain. Let's get some vocabulary out of the way. A **sheave** is basically a pulley. It has a groove around its circumference to support and contain a rope. There is a bearing at its center to permit rotation. A block is an assembly that consists of one or more sheaves in a housing. A **spot block** is designed for a temporary and easily movable connection to the **grid iron** on the ceiling or other theater structure. A **head block** is a pulley mounted to overhead steel at the top of the fly loft. The head block helps change the direction of multiple ropes simultaneously. A **loft block** is a pulley mounted to the grid iron that supports changes in the direction of a rope between the load and the head block. Figure 11.15 illustrates how all the parts we've just talked about go together.

■ **Figure 11.14** Sandbags on the floor backstage, waiting for their next purpose.

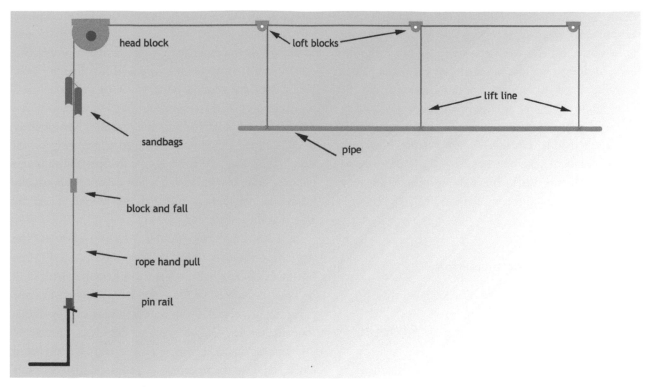

■ **Figure 11.15** Diagram of a working hemp house.

The rope attaches to the pipe with a clove hitch. Remember the clove hitch? Then, the rope goes straight up to the loft block. The rope could also go to a spot block if you need something changeable. All the blocks have pulleys, so the rope goes into the block to make a 90-degree turn. Owing to the width of the rope, the groove is U-shaped. Usually, three or five ropes are attached to the pipe. After going through their individual blocks, they all run through the head block, where they turn direction again. The various blocks have to have enough sheaves to accommodate the number of ropes per pipe. Once the ropes come out of the head block, a sandbag is attached. Then, the ropes continue down to the pin rail, where they are belayed to secure them. The sandbag(s) should be close in weight to the total weight attached to the pipe *plus* the weight of the pipe itself!

If you are dealing with something that is extraordinarily heavy, you can add a block and fall for an additional mechanical advantage. A block and fall is a piece of equipment that simulates the standard blocks we've been discussing, allowing multiple ropes to come in through the top. The difference is in the "fall" side, as it reduces the number of ropes coming back out down to

one. This reduces the number of ropes to one and also the overall weight to make it workable for one stagehand to move the pipe. Think of it this way: Five ropes go into the block, and one rope comes out of the fall. The ropes coming out of the head block are now tied off to the top of the block and fall. The bottom of the block and fall is fixed to the pin rail.

> This hemp system has smells and feels and sounds and it's like a full sensory experience. You can feel flex in the floor … and anything that gives you a little weird feeling is to be paid attention to!
>
> —Jason Adams,
> 1869 Bardavon Opera House

Keep in mind the goal is to balance the weight, to keep it at whatever height it is needed, while making the pipe a little lighter to help get it moving when it needs to. If you have to choose, you always want the pipe to be slightly heavier than the sandbags, so the pipe is more likely to drift down to the stage slowly rather than up to the roof. This helps when you are flying pipes into the floor and doesn't really affect anything when the pipe is tied off. A dead lift is tough, meaning trying to lift the full weight of the pipe with no help from any kind of counterweights. You can't physically get enough hands around the rope to actually lift heavy items. Plus, each stagehand has to take one hand off the rope to move their hand higher up before pulling again. This gives every other stagehand more weight to hold.

Sample Rigging Conversation

Loader: Clear the rail; loading weights.
Operator: Rail clear. OK to load.
Loader: Loading complete. OK to check
           for balance.
Operator: Thank you. Checking for balance.

SINGLE PURCHASE

Before we change topics to single and double counterweight systems, let's introduce some more vocabulary. We are now changing from using synthetic rope to using wire rope (Figure 11.16). Wire rope consists of a number of wire strands twisted on the diagonal around a core. You can see how strong it can be! A thimble is a grooved fitting around which a wire rope is bent to form an eye. It supports the rope and prevents it from kinking and weakening. To hold the thimble in place, you use a wire rope clip. This is a U-shaped bolt and a pad with two holes for sliding up the bolt. Two small nuts are used for holding the pad in place. The wire rope comes out of the thimble and doubles back on itself. Both pieces of rope go between the bolt and the pad. Once the nuts are tightened, the wire rope stays securely in place.

Another option for the wire rope clip is a crimping tool. Tools are designed to create the maximum holding around the wire when using a matching compression sleeve. It's fairly easy. Simply slide the sleeve onto your wire rope and then slip the end back through the sleeve, leaving an eye of whatever size you wish. Place the sleeve in the jaws of the tool and squeeze. The tool compresses

the sleeve and the wire rope for a permanent solution to wire rope ends.

The arbor is a carriage or rack that contains weights, usually flame cut steel. The cast iron is called pig iron. No, it does not contain pork. No it isn't shaped like a pig. Pig iron gets its name from the days when iron ore production required melting the ore and then pouring it into shaped sand that resembled a pig lying on its side. The locking rail is where the fly operator adds and removes counterweights from the arbors. It is usually located so that they can change the weights when the pipe is at the lowest level.

In both single and double purchase systems, the rigging overhead is identical. Wire rope goes up to the loft block. Blocks can be shaped differently, depending on how they are to be hung and how many ropes must pass through them. As wire rope is thinner than synthetic rope, it uses a V-shaped track in the blocks instead of a U-shaped one. The wire rope goes through the head block and down to the arbor. A wire rope then connects directly to the arbor. The operating line is a big, thick, synthetic rope that attaches to the bottom of the arbor

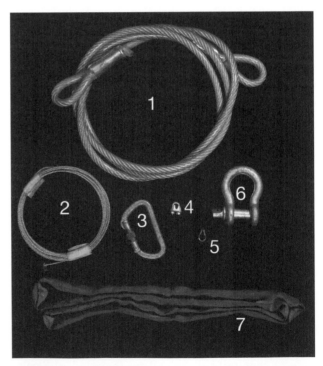

■ **Figure 11.16** (1) 5/8-inch wire rope sling, (2) 1/8-inch wire rope, (3) locking carabiner, (4) 1/8-inch wire rope clip, (5) 1/16-inch thimble, (6) 5/8-inch shackle, and (7) 3-foot span set.

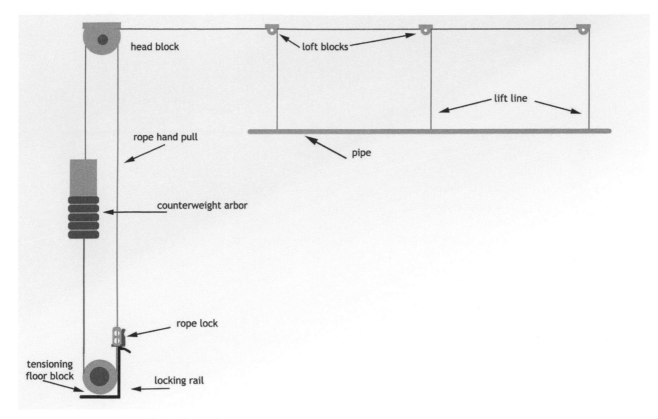

■ **Figure 11.17** Diagram of a single purchase system.

and goes around to the head of the block. Pulling on the hand pull raises and lowers the pipe the hard way.

In a **single purchase** setup, the locking rail is on the stage floor (Figure 11.17). This means you lose a lot of stage space in the wings to accommodate the arbors. The advantage of the single purchase system is that the counterweight requires a 1:1 ratio. You add one pound on the pipe for every pound of arbor weight. Also of note is that the counterweights travel the same distance as the pipe!

DOUBLE PURCHASE

A **double purchase** system puts the locking rail halfway between the stage floor and the loft blocks (Figure 11.18). This saves valuable backstage floor space. There is an extra pulley, both above and below the arbor, to double the wire rope length. This is necessary to make the system work properly. The pipe travels 1 foot for every 2 feet the rope has to travel. The ratio for a double purchase system is 2:1. You need to use twice the amount of weight of what is hung on the pipe. The advantage is that you lose

no floor space. This is often the major deciding factor in which type of system to use.

WINCHES

Let's look at automated systems next. **Winches** are geared mechanisms that can be either hand-operated or motorized. They are used to raise or generally move heavy equipment. The internal gearing produces a mechanical advantage in both speed and load capacity. This is somewhat similar to the single versus double purchase systems in terms of weight advantages. As a transition between counterweight and winches, let's look at the counterweight assisted-winch setup. This is a motorized winch that is retrofitted into existing manually operated systems that use counterbalancing weights. The counterbalancing weights are fixed at 50 percent of the maximum capacity of the set. The winch is rated at 50 percent of the maximum capacity of the set. The winch operates the line set at any load from 0 to 100 percent of its rated capacity, without the need to ever adjust the counterbalancing weights.

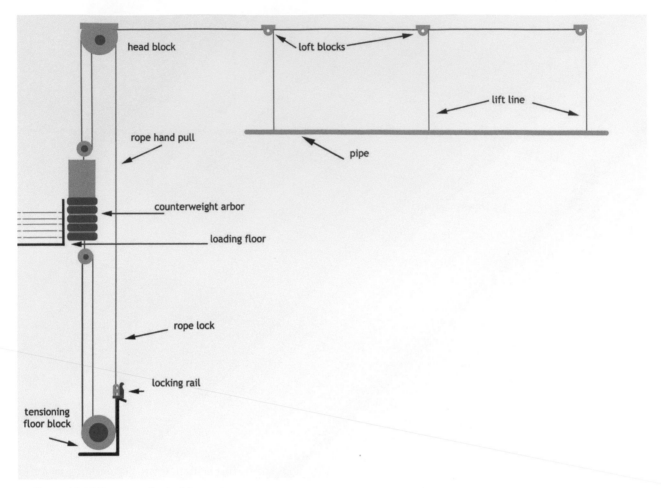

■ **Figure 11.18** Diagram of a double purchase system.

Fully motorized systems contain one of two types of winches: Single drum winches and line shafts. A drum winch system has a head block and loft blocks, just like a regular counterweight system. This is a good way to motorize a system and balance the costs. The line shaft winch has a drum for each lift line, which eliminates the need for blocks. The biggest concern with the line shaft system is the cost. If your system has 30 line sets, you need 150 drums, or five per line set. The secondary concern is having the room for fitting the system into your existing space.

Motorized systems like these can be run by computer software. Tell the system you want the height of a specific line set pipe to be 6´ above the deck, hit a button, and it happens. Wow, that's great! However, it creates another safety concern. The controller for the system needs to be in view of the stage *or* there must be a video system with a monitor near the control station. I cannot say this strongly enough! You can't responsibly hit a button to bring a pipe to the deck when you don't know if anyone or anything is in the way. Communication. It's a powerful thing.

TRUSS

A truss is our next concept in the area of rigging. A **truss** is two or more pieces of pipe fabricated together with cross bracing (Figure 11.19). This is used in place of standard pipes when you have extremely heavy loads to lift or there are extended distances between lift lines (Figures 11.20 and 11.21). Trusses come in a variety of shapes and lengths. There are flat trusses, triangular trusses, square trusses, and then any kind of custom shape you can think of (Figure 11.22). Let me also explain that there is a major difference in rigging a truss for a theater versus an arena. Let me start by saying

■ **Figure 11.19** Different styles and sizes of truss.

■ **Figure 11.20** Hick, a rigger for the 1869 Bardavon Opera House, stands next to a 1-ton chain hoist box during a load-in.

that the arena we are now talking about is *not* the arena theater we have discussed in previous chapters. It is an arena stadium where you go see a music concert. Now, in a theater, a truss usually is rigged not much higher than a normal pipe. It is used to supplement the pipes in places where pipes can't easily be placed. In an arena, that is not the case, as most arenas have no pipes at all. Arena rigging is a work horse providing all the hanging positions. It can also be much higher given arena

architecture. Riggers that do this work are called either upriggers or downriggers who do the work designated by their respective titles.

A 12″ × 12″ truss is manufactured from 2″ diameter and 1″ diameter aluminum tubing. An 18″ × 12″ is a bigger variation manufactured the same way as the 12″ × 12″ but has the added advantage, owing to its width of 18″, of being able to accommodate two lighting bars back to back (Figure 11.23). Also, the truss is slightly

■ **Figure 11.21** A box truss with chain hoist attached, waiting to be raised.

■ **Figure 11.22** A curved box truss at Production Resource Group.

stronger over longer spans. It is made from an aluminum alloy of 2″ tubes and 1″ tubes for the diagonals. A third standard size option is the 20.5″ × 20.5″ truss. It is for those ever-increasing load requirement situations. The truss pieces can be connected together with bolts to increase the length. This truss can also be specified with castor wheels.

The pre-rig truss has a different purpose. It is 30″ × 26″ in size (Figure 11.25). It is manufactured from 2″ diameter aluminum tube for the main tubes and 1″ for the diagonals. Each truss piece has four castor wheels for easy maneuverability and bolts for connecting of truss pieces. The footprint of this truss is rather large but worth it, and you will read why next. Each truss is designed to

GP 18 x 12

18" x 12" manufactured the same way as 12" x 12", but has an added advantage, due to its width of 18" of being able to accommodate 2 lighting bars back to back. Also the truss is slightly stronger over longer spans. It is made from 6061T6 or 6082T6 alloy 2" x 0.125" tubes for the main chords and 1" x 0.125" tubes for the diagonals.The truss can be used with Ground Support System with suitable sleeve blocks and towers.

PRODUCT CODE	DESCRIPTION	WT lbs
B0600	10' Section	61.5
B0601	8' Section	52.5
B0602	5' Section	37.5
B0603	2' 6" Section	24
B4600	3m Section	61.5
B4601	2.5m Section	53
B4602	2m Section	42
B4603	1.5m Section	37.5
B4604	1m Section	28.5
B4605	0.5m Section	19.5
B4608	4 Way Corner Block	22
B46	5 Way Corner Block	
B4	6 Way Corner Block	

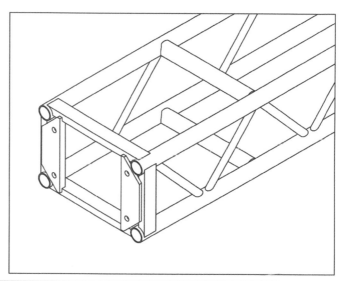

Allowable Load Data	Maximum Allowable Uniform Loads		Maximum Allowable Center Point Loads	
Span feet (meters)	Loads pounds (kgs)	Maximum deflection inches (mm)	Loads pounds (kgs)	Maximum deflection inches (mm)
10 (3.048)	6140 (2785)	0.276 (7)	4497 (2040)	0.20 (8)
20 (6.096)	3100 (1406)	1.10 (28)	1550 (703)	1.10 (28)
30 (9.144)	1726 (783)	2.20 (56)	864 (392)	2.20 (56)
40 (12.192)	855 (388)	2.95 (75)	427 (194)	2.95 (75)
50 (15.24)	425 (193)	3.70 (94)	214 (97)	3.70 (94)

LOADING FIGURES show maximum loads between supports in addition to the self weight of the truss. Information extracted from the structural report by Broadhurst, Goodwin, and Dunn
suit maximum shear capacity. All loads include 20% overload factor for dynamic effects.

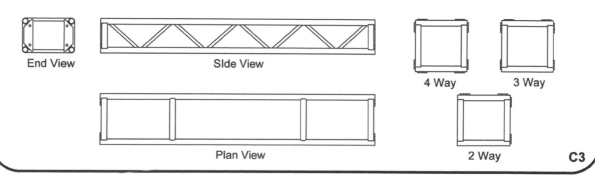

End View   Side View   4 Way   3 Way

Plan View   2 Way   C3

■ **Figure 11.23** James Thomas Engineering's general purpose 18˝ × 12˝ truss.

GP TRIANGULAR

ENGINEERING

23 1/4" x 60 degree equilateral triangular truss is designed and manufactured for high strength, in relation to storage space required. The main chords are 2" x 0.125" tube and the diagonals are 1" x 0.125" tube in either 6082T6 or 6061T6. The truss can be used with a Ground Support System with appropriate Sleeve Blocks and Towers. Each section is complete with bolts.

PRODUCT CODE	DESCRIPTION	WT lbs
B0500	10' section	66
B0501	8' section	53
B0502	5' section	35
B4500	3m section	66
B4501	2.5m section	53
B4502	2m section	44
B4503	1.5m section	35
B4504	1m section	26.5
B4505	2 way corner block	35
B4506	3 way corner block	39.5
B4507	4 way corner block	44
B4508	Flat pivot section	39.5

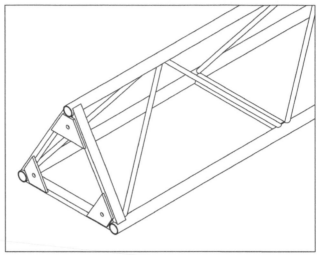

Allowable Load	Maximum Allowable Uniform Loads		Maximum Allowable Center Point Loads	
Span feet (meters)	Loads pounds (kgs)	Maximum deflection inches (mm)	Loads pounds (kgs)	Maximum deflection inches (mm)
10 (3.048)	5600 (2540)+	0.1 (2)	2800 (1270)+	0.1 (2)
15 (4.572)	5600 (2540)+	0.34 (8)	2800 (1270)+	0.34 (8)
20 (6.096)	4700 (2131)	0.70 (17)	2350 (1065)	0.70 (17)
25 (7.62)	3700 (1678)	1.09 (27)	1850 (839)	1.09 (27)
30 (9.144)	3000 (1360)	1.57 (39)	1500 (680)	1.57 (39)
40 (12.192)	2100 (952)	2.8 (71)	1050 (476)	2.8 (71)
50 (15.24)	1300 (589)*	3.75 (95)	650 (294)*	3.75 (95)
60 (18.288)	700 (317)*	4.50 (114)	350 (158)*	4.50 (114)

LOADING FIGURES show maximum loads between supports in addition to self weight of truss. Information extracted from structural report by Jessie Mise. + Denotes load limited to suit maximum shear capacity. *Denotes load limited to a maximum deflection of (span /160). All loads include a 20% overload factor for dynamic effects.

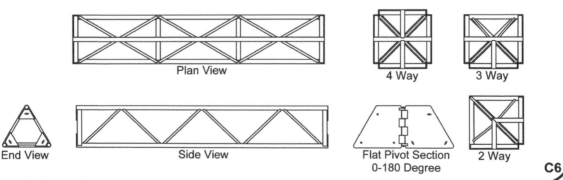

Plan View

4 Way   3 Way

End View   Side View

Flat Pivot Section
0-180 Degree   2 Way

C6

■ **Figure 11.24** General purpose triangular truss.

ENGINEERING

PRE-RIG TRUSS

Pre-Rig truss is 30" x 26" in size. It is manufactured from aluminium tube 6082-T6 with 2" x .125" wall thickness for main tubes and 1" x .125" wall tube for the diagonals. Each truss piece has 4 castor wheels for easy maneuverability and bolts for the connection of truss pieces.

Each truss is designed to carry 2 lighting bars complete with lanterns. The lighting bars are stored internally in the truss and can be lowered to the working position when in use. This design reduces the amount of space required for lighting and rigging in the truck. Each truss is also designed to carry a varying amount of lanterns, the 10' section carries 2 bars of 8 lanterns, 7' 7" section carries 2 bars of 6 lanterns, 5' section carries 2 bars of 4 lanterns, and the 3' 9-1/2" section carries 2 bars of 3 lanterns. This feature enables great flexibility in the truss design.

The Pre-Rig truss accepts a modified lighting bar which have 2 sleeved holes in them. The lighting bars are located inside the truss by guide rods. In the storage position the bars are securely held in the truss by shank hooks. The whole system can be used with our Ground Support System by using suitable sleeve blocks and towers.

PRODUCT CODE	DESCRIPTION	WT lbs
B0300	10' section (empty)	111.3
B0301	7' 7" section (empty)	91
B0302	5' section (empty)	77.15
B0303	3' 9 1/2" section (empty)	57.35
B0304	6"-12" make up piece (empty)	-
B4300	2 way corner block	52.9
B4301	4 way corner block	61.75
B4302	Universal pivot section 0-270 degree	59.5
B4303	Universal pivot section 0-90 degree	59.5
B4304	Horizontal load-bearing pivot section	123.5
B4305	Vertical load-bearing pivot section	123.5
B4306	P.R.T. to G.P. adapter	28.65

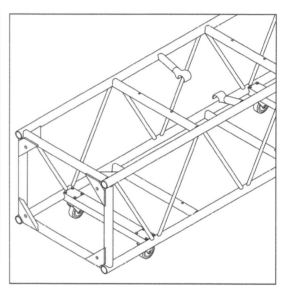

Par 64 lanterns in storage position

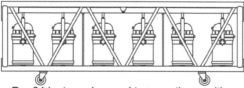

Par 64 lanterns lowered to operating position

To lower lanterns from storage to operating position, simply pull tab on shank hook with one hand whilst holding the lighting bar with the other hand. Then lower the lanterns into operating position.

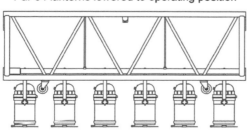

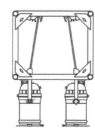

C12

■ **Figure 11.25** James Thomas Engineering's pre-rig truss.

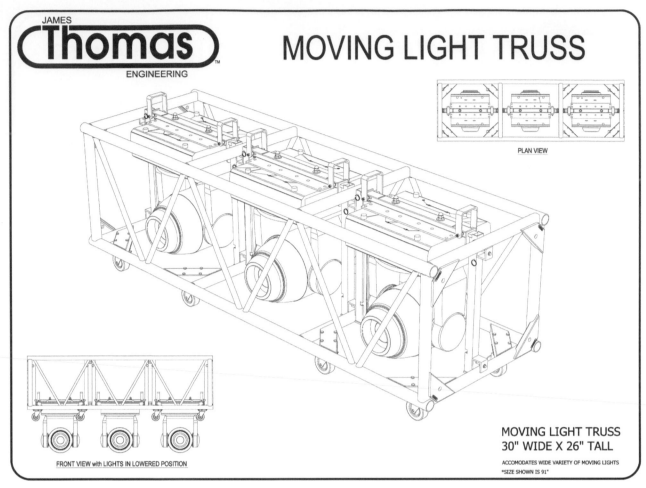

JAMES Thomas ENGINEERING

MOVING LIGHT TRUSS

PLAN VIEW

FRONT VIEW with LIGHTS IN LOWERED POSITION

**MOVING LIGHT TRUSS
30" WIDE X 26" TALL**

ACCOMODATES WIDE VARIETY OF MOVING LIGHTS
*SIZE SHOWN IS 91"

■ **Figure 11.26** James Thomas Engineering's moving light truss.

carry two lighting bars complete with lights. The lighting bars are stored internally in the truss and can be lowered to the working position when in use. This design reduces the amount of space required for lighting and rigging in the truck when transporting to the theater or for a tour. Each truss is also designed to carry a varying amount of lighting fixtures: The 10′ section carries two bars of eight lights each; the 7′ 7″ section carries two bars of six lights; the 5′ section carries two bars of four lights; and the 3′ 9½″ section carries two bars of three lights. This feature enables great flexibility in the truss design.

The pre-rig truss is great when you have the room for the bigger truss profile. Unfortunately, some situations can't accommodate that size. A smaller one was designed that accepts a modified lighting bar. The truss is 20.5″ wide × 20.5″ deep × 96″ long standard. The lighting bars are located inside the truss by guide rods that allow for quick installation of the bar within the truss. For transportation, the bars are securely held in the truss by shank hooks. The smaller size of this truss allows the use of pre-rig lighting bars with short-nosed or smaller lights. It is ideal for when a small truck pack is required.

The moving light truss has been designed around the pre-rigged truss size (Figure 11.26). The basic truss is 91″ × 30″ × 26″ in size, although of course other sizes are available. It is manufactured from 2″ aluminum tube for main tubes and a 1″ for the diagonals. Each truss piece has eight castor wheels for easy maneuverability and bolts for the connection of truss pieces. You may wonder about the casters. Well, once you start putting lights into the truss for storage, transport, and usage, it gets pretty heavy!

Each truss as described is designed to carry three moving light fixtures. The moving lights are stored internally in the truss and can be lowered to the working position when in use. This design reduces the amount of space required for lighting and rigging in the truck since rigging and lighting equipment share the same space.

Towers provide the equipment to support a truss rig in venues where the flying points are either not strong enough or just not in the right place. Support tower systems have really come into their own, with specialized designs to better support heavy loads. Thomas offers a variety of support towers including 12″ × 12″, 15″ × 15″, and 20.5″ × 20.5″ Super Towers. These ground support towers are capable of supporting from 2000 pounds to more than 4 tons. Maximum heights have a great range depending on the configuration, with a range from 14′ to 60′ using multiple towers.

James Thomas Engineering created SuperTruss, which is designed to offer all the advantages of the 20.5″ truss in the much smaller footprint of a 12″ × 12″ layout (Figure 11.28). The 12″ × 12″ SuperTruss provides a substantial increase in load-bearing capacity over the existing general-purpose 12″ × 12″ truss. The 18″ × 12″ SuperTruss provides a substantial increase in load-bearing capacity over the general-purpose 18″ × 12″ truss. All of this is achieved through material selection and engineering.

The ProPlus rescue system™ from Sapsis Rigging, Inc., needs to be mentioned as well (Figure 11.29). The rescue system was designed by and for entertainment industry professionals. This versatile lifting and lowering system is a cost-effective rescue system for people working at heights. The ProPlus rescue system is lightweight, compact, and can be set up quickly. With a 3:1 mechanical advantage ratio, the system can be easily operated by one person. No special tools are needed to install or remove, and all components are reusable.

Designed for assisted rescue from the deck or from the truss, the system can be mounted on a grid, on a truss, or in the high steel.

The ProPlus rescue system consists of

- A manually operated controlled descent device
- A 15′ (extended) telescoping rescue pole with rescue clip
- Carabiner for use with the rescue pole
- Scaffold hook for system anchorage
- Synthetic rescue ladder for use in an alternate rescue scenario
- 100′ × ½″ Showbraid synthetic rope
- Rescue 8 with ears
- Storage bags with attachment straps
- Utility gloves
- Operating manual
- ProPlus T-shirt

The next component to rigging is **span sets**, generically known as *round slings*. They are continuous loops of synthetic fiber or steel-galvanized aircraft cable in a canvas-like (polyester) sheath. The number of loops used determines rating or weight capacity. For example, you would calculate the weight the of truss, the lighting equipment, and all the cabling.

A wire rope sling is an alternative to the span set. A wire rope sling is made from larger gauge wire rope and is fabricated with a large eye and thimble at each end. There is no fabric covering however, so keep that in mind when choosing which to use for a given task. Slings come in varying lengths, or you can make your own.

Span sets come in a series of standard lengths. If a span set is not long enough, there are techniques to shackle two span sets together for more length and flexibility.

To use the span set or wire rope sling, you need a shackle. The **shackle** is a U-shaped device with holes at each end to accommodate a pin or bolt in order to secure it. There are three different standard configurations for using a span set with a shackle. The strongest of these is called a *basket*. This is made by creating a U shape out of the span set. It gives you four points of contact. The next configuration is to use the span set straight. This gives you two points of contact. The last is the choke. You wrap one end around and put one through the other. This is

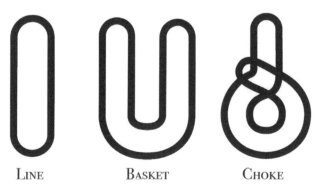

LINE   BASKET   CHOKE

■ **Figure 11.27** Span set configuration options.

SUPERTRUSS
12 x 12

The revolutionary truss designed to offer all the advantages of the 20.5" Supertruss in a 12" x 12" layout. The 12" x 12" Supertruss provides a substantial increase in load bearing capacity over the existing GP 12" x 12" truss. The main chords of the truss are made from 2" x 0.157" 6061-T6, and the diagonals are 1" x 0.125".

PRODUCT CODE	DESCRIPTION	WT lbs
B1260A	12' Section	87
B1261	10' Section	72
B1262	8' Section	67
B1263	6' Section	51
B1264	5' Section	42
B1265	2' 6" Section	27
B1200A	60 Degree corner gate	14
B1201	90 Degree corner gate	8
B1203	135 Degree corner gate	5
B1204A	3 Way gate/ 120° gate	8
B1204B	3 Way gate with lifting point	8
B1208	Square support plate	4
B1211	12" Super-truss to GP 12" x 12" adaptor gate	7
G6671A	12" Supertruss pin extraction tool	7

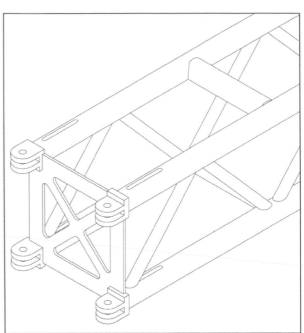

Allowable Load Data	Maximum Allowable Uniform Loads		Maximum Allowable Center Point Loads	
Span feet (meters)	Loads pounds (kgs)	Maximum deflection inches (mm)	Loads pounds (kgs)	Maximum deflection inches (mm)
10 (3.048)	8496 (3854)*	0.20 (5)	7348 (3333)	0.20 (5)
20 (6.096)	7255 (3291)	1.50 (38)	3628 (1646)	1.50 (38)
30 (9.144)	3324(1508)	2.20 (56)	1662 (754)	2.20 (56)
40 (12.192)	1695 (769)	2.95 (75)	848 (385)	2.95 (75)
50 (15.24)	888 (403)	3.70 (94)	445 (202)	3.70 (94)

LOADING FIGURES show maximum loads between supports in addition to self weight of truss. Information extracted from structural report by Broadhurst, Goodwin & Dunn for Super-truss manufactured after November 1993. * Denotes load limited to suit maximum shear capacity. All loads include 20% overload factor for dynamic effects.

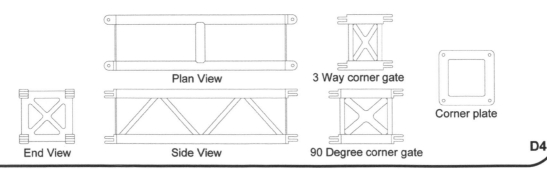

Plan View

3 Way corner gate

Corner plate

End View

Side View

90 Degree corner gate

D4

■ **Figure 11.28** James Thomas Engineering's SuperTruss.

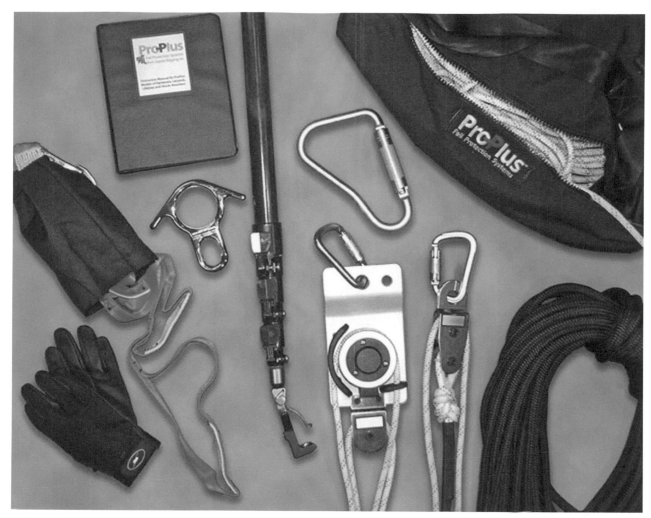

■ **Figure 11.29** Sapsis Rigging, Inc.'s ProPlus rescue system.

not as strong as the other options since a bend weakens the line of the span set.

Now that you have a good holding point for your span set, you are ready to lift your truss into place. But how? This is where the chain hoist comes in really handy. A chain hoist is a mechanical device used for lifting heavy loads of objects and equipment. There are three types of chain hoists: Air, manual, and electric. The manual one and the air one are designed with reduction gears, hook pivots, and swivels. Suspended by a top hook, or by a push or geared trolley, these devices move objects slowly and carefully while making height adjustments. The attached load is well secured so it can be left fixed without requiring a great deal of supervision. The electric chain hoist, on the other hand, is generally used for lifting heavy-duty industrial loads. It allows the user to

pull from the side as well as vertically. In theater, we tend to use the electric hoist most commonly.

> The only thing that can ever go wrong in a fly rail or rigging system is operator error! Your best friends are in danger of you killing them at any minute!
>
> —Jason Adams,
> 1869 Bardavon Opera House

I cannot stress enough how dangerous rigging systems can be if they are not used properly. Regular inspection prevents a lot of problems. The person operating the system needs to be trained properly and pay attention to every part of the system. The initial installation needs to be done with strict observance of the manufacturer's guidelines, of course. Regular inspection should be a continuous process during the use of equipment, as well as once or twice a year for a complete maintenance inspection. With that said, if you do the job well, there will be time to relax between cues (Figure 11.30).

■ **Figure 11.30** At the end of a long call, the riggers get a chance to relax!

CHECK YOUR KNOWLEDGE

1. Explain why you might choose to use synthetic rope over natural rope.
2. Predict which knot you might use the most. Defend why.
3. Each type of rigging system has pros and cons. Argue for and against each of the three major types with specific examples.

- Arbor
- Belaying
- Block and fall
- Bowline
- Chain hoist
- Clove hitch
- Coiling
- Counterweight
- Dead lift
- Double purchase
- Fly loft
- Grid iron
- Half hitch
- Head block
- Hemp house
- Line set
- Line set inventory
- Locking rail
- Loft block
- Monkey's fist
- Operating line
- Overhand knot
- Pin rail
- Sandbag
- Shackle
- Sheave
- Single purchase
- Span set
- Spot block
- Square knot
- Thimble
- Truss
- Winch
- Wire rope
- Wire rope clip

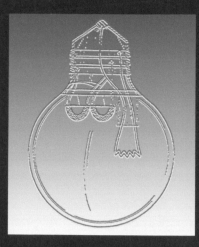

STUDY WORDS
Chapter 11

House to Half ...
Lighting

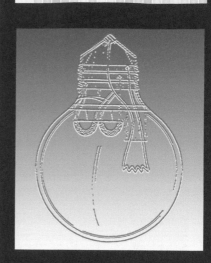

From all things scenic to lighting, this chapter discusses lighting. In the same format as other chapters, we discuss some of the history for lighting through a variety of developments straight to today's fixtures. Conventional lighting (meaning nonmoving lights) and intelligent lighting (meaning the fixture is controlled remotely) are both viable options in today's theater. In some ways, this is one department where both old and new technologies can coexist on the stage seamlessly.

As with other chapters, we start by taking a look at theatrical lighting in history. So, I guess, we all know it started with the sun. I'm not kidding. The Greeks and Romans performed all their shows outside. They based the starting time for the show on the position of the sun in the sky. Once the theaters were moved indoors, in Shakespeare's time for example, the use of candles started to come into play (Figure 12.1). The candles were used both as props and for overall ambience within the theater.

The Chestnut Street Theater in Philadelphia used candles on booms for side light and employed rope and pulley mechanisms to move them on and off stage. Additionally, productions were scripted according to lack of illumination because the audience couldn't see upstage. So, imagine reading a script and seeing, "look here comes John," and then John enters up left.

■ **Figure 12.1** Candle, the original indoor light.

Playwrights have always adapted to the needs of the stage!

The first **footlights** were candles. Footlights were named for exactly what they sound like—lights near your feet. Footlights are traditionally located on the downstage edge of the stage or apron. They point upstage toward the back wall, aiming up into the actors' faces from below. The "invention" of footlights was a changing point for lighting in the theater. Suddenly, there was some control over the lighting. This was a first. Putting candles on the edge of the stage wasn't enough. It was figured out pretty quickly that, if you put some sort of reflector behind the candle (meaning between the audience and the candle), the light would become brighter. It also wouldn't blind the audience as the actual light source was now shielded from direct view. These reflectors became decorative in addition to useful, and that is how we primarily remember them.

This little taste of control over the lighting wasn't enough though. The next step was to put a glass of

■ **Figure 12.2** *Henry V* by William Shakespeare, directed by Saheem Ali; sets by Melanie May, costumes by Desira Pesta, and lights by Tim van't Hoff. Tisch School of the Arts Graduate Acting in collaboration with Design for Stage and Film.

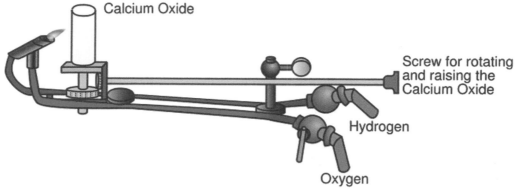

Figure 12.3 How limelight actually worked.

colored water between the footlight and the actors. This changed the color of the light that was projected onto the stage. Then, of course, the audience wanted it brighter, in different locations—more control, more control, more control.

What a surprise! Enter the wonderful world of gaslight. As gaslight began to be piped into buildings, people working in the theater suddenly got some great ideas. And, this leads us to the invention of limelight. It was first used at the Covent Garden Theatre in London in 1837. Limelight is an intensely bright light created when a gas flame is directed at a cylinder of calcium oxide, or lime (Figure 12.3). Let's hear it for chemical reactions!

Enter Thomas Alva Edison to shed some additional light on the subject. Or rather Joseph Swan. Who, you might ask? Well, Sir Joseph Wilson Swan was a physicist and chemist in England, born in 1828. In 1850, he began working on a light bulb, using carbonized paper filaments in an evacuated glass envelope or bulb. By 1860, he was able to demonstrate a working bulb and obtained a UK patent covering a partial vacuum, carbon filament incandescent light bulb. Unfortunately, the lack of a good vacuum and an adequate electric source resulted in an inefficient bulb with a short lifetime.

Fifteen years later, in 1875, Swan returned to consider the problems he had with the light bulb. The most significant feature of Swan's newly improved bulb

Figure 12.4 *Henry Box Brown* by Tony Kushner, directed by Mark Wing-Davey; sets by James Bolenbaugh, costumes by Olga Mill, and lights by Dante Smith. Tisch School of the Arts Graduate Acting in collaboration with Design for Stage and Film.

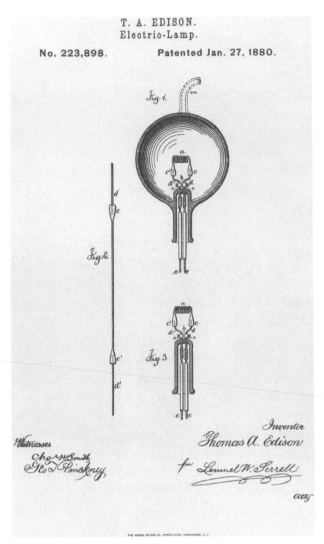

T. A. EDISON.
Electric-Lamp.

No. 223,898.   Patented Jan. 27, 1880.

Fig. 1.

Fig. 2.

Fig. 3.

Inventor
Thomas A. Edison

Witnesses
Chas H. Smith
Geo. T. Pinckney

per Lemuel W. Serrell

atty

THE NORRIS PETERS CO., PHOTO-LITHO., WASHINGTON, D. C.

■ **Figure 12.5** Thomas Edison's original patent.

Theatre Traditions: Ghost Light

Many theaters have ghosts, according to resident theatre personnel, who will tell you they've seen or heard uncanny visitors, and some insist that, to ward off bad-luck spirits, there must always be a "ghost light" illuminating the stage when it is not in use. It is turned on as the actors and crew leave and burns all night. If the stage is dark, the superstition has it, ghosties can run free. Or, perhaps, we leave a light on so they can perform.

To me, the reason is less ghostly and more a statement of intense belief: We must be sure that a real light is always on so that the metaphorical light of the theatre will never disappear. *Dark*, let us recall, refers to a time when there is no show (i.e., "We perform Tuesday through Sunday, but Monday is dark."). We want our art never to become "dark" but instead to remain brightly alive. Or, the stage should never be left dark. A light should always be on to keep the ghost company as well as happy. The light left on the stage is referred to as the *ghost light*. Or, a burglar fell off the stage, broke his or her leg, and sued the theatre. Take your pick!

was that there was little residual oxygen in the vacuum tube to ignite the filament. This allowed the filament to glow almost white-hot without catching fire, producing a much brighter light than originally. However, his filament had low resistance and therefore needed heavy copper wiring, which was expensive. Swan received a second British patent in 1878, about a year before Thomas Edison (Figure 12.5).

In America, Edison worked from copies of the original Swan patent, trying to make them more efficient. Though Swan had received a patent in England, Edison obtained patents in America for a direct copy of the Swan light (Figure 12.5). In 1878, Edison applied the term filament to the element of glowing wire carrying

the current, as had Swan. At this point, Edison's main goal was to improve the longevity of the lamp so that it would have commercial possibilities. Edison took the early features and set his workers to the task of creating longer-lasting bulbs. By 1879, he had produced a new concept: A high-resistance lamp in a very high vacuum, which would burn for hundreds of hours (Figure 12.6). Edison said, "We will make electricity so cheap that only the rich will burn candles."

Edison then started an advertising campaign claiming that he was the real inventor. Swan, who was less interested in making money from the invention, agreed that Edison could sell the lights in America while he retained the rights in Britain. To avoid a possible court

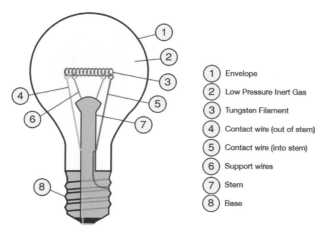

■ **Figure 12.6** Light bulb diagram showing individual components.

1	Envelope
2	Low Pressure Inert Gas
3	Tungsten Filament
4	Contact wire (out of stem)
5	Contact wire (into stem)
6	Support wires
7	Stem
8	Base

battle with Swan, Edison and Swan formed a joint company called *Ediswan* to manufacture and market the invention in Britain. Well, Edison wasn't done yet; read on. A little thing called neon lighting was first demonstrated in a modern form in December 1910 by Georges Claude at the Paris Motor Show.

The next development we talk about is the fluorescent lamp. It wasn't until 1934 when the first commercially produced fluorescent lighting would hit the market. A fluorescent lamp is a gas-discharge lamp that uses electricity to excite mercury vapor. The excited mercury produces shortwave ultraviolet (UV) light that causes a phosphor to fluoresce, producing visible light. Ugh, what a description. But you get enough of the idea, so let's move on. Unlike incandescent lamps, fluorescent lamps always require a ballast to start and properly control the flow of power through the lamp. A fluorescent lamp converts electrical power into useful light more efficiently than an incandescent lamp. Compared with incandescent lamps, fluorescent lamps use less power for the same amount of light and last longer. Thomas Edison briefly pursued fluorescent lighting for its commercial potential. He invented a fluorescent lamp in 1896 that used a coating of calcium tungstate as the fluorescing substance, excited by X-rays. He received a patent in 1907, but it was not put into production. Edison had little reason at this point to pursue an alternative means of electrical illumination.

Nikola Tesla, from Croatia, made similar experiments in the 1890s, devising high-frequency powered fluorescent bulbs that gave a bright greenish light, but, as with Edison's devices, no commercial success was achieved. Although Edison lost interest in fluorescent lighting, one of his former employees, Daniel Moore, was able to create a gas-based lamp that achieved a measure of commercial success. In 1895, Moore demonstrated lamps 7–9 feet in length that used carbon dioxide or nitrogen to emit white or pink light, respectively. As with future fluorescent lamps, there are pros and cons to each type of lamp. After years of work, Moore was able to extend the operating life of the lamps by inventing an electromagnetically controlled valve that maintained a constant gas pressure within the tube. Although Moore's lamp was complicated, expensive to install, and required very high voltages, it was considerably more efficient than incandescent lamps and it produced a more natural light. That is right, fluorescent was more natural than early incandescent!

KELVIN TEMPERATURE	BENCHMARK
1700 K	Match flame
1850 K	Candle flame
2800–3300 K	Standard light bulb
3400 K	Theatre lamps, photofloods
4100 K	Moonlight
5000 K	Horizon daylight
5500–6000 K	Typical daylight
6500 K	Overcast daylight

The next development is the halogen light bulb—also known in theaters as tungsten-halogen. It is an incandescent lamp with a tungsten filament. The filament is sealed into a compact, transparent, quartz envelope, filled with an inert gas and a small amount of halogen. The halogen increases the lifetime of the bulb by re-depositing tungsten from the inside of the bulb back onto the filament. Another benefit is that the halogen lamp can operate at a higher temperature. Thus ends the age-old question: Is it tungsten, halogen, or quartz? Well, actually it's all three!

Today, lamps come in all sorts of options. But first, a quick reminder to never, ever touch the glass envelope with your bare fingers. The oils on your skin will create a heat barrier on the glass and significantly shorten the life of the lamp! Now, the envelope shape has a whole

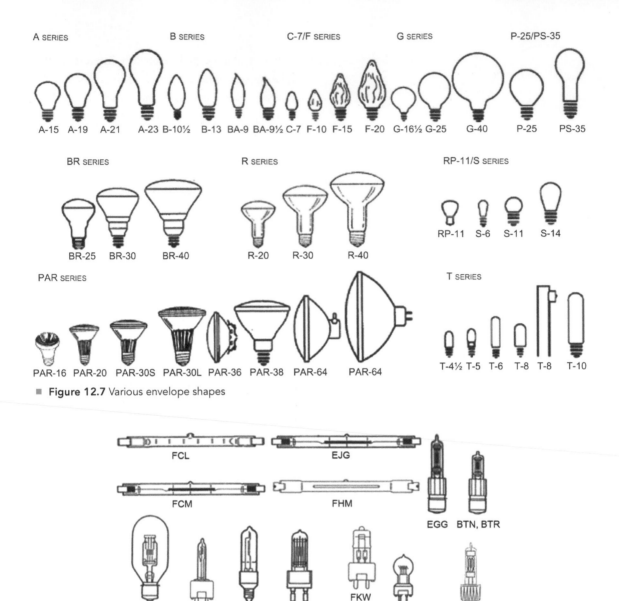

■ **Figure 12.7** Various envelope shapes

■ **Figure 12.8** Standard theater lamp types.

range of possibilities, and so do the base and wattage. When you combine these three parts, you find that bulbs are actually very specific for the fixture you want to put them in. They are also specific for the purpose you have in mind. It is important to know the options so you can properly choose what you want and also so that, if you need to replace a bulb, you know which one to use. Take a look at Figures 12.7 and 12.8 to see some charts of the most commonly used envelope and base shapes.

The next thing to talk about is the Kelvin scale. Color temperature is a part of all visible light. It is important in lighting, photography, film, and many other fields. The color temperature of a light source is determined by comparing the quality of the color with that of the perfect black. Yellow–red colors are considered warm, and blue–green colors are considered cool. Well, that is nothing new. Confusing though is how the Kelvin scale is set up. The higher Kelvin temperatures are considered cool, and lower color temperatures are considered warm. Always keep in mind when choosing a lamp that cool light produces higher contrast, and warm light is considered more flattering to skin tones and clothing. The Kelvin scale ranges from 1,000 to more than 10,000. Some basic benchmarks along the scale are shown in the table on page 297.

■ **Figure 12.9** *42nd Street* tour, 2016. Lighting designer, Ken Billington; scenic designer, Kacie Hultgren (in combination with original set designer Beowulf Boritt); and costume designer, Roger Kirk. Notice the combined composition of staging, scenery, and lighting.

ELECTRICITY

OK, before we go any further, we have to talk about electricity. I can't put it off any longer. It won't be that bad, so let's just do it and get it out of the way. Let's start with current. There are two kinds: Direct and alternating. **Direct current** (DC) is an electric charge that flows in one direction. DC is produced by such sources as batteries and solar cells. DC may flow through a conductor, such as a copper wire, but can also flow through semiconductors and insulators. On the other hand, **alternating current** (AC) is an electric current whose direction reverses cyclically. AC is the most efficient transmission of energy and is the type used in residences and commercial buildings.

The system of three-phase alternating current electrical generation and distribution was invented by Nikola Tesla (more on this later). He made many careful calculations and measurements and found out that 60 Hz (Hertz are cycles per second) was the best frequency for alternating current power generation. He preferred 240 volts, which put him at odds with Thomas Edison, whose direct current systems were 110 volts. Perhaps Edison had a useful point in the safety factor of the lower voltage, but DC couldn't provide the power to a similar distance from the source that AC could.

When the German company AEG built the first European generating facility, its engineers decided to fix the frequency at 50 Hz, because the number 60 didn't fit the metric standard unit sequence (1, 2, 5). At that time, AEG had a virtual monopoly, and its standard spread to the rest of the continent. In Britain, differing frequencies proliferated, and only after World War II was the 50-cycle standard established.

■ **Figure 12.10** *Hedda Gabler* at NYU's Department of Graduate Acting and Department of Design for Stage and Film in 2005. Director, Cigdem Onat; scenic designer, Veronica Ferre; costume designer, Sarah Greene; and lighting designer, Dans Sheehan.

Originally, Europe was 120 volts too, just like Japan and the United States are today. It was deemed necessary to increase voltage to get more power with less loss and voltage drop from the same copper wire diameter. At the time, the United States also wanted to change, but, because of the cost involved to replace all electric appliances, it decided not to. At the time (1950s–1960s), the average US household already had a fridge and a washing machine, but this was not the case in Europe.

The result is that the United States is still evolving from the 1950s and 1960s and—mostly in older buildings—still copes with such problems as light bulbs that burn out rather quickly when they are close to the transformer (too high a voltage) or light bulbs that don't burn at their brightest (lack enough voltage at the end of the line). Currently, all new American buildings are wired for 240 volts. The voltage is then split into two 120-volt lines using the hot wires and sharing the neutral between them. This is the best of both worlds, where you can have

120 and 240 in your home or business. Major appliances, such as virtually all drying machines and ovens, as well as most stationary woodworking tools in your scene shop, are now primarily connected via 240 volts.

Electrical power, in general, is defined as the rate at which electrical energy is transferred by an electric circuit. The unit of measurement for this is the wattage (W). Voltage (V) is the difference in electrical potential between two points of a circuit. In the United States, the standard voltage is 120 V and 240 V but can range anywhere from 110 V to 240 V. In Europe, it is almost exclusively 220 V (240 V in the UK). The ampere (A), usually shortened to *amp*, is a unit of electric current, or amount of electric charge per second. Every theater has a different amount of amps available for you. It is always good to know what is available before you begin to plug things in. You often have two of these three measurements and need to determine the last one. Consequently, the following three formulas apply to electricity for our needs. They are often referred to as the West Virginia formulas for somewhat obvious reasons.

W = VA
V = W/A
A = W/V

In your travels, you are likely to encounter two power types. First is single-phase power. You probably have this in your home, as it is most often used in residences and in more rural areas. You can tell single-phase power by looking at the main power feed lines coming into the breaker panel. You'll find two hot wires (typically one black and one red), a neutral wire (the white one), and a ground wire (the green one). Each hot wire, when measured with the neutral, equals the two halves of AC and can be metered about 120 V. If you measure the two hot wires, one to the other, you get about 240 V. When I say about 120 V or 240 V, this is because, in a perfect world, it would be exact. In actuality, you're likely to find between 110 and 120 V, and 220 and 240 V, depending on how much power is being used and, well, how the local power company is getting power into the building.

The ground wire is there as a safety in case of some sort of short circuit.

Next to discuss in detail is three-phase power. You can tell three-phase power because it has three hot wires (black, red, and blue) along with the neutral and ground. Three-phase power is found more often in urban areas where there is industry or manufacturing. This is because there is a greater likelihood of motors and other equipment that require more overall power, which justifies the extra expense of installation. Each hot wire measured to neutral is about 120 V while, when measured to each other (black to red, red to blue, black to blue), it is about 240 V. The neutral and ground wires work the same way here as in the single-phase system. Always be extremely careful around breaker panels since it is possible for *you* to be the short circuit.

There is no standard voltage throughout the world, and the frequency—that is, the number of times the current changes direction per second—also has no standard (Figure 12.11). Moreover plug shapes, plug holes, plug sizes, and sockets are also different in many countries (Figures 12.12 and 12.13).

Let's move on to types of cable or, more specifically, the wire that makes up a cable. Since we chatted about

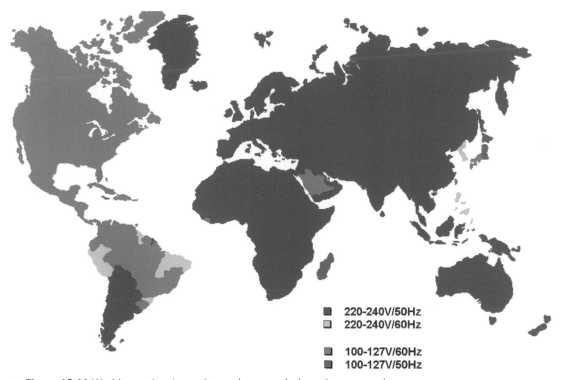

■ **220-240V/50Hz**
□ **220-240V/60Hz**

■ **100-127V/60Hz**
■ **100-127V/50Hz**

■ **Figure 12.11** World map showing various voltages and where they are used.

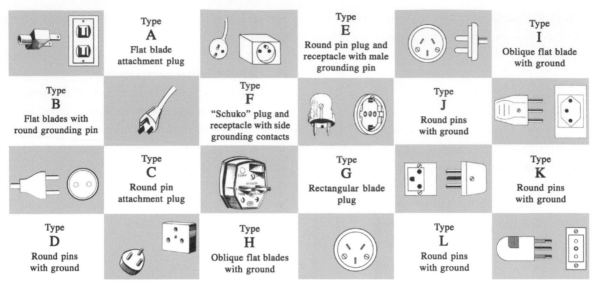

Figure 12.12 Electrical plug types used around the world.

Type of Plug by Country

Country	Plug Type
Afghanistan	D
Albania	C
Algeria	C, F
Angola	C
Argentina	C, I
Australia	I
Austria	C
Bahamas	A, B
Bahrain	G
Bangladesh	A, C, D
Barbados	A, B, F, H
Belarus	C
Belgium	A, C, E
Belize	A, B, H
Benin	D
Bermuda	A, B
Bolivia	A, C
Botswana	C, D, H
Brazil	A, B, C
Brunei	G
Bulgaria	F
Burkina Faso	B, E
Burma	C, D, F
Burundi	C, E
Cameroon	C, E
Canada	B

Country	Plug Type
Canary Islands	C, E
Cape Verde, Rep. of	C, F
Cayman Islands	A, B
Central African Republic	C, E
Chad	E
Chile	C, F, L
China, Peoples Rep. of	C, D, G, H
Colombia	A, B
Congo, Dem. Rep of (form. Zaire)	E
Congo, Peoples Rep. of	C, E
Costa Rica	A, B
Cyprus	G
Czech Republic	E
Denmark	C, K
Djibouti, Rep. of	C, E
Dominican Republic	A
Ecuador	A, B, C, D
Egypt	C
El Salvador	A, B, C, D, E, F, G, I, J, L
England	A, C, H
Equatorial Guinea	C, E
Eritrea	C
Ethiopia	C
Fiji	I
Finland	C, F
France	E

Country	Plug Type
Gabon	D, E
Gambia, The	G
Germany, Fed. Rep. of	F
Ghana	D, G
Gibraltar	C, G
Greece	C, F
Greenland	C, K
Grenada	G
Guatemala	A, B, G, H, I
Guinea	C, F, K
Guinea-Bissau	C
Guyana	A, H
Haiti	A, B, H
Honduras	A
Hong Kong	H
Hungary	C, F
Iceland	B
India	C, D, G
Indonesia	C, E, F
Ireland	G
Israel	C, H
Italy	L
Ivory Coast	C, E
Jamaica	A, B, C, D
Japan	A, B, I
Jordan	C, F, G, L
Pakistan	B, C, D

Country	Plug Type
Lesotho	D
Liberia	A, B
Luxembourg	F
Macedonia	C, F
Madagascar	C, D, E, J, K
Malawi	G
Malaysia	G
Mali, Rep. of	C, E
Malta	G
Mauritania	C
Mauritius	G
Mexico	A, B
Monaco	C, D, E, F
Morocco	C, E
Mozambique	C, D, F
Namibia	C
Nepal	C, D
Netherlands	F
New Zealand	H
Nicaragua	A
Niger	A, C, E
Nigeria	C, D, H
Northern Ireland	A, C, H
Norway	C, F
Oman	H

Country	Plug Type
Qatar	D, G
Romania	C, F
Russia	C
Rwanda	C, J
Saudi Arabia	A, B, G
Scotland	A, C, H
Senegal	C, D, E, K
Serbia-Montenegro	F
Seychelles	D,
Sierra Leone	D, G
Singapore	B, H
Slovak Republic	E
Somalia	C
South Africa	D
Spain	C, F
Sri Lanka	D
Sudan	C, D
Suriname	C, F
Swaziland	D
Sweden	C, F
Switzerland	C, E, J
Syria	C
Tajikistan	C, I

Country	Plug Type
Tahiti	A
Taiwan	A, B
Tanzania	D, G
Thailand	A, B, C, D, E, G, J, K
Togo	C
Trinidad and Tobago	A, B
Tunisia	C, E
Turkey	C, F
Turkmenistan	B, F
Uganda	G
Ukraine	C
United Arab Emirates	C, D, G
Uruguay	C, F, I, L
Uzbekistan	C, I
Venezuela	A, B, H
Wales	A, C, H
Western Samoa	H
Yemen, Rep. of	A, D, G
Zambia	C, D, G
Zimbabwe	D, G

Figure 12.13 Alphabetical list of countries and what plug type they use.

lamps, wattage, voltage, and amps, now we need to figure out how to plug in this stuff. The AWG, or American wire gauge, is a standardized way of measuring wire and determining how much electricity it can carry before burning. The following lists the most common wire gauges used in the theater. When a zero specifies the gauge, it is pronounced "aught." For example, the first line in the chart would be "four aught."

AWG	MAX AMPS AT 120 V
0000 (4/0)	400
00 (2/0)	200
0	175
1	150
2	125
4	100
6	80
8	50
10	30
12	20

FIXTURES

Now that we have laid the groundwork with all this background information, we can move on to lighting fixtures (Figure 12.14). Let's do just one more thing first, but don't worry, it will be much easier than electricity was. Let's talk about the basic parts of a fixture so that we can reference them throughout the next section of this chapter (Figure 12.15). At the front of the fixture is an accessory holder. Directly behind that there may be a lens. Similar to the lens on a camera, the lens on a fixture helps to focus the light coming out. Each style of lens is a little different, designed to produce a different kind of light beam, and some fixtures don't even have them. The main body of the fixture is next. It may be completely open and be the only way the light gets shaped as it moves from the lamp out the front opening. Or, it may have additional lenses or shutters to help shape the beam. On the outside, the middle of the fixture has mounting hardware attached, either a yoke for hanging or a

trunnion for sitting on the floor. This is the place in the fixture where most of the locking bolts exist, which you need when you focus. Focus is the process of aiming the lights to the place the designer wants. This can include a number of different adjustments, depending on the type of light involved.

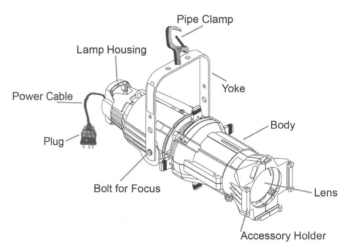

■ **Figure 12.15** Diagram showing fixture parts.

■ **Figure 12.14** Lighting load-in.

If there is a yoke, it will have a pipe clamp bolted on that allows you to hang the fixture on a pipe. Continuing toward the back of the fixture is the lamp housing. The light bulb, or lamp as it is called in the theater, lives here, and so does the socket for the lamp. At the very back is the possibility of a reflector. Again, shapes change, but the premise is the same. The reflector bounces the light from the lamp around, gaining brightness, until it comes out the front of the fixture. On the outside is a power cable with a plug on it.

There are some basic categories of fixtures based on their individual qualities. I do have to put in one more bit of techno-speak before we go on. When you are looking at the product specification sheets supplied by manufacturers about their fixtures, you'll see the phrases *beam angle*, *field angle*, and *beam spread*. If this sounds confusing, don't worry, it is actually pretty simple, and they are all measured in degrees. First, the easiest part: Field angle and beam spread are the same thing. Every light fixture has a beam of light that comes from it. That is the point after all. The light is shaped as it comes out the front of the fixture. These terms are based on a percentage of the maximum intensity of the beam at its center. The beam angle, where you get the best quality of light, is measured at a level of 50 percent of the maximum intensity of the beam. The beam spread (wider than the beam angle) is measured where you get down to 10 percent of the maximum intensity of the beam. In the case of an Altman Lighting 20-degree Shakespeare®, the beam angle is 13 degrees, while the beam spread is considered to be 20 degrees. Keep in mind that there is usually some light beyond the measured beam spread (that last 10 percent). The quality of the remaining light is unpredictable at best, so just ignore it for now.

Now, back to lighting fixtures. The beam projector is still one of my favorite fixtures, even though it is not in common use today (Figure 12.16). A beam projector is an open-face fixture that produces a narrow beam of light. It does this through the use of two reflectors. The primary reflector is the back of the actual fixture and is a somewhat flattened parabolic reflector. In front of the lamp is a secondary reflector that is spherical. The spherical reflector reflects light from the lamp toward the parabolic reflector in the back. The parabolic reflector organizes the light into nearly parallel beams. The result is an intense shaft of light. Beam projectors have a

■ **Figure 12.16** Beam projector.

history of creating a "fingers of God" effect. They were made in two sizes, both of which are defined by the size of the front opening. Beam projectors have fallen out of use today, but, if you ever get the opportunity to try them out, I highly recommend it!

The scoop light is our next fixture and is probably familiar to most of you. Scoops are elliptical reflector floodlights (ERFs), meaning they have no lens (Figure 12.17). The housing for the light has an ellipsoidal shape. There is no reflector in a scoop; however, the inside of the housing is usually painted white to help reflect the light forward. The lamp enters the scoop at the narrow end of the ellipsoidal. To focus the scoop, you have only two options: You can pan or tilt the entire scoop. The quality of the light from a scoop is very soft and gentle, creating an even wash. It has often been used as a work light. Scoops come in a number of different sizes, based on the size of the open end and ranging from 10 to 18 inches.

The Fresnel is a soft-edge light (Figure 12.18). It can create an even wash or a small, focused spot. The Fresnel has a spherical reflector in the back that is attached to a slide in the bottom of the fixture. Also attached to the slide, in front of the reflector, are the socket and lamp. This slide is what allows the Fresnel to be focused. By adjusting the slide forward and back, you change the relationship of the reflector and lamp to the lens. When the lamp is toward the front and closer to the lens, the light output will be a spot; further away from the lens,

■ **Figure 12.17** Scoop.

■ **Figure 12.18** Fresnel.

the light will grow larger. And, speaking of the lens, the Fresnel lens is what makes this fixture special (Figure 12.19). A French physicist by the name of Augustin-Jean Fresnel invented the lens that still carries his name. He was trying to make a thinner lens that would be lighter and less expensive. He divided the lens into a series of concentric circles that step in toward each other. Take a look at Figure 12.19. This design achieved his purpose, making the lens much lighter while the light output was not sacrificed. The original use for this lens was in lighthouses, and they are still used for that purpose. Fresnels come in a wide range of sizes, from as small as 3 inches all the way to 24 inches!

Our next fixture is the ellipsoidal reflector spotlight (ERS). Its official name tells you a bit about it. For starters, it has an ellipsoidal reflector. This fixture also has something new for us to talk about. It has two lenses. Yes, two lenses! This means you can change the edge beam from sharp to blurry by changing the distance between the two lenses. This feature makes this fixture one of the most flexible in our inventories. It is usually the most-used fixture in all of the theatre.

Ellipsoidals, for short, come in a range of focal lengths, which means the width of the beam at a certain distance from the light. There are also ellipsoidal zooms that have an adjustable range. There are differences between manufacturers and between newer and older styles. But the basic idea and workings of the ellipsoidal remain the

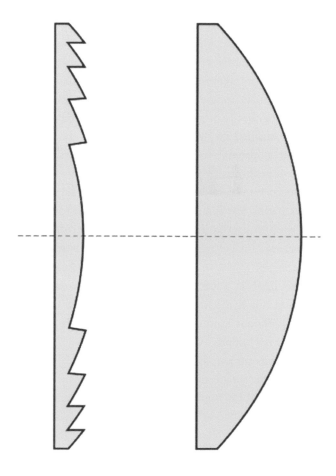

Fresnel Lens   Standard Lens

■ **Figure 12.19** Fresnel lens diagram.

■ **Figure 12.20** Old and new style ellipsoidals.

same. Ellipsoidals are also capable of projecting various designs, known as *templates* or *gobos*. We talk about these later in the chapter, but just remember this great option when you use them. Yet another feature that makes the ellipsoidal unique is that it has shutters. **Shutters** are shaped pieces of metal inside the ellipsoidal with a handle attached on the outside. By pushing the shutter into the ellipsoidal, you can mask a portion of the light that comes through the lens (Figure 12.20). This allows you to frame objects or people. Newer ellipsoidals have a lens barrel that is interchangeable and that rotates so that shutters can be aligned to an object as needed. This is awesome for getting the perfect shutter cut at a truly weird angle.

The PAR is a fixture named for its type of lamp. Actually, this is the first fixture we've discussed that has a very different kind of lamp. The PAR fixture takes a PAR lamp. Sounds obvious, but the question is why? **PAR** stands for parabolic aluminized reflector. The lamp and the reflector are sealed together with a lens. Think of some styles of car headlights—they work the same way.

This "combination" lamp is then inserted into the back of a tube, or "can," which can help shape the beam of light (Figure 12.21). The lamps come in a variety of configurations with different lenses, from very narrow to very wide, meaning that simply by changing the lamp you can get a variety of beam sizes from the same fixture. Most PAR beams produce an oval shape. This oval can

be rotated to change the direction of each beam's axis by physically rotating the lamp. This makes them very useful for creating alleys of light on stage. These fixtures have been around for a long time but are still used today. Newer varieties separate the lamp from the lens, making it very similar to the other fixtures we discussed so far and modern car headlights that did the same thing. The optics on these newer fixtures are much more efficient than their older cousins, and, by having to keep only thin lenses around, they save you a ton of space. It's also way more energy efficient and a better quality of light!

It used to be that, if you wanted to light a large area like a cyc, you'd have to use a whole bunch of fixtures and a boatload of cables. Well, someone clever figured out that, if you take several fixtures and build them together into one fixture, you could save a lot of time and cost in your setup. This led initially to fixtures called *far cycs*, but they were huge and very bulky. From this idea, the **strip light** was invented. Think of one long fixture with several lamps in it (Figure 12.22). Most strip lights come with one, two, three, or four separate circuits so you can have multiple colors in the same fixture. They can be hung with clamps on a pipe over the stage or put on the floor using **trunnions**. Strip lights are great for creating large swaths of color and are also wonderful for color mixing. Since it's one fixture with several lamps, you know they're all going to be on the same angle, making your focus way faster, too! You have many lamp options here, too.

■ **Figure 12.21** Old and new PAR cans.

Depending on what strip lights you choose, they could vary from 20 watts per lamp up to 2000 watts per lamp.

Now that we've gone through the bulk of the conventional fixtures, are you ready to have some real fun? Over the years folks have said, "Wouldn't it be cool if I could only …?" To answer this question, manufacturers have come up with a variety of specialty fixtures. We discuss some of them next to get your creativity flowing. But don't get me wrong. The lights we just talked about are the workhorses of the theater.

■ **Figure 12.22** Old and new strip lights.

Ultra violet lights get a lot of use in the theatre. They make things glow. You've probably seen these in use many times. UV gives a special purplish glow to white gloves or other garments on what looks like a dark stage. It can also add an extra punch to a lit stage where costumes or set pieces have been treated with UV-sensitive paints or dyes. There is even special UV makeup. If you've ever seen any of the Blue Man Group© shows or commercials, you know what I mean. *Very* cool effects! UV fixtures come in a wide variety of sizes and shapes to provide many different uses. Remember the UV part of the light is the lamp, not the fixture. UV fixtures can be a small or large fluorescent or a high-intensity discharge type to be used in even larger areas. They are made in flood styles and spot styles. UV ellipsoidals can do all of the things a regular ellipsoidal can do but with the added benefit of also being UV. Fresnels can be made as UV fixtures as well, giving you a variable-size beam of light from one specialty fixture. I've even seen follow spots with UV filters on them in place of a UV lamp, so you can move the effect from place to place on the stage.

Fluorescent lights, when they're not being UV lights, are more versatile than many people give them credit for. They can be used to fill in tight areas on a set, such as behind windows and doors or maybe on Juliet's famous balcony. Modern fluorescents can also be dimmed for added flexibility. Fluorescent lamps can have different color temperatures to make the light cooler or warmer. They can also be gelled to make them even more variable.

LED fixtures have become the wave of the future. Although LED (light-emitting diode) technology has been around since the early 20th century, building them reliably into theatrical fixtures is fairly recent. These fixtures come in a single color or multiple colors. The most common type today is the three-color fixture. The three colors are—and this should be familiar—red, green, and blue. If you recall the color wheel we discussed earlier, you can mix these three colors and get pretty much any color. The math tells us that you can get approximately 16.7 million colors. Some companies are also adding white or amber for more mixing options and so you can alter the color temperature.

> So much modern scenery is about how you light it. Many plays are written with 20–40 scenes and you really can't make all those places with hard physical scenery so you're dependent upon creating a lot of those places with light and color and shapes.
> —Derek McLane,
> **American scenic designer**

LED fixtures come in a variety of sizes and shapes—from small fixtures, to hideaway fixtures in very tight places, to strip-light versions that are incredible for washing a cyc in saturated color (Figures 12.23–12.28). Most companies are building them into automated fixtures. Some are even flexible so you can go around curves on a set. Some can be set up to run on their own, but most are controlled through your light board. Possibly one of the coolest things about LED fixtures is that they are very low wattage, which means that you can put a lot onto one electrical circuit. They operate at a low temperature because of the wattage, making them perfect for use where heat may be a problem for people, scenery, or soft goods. LEDs don't eat up dimmers, since all the dimming is achieved by digital control. The only drawbacks, sort of, are that they are still fairly expensive and they tend to degrade toward the end of their life—

ten years. However, what they save in electricity and dimmers can make up for that on a 50,000-hour lamp!

LED fixtures are shown in Figures 12.23 and 12.27 with their comparable incandescent fixtures. As always, keep in mind that the fixture and the light source are two separate items. When choosing a lighting unit, you now have many more options than ever before.

Another versatile and fun fixture is the automated or moving light. These fixtures also come in a wide variety of styles for particular purposes. The two main types are spot versus wash fixtures. This means pretty much what it sounds like and what we've learned on other fixtures. Spot fixtures are focusable fixtures that can produce a hard-edge beam like an ellipsoidal, while the wash fixture is designed to cover an area in a soft-edge beam more like a Fresnel (Figures 12.30–12.37). If you've ever been to a rock concert, you've certainly seen these in use, and they are being used more and more in traditional theatre productions. The main differences in these fixtures are in their features, as everything is accessed via digital multiplex (DMX). They can be as simple as an ellipsoidal or PAR mounted into a moving yoke, like City Theatrical's **Auto Yoke®** (Figure 12.38), or they can have so many bells and whistles that it would make your head (and the light) spin.

Some of the fixtures have color mixing built in, so you can achieve virtually any color (similar to LEDs), as well as a bunch of gobos to project different patterns. You can even spin the gobos for some great motion effects. All the fixtures pan and tilt remotely. They can be programmed to do all sorts of movements. Some designers keep them moving almost all the time (usually with a whole bunch of haze in the air so the audience can see the light beams), while others use them to create specific looks on the stage. Think of it this way. Scene 1 takes place in a castle, so you use the gobos in the fixture to create the look of stone on the stage floor and maybe the walls as well. Then, you go to Scene 2, which takes place out in the forest. Simple. You take the next cue, and the fixtures readjust focus and change their beam size and color. The gobos change to a leaf pattern, slightly out of focus, and there you are in the middle of the forest. The possibilities are absolutely endless.

■ **Figure 12.23** Robert Juliat Fresnel (left) and Robert Juliat LED Fresnel (right).

■ **Figure 12.24** Altman Spectra (LED) PAR.

■ **Figure 12.25** Robert Juliat Plano-Convex wash fixture.

■ **Figure 12.26** Robert Juliat profile fixtures.

Figure 12.28 ETC ×7 LED strip light.

Figure 12.27 Robert Juliat cyc light (top); Altman's Spectra (LED) cyc (bottom).

Figure 12.29 *Machinal*, James Madison University, October 2014.

■ **Figure 12.30** Altman's AltSpot follow spot.

■ **Figure 12.31** Strong's Super Trouper follow spot.

■ **Figure 12.32** Lycian's M2 follow spot.

■ **Figure 12.33** Lycian's 1275 follow spot.

■ **Figure 12.34** Robert Juliat's Super Korrigan follow spot.

■ **Figure 12.35** Martin MAC 2000® wash moving light.

■ **Figure 12.36** Robe Robin 1200 LED wash moving light.

■ **Figure 12.37** Martin MAC 2000® profile moving light.

■ **Figure 12.38** City Theatrical's Auto Yoke.

DIMMERS

Now that we have covered the basics of lighting fixtures, we have to talk about what you plug those fixtures into. I am talking about dimmers, used in conjunction with non-LED fixtures. Dimmers come in almost as many configurations as light fixtures. Their essential function is to raise and lower the brightness level of a fixture. Modern-day dimmers are rated by their capacity. This capacity can range from 600 watts to 12,000 watts, but the most common ones you find in a theater are 1200 and 2400 watts. The number of dimmers in the system can be as few as one or as many as several hundred, up to well over 1000.

Dimmers, like light fixtures, have a history. The first dimmers were mechanical devices that were lowered in front of candles to dim them. By 1900, saltwater dimmers had been developed. These worked by increasing or decreasing the salinity in a vat of water to increase or decrease the conductivity and thereby raise or lower the light level. Be glad you don't have to do this anymore. It was inexact and could be pretty messy, not to mention the whole water and electricity not mixing thing. Then, in about 1910, resistance dimmers were developed. They were huge Frankenstein-looking things that worked by

> It's exciting that the computer age is allowing us to realize the kind of movement in light and the flexibility we want to achieve. We can make light move in ways we never could before. And we haven't even begun to tap what computers can do.
>
> **—Tharon Musser,**
> **American lighting designer**

changing the resistance on the wires using a big lever. Dimmers today are tiny in size by comparison and huge in capacity.

The year 1933 was a big year for dimming. It saw the advent of the autotransformer. Autotransformer dimmers, which really aren't much different (in concept, anyway) from the wall dimmer you may have at home that works by turning a knob, came in different capacities and configurations. When you move the handle on an autotransformer, inside it moves a brush along a coil, varying the amount of electricity getting through to the lamp. On a larger system, which could be 24–30 dimmers, you sometimes needed several people to run a show and move all the handles (Figure 12.39). There are still some places today that are using autotransformers. They are a dimmer and controller wrapped up in one and they're pretty tough to kill.

> I want my students to see more deeply. The gear doesn't matter so much, all that is changing so fast anyway. I want them to ask why, to see the underlying power dynamics, to consider the colors that are under the main color. After that, to begin to see lighting design in relationship to, in dialog with, the entire world of visual art, so that they realize that it is not about a "method," but a poetic visual language that has its own potential for expression.
>
> **—Clifton Taylor,**
> **American lighting designer**

Figure 12.39 Very scary old circuit panel.

Figure 12.40 ETC Sensor® installation dimmer rack.

In 1958, we got the SCR, or silicon controlled rectifier. This innovation allowed manufacturers to make things much smaller and lighter by comparison. The big difference is that these dimmers now required a separate controller. We talk about controllers soon. SCR is basically the same technology used today. Today's dimmers have gotten even smaller and much cleverer. Actually, the dimmer itself isn't necessarily all that smart. It is the way it is controlled. The newer dimmer racks have electronics installed in them that can do all sorts of things, from turning on an individual dimmer to giving you readings on exactly how many volts are coming into it and exactly how much is going out, and so on (Figure 12.40). The long and the short of it is that, when you ask the dimmer to raise the brightness of the light, it should do it, no matter what type of dimmer it is.

CONTROL

Controlling dimmers has changed over the years. The concept, however, has always been the same. The first dimmers were manual, meaning that you had to raise and lower a direct control to raise and lower the brightness of a light. Eventually, that handle evolved into a signal cable and a separate indirect controller. These controllers used a low-voltage DC electrical signal to tell the SCRs what to do (Figure 12.41). The DC signal was raised and lowered by moving a potentiometer (pot). Sometimes, these were moved in a circle; sometimes, they were moved straight up or down. Think about the dimmers in your home attached to the wall. (These are direct control.) Same thing! With the straight ones, and these are still used today, you would literally raise and lower the handle to raise and lower the level on the light. In the 1970s, the DC signal was changed to a multiplexed signal called AMX, or analog multiplex. This was essentially a computer signal. Modern controllers use DMX, or digital multiplex. While DMX is the standard control signal today, some manufacturers have started using Ethernet (both wired and wireless) for controlling dimmers and lights.

While we were getting upgrades in control signals, the complexity of the lighting controllers and what they could do grew by leaps and bounds. Early control boards could control only the pots. Today, controllers are computers capable of programming anything you can

■ **Figure 12.41** ETC Eos® lighting console.

■ **Figure 12.42** Avolites Pearl 2010 moving light controller.

think of creating. Newer controllers have really opened up possibilities for designers, including controllers that are software able to run on a laptop (Figures 12.42–12.44). Ideas that designers could only imagine before can now be accomplished with the push of a button. Keep in mind that a whole lot of programming needs to happen first, though. There are technicians who specialize in certain types of controllers, since the complexity of each can be so great.

EXPENDABLES

Even the best set up theater needs to replenish its supply of gel and other items on a regular basis. These items are officially called *expendables*. Expendables are any of the items that are used for one show, then discarded—hence the name. This can include gel, gobos, tapes, tie line, batteries, and so on. Some theaters have a specific supply house they work with to order expendables or they may purchase them from a lighting rental shop when they get rental equipment for the next show.

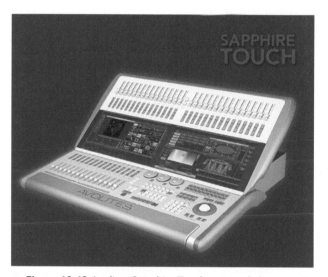

■ **Figure 12.43** Avolites Sapphire Touch moving light controller.

> It's been very exciting to see that happen. It's exciting to see that lighting is becoming known as an art form and not just a director saying to an electrician, "Can I have some moonlight through that window?"
> —**Tharon Musser, American lighting designer**

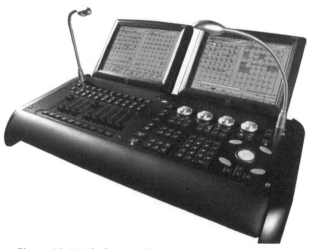

■ **Figure 12.44** Whole Hog II® moving lighting console.

ACCESSORIES

We have discussed all sorts of fixtures, both old and new. Designers have a tendency to first create their designs in their imaginations. Thankfully, many manufacturers are out there who make a good living from translating those visions onto the stage. As Gary Fails of City Theatrical says, "It's all about the accessories."

Each of the following accessories is great in its own right. There may be other ways of accomplishing the effect, usually higher-end ways, but sometimes the simpler ways are best. Let's start small. Many products made to add onto or into light fixtures help us do fun things with the light beam. First is the color frame. Simply put, this is a metal or cardboard frame that holds gel in place. It goes into the accessory slot on the front of a fixture. The next is a donut, a piece of metal the same size as a color frame with a hole. It is designed to help a sharp ellipsoidal with a template look even sharper. The top hat, or high hat, gets its name because it looks like an old-fashioned gentleman's top hat, with the exception of being open at the top. It helps reduce flare and cut out some of the excess light, such as the light beyond the beam spread.

The **Beam Bender**® and the **Image Multiplexer**® are pretty cool tools. The Beam Bender goes in front of a fixture and has an adjustable mirror on it. The idea is to light some of those hard-to-reach spots by focusing the light into the mirror. The mirror then bounces the light

■ **Figure 12.45** City Theatrical's VSFX3 effects projector.

out at a 90-degree angle, making it seem like you can light around corners! The Image Multiplexer goes in the accessory slot of an ellipsoidal. It splits the light beam into several beams, sort of like a kaleidoscope. Just add a gobo to the multiplexer and see what happens!

Barn doors go in front of soft-edge fixtures, such as Fresnels or PARs, to allow you to block parts of the light beam. This works great when you have a Fresnel or a PAR that is spilling onto a border and you want to block a little of the light without having to lose what that light is doing elsewhere on stage. This works sort of like an ellipsoidal shutter. It's not as crisp as a shutter, but it works in a pinch.

There is an accessory slot in ellipsoidals, also known as the *drop-in slot*, right near the framing shutters, that will accept a wide variety of things. The mulitplexer we just talked about uses this same slot. Fixtures used to have an iris installed, but most of the ones made today do not. You can use a drop-in iris, either manual or mechanical, to make the projected beam of light smaller while still keeping it round. Special gobo holders fit in the drop-in slot to allow you to use glass gobos instead of metal ones. To have even more fun and create basic moving images, you can use a gobo rotator that spins one or more gobos around at variable speeds. Rotators are, of course, DMX controlled!

A step up from the drop-in slot gobo holder is Rosco's iPro Image Projector®. This accessory allows you to project photographic images that have been printed on acetate. This is awesome for projecting realistic images such as an actual forest or a picture of someone or, well, pretty much anything. GAM Products makes a really cool device for the drop-in slot called the Film/FX®. With this, you can project moving images such as clouds floating through the sky. As you can see, these accessories really open up options for lighting design and effects.

For the most part, we have talked about hanging lighting fixtures on pipes. While this is the typical situation, you didn't think I'd leave it at that, did you? There are many options for mounting a fixture. You can use extenders that hang a fixture lower or higher than a regular pipe clamp to give you maximum flexibility in making the fixture hang just where you need it to be. These are also good for those times when the set is high, and you need to get above part of it with a fixture. Another mounting option for fixtures is the pipe and

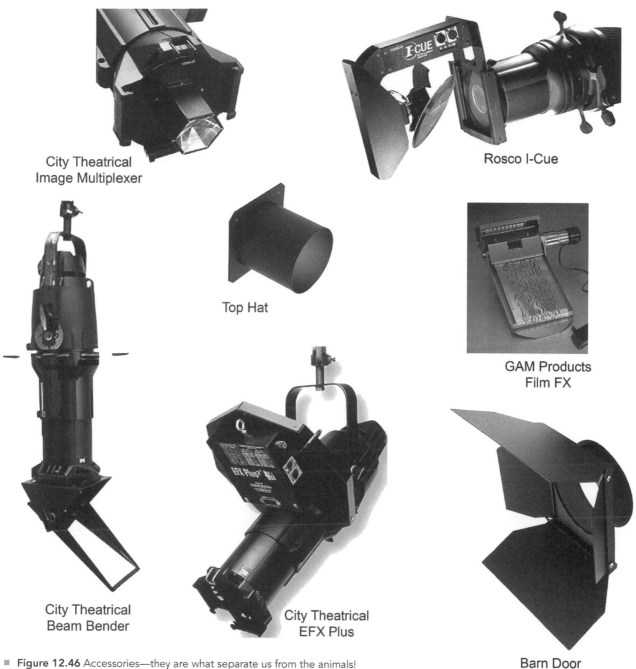

City Theatrical
Image Multiplexer

Rosco I-Cue

Top Hat

GAM Products
Film FX

City Theatrical
Beam Bender

City Theatrical
EFX Plus

Barn Door

■ **Figure 12.46** Accessories—they are what separate us from the animals!

base. While the pipes normally found in a theatre are hung horizontally, sometimes you need to go vertical. The way to do this is with a boom. Typically, you use a 25-pound or 50-pound base that is threaded to accept a pipe of whatever length you need. You can then hang a fixture anywhere along the height of the pipe. To keep the light consistent with other lights hung on regular pipes, you can use a sidearm. This is a small piece of pipe with a C-clamp. This gets used a lot for dance, where you want a lot of sidelight at several heights. It is also great for putting lights out in the auditorium or somewhere that has no hanging position already. Some bases even have wheels on them, so they can be moved around during a performance. Take it one step further. Use two booms with a horizontal pipe between them. Now you've made a goal post! The possibilities are endless. You can mount a light anywhere you can safely figure out how to hold it in place!

PAPERWORK

The light plot, as you know from Chapter 5, shows all the fixtures in their exact locations. This must include the front of house (FOH) hanging positions (Figure 12.48). Front of house means anything downstage of the proscenium or over the audience. Since the FOH is usually quite large, it is common practice to compress the space between the FOH hanging positions, as well as between the pipes and the proscenium. This is done to help all the pipes fit onto one page of drafting! If the FOH is extensive, it can be moved to its own page of drafting.

The light plot shows more than just the lighting fixtures (Figure 12.49). *It shows the centerline—in case I forgot to mention how important that is!* The hanging positions, lighting equipment—each individual fixture—and any additional accessories are shown. The symbols used to represent the fixtures are approximately the correct shape and size, in the scale of the drawing, of the real fixtures. This is very important. If you use a symbol that is 6 inches to represent a fixture that is 18 inches, chances are your lights won't actually fit in the air when they are being hung. The standard default spacing for fixtures is 1 foot 6 inches, or 18 inches. This is commonly used and based on fixture sizing and the ability for the electrician to get his or her hands in between everything to focus and tighten the lights. If larger fixtures are used, you will obviously need more room.

The light plot needs to have a key to all the symbols you use so that everyone can understand what each symbol actually means. Without the key, the light plot is useless to everyone except the person who created it. Dimensions need to be on the light plot as well. Critical dimensions include spacing between units, as I already mentioned, but also dimensions to locate all the pipes, not only US to DS and SL to SR, but also in terms of height. Take a look at Figures 12.47 and 12.48 for more details.

Once the lighting designer gets into the theatre, he or she and the assistants make magic sheets (Figures 12.49 through 12.51). They are a quick reference for the design team to be able to find the channel number quickly and easily when they want to use that light in a cue. A cheat sheet is usually a compressed number list, and a magic sheet is more of a visual reference.

The more complex a design, the more drawings will be needed to get all the details across to the electrician. Often, several drawings are needed to fully indicate the placement of all the built-in fixtures. Figure 12.52 should give you an idea of this.

> If I'm a good designer today it's because I learned so much from Tharon—I always say I went to Musser U.
>
> **—Ken Billington,**
> **American lighting designer**

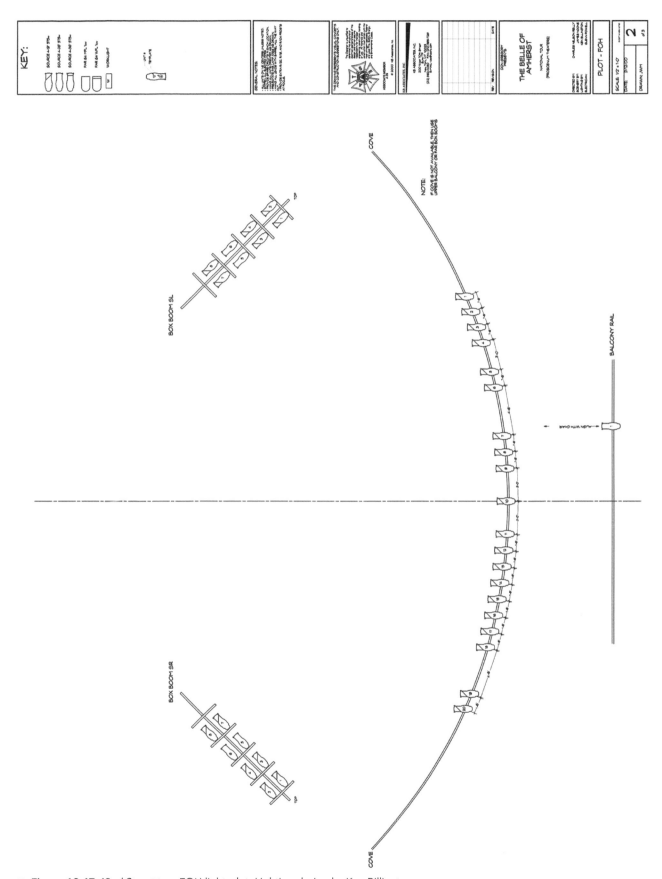

■ **Figure 12.47** *42nd Street* tour FOH light plot. Lighting design by Ken Billington.

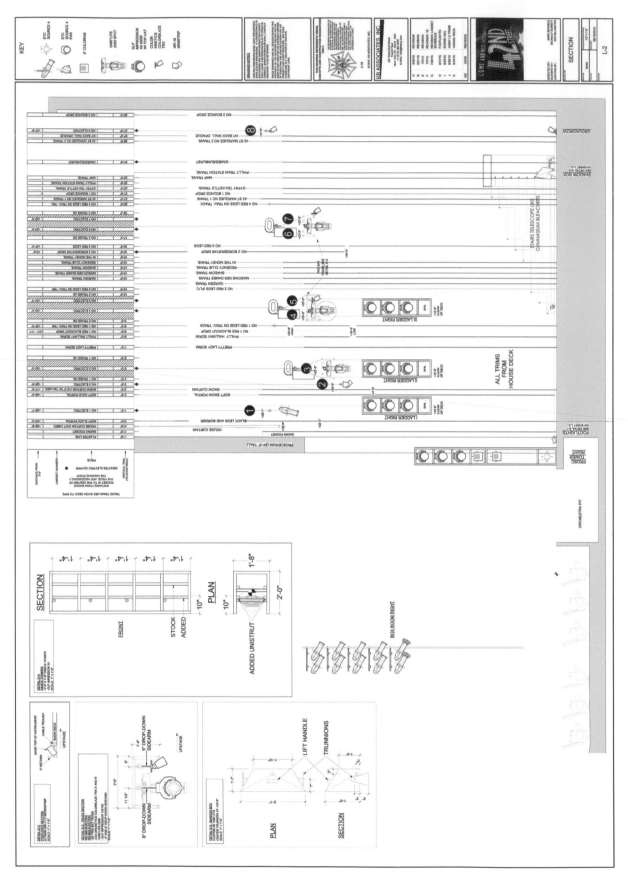

■ **Figure 12.48** *42nd Street* tour lighting section. Lighting design by Ken Billington.

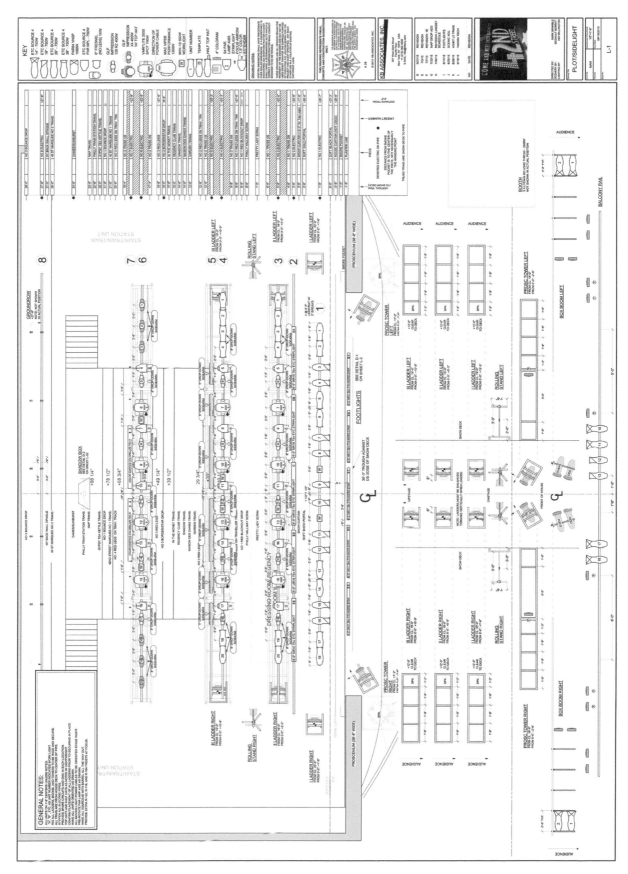

■ **Figure 12.49** *42nd Street* tour light plot. Lighting design by Ken Billington.

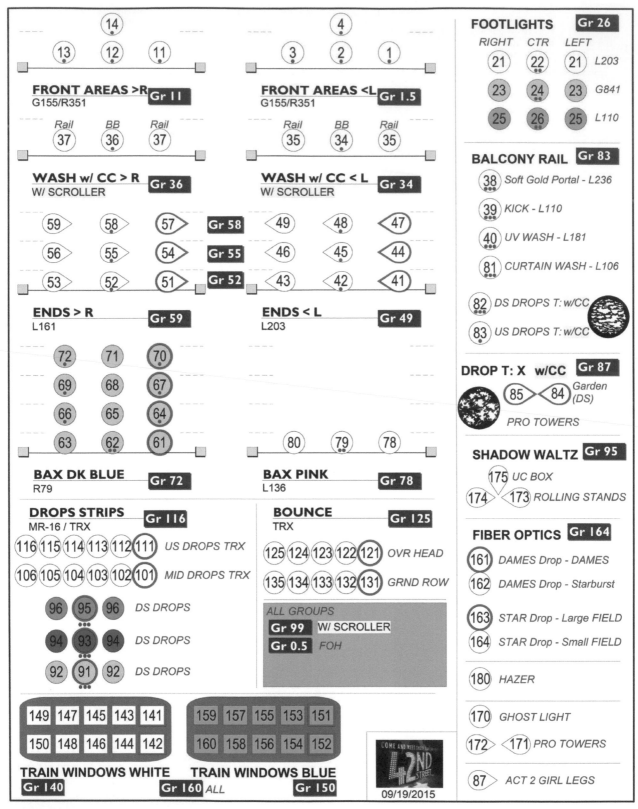

■ **Figure 12.50** *42nd Street* tour lighting magic sheet.

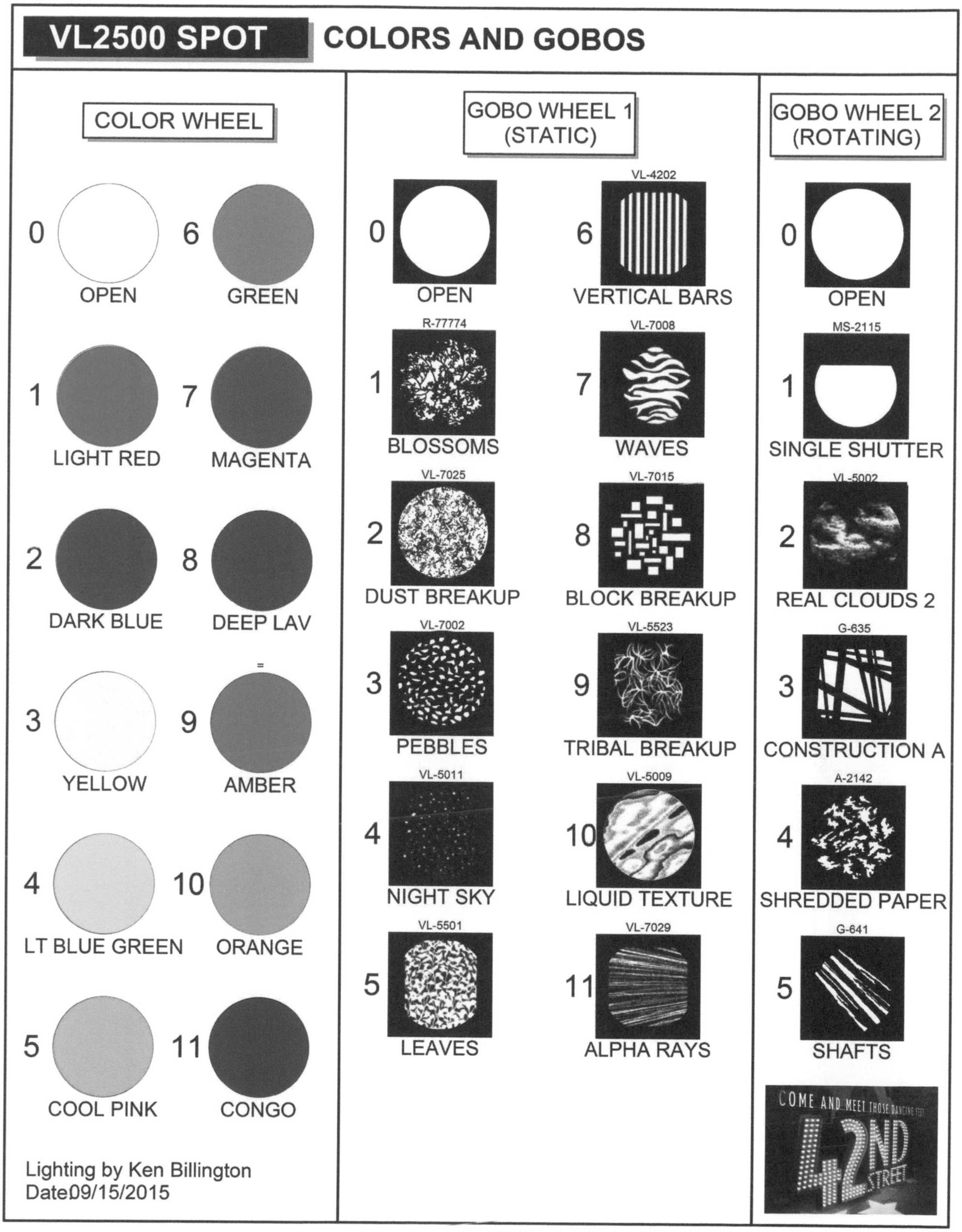

VL2500 SPOT COLORS AND GOBOS

COLOR WHEEL

0 OPEN
6 GREEN
1 LIGHT RED
7 MAGENTA
2 DARK BLUE
8 DEEP LAV
3 YELLOW
9 AMBER
4 LT BLUE GREEN
10 ORANGE
5 COOL PINK
11 CONGO

Lighting by Ken Billington
Date09/15/2015

GOBO WHEEL 1 (STATIC)

0 OPEN
6 VL-4202 VERTICAL BARS
1 R-77774 BLOSSOMS
7 VL-7008 WAVES
2 VL-7025 DUST BREAKUP
8 VL-7015 BLOCK BREAKUP
3 VL-7002 PEBBLES
9 VL-5523 TRIBAL BREAKUP
4 VL-5011 NIGHT SKY
10 VL-5009 LIQUID TEXTURE
5 VL-5501 LEAVES
11 VL-7029 ALPHA RAYS

GOBO WHEEL 2 (ROTATING)

0 OPEN
1 MS-2115 SINGLE SHUTTER
2 VL-5002 REAL CLOUDS 2
3 G-635 CONSTRUCTION A
4 A-2142 SHREDDED PAPER
5 G-641 SHAFTS

COME AND MEET THOSE DANCING FEET
42ND STREET

■ **Figure 12.51** *42nd Street* tour moving light magic sheet.

PAULUHN "NHID" HIGH
PRESSURE SODIUM LIGHT
[150 WATTS]
(SEE ATTACHED CUT SHEET)
MOUNTED ON 18" ARM
FOCUS: WALL WASH
CHANNEL: 283

PAN LIGHT SET PRACTICAL
(AS PER SET DESIGNER)
[CLEAR A-LAMP 100 WATTS]
CHANNEL: 282

PLAN VIEW OF SODIUM LIGHT

(a)

PAULUHN "723" INCANDESCENT
[100 WATTS]
WITH ALUMINUM GUARD,
CLEAR LAMP AND CLEAR
GLOBE
(SEE ATTACHED CUT SHEET)
MOUNTED DIRECTLY TO WALL
CHANNEL: 284

PLAN VIEW OF LAYOUT

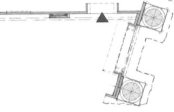

(b)

PAULUHN "NHID" MERCURY VAPOR
LIGHT [175 WATTS]
(SEE ATTACHED CUT SHEET)
MOUNTED ON 12" ARM
CHANNEL: 290

PAULUHN "NHID" HIGH PRESSURE
SODIUM LIGHT [250 WATTS]
(SEE ATTACHED CUT SHEET)
MOUNTED ON LEDGE
FOCUS: CAESAR BANNER
CHANNEL: 291

PANI P500 PARABOLIC SPOTLIGHT
[500 WATTS/24 VOLT]
(SEE ATTACHED CUT SHEET)
MOUNTED ON WINDOW LEDGE
FOCUS: CINNA SPECIAL (?)
CHANNEL: 289

ELEVATION

PLAN   BLIND WALL

PLAN VIEW OF LAYOUT

(c)

PANI P500 PARABOLIC SPOTLIGHT
[500 WATTS/24 VOLT]
(SEE ATTACHED CUT SHEET)
MOUNTED ON SET WALL FOR ACTOR USE
[VARIOUS FOCUS]
CHANNEL: 286

PAULUHN "723" INCANDESCENT [150 WATT]
WITH ALUMINUM GUARD, YELLOW LAMP
AND CLEAR GLOBE
(SEE ATTACHED CUT SHEET)
MOUNTED DIRECTLY TO WALL
CHANNEL: 285

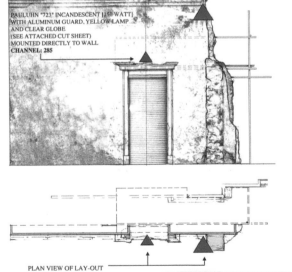

PLAN VIEW OF LAY-OUT

(d)

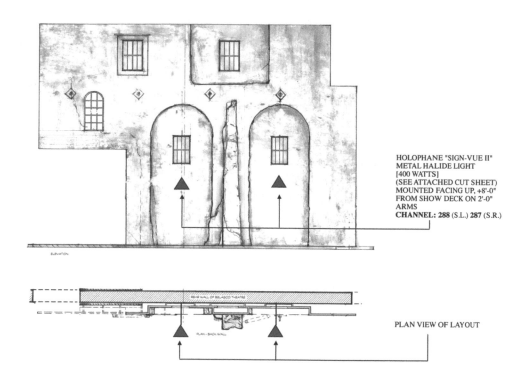

HOLOPHANE "SIGN-VUE II"
METAL HALIDE LIGHT
[400 WATTS]
(SEE ATTACHED CUT SHEET)
MOUNTED FACING UP, +8'-0"
FROM SHOW DECK ON 2'-0"
ARMS
CHANNEL: 288 (S.L.) **287** (S.R.)

PLAN VIEW OF LAYOUT

(e)

■ **Figure 12.52** *Julius Caesar* detail drawings.

EXERCISES

EXERCISE 1

Discuss the differences between beam angle, field angle, and beam spread.

EXERCISE 2

Describe the different accessories you can use with an ellipsoidal and what each does to affect the beam.

CHECK YOUR KNOWLEDGE

1. Explain the difference between single-phase and three-phase power.
2. Recite the West Virginia formula. Describe why it is so important.
3. Categorize the different types of lighting fixtures based on the qualities of light they produce.
4. Restate the options for dimming that have been available over the years. List why each advancement was better than the last.

- Accessory slot
- Alternating current
- Ampere
- AMX
- Autotransformer
- Auto Yoke®
- AWG
- Ballast
- Barn door
- Beam angle
- Beam projector
- Beam spread
- Booms
- Conventional lighting
- Dimmer
- Direct current
- DMX
- Donut
- Ellipsoidal reflector spotlight
- Filament
- Fluorescent
- Focus
- FOH
- Footlights
- Fresnel
- Fresnel lens
- Gel
- Gobo
- Ground
- Halogen light bulb
- Incandescent light bulb
- Intelligent lighting
- Kelvin
- Lamp
- Lamp housing
- LED
- Lens
- Lighting controller
- Limelight
- Magic sheet
- Pan
- PAR
- Pipe clamp
- Quartz envelope
- Reflector
- Scoop
- SCR
- Shutters
- Single phase
- Strip lights
- Three-phase
- Tilt
- Top hat
- Trunnion
- Voltage
- Wattage
- West Virginia
- Yoke

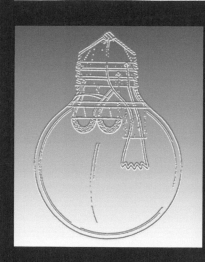

STUDY WORDS

Chapter 12

Is This Thing On?

Sound

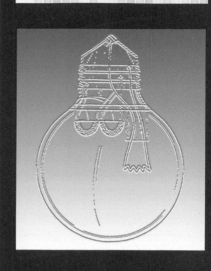

Students will acquire:

- An overview understanding of the major aspects, techniques, and directions in the area of sound.

- Fundamental, conceptual understanding of the expressive possibilities of theatre.

- A working knowledge of technologies and equipment applicable to the area of sound.

We dealt with the visual, let's move on to the aural! There are many aspects to what sound can do for a theatrical production. At the very least, sound can reinforce the spoken word. Sound can also add direction and effects, just to name a few. With the advent of digital technology, the impact sound can have has drastically improved. Sound can now follow a performer around the stage or around the entire theatre. Digital delays can ensure that audiences of 50–50,000 all hear the same thing at the same time.

Picture it. The audience is gathered, with a soft undertone of conversation and the rustle of programs. The house lights dim, and then it goes totally black and silent. The audience is now in that bridge between reality and theatre. Anything is possible now. In reality, it is not totally black of course. There are exit signs and light leaks from latecomers opening doors. Neither is it silent, because there are hundreds of fans cooling electronics used in all of the equipment needed to create the magic of modern theatre productions. Every department in the theater uses computers in some aspect. There are electronics in the consoles, the lights, the dimmers, the amplifiers, switches, and all manner of processors all over the theater.

With the advent of digital technologies, people's ears have grown more acute, or at least their hearing has. The general public is accustomed to hearing sound that is very crisp. Now, everyone wants to hear everything as if they are wearing digital headphones. So, basically, the audience's expectations have gone up—way up. This means the sound designer in today's theatre has ever-expanding components to their design. Depending on the production, the designer's responsibilities can range from the simple playback of sound effects, to reinforcing the performers' voices, to providing an intercom package, and far beyond!

These days, sound systems are very quiet and can do extremely complex things, primarily because they are digital and can therefore be controlled by computers. The possibilities are endless.

> For better or for worse, the story is the most important thing. It is up to me to enhance that, but never overshadow it.
>
> —Kai Harada,
> American sound designer

SOUND SYSTEMS

Let's talk about a basic sound system (Figure 13.1). This introduces you to each of the three main areas of the sound system: Input, output, and processing. The **inputs** in our sample system are microphones. The microphones are connected to inputs on the **mixing console**. The console provides pre-amplification, which amplifies the microphone-level signals to a consistent level, or line level. The signal then goes through equalization, which provides the means to control each microphone individually. Level control is the last step in the processing. The console takes the processed signal and routes it to the **amplifier**. The amplifier boosts the signal to an adequate level that drives the loudspeaker, which is an example of an **output**. The loudspeaker converts the signal into sound waves that people can hear.

There are other kinds of inputs than microphones, obviously. Here's a short list of the history of inputs:

- Phonograph
- Mag tape (8-track reel-to-reel cassette)
- Compact disc (CD)/compact disc recordable (CD-R)
- DAT (digital audio tape and associated formats)
- Minidisc
- Wav/MP3

Sound equipment has many variations and alternatives. Let me give you some ideas for each of our three categories. Inputs can be microphones, contact pickups, magnetic pickups, laser pickups, and optical pickups. **Signal processors** can be mixing consoles, equalizers, reverberation, delay, and amplifiers. Outputs can be loudspeakers (woofers, midrange, and tweeters), headphones, or infrared hearing assist devices. There are variations on all of these options. The last part of choosing equipment is to consider the right speakers, the

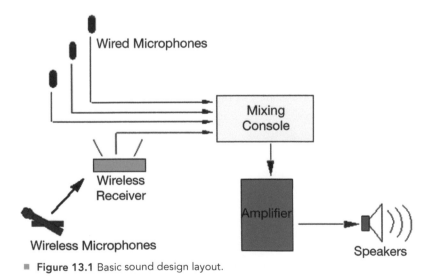

■ **Figure 13.1** Basic sound design layout.

right microphones, the right mixing system, and, most important, the positioning of all of these.

WORLD CLOCK

In the digital domain, all digital devices that deal with audio need to be referenced to the same world clock known as the master clock. The lighting, rigging, and projection departments may also have similar needs. Without this synchronization, the system can exhibit clicks or dropouts or does not function at all. It is an absolutely necessary piece of our digital world. The world clock can be generated from external devices or internally by one of the system devices. There has to be a master clock that is chosen to be used for your digital audio. Sometimes, the master audio clock will need to be slaved to a grand master clock—for example, when providing audio for video or, say, in a studio with multiple recording locations. A master clock is required to tie all the pieces together.

MICROPHONES

Let's start talking about specific equipment. We start with input devices. As I already mentioned, these include microphones and different kinds of pickups. A microphone is a device for converting acoustic sound into electrical energy. The two main types of microphones are dynamic and condenser. Dynamic microphones are good all-around microphones, which are both durable and affordable. Condenser microphones are more versatile,

more costly, and less durable. Condenser microphones are the choice for the theatre, given their range in quality for many purposes. Their durability issues, though, mean backups must be on hand.

There are differences between the various styles of microphones (Figure 13.2). The handheld microphone was once the most prominent design. It is still used today, although only for effect during obvious "performance" sequences within a play. Almost exclusively, the lavalier microphone has replaced the handheld. Lavaliers are very small and designed to be clipped to clothing or hung around the neck. As the need for sound design in the theatre has grown, lavaliers can now be attached in the hair or wigs, behind the ear, and even sewn into costumes—all to try to hide them while still maintaining adequate usage. The big concern with lavaliers is moisture, as perspiration can cause major issues with these tiny microphones. Hence, the need for backups!

Contact pickups are "like" microphones. They are attached to musical instruments and pick up sound through vibrations instead of from the air. Pressure-response microphones are usually mounted to a flat surface with the attached plate that increases gain.

The impedance of a microphone is the amount of resistance a microphone has to an audio signal. The lower the resistance, the fewer problems the microphone may have using longer cables and dealing with noise interference. Generally, low impedance means a better-quality microphone, which therefore becomes a perfect choice for the theatre.

■ **Figure 13.2** Different microphone styles and types.

Theatre Traditions: Cats

Cats, on the other hand, are thought to be lucky in the theatre, that is, as long as they are content to watch plays from the wings. A black cat is supposed to be an even more infallible source of good luck. It is said that, all around the theatre world, dark felines are treated with the greatest care and consideration. If a cat crosses the stage though, it is thought to be a terrible omen.

Gain in a sound system is what we usually think of as volume. However, it is a little different than volume. Gain is the amount of amplification available within the sound system. If set up properly, meaning the system, microphones, and speakers, gain can be maximized, which means you have the most latitude for volume and effects within your microphone. If you think about it, the number of inputs trying to simultaneously use the output divides the potential gain. So, it is important to have open and ready to use only the microphones and contacts that need to be used for a given portion of the show.

So, now that you have all this information, how do you choose a specific microphone?

Handheld microphones have much more latitude in gain than lavaliers. However, most shows want to use the much smaller microphone for aesthetic reasons. The standard is rapidly becoming the lavalier with a wireless transmitter. Sennheiser introduced the MKE-2 lavalier in the early 1980s as a major innovation. It is the smallest, highest-quality lavalier to date.

Most microphones used in theatre are wireless (Figure 13.3). That means they need a transmitter and a receiver. Wireless microphones operate on radio frequencies. Bluetooth also operates on radio frequencies, but is not used in theater owing to its low quality and short range. Most transmitters and receivers can be used on a range of frequencies, so that local issues, such as television, radio, and taxicabs, can be worked around. If you use a frequency that is already in use or very close to another that is in use, it can cause everything from a hiss, to just plain not working, to interference such as hearing the other frequency.

Lavalier microphones were developed for television news. Originally, they were hung around the newscaster's neck on some kind of a loop or clipped on their clothing (Figure 13.4). Lapel and chest mounts can be used as long as they are taped securely in place. If the microphone needs to be placed between the skin and the costume, the only tape option is to use medical tape. Medical tape has a secure adhesive while being gentle on the microphone

Figure 13.3 Sennheiser wireless microphones.

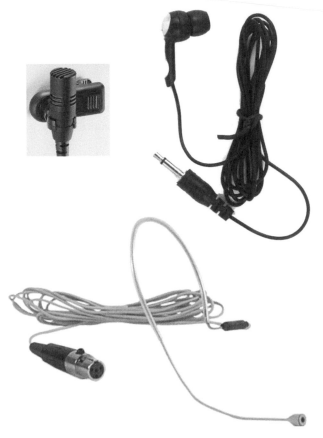

Figure 13.4 Lavalier mounting options.

and the skin of the actor. If the lavalier is to be worn behind the ear, an ear loop holds the microphone in place while a thin boom brings the microphone around and in front of the mouth. This is obvious to the audience, but, if the director doesn't mind, it is a good and easy placement.

The forehead lavalier is the best and most popular method in the theatre today. This allows the microphone to land in the middle of the forehead. It uses the natural resonance of the skull. There are a number of ways to secure this in place, depending on the use of hairpieces or hats. The worst thing for the lavalier is if an actor is wearing a hat; the second worst thing is the noise from moving lights. To use microphones on a group of people, such as a chorus, a technique known as area mic'ing is used. An array of floor or hanging microphones is used, and the sound operator raises and lowers the gain as needed. Since so much of theatre can take place on the centerline, it is good to use an odd number of array microphones. This gives you the most options in which microphones to use at what time during any given musical number.

> What I've discovered through the preview period is that, if the show is good enough on its own, it doesn't *have* to be loud all the time—kids will shut up if they're interested enough.
> —Kai Harada, American sound designer

SOUND BASICS

Let's talk for a moment about some basic sound ideas. Acoustics refers to the inherent sound qualities of a room in regard to the overall audio quality when no reinforcement is in use. Ambient noise is the sound in a room when there is no planned audio source. So far, so good? OK. Sound reinforcement happens for a variety of reasons. The auditorium where the show takes place may have bad acoustics, the audience may be too large to hear someone speaking on stage, or maybe the performer never learned to properly project his or her voice. Today's performers are not always trained to project their voices the way they once were. Proper voice support in the 21st century is augmented with vocal reinforcement. Gone are the days when musicals were done without any sound reinforcement. Vocal reinforcement is an everyday occurrence now. Every actor knows about body microphones. Orchestral reinforcement works on the basis that every part should be heard, and that everything should blend together and be cohesive. The sound operator and the orchestra working together can achieve this goal. Please, please, please, always remember louder *does not* mean better!

To start with, sound amplification is the conversion of analog signals to electrical energy, which can be as simple as air vibrating a microphone element. We are in the electronic stage of audio. This has been the basis for audio for decades. The signal can now be manipulated at the sound console by faders, capacitance combined with equalization, and so forth.

The manipulation of the digital signal is then done by a device known as a DSP, or digital signal processor. This DSP can be controlled by a purpose-built control surface that has knobs and faders that mimic the analog consoles—perhaps to satisfy the old guys who need to have something familiar to work with—but it still gives the operator in the back of the theater the ability to grab and fix a problem in an instant, which is essential to live performances. Anything can and will happen, and the sound person needs to have tools at their fingertips.

At this stage, we need to be aware of sample rates and bit depths. Think of sample rates as how many times an analog signal is sampled or a digital picture of the sound wave is taken. Bit depth defines the magnitude of the digital picture taken. Basically, though, the sample rate defines how accurate the picture is, especially in detail in higher frequencies. The higher the sample rate, the more the detail. The larger the bit depth, the greater the dynamic range, sometimes referred to as signal-to-noise ratio. Signal-to-noise is simply the difference between quiet and loud. If you put your ear near a speaker that is at full volume but there is no signal present, you will hear a background hiss. This is the noise. Now play Bruno Mars at full volume, and you have signal. The difference is your signal-to-noise ratio, or rather dynamic range. Once the signal is digitized, it can then be manipulated by a DSP.

Let's look at a basic concept in sound design to apply this new information to. What is the difference between amplification and reinforcement? This is a critical part of sound for the theatre, and we had better know the difference. *Amplification* means simply making it louder. That equals putting a huge stack of speakers on either side of the stage and cranking the volume. Reinforcement is much more subtle. Reinforcement is all about pushing and pulling the sound to create the right environment. Amplification is obvious; reinforcement should not be. Amplification is easy to notice; reinforcement—when well done—should be a seamless addition to the performance.

Another factor contributing to the differences in theatre sound for today's productions is ambient noise. There is a great deal more street noise in most areas than ever before. Most theaters are also air conditioned, which in turn adds another level of sound to the background. New technology in other design areas, such as lighting and rigging, brings noise from motors and fans. All these factors conspire against the actors, the audience, and the designers. These issues must be addressed for the sound design to properly do its job. Of course, the director can help through staging, and the conductor can help by controlling the musicians—but the sound department ultimately is responsible for the final way the show sounds.

RECORDED OR LIVE?

One question that sound designers must ask themselves constantly is: Should a cue be live or should it be recorded? Advantages to recorded cues include being cheaper, less space being needed, and being able to have sounds that would be impossible in real life.

- Cheaper: If you have a music cue, it almost always will cost less to use the recording of an existing work than to have a live musician perform the cue
- Less space needed: Items needed to produce sounds all require at least a little space, or in some cases a lot How much space would a car take up just to hear the sound of an engine revving up for one cue?
- Impossible sounds: I don't know about you, but I've never seen a dragon performing a live roar on stage

Recorded sounds have many advantages, but they have some disadvantages as well. The biggest is that all recorded sounds must come out of a speaker, which can separate the sounds from the live events on stage. Recorded sounds are less adaptable to the exact action happening during a performance on a particular evening; maybe the sound of a crash should be bigger and longer one night and smaller and quieter on another.

Live sounds produced during the performance are called live Foley in honor of Jack Foley (1891–1967), who was the leading pioneer in sound in the early film industry. Many plays use at least a few live sound effects, such as door slams, telephone rings as phone calls, and gun fire using blanks. When the director wants an actor to produce a specific sound, frequently the sound designer will be consulted to figure out what the actor should slam down on a desk or how to cut a melon to get the right sound.

Another type of performance has been on the rise recently: Live radio plays. In these performances, the stage is made to look like a radio station (frequently one from the past), and, while the actors perform their roles with a script and microphone in front of them, another person is the Foley artist who produces most of the sounds needed for the production. The Foley artist will be at a table (Figure 13.5) with sound props and microphones all set up to execute the required effect when needed.

Some of the sound effects that happen frequently include footsteps, doors opening and closing (Figure 13.6), and storm effects such as wind and thunder. Other times, Foley artists get to create more unusual effects such as death rays using a slinky or a bone snapping by breaking celery. The rest of the cast can get into the action as well; one famous effect is talking into a coffee mug to make it sound like you are on the other end of a phone.

The audience usually enjoys seeing how the sound is created as much as they enjoy watching the performers.

MIXING CONSOLES

Next, we talk about the mixing console, which is where the design is implemented. Levels are adjusted both for inputs and outputs. These can vary on a daily basis, as humidity can affect the tonal quality. All consoles work

Figure 13.5 Foley table set up and ready for the show to begin.

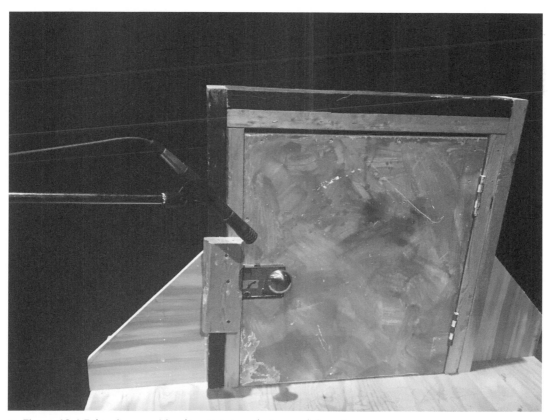

Figure 13.6 Foley door used for door opening, closing, and slamming.

■ **Figure 13.7** Analog console.

on the same principle. They take inputs, process the signal, and transfer the audio to the outputs. It sounds simple, but there are still many variations that can happen. Consoles allow for only a certain number of inputs and outputs. The individual console also limits the types of adjustments you can make to the audio signal. These combinations of variations are what determine the right console for a show.

Analog consoles are generally used today for smaller-budget shows (Figure 13.7). As they are the "older" style now, they are generally simpler to operate and less expensive to rent. These boards are large, owing to their technology. They are also simpler inside because they don't need all the digital processing and conversions. To operate the analog console, you move the faders up and down, as well as rotate the dials. The drawback is that there is generally no onboard equalizer, delay, or any other effects. This means, if you want them, they cost additional money, and you have to find a place to put them.

Digital consoles are the newest technology, and they are continuing to develop (Figure 13.8). Overall, digital consoles have more flexibility and are smaller physically, options are limitless, bandwidth is more than double, and all the effects are on board. Other benefits are that the amount of outboard gear is cut down, and there is never a need to repatch cables due to a lack of inputs or outputs.

With more control comes a price, in a way. How many faders can you move simultaneously? *Relative mixing* is a term that means individual faders are proportionally controlled by a master fader. That means you move one master fader, and all other faders associated with it will move proportionally as well.

The next step is computerized mixing on a digital console. Similar to a lighting controller, this type of digital console can record scenes or cues with all the nuances of input, output, and effects. You can then recall it with the touch of a button! The more the computer can control, the smaller the overall size of the digital console needs to be.

The software has already gone to the next level. It can also control the manual faders via motors. When a scene is recalled, the software actually moves the physical faders to reestablish their positions when the scene was recorded.

SIGNAL PROCESSING

Signal processing is our next topic. Equalizers and effects processors are examples of this. They all change the input signal before it heads to the output signal. Effects processors are something we haven't really talked about yet. They are capable of time delay, echoes, reverberation, and much, much more. We generally tend to use

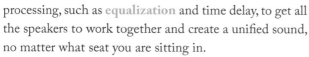
Figure 13.8 Yamaha CL5 digital console.

Figure 13.9 Avid S6L digital console.

processing, such as equalization and time delay, to get all the speakers to work together and create a unified sound, no matter what seat you are sitting in.

Equalizers are the most common use for a basic signal processor. Think of them as a filter. Equalizers help tune specific sources to a similar base level. If an equalization attempt does too much correction, it can tend to distort the resulting audio. You should try to keep it to the minimum correction needed to do what you want, without overdoing it.

As the system gain is increased, distortion shows up first on any sources where you have over-equalized. All this means is that you need to use the tools the way they were intended. You can push it to the extremes, but the equipment lets you know fairly quickly if you've gone too far.

Reverberation is basically reflected sound that has blended with the original sound. This happens normally. Sometimes, you want to try to reduce it. Sometimes, you want to enhance it even more. Delay effects are just what the words sound like. They input the audio and hold onto it for a certain amount of time before giving it to the output. This is pretty cool—here is why! If you are in a large auditorium, and the speakers are fairly far apart, a delay can make sure the sound comes out of all speakers at the same time.

> People's eyes and ears must go to the same place. Time is the most important thing in a sound system.
>
> —Tim Mazur,
> American sound designer

There are literally hundreds of types to choose from in the mixer console world. If you are renting, you need to find out what is available. Things that may influence you are all the different traits we just discussed. These also include your budget, the space allowed in the auditorium, and the experience of your sound technician.

SPEAKERS

Let's do a little introduction to speakers. There are four types: Tweeter, midrange, woofer, and subwoofer (Figure 13.10). A tweeter is a type of speaker designed specifically to reproduce high frequencies. A midrange is designed specifically for, yes, you guessed it, the midrange frequencies. A quick note: The human voice resides primarily in the midrange. A woofer is designed to reproduce low frequencies. A subwoofer is designed specifically to reproduce very low-frequency sounds.

Subwoofer

Woofer   Mid-Range   Tweeter

■ **Figure 13.10** Subwoofer, woofer, midrange and tweeter speakers.

These types of speakers are used in many combinations, based on your location and the needs of the production.

A **line array** is multiple speakers hung together, either vertically or horizontally, so that they can act as one huge speaker (Figure 13.11). Each speaker in an array has a very narrow spread of sound. A **cluster** is similar to an array; however, it is almost always hung on center right above the edge of the stage. A wedge is a kind of speaker cabinet (Figure 13.12). It refers to one that is shaped with an angled bottom, placed on the floor; the result is the speaker points up, usually at a 30–45-degree angle. The actors use the wedge to hear themselves isolated from the balanced mix coming out of every other speaker. Last, the sweet spot is the best location in the house. Optimally, it is the place where everyone in the audience is equidistant from each speaker, but that is hard to do in many of today's theaters.

I did do a show once in which the director ran up to me in a frenzy, and said, "The lighting is dark, the actors can't act, the singers can't sing, the set looks miserable; you are our only hope! We need more thunder cues!" I complied, although that, to me, is putting a band-aid on a gaping wound.

—Kai Harada,
American sound designer

■ **Figure 13.11** Speaker array at the 1869 Bardavon Opera House.

■ **Figure 13.12** Speaker array on left and wedges in the center for an outdoor concert.

CONNECTORS AND CABLES

How do we connect all this stuff? Well, there are connectors and there are cables. We will take a look at each of the various types. The granddaddy of all audio connectors is the banana plug (Figure 13.13). Although it can come in various sizes, the ¼″ and 1/8″ have become the most common. These plugs are single wire. They are often color-coded red and black.

The XLR is a connector that can have three pins or more. This connector is one of the most commonly used connectors in the sound world today. Originally called the *X series* when it first came out, the *L* represents the added latch, and the *R* is for the rubber surrounding the internal contacts. The BNC connector is a coaxial connector. It has a miniature bayonet-locking connector. The threaded version of this connector is the TNC connector. The threads replace the bayonet. Both these connectors are locking, which makes them infinitely useful—in addition to the XLR—in theaters where cables may be tripped on or pulled inadvertently.

So much for connectors; let's talk about cable. Coaxial cable, as shown in Figure 13.14, is made up of a single copper core (D), surrounded by a layer of insulation (C), covered by a copper shield (B), and then a flexible plastic jacket (A). Multipair cable has a single outer jacket and insulation with many internal balanced, or twisted-pair, lines. Twisted-pair cable has two center conductors twisted together. Many twisted pairs can share one insulation and jacket. All balanced audio cables are twisted-pair cables with a shield, which further protects the signal being transmitted from introduced noise. A shield is a different kind of insulation that is conductive to protect against electromagnetic and electrostatic fields. This helps keep the buzz and hum away from the system. Last, we look at a snake (Figure 13.15). That is right, an audio snake. Picture several complete audio cables held together in a common jacket. These are awesome for loading in a temporary show.

Digital audio has reduced the amount and complexity of the cable needed. Cable labels are most important. Technicians must be clear as to when and where a cable is going to be terminated. Many departments will share cable runs with audio, and they often use the same type of cable.

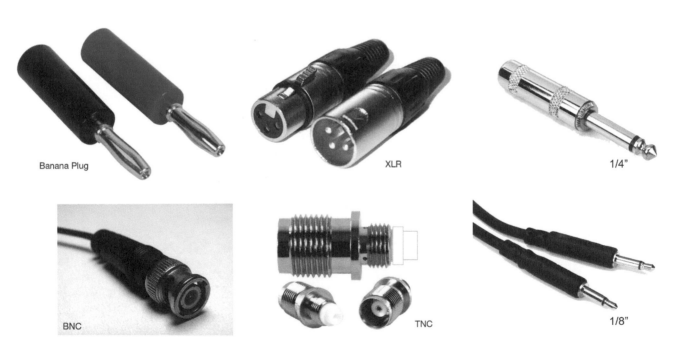

Banana Plug   XLR   1/4"

BNC   TNC   1/8"

■ **Figure 13.13** Various connectors.

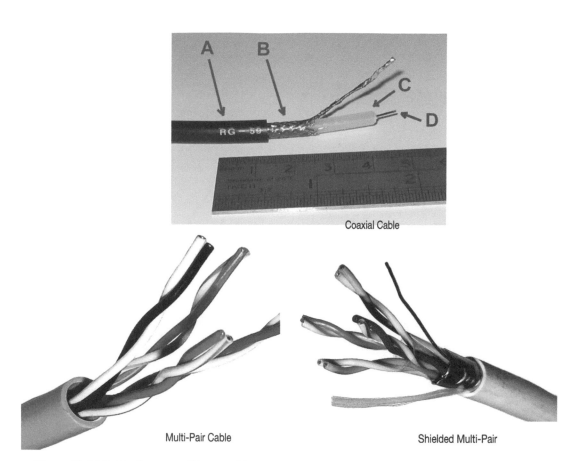

Coaxial Cable

Multi-Pair Cable

Shielded Multi-Pair

■ **Figure 13.14** Cable diagram—different cable types.

■ **Figure 13.15** Audio snake.

HEADSETS

Let's talk headsets next. For a show to run smoothly, everyone behind the scenes must be able to communicate easily. This usually requires a combination of wired and wireless headset stations on multiple channels (Figures 13.16 and 13.17). All wired and wireless communication needs to flow through a base station of some kind. The wireless belt pack and wired intercom connection on the rear panel of the base station should have their own full-duplex port. Some manufacturers, such as Clear-Com, offer the voice communication from each to be sampled, mixed, and then rerouted throughout the system as desired.

■ **Figure 13.16** Clear-Com wireless communication system.

■ **Figure 13.17** Another model and style of Clear-Com wireless communication system.

The base station needs to support as many wireless belt packs and intercom connections as the show needs. It also needs to have multiple channels as required to give privacy to different departments to talk. LED indicators and a front-panel fluorescent display are nice to show status and battery information. It is important that each belt pack have its own way to be individually addressed by the base—allowing multiple combinations of belt-pack-to-belt-pack and small-group conversations to happen simultaneously.

Some models offer many extra benefits, such as programmable software menus on the base, accessible via the display, and a push-to-enter rotary encoder. All aspects of the belt packs, rear-panel connectors, and creation of communications routes and groups can be addressed. Each belt pack and rear-panel connector can be labeled with a five-character name, which appears on the base station and belt pack displays, uniquely identifying the system users. Relative levels among belt packs and input and output levels for the wired connections are also under software control. This is a long way from a tin can on a string!

ASSISTED-HEARING DEVICES

Our last topic in this chapter is assisted-hearing devices. The first infrared listening system was introduced by Sound Associates on Broadway at the Lunt-Fontanne Theatre to aid hearing-impaired patrons in 1979 (Figure 13.18). An infrared listening system provides amplification for hearing-impaired patrons through wireless receivers. The sound is transmitted to the receivers using infrared light, which is invisible to the naked eye. ShowTrans by Sound Associates was the next stage in this product's development in 1998, and it added multilingual, scene-by-scene commentary via infrared transmission. This is not a word-for-word translation of the show. Instead, the system gives the audience member detailed plot information. The lighting control board can trigger these translations. Each time a lighting cue is executed, the translation software knows to begin the next set of lines.

D-Scriptive by Sound Associates was the next advance. It added a fully automated audio description for the visually impaired audience members, which includes a detailed account of all onstage action including

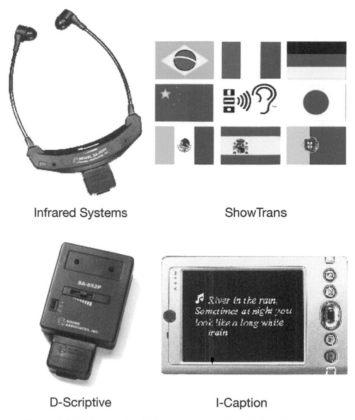

Infrared Systems

ShowTrans

D-Scriptive

I-Caption

■ **Figure 13.18** Infrared assistive devices by Sound Associates.

choreography, blocking, lighting, sets, and costume changes. The newest advance is the I-Caption system, also by Sound Associates, which is a state-of-the-art wireless visual aid that provides verbatim real-time closed captions for theatrical performances. By displaying dialogue, lyrics, and sound effects on a handheld device, hearing-impaired patrons can better understand a production or event. The I-Caption System can also be expanded to incorporate subtitles, showing the text in multiple languages and playing audio segments. All of these assistive devices help the theatre take a major step forward to accessibility for the handicapped.

NETWORKS

You've got all this equipment; that's great. How do you get all the components to talk to one another? At some point, you will need to network your audio stream, head amp control, console control, and even WiFi for remote control of your console. This gets very technical very quickly.

Digital audio consoles and their associated components have the ability to connect over dedicated networks and sometimes even over open local area network (LAN) built into existing buildings. Most newer consoles can be remote controlled by tablet-based apps over dedicated wireless fidelity (WiFi) networks.

IP ADDRESSES

The internet protocol (IP) address is either manually assigned or assigned by DHCP, or dynamic host communication protocol. If DHCP is used, there can only be one DHCP server on the network. There can be no duplicate addresses on a network. This may sound familiar to you. It's identical to the IP address on your laptop or tablet. That's the extent of what we'll address in a fundamental book. There is so much more you can dive into if this topic interests you.

EXERCISES

EXERCISE 1
LISTENING

Before you can create sound for the stage, you have to know what things really sound like, and which sounds you will encounter. Find an environment, be it a street corner or the middle of a forest, and listen for ten minutes; write down what you hear. Did you hear any sounds that you were not expecting? Were any sounds absent that you did expect? Did you have any other impressions?

EXERCISE 2
FOLEY

Each student will bring in materials to create a live Foley sound effect (maybe cellophane to crumple and sound like a fire, or celery to snap and sound like a breaking bone). The Foley effects will be performed behind a screen, and the rest of the class will need to guess what the Foley effect was supposed to be and how the Foley effect was achieved. What Foley effects worked the best?

CHECK YOUR KNOWLEDGE

1. Explain the reason sound design has become so much more important in recent years. Provide examples.
2. Identify the major components needed for a complete system with descriptions of the use for each piece of equipment.
3. Predict the next step in sound design and illustrate how it will integrate with other departments.

- Acoustics
- Ambient noise
- Amplifier
- Area mic'ing
- Banana plug
- BNC
- Cluster
- Coaxial cable
- Condenser microphone
- Contact pickup
- Dynamic microphone
- Equalization
- Gain
- Impedance
- Input
- Lavalier
- Line array
- Live Foley
- Midrange
- Mixing console
- Multi-pair cable
- Output
- Pressure response microphone
- Shield
- Signal processor
- Snake
- Subwoofer
- TNC
- Tweeter
- Twisted-pair cable
- Woofer
- XLR

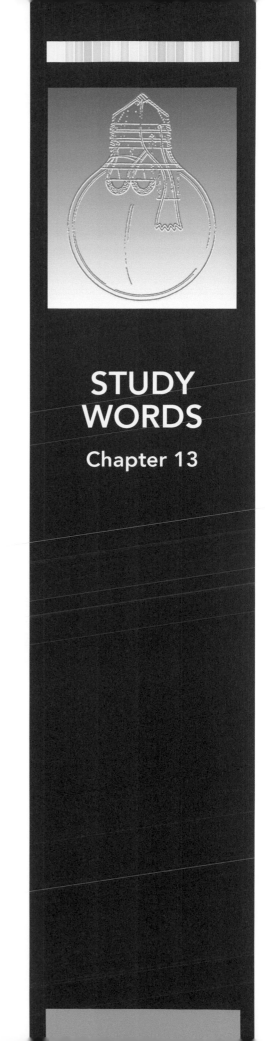

STUDY WORDS
Chapter 13

PART
FOUR

Costume and Makeup

CHAPTER 14: All Dressed Up with Someplace to Go
Costumes

CHAPTER 15: Accessories and Other Stuff
Costume Crafts by Denise Wallace-Spriggs

CHAPTER 16: Put on a Happy Face
Hair and Makeup

All Dressed up with Someplace to Go

Costumes

This chapter is all about costumes. Always start with "What can you afford?" Remember good–cheap–fast? As much as we would like it to be all about the concept, it can really be about the money available versus what costumes may be in stock. Are you building the full set, leads, or just bits and pieces? If you are doing a redesign, always question if it could be conceptualized inside the existing design. Evaluate the existing design, if one exists, and try tweaking for characters and overall unification. The springboard for the concept of a design can come from any design element. Sometimes, the concept just springs from a fabric choice or a color.

The costume designer provides the shop with costume sketches (Figures 14.1 and 14.2). There is one sketch per costume or character, whichever is required for the show. Each sketch shows the front as well as back or side details, accessories, and fabric swatches. This is the first chance the shop has to see what it is about to build. Usually, the entire show's renderings are posted on a shop wall, so that everyone can reference them together as needed throughout the entire process.

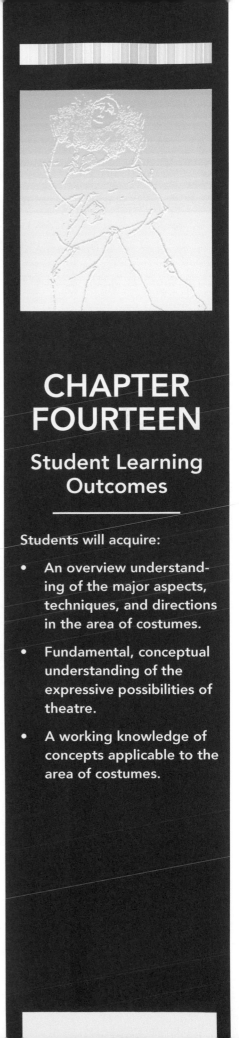

CHAPTER FOURTEEN

Student Learning Outcomes

Students will acquire:

- An overview understanding of the major aspects, techniques, and directions in the area of costumes.

- Fundamental, conceptual understanding of the expressive possibilities of theatre.

- A working knowledge of concepts applicable to the area of costumes.

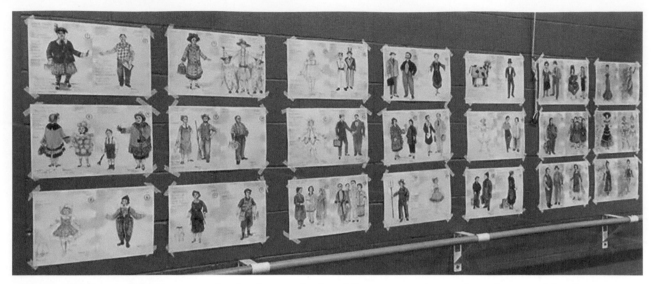

■ **Figure 14.1** Campbell Baird's costume sketches for a production of *Gypsy*, mounted on a rehearsal room wall for all to see.

■ **Figure 14.2** Two of Campbell Baird's costume sketches for a production of *Gypsy*.

It's always a group effort ... I develop the designs by working with the director and choreographer and, if there is one living, the author. That's how it all begins. And then you get to the actor, and they bring in their elements. It's like cooking! I feel like Julia Child sometimes!

—William Ivey Long,
American costume designer

FABRICS

One of the first choices a costume designer makes is with regard to fabric. So many fabric options are available today. Also, many techniques can add additional design, texture, or color to a fabric. Fabrics are chosen for a number of different reasons. For example, in dance, the "must have" fabrics are tulle, netting, spandex, chiffon, and georgette. There are others, of course, but you cannot do dance without these.

Let's take a look from the perspective of natural fabrics versus synthetic fabrics. Natural fabrics can be divided into four basic categories: Wool, cotton, silk, and linen. Wool fabric often brings to mind cozy warmth or being slightly scratchy. Wool fiber comes from a variety of animal coats. Wool is also processed in different ways; some wools are even extremely soft.

The wool fibers have natural crimps or curls that create pocketed areas, making the fabric feel spongy. This also creates warm insulation for the wearer. Wool can absorb up to 30 percent of its weight in moisture, either from rain, snow, or perspiration, without feeling damp. All these traits combine to make wool the most popular fabric for tailoring fine garments or outdoor wear. Wool is also dirt resistant and flame resistant and, in many weaves, also resists wear and tearing.

Cotton is often thought of as cool, soft, and comfortable. The cotton fiber is from the cotton plant's seedpod. The fiber is hollow in the center and, under a microscope, looks like a twisted ribbon. The fiber absorbs and releases perspiration quickly, thus allowing the fabric to "breathe." "Absorbent" cotton retains 24–27 times its

own weight in water and is stronger when wet than dry. Cotton can stand high temperatures and takes dyes easily, which is often important in theatrical design. Chlorine bleach can be used to restore white garments to a cleaner white, but this same bleach may yellow chemically finished cottons or remove color in dyed cottons (Figures 14.3 and 14.4).

Silk is a fabric that has its own reputation. When you hear the word *silk*, what do you visualize? For centuries, silk has had a reputation as a luxurious and sensuous fabric, one associated with wealth and success. No other fabric generates quite the same reaction. Silk is a natural protein fiber taken from the cocoon of the silkworm, which makes it very expensive. Silk is one of the oldest textile fibers known to humans. Silk absorbs moisture, which makes it cool in the summer and warm in the

■ **Figure 14.3** *Othello*, as produced by the Shakespeare Theatre Company in 2005. Avery Brooks as Othello; director, Michael Kahn.

■ **Figure 14.4** *Othello*, as produced by the Shakespeare Theatre Company in 2005. Avery Brooks as Othello and Colleen Delany as Desdemona; director, Michael Kahn.

winter. Because of its high absorbency, it is easily dyed in many deep colors. Silk retains its shape, drapes well, caresses the figure, and shimmers with a luster all its own. Its reputation is well earned.

Linen is often confused with cotton or at least with being made of some part of the cotton plant. Linen is actually made from flax or, more specifically, a fiber taken from the stalk of the flax plant. It has a natural luster from the inherent wax content of the plant. Linen is an elegant, beautiful, durable, and refined luxury fabric. Linen is the strongest of the vegetable fibers and has two to three times the strength of cotton. Not only is linen strong, it is also very smooth. It is highly absorbent and a good conductor of heat, like most natural fibers. Linen is naturally off-white or tan. It can be easily dyed, and the color does not fade when washed. Linen is one of the most durable fabrics as well.

As a designer, it's my job to see that the clothes do not hinder the performer.
—Patrick Rocheleau, American costume designer

Man-made fibers are a whole different category. Man-made fibers are the result of extensive research by scientists to improve on naturally occurring animal and plant fibers. Before these fibers were developed, artificial (manufactured) fibers were made from cellulose, which comes from plants. All these developments happened during times of war—out of necessity. As certain materials were rationed, these developments were necessary to our culture. Rayon, acetate, nylon, and polyester are just a few of the synthetics we discuss.

Let's start with rayon. Rayon, introduced in 1910, is a very versatile fiber and has many of the same comfort properties as natural fibers. It can imitate the feel, texture, and drape of silk, wool, cotton, or linen as its basis is cellulose. The fibers are easily dyed in a wide range of colors. Rayon fabrics are soft, smooth, cool, comfortable, and highly absorbent, but they do not insulate body heat, making them ideal for use in hot and humid climates.

Acetate, introduced in 1934, is low in cost, has good draping qualities, and is derived from cellulose. Acetate is used in fabrics such as satins, brocades, and taffetas to accentuate the fabric's luster, body, drape, and beauty. It is soft, smooth, dry, and crisp. It breathes, wicking away moisture and drying quickly, but offers no heat retention. Contemporary acetate is an environmentally friendly fabric, as it is made from the wood pulp of reforested trees. Deep brilliant color shades are possible through dyeing.

Nylon, introduced in 1935, has the ability to be very lustrous, semi-lustrous, or dull and is one of the first artificial fibers to be derived from petroleum. Nylon was intended to be a synthetic replacement for silk and substituted for it in many products after silk became scarce during World War II. It replaced silk in military applications, such as parachutes and flak vests, and was used in many types of vehicle tires. Nylon fibers are used in a great many applications, including fabrics, bridal veils, carpets, musical strings, and various kinds of rope.

Last, there is polyester, discovered at about the same time as nylon. Polyesters are the most widely used human-made fiber in the world and are sourced from crude oil. Polyester fabrics are used in consumer apparel and home furnishings, such as bed sheets, bedspreads, curtains, and draperies. Polyester fiberfill is also used to stuff pillows, comforters, and cushion padding. Polyester fabrics can have a "less natural" feel when compared with similarly woven fabrics made from natural fibers. Owing to this, polyester often gets a bad reputation. However, polyester fabrics may exhibit other advantages over natural fabrics, such as improved wrinkle and stain resistance. As a result, polyester fibers are sometimes spun together with natural fibers to produce a cloth with blended properties.

So, as you can see, before we even talk about color and pattern of fabric, there are a lot of choices to consider, and we've only discussed a few (Figure 14.5). What type of fabric properties are you looking for? This is a major question to be answered before you ever go shopping for fabric and needs to be considered in conjunction with the costume's pattern. Shopping might not be as much of an option, depending on the costume shop's in-house stock of fabric and/or costumes pieces (Figure 14.6). Remember that most fabrics need to be pre-washed before you cut and assemble them into a garment. This allows them to preshrink before fabrication, which basically means your sizing will be, and remain, more accurate.

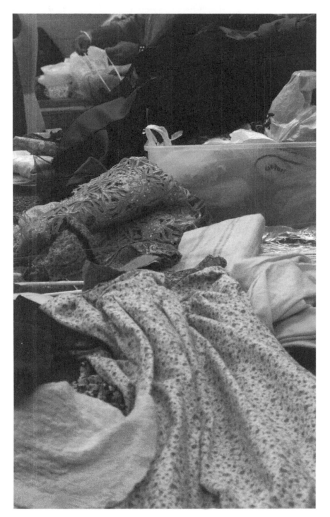

■ **Figure 14.5** A variety of fabric choices.

■ **Figure 14.6** Organized swatch books of all in-house fabrics listing amount of yardage available.

TOOLS AND ACCESSORIES

Let's talk about basic tools for a little bit. There are many small tools and a few bigger tools. The smaller tools are something that most costume shop workers carry with them from job to job. Once you develop a preference for a specific pair of scissors, you won't leave home without them. So, here goes.

Measuring tapes are a very important part of the costume shop (Figure 14.7). These are similar in concept to the scenic tape measures, yet different in fabrication. Huh? Well, basically, they are a soft, flexible measuring tape. People are soft and have curves; wood doesn't. This is one example where similar, if not identical, tools are used in different departments of theater design.

Use your measuring tape to take all the appropriate measurements for the performer. More detail on this later. Once you have the actor's measurements, you work with a pattern. You either work with an existing pattern, create your own, or use some mixture of the two. If you have a pattern, it gives you each piece of the finished garment separated from the other pieces, so that you can lay them out on fabric to begin cutting. Think here of a jigsaw puzzle. Many individual pieces when put together

■ **Figure 14.7** Measuring tape.

properly form something completely different looking from the pieces.

If you are creating a pattern from scratch, you will most likely use a sloper. A sloper is a basic pattern shape that comes in a variety of sizes (Figure 14.8). Slopers also come in many standard pattern shapes. They will help you to get started with a custom pattern by letting you more easily fit the pattern pieces together as you are

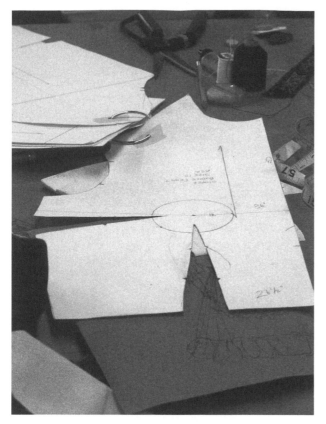

■ **Figure 14.8** Sloper.

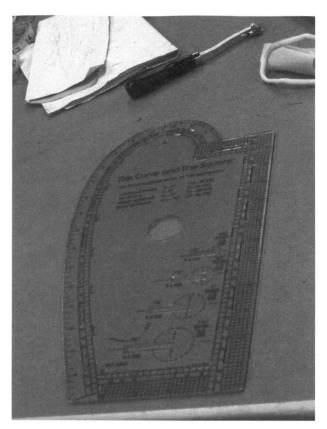

■ **Figure 14.9** Patterning template.

making adjustments for size and design. As you make these adjustments, a patterning template helps you ease the transitions between pattern pieces (Figure 14.9).

Next up are the pins. This may seem really obvious, but there are many kinds of pins—some with different purposes and some that are slightly different sizes based on preference. Differences in a pin can vary from having a flat metal head to a round plastic head, and the length of the pin can change from short to very long for quilting. A pincushion holds the pins all in one place. It is usually a soft, stuffed shape that you stick the pins into. The coolest thing I've seen in a long time is the magnetic pincushion, and they are becoming more common (Figure 14.10). It's sort of obvious how it works, but wow! What a great idea.

Once the pattern is created and pinned to the fabric, you get to cut it out. Scissors are not new to us, but the scissors you use for fabric are much different (Figure 14.11). Sewing scissors are usually much more expensive than regular scissors because they are made to be adjustable and sharpened as required. There are great

■ **Figure 14.10** Magnetic pincushion.

■ **Figure 14.11** Scissors.

Figure 14.13 Buttons organized in sets of identical multiples.

Figure 14.12 Various thread spools organized for ease of finding what you need.

scissors for those of us who are left-handed. Getting a pair of scissors that fits your hand properly and has a good cutting edge is critical. Cutting any kind of paper will dull scissors' blades faster than anything else I know of. Never let anyone use your sewing scissors to cut anything other than fabric. If possible, never let anyone else use your good scissors! Many scissors now even have handles that work fairly well for right- or left-handed people.

Continuing in some sort of semi-logical order, let's talk about thread (Figure 14.12). There are almost as many types as there are colors. Thread comes in cotton, rayon, polyester, silk, and so forth. You get the idea. And, the colors are endless. Many manufacturers have their own color list. You can get almost any kind of thread in any color you can think of. The important part of choosing a specific thread is to know what you will be sewing, so that you make sure to match the thread's properties to the fabrics. There are threads for regular sewing, mending, quilting, and embroidering. Just because a thread says it is for a specific purpose, doesn't mean you can't use for it something else. You just have to make a small sample to try it out.

Notions, zippers, lace, appliqués, beads, and all sorts of other accessories complete the costume and make it truly unique (Figures 14.13 and 14.14). These are some of the hardest items to find when you are looking for something very specific, and this can become the most time-consuming part of making a costume. Most shops

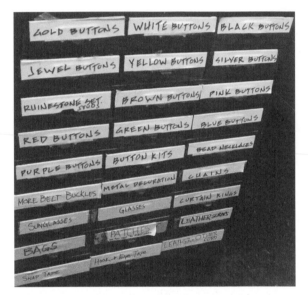

Figure 14.14 Buttons organized by color.

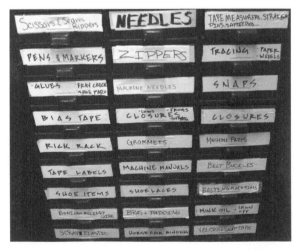

Figure 14.15 A great way to store a variety of different accessories in order to easily find them as needed.

have a stock of accessories, just waiting for the right costume. It is important to store these items in a safe and organized way (Figure 14.15). If you can't find them when the time comes, they don't get used and end up just wasting storage space.

Seam rippers are almost as important as any other tool (Figures 14.16 and 14.17). Once you have sewn anything, from a single seam to a whole garment, there will always be times when you need to open a seam up again. Changes happen. The seam ripper is your best tool for this since it is specifically designed for it. If you try to open a seam with a pair of scissors, you will have a much higher possibility of cutting the fabric rather than just removing the thread. Similar to scissors, you end up finding a favorite kind of seam ripper and want to have it with you all the time.

Once the garment is made, you need to hold fittings to finesse the fit to the specific actor or actress. Tailor's chalk is perfect for marking where you need to adjust the fit, either larger or smaller (Figure 14.18). Of course, you can also use chalk to make markings before you cut and assemble. The reason tailor's chalk is so good

for this purpose is that, when you no longer need the markings, the chalk can be brushed away without leaving any residue. During fittings, it is much faster to mark a garment with chalk than to have an actor stand there while you insert pin after pin after pin.

While we're on the subject of chalk, a great use for it is to mark a hem during the fitting process. The problem with hems, especially full ones, is that it is very difficult to get them hemmed evenly. This is even more of an issue if a skirt is bustled. There is no way to mark the hem unless it is on the performer *and* bustled. Enter Mr. Puffy! **Mr. Puffy** is used basically the same as a chalk line for scenery, but works very differently (Figures 14.19 and 14.20). Tailor's chalk, ground to a powder, is put into a small container with a very focused spout. A hose is attached to the container, controlled by a squeeze ball. The whole thing is mounted on a stand that is measured and marked, so you know how high it is off the ground. Squeeze the ball while your actor turns slowly in a circle and, *poof*, your hemline is marked. I'm sure Mr. Puffy has another name, but this is the only name I've ever heard him called, and I like it!

■ **Figure 14.16** Seam ripper.

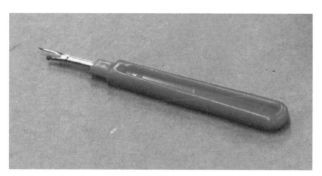

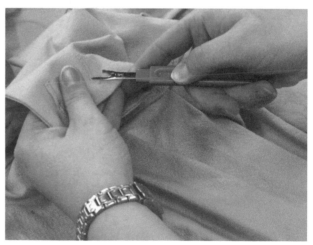

■ **Figure 14.17** A seam ripper being used to open a newly finished buttonhole.

■ **Figure 14.18** Tailor's chalk comes in a variety of colors, so you can easily use the color that shows up best on each individual fabric.

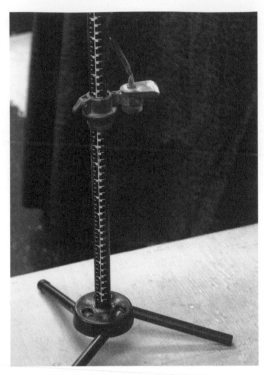

Figure 14.19 Mr. Puffy close up.

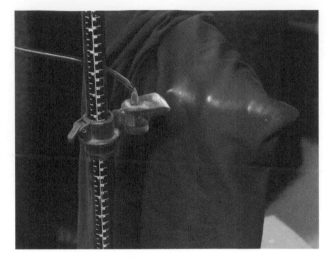

Figure 14.20 Mr. Puffy in use to mark a bustled hemline.

Theatre Traditions: Baby Doll

When baby dolls are off stage during a performance, set them face down on the props table instead of face up. This superstition comes from China. It is believed that, if a baby doll is left face up, its spirit (kind of like a poltergeist) will emerge from its eyes and do poltergeist-like things in the theatre.

MEASUREMENTS

Now that we have the basic small tools covered, let's talk for a minute about the actors' measurements. All the actors must have their measurements taken by a member of the costume department. *Do not* take their word for it that they are a certain size, dimension, or weight. First off, most people don't know how to properly measure themselves for the purpose of making clothing. Second, we all have our own idea of what our body looks like.

WOMEN'S MEASUREMENT INSTRUCTIONS (Figure 14.21)

Bust:	The fullest point of the bust, under the arms and around the widest part of the back.
Chest:	Just below the bust measurement, usually corresponds to bra size.
Waistline:	The natural waistline is the narrowest part of the body. Firmly measure with your fingers on the outside of the tape.
Outer leg:	From the waistline to the anklebone.
High hip:	Measure around the high point of the hip bones, usually 3–4 inches below the waistline.
Bodice front:	From the nape of the neck, down over the bust and to the bottom edge of the waistline. (The nape is where the neck turns toward the shoulder.)
Height:	In bare feet, measure from the top of the head to the bottom of the feet.
Weight:	Use an accurate scale and remember, all of this information is confidential!
Shoe size:	Wide, medium, or narrow, plus size.

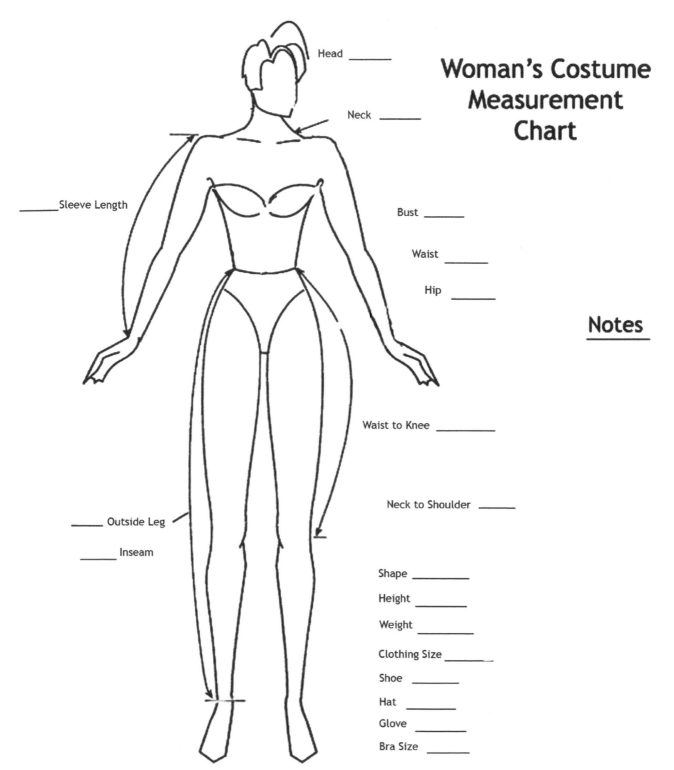

Head _____

Woman's Costume Measurement Chart

Neck _____

_____ Sleeve Length

Bust _____

Waist _____

Hip _____

Notes

Waist to Knee _____

Neck to Shoulder _____

_____ Outside Leg

_____ Inseam

Shape _____

Height _____

Weight _____

Clothing Size _____

Shoe _____

Hat _____

Glove _____

Bra Size _____

■ **Figure 14.21** Form to use when taking down women's measurements.

Just because you can squeeze into a size 6 pair of jeans, without being able to breathe or sit down, doesn't mean they fit! Men's and women's measurements are taken slightly differently. Let's go into them one at a time.

> You can lead a horse to water and you can even make it drink, but you can't make actresses wear what they don't want to wear.
>
> **—Edith Head,**
> **American costume designer**

Depending on the actual costume designs, you may need to add other specific measurements to those noted. Once the actors have been measured, the next step is to keep track of which actors/characters are wearing which costume pieces and accessories. Yup, this means more paperwork and yet another form (Figures 14.23 and 14.24). Just like the other departments, you will be creating a binder full of information for constant reference. Small accessories can get lost so easily that tracking their use is very important.

Also, every character should have an accessory bag, sometimes known as a ditty bag (Figure 14.25). This is not an item you can easily buy. Costume shops usually make them during down time between shows using leftover muslin. A hanger is sewn into the top of the bag, and a series of pockets are created down below. This allows the accessory bag to hang with the actor's costumes. It keeps everything in one place, which means fewer crises before the show and easier maintenance after the show.

At one time, the cutter and draper were two separate positions in the costume shop. The cutter was a person who used patterns, or created patterns, and cut the pattern from the fabric. And the draper was a person who, instead of using a pattern, created a design by draping the fabric onto the actor or a mannequin. With that technique, marking and pinning defined where the fabric needed to be stitched. This was all done on the actor or mannequin, with no pattern. Obviously, this was very specific to the actor's body. Mannequins come in different sizes and are adjustable so that you can truly

MEN'S MEASUREMENT INSTRUCTIONS (Figure 14.22)

Chest:	Measure the widest part of the chest just below the armpits and around the back.
Waistline:	Measure the circumference of the waist. If the actor wears his pants at or below the waist, indicate the distance from his navel and in which direction (below or above).
Outer leg:	Measure from the waist down to the anklebone.
Inner leg:	Measure from the crotch down to the anklebone.
Crotch length:	Measure from the waistline at the center back all the way around to the waistline at the center front.
Back width:	Measure across the broadest part of the back from armpit to armpit.
Neck:	Measure comfortably around the base of the neck. The actor should be able to move his neck and swallow.
Shoulder:	Measure from the base of the neck to the outermost point of the shoulder.
Arm:	With arms slightly bent, measure from the outermost point of the shoulder down to the wrist bone bump.
Height:	In bare feet, measure from the top of the head to the bottom of the feet.
Weight:	Use an accurate scale, and remember all of this information is confidential!
Shoe size:	Wide, medium, or narrow plus size.
Head size:	Measure around the forehead holding the tape taut.

simulate the size and shape of the actor. Oftentimes, padding is added to different parts of the mannequin to better simulate the actor's body. Certain designs still call for this, but not nearly as much as there used to be. So, gradually, the two positions became combined.

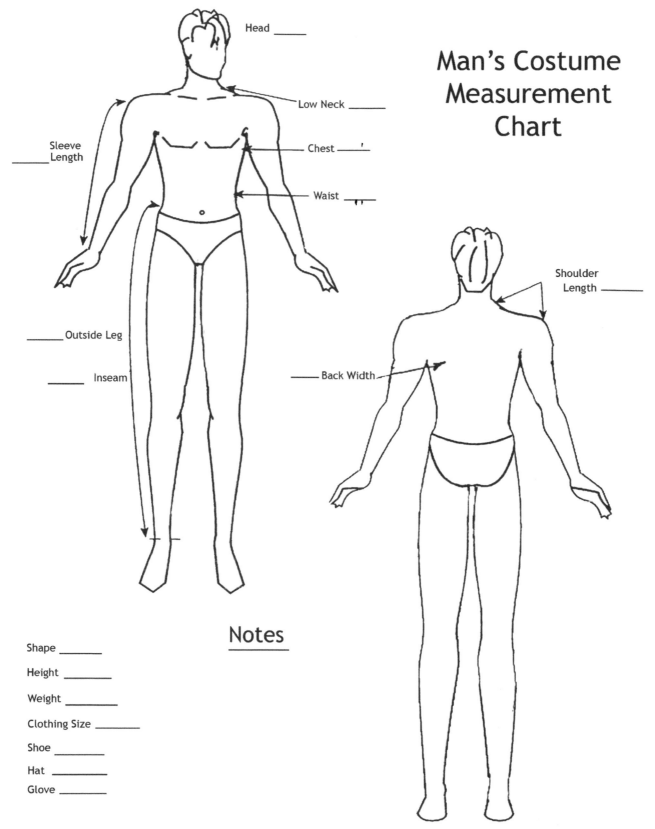

Man's Costume Measurement Chart

Head _____

Low Neck _____

Sleeve Length _____

Chest _____

Waist _____

Outside Leg _____

Inseam _____

Shoulder Length _____

Back Width _____

Notes

Shape _____

Height _____

Weight _____

Clothing Size _____

Shoe _____

Hat _____

Glove _____

Figure 14.22 Form to use when taking down men's measurements.

Actor's Name:		Character:	
Scene			
Undershirt/T-shirt			
Corset			
Bum Roll			
Bustle			
Petticoat			
Tights			
Stockings			
Shoes/Boots/ Footwear			
Bodice			
Skirt			
Bustle Drape			
Apron			
Shawl			
Hair Ribbon			
Hat/Bonnet			
Gloves			
Jewelry			
Parasol/Cane/ Walking Stick			
Pocketbook			
Other (Costume Props)			
Wig/Hair Piece			
Makeup			

■ **Figure 14.23** Form to use when tracking women's costume pieces.

Actor's Name: Character:

Scene			
Undershirt/T-shirt			
Dance Belt			
Socks			
Shoes			
Spats			
Shirt			
Overshirt/Dress shirt			
Vest			
Coat/Jacket			
Pants			
Apron			
Suspenders			
Tie			
Hat/Cap			
Gloves			
Jewelry			
Cane/Walking Stick			
Wallet			
Other (Costume Props)			
Wig/Hair Piece			
Makeup			

■ **Figure 14.24** Form to use when tracking men's costume pieces.

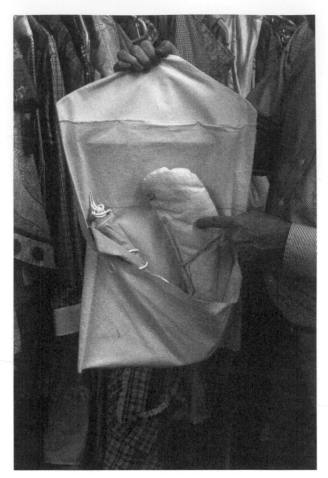

■ **Figure 14.25** Ditty bag for accessories. These are a great way to keep every costume piece for any given character together.

The lighting can make it or break it. You pick a color and you think, "This is going to be great!" And then you get it on stage and you think, "Oh, my, what was I thinking?" Black costumes are a particular problem, due to the many colors and multistep process used to dye the cloth. Certain lights, particularly lavender tints, can pierce through black dye to reveal other colors that had been on the fabric before, ruining the effect. You have to do lots of color testing, but the whole process is "fun."

—**William Ivey Long,**
American costume designer

SEWING

It is now time to begin sewing. Finally. Who knew there was all this work to do before you could even stitch your first stitch? Let's chat briefly about hand sewing. Many of the basic principles of hand sewing also apply to machine sewing. There are different types of needles to use depending on what fabric you are sewing. Some things that are frequently sewn by hand are basting stitches, buttons, hems, and of course *mending*. Certain kinds of appliqué and embroidery are also done by hand. There is a specific talent to hand stitching!

Sewing machines have only been around since the early 1800s and were not common until the middle of the 19th century. But people have been sewing by hand for centuries, and there are many instances in garment construction where hand stitching is still necessary. Sewing with a machine is faster, which is why there are many different kinds of sewing machines; some are simple and straightforward, while others are more complicated and have specialty things they do, such as embroidery. There are lots of manufacturers. If a costume shop has several sewing machines, it will most likely set each one up for a different task. One might be for straight sewing, while another is set up to only create buttonholes (Figures 14.26 and 14.27).

Let me pause here for a second. In extremely complicated costumes, a test garment is made out of muslin. The whole process of patterning, cutting, sewing, and fitting is still done, and great attention is paid to the details. Muslin is a cotton fabric that is relatively inexpensive. Once the muslin garment has been properly fitted to the actor, the muslin is taken apart, and the pieces are used as a pattern to make the actual costume out of the real fabric.

There is a stitch called *overlocking* that we should discuss. If you happen to be wearing a T-shirt, turn it inside out and look at the seam—most likely it was seamed with an overlocking stitch. This stitch sews over the edge of one or two pieces of cloth for edging, hemming, or seaming. Usually, an overlock sewing machine, or serger, will cut the edges of the cloth as it is fed through, though some are made without cutters. The inclusion of automated cutters allows sergers to create finished seams easily and quickly. A serger differs from a regular sewing machine in that it utilizes loopers fed

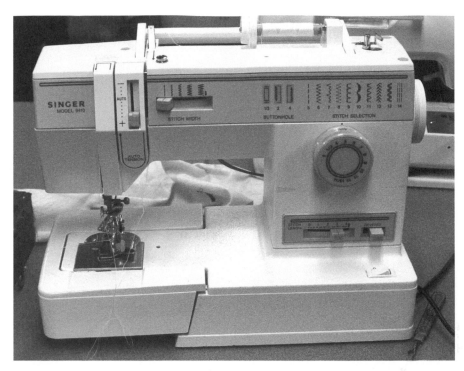

■ **Figure 14.26** Sewing machine set up for regular stitching.

■ **Figure 14.27** Sewing machine set up for buttonholes.

by multiple thread cones rather than a bobbin (Figure 14.28). Loopers create thread loops that pass from the needle thread to the edges of the fabric so that the edges of the fabric are contained within the seam (Figure 14.29). Overlock stitches are extremely versatile, as they can be used for decoration, reinforcement, or construction.

OK, so—fittings. Once you've sewn the costume, or at least a part of the costume, you schedule a fitting with the actor, usually during a rehearsal as time is always at

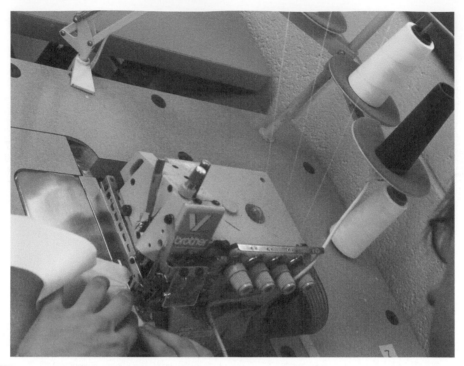

■ **Figure 14.28** Serger with three loopers.

■ **Figure 14.29** Seam created by a serger.

a premium. The main purpose at this time is to have the actor try on the pieces that are ready to see how they fit, as well as how they look on the actor. The costume designer is on hand to oversee all of this, especially for the principal characters. This is also a time when the designer may work out any accessories or decorative items that may be needed. Be ready to help the actor get into the costume for the first time, and also to take lots of notes!

Take a look at Figures 14.31–14.36 to see how a period costume is tried on in stages. The fit is checked at each step along the way.

■ **Figure 14.30** *Midsummer Night's Dream.* JMU, director: Oliver Meyes; scenic design: Richard Finkelstein; costume design: Kathleen Conery; associate costume designers: Skyler James and Sophie Sons; lighting design: Catherine Holcomb.

Your dresses should be tight enough to show you're a woman and loose enough to show you're a lady.

**—Edith Head,
American costume designer**

Once the costume has been fitted to the actor, much of the trim work can be positioned with the aid of a mannequin without the actor needing to be present (Figures 14.37–14.39). This saves the actor time away from rehearsal and allows the shop to keep working on several projects with mannequins simultaneously.

Accessories come in so many types and styles, in addition to specialty items. Simple accessories include jewelry, shoes, wigs, hats, and gloves. There is a whole new chapter coming up next called Costume Crafts that goes into great detail about this and much more. If what is needed is basic, or easily attainable, the costume shop can provide it. Most costume shops have a stock of these types of items that can be easily adjusted to work with the design (Figures 14.40–14.42).

Costumes that need to do a "trick" of some kind may also be created elsewhere, depending on what the trick entails. The other option is to rent items like this or, for that matter, rent the entire show. If you are going to rent all the costumes, the costume designer must be

■ **Figure 14.31** Fitting a corset.

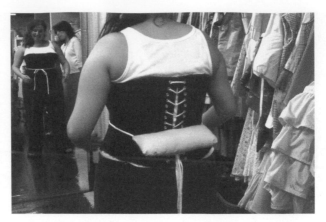

■ **Figure 14.32** Trying on a bum roll.

■ **Figure 14.33** Fitting an underskirt and bustle.

■ **Figure 14.34** Adding in the skirt and scarf.

Figure 14.35 Blouse and decoration.

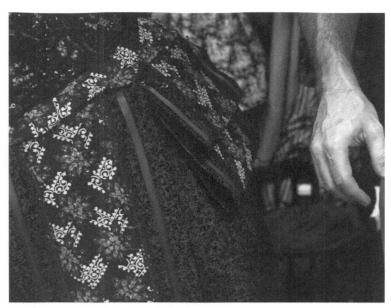

Figure 14.36 Bustle detail.

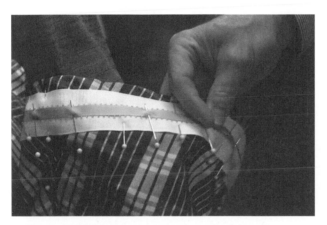

Figure 14.37 Pinning trim is the time when the exact placement is determined.

Figure 14.38 Pinning ruffle.

Figure 14.39 Costume with all trim pinned in place and ready to be sewn.

■ **Figure 14.40** Jewelry organized, stored, and ready for its next use.

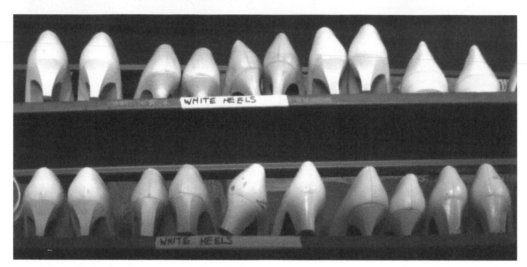

■ **Figure 14.41** White heeled woman's shoes. One of many categories of shoes a costume shop is liable to have.

■ **Figure 14.42** A few wigs that have been pulled for a production. When ready, they will be kept on "heads" to help keep their shape.

careful when selecting costumes, to make sure they work together on the stage. Many rental houses allow you to make minor alterations, and this can be the key to unifying a rented design.

There are many shortcuts that can be taken to achieve a period feel without building an entire costume from scratch. For example, modern men's shirts with a proper collar design can be altered to have the appropriate period cuff to work within a costume designer's idea (Figure 14.43). This saves both time and money. If the look works, do it! Here are some specialty items that can be created in the costume shop provided enough time and budget are allowed (Figure 14.44).

One topic I really haven't discussed is fantasy costumes. These can be done for dance, theatre, or opera. The idea is that you are catering to the specific needs of character creation in a different way than usual. All of your choices, from fabric, to patterns, to cutting, to sewing, to fitting, are slightly different than when making a more traditional costume. Each of these situations is slightly different from any other and caters to the needs of that individual production.

OK, do you want a four- or five-layer romantic, all tulle, one layer of net, full romantic or less tutu that is 12′ from the floor or shorter? Perhaps you'd rather have a classical 8–16″ layered tutu, English, Russian, or Karinska powder puff. Are we mixing romantic and classical tutus, which can often feel like two different worlds? The rough part about implementation is dancers are used to working in tights and leotards. Anything resembling real clothes limits motion to some extent. The design and construction to make these costumes must be as flexible as possible. Fitting and getting the dancers' input are critical. Dance is about expressive movement. As a designer, it's your job to see that the clothes do not hinder the performer.

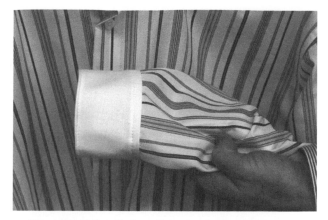

■ **Figure 14.43** Detail of a cuff that has been added to a modern-day men's shirt to give it a period feel.

■ **Figure 14.44** A wonderfully done turkey hat, created at Muhlenberg College's costume shop.

■ **Figure 14.45** *PACK*, 2022. New Voices in Dance Contemporary Dance Ensemble. Choreography: Shane O'Hara and the cast; lighting design: Gordon Olson; and costume design: Elizabeth Wislar, Cast: Leah Baines, Sarah Carrington, Caroline Christie, Amelia Danehy, Taylor McGovern, Samantha McGowan, Emily Moreira, Kelsey Nihill, Ashley Robbins, Shelbi Shelton, Annie Weigh, Lizzy Wyatt. James Madison University, School of Theatre and Dance. Artistic Director: Ryan Corriston.

■ **Figure 14.46** *Animal Farm* by George Orwell/Peter Hall. Directed by Scott Illingworth, sets by Yu-Ting Lin, costumes by Rodrigo Munoz, and lights by Michael Cunningham. Tisch School of the Arts Graduate Acting in collaboration with Design for Stage and Film.

■ **Figure 14.47** *Head over Heels*, James Madison University, November 2021. Directed by Kate Arecchi, choreographed by Ashleigh King, scenic design by Richard Finkelstein, costume design by Sabrina Simmons, and lighting design by Emily Becher-McKeever.

■ **Figure 14.48** *The Caucasian Chalk Circle* by Bertolt Brecht. Directed by Tazewell Thompson, sets by Yu-Hsuan Chen, costumes by Jessica Posteraro, and lights by Jennifer Hill. Tisch School of the Arts Graduate Acting in collaboration with Design for Stage and Film.

■ **Figure 14.49** PatternMaker screenshot of "costume" options.

SOFTWARE

We finish up this chapter by talking about software that can make all of this easier. A number of software packages on the market help you through the patterning process. The software does not help you design, choose fabric, or sew, but it can be a huge aid in pattern creation. If your shop does not have a set of slopers or someone who is able to create patterns, then this is the right path for you to consider.

Some of the pattern software packages available today are PatternMaker® and Garment Designer, to name just a couple. All have websites, and most have a demo version you can download to try! Most software programs have a series of standard patterns or slopers. You input the actor's measurements, select the different

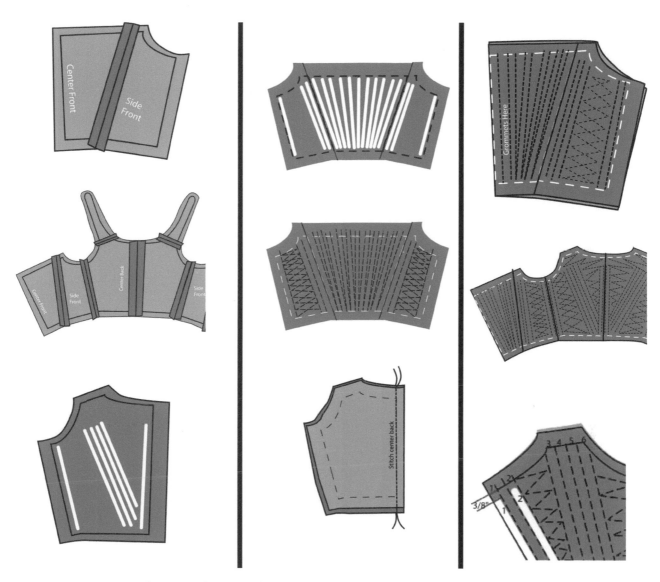

■ **Figure 14.50** PatternMaker images from a step-by-step instruction for a corset.

pattern pieces you are interested in using, and—*boing!*—pattern pieces can be printed out. Well, it's not quite that easy, but it is close. PatternMaker, for example, gives you a great deal of flexibility without costing a small fortune. Figures 14.49 and 14.50 show a couple of images from PatternMaker.

I could tell you all about the software in more detail, but the only way for you to really get a feel for it is to try

it. This is the case with any tool, not just software. The feel in your hand, or under your control, is completely different than a verbal description. So, go out there, find software to try, and decide for yourself.

EXERCISES

EXERCISE 1

Choose a photo from a magazine as a costume sketch. Go to a fabric store and find swatches you would use if designing the costume.

EXERCISE 2

Using the same image as above for research, create a costume sketch.

EXERCISE 3

Make a ditty bag out of muslin.

CHECK YOUR KNOWLEDGE

1. Explain the proper way to take measurements for men and women.
2. List the fabric types, including the properties that make them unique.
3. Identify different tools from this chapter that are similar or the same as tools in other chapters so far.

- Acetate
- Cotton
- Cutter
- Ditty bag
- Draper
- Linen
- Looper
- Measuring tape
- Mr. Puffy
- Nylon
- Overlocking
- Patterning template
- Patterns
- Polyester
- Preshrink
- Rayon
- Seam ripper
- Serger
- Silk
- Sloper
- Tailor's chalk
- Wool

STUDY WORDS
Chapter 14

Accessories and Other Stuff

Costume Crafts

by Denise Wallace-Spriggs

Costume crafts are to the costume department as props and scenic painting are to the scenery department.

Costume crafts is a subdivision of the costume department. The costume crafts artisan works under the costume director and also takes direction from the costume designer. The duties of the craft artisan can include many of the processes for building a costume, except draping or sewing the garment. Those duties may include millinery, shoemaking or modification, fabric dyeing and painting, distressing, masks, armor, body padding, and accessories. Occasionally, the crafts artisan will make wigs or work closely with the wigmaker to achieve a design. Costume crafts artisans must also see to it that tasks are performed in a safe environment and so they need training in hazardous materials safety and personal protective equipment (PPE), such as respirators and eye protection.

Costume crafts artisan is one of the usual job titles for the person who performs this job. Sometimes, the jobs are split up into separate job titles; for instance, many large opera companies, such as Santa Fe Opera, have a dyeing department, as well as separate departments for millinery and for crafts. Theaters combine most of these skills into one position or, at the very least, into one department. Alternative titles for the job include **crafts person and crafts person/dyer.**

CHAPTER FIFTEEN

Student Learning Outcomes

Students will acquire:

- An overview understanding of the major aspects, techniques, and directions in the area of costume crafts.

- Fundamental, conceptual understanding of the expressive possibilities of theatre.

- A working knowledge of concepts applicable to the area of costume crafts.

Let's have a look at some of the skills that a crafts artisan needs to have.

MILLINERY—MAKING HATS

As part of a costume design, hats really help tell the story. They help to fill out the world of the play. Hats can denote historical period, occupation, class, and even the weather. They punctuate the silhouette of the look and can even have a silhouette of their own. Often, a hat will help a character to make an entrance or exit. It might be swept off the head and hung on a peg, or tossed in the air to complement the action. Whatever part it is playing, a hat is very important on the stage.

The milliner is responsible for making hats as well as cleaning, modifying, trimming, and fitting the hats for a stage production. Millinery refers to the work of a hatmaker who makes hats for women. Hatter is the term used for one who makes hats for men. In the theater, however, the milliner is responsible for hats for everyone.

Millinery requires some specialized equipment. Let's have a look.

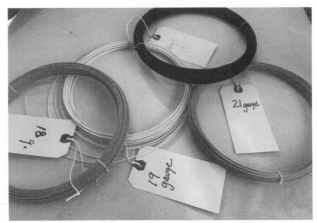

■ **Figure 15.1b** Types of millinery wire, paper covered, rayon covered in black and white, in several typical gauges.

■ **Figure 15.1a** Hat-making supplies: Buckram, hat blocks, grosgrain ribbon, and a canvas block.

■ **Figure 15.1c** Milliners' needles.

EQUIPMENT AND TOOLS

Millinery Tools

For making hats, there is some need for specialized tools such as hat blocks and steamers, but many of the tools and equipment are the very same that are used to make costumes: Steam irons, sewing machines, needles, and cutting tools.

Blocking a Hat

The word "blocking" refers to shaping materials over a wooden mold called a hat block. (What other definitions of "blocking" have you come across this semester?)

Hat blocks are most often hand-carved wooden tools, but these days you can use blocks made of many types of plastics, soft and rubbery types, or vacuum-formed hard plastics. Many artisans are 3D printing them. The

Milliner originally comes from the word "Milener," which used to mean a person from Milan, in northern Italy, in the early 16th century. It was used to refer to the Italian merchants who sold bonnets and accessories. We now use the term to describe those who make hats. In other parts of the world, they might use the word "modist," which comes from French. In Britain and other anglophone countries, the term "model milliner" is used for those who make custom-made hats. In hat-making, we do not use the word "couture," which is reserved for garments.

■ **Figure 15.2a** Head block, canvas block, hat block.

■ **Figure 15.2b** Crown block and brim block.

■ **Figure 15.3** Stock image of a conformateur. A conformateur is an old-style tool for finding the exact shape of the head. This tool was, and still is, used when making very stiff hats, when it is very important to fit the shape of the head for comfort and wearability. These tools are very rare.

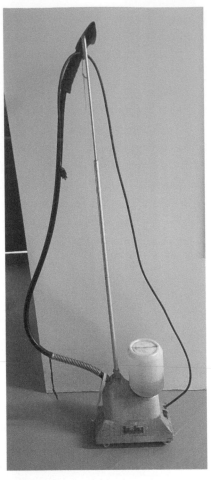

wooden ones are most useful because they can be pinned into and they have a groove, called a rope line, to fit a blocking cord into when tying the materials to the block for drying. Some craft artisans use canvas blocks like the type that wig makers use.

An artisan can block felt, straw, or buckram over the hat block. There are also newer materials, such as Fosshape, that can be blocked over the forms. Fosshape is a thermo-formable material that has become popular all over the world to make hats, costume props, and cosplay items.

Steaming

The milliner's most important tool is steam. The steam loosens the fibers of the material, which allows them to be stretched over the block. Steam is achieved in many ways. You can use a drapery steamer, a handheld garment steamer, a wallpaper steamer, a tea kettle, or a good steam iron. Some hatmakers have a steam cabinet built right into the work table.

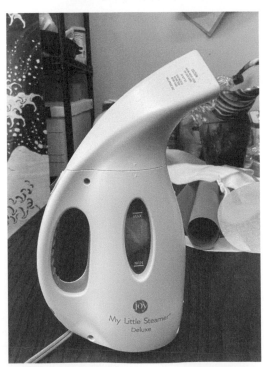

■ **Figure 15.4b** A small hand-held clothing steamer is an inexpensive steaming alternative.

■ **Figure 15.4c** Types of hat stretchers.

■ **Figure 15.5** Felt capeline choices at the Manhatco Stockroom in NYC.

MATERIALS FOR MAKING HATS

The names of hat-making materials vary around the world. Not only are they called by the word translated into each language, but the terminology can vary as well. Millinery has become quite international, and these terms are being shared by hatmakers all over the world, from Europe to Australia, North America to Africa.

Hat-Making Fabrics

Some hat-making materials are sold by the yard or on a large roll. One such fabric is buckram. Buckram is a stiff fabric. It is coarsely woven of cotton fibers and made very stiff with starchy glue. It is also known as English blocking canvas. The glue is dissolvable in water. Buckram can be blocked over a hat block by dampening it and stretching it over the block. If you are going to

■ **Figure 15.6** Block covered with plastic wrap and one covered in foil.

■ **Figure 15.7** Rolls of differing weights of buckram.

■ **Figure 15.8a** Sinamay hat built for *The Corn in Green* at the Huntington Theatre Company; designer Robert Morgan.

■ **Figure 15.8b** Sinamay hat.

block buckram fabric over a block, it is best to protect the block by covering it in plastic wrap or aluminum foil to keep the block clean and to allow the blocked shape to come off the block after it is dry. Otherwise, the dissolved glue will have adhered to the block!

Buckram is a very versatile material because it is so stiff. It can be used to make a cut and wired frame to be covered in fabric. This type of hat-making does not require a block and can be used to make many types of theatrical hats, such as bonnets and top hats.

Other specialty foundation fabrics such as Dior net (also known as Paris net), tarlatan (called crinoline in the USA), chicken net, and cape net have been in and out of fashion for hat manufacture, but we see them in many vintage hats. The most sought-after foundation fabric is esparterie, also known as sparto cloth, sparterie, and willow. It is a fabric woven of a type of willow grass and layered with a fine, stiffened cheesecloth. It holds a shape like no other material. Unfortunately, it is so very rare. There is a modern version being sold today; it is made of paper.

Some hat-making fabrics are made of straw-like materials such as raffia, sinamay, pinak pok, and buntal. These fabrics are most often made up into hats that showcase the natural fibers. Sinamay has been very popular for fancy wedding hats all over the world. In some countries, it is referred to as banana fiber, because it is made from the fibers in the leaves of a type of banana plant.

Hat Bodies

Hat bodies are premade shapes to block hats from. They look a bit like a hat already. Hat bodies can be made of straw or felt and come in different finishes and shapes. The hood shape is for blocking small-brimmed hats or hats without a brim. In another country, this type of body may be referred to as a cone. It looks a bit like an upside-down rounded cone. The cartwheel, so called for its rounded "wheel" shape, is for blocking wide-

■ **Figure 15.8c** A wide-brimmed sinamay hat made for Kate Burton in *The Seagull* at the Huntington Theatre Company; designer Robert Morgan.

■ **Figure 15.8d** A wide-brimmed sinamay hat waiting to be trimmed.

brimmed hats. The flare shape is in between a hood and a cartwheel.

Felt bodies come in many types of finishes, such as the velvety velour finish, which is called peach bloom outside the USA, or salome, a smooth brushed finish. They come in many colors according to what is in fashion at the moment.

Straw bodies is a blanket term used to talk about woven bodies that are mostly used for making

summer-style hats. They are called "straw" but can be manufactured from grasses, leaf fibers, stems of plants, and even coated paper. Straws also come in lengths of braid. They can be called bundle straw or plait. This type of straw can feature novelty elements and is sewn in a coil by hand or machine.

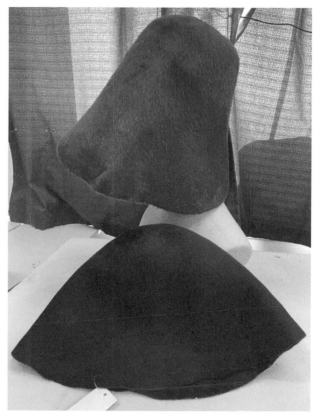

■ **Figure 15.9a** Two felt hoods (or cones), melusine and wool.

■ **Figure 15.9b** Visca straw flair shape and fancy sisol straw hood shape.

MEASUREMENTS

Now that we have talked about the materials and tools, it is time to have a look at some hat-making procedures. The first step is measuring the head.

How to Measure the Head

Before you can make a hat, measurements must be made. These measurements can be used to make a pattern. Making a pattern for a hat is very similar to making one for a garment. The main difference is that, when making a hat, there are fewer essential measurements. The measurement around the head is the most important. It is referred to as the head circumference. Once the measurements are recorded, a milliner will make a pattern and then a mock-up.

■ **Figure 15.10a** Front view showing how to measure for a hat.

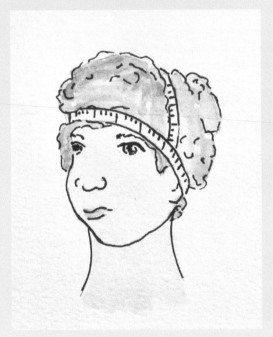

■ **Figure 15.10b** Three-quarter view showing how to measure for a hat.

PATTERN AND MOCK-UP

Whether you are building a cut and sewn hat or a covered buckram hat, patterning skills are important. Most often, the craft artisan will work in paper to determine the shape and size of the desired hat. A paper or fabric mock-up is made in order to work out all the ideas in inexpensive materials, before cutting into the fashion materials.

The mock-up brings to life the idea of the hat and can be tried on the actor in a costume fitting. The designer will work closely with the milliner to establish the correct placement, fit, and silhouette. After the hat is fit, pattern corrections are made, and work on the hat can begin.

■ **Figure 15.11** Paper hat mock-up.

■ **Figure 15.12** Cut and sewn hat.

CUT AND SEWN HATS

A cut and sewn hat begins with the fabric. Choosing a fabric that has the proper hand to achieve and hold the shape is most important. If the fabric is too soft or thin or has too much drape to make the hat, a milliner may opt to add interfacing or starch, which can add body or stiffness to the chosen fabric.

Once the fabric has been prepared, it is laid out for cutting. The nature of a cut and sewn hat is in its very name—it is first cut out of fabric and then it is sewn together. Newsboy caps, chef's hats, baseball caps, and some cloche hats are examples of cut and sewn hats. This is often the introductory hat made by a hatmaker in training. Patterning and sewing skills are required.

COVERED BUCKRAM FRAME HATS

Using the foundation materials that were described previously, a buckram frame hat has much in common with a cut and sewn hat; however, it is stiffened by the layers of buckram that define its shape. Fabric is sewn to the shape, and the parts are assembled into the final hat. Because many historical types of hats are made with buckram, it is very popular for costumes.

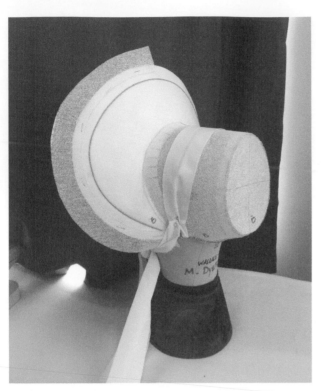

■ **Figure 15.13a** A buckram mock-up for a fitting.

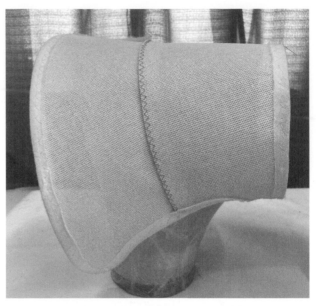

■ **Figure 15.13b** A buckram frame awaiting a fabric cover.

■ **Figure 15.13c** Buckram brim with fabric pinned on and ready to stitch.

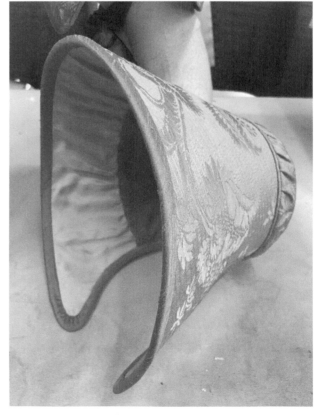

■ **Figure 15.13d** Buckram frame covered in fabric.

■ **Figure 15.13e** Completed buckram bonnet.

SHOES

The costume craft artisan is called upon to make the shoes that are chosen fit the design. This can include painting the shoes to the color of the design, rubbering the soles of the shoe, stretching them for the comfort of the actor, relining the leather insole, and cleaning up a dusty pair that has been in costume stock for a while.

For safety reasons, shoes for the stage usually need to have thin rubber applied to the sole. Soles are often leather and are just too slippery! Sometimes, the rubber is referred to as "Cat's Paw," a term taken from the name of a company that manufactures the rubber sheets. Rubbering can be done in-house by the craft artisan,

■ **Figure 15.14** Shoe paint with primer and after final coat of paint.

■ **Figure 15.15a** Prepping for shoe rubber.

■ **Figure 15.15b** Rubber glued.

or is sometimes sent out to the local cobbler. Adding rubber to the shoes helps the actor to keep a sure footing on stage surfaces.

Much of the modifying of shoes falls under the heading of distressing. For example, let's say that the show is set in the 1930s dust bowl. If the craft team is presented with a brand-new pair of black shoes, but the designer would like them to be brown and look old and worn, the team will employ various techniques to break them down. They will use paints that are formulated to adhere to shoes and be flexible. (Some paints, such as

fine arts acrylic paints, are too stiff to use on a shoe and will crack off after use.)

Most theater companies do not have a cobbler on staff who can build shoes from scratch. Simple slippers, cuffs, extensions on boots, or additions of buckles, shoe bows, or taller tongues to go with a specific period of dress are often done by the craft team. Shoes can be sent to the local cobbler for repairs that require specialized machinery or tools. For more complex or specific footwear, there are businesses that specialize in building shoes for the theatre.

Ballet companies will usually have a person or department that is dedicated to shoes and slippers. They order the shoes and make sure that each dancer has enough shoes to last the run of the ballet. They will also dye or paint the shoes. As for fitting the ballet shoe to the foot, if a dancer wants a perfect fit, they should do the alteration to their own shoes, and so, early in their careers, they learn to sew on the ribbons and make any alterations themselves.

> My job is to make the brown shoes black, make the black shoes brown, make the clean shoes dirty, make the dirty shoes clean.
> —**Denise Wallace-Spriggs,**
> **crafts artisan,**
> **Huntington Theatre Company**

Figure 15.15c Rubber glued and ready to pound and trim.

Figure 15.15d Final tweak before finish.trim.

Figure 15.16a A boot before distressing.

Figure 15.16b Distressed boots.

DYEING AND FABRIC MODIFICATION

One of the main jobs of the costume craft department is dyeing and fabric modification. There are so many fabrics that are available on the market these days that you might wonder why you would ever need to dye it. The thing is, a costume design has quite specific needs for the weight and the "hand" of the fabric. The term hand refers to the way that the fabric feels in your hand. For instance, it may feel stiff, soft, or drapey. The weight and the hand are the most important attributes of the fabric. In order for the costume team to construct the garment to the specifics of the designer, they will need the fabric to be just right. It is easier to change the color than to change the hand, so that is where the dyer steps in.

Many theatre companies use high-quality natural fibers in order to be able to control the color with dyes. Some man-made fibers are quite difficult to dye in a non-industrial setting. The dyer's job is to change the color or pattern of the cloth. They will make swatches for the designer to choose and approve. Once the colors are chosen, the dyer will need to match the swatch color very closely, and sometimes exactly, so they keep very careful records of the dye recipe. Even with the time constraints of a costume build, a dyer cannot take shortcuts when recording the swatch recipes. When you have accurate records, the dyeing goes much faster. In the theatre context, we are looking for repeatable results. The dyer will need to control for many variables, such as: weight of the fiber, temperature and volume of the dye bath, amount of dye being used, time the fabric is in the dye bath, and any other chemicals that are used in the bath.

A well written recipe will help the dyer translate the tiny amount of dye that is on a small swatch to the amount that you will need for the total amount of yardage. To do this, the metric system is used to calculate the depth of shade. This refers to the intensity and value of the color and is expressed by the formula:

$$\text{Depth of shade} = \frac{\text{weight of dye}}{100 \text{ grams of fiber}}$$

This formula gives what is called the on weight of goods calculation, or the OWG. If a formula is for 1 percent OWG, it means that that, for every 100 grams of fabric, you will use 1 gram of dye; 0–1 percent is a light value; 2–4 percent is a dark value.

Dyes can be natural, or man-made. Natural dye can be derived from animal, vegetable, or mineral sources. They are generally less predictable than man-made dyes. Manufactured dyes can help ensure repeatable results.

Fabric yardage is not the only thing that comes through the dye room. Quite often, complete garments need to be dyed. These could be items that have been freshly made by the costume team or purchased items. There are special challenges in dyeing whole garments, not the least of which is the fact that air pockets can get trapped in the sleeves, pockets, and legs of the garments The air pockets make it hard to keep the fabric under the surface of the bath to promote even dyeing. Stirring the

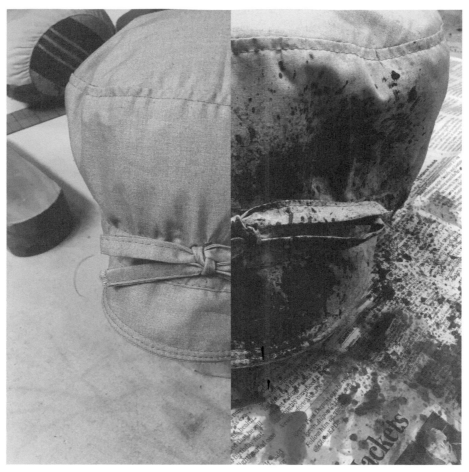

■ **Figure 15.18** Before and after cap distressing.

fabric and poking it so the trapped air gets released are referred to as "burping" the bath.

In addition to dyeing fabric, the dyer is often responsible for fabric modification and distressing. Fabric modification can include painting, printing, and pleating. Craft artisans will use brushes, silk screens, stamps, and stencils to print patterns onto fabrics before or after the costumes are made.

Distressing of garments is the technique of using paint and tools to break down the garments to make them look worn or old. They can also have special effects, such as blood or dirt stains, added to them. With so many contemporary productions happening lately, the costume craft artisan is often asked to make brand new garments look less new, and sometimes very worn and old looking, even if they have just been made. In the film industry, these artisans are called breakdown artists or agers/dyers.

MASK MAKING

Since the very first dramas were performed in Ancient Greece (or maybe earlier?), masks have been a part of the theatrical experience. The very first costumes for the stage involved wearing a mask. The heavy carved wood and leather mask of old has made way for masks made of materials of every description. Contemporary masks can be made of molded leather, thermoplastics, papier-mâché, fabric, plastic, or paper. You name it, and you might be able to make a mask with it! A mask can cover all or part of the face; it can change the performers look to change or enhance a character. It can be neutral, comic, or scary. When masks are called for in a performance, they come to the work table of the craft artisan.

CASTING

One of the first things that the artisan needs in order to build a mask is a face to mold it over. A premade shape can be used, such as a pre-existing mask that has been reinforced, but one of the best ways to get a shape that fits well is to make a casting of the performer's face.

Casting the actor requires preparation and planning. All of the tools and supplies should be laid out carefully and ready to use, because, once the process begins, you do not want to stop to measure or cut open bags or search for the scissors. Your hands will become sticky, and it will be hard to go searching for your stuff.

There are a few ways to cast a face. Alginate casting and plaster casting are two popular methods. Alginate might be familiar to you if you have ever had to have

■ **Figure 15.19a** Model Zarah Avalon in protective plastic layer.

Things to keep in mind when you are setting out to make a face cast:

- How much product will you need. A face cast requires about 1.5–2 rolls of 3″ bandages.
- **Barrier creams** can be useful to protect the skin of the model. Use a good slather of barrier cream, let dry, do another, and let dry.
- Apply Vaseline on eyebrows and lashes to act as a **release agent** and keep them from being ripped out when the cast is removed.
- Once the Vaseline goes on, the model cannot open their eyes.
- It is very difficult to work on a face with facial hair. You will need to use lots of Vaseline.
- A trash bag is a good layer to protect the model's clothing.
- Tape a plastic grocery bag to the hairline.
- Do not forget to coat the inside of the mold with soap as a release agent before you make a cast of it.

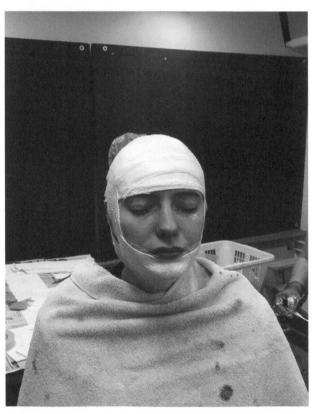

■ **Figure 15.19b** Wrapping the face in plaster bandages.

■ **Figure 15.20a** Preparing the plaster to fill the negative mold.

■ **Figure 15.20b** Final "positive" cast.

impressions made of your teeth at the dentist. It comes as a dry powder and is mixed with water and stirred until it begins to thicken. When using alginate, you will need to work quickly, since it can set in from two to ten minutes. The alginate can be smoothed over the face of the performer. When it is set and removed, you will have a negative mold of the face.

There are, of course, many other ways to cast the face for mask making. One of the simplest and most straightforward is by using plaster bandages.

THE COMFORT OF THE MODEL

When casting the face of the model, be sure to consider their comfort. During most of this process, the model will not be able to see what is going on and, for part of it, they will not be able to speak. Consider setting up a communication system. You could use hand signals, if the model can see; if not, you will need to develop a system that can be understood by all. Make sure the room that you are working in has a comfortable temperature. The materials that are being used can make a person quite chilly. You will need a water source or a bucket of warm water. The warm water will speed the process. To slow the process, use cooler water.

TYPES OF CASTING

Once you have your negative mold, this can be filled with a casting material such as plaster to form a positive cast of the face. Dump casting is the process of filling a mold with liquid plaster, whereas slush casting is when you use small amounts of plaster in layers in the mold by swirling it around. This type of casting creates a hollow-backed cast that is lighter in weight than a dump cast. Also, it uses less material. It is good to add a layer of burlap or other open-weave fabric to give it some structural strength.

■ **Figure 15.21** Unmolding the cast.

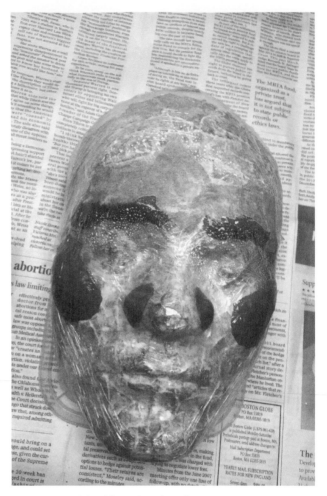

■ **Figure 15.22** Adding plastalina clay to a positive cast to change the shape.

SCULPTING OR MANIPULATING THE SHAPE OF THE FACE

When you have a cast of a face, you can manipulate the look of the face by sculpting on it with clay. In this way, you can use one cast to make many masks. Plastalina is a good type of modeling clay to use for this purpose. If you are going to work with heat-activated materials, such as thermoplastics, you may need to cast the sculpted form again to make a negative and then a positive, since plastalina will melt and deform when heat is applied to it.

FITTING THE MASK

You can make a mock-up in papier-mâché in order to look at the shape of the mask before it is made with the final materials. Then you can make any changes to the mold that are needed and move on to making the real thing.

Wet leather can be used to make a mask. It is best to shape it over a carved wooden mold since you will need to hammer it into the final shape as it is drying. Papier-mâché can be used to make the final mask. It can be sanded and painted to mimic many types of materials. But really, you can make a mask out of almost anything you can imagine. Once you have a cast or two, they can be adapted to use for many faces.

STAGE ARMOR

Making stage armor is one of the specialty costume areas that some craft artisans work in.

Because historic battle armor was made to protect the wearer by deflecting weapons, the pieces were usually stiff and often quite heavy. Heavy, inflexible armor is inappropriate for the stage. It is difficult for an actor to move in, impossible to make quick changes, and often very noisy. Stage armor needs to be easy to wear but tough enough for the stage. Craft artisans and cosplayers all over the world have been developing techniques to make armor from many historical periods using leather, thermoplastics, felt, or foam.

■ **Figure 15.23** Vacuum-formed armor front and back plate, from Tobins Lake Studios, one with papier-mâché reinforcement.

Approaching an Armor Project

Before beginning an armor project, the craft artisans will ask themselves and their designer a few questions:

- What is the specific time period for this costume?
- Is this armor going to be in a quick change?
- What will be worn under the armor?
- What will the surface look like?
- What materials will it be made of?
- What noise will it make when the performer is moving?

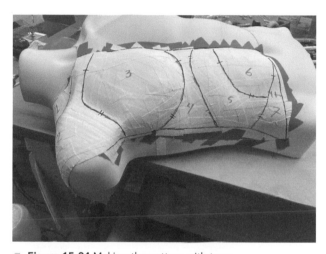

■ **Figure 15.24** Making the pattern with tape.

One of the most straightforward ways to make stage armor is to use preformed shapes. Companies such as Tobins Lake Studios sell lightweight vacuformed armor parts that come in a plain white color and can be used as a substrate to cover and paint. You can choose from many historical periods. They have pieces from helmets and leg greaves to breastplates and gorgets.

If making the form of the piece from scratch, it is best to have a mannequin to mold the armor pieces over. A prototype, called a mock-up, is made using an inexpensive material that can hold the shape. Some prototype materials are felt, canvas, thin EVA foam, and cardboard with tape.

FITTING THE MOCK-UP

Once the armor parts are mocked up, they can be tried on the performer in a fitting. In the fitting, the armor should be fit over any parts of the costume that will be worn under it. The performer should try out any movements that they may be using on stage to make sure that the stiff armor will not inhibit these moves. It is very important to get it right in the fitting since it will be difficult to make changes later in the process.

ALTERING THE MOCK-UP

If the changes to the mock-up are extensive, it is best to make a second prototype. It is worth the time to get the fit right at this point. The prototypes can be sent to the rehearsal room for the performers to use. This way they get used to how the piece might affect the way they move. They can also practice getting in and out of it.

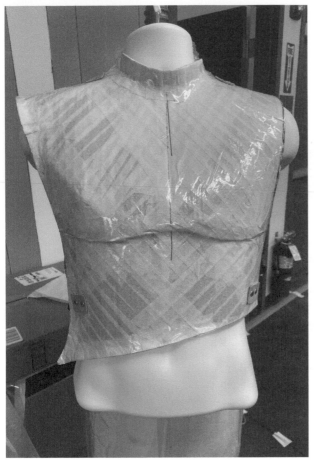

■ **Figure 15.25** Armor mock-up made with cardboard and tape.

EXAMPLES OF SOME TYPES OF STAGE ARMOR

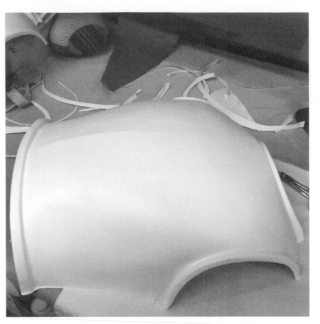

■ **Figure 15.26a** Vacuformed chest plate.

■ **Figure 15.26b** Applying papier-mâché over a vacuformed chest plate.

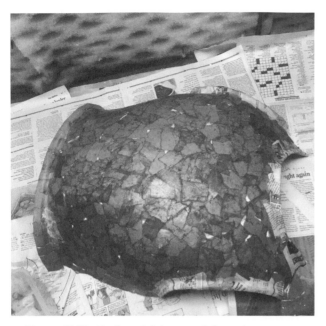

■ **Figure 15.26c** Papier-mâché-covered chest plate.

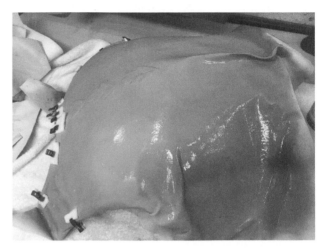

■ **Figure 15.26d** Covering chest plate with wet leather.

■ **Figure 15.26e** Finished leafed and painted chest plate.

MAKING THE ARMOR

Some materials are quite thin, and it is best to build them onto a substrate or line them with a material that will bulk them up a bit. EVA foam is a good base to work thermoplastics over.

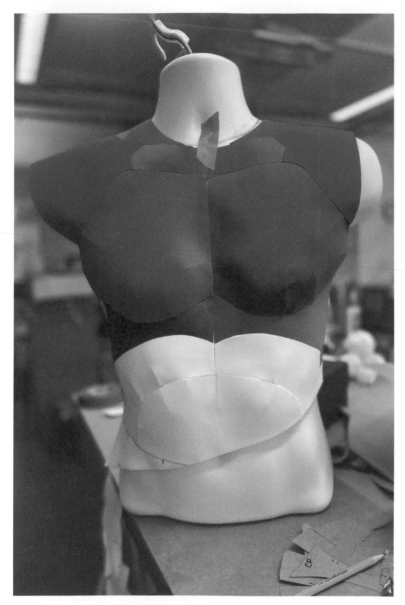

■ **Figure 15.27** EVA foam understructure for thermoplastic armor.

Types of Armor

- Lamellar: Made of pieces of hardened leather, **hides**, and fur sewn to a backing. This is the oldest type of armor.
- Chainmail: **Chainmail**, also called mail, began as an outgrowth of **lamellar**. Metal rings were sewn to a backing of cloth or leather. This practice evolved to linking the rings together to protect the wearer from arrows and spears.
- Plate: Plate armor is still seen today in the form of the padding used for many "high-impact" sports.
- Futuristic: Contemporary cosplayers and craft artisans build armor pieces based on **futuristic** ideas from anime, films, and their own imagination. The shapes and ideas for these pieces often are influenced by the historic armor shapes. They are often made of thermoplastic materials.

Working with Thermoplastics

Thermoplastics are materials that can be manipulated by heating them gently and molding them. They can be molded over a form or free-form. Costume craft artisans use them for many things including armor, crowns, jewelry, and more.

Figure 15.28a Heating thermoplastic with a heat gun.

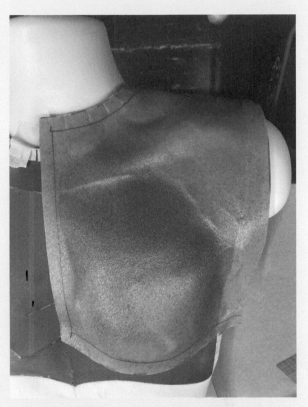

Figure 15.28b Forming the thermoplastic over the understructure.

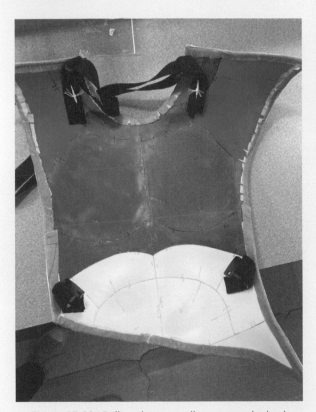

Figure 15.28c Rolling the seam allowance to the back.

Many artisans like to use felt or pigskin as the lining. The felt is comfortable, while the pigskin can be cleaned fairly easily.

■ **Figure 15.29a** Gluing a leather lining to a leather vambrace.

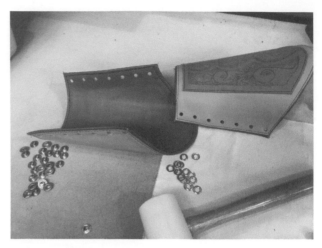

■ **Figure 15.29b** Inside and outside of the vambrace, before finish work.

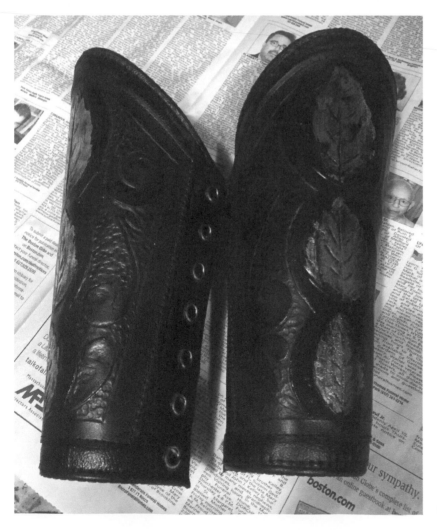

■ **Figure 15.29c** Finished vambraces.

SURFACE FINISHES

Careful testing should be done on the paint treatments and surface finishes. Some finishes do not sit well with others. Testing them is important to make sure that they do not crack or rub off.

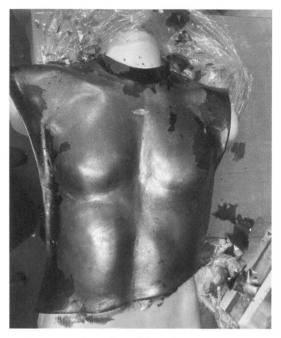

■ **Figure 15.30** Finishing failure due to incompatible paints.

■ **Figure 15.31a** Testing swatch for finishing coat.

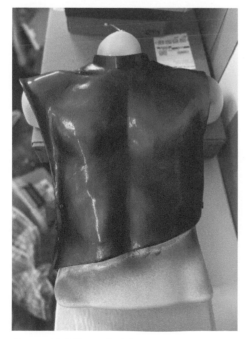

■ **Figure 15.31b** Applied finish coat.

■ **Figure 15.31c** Successful finish on chest plate for *Hurricane Diane* at the Huntington Theatre Company; designer, Hahnji Jang.

BODY MODIFICATION PADDING

Modifying a performer's body can be done in many ways. Corsetry, high heels, temporary tattoos, and the use of wigs are a few. A common way to change the look of the body is by using body padding. Some types of body paddings are: bellies, humps, muscle padding, and pregnancy pads.

Note: There are other times that padding is used in costuming that is the purview of the draper's team, such as: hip and bum rolls that fit under petticoats for gowns of certain periods, chest padding in a doublet, shoulder pads in garments, and bust pads. Generally, the craft artisan does not deal with these.

Thinking Your Way through a Body Pad

- Does the actor wear it throughout the performance? Or do they change in or out of it?
- If they change, is it a fast change?
- How much weight, or "baby," needs to be added for the actor to work with?
- Do you have visual research?
- Does the pad need to washable? Will it be washed after every performance?
- Think about drying it. How long will that take? Will it go into a dryer or hang dry?

Answering the above questions will help the artisan decide what the pad should be made of and what the construction will be.

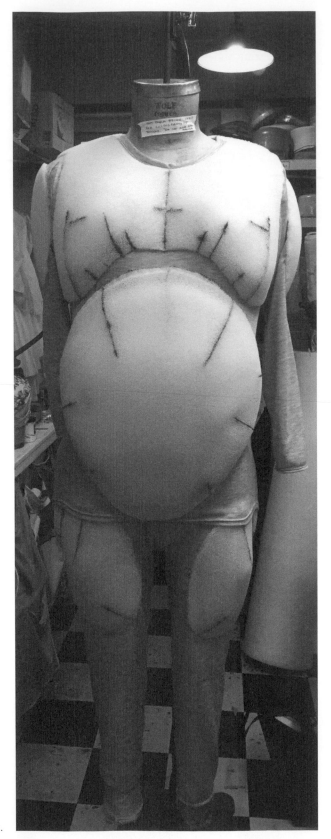

■ **Figure 15.32a** Full body padding mounted on wicking undergarments.

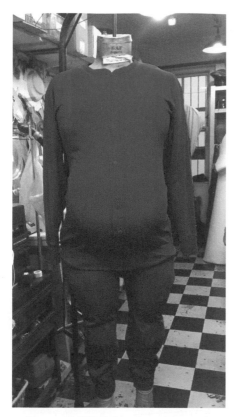

Figure 15.32b Full body padding with outer garment applied over the padding, front view.

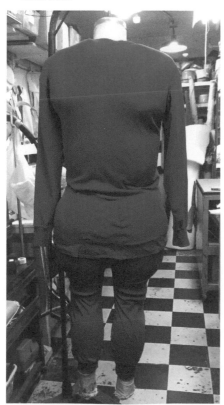

Figure 15.32c Full body padding with outer garment applied over the padding, back view.

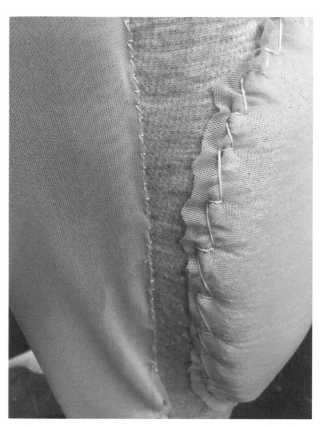

Figure 15.32d Detail view of the stitching used to sew the individual pads onto the undergarment.

RETICULATED VS POLYURETHANE FOAM

Reticulated foams such as air conditioner foam or Dryfast™ foam are open-cell foams. They are lightweight, airy, and have a net-like structure to the air cells. They can hold their shape quite nicely. Dryfast™ and other types of reticulated foams for outdoor furniture are designed to shed moisture such as rain. Air conditioner foam is another type of reticulated foam, but it does not shed moisture in the same way. If your padding needs laundering on a regular basis, a fast-drying type is a good foam to choose. If constructed well, it can be washed on a gentle program in the washing machine. The spin cycle will spin out most of the water, or it can also go into a dryer, on a low setting.

Polyurethane foams are readily available at many upholstery or sewing stores. Companies are beginning to manufacture some eco foams that are better for the environment. Polyurethane foams can be heavier in feel and often feel softer. They also hold moisture and take a long time to dry. If your padding does not need to be washed often, you can use polyurethane foam.

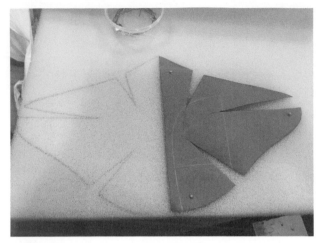

Figure 15.33a Pattern piece cut out of Dryfast™ foam.

Figure 15.33b Cutting foam with electric knife.

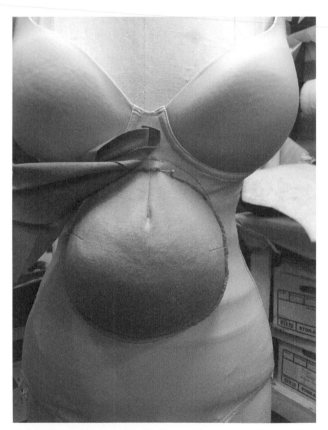

Figure 15.33c Weighted stuffing pouch.

Figure 15.34 Glued foam belly piece.

POLYESTER BATTING: QUILT TYPE VS UPHOLSTERY TYPE

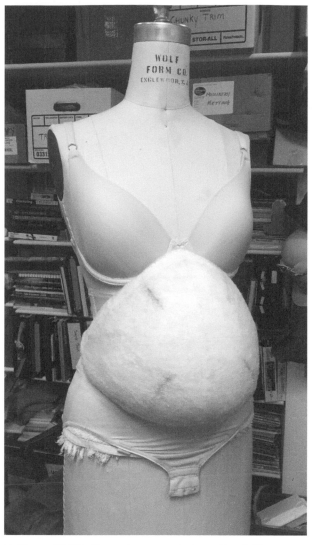

■ **Figure 15.35a** Foam piece mounted over the stuffing.

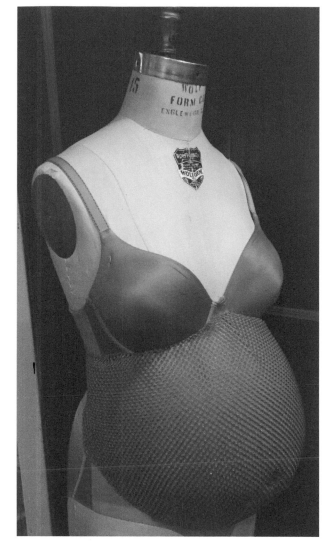

■ **Figure 15.35b** Finished pregnancy pad.

There are many types of batting. Some batting is purpose-made for quilting and crafts. A sturdier type can be bought from upholstery suppliers. It has a firmer spring and holds its shape longer. Most types of batting can be peeled apart in layers to make finer gradations in your padding.

One reason to use batting to make your padding is that it is readily available at many craft and sewing suppliers. If it is quilted together lightly, by hand, with a net-like structure similar to a tailor's pad stitch, it can hold through many washings.

SMOOTHING LAYERS AND COVERINGS

For quilted paddings, it is a good idea to add a layer of batting over the top, to smooth out any of the indentations made by your stitching. Over the top of that you will need to make a covering layer. Often a knit fabric is used, since it can stretch nicely over the dimensions of the shape. You will want your padding to appear smooth under the costume.

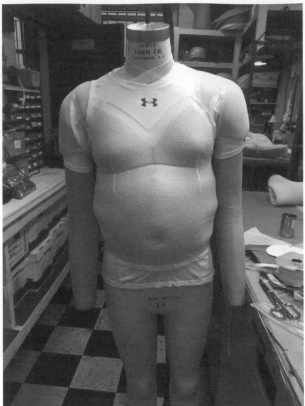

■ **Figure 15.36a** T-shirt-based, zipper-back padding, front view.

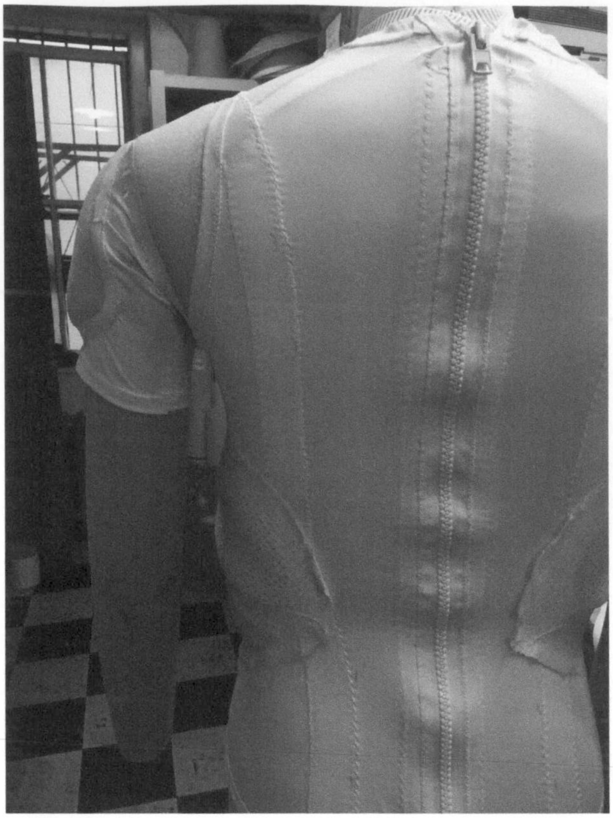

■ **Figure 15.36b** T-shirt-based, zipper-back padding, back view.

PADDINGS ON A T-SHIRT BASE

One easy way to make a padding for the torso is to build it on a T-shirt. A moisture-wicking shirt will help to keep the performer more comfortable on stage. You can sew a zipper up the center back. If you are adding a shape to the back, such as a hump, you can sew the zipper into the front. T-shirt-based paddings are great for tummies. To make a muscle pad, it is good to use a long-sleeved base.

Fitting the garment to the performer with darts will help to keep the padding in its proper place. A strap at the crotch can help to keep the pad from riding up during the action of the play.

ACCESSORIES/JEWELRY

Accessories might be considered incidental in everyday clothing, but, for a costume, an accessory can be the detail that helps to complete the story that the garments are trying to tell! A ruff, fastened around the neck, shows the audience that the play is set in the Tudor period. A lacy parasol will indicate a scene set in the Victorian or Edwardian period. In addition to pinpointing a time period, accessories can show where in the world the play is set.

Costume accessories can include a wide variety of items such as: parasols and umbrellas, gloves, mittens and mitts, purses and bags, belts and baldrics, sword belts and scabbards, and jewelry.

PROP OR COSTUME?

With parasols and umbrellas, we begin to come up against the age-old question, "Is it a costume? Or is it a prop?" To answer this, we have consulted with prop and

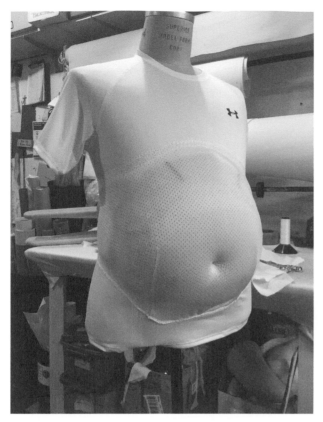

Figure 15.36c T-shirt-based, zipper-back padding, front view.

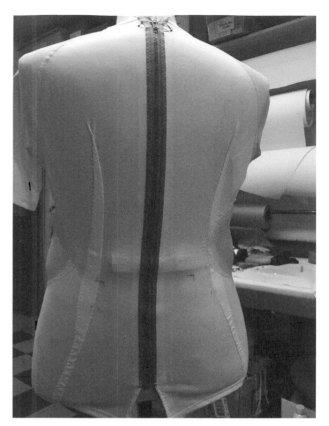

Figure 15.36d T-shirt-based, zipper-back padding, back view.

craft artisans from around the country, and the consensus seems to be that each theater sees things a bit differently. One guideline is "If you wear it, it is a costume. If you carry it, it's a prop." But what of things such as parasols that match a costume? At many theaters, the parasol comes from the costume department, because it has to coordinate with the look of the garments, whereas an umbrella is more universal in its function and has a more generic look, and so, at most theaters, it would be called a prop, stored with props, and might be under the purview of the props running crew backstage.

Other pieces that come up for this question are bags, purses, and luggage. Most luggage is considered a prop, unless the costume designer gets the notion to coordinate it with a costume and draws it in their rendering plate, and then it would be likely to go on the list of the costume craft department. Purses are usually costumes, but some bags can end up in the props department, such as money purses and backpacks.

The thinking may be different from venue to venue. For instance, at a regional theater that has individual

departments for each specialty (costume crafts and props), the areas will develop a system to divide the workload that makes sense for them. Often, they will work together on cross-over pieces such as luggage that matches a costume. The suitcase might come from prop storage, but be decorated by the craft artisan. If it needs to be filled with clothing, that could come from the costume department. What about smaller theaters that do not have a costume or prop shop, or a commercial venue, such as a Broadway house? In those cases, the designers work with the costumer and the head of props to contract out to the appropriate business or artisan who will do the work on a freelance basis.

When weaponry is concerned, there is most often coordination between the two departments. For instance, the gun belt or sword belt would need to be fitted to the performer, so they are costumes, but the scabbard and sword, as well as firearms, are props. When handling firearms, even ones that shoot blanks, extreme care must be paid to their safe handling. They should be stored in a safe. Anyone responsible for the prop gun

■ **Figure 15.37a** Necklace beaded in the Zulu style for *Nomathemba*, by Joseph Shabalala, at the Huntington Theatre Company.

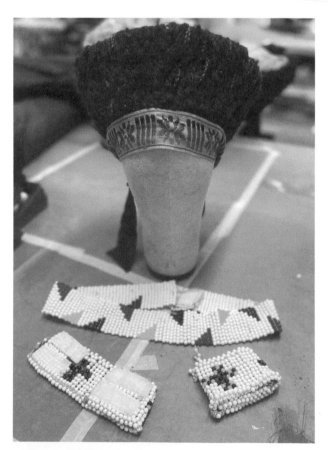

■ **Figure 15.37b** Zulu-style headdress, built of wool twisted with synthetic hair over a wire frame. Beaded bracelets from South Africa, with quick-change Velcro tabs added.

■ **Figure 15.37c** Another view of the Zulu-style headdress.

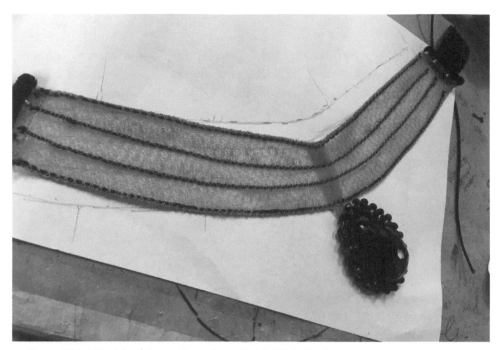

■ **Figure 15.38** Mesh-back jet necklaces from *A Little Night Music.*

will need special safety training, and often a gun license is required.

There are many specialty businesses that deal in particular types of accessories and can build custom pieces for a production. A designer can contract these artisans or businesses to build custom-made gloves, shoes, corsets, or wigs, to name a few.

The theatre is particularly hard on jewelry. Pieces that last for years in the ordinary person's wardrobe sometimes cannot stand up to the abuse that they might be put through on stage. Let's take for example a multi-strand beaded necklace that is involved in a quick change. The strands of beads can easily become tangled, and a weak string could break, scattering beads everywhere, so that now we have a tripping hazard. Special care should be taken to restring beads with a knot between each bead so that, if the string should break, only one bead would end up on the floor. Another approach is to mount the necklace on a sheer base, such as illusion net or some other type of mesh. The mesh can be dyed to match the performer's skin tone so that it cannot be seen from the audience. Another use for net or mesh is to cover a bejeweled piece such as a brooch or tiara so that it will not catch on the costume or wig, but the sparkle can be seen through the net.

LEATHER WORK

Craft artisans use leather in so many applications; masks, accessories, and stage armor are the big categories. But it can also be used as a support material in other ways. Often, leather is used as a repair material. In order to maintain, refurbish, or augment shoes for productions, a knowledge of leather and how to work with it is essential.

Let's have a look at some of the ways leather and leather substitutes are used by the craft artisan.

THE FIRST CHOICE: LEATHER TYPES AND WEIGHTS

The first thing that we need to have a look at is the type of leather that we will use. Leather is a material made from the skin of an animal by tanning or a similar process. The tanning process converts animal skin into leather by soaking it in a liquid containing tannic acid, or by the use of other chemicals. There are two major types of tanning processes, chrome tanning and vegetable tanning. Chrome tanning uses chromium sulfate. Leather tanned this way is used mostly for garments. Vegetable tanned leather is an ancient form of preparing leather with tannic acid from vegetation, often oak leaves. Sometimes the leather will be called oak tanned.

Vegetable tanned leather is the type that can be molded and carved. It is the type for making masks, tooled belts, and often armor pieces, because it can hold a shape after it is wet and molded.

MAKING THE PATTERN PIECES

Patterning for leather pieces is very much the same as garment patterning. The craft artisan needs to take into account the stiffness and thickness of the leather, because it moves differently than most fabrics.

TOOLS

Special tools are required to work with leather. Many are similar to dressmaking tools, but they are heftier in order to handle the thickness of the hides. Leather shears are manufactured to allow for the kerf of the materials. Kerf refers to allowance made for the thickness of materials. Leather needles have a cutting point to go through tough skins. They actually look like tiny spears.

PREPARING THE GOODS

In order to tool designs into the leather, the surface needs to be prepared by dampening. This is called casing the leather. Once the water, or casing solution, soaks into the leather, we can use special knives and stamps to tool a pattern into the leather.

SURFACE DESIGN AND TOOLING

Tooling is very much like embossing but on a smaller scale. Designs and patterns are pressed or hammered into the surface.

■ **Figure 15.39a** Cutting in the design for tooled leather with a swivel knife.

■ **Figure 15.39b** Tooled leather.

STITCHING TECHNIQUES

Because leather is often much tougher and thicker than fabric, special needles and machines are used. A walking foot sewing machine can be helpful. It has a special foot that lifts up and comes down with each stitch, grabbing the material and moving it along. When stitching heavyweight leathers by hand, a leather worker will punch stitching holes with a punch and then stitch through the holes using two needles, one for each side of the seam. If we are stitching through very soft or thin leather, such as the type we use to make gloves, a glover's needle is used to punch through the hide as we stitch.

HARDWARE

There are hundreds of types of specialized hardware for use with leather. Where shall we begin? Here are three of the most commonly used. Grommets are set with a grommet die in order to reinforce a hole in the leather with a metal tube. Rivets are two-part metal hardware used to join pieces, instead of, or in addition to, stitching. Chicago screws are like rivets, but they are threaded so they can come apart. They are great to use for fittings because they are easily removed.

FINISHING DETAILS

In addition to tooling and embossing, the surface of the leather can be worked or designed with paints, dyes, and finishers. Leather dyes are a bit different from dyes that are used for fabric. They are designed to be applied to the surface, with a brush, spray, or dauber, and left to dry. Unless they are being processed in an industrial setting, they are not set in a dye bath. In this way they are very much like paint, but they do not contain a binder (or glue) to hold them to the surface. Instead, finishers are applied over the top, which help to bind them. These finishers can be shellac-based resins, oils, or clear acrylics. They come in matte, satin, and high gloss.

Leather paints are developed to adhere to the surface of the leather and are very flexible to allow for movement of the leather piece without cracking.

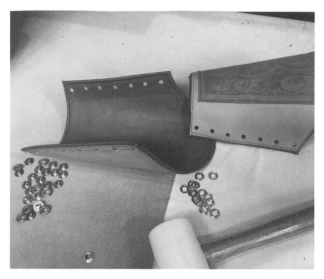

■ **Figure 15.40a** Setting grommets through the punched holes in leather vambraces.

■ **Figure 15.40b** Grommets set into finished vambraces.

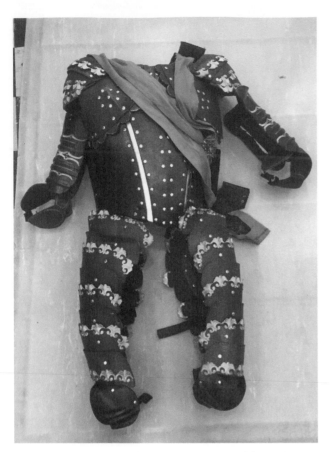

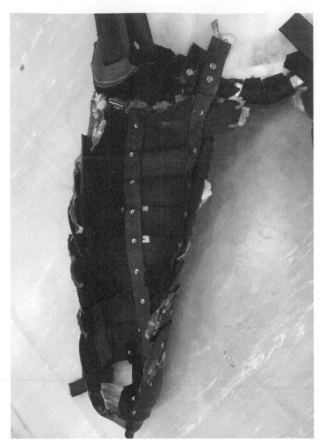

■ **Figure 15.40c** Quick change suit of armor held together with rivets.

■ **Figure 15.40d** Inside view of riveted armor.

■ **Figure 15.40e** Leather buckle tabs will hold a chest plate to a back plate.

Figure 15.40f
Punching holes with
a hand-held hole
punch to set the
rivets for the buckle
tabs in a back plate.

Figure 15.40g
Finished plate armor
(modeled by
Marshall T. Spriggs).

EXERCISES

EXERCISE 1

Build a cockade using ribbon and a button.

EXERCISE 2

Clean and polish a shoe, using rag, shoe polish, a spray bottle of water, and a shoe brush.

EXERCISE 3

Distressing: Tea dye a hankie using a cotton handkerchief, a bowl of hot water, and a teabag.

CHECK YOUR KNOWLEDGE

1. Discuss the different kinds of tanning and why they exist.
2. What are the different styles of armor? Choose a different play or musical where each type would be appropriate.

- Ager/Dyer
- Alginate
- Barrier cream
- Breakdown artists
- Burlap
- Burping
- Casing the leather
- Cast
- Chainmail
- Chicago screws
- Chrome tanning
- Cobbler
- Depth of shade
- Distressing
- Dump casting
- Dyeing
- Fabric modification
- Finish
- Futuristic
- Glover's needle
- Gorgets
- Grommets
- Hand
- Hide
- Kerf
- Lamellar
- Leather
- Leather needles
- Leather shears
- Leg greaves
- Mold
- On weight of goods (OWG)
- Papier-mâché
- Plaster bandage
- Release agent
- Repeatable results
- Rivets
- Ruff
- Shellac
- Slush casting
- Swatches
- Tanning
- Thermoplastics
- Walking foot

STUDY WORDS
Chapter 15

Put on a Happy Face

Hair and Makeup

CHAPTER SIXTEEN

Student Learning Outcomes

Students will acquire:

- An overview understanding of the major aspects, techniques, and styles in the area of hair and makeup.

- Fundamental, conceptual understanding of the expressive possibilities of theatre.

- A working knowledge of concepts applicable to the area of hair and makeup.

In our eternal search for the next logical step, we made it to hair and makeup! Let's begin with makeup. We will look at the history of makeup in general and then get more specific regarding performance makeup. We will discuss some additional information about hair and wigs toward the end of the chapter.

Makeup, and the concept behind it, has changed greatly over the years. Makeup goes back to Egypt and before. Women of the time would use a product called *kohl* as an ancient eye makeup. Kohl was made by grinding several natural ingredients together and making a powder. This could be used as an eye shadow or, with water added, as an eyeliner or mascara.

Organized makeup as we know it came into fashion during the 1920s and 1930s, when a man by the name of **Max Factor** became associated with the world of Hollywood makeup. Yes, that is right, Max Factor was a real person. And his son, Max Factor, Jr., continued his father's tradition. Max Factor created the first makeup for the movies and coined the term *makeup*, based on the verb *to make up* one's face. Prior to this, all performers were pretty much on their own for what they used. Max and his company are credited with many cosmetic innovations, such as the first motion picture makeup in 1914, lip gloss in 1930, pancake makeup (the forerunner of all modern cream makeups) in 1937, Pan Stik makeup in 1948, Erace (the original coverup) in 1954, and the first "waterproof" makeup in 1971. How is that for one man's history?

Ben Nye is another makeup pioneer, and his company has been very helpful in providing me with in-depth information both on tools and techniques. Ben Nye began his career as a Hollywood makeup artist, beginning in the 1930s. By the time he retired, his ethnic foundations and unique colors had become standards in most makeup departments. He began formulating his own makeup brand ten years after his retirement. Today, his son Dana runs the company Ben started in 1967.

DESIGN

Hair and makeup design only partially follows the design process outlined in earlier chapters. Let's discuss the process in depth, starting with research. Before beginning your own research, you should discuss with the director and other designers what their concepts are. If other designers already have sketches, make sure to see those. Are the sets and costumes being rented? This can also make a big difference to how you proceed.

At the first rehearsal, take headshots of all the actors. These photos can be used as a base for makeup plots and even hair/wig plots. Make sure to notate their height. Speak with stage management and determine the amount of time each actor will have for pre-show prep time. Begin your in-depth notes with hair length, style, texture, and color. Color assessments can be made using samples from an industry hair color wheel. Measure each actor's head circumference in case wigs will be used.

Begin with your historical research. Use either reliable imagery or references of real individuals. Don't depend on photos from other productions, as their research may be flawed. If you are dealing with a celebrity, extra research is needed. Research images of past roles to establish their "comfort zone" for attractiveness, style, and colors. This is one area where the actors' input is key. Statements like "I had to wear a blonde wig once and hated it," "I am terrible with (or love) makeup," or "I'm

■ **Figure 16.1** *The Tempest*, by William Shakespeare. Produced in 2016 by James Madison University School of Theatre and Dance. Directed by Ben Lambert, set design by John Burgess, costumes designed by Pamela Johnson, lighting design by Stuart Duke, Caliban played by Melissa Carter.

worried I'll seem too young in this part" are all valuable things to remember and consider when designing.

Your design must always keep in mind who will be implementing the design. Will it be the actor or a makeup artist? This makes a big difference to what can be achieved. Another important thing to keep in mind is how active the character is. Does the makeup need to be waterproof? Durability is very important since touchups have to happen quickly and almost always backstage in the dark.

MAKEUP STYLES

There are three general styles that makeup can be grossly categorized into. The first is **natural** makeup. Think of this as appropriate street makeup for the character. It enhances the face to project from stage to audience and have detail read from further away under stage lighting. Natural makeup can also be glamorized. This might include characters who are super models or socialites who routinely wear heavy fashion makeup.

The second is considered **character** makeup. It modifies the actor's face to better reflect character. This can include aging—either older or younger, scars, disabilities, facial hair, and pretty much anything that a character's face might have developed during its life span. Character makeup also includes makeup designed to look like a period other than the current one. Does the show take place in the 1920s? In the 1980s? These are "periods" that can be represented by specific makeup applications and designs.

Let me introduce a new word. Physiognomy. The easy definition is physiognomy is judging a book by its cover. It is the assessment we all tend to make about people's character, personality, and even emotions based on their outer appearance—especially the face. We make associations, even judgments, concerning hair color, face shapes, brow thickness and placement, nose prominence, even down to such a detail as eyelash length! Modifying the actor's face using physiognomy can actually affect how the audience reacts to and perceives the character.

The third, and last, category is often called "**stylized**." This includes anything that shifts away from reality in order to support a directorial concept or to support the design concepts of yourself or other designers. Common

examples of stylized makeup for theater would be animal makeup, cartoon-like makeup, exaggerated or satirical makeup. Additional examples are witches, ghosts, and all other-world characters.

CHARACTER ANALYSIS

Now that we've identified the different types of makeup styles, let's discuss the details of character and how to determine what is the appropriate style for each individual situation you may encounter. There are five classifications for character analysis: Heredity, environment, age, temperament, and evolution. Let's look at each one individually below.

Heredity refers to the characteristics intrinsic to the person/character at birth. What race/ethnicity are they? What is the shape of their face and individual features? What is the coloring of their skin and hair? Do they have any physical imperfections or defects? All of these details combine to form the physiognomy of the individual.

Environment is the next classification to consider. Some of these attributes can be quite subtle. Consider the climate of where the individual was born and raised. Land is the first example: Country, rural, suburban, urban, city. All of these will affect how the person looks. What do they do for employment? Do they work inside, outside, or a combination of both? Is their work stationary or active? Consider what they enjoy doing for leisure. Stationary versus active enjoyment says a great deal about a person. Are they financially wealthy, comfortable, struggling, or poor? What time period do they exist within?

Next is age, and it's not as simple as you might think. What is the actual age of the character? That's the easy part. What is the "apparent" age of the character? This is more difficult. Depending on how the character has lived, they may appear younger or older than their actual age. This says a lot about a character. In reality, we say someone has "aged well" or they have "lived hard," both of which means they don't look their age, one for the better and one for the worse.

Temperament is sometimes a difficult thing to determine. Often you will need to discuss this with the director and the actor. We are now discussing the overall disposition and mentality of the character, the general personality. How do they approach life? Do they simply accept things as they come? Are they an introvert or an extrovert? What is their fashion mentality? Are they aware of and interested in fashion? Do they defy current trends? What are their preferences, and how do they see themselves?

Lastly, let's look at the evolution of a character. This is where the details become critical. How does the character change throughout the play? Do they grow older? Do they become a health nut? Do they develop ownership of who they are? Do they lose all hope, or do they bask in the glory of success? In every play, your main characters are always in a different place at the end of the play than they were at the beginning of the play. Regardless of the shift, the hair and makeup should help to convey, or at least support, this evolution in some visual way to the audience.

FACIAL SHAPES

The next thing to talk about when makeup is the subject are the different face shapes. The face is always balanced. We might not like the balance, but it's always balanced. Analyze the face; take it apart. We are always taking an existing face and using it as a base. The question to ask yourself is: What can I do to help the actor create the character better? Makeup does its entire design all in the size of the face. It is a much tinier scale than any other design, so detail and subtlety become key. We always want to be able to see the eyes! They are the window to the soul after all. Double check the wardrobe, check character research, and talk to costumers, lighting designers, and hairstylists. It's an ensemble that all has

to work together, and all the individual pieces have to add up.

There are six different facial shapes—oval, heart, pear, square, round, and long (Figure 16.2)—and each has its own specific needs when applying makeup. An oval face is usually considered "perfect," because it is absolutely symmetrical. It has wider cheekbones and is narrow down toward the jaw line and chin and also narrow up toward the forehead. A heart face, which can also be called a *triangle*, is very unusual. It is broader at the forehead and then tapers into a small, narrow chin. A pear face is wider at the cheeks and jaw but has a narrow forehead. A square shape is actually the most common facial shape. It is equally wide at the forehead, cheeks, and jaw line. A round shape is fuller and usually makes a person look younger than they are. It has a round forehead and a round chin, with wide, full cheeks. The long shape is similar to an oval face shape but has higher cheekbones and a high forehead.

PROCESS

For both hair and makeup, the process is similar. After compiling research, determining the style, and doing the character analysis, the next step is to design each character's look taking into account the actor who will be portraying the character. This is called creating a design plot. There are several ways to do this depending on what will be most helpful to you, as the designer, to the director and actor for understanding what you intend, and to whomever is going to implement the design.

Internet reference images can be used, if you have found excellent images that clearly convey the design

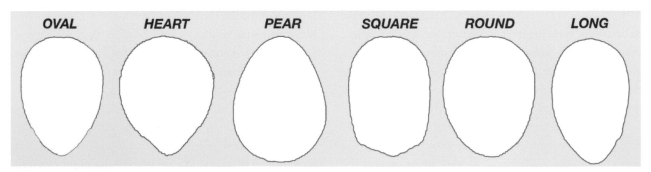

■ **Figure 16.2** Various facial shapes.

concept, and if the actor seems comfortable enough with makeup. **A full sketched design plot** works for simple, but slightly more involved, makeup designs that require some more detail in clarifying color, placement, and the overall desired effect. **A half-face sketched/ half-face charted plot** can be used for more involved designs. The "charted" half can clarify the layering of colors by breaking down each color into compartments, or have each element labeled to clarify the product/color to be used. A **"before & after" plot** is useful for more complicated and/or feature-altering designs. Use the actor's headshot from the first rehearsal and draw the makeup design over their own face, using colored pencils or acrylic paints. This is also really helpful when you need the actor to better understand how the end result should look on their face and/or how the feature-altering designs work in relation to their own features. With a **half-face "after"/half-face charted plot**, one side shows the end result, and the other side shows a breakdown of what products go where. The cons of the "before & after" plot are that the actor doesn't have any "how to get there" assistance; this plot is helpful with that problem.

MAKEUP AND TOOLS

Let's start talking about the tools and makeup of today. There are several manufacturers of stage makeup. Similar to paint from Chapter 10, there are differences between the makeup you buy at the local pharmacy or department store and stage makeup. One of the main differences is that stage makeup is intended to be applied and removed frequently. Stage makeup also lacks perfume. It is, therefore, easier on your skin and any allergies you may have.

Makeup tools are fairly easy to talk about. Makeup brushes, like paintbrushes, come in a number of shapes and sizes. They are also composed of a handle, bristles, and a ferrule, just like the paint brushes we discussed in Chapter 10. There are a variety of shapes of brushes which fall into two main categories—creme versus fluff. Creme, or wet, brushes are flat, angle, dome, and round. Fluff brushes are detail, foundation, contour, and blush. Brushes can be used in whatever way you need to achieve your goal. Here are a few examples, but know that you can use them any way that works for you.

Flat brushes are great for blending (Figure 16.3). The shape gives you great control when moving the makeup around. You can really control how much makeup you remove versus how much you add. Angle brushes are for very precise work. Applying eye shadow, eyeliner, brow coloring, and lipstick are all good options for the angled brush. Dome brushes, with rounded corners for soft edges, are ideal for under-eye concealer as well as eye shadow (Figure 16.4). Round brushes are good for lining eyes, etching brows, and applying fine details to effect makeup (Figure 16.5).

Now, wait a minute. Didn't you say the same for dome brushes? Well, yes. But think about it for a second. Everybody uses brushes in different ways. And the eyebrow, for example, has places where you will need a wider brush and places where you will want a smaller brush. Whoever said you could only use one brush for each purpose? Not me!

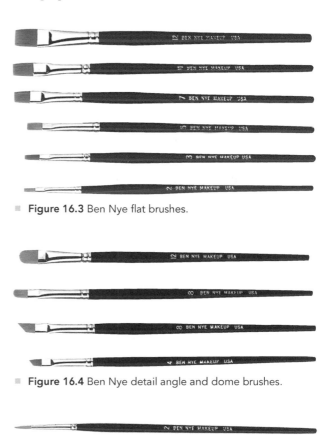

■ **Figure 16.3** Ben Nye flat brushes.

■ **Figure 16.4** Ben Nye detail angle and dome brushes.

■ **Figure 16.5** Ben Nye round brushes.

Detail brushes come in a variety of shapes. Small powder brushes are soft and rounded, which gives you great control when adding pressed-powder colors to cheeks and eyes. The tapered-point brush is good for contouring eye shadows or applying powders that sparkle or have glitter. The petite shader is a small rounded brush for use when delicate powder detailing is important. The medium blender is a soft, but firm, chiseled-end brush for the precise finishing of powders. Last, the lip brush is a finely tapered brush with a petite shape for applying lip colors and glosses.

Foundation brushes and contour brushes come in a variety of sizes, all with the same shape (Figure 16.6). They are rounded, with tapered edges that make them perfect for applying creme-style foundations and pressed-powder colors. Rouge brushes come in several different options. The professional rouge brush has a full shape for the quick application of powders to the face and body. The touch-up brush is beveled for precise application of powder, especially around the eyes. The angle contour is great for touch-ups. The contour shader is great for contour powder and shimmer powders, where you want a little extra control. The powder brush is full and luxurious for adding powder or removing excess powder without disturbing makeup. Natural hair smudge brushes are a new design, with dense, short bristles that quickly soften or blend eye makeup. Are you starting to see the flexibility offered by the wide variety of brushes available?

■ **Figure 16.7** Ben Nye sponge brushes.

Brushes are not the only way to apply makeup. There are a few other tools we should discuss. Sponge applicators, for single use, can be very helpful as they give you a huge amount of control (Figure 16.7). Spatulas are used for mixing makeup and applying thicker products such as nose or scar wax and gel effects. New designs include the tapered blade spatula and the blending spatula. Spatulas are used in conjunction with plastic palettes. Palettes are great for mixing colors to get the perfect color and they are easy to clean. Powder puffs are usually round and always soft. Some are even washable. They are great for applying powder very specifically and for blotting excess powder away from the face. Foam sponges come in different shapes and sizes (Figure 16.8). They are ideal for applying creme makeup. To use, dampen them first. They are gentle on the skin, and you will end up using less makeup in the long run. The makeup also blends more easily and wears better. Stipple sponges are made of nylon and come in square shapes. New designs include a fine-pore and a medium-pore stipple sponge. These sponges are great for adding texture

■ **Figure 16.6** Ben Nye foundation brushes.

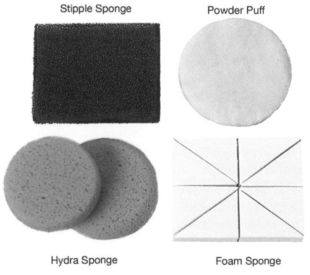

Stipple Sponge Powder Puff

Hydra Sponge Foam Sponge

■ **Figure 16.8** Ben Nye multi-purpose sponges.

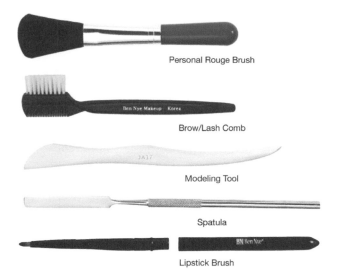

Personal Rouge Brush

Brow/Lash Comb

Modeling Tool

Spatula

Lipstick Brush

■ **Figure 16.9** Other Ben Nye brushes, combs, and tools.

■ **Figure 16.10a** Ben Nye creme foundations.

■ **Figure 16.10b** More Ben Nye creme foundations.

such as beards, bruising, and road rash, to name a few effects.

That should give you a basic idea for the tools (Figure 16.9). Let's move on to makeup. There are many variations within each category. We discuss foundation, concealers, face powders, cheek colors, eye shadows, eyeliners, eye pencils, mascara, lipsticks, lip pencils, and lip glosses. We also look at hair and character effects, bloods, latex, modeling wax, adhesives, removers, sealers, and cleansers. Wow, that is a lot of stuff. Let's get going!

Creamy matte and color-cake foundations glide on easily when using a foam sponge (Figure 16.10). They come in cakes or sticks that are easy to apply. They are long lasting and provide a flawless finish. Foundations come in a wide range of colors to match any skin tone. If, by chance, you can't find the exact color, you can mix them using a spatula and plastic palette to create a new hue. Creme foundations need to be set with powder, but more on that in a minute. Concealers blend away

We all want to have a thriving world where all people will be able to enjoy theatre for generations to come.

—Eric Nye,
Ben Nye Makeup

■ **Figure 16.11** Ben Nye concealer and neutralizer crayons.

temporary and permanent imperfections. These can include birth marks, blemishes, and tattoos. Concealers are highly pigmented, which helps them to create an even tone to the skin. This is the inherent difference between a foundation and a concealer. Concealers are the perfect way to cover up tattoos. Since tattoos have become much more popular, the need to cover them up

for specific characters is frequent. Neutralizers correct specific differences within the natural skin tone, as opposed to just covering something up.

Cheek colors come in a variety of hues from the palest to the truly strong (Figure 16.12). Cheeks can be done in powder or creme. Keep in mind that the character may need just a gentle enhancement of the actor's normal look, or you may be creating a fantasy character. Cheek colors can help with all of this, including contouring with darker shades for special effect. Powder cheek color is most often applied by gently dusting the color over the cheeks with a rouge brush. Creme color is applied with a sponge or even fingertips. Palettes can be geared toward a single skin tone or can be more broadly aimed for any and all to use.

Face powders come in variations from completely translucent to heavily pigmented (Figure 16.13). Translucent is colorless and will work for everyone. Powder sets creme foundations for a durable, soft, matte finish. A range of colors is available to match any foundation and skin tone for additional coverage. In addition, there is white powder for use when you are using a white foundation for effect.

Eye shadows, similar to cheek colors, are pressed powders with pigment (Figure 16.14). The colors for eye shadow are almost endless: Beiges, pinks, browns, purples, blues, greens, grays, and blacks. These colors are overall more intense than the cheek colors. Here is the cool thing. Cheek colors and eye shadows can be used interchangeably. That is right—if you want to use navy blue as a cheek color and you happen to have that color as an eye shadow, go ahead and use it.

Liquid eyeliner (Figure 16.15) packaging looks a lot like mascara. Inside the container is a small, fine brush that reloads every time the brush is put in. Liquid eyeliner gives a very precise line. It is smudge resistant and also comes as water resistant and waterproof—and comes in a variety of colors!

Eyebrow pencils are great for enhancing brow contours or for completely changing the shape (Figure 16.16). They are also great for filling in any minor thin spots in eyebrows. Pencils come in colors from white to black, with a range of browns in between. Mascara is used to coat eyelashes to make them appear thicker, longer, or curlier. The many different formulas enhance eyelashes in different ways and to different degrees. Mascara comes in

Figure 16.12 Ben Nye cheek colors.

Figure 16.13 Ben Nye face powders.

Figure 16.14 One of many Ben Nye eye shadow collections.

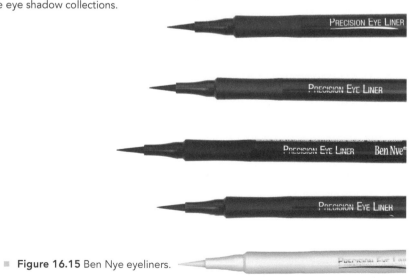

Figure 16.15 Ben Nye eyeliners.

■ **Figure 16.16** Ben Nye mascara, eyebrow pencils, and powdered eye liner.

■ **Figure 16.17** Ben Nye lipsticks and lip pencils.

brown, black, and, more recently, a wide range of colors to match eye shadows. It also comes in white, for aging, and clear for a simpler look. Mascara can be used on all facial hair to enhance and help style it.

Lipsticks are perhaps the most used cosmetic (Figure 16.17). Everyone knows what lipstick is, right? Moist, creamy color for your lips. Every color, from a perfect match to the wildest color you can think of. Lipsticks come in a standard lipstick package or you can get them in a palette. Either way, applying lipstick with a brush is more precise and lasts longer. Lipsticks come in matte, gloss, and iridescent. The combinations are endless. Lip balm is usually used as a protection against the weather.

Figure 16.18 Ben Nye creme colors.

Theatre Traditions: Lipstick

When applying makeup, an actress regards it as a sign that she will receive a good contract if she accidentally smears some lipstick onto her teeth.

Lip pencils help contour lips. You can also alter the shape of lips with a pencil. Pencils are coordinated with the colors of lipsticks. You have the choice of a natural look, by matching the pencil and lipstick colors, or going for something more dramatic, by using a pencil that is lighter or darker than the lipstick color. Lip glosses come in clear, tinted, and shimmering. They are not meant to be as colorful as lipstick. Glosses are more delicate looking when used alone. When combined with lipstick, they create a layered effect that is stunning.

Creme colors began life as creme rouge for your cheeks only (Figure 16.18). They exploded off the chart in terms of color and are now used for rouge and so much more. Creme colors can also be used for such ideas as highlights and shadows for creating contouring and aging details, and rich colors for the more whimsical, dramatic, and magical. This is truly an area where your imagination is the only limit.

Liquid face paints are highly pigmented paints used for face painting and more (Figure 16.19). They come in a wide variety of colors. Aqua paints are similar to liquid paints in their uses. They come in cakes and need to be used with a brush and water. Both of these are created

not only for faces but also for bodies. Sparkles and glitter come in various colors for multiple uses. These are loose, small pieces of sparkle and glitter that are applied over wet liquid makeup or with a special glue.

Clown white is a foundation that covers your entire skin tone with opaque white (Figure 16.20). It can be used by, well, clowns, but also if you are creating a geisha look or for certain aging looks. Creme shades in bright colors are packaged together and often called a *clown series*. Keep in mind that the most important thing isn't the product, but how you use it. These are creme shades in bright colors. Use them any way you can, for whatever purpose. And maybe even to make a clown face!

Creme shades, as we discussed already, come in a wide variety of colors. Now, let's take a look at how we

Figure 16.19 Ben Nye liquid aqua face paints.

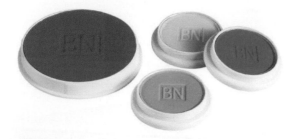

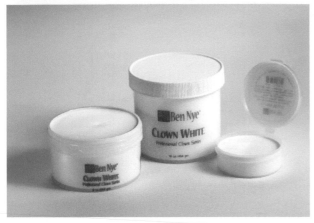

Figure 16.20 Ben Nye clown colors.

Figure 16.21 Ben Nye effects wheels.

Sustainability

The Ben Nye Company understands the importance of sustainability for communities around the globe, and we incorporate this into our manufacturing principles. A key focus of our sustainability efforts is reducing waste. While tenets like recycling are beneficial, we believe it is much more environmentally friendly to be able to reuse products and in turn, limit waste. Efficient production and minimalist design are other areas of importance, which reduce demand for sourcing raw materials.

We design our products to maximize their longevity. They are manufactured to be durable so they can withstand the high-intensity working conditions of professional artists. Nearly all of our palettes, either creme or powder, are refillable. This makes it so one doesn't need to buy a whole new product to get more of their favorite shade.

Even the majority of our single color products feature magnetic cases that are easily refillable. Refills are available for the entire line of Eye Shadows, Blush, Lumière, MagiCake, and Eyeliners. Liquid products are also available in larger refill sizes so smaller, kit-oriented bottles don't need to be thrown out. Products like our Studio Color Palettes feature a compact case that minimizes materials required to produce. And when a product does meet the end of its usable life, just about all the containers we use can be recycled.

—Eric Nye

can combine them in different configurations for a wide range of effects. Effects wheels often have four shades of creme color that work together to create specific effects, such as bruises, cuts, abrasions, burns, blisters, age, severe exposure, monsters, camouflage, and even death (Figure 16.21). They are totally cool! As always, remember that your imagination is the only limitation.

Special FX is the last category of makeup we will discuss. It is a huge category and really needs a class all of its own. We will only touch on some of the things you can do. Just know this is the tip of the iceberg. First off is blood. Blood can come in different colors, from bright red to dark red. It can also be thin and watery or thick and starting to congeal. The darker and thicker it is, the closer to being a scab. Ben Nye has a product called Fresh Scab that is amazingly realistic.

Ben Nye has a category of effects makeup called Grime FX. It includes Coal, Death, Dirt, Grease, Grit, Plains Dust, Slime, and Stone. They come in a water-based liquid and also in a powder. Each will effectively distress skin, costumes, prosthetics, and hair, which can provide realistic details that convey a character's authenticity.

HAIR

The question is always the same with regards to hair: Wig or actor's own hair? This is influenced by many things such as budget, the demands of the show, how natural the hair must look, available time investment, access to wig stock, and of course the actor's own hair style and color. If an actor playing multiple characters needs to wear a wig for one character, they usually need a wig for all their characters because there is usually not time for an actor to do the needed prep between scenes.

There are three basic options for each character. Use all of actor's own hair is the first option. This option only works if the actor's own hair is the right color, length, and cut for the character, and if the character hair does not need to change much during the show or, if it does, it is a change that is manageable by the actor and realistic with the offstage time needed for the change. The second option is to use part of the actor's own hair and supplement as needed. This could mean using a fall, a wiglet, a switch or braid, or clip-in extensions. Regardless of which is used, all of them require that the hair piece is a good color and texture match to the actor's own hair. Third, and last, use a wig.

You have three basic wig options to choose from: a **hard-front wig**, a **lace-front wig**, or a **fully hand-tied wig**. Let's explore each. A hard-front wig does come in several options. A fully "exposed" hairline on a hard-front wig is the first option we will discuss. If the character is supposed to look like they are wearing a wig, this is okay. A softened or hidden hairline on a hard-front wig is another option. Hard-front wigs will look "wiggy" unless the front hairline of the wig is hidden through some type of bangs or softened through adding sporadic tendrils or curls along the hairline to hide the hard-edge

front. Incorporating an actor's own hairline into a hard-front wig is the last option for this type of wig. If you choose a wig that matches the actor's hair, you can place the wig just behind the actor's own hairstyle to hide the hard front. This means that the actor must curl and/or pin their own hair into the wig.

A lace-front wig has had the front section of a hard-front wig removed and replaced with lace. Hair that matches the rest of the wig is then tied into the lace. These wigs have a very natural-looking hairline and therefore are great if the hairstyle of the wig must have an exposed hairline. Attaching hairs one by one onto lace is a time-intensive, and therefore expensive, process. Lace-front wigs are much more expensive than hard-front wigs for this reason. A fully hand-tied wig is the third wig option, being the most realistic and most expensive. These wigs are completely hand-tied on a lace backing and can cost thousands of dollars.

One other thing to consider with wigs is the type of hair used. Human hair is more expensive. However, human hair is unique in that it can be wet set, can be dyed, and you can use heat for styling such as a curling iron. Synthetic hair is understandably less expensive. Synthetic hair sets with steam or boiling water, which is a more durable set. However, it won't take hair dye or the use of heat from a curling iron.

Hair dye for natural hair is easy to get at the corner drugstore, right? Well, yes, but it doesn't just wash out. Liquid hair colors can be brushed in for fabulous effects, and they wash right back out when you are done (Figure 16.22). There is no damage to your hair either. There are a number of colors, and you can combine them for variations. Character powders are pigmented for very specific reasons. Plains dust looks like real dirt. Stipple this powder on to create "dirty" characters. Plains dust is a pale powder that can be used for aging. Charcoal powder can be used to simulate grease stains, powder burns from a gun, and much, much more.

Let's move on to blood and gore. Stage blood has come a long way (Figure 16.23). Commercial stage blood has many realistic qualities, including color and viscosity. Fresh Scab is a new product that looks partially clotted! Blood can also come in a peppermint flavor so that, if the blood must be put in the mouth, it is at least palatable. Staining can occur on skin and fabrics, so be careful of this and test ahead if needed.

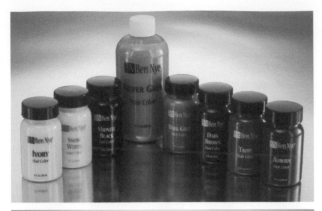

Figure 16.23a Ben Nye stage blood.

Figure 16.22 Ben Nye liquid hair color and tooth colors.

The Graftobian Makeup Company makes an F/X Powdered Blood that is activated by water. It is pretty cool! Here is how it works. Let's say you put some of the blood powder on your arm. Then someone "attacks" you with a fake knife, and the blade is wet. As the knife is dragged across your arm, the blood powder mixes with the water and turns into realistic-looking blood. It looks like you are being cut, and the blood is coming out of an unseen wound!

Nose and scar waxes are very cool (Figure 16.24). They are pliable yet firm and can create a number of injuries. They are easy to shape into exactly what you need. They stick to the skin on their own, but applying them with spirit gum allows for longer wear. Wax is always covered with makeup after it is applied, to make it blend in with the other makeup for a seamless effect. For more advanced effects, liquid latex is a great product. First off, always check to see if an actor has a known allergy to latex. Even if he or she has never had a reaction, try a small amount of latex on the skin and monitor it carefully for any signs of a reaction, as we discussed in Chapter 6. For certain types of aging or injuries, you can apply the

Figure 16.23b Ben Nye Fresh Scab.

latex with a brush while holding the skin taut. When the skin relaxes, the latex causes wrinkles and puckers. It can be that easy, but again the effect must be covered with makeup to be complete.

■ **Figure 16.24** Ben Nye nose and scar wax.

Let's talk next about adhesives. But, first, always do a test, as some adhesives can cause dermatologic irritation, especially on the face. We talked about glitters needing adhesives and wax needing adhesives. Glitter glue is specifically designed for glitter and sparkles. Spirit gum is sticky when wet but dries to a flat finish. It is used to attach various hairpieces such as beards and mustaches, as well as prosthetic pieces made from latex, foams, plastics, and the like. The gum is applied, then allowed to partially dry. When still slightly tacky, place the material on it that you are trying to adhere.

Removers are just as important as adhesives and similarly come in a number of types, depending on what you are trying to remove (Figure 16.25). Spirit gum remover is specifically made to, well, remove spirit gum and only spirit gum. Other removers are meant to remove a variety of products. Follow up the use of any remover with a cleanser that is delicate on the skin. Massage a cleanser into the skin and then gently wipe it away and, last, follow up with a good-quality moisturizer. The other cleanser type is for brushes. All of your tools should be cleaned after every use. This is really important not only for the longevity of the brushes but, more important, for the health of the actors you are using the brushes on. Dirty brushes can transfer bacteria and illnesses. It is best to have one set of brushes per actor, if at all possible.

■ **Figure 16.25** Ben Nye removers, adhesives, and cleansers.

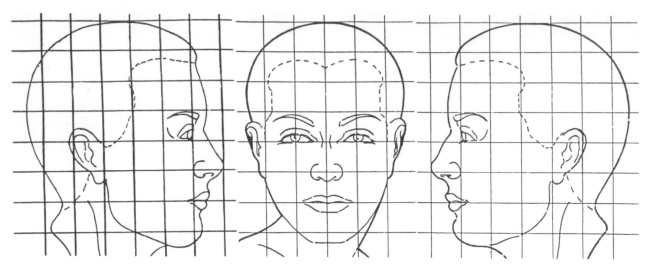

■ **Figure 16.26** Linda Mensching's makeup chart.

MAKEUP APPLICATION

OK, relax for a minute. We've gotten through all the tools and types of makeup. Exhausted? Excited? Well, next we need to figure out what to do with all that stuff you just read about. We learned about the face shapes. The next thing to do is figure out what the makeup will look like. Makeup designers usually keep a morgue of photos showing different people and character types. They will often then do sketches of the finished makeup design. When applying makeup, it is important to chart what you create, mostly so you, or the actor, can recreate it for the next performance. The chart in Figure 16.26 is used to document the makeup you apply when you need to do the same makeup again. Notice the grid, which makes it easier for others to pick up your notes and create the same design.

The application of makeup happens in a very specific order. But, here is the thing. The order does depend on what type of makeup you are applying. For basic street makeup, whether or not it is "enhanced" for the stage, the steps are as follows:

- **Foundation:** Blend on a palette if needed. Gently pat the sponge on forehead, nose, and cheeks. Patting doesn't pull skin the way rubbing does. Always work in an upward motion to help fight gravity. You are going for an even look, but be careful not to blend it all away.

- **Concealer:** If trying to conceal dark circles or marks, the color should be slightly lighter than regular foundation, because it has to counterbalance the darkness. Don't change the hue for the rest of the skin, just use a slightly darker version.

- **Powder:** This sets the makeup. That means the makeup below the powder stops moving around or blending with the makeup above the powder. Make sure you are happy with the makeup before you powder! You use powder after the foundation and concealer, then again after the cheeks and eyes. And of course at any other point where you need to "lock in" the makeup.

- **Cheeks:** Both highlights and shadows can be done at the same time. Use two cheek powders for shadowing if the actor's facial structure might have a tendency to get washed out by lighting.

- **Eyes:** There are so many variations in shadow, highlight, liner, lashes, and brow techniques that it is impossible even to summarize. Look at the makeup you love. Study it and break it down. Figure out how it was done, then you will know how to apply it for yourself. Don't underestimate the power of a well-shaped eyebrow. It frames the eye.

- **Lips:** Lip liner and lipstick not only color the lips but help define and shape them. Even if color is not desired, a clear gloss or balm makes an actor more comfortable onstage, where the air is sometimes drier.

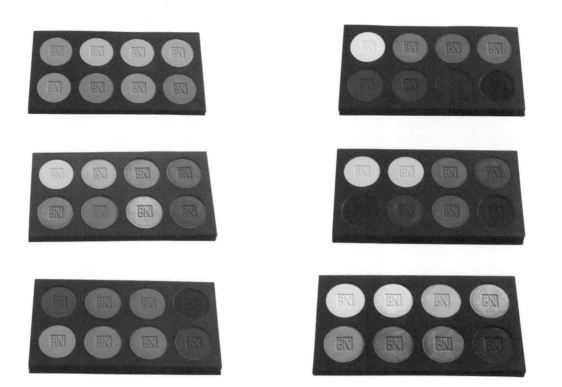

Figure 16.27 Palettes of combined colors can come in handy for original applications as well as touchups.

Figure 16.28 Kits are also available for a variety of complexions, specific needs, and effects.

■ **Figure 16.29** Makeup techniques varying to the extreme shown over the next several pages. All have different starting points, outcomes, and effects.

■ **Figure 16.29** continued

Ben Nye has obviously been very generous with me in sharing product samples and insights. The photos in Figure 16.29 are courtesy of another generous person, Paul Hadobas. They are process photos of makeup applications. This is a great opportunity to see the difference makeup can actually make, as well as to study the individual steps. Check them out!

Sometimes, makeup is part of what helps an actor get into character. The days are over of makeup being hugely different between street and stage. Heavy shadowing is gone, unless it is for a special effect. Lighting has changed, and makeup has had to change with it. In film and television, high definition has also eliminated the need for heavy makeup. Lighting can make or break the makeup design. Everybody has to work together.

EXERCISES

EXERCISE 1

Take a headshot of yourself with no makeup. Then use the headshot to create a makeup plot for a basic stage makeup design.

EXERCISE 2

Create a makeup plot for aging makeup using your headshot.

EXERCISE 3

Create a makeup plot for fantasy makeup using your headshot.

CHECK YOUR KNOWLEDGE

1. List and define the three styles of makeup.
2. Explain why character analysis is an important part of the design process.
3. Predict how an actor's natural facial shape can work for and against a character. Explain how makeup can compensate for this.
4. List different types of brushes and their specific uses.
5. Describe the three different styles of wigs, listing pros and cons for each.
6. Analyze why makeup and hair have so many different emerging trends.

- Adhesives
- Angle brush
- Cleansers
- Concealer
- Detail brush
- Dome brush
- Facial shapes
- Flat brush
- Foam sponge
- Foundation
- Foundation brush
- Liquid latex
- Palette
- Physiognomy
- Powder puff
- Removers
- Round brush
- Scar wax
- Spatula

STUDY WORDS

Chapter 16

PART
FIVE

Video and Special Effects

CHAPTER 17: Projections, LED, Screens, and Content—Oh My
Video

CHAPTER 18: The Magic Behind the Curtain
Special Effects

Projections, LED, Screens, and Content—Oh My

Video

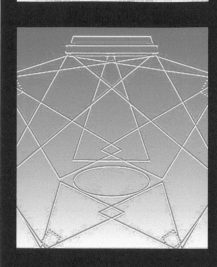

Let's move on and take video and projections to the next level. This is where a great deal of the new technology is happening today. What is so amazing is that video can be scenery, lighting, and special effects! So, a new department dedicated to video of all kinds needed to be formed. That made room for another designer on the team, one who is focused on the video and only the video. As usual, we need to start with some history before we get to the newest examples.

The youngest department within theatre and live events is video. The term video is a catch-all term that encompasses many technologies and departments, such as projections, screens, content, and more. While video certainly isn't exactly what we would call "new," as compared with lights, sets, sound, and special effects, it certainly is the youngest discipline. The video department has benefited greatly from the technological age we live in. Just as lighting has come on leaps and bounds in the past decade with the advent of the light-emitting diode (LED), video has also seen some tremendous technological shifts and huge adoption in the past two decades. The world of video is complex, dynamic, and ever evolving.

Video started out in the theatre world as projected scenery. Originating back in the 17th century, the first "video projectors" actually projected static images, cut-out scenes where a candle was placed behind the cutout, displaying the image on a wall. Fast-forward to 1849 when lantern slides were invented. These were glass slides that were derived from photographs; however, they were still static. The standard for early video projection, 35-mm film, was invented around 1935, allowing for the projection of moving images, mostly in movie theaters, or academic settings. Analog film projections were used in theatrical and live events sporadically, projecting animated scenery or edited sequences on scenery or fabrics for many years. Digital projectors were first debuted in 1988.

EARLY PROJECTIONS

As the theatre became a little more modern, a number of inventions took effects to the next level. The following are certainly not modern by today's standards, but they were cutting edge at the time. We now call them *vintage*!

A guy named Adolf Linnebach originally developed the Linnebach projector in the late 19th century (Figure 17.1). This was the first time there was a way to project images as part of the scenic design. Here is how it works. A deep box is made and painted entirely black inside. Then, a high-intensity, concentrated light bulb is placed inside the box, near the back. One side is open and contains a glass "slide." The slide is hand painted with the image to be projected. That's it. Really. There is no lens; the size of the projection is controlled by the size of the glass in combination with the distance from the box to the surface projected upon. Owing to the lack of a lens, the only way to sharpen or soften the glass image is to move the lamp closer or further away. Since there is limited room to do this, you can see how, as time passed, we looked for something more flexible.

The next improvement over the Linnebach was the scene machine (Figure 17.2). It has a lens! This meant you could control the focus and size of the projected image. The wattage of the lamps got higher and became much brighter as well, which meant you could project denser designs across longer distances. The images were created out of steel patterns or were painted on heat-resistant glass. Since the focusable lenses and higher-wattage lamps create more heat, the heat resistance of the image became crucial. The images were still static

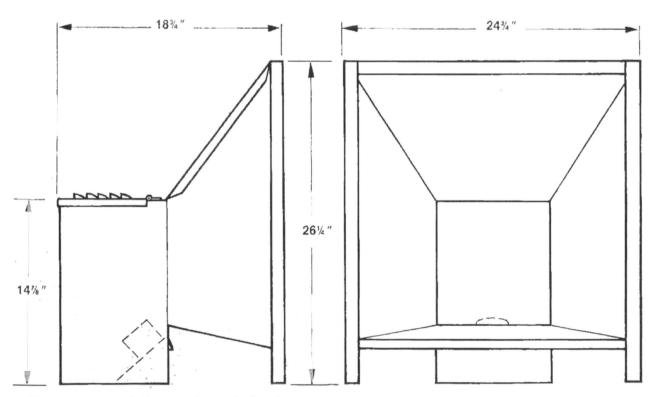

■ **Figure 17.1** Front and side views of a Linnebach projector.

■ **Figure 17.2** GAM Products scene machine.

though; no movement was added as part of the new invention. Subsequently, attachments were invented to create spinning effects. This was somewhat successful and certainly had a "wow" factor as the first moving projection.

There was a time when the only way to do a projection was to use a regular slide projector like a Kodak Carousel (Figure 17.3). This was the standard for a long time. Then, we started using two projectors and developed the ability to crossfade between them. Slowly, we added more and more projectors to the design, as the ability to control and align them developed. It seems like such a simple concept now, but it was once the state of the art. One thing to always remember is that today's state of the art is tomorrow's vintage!

The next vintage effect is the lobsterscope (Figure 17.5). Think of it as the predecessor to today's strobe. The idea is to take a focusable light and mount a motor on the front of it. Attached to the motor is a metal disk with two slits cut into it. Turn on the motor, and the disk and the light together make a strobing effect. This was *very* popular to create the effect of a moving train or a television's reflected light. Other uses included time passage or slow motion. The neat thing with this effect is

■ **Figure 17.3** Kodak Carousel slide projector.

■ **Figure 17.4** *Dr. Faust* at the Metropolitan Opera in 2001. Director, Peter Mussbach; scenic designer, Erich Wonder; costume designer, Andrea Schmidt-Futterer; and lighting designer, Konrad Lindenberg.

■ **Figure 17.5** Lobsterscope disk.

that you can color the light and also dim it. This added a great deal of variability to its look and was amazing for its time.

Let's look next at a much more complicated effect that has its roots during the same time frame. How do we make a ghost appear and disappear? Keep in mind here that we are not talking about today, but 100 years ago or more. How do you turn the reflection of one actor into another? Well, a chemist by the name of John Pepper first saw a technique developed by Henry Dircks in the late 19th century. Dircks's idea was visually successful, but it would never work in the theatre, since it was too complicated and large. Pepper instantly knew how to make it much easier to work with, and it became known as Pepper's ghost. Here is how it works.

For the illusion to work, the viewer must be able to see onto the main stage, but *not* into the secret off-stage area that is hidden by a mirror (Figure 17.6). The trick is to hide the edge of the glass that separates the areas. Both areas should be identical to, yet mirror images of, each other. The off-stage area should be painted completely black, and you need to use lighter-colored props and

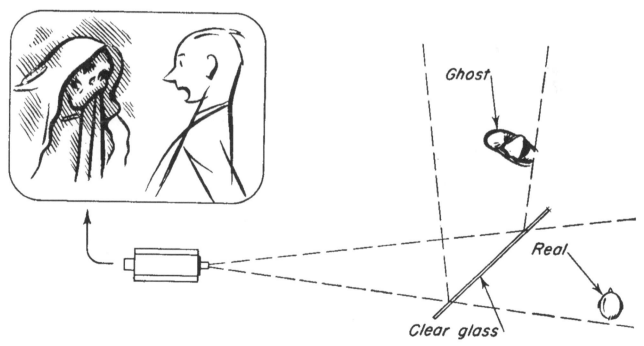

■ **Figure 17.6** Easy diagram for creating a ghost effect when you have some control over the situation.

furniture because the reflection will naturally be a little bit darker. When the light is turned on the secret area, it reflects in the glass, making the reflections appear as ghostly images on the main stage.

Geoff Dunbar used a similar, yet updated, technique during a production of *Spirit Lodge* (Figure 17.7). A projector was used to project a film loop onto a rear projection screen that was suspended over the heads of an audience. The audience was constrained to a tight viewing angle. All viewers viewed the virtual image in roughly the same position, and that image was superimposed over an actual theatrical set and actor. With no lights on the set, the audience would see *nothing* except a projected image. With lighting, they would see a magical "How did they do that?" kind of show.

The lighting works this way. When smoke rises from the campfire, lights inside some fake logs illuminate the actor and the logs for an appropriate amount of time. Then, they dim, and lights at the smoke hole above illuminate the hole as the animated smoke passes through it. And so on. As the crow "flies" around the room, lights in various positions track it, so that, in the end, when the "crow" lands on the actor's hand, the hand is illuminated to reinforce the image.

Let's take a look at one person's journey in this part of the business. Anne Johnston started working for Production Arts (PA) located in NYC in 1985 and worked in the office. It was supposed to be her "day job" while she stage-managed at night. Anne took an instant liking to projections, as it was so different from lighting and 3D scenery. PA was the only shop to have access to Pani projectors, as they were Austrian made and in limited supply; at the time, they were the state-of-the-art projectors (Figures 17.8 and 17.9).

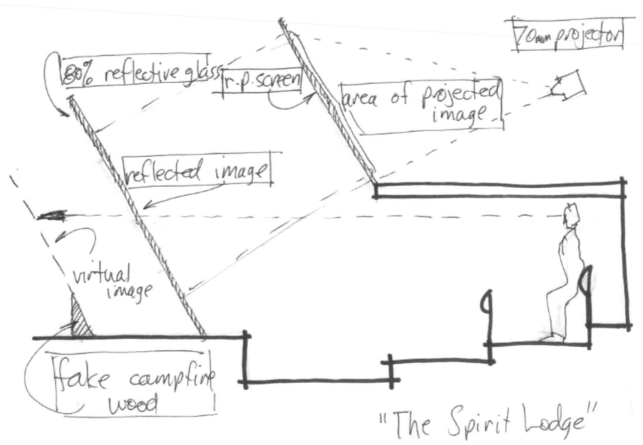

■ **Figure 17.7** Geoff Dunbar created this section while working on a production of *The Spirit Lodge*.

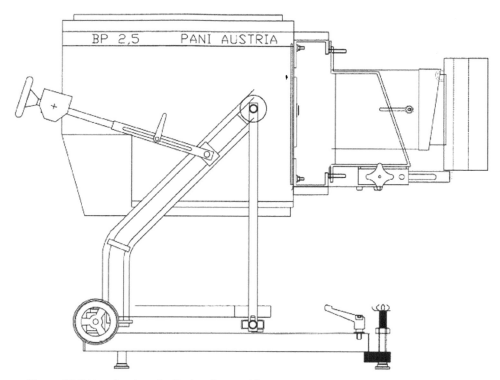

■ **Figure 17.8** Line drawing of a Pani projector, side view.

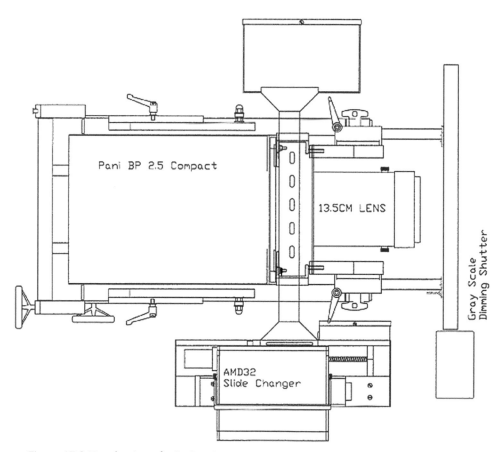

■ **Figure 17.9** Line drawing of a Pani projector, top view.

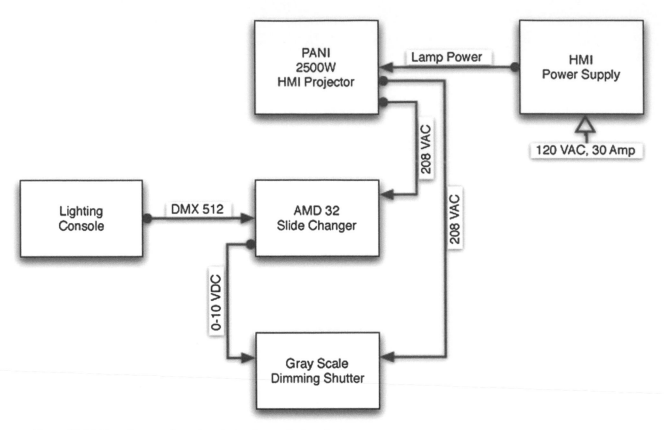

■ **Figure 17.10** Riser diagram shows how to hook up a Pani projector.

A typical equipment list for a Pani projector includes much more than just the projector. Take a look at the box and see how many other items have to be specified. As the technology advances, the equipment lists get longer. That is not a problem, just something to be aware of. If you are the one writing the equipment list, make sure you understand the technology and all that it entails.

1 Pani BP 2.5 compact HMI projector
1 Pani 2500-watt HMI power supply
1 Pani AMD 32 random-access slide changer
1 Pani G405/PCS gray scale dimming shutter
1 Lighting control console with DMX 512 outputs
1 100-foot power supply extension
1 5-foot three-pin XLR analog control cable
1 50-foot DMX 512 control cable

Madonna's *Who's That Girl?* tour in 1986 wanted to use projectors, so the group came to PA. Anne had to figure out road boxes for shipping, coordinating spare lamps and fixtures, as well as onsite technical support. The new projection department of PA was learning quickly, and Anne was now working full time. The next call was from The Rolling Stones for their 1989 Steel Wheels Tour, and the rest, as they say, is history. Anne continues to work in the industry, helping to design and develop new technologies as they are called for!

Remember when I said, if you have an idea, the technology would be developed to help you create that idea. Well, Pani didn't make an automatic slide changer for its projectors at this point, so PA started developing and building its own accessories for the projectors. The first was the automatic slide changer. It also developed the ability to control the projectors via DMX, so the lighting board could control everything together.

The next major development in projectors came from a French manufacturer, PIGI. PIGI projectors added a new feature, film. This had never been seen before, and it was amazing to witness for the first time. The rotating double scroller added the ability to change the orientation of the projection at will. The PIGI system could also be controlled through computer software. This became a major step in the process toward today's projections.

Enter the world of video projection! Most dedicated projectors have slowly been phased out. They are still in use, but the larger shows are going all-digital with their projections. Digital projection gives way more control and, in combination with moving lights, gets the best of both worlds. Most technicians from the projector departments are being cross-trained onto digital equipment. It is the inevitable next step. In fact, digital projection and its playback has become so affordable and ubiquitous, college productions use video as a design element alongside lighting on a daily basis.

The toughest part of new technology for the rental shops is to know which equipment to invest in. Think about it. If your laptop computer becomes obsolete in 18 months, doesn't the same happen with higher-end equipment? Of course, it does! European theaters are different, in that they tend to own the equipment, as opposed to for-profit American theaters, which tend to rent it. If you own it, you keep using it until it stops working. European theaters also have stagehands on staff, so it is easier to get familiar with the equipment.

WHAT'S IN A TITLE?

Originally, the person who was responsible for all things video in the theater was actually the scenic designer, because, at least initially, projections were often used to animate or augment scenery. As the scenic designer already had an eye for this discipline, this made sense. However, in the concert and live event world, video usually fell under the lighting designer's responsibility, as

■ **Figure 17.11** *Equus*, James Madison University, September 2017. Directed by Ben Lambert, scenic and projection design by Richard Finkelstein, costume design by Pam Johnson, and lighting design by Kelly Rudolph.

most concerts don't employ a scenic designer. Over the years, as technology expanded and executing video in live events became more complex, video became its own department, with a myriad of specialized personnel that varies project to project. Here are just some of the roles in today's video department.

VIDEO DESIGNER/PROJECTION DESIGNER/ CREATIVE DIRECTOR

While projection designer is a common term for the designer of video in theatre, it is a misnomer. A video designer in theatre *may* use projectors in their design, but they may also use LED screens, televisions, or a myriad of other video output devices. Therefore, we will call the lead creative designer the video designer moving forwards. The video designer is responsible not only for the layout of the various output devices, but also for the overarching narrative of the imagery that must be produced. The rest of the team members work to fulfill the vision of the video designer

ANIMATOR/CONTENT CREATOR

An animator/content creator is someone who takes the video designer's vision and brings it to life by actually creating the graphics that get displayed on the various output devices (screens). Animators typically specialize in certain types of content (2D, 3D, live reactive, animated, shot, etc.) and get hired for their specific aesthetic, just like a designer is hired for their specific style. Animators typically work in the office and don't frequently end up in the theater or the venue.

CONTENT/MEDIA MANAGER

This role is typically found on large projects where you have multiple content creators involved. When you have lots of pieces of video content (also sometimes called "assets" or "media") coming in from various creators, often all over the world, you need someone to manage all the assets. The content manager's job is to make sure all the assets are the correct size, resolution, aspect ratio,

named correctly, etc. It is also vitally important that all of the assets have proper copyright to be displayed publicly, and the content manager will work with asset rights holders to secure that. Once the assets "pass," the content manager hands the assets off to the video programmer.

VIDEO PROGRAMMER

The video programmer is the right hand of the video designer. They are responsible for taking the assets created by the animators and sequencing them correctly inside a big fancy computer called the media server. The programmer tells each piece of video content when it's supposed to play, through which projectors or on which LED walls, and if there are any other effects required. The role is half-artistry and half-nerd!

VIDEO ENGINEER/VIDEO CREW CHIEF

This person is responsible for the technical execution of the video system. They take the design documents from the designer and build a system of projectors, LED screens, televisions, cables, boxes, widgets, cameras, converters, etc. to make a fully working system.

TECHS

An LED tech is someone who specializes in the installation and maintenance of LED walls. A projectionist/projector tech is someone who specializes in the installation and maintenance of projectors. A media server tech is someone who specializes in the installation and maintenance of media servers.

SCREENS PRODUCER

On large shows, typically TV or large commercial projects, a screens producer will wrangle all the technical parts of video under their umbrella. All the technicians, the media server programmer, and the engineer will answer to this person. They are the glue between the video designer and the rest of the team.

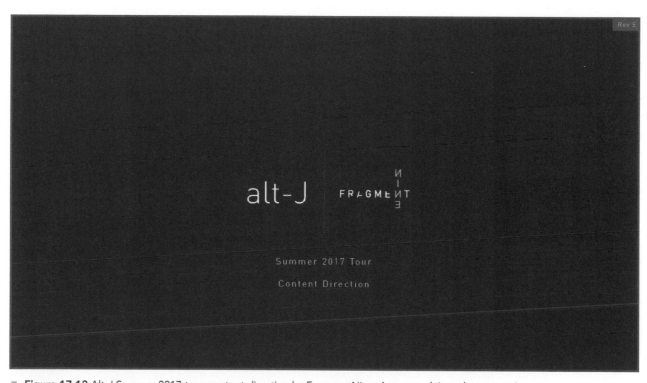

■ **Figure 17.12** Alt-J Summer 2017 tour content direction by FragmentNine. A rare peek into the process!

The overarching goal for this show is to place the band, and their audience, inside an immersive, linear, digital, reactive world. The architecture of the rig has been designed as a modern forest/hearth that expands and contracts with the ebb and flow of the music.

All content and lighting decisions should emanate from the singular volume of "line". Embrace the negative space inherent in the design.

Stylistically, we tend towards 2d, graphical, textural, fractal animations that are exquisitely timed to the music. The style guide below is meant to elicit emotion or convey the feeling of the environment we'd like to create. However, never take it literally. IE: if we say "dark brooding forest" — we don't every want to see trees and leaves. But maybe its variegated width 2d lines with a slowly moving 2D texture behind.

We just recently got a new set list, so there are a few ??? songs and we welcome your input.

This show will be on d3, and is incorporating Kinect cameras on each musician as well as Notch. If you feel any of these aspect could help elevate a look you are working on, your input is welcome and we will work with you or others to implement these tools if necessary.

Ultimately we are excited to work with you because we respect and admire your work as an artist and hope for this project to be a dialogue between us and not just mindless content creation because artistic collaboration makes for a better end product and hopefully gives you more ownership and pride in your work.

-Jeremy and Jackson

FRAGMENT

For reference, this is what we've done in the past

FRAGMENT

■ **Figure 17.12** continued

These are graphic styles that we like

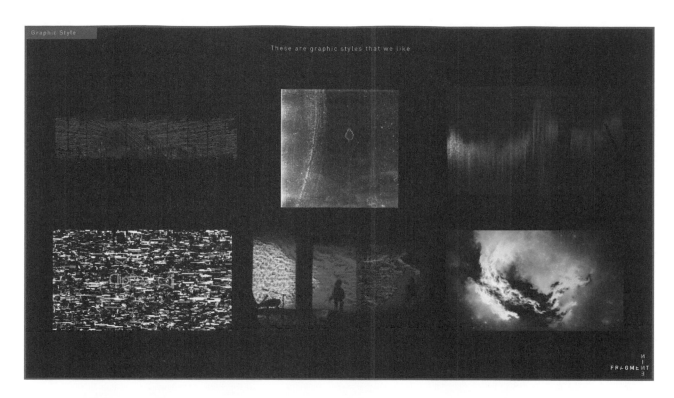

FR∧GMENT
NINE

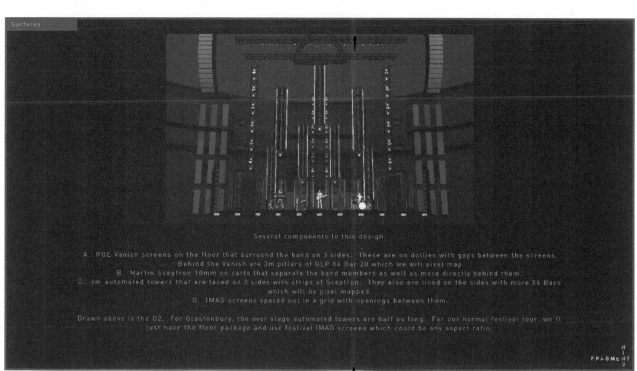

Several components to this design:

A. ROE Vanish screens on the floor that surround the band on 3 sides. These are on dollies with gaps between the screens.
Behind the Vanish are 3m pillars of GLP X4 Bar 20 which we will pixel map.
B. Martin Sceptron 10mm on carts that separate the band members as well as more directly behind them.
C. 6m automated towers that are faced on 3 sides with strips of Sceptron. They also are lined on the sides with more X4 Bars
which will be pixel mapped.
D. IMAG screens spaced out in a grid with openings between them.

Drawn above is the O2. For Glastonbury, the over stage automated towers are half as long. For our normal festival tour, we'll
just have the floor package and use festival IMAG screens which could be any aspect ratio.

FR∧GMENT
NINE

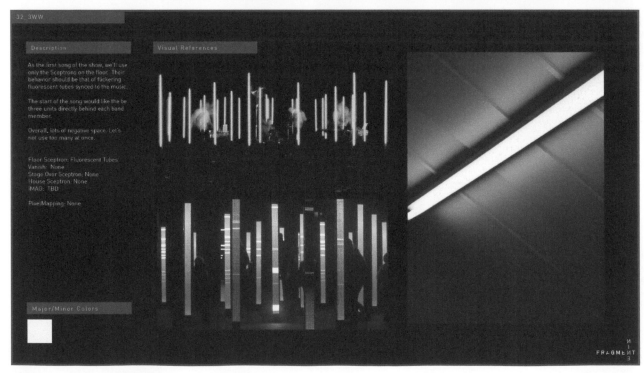

■ **Figure 17.12** continued

6. Something Good

Description

This will be the first time we reveal the upstage Vanish screen.

Some sort of linear static that is as frenetic as the the drum kit would be a good way to start.

For the "piano trills" we should find a way to wipe around the entire environment, potentially also including the pixel map of the X4 Bars.

Stay very mono-tone for the entire song.

Floor Sceptron: Static
Vanish: Static
Stage Over Sceptron: Blank
House Sceptron: Blank
IMAG: Static Notch?

PixelMapping: On Wipes

Might be we utilize the horizontal laser cage here.

Visual References

Major/Minor Colors

FRAGMENT

3. Tessellate

Description

For the O2 show, we will have a large triangle descend from the roof and be the primary focus of the song.

However, for other shows, lets live in a connected nebulous world. Sort of like 3D nerves or dots connected by lines, that sort of effect. We want to hint at the idea of "geometry" which they are talking about, but we never want to be too overt.

Floor Sceptron: Nebulous
Vanish: Nebulous
Stage Over Sceptron: Nebulous
House Sceptron: Nebulous
IMAG: Fractal

PixelMapping: None

Automated triangle of light.

Visual References

Major/Minor Colors

FRAGMENT

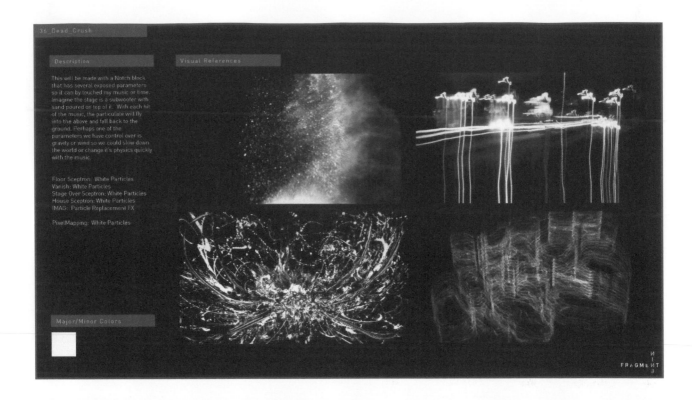

■ **Figure 17.12** continued

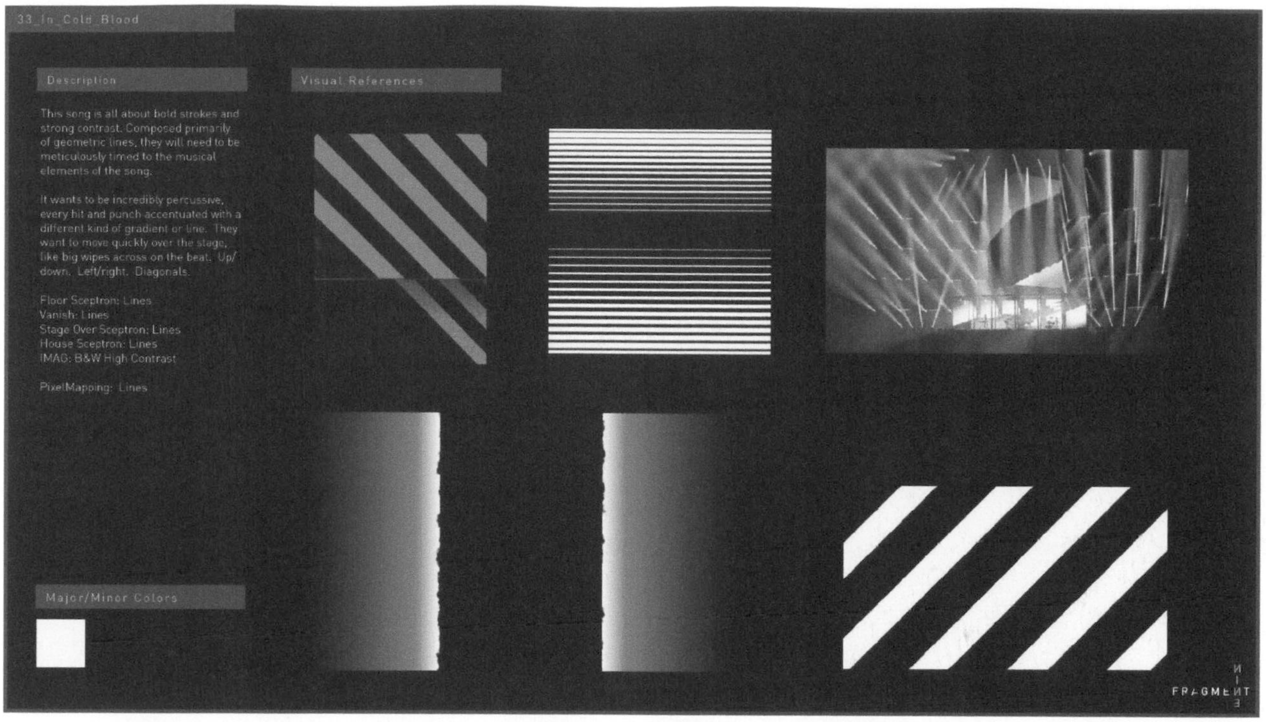

33_In_Cold_Blood

Description

This song is all about bold strokes and strong contrast. Composed primarily of geometric lines, they will need to be meticulously timed to the musical elements of the song.

It wants to be incredibly percussive, every hit and punch accentuated with a different kind of gradient or line. They want to move quickly over the stage, like big wipes across on the beat. Up/down. Left/right. Diagonals.

Floor Sceptron: Lines
Vanish: Lines
Stage Over Sceptron: Lines
House Sceptron: Lines
IMAG: B&W High Contrast

PixelMapping: Lines

Visual References

Major/Minor Colors

FRAGMENT

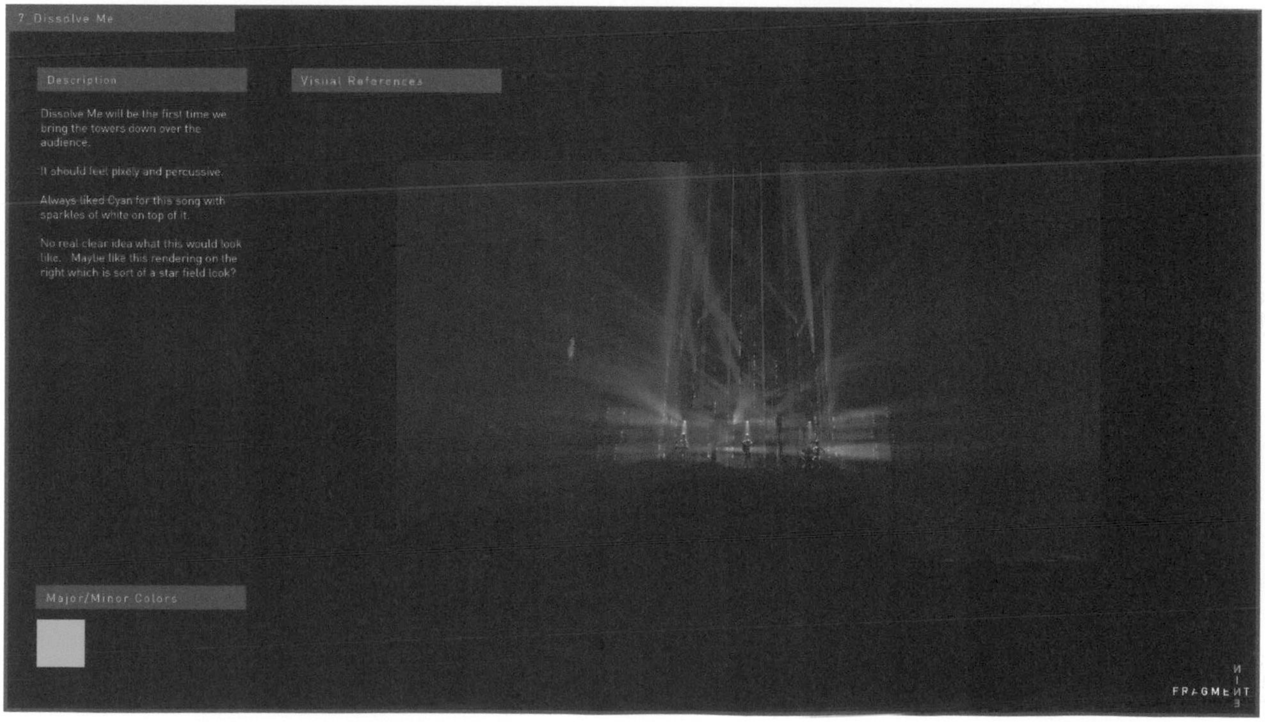

7_Dissolve Me

Description

Dissolve Me will be the first time we bring the towers down over the audience.

It should feel pixely and percussive.

Always liked Cyan for this song with sparkles of white on top of it.

No real clear idea what this would look like. Maybe like this rendering on the right which is sort of a star field look?

Visual References

Major/Minor Colors

FRAGMENT

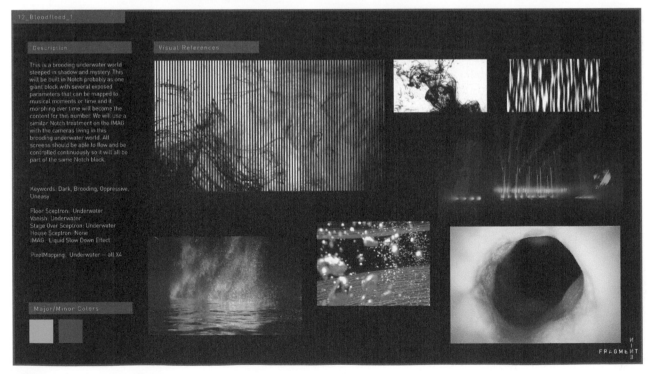

■ **Figure 17.12** continued

Description

CTO-ish — see picture way bottom left, this is the pallet. Should be nuanced shades of CTO, not one solid color.

Think thin, vertical geometric "forest" encompassing the band. The top left image is what the final result of two layers will look like on the vanish. The vanish will mimic the Sceptron so that we are in this forest world everywhere you look and seemingly never-ending. We need two layers, the bottom is a organic, fractal, breathing texture that undulated in sync to the music perhaps. The bottom left is a starting point for this texture. This will be played on both the Sceptrons and Vanish. We then need a mask for the Vanish to make it look like the Sceptrons. Probably 1-2px wide with slight bulges here and there so it is a bit "noisy".

Drum frills @ beginning will be the underlying laying becoming more positive so the forest shape stays the same but grows in weight around them. Other moments in the song will change this "weight" of the forest.

Some sort of weird shift for the "angel bridge". TBD

Bottom Right image is sort of something that end result would want to look like, but the upstage walls more like the hanging structure and generally more negative.

Visual References

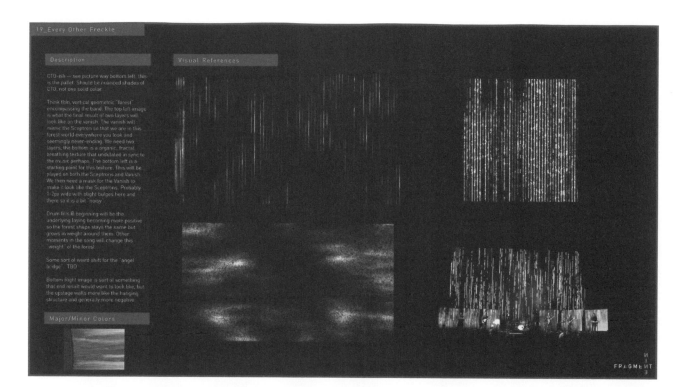

Major/Minor Colors

FRAGMENT

Description

Vertical laser cage — no video content.

IMAG: Clean/Sepia FX

Visual References

Major/Minor Colors

FRAGMENT

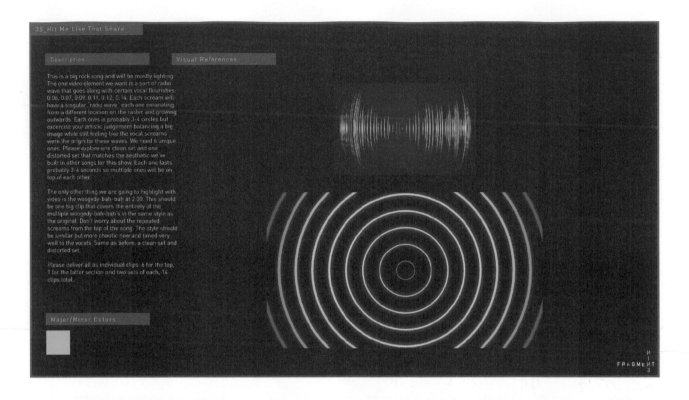

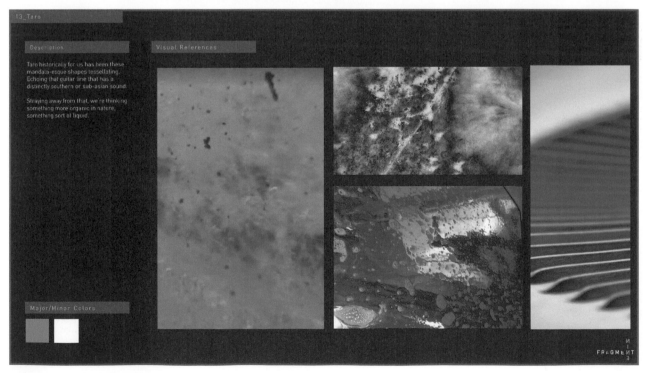

Figure 17.12 continued

Description

Magic mirror maze, camera feedback, silhouettes

Breezeblocks is a trip through a magic mirror funhouse. Using Kinect's and notch, we'll play with mapping silhouettes on different surfaces. There may be some grungy clips that need to be played underneath.

Visual References

Major/Minor Colors

FRAGMENT

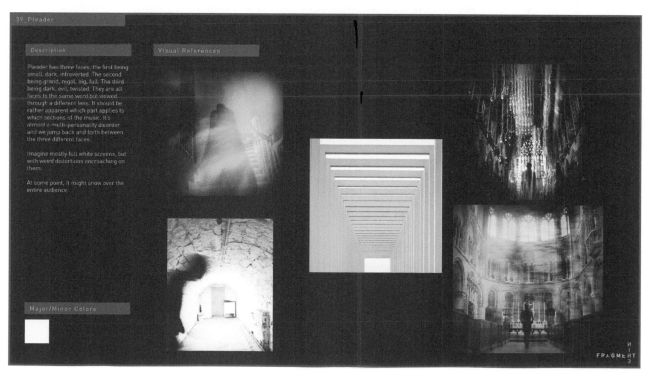

Description

Pleader has three faces, the first being small, dark, introverted. The second being grand, regal, big, full. The third being dark, evil, twisted. They are all faces to the same word but viewed through a different lens. It should be rather apparent which part applies to which sections of the music. It's almost a multi-personality disorder and we jump back and forth between the three different faces.

Imagine mostly full white screens, but with weird distortions encroaching on them.

At some point, it might snow over the entire audience.

Visual References

Major/Minor Colors

FRAGMENT

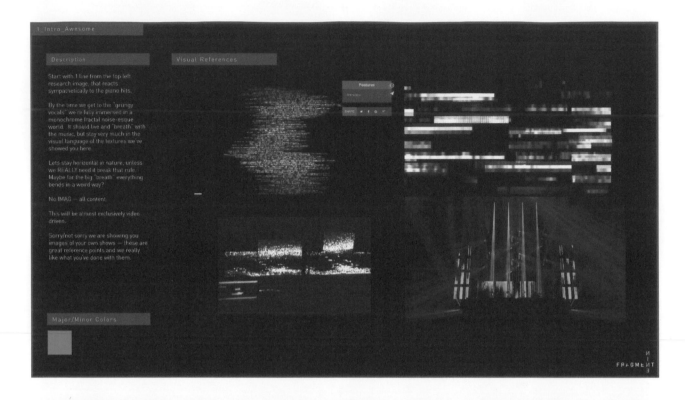

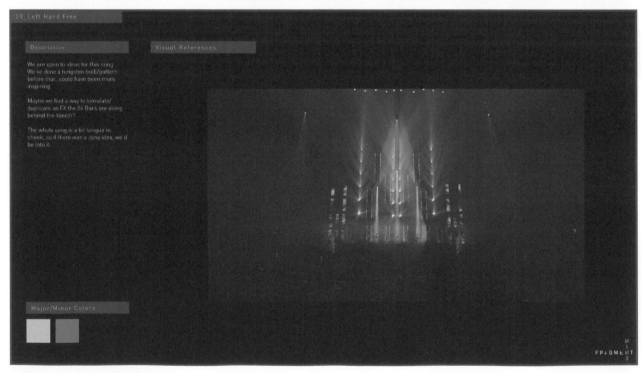

Figure 17.12 continued

Description

This song is about the interplay between two opposing forces: vertical and horizontal.

Introducing the horizontal laser array for the first time, we will be alternating between that array and the riser laser cages which shoot vertically. Content should echo this "jail cell" alternating effect and should not over power the lasers. Strobing, static lines, almost like they are bursting with energy but can't move, might be a cool way to think about it. Think of it like we are trapped in a box. Maybe we "open" the center to see the band's faces at times, but top and bottom are always full content, or something. Play with the box.

End of the set, balls to the walls.

Visual References

Major/Minor Colors

FRAGMENT NINE

HARDWARE

PROJECTORS

Nowadays, projectors come in lots of different flavors. What started out as a pretty limited option has exploded in the past ten years. Typically, projectors comes in either HD (1920 × 1080) or 4K (3840 × 2160) pixels (resolution—we'll get to this later). They also come with either lamps or lasers as the source that emits the light from the projector. Laser projectors are pretty new and, while incredibly bright, are also super expensive, though getting cheaper every year—a 10k projector can now cost half of what it did in 2010. Another note on projectors is how heavy they are; if they need to be hung in the air, specialty rigs have to be executed for each projector. Additionally, they make a *lot* of noise, cooling down the light source with a continuous fan—something that goes unnoticed at a rock show, but is detrimental in a 200-person black box!

One unique thing about projectors is that you can put a lot of different lens options in them. This means you can use the same body to project an image both super close up and super far away, just with different lenses. One bad thing about projectors is they are usually really power-hungry. And, while you might think new projectors are bright, as compared with LED walls, lights, even ambient light in a room, they aren't very bright at all. Think about your TV as compared with a projector in the classroom—same thing. To get enough brightness on certain shows, you need to "double stack" or even "triple stack" projectors on top of one another, all pointing at the same place.

The surface that you are trying to project on has a huge impact on what projectors and how many are needed as well. Some surfaces reflect light well (we call these "high gain" surfaces), such as purpose-built projection screens or white walls. Some surfaces, such as concrete, are terrible at reflecting light (low gain), and so many more projectors must be used to achieve the same amount of brightness on low-gain surfaces compared with high-gain surfaces. One cool thing you can do with projectors you can't do with LED is, well, project! This means you can project onto buildings, onto curves, onto balls, etc. To do this, which is actually called projection mapping, it gets really complicated really quickly, and so we'll skip that for this edition. The long and short of it is

that there are lots of options with projectors, but in most instances they aren't just "plug and play."

LED

In 1968, the first LED screen was invented at Hewlett Packard, a computer company. At some point, the entertainment industry adopted the technology to create LED screens as we know them today. Initially, the size of LED screens was pretty limited, they had terrible colors, and they were super heavy. You get the idea. Today, they are light, gorgeous, come in a ton of different shapes and sizes, etc.

Commonly, LED screens are manufactured into what we call "tiles," which is a frame that holds individual LEDs spaced at a specific distance apart, generally in a square or rectangular frame. Tiles are typically .5 m (meter) or .6 m square, although you can also get 1 m square, 1.2 m square, .5 × 1 m, .6 × 1.2 m, and plenty of other variations. You can even buy curved ones, triangle ones, or strips. You can even have them custom-made to any shape or size you desire. Tiles come in a variety of "pixel pitches," which is the distance between the actual LEDs within each tile. It is typically expressed in millimeters. The lower the pixel pitch, the smaller the distance is between pixels, which typically results in a better-looking image. For example, a 5-mm LED tile wall has individual LEDs every 5 mm. A 25-mm LED tile will have LEDs spaced out every 25 mm. For the same tile size of .5 m × .5 m, the 5-mm pitch tile would have 10,000 LEDs per tile, whereas a 25-mm pitch tile would only have 500 LEDs per tile. This is a *huge* difference in what we call "resolution."

When you connect multiple tiles together, we call this an LED "wall." A wall can be almost any size. Walls can be square, rectangular, columns, etc.—the options are endless. However, walls can get really heavy really fast, so make sure you check with the venue and rigger to make sure it can support the weight!

BONUS CONCEPT: SCREENS

Projectors and LED walls often end up being used on shows at the same time. Because they are basically the same thing, just a different way of displaying imagery (emissive vs projected), we tend to call them both "screens."

MEDIA SERVER

The media server is a fancy computer with big hard drives and a lot of connectors. It stores all the video content on its drives, and then plays it back when the video programmer has asked it to be played back. Typically, it listens to DMX from the lighting console for its commands and then it outputs a variety of video signals [high-definition multimedia interface (HDMI), DisplayPort, serial digital interface (SDI), etc.]. Servers can be very basic or very complex, depending on the needs of the show. Often, multiple servers are chained together on larger shows such as when you have multiple screens.

Some media servers will interface with the light board and the sound board in order for all the cues to play at once, while others will not. Media playback can be proprietary and made for a specific purpose, or commercially available. The latter includes QLab, Isadora, WatchOut, and others. Some of the playback will work in a Windows environment only; some in that and Mac.

And, while we are on media servers, please know how important it is to *always* have a backup server! Did you ever write a paper for class and not have auto-save turned on, and then your computer crashed, and you lost the whole thing? If you have an automatic cloud backup, you will have a solution quickly. Same with video media: In the event of a computer issue, switching to a backup server will ensure your production goes smoothly.

OTHER GACK

There are plenty of other bits and bobs and cables that go into making a video system work. For now, we're going to ignore them and stop here.

> A truly successful production is when collaboration happens and no one makes assumptions … Then work can be more unified—or not depending on what the team is going for. If everyone does their homework, and shares their ideas … the work is done and you go to the theatre and "plug it all in" … until script changes—the work is done.
> —Michael Clarke,
> American video designer

SOFTWARE
RESOLUTION, CODECS, AND FRAME RATES

Resolution
Resolution is an abstract term that describes the density of pixels within a given screen. It is typically expressed as $X \times Y$, where X is the horizontal direction and Y is the vertical direction. We are familiar with HD and 4K, like your TV. HD is 1920 pixels wide × 1080 pixels tall. This is the "resolution" of your TV. However, because we can make LED walls of any shape we want, and we can stack projectors to project on the side of a building, we often go beyond the bounds of HD and 4K in the video department. The resolution of the show, which may actually be multiple resolutions (multiple screens), can get pretty whacky.

Codecs
This is a term that describes how the video content is encoded, or how the actual bytes of the video file are arranged. Annoyingly, certain media servers will only play certain codecs, so be careful. Certain codecs are good for some things and not others. Some are good for really beautiful images; some are really good at keeping the file size small. Your content/media manager or your programmer can usually help decide what codec should be used on your show.

Frame Rate
In actuality, video content isn't a moving image. It's a succession of still images that are all slightly different from one another played back so fast that the transition between them appears so smooth that you as an audience member think the transition between still images is seamless. Typically in the US, we have adopted a standard of 29.97 frames per second, so 29.97 individual still images are being displayed every second on a screen to show you a moving image. Frame rates can vary by project or location around the globe.

Theatre Traditions: Church Key

The monks made their own ale. To keep the recipes secret, the monasteries were locked. Since the new bottle opener looked a bit like a skeleton key, it was referred to as a *church key.*

VIDEO CONTENT

Once you have defined your screens (LED vs projector, skinny vs tall, flat vs curved), then you need to start thinking about the imagery actually being displayed on your screens. Video content can be something you recorded on your iPhone, something custom made by an animator, something filmed by a live camera, live generated graphics, or even a still image. Typically, you want to edit or manipulate the video content in some way to make sure it's the right length and looks like it's in the style of the show. If it's being custom-made by a content creator, then you must tell them how your screens are laid out in 3D space and what resolution each screen is. Someone on the video team will make what is called a "raster," which is a 2D guide that defines where the screens are, what their resolution is, what their names are, etc.

The true artistry of the video designer comes through the content creators. A lot of trust must be put in them, and the relationship between the video designer and content creators must be strong. Sometimes, a video designer will make their own content, but typically they have too much to do, and so they must have a team of creators/animators helping them.

Flow of a Video Production for a Show

- The video designer comes up with an idea of how they want to use video on a show
- The video designer specifies where they want to use projectors vs LED walls
- The video crew chief or screens producer will work with the video designer to determine exactly which LED tiles and which projectors are necessary for the desired effect
- Someone on the production team makes rasters based on the arrangement of LED tiles and projectors
- The video designer communicates with content creators what the look and feel of each part of the show wants to be
- Content creators deliver their assets to the content manager, who double checks files and loads them onto the media servers
- The media server programmer programs the pieces of content in sequence as designed by the video designer
- Load-in happens, and the projectors get hung by the LED technicians and the projectionists
- Rehearsal happens, where the video designer communicates desired changes to both the media server programmers and the content creators
- Show time!

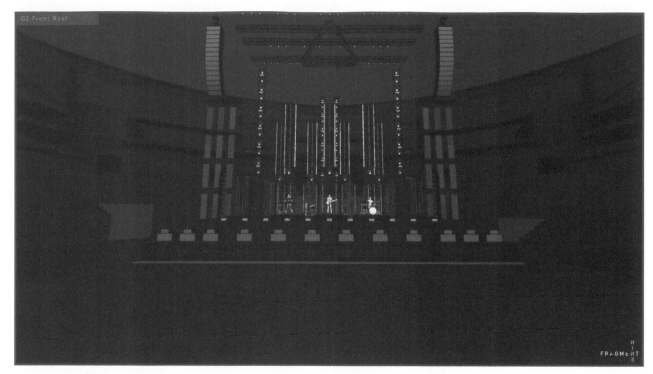

■ **Figure 17.13** Alt-J Glastonbury Festival previsualization of truss moves by FragmentNine.

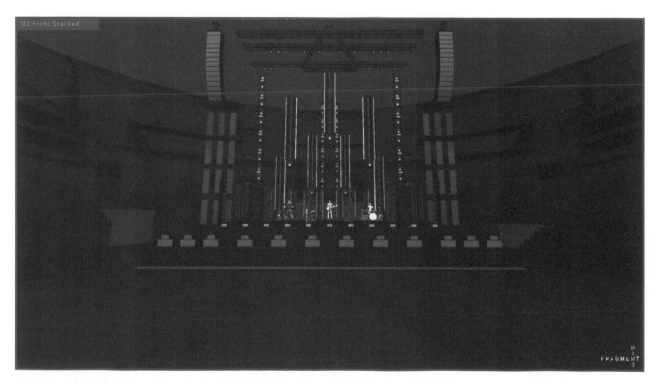

■ **Figure 17.14** Alt-J Glastonbury Festival previsualization of truss moves by FragmentNine.

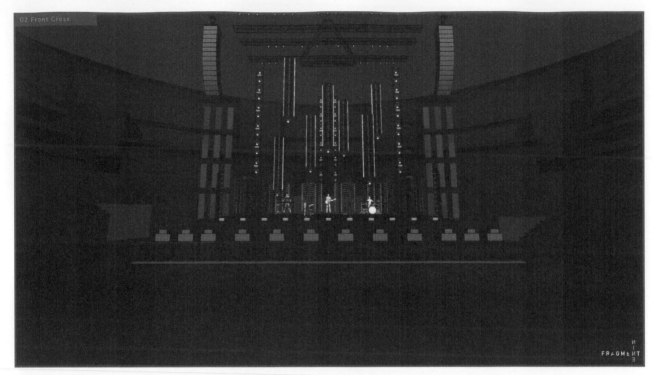

■ **Figure 17.15** Alt-J Glastonbury Festival previsualization of truss moves by FragmentNine.

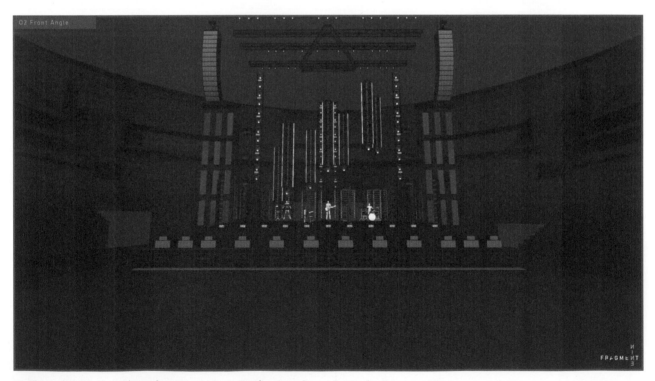

■ **Figure 17.16** Alt-J Glastonbury Festival previsualization of truss moves by FragmentNine.

■ **Figure 17.17** The first documentation received from a scenic designer will typically include 3D renderings of the set. These were prepared by Jorge Dominguez, set designer for the 2016 production of *Premios Juventud* for Univision. This image was prepared in VectorWorks.

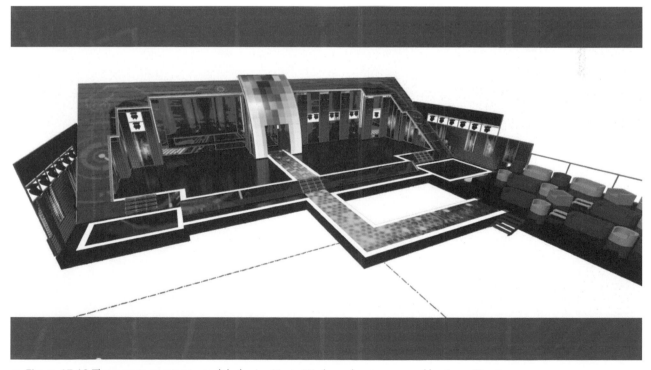

■ **Figure 17.18** These were computer modeled using VectorWorks and were prepared by Jorge Dominguez, set designer for the 2016 production of *Premios Juventud* for Univision.

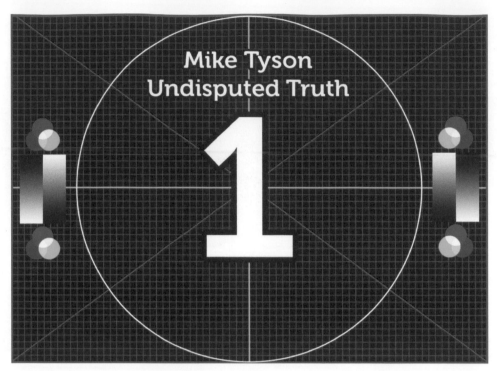

■ **Figure 17.19** A pattern, color, and gradient test slide for video. An image such as this is used to calibrate video sources to look as one.

■ **Figure 17.20** Alt-J @ London O2 Arena 2017. FragmentNine won the 2019 Knight of Illumination award for this production design.

■ **Figure 17.21** BTS @ Citi Field 2018 by FragmentNine.

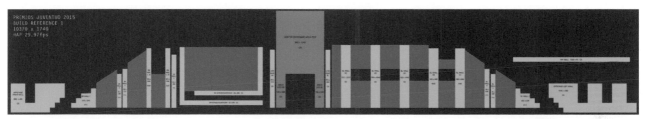

■ **Figure 17.22** For content production, a single raster covering every screen surface in one plane is an essential design tool. Here are the screens from Univision's *Premios Juventud*. While the screens are made of many types of LED product and projection, all surfaces are unified to one **pixel density** so image sizing will remain consistent.

■ **Figure 17.23** A chart for tracking all the naming conventions for the People's Choice Awards 2017, with set design from Steve Bass.

	Tile count	Tile type	Tiles Wide	Tiles High	Native Pixels Width	Native Pixels Height	Signal Pixel Density W	Signal Pixel Density H	Grid Code
MAIN SCREENS									
HERO	252	SV-9	21	12	1344	768	1512	864	I
SIDE SR	84	SV-9	12	7	768	448	864	504	B
SIDE SL	84	SV-9	12	7	768	448	864	504	P
HOUSE SR & SL	n/a	house			1920	1080	1920	1080	
COLUMNS									
DS Column SR	7	SV-8	1	7	72	1008	72	1008	A
Column B SR	6	SV-8	1	6	72	864	72	864	D
Column A SR	8	SV-8	1	8	72	1152	72	1152	F
US Column SR	8	SV-8	1	8	72	1152	72	1152	G
US Column SL	8	SV-8	1	8	72	1152	72	1152	K
Column A SL	8	SV-8	1	8	72	1152	72	1152	L
Column B SL	6	SV-8	1	6	72	864	72	864	N
DS Column SL	7	SV-8	1	7	72	1008	72	1008	Q

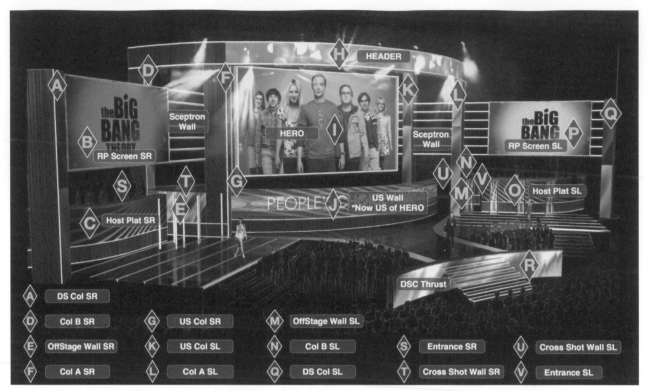

■ **Figure 17.24** Video screens dominate scenic design. Clear screen naming is a simple and valuable tool to share among teams. For the People's Choice Awards 2017, this set design from Steve Bass uses the names provided on his scenic documentation, as well as a letter code system to shorthand screen referencing.

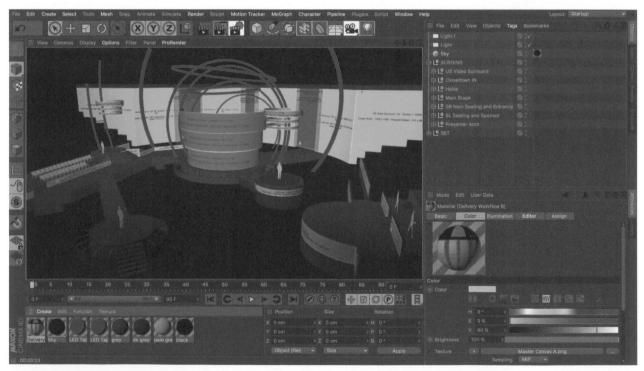

■ **Figure 17.25** Tools such as Cinema4D are great for prepping 3D assets for sharing. Here is the 2017 set for the CMT Music Awards designed by Anne Brahic. Her scenic model has been optimized for use by the screens team and UV mapped with the requested delivery files for preview.

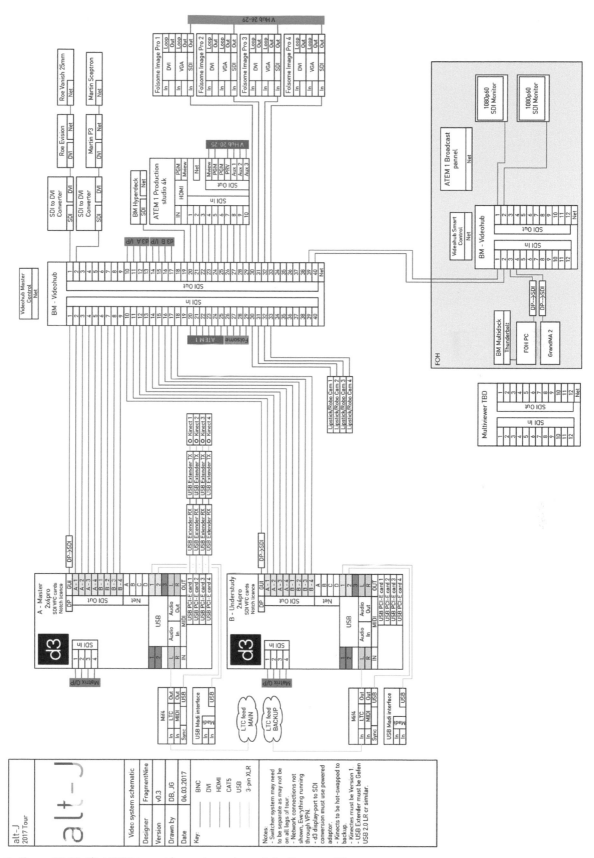

Figure 17.26 Alt-J 2017 tour video system schematic by FragmentNine.

EXERCISE

Create a montage of photos telling a story based on the play your school is currently doing.

CHECK YOUR KNOWLEDGE

1. Explain how projections first started to be used as an effect and in what industry. Discuss why they were not used in early theaters.
2. Define the difference between a video designer and a screens producer.
3. Create a scenario where projections can be used beyond their current applications. Describe your idea in detail.

- Content creator
- Creative director
- Digital projection
- Media server
- Pani
- PIGI
- Pixel
- Pixel density
- Raster
- Road box

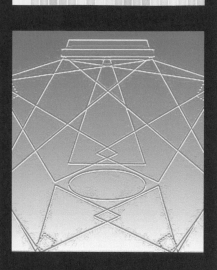

STUDY WORDS
Chapter 17

The Magic behind the Curtain

Special Effects

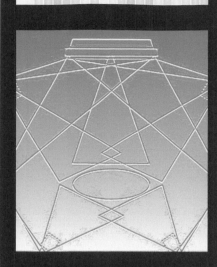

Student Learning Outcomes

Students will acquire:

- An overview understanding of the major aspects, techniques, and styles in the area of special effects.

- Fundamental, conceptual understanding of the expressive possibilities of theatre.

- A working knowledge of concepts applicable to the area of special effects.

We explore a variety of effects in this chapter (Figure 18.1). Effects can fall into any of the departments we already discussed, or the production may add an effects department if there is a need for many specialized effects. A prop may need to explode into flames, the stage may need to rain or snow for a certain scene, or a character might need to fly through the air. All of these effects can be handled in a variety of ways, depending on the theater space and the budget. Bringing in an expert in special effects is sometimes the only way to safely do these things. Other times, if the effects are done simply enough, someone already on the production team can set them up and supervise them.

Effects are a brand-new concept in theatre, right? Wrong! Let's pause for a minute and think back into theatre history. Did the Romans and Greeks use special effects? Well, of course, they did! Effects are *not* a new idea. What is new, however, is the implementation of our ideas (Figures 18.2 and 18.3). The more theatre tries to emulate film, the more the audience expects, with the advent of new technologies opening up almost limitless possibilities for designing new effects ideas. Some effects become more magical and mysterious, triggering our imaginations into high gear, while others become overly realistic and filmic.

■ **Figure 18.1** At the moment of explosion, a cross explodes during a production of *Laughing Stock*.

■ **Figure 18.2** Alt-J @ The Anthem 2022. This design featured a transparent hologauze fabric stretched across a frame that we call "The Fish Tank," by FragmentNine.

■ **Figure 18.3** *Tote Stadt* at New York City Opera in 1971. Director, Frank Corsaro; slide and projection designer, Ronald Chase; and costume designer, Theoni Aldredge.

The interesting thing about stage effects is that using the real thing doesn't always work. Think about it. Your audience is usually at least a minimum of 20 feet away from the stage and sometimes as much as hundreds of feet away. The effect has to be seen from many distances and still work from every seat in the house. There are many different ways to create an effect in order to achieve the desired result.

VINTAGE EFFECTS

NATURE

Let's look at some of the more classic effects in theatre before we move on to the newer generation. The "older" effects were meant to recreate nature. Wind, thunder, rain, snow, and fire are just a few of the effects that come to mind initially. The techniques used 100 years ago can

■ **Figure 18.4** Vintage thunder-making machine.

still work today, especially if you are on a small budget. Wind was easy, and it still is. Any ideas? Yup, use a fan! It can be that easy. Of course, you want to use a quiet fan; otherwise, it will sound like the aliens are landing a spaceship backstage. And the fan needs to match the type of wind you need. You can create anything from a gentle summer breeze to a tornado.

Thunder is one of my favorite old-time effects (Figure 18.4). All you have to do is find a long, thin piece of sheet metal. Drill of couple of holes in the short end and attach a piece of wood that can work like a handle. Drill a couple of holes in the other short end and hang it in the air so that the bottom is just above your head but still reachable. All you have to do is grab the wooden handle and give it a gentle shake. Once you have practiced a bit, start it slow, speed up, and slow it down again. It's a cool effect!

Rain was originally a little tougher (Figure 18.5). A trough would be created with holes drilled in the bottom. The trough was hung in the air at a slight angle to allow gravity to help out. At the high side of the trough, a stagehand would be on a ladder with a bucket of water

■ **Figure 18.5** I found this image in a *very* old book. I can't believe anyone actually created a rain effect like this!

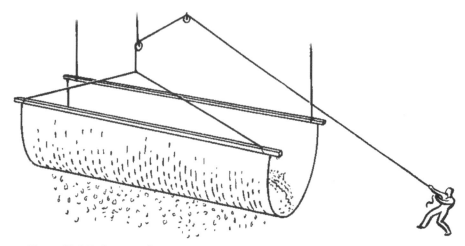

■ **Figure 18.6** Early snow effect.

and would slowly pour the water into the trough. The trough changed to either a garden hose or a piece of small conduit, but the idea is the same. The difficulty with this is getting the rain to stop on command! Water often has a mind of its own. Do not forget to provide proper drainage for your stage or, the next day, you will have to replace the entire stage deck!

Snow effects have been around forever (Figure 18.6). Snow shares the same problem as rain in that the snow doesn't stop on command. The original snow bags were long horizontal bags or slings with holes at the bottom. They would be filled with confetti, bleached cornflakes, or any other material that would fall to the floor gracefully. The bag was hung horizontally, with strings attached to shake it from the floor to release the "snow." Of course, this type of snow doesn't melt, but we always seem to just ignore that aspect.

FIRE

Fire—well, original fire effects actually used real flame (Figure 18.7). That is one of the reasons there were so many theater fires early on. Once theatre designers figured out this was a *bad* idea, they started to create fire effects with lighting. Three lights would be hidden in the fireplace, or other appropriate place, with each light gelled to a different color. The colors most often used were amber, orange, and red. Then, a small fan with several flame-shaped pieces of fabric would be placed in the middle of the lights. Turn on the fan and the

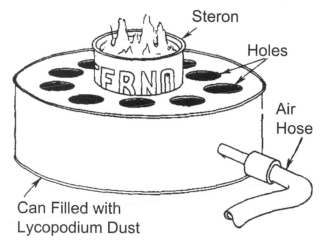

Steron

Holes

Air Hose

Can Filled with Lycopodium Dust

■ **Figure 18.7** A *very* early fire effect, before we got smarter.

lights, which would be sequenced on and off in rapid succession to make it look like the flame was flickering. It's much easier to achieve this with computer lighting controllers.

MODERN EFFECTS

OK, enough of history you say. You want to know about today's effects. OK! So much information is out there. Every day, new ideas create the need for new technological ideas. Don't let the rest of this chapter limit your imagination. Keep in mind that every piece of machinery or technology was created because someone had an idea. Today, there are many choices, from the simplest to the most extremely advanced. Let's start by looking at today's effects that replaced some of the

■ **Figure 18.8** *Medea*. Directed by Tom King, with costume design by Jenner Brunk. Medea is played by Elise Boyd. James Madison University, 2003. Scenic and lighting design by Richard Finkelstein.

vintage ones. Keep in mind that, in the previous chapter, we already focused solely on modern projections and the complexities they have achieved.

> Theatre used to be about imagination; now if you're not careful all you look at is the big screen closeup of the star's face. That's TV!
> —Anne Johnston, projection innovator

NATURE

Wind is still created with fans. However, today's fans can vary in speed and direction for a more realistic movement across the stage. The lighting department is still the one responsible for creating and controlling wind effects when they are simple. Given the variety of new DMX-controlled fans, it is simpler than ever to program your breeze or tornado through the lighting control board.

The sound designer is usually the one to create thunder today. Mostly because we have advanced far beyond hanging a piece of metal in the air and shaking it! With the advances in speaker size and placement as well as sound mixing boards, thunder can come from any specific location and move across the stage or throughout the auditorium. This flexibility can be amazingly realistic—if that is what the designer wants.

Lightning was never dealt with very well during the "vintage" times. To today's sensibility, what they tried back then is actually funny to us now. Always know that we are limited by what exists unless we have the resources to invent something new! Today, lightning can be done very effectively using a combination of equipment such as strobes and projections. The advances in lighting control boards have allowed for complicated cueing and triggering of various equipment that can give us quite the lightning storm. Newer light sources that turn on and off instantaneously create this effect better than ever.

Strobes come in many, many varieties, and all have their uses. Martin makes the Atomic line of strobes. These fixtures are LED-based with red, green, and blue LEDs. Martin has also created a scroller for their strobe so you can layer color on top of the LED source.

Moving to bigger units, Luminys makes a series called LightningStrikes®. They have nine different models in this line. These are some of the brightest on the market. They have so much flexibility that you can create almost any effect you can imagine. Basically, there is something for almost every idea you can dream up.

Remember when I said ideas could generate the technology. Well, remember the musical *Singin' in the Rain*? That show forced the issue of how best and most safely to do rain onstage. A full stage deck was built with a drain in it for the rain to pass into. Overhead, there was a complicated plumbing setup with multiple pipes to produce the rain. Off stage there was a pressurized water tank that fed the overhead pipes and recycled the water from the deck. The water was also temperature-controlled for actor safety—not too hot and not too cold, just right.

Snow has come a long way since the simple snow bags I described earlier! Although we can still use the snow bag idea, there are now many other options with a variety of distribution effects. You can rent or buy a snow machine (Figure 18.9). The machine takes a liquid formula and turns it into snow at the same time it blows the snow out of the machine with a fan. Most machines work only when the temperature is more than 40ºF. The nice thing is that, once the snow melts, it reverts

■ **Figure 18.9** Little Blizzard snow machine.

back into the liquid formula leaving almost no residue. That means no cleanup either! However, they were very loud. The newest of the machines can vary the size of the snowflakes, the speed at which they are generated, and the distance that they blow. And they do all of this while being quiet. All of this can be very realistic, if that is what you are going for, or stylized.

FIRE

Real fire is always a danger on stage, which is why many cities and towns have regulations governing its use. You will need training to become certified and obtain a license to use fire effects. This is truly a specialized area. You can buy products to create flames and smoke, but most of those require you to have a special effects license before you can even purchase the supplies, never mind operate the equipment. With all that said, there are still ways to create a simulated fire on stage. Most of the best ones are packaged units that you simply plug in and control via a remote control or the lighting board.

FOG AND HAZE

The developments lately in fog and specifically fog fluids are amazing. Early fog fluids were mineral-oil-based. Water-soluble foggers have long since replaced them for good reason. A number of factors went into this transition. First, the oil would often coat the stage when the fog dissipated, leaving it slippery and dangerous. The mineral oil also didn't agree with singers' voices, which is

■ **Figure 18.10** *Ghosts of Versailles* at the Metropolitan Opera in 1991. Director, Colin Graham; scenic and costume designer, John Conklin; and lighting designer, Gil Wechsler.

a major worry. Lastly, the oil was combustible. All of this combined to make for a very dangerous situation. Water-soluble fluids solved all these problems! The basics of how any fog machine works are relatively simple (Figure 18.11). Fog fluid is moved into a heater by an internal pump. The heater maintains a high temperature at which the fluid vaporizes. As the fluid changes to vapor and rapidly expands, it is that expansion that forces the new vapor through the nozzle of the machine. When the vapor mixes with cooler air outside the machine, it instantly forms an opaque aerosol—the effect we call *fog* or *smoke*.

There are many manufacturers of fog machines today. The main factor is whether the fog hangs in the air or on the ground. Every machine is a little different and has different features. These features can control the start and end of the fog, overall quantity of flow, and the speed at which the fog dissipates. Fog dissipation is more important than you might at first think. You create this amazing environment on stage filled with fog,

■ **Figure 18.11** Rosco V-Hazer.

but the next scene takes place in a completely different location—with *no* fog. How do you get rid of the fog quickly? Certain fog juices are meant to last longer, and some are designed to dissipate more quickly. Some machines even have a timer that you can set for turning them on and off. What we've been discussing is fog that hangs in the air.

■ **Figure 18.12** A 55-gallon dry ice fogger.

If you want your fog effect to stay close to the stage floor, you will need dry ice. First, let me say a word of caution. Dry ice can be tricky to deal with, and there are safety protocols to be aware of. Dry ice is basically solid carbon dioxide at a temperature of $-109.3°F$ or $-78.5°C$. That is *negative!* So be careful. You can't just pick it up with your hands; you have to use gloves. It burns your skin with only momentary contact! Additionally, dry ice melts within 24 hours on its own, even if you keep it in a cooler, so, if you decide to use dry ice, make sure to check and budget for easily accessible daily pick-up of the materials!

You put the dry ice in a large container and pour water over it; it instantly starts to melt, giving off a dense fog. Dry ice machines are typically shop-built and made from a 55-gallon drum (Figure 18.12). You put water in the bottom, where there is a heater element. You put the dry ice in a basket at the top. When you are ready for fog, you lower the basket into the water, and a hole in the side of the drum connects to a hose that points the fog in a specific direction. When dry ice fog dissipates, no residue is left on the stage or in the air.

Haze is yet another kind of fog that can be created with today's machines. Haze is about revealing light beams more than it is about being seen on its own. Haze is a water-soluble liquid that, when heated, turns to haze. Sound familiar? It works just like the foggers we've discussed; the difference is in the fluid.

BLOOD

We've addressed blood in the makeup chapter that allows for small applications. But what happens if you need a lot of blood? Well, first let's discuss some of the attributes of blood. Most importantly, blood will steal focus. The audience will be drawn to it. So use it judiciously and make sure it is necessary!

The next thing to keep in mind is the color. Bright red blood tends to imply "fresher" blood and will give more of a shock factor to the audience, especially if used unexpectedly. Dark red blood is better for older injuries, scabs, or blood that has pooled. Also relating to color, think about the color of the costumes, scenery, and lighting being used in conjunction with the blood.

Blood can be bought in large quantities—up to 5-gallon containers—at a time depending on what you need. Creating your precise effect may require tinting the blood your purchase or thickening/thinning it. Always do this with the amount you need for the day; don't mix ahead. Talk to the manufacturer to be sure of how best to achieve the results you want. In general, you can usually thin blood with water and thicken it with xanthan gum. You can adjust the color with dyes, *but* that will affect whether it washes out or not!

CONFETTI

Confetti blowers, sometimes called confetti canons, are another product in the world of special effects. This is a very specialized effect that needs that right situation within a production in order to make sense. The blowers are fairly loud also, so this effect is in no way subtle!

With the ability to shoot confetti at a rate of ½–1 pound per second and up to 50 feet high, you can fill almost any venue. No electricity is required as these run on CO_2, which makes these units extremely versatile and simple to use. An operator is required to manually control the flow of CO_2 gas. There is now a variety of confetti available in terms of colors and materials.

PROJECTION SEGUE

Here we will discuss early projection ideas and what I term "simpler" projections. Simpler projections may be a single image or possibly a few images that crossfade between one another. Nothing too fancy. The previous chapter is where we dealt with higher-end projections that are used in complicated configurations with much more equipment and computing power. So, hang in there while we look at some such simpler solutions.

The Rosco X-Effects LED projector provides large-scale rippling light effects (Figure 18.13). Rotating two X-size glass gobos off center of the optical path creates the effect. This results in a projection with linear motion for creating reflected water, blowing fire, cascading rain, northern lights, and other animated lighting effects.. The lens is available in 1400 or 3000 lumen of output of 45 and 90 watts of power. There are two models, a 5500 kelvin and an RGBW version—both are LED-based.

You can also use a PowerPoint slide show connected to a projector and be done, if that is all you need. I designed a production of *Personals* that used this method (Figures 18.14 and 18.15). We built a large back wall that

■ **Figure 18.13** Rosco X-Effects LED projector.

was framed to look like the columns from a newspaper. I imported the design drawing into Photoshop to create the template or matte. Then, all the graphics were inserted into it.

Using this simple method, you can project still images, video, or video with audio. You need someone to run the computer and advance the slides on a cue from the stage manager (Figure 18.16).

With any technology, you have to be willing to make a leap of faith. That doesn't mean you jump with your eyes closed. You have to do your research and be informed about the technology. It is only a tool. And, any tool, as we know, is only as good as the person who uses it!

Just because you can, doesn't mean you should!

—Curt Ostermann, American lighting designer

The projection world has gone in two directions. We discussed a little of this, but let's go into more depth. There is still the concept of traditional projection; then, there is fully digital scenery. Still projections to a rear projection screen or TV set are still possible and used frequently. These can include a static backdrop, a skyline, a grotto, and so forth. The computer technology available today can create all sorts of projection effects. At a very

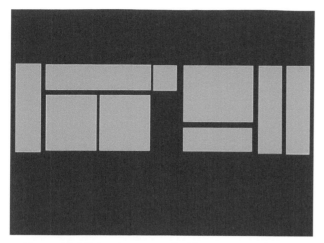

■ **Figure 18.14** Template created of the projections for a production of *Personals*.

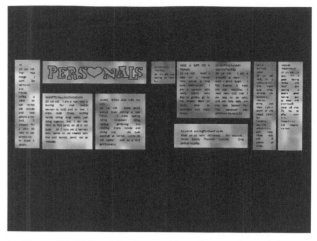

■ **Figure 18.15** Graphics inserted into the template of the projections for a production of *Personals*.

■ **Figure 18.16** A production at the 1869 Bardavon Opera House using supertitle projections.

high level, this replaces the lobsterscope effect. Digital projections have come so far that they are now amazing and beautiful and can be used in abstract ways as well as realistic ones. The projections have become more of a lighting effect when used this way.

The first try with almost any new technology is not a good experience. The key to much of the success is working with the manufacturer. If the manufacturer's responsiveness to our needs is good, then the technology can continue to develop and become a great tool for us in the theatre. Now that you have all this information, how do you use it? Ultimately, it's up to you and your imagination.

One last effect to discuss is **flying**. Have you ever seen a production of *Peter Pan*, *Angels in America*, *Billy Elliot*, *Chitty Chitty Bang Bang*, *Spamalot*, or *The Lion King*? If you have, you've most likely seen the work of the best-known theatrical flying company—Flying by Foy. In addition to theater, Flying by Foy has also worked on projects for the National Aeronautics and Space Administration (NASA) space program, the Smithsonian, and the Olympics! Let me explain a little.

Peter Foy revolutionized the concept of safely flying performers. His artistic vision used innovative techniques while patenting his own ingenious mechanical inventions. Let me be very clear here: No one should ever suspend performers in the air without consulting with professionals or hiring professionals! Foy's first success came with something called the inter-related pendulum. This invention meant a performer could move in two different directions simultaneously. The floating pulley allowed flying in spaces where there is a low ceiling. This was unheard of prior to this invention. The multi-point balance harness has adjustable points of attachment that enable the actor to maintain a specific position during flight. The inter-reacting compensator was designed to be less evident to the audience, helping to create the illusion in a less conspicuous manner.

The latest innovation is the Aereographer, which combines a visualization environment with a real-time physics engine to create rendered simulations of automated flying sequences. Any 3D flight path can be accurately simulated on any combination of pendulums and tracks before ever setting foot in the theater. During rehearsals, the flying can be quickly and easily modified—eliminating the tedious, time-consuming re-

cueing delays commonly experienced using conventional programming techniques. The flying simulation then seamlessly connects with Foy's high-speed Pegasus® winch systems to run the new sequence with live performers.

EXERCISES

EXERCISE 1

Create a snow effect using one of the methods discussed. It can be realistic or stylized, as you wish.

EXERCISE 2

Create a ghost effect for the stage.

EXERCISE 3

Using Shakespeare's *The Tempest,* design on paper how you would go about creating the storm with all the technology available to you, regardless of budget.

CHECK YOUR KNOWLEDGE

1. Choose a vintage effect listed in the chapter and rethink it for today's audience. How can you update it to make it better received by a current audience?
2. Choose an early projection effect listed in the chapter and rethink it for today's audience. How can you update it to make it better received by a current audience?
3. Compare one of the projection segue effects with a projection from the last chapter. Explain why one is not better or worse than the other.

- Dry ice
- Fog
- Haze
- Linnebach projector
- Lobsterscope
- Pepper's ghost
- Scene machine
- Strobe

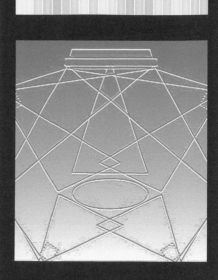

STUDY WORDS

Chapter 18

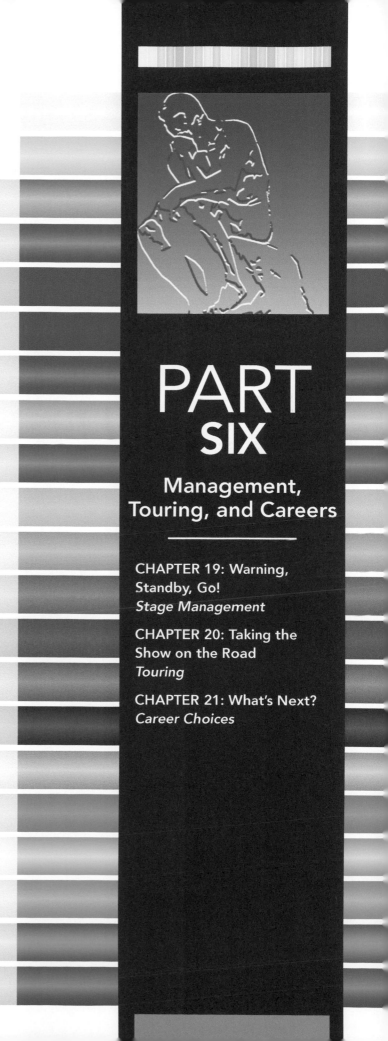

PART
SIX

Management, Touring, and Careers

CHAPTER 19: Warning, Standby, Go!
Stage Management

CHAPTER 20: Taking the Show on the Road
Touring

CHAPTER 21: What's Next?
Career Choices

Warning, Standby, Go!

Stage Management

CHAPTER NINETEEN

Student Learning Outcomes

Students will acquire:

- An overview understanding of the major aspects, techniques, and styles in the area of management.

- Fundamental, conceptual understanding of the expressive possibilities of theatre.

- A working knowledge of concepts applicable to the area of management.

Now that we have all the technical things done, what next? Well, as Mickey Rooney once said to Judy Garland, "Let's do a show!" The culmination of working in the theatre is the actual performance. I don't think we'd ever get much of an audience if all we did was put the fabulous set on stage and do some really cool lighting cues. The audiences have come to expect performers as well!

This chapter goes into the details of stage management, but we will also briefly discuss production management. These two positions are the liaisons between the pre-production and production phases of a show. A production manager is responsible for organizing and realizing all the physical aspects and logistics of the show. This includes working with the individual designers and shops regarding schedule, budget, production meetings, personnel, and transportation, to name a few. The stage manager (SM) is responsible for guiding the show through the rehearsal process and maintaining the artistic integrity of the show through the performances.

In some places, the SM is responsible for organizing and helping with auditions, but typically their duties begin a week or so before rehearsals, preparing the schedules, scripts, and other items needed in the rehearsal room. They work with the director to determine the rehearsal schedule, call and facilitate the rehearsals, facilitate communication between everyone involved in the show, and run the technical rehearsals; then, they call the cues and facilitate the backstage activity during performances while ensuring the directors' and designers' intentions are upheld. Without the SM, we would never get as far as *house lights to half*. SMs must be highly organized and keep detailed documentation of all aspects of the show, and they need to work well with a variety of artistic temperaments in situations that can sometimes be very stressful. The SM needs to be comfortable acting in place of the director once the show is open and needs a modest knowledge of all technical areas to be able to facilitate the needs of the designers and crew.

Stage management is a unique job within the industry. No other job goes through so many different phases within the production timeline, with so many varying responsibilities. The cast and crew look to the SM as the guiding beacon. A good SM helps create a physically and emotionally safe place for performers and creatives to work by documenting anything that detracts from that and forwarding the information to the appropriate people for them to take action. SMs need to know when to keep something confidential and when situations should be handled by company management or human resources.

STAGE MANAGER KIT

Most SMs have a personal **SM kit** filled with the items they need to do their job. This may include personal office supplies, favorite writing tools, a scale ruler for measuring drawings, a laptop, small speakers, snacks, or any other things that help them to work well. They can use anything that will hold the items and is easy to transport such as a fishing tackle box or a rolling bag of some kind. The theater company should supply the following items for the use of the SM and the entire company, as well as any scripts needed:

- Three-ring binders
- Pencils
- Erasers
- Highlighters
- Pads of paper
- Post-it notes
- Paper clips
- Stapler
- Printer

The SM also needs access to a standard first aid kit and should know enough about first aid to be able to assist an injured person until the emergency medical technicians (EMTs) arrive. An automated external defibrillator (AED) should also be available.

The SM's primary duties are about documentation and communication, and so they are somewhat ruled by paperwork and forms. Every SM has their favorite designs they have developed through years of experience. Keep in mind that every production is unique, and so not all forms are needed for all shows, and some shows need newly customized forms. At the very least, these samples will get you started. Don't be afraid to alter or create forms as needed for your specific needs or tastes. Also keep in mind that some of the following information is based upon Actors' Equity Association (AEA) guidelines. However, and it's a big however, AEA has many different contracts with different stipulations; alternatively, you might be working nonunion. All or some of the following may be applicable to your production situation.

AUDITIONS

The SM should always arrive early, but this is especially true when they are involved with auditions. They need to organize the space: Setting up a table and chairs for the director and producer, a holding area for the actors, a space for the actual auditions, and a table to greet actors and hand out the audition forms (Figure 19.1). Most actors will have a résumé and photo. Attach these to the audition form. Some directors like to take photos at the audition, and so a digital camera and small color printer may also be needed. The goal is to remember the actor's face after they have left the auditions.

Take a look at the sample audition form in Figure 19.1. Contact information and schedule conflicts are critical to casting for obvious reasons. Also notice the paragraph and signature line at the bottom of the page. Think of the audition form as a contract. If the actor is willing to sign on the line, it means they agree to the ground rules that have been established for this particular production.

Once auditions are over, the forms and any other documentation should be handed over to the director or producer. Depending on the SM's relationship with the director, you may or may not be a part of the casting process. If you are a part of the casting process, you will be asked for your opinion about various actors. Some of your input can be observations you made while running the audition. Details of import may include whether the actor arrived on time. Did the actor seem prepared? Were they courteous? Talent is an important part of casting, but so is selecting people who will work well with one another. If you observe something that causes you concern, share that information with the director and producer.

REHEARSALS

The SM's first step once the show is cast is to create a contact sheet. The contact sheet needs to show everyone involved with the production. Depending on the production, and more importantly the venue, there are two different styles of contact sheets. A production contact sheet is used primarily by schools and community theaters (Figure 19.2). A company contact sheet is used by professional theatre companies that have many more people involved (Figures 19.3–19.5). The production contact sheet sample (Figure 19.2) does not include addresses and may not include phone numbers or emails for all of those involved. The SM should ask each person what information they are willing to share with the company. The producer, director, SM, and HR should have contact sheets with all of the information for everyone, but the rest of the company does not need that level of detail. The SM may also want to put some mark to indicate if the individual has a health situation such as a pacemaker or diabetes that emergency medical personnel would find helpful, but again this information must only be shared with appropriate medical personnel when the need arises. The company contact sheet allows for the possible involvement of a separate producer or technical shops, and they are therefore included. Think

Laughing Stock

AUDITION FORM

Performances:
Thursday, March 1 through Saturday March 3 at 8pm
Sunday, March 4 at 2pm

NAME: _____

PHONE: _____

EMAIL: _____

Please list below your class/work schedule...and any other weekly commitments:

	Sun	Mon	Tues	Wed	Thur	Fri	Sat
9a-12p							
12p-3p							
3p-6p							
6p-9p							
9p-12a							

Please Note:

Rehearsals will most likely be during 2 weekday evenings, and 1 weekend afternoon. Load-in will be on Saturday, February 24. Cue-to-Cue will be on Sunday, February 25. Technical rehearsals will be Monday, February 26 through Wednesday, February 28th.

Role you would like to audition for: _____

If auditioning for a specific role, will you accept a different role: _____

I agree to the above schedule of rehearsals and performances for Laughing Stock. I understand that this production is striving to achieve the highest standards of performance and I agree to make all arrangements with other classes and/or my work schedule to participate in the all listed rehearsals and performances. I also understand that should I miss rehearsals or not maintain a professional work ethic, I may be released from my role.

Signature: _____   Date: _____

■ **Figure 19.1** Sample audition form.

of the contact sheet as your "speed dial" for the show. Any information you might need should be there. You can even include rehearsal and performance spaces as on the company contact sheet. Feel free, as always, to alter these samples and make a hybrid version as needed for your own use. This list becomes your distribution list for all paperwork generated in the future, to include script changes, schedule updates, etc.

The rehearsal schedule is the next thing that needs to be published to the entire company (Figures 19.6 and 19.7). You will work closely with the director to create this. The rehearsal schedule becomes your master calendar. It should show dates, times, places, and which members of the cast are required to attend. Be prepared to revise the schedule repeatedly throughout the rehearsal process as frequently as needed. Make sure to include a date, and possibly a time, on the revisions for all paperwork so that everyone knows which contact sheet or schedule is the most current. This is one of those times that can become frustrating, given the amount of

Show Name
Production Contact Sheet

TITLE	NAME	EMAIL	CELL PHONE	HOME PHONE
Director				
Asst. Director				
Musical Director				
Choreographer				
Scenic Designer				
Lighting Designer				
Costume Designer				
Sound Designer				
Effects Designer				
Production Stage Manager				
Stage Manager				
Wardrobe				
Property Manager				
Hair/Makeup				
CHARACTER	NAME	EMAIL	CELL PHONE	HOME PHONE

■ **Figure 19.2** Sample production contact sheet.

Show Name
Company Contact Sheet

SEND PACKAGES/ MAIL TO:

<NAME>
Theatre Name/Production Name
Mailing Address
City, State, Zip

(212) 555-1234 Box Office
(212) 555-2000 Stage Mgmt Office
(212) 555-2100 Backstage Security
(212) 555-1235 Opening Night Tickets

Role/ Position	First	Last	phone	email	Personal/ Company Address	Representative Contact
Company Staff						
Artistic Director						
Managing Director						
General Manager						
Associate Producer						
Assoc. General Manager						
Company Manager						
Asst. to General Manager						
Casting Director						
Director of Marketing & Communication						
Creative						
Playwright						
Director						

■ **Figure 19.3** Sample company contact sheet.

Creative						
Asst. Director						
Musical Director						
Choreographer						
Scenic						
Scenic Designer						
Associate Scenic Designer						
Asst. Scenic Designer						
Lighting						
Lighting Designer						
Assoc. Lighting Designer						
Asst. Lighting Designer						
Costume						
Costume Designer						
Assoc. Costume Designer						
Asst. Costume Designer						
Hair Designer						
Makeup Designer						
Sound						

■ **Figure 19.4** Another company contact sheet.

Sound Designer						
Associate Sound Designer						
Asst. Sound Designer						
Stage Management						
Production Stage Manager						
Stage Manager						
Cast						

■ **Figure 19.5** Yet another company contact sheet.

Laughing Stock Rehearsal Schedule

Day	Date	Time	Place	Scene(s)	Notes
Sunday	01/28/07	12pm - 4pm	DHT	*2-4, 2-5*	
Sunday	01/28/07	5pm - 9pm	DHT	*1-3, 1-6*	
Wednesday	01/31/07	6pm - 10pm	DHT	*1-9, 2-2*	
Friday	02/02/07	5pm - 9pm	DEL	*1-1, 1-7,* Shakespeare	
Sunday	02/04/07	12pm - 4pm	DHT	*1-2,* Shakespeare	
Sunday	02/04/07	5pm - 9pm	DHT	*1-4, 1-9*	
Wednesday	02/07/07	6pm - 10pm	D205	1-3,2-3, 1-5	
Friday	02/09/07	5pm - 9pm	DEL	*2-1, 1-8*	
Sunday	02/11/07	12pm - 4pm	D209	1-6, 2-4	OFF BOOK
Sunday	02/11/07	5pm - 9pm	D209	2-2	
Wednesday	02/14/07	6pm - 10pm	D205	Snow Day	
Friday	02/16/07	5pm - 9pm	DEL	*2-1, 2-3,1-2, 1-1*	
Sunday	02/18/07	12pm ·4pm	D209	1-4,2-5	
Sunday	02/18/07	5pm - 9pm	D209	1-5,2·2	
Monday	02/19/07	12pm - 4pm	DHT	Runthrough Act 1	*President's Day*
Monday	02/19/07	5pm - 9pm	DHT	Runthrough Act 2	*President's Day*
Wednesday	02/21/07	6pm - 10pm	D205	Runthrough Acts 1&2	
Friday	02/23/07	5pm - 9pm	DEL	*As Needed*	
Saturday	02/24/07	10a-8pm	DHT	Load-in	
Sunday	02/25/07	12pm -6pm	DHT	Cue-to-Cue	
Sunday	02/25/07	7pm - 10pm	DHT	Tech Rehearsal-Costume Parade	
Monday	02/26/07	6pm -10pm	DHT	Dress Rehearsal	
Tuesday	02/27/07	6pm -10pm	DHT	Dress Rehearsal	
Wednesday	02/28/07	6pm -10pm	DHT	Invited Dress	
Thursday	03/01/07	6pm	DHT	Opening Night	
Friday	03/02/07	6:30pm	DHT	Performance #2	
Saturday	03/03/07	6:30pm	DHT	Performance #3	
Sunday	03/04/07	12:30pm	DHT	Performance #4	
Sunday	03/04/07	5pm - 8pm	DHT	Strike	

■ **Figure 19.6** Sample rehearsal schedules. Everyone has a preference for what the schedule should look like.

March 30 to April 5, 2008

	Sunday 30	Monday 31	Tuesday 1	Wednesday 2	Thursday 3	Friday 4	Saturday 5
9:00 AM							
10:00 AM		Character work-Leads only	Block Act 2, scenes 3-5		Work Through Act 1		
11:00 AM	Musical Rehearsal-Full Cast					Run Through w/Designers	
12:00 PM				Dance Rehearsal-Full Cast			
1:00 PM		Lunch	Lunch		Lunch		
2:00 PM		Ensemble choreography	Fight rehearsal		Work Through Act 2		
3:00 PM							
4:00 PM							
5:00 PM							

■ **Figure 19.7** Here is another version of a rehearsal schedule.

revisions possible. Changes can be due to a number of things: People's schedules can have unforeseen conflicts, or more rehearsal time may be needed for a particular scene. I always believe that every schedule I publish is "tentative" until the show is open. Then, we have a final schedule.

Before rehearsals actually begin, you will need to set up the rehearsal space. If the SM is lucky, there will be a dedicated rehearsal space. One of the first things done is to tape the floor by using a scale drawing of the set designer's ground plan and recreating exactly all the important details on the floor of the rehearsal space using ½″ gaffer's tape, also called spike tape. Important details include things such as walls, doors, stairs, platforms, and windows. This is essential for accurate blocking.

The first rehearsal is one of the most hectic days during the whole production. Usually, many guests are invited to the first rehearsal, and there are many introductions and presentations. The producers are often in attendance. The designers are invited to attend, and the set and costume designers usually make presentations about their designs to give actors an idea of what will be created. Often, department heads from the various shops will be in attendance—especially costumes, hair, and makeup. If it is a union show, there will also be a brief meeting of the union members.

The SM needs to predict what they will need during rehearsal from the different departments. Sets, costumes, and props are the most common departments to deal with on this issue, although any item required should be available. They create a list of what will be needed in enough time for things to be procured and delivered to rehearsal. Needs may change as rehearsals begin. Items can always be added as you go, but the more you think

SP4 CAST CREW CONTACT LISTING

Live and Unrehearsed

Sign In Sheet
Thursday, September 11th 7:00 pm – 10:00 pm

ACTOR NAME	CHARACTER	SIGNATURE

■ **Figure 19.8** Sample sign-in sheet.

through ahead of time, the smoother rehearsals will progress. Typical items are shoes, rehearsal skirts, and substitute props—the real ones will be saved until tech.

Once rehearsals begin, the SM tracks many things simultaneously. The first thing each day is to determine who is present. If actors are late, they need to be contacted to find out where they are and when they expect to arrive. A sign-in sheet (Figure 19.8) posted near the door is a quick way to keep track of missing actors and crew. A policy should be in place regarding lateness and the ramifications for the actor or crew member. This should be decided by the director, with escalating steps of consequences for repeat offenders. The SM documents the arrival time of latecomers but is not the disciplinarian. Remember, this is show business—not show fun.

During each day's rehearsal, the SM keeps notes for each department (scenery, costumes, lighting, props, etc.) and shares them in the daily rehearsal report (Figure 19.9). These notes include any changes or additions to the lists based on the script that may come up during the rehearsal. A script change, the addition of a prop, rescheduling rehearsals, specific requirements for lighting or costumes, a sound cue that will be needed, anything like that is noted. Should it be determined that a quick-change area is needed backstage for costume or other reasons, this should be listed on the report. If the show will need live fire—anything from a candle to a cigarette, gun, or explosion—this is critical information that must be shared immediately as it usually requires additional personnel and permits. All the information needs to get to all the right people. The SM is responsible

A Midsummer Night's Dream

Rehearsal Report

Day: Sunday **Date:** April 18 **Rehearsal:** #1	**Start time:** 7:00 pm **Break:** 8:20–8:30 **End Time:** 9:57
Attendance: TC, SB, MMS until 9:05, DS, BLO	**Prod. Attendance:** KLT, EAK, SW, EW, JA
Today's Schedule: block and work Ii	**Tomorrow's Schedule:** block and work Iii
Set:	**Props:** guitar (EAK has one we can restring and teach SB to play), blanket, poetry book, picnic basket, picnic food (tbd—grapes?)
Lighting:	**Sound:** song for introduction to characters for opening sequence, SB song?
Costumes:	**Box Office:**
Rehearsal Notes:	**Misc:** tomorrow start at 8pm; Wednesday don't start until 9pm; fill open roles at 7pm

■ **Figure 19.9** Sample daily rehearsal report.

for disseminating all this information to the department heads. Emails are sent at the end of each rehearsal day. It is good practice to include the rehearsal schedule and plan for the next day in the daily report: That way, while you are updating the master rehearsal schedule, you don't need to resend it to everyone in the company should there be significant changes. Any questions that arise are directed to the SM, and so the notes need to be concise but specific. For example, "May we have a large latte mug for Jo in scene 4?" under "Props" is a better note than "We need a cup for Jo" written in General Notes.

The SM is the archivist of the show. Their files are the master copy of everything that people will reference. They keep every piece of paper, even little notes on napkins, as they never know what may be needed in the future.

Tasks will start coming fast and furious now. The SM needs to make a spreadsheet of all the acts and scenes and sub-scenes in the play along the left side, with a list of all the characters along the top in order of appearance in the show. An X goes in the box if the character is in that scene. This matrix is called a French scene breakdown (Figure 19.10). A French scene breakdown is invaluable in mapping the progression of a play. By looking at a French scene breakdown without knowing the play, it's possible to understand major scenes and central characters, as well as analyze the sequence and duration of scenes that constitute the overall rhythm of the play. This is a critical piece of paperwork, since all rehearsal call sheets are based on it, and so it is imperative that it be triple checked for accuracy. The director will use this as a part of their process, potentially changing or adapting it as the need arises. If the script is changed in any way, this breakdown needs to be updated. This may also be helpful for the wardrobe running crew when they

are planning quick changes, or the audio crew if mics need to be shared.

Although we don't really like to talk about accidents in the theatre, they do occasionally happen. Ideally, you will never deal with anything major, but even small accidents must be documented. Should a mishap occur, the first thing to do is evaluate the situation to see if a doctor or ambulance is required. Even if the accident is minor and does not require professional medical intervention, the SM still needs to document what happened, when, why (if known), and who witnessed it. The producer will need the state's accident report completed to file with the state workers' compensation organization (Figure 19.11). There may be additional paperwork for the unions, Occupational Safety and Health Administration (OSHA), or other entities. It is the responsibility of the employer, not the SM, to complete these forms, but the SM often has information that can ensure they are completed accurately. Obviously, the most important thing is to get the injured person the help they need; then—and only then—fill out the necessary paperwork.

For small incidents such as scratches or bruises, the SM or another company member who has appropriate training may assist the injured person, if and only if the injured person consents. The best option is to keep a well-stocked first aid kit and selection of common over-the-counter medicines so that those who need them can select and administer the treatment for themselves. Ice packs, bandages in assorted sizes, pain relief, and stomach medicines are commonly used items. There are many medical and legal ramifications on this subject should something go wrong, so only offer assistance you have the training to give. Have plans in place for all contingencies—that is the best advice. Sometimes, in the aftermath of an accident, it is rather hectic. It is your job

Laughing Stock Characters by Scene

	Dracula	Charley's Aunt	Hamlet	Act 1-1	ACT 1-2	ACT 1-3	ACT 1-4	ACT 1-5	ACT 1-6	ACT 1-7	Act 1-8	Act 1-9	ACT 2-1	ACT 2-2
Gordon Page			Hamlet	x	x	x	x	x	x	x		x	x	
Jack Morris	Harker	Fancourt	Horatio	x		x	x		x					x
Susannah Huntsmen	Peasants		Player King		x	x	x		x					x
Mary Pierce	Mina	Kitty	Ophelia		x	x			x		x			x
Tyler Taylor	Dracula	Jack	Laertes		x	x	x		x		x		x	x
Vernon Volker	Dr. Seward		Claudius		x	x			x		x			x
Richfield Hawksley	Van Helsing	Spettigue	Polonius/Gravedigger		x	x			x		x		x	x
Daisy Coates	Peasants	Donna Lucia			x	x	x		x					x
Craig Conlin						x	x	x	x	x			x	
Sarah McKay						x	x	x	x			x	x	x
Henry Mills						x	x	x					x	
Brooke Oakes	Workman	Brasset				x			x				x	x
Karma Schneider	Peasants	Amy	Player Queen			x	x		x					x
Ian Milliken		Charley	Lucianus			x			x					

■ **Figure 19.10** French scene breakdown, characters by scene.

Accident Report

Employee(s) name(s): _____

_____

Time & date of accident/incident: _____

Job title(s) and department(s): _____

_____

Supervisor/lead person: _____

Witnesses: _____

_____

Brief description of the accident or incident: _____

_____

_____

Indicate body part affected:

Did the injured employee(s) see a doctor?   ( ) Yes ( ) No

If yes, did you file an employer's portion of a worker's
compensation form?   ( ) Yes ( ) No

Did the injured employee(s) go home during their work shift? ( ) Yes ( ) No

If yes, list the date and time injured employee(s) left job(s): _____

_____

Supervisor's Comments: _____

_____

What could have been done to prevent this accident/incident? _____

_____

Have the unsafe conditions been corrected?   ( ) Yes ( ) No

If yes, what has been done? _____

_____

If no, what needs to be done? _____

_____

_____

Employer or Supervisor's signature: _____

Date: _____

Additional comments/notes: _____

_____

_____

■ **Figure 19.11** Sample accident report from OSHA.

to keep everyone calm, deal with the situation, and get everyone focused again on rehearsal as soon as possible.

Let's talk about putting together the stage management script together. SMs use a three-ring binder with divider tabs and print the script single sided on letter-size paper, either by enlarging a published script or printing from a digital copy. Some publishers are now offering these pre-made. Should the script get updated during rehearsals, the SM will update their script and provide updated pages for everyone else. Some SMs like to use post-it notes as flags to mark scenes or

French scenes along the right-hand side. The divider tabs keep the reports, information from designers, and other documentation in order.

A big part of the SM's job during rehearsals is to record the blocking, the actors' movements, in their script. To do so, many SMs will use pages in their show binder that have a miniature black and white version of the scenic plot drawing on the top half of a page with lines below and place one page opposite each page of script. It is important to notate this for several reasons. The first is that the actors are trying to remember their

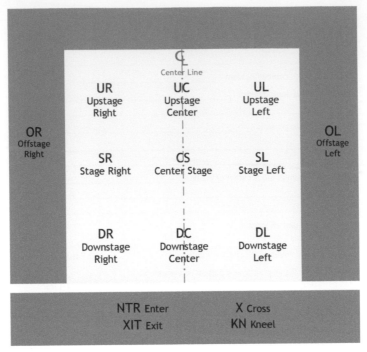

Figure 19.12 Symbol key for taking blocking notes.

me for it. *(SHE gets up.)* Give da boys an ice cream cone, Bella. Den come inside and finish my legs.

stand

L begins X to L door

EDDIE. *(Without anger.)* ... You're right, Momma. I am the weak one. I am the crybaby ... Always was. When you wouldn't pick me up and hug me as a child, I cried ... When my brother and sister died, I cried ... And I still haven't stopped crying since Evelyn died ... But you're wrong about one thing. She never turned me against you. She turned me towards *her* ... To loving, to caring, to holding someone when they needed holding ... I'm sorry about not bringing the boys out here more. Maybe the reason I didn't was because I was afraid they'd learn something here that I tried to forget ... Maybe they just learned it today ... I'm sorry I bothered you on your Sunday. I'm sorry I imposed on your rest. I'm sorry about what they did to you as a child in Berlin. I'm sure it was terrible. But this is Yonkers, Momma. I'm not angry at you for turning me and the boys down. I'm angry at myself for not knowing better ... Take care of yourself, Momma ... Never mind the ice cream cones, Bella. I used up all my obligations for this year. *(HE crosses to the door.)* Come on, boys. We're going.

boys slowly back UP – R

XC to Momma momma sits

Momma sits on sofa

X to Momma

to sofa R

boys X sofa L

Bella X behind sofa L

eddie begins to stop DS

(JAY and ARTY are too dumbstruck to move, to have been in the middle of all this.)

EDDIE. ... I said let's go.

begins X to L door

Figure 19.13 Sample blocking notes from a script.

lines, develop their characters, and many other things. Remembering blocking is often difficult, and so they may need a friendly reminder of when they move and to where. Throughout rehearsals, blocking may change several times, so always work in pencil and always carry a *big* eraser. Blocking changes can be confusing for everyone, actors and directors alike. The SM should *always* have the most up-to-date version. Another reason for taking down the blocking is for actor understudies, replacements, or touch-up rehearsals, especially during longer-running shows. The SM is the person who works with the new actors to help provide a seamless transition between old and new cast members.

Blocking notation can be written in a wide variety of ways. A standard notation is taught in stage management classes (Figures 19.12 and 19.13). The symbols are used in conjunction with arrows and the initials of the characters as needed for clarity. The standard symbols are important to use, so that anyone else can pick up the book and understand it. If each SM were to create their own notations, that would be more difficult. Should the SM have to miss a rehearsal or performance, then the assistant SM or director will be at a major loss. Since the goal of the SM is to organize the production and keep it moving forward in an orderly way, using your own notation is not a good idea. Many shows may need a unique blocking note for some odd object in that show. Keep a "key" of all blocking symbols, their meanings, and any character abbreviations in your show book so there is no confusion.

Throughout the course of rehearsals, the SM makes notes including not only hand props, which the actors handle, but also scenic props, such as furniture or specific pieces of scenic dressing mentioned by the script or used through the actors' actions. The SM must keep good notes about the hand props. They can change almost as frequently as the blocking. They make a spreadsheet of which actor(s) uses a prop, where they enter from, when the prop is needed, which scene the prop is in, and when and where the prop comes back offstage. Also, and very important, how does the prop get offstage if the original actor doesn't carry it? Often, this crucial detail is forgotten until the technical rehearsals. This coordination is very important, and that spreadsheet will be the basis for a **prop breakdown** (Figure 19.14). Again, remember that the designers and technicians don't know what is

Laughing Stock Prop Breakdown

Act 1-1	
Gordon	flashlight
Act 1-2	
Gordon	pictures/resumes
Gordon	scripts
Mary	flyer for "Epic of Gilgamesh"
Mary	bag
Tyler	script
Vernon	briefcase
Gordon	cell phone
Act 1-3	
Craig	handouts - thick and impressive
Henry	script
Sarah	gin and tonic
Act 1-4	
Act 1-5	
Henry	Ethel's will
Henry	hat box with skull
Act 1-6	
Jack	rehearsal skirt and wig
Gordon	hat box with skull
Braun	tea service w/4 cups, sugarer, creamer
Richfield	hat that can hold liquid
Sarah	stop watch
Act 1-7	
Craig	several trays of coca-cola products
Act 1-8	
Tyler	cape
Tyler	vampire teeth
Richfield	script
Act 1-9	
Gordon	ghostlight
Act 2-1	
Gordon	cell phone
Craig	several garbage bags of empty coca-cola products
Henry	roll of fabric
Henry	tiny pencil
Apprentices	straight ladder
Richfield	script
Act 2-2	
Peasant woman	crucifix
Dracula	teeth
Dracula	door
Dracula	claw-like hand
Harker	change
Harker	eye drops
Harker	journal
Seward	newspaper "The Whitby Daily Telegraph, 8 August 1892"
Mina	diary, pen
Mina	letter from Professor Szgany
Harker	gun that doesn't fire
Braun	tea service
Mina	broken lighting instrument
Dracula	door
Van Helsing	exploding cross
Seward	pry bar
Karma	mallet and stake
Act 2-3	
Gordon	Hamlet costume
Company	Chairs
Company	Costume Rack
Company	Props Table
Act 2-4	
Brooke	cardboard box w/cantaloupe and magic marker
Sarah	tea
Henry	skull
Craig	pencils
Sarah	ghostlight
Act 2-5	
Henry	hatbox
Sarah	2 drinks
Henry	skull
Susannah	dip on her head

■ **Figure 19.14** Sample prop breakdown.

Laughing Stock Costume Breakdown

			costume provided	personal clothes	accessories
Gordon Page					
	1-1	black pants, turtleneck, leather jacket		black pants, turtleneck, leather jacket	
	1-2	black pants, plain black T-shirt, leather jacket		black pants, plain black T-shirt, leather jacket	
	1-3	khaki pants, polo shirt	blue ss shirt	khaki pants	
	1-4	khaki pants, polo shirt		khaki pants, green polo shirt	
	1-5	khaki pants, polo shirt	maroon ss shirt	khaki pants	
	1-6	khaki pants, polo shirt		khaki pants, green polo shirt	
	1-7	khaki pants, polo shirt		khaki pants, polo shirt	
	1-9	khaki, polo, blazer		khaki, green polo, blazer	
	2-1	khaki pants, polo shirt		khaki pants, green polo shirt	
	2-3	tux pants, white shirt, black jacket		tux pants, white shirt, black jacket	
	2-4	Hamlet in Hamlet performance	beige/aqua tunic	black pants, white T-shirt	
	2-5	tux pants, white shirt, black jacket		tux pants, white shirt, black jacket	
Jack Morris					
	1-1	jeans, coat, hat, gloves		jeans, turtleneck, coat, hat, gloves	
	1-3	shorts, T-shirts		shorts, T-shirts	
	1-4	Harker of Dracula rehearsal	maroon pineapple shirt	shorts	
	1-6	Fancourt in Charley's Aunt rehearsal	dress, wig, hat, shoes, fan	jeans	
	2-2	Harker of Dracula performance	plaid vest	brown pants, green turtleneck	
	2-3	shorts, T-shirts		shorts, T-shirts	
	2-4	black jeans	navy tunic	black jeans	
	2-5	suit, dress shirt	blue sailboat shirt	blue or khaki pants	
Susannah Huntsmen					
	1-2	flowy dress	dress from costume stock	spaghetti strap top	
	1-3	spaghetti strap top, skirt	katia's dress		
	1-4	Bride of Dracula rehearsal	brown velvet hippie	khaki pants/skirt	
	1-6	flowy sleeves, pants	crocheted dress		
	2-2	Bride of Dracula performance	black skirt, cravat	white blouse	
	2-4	black pants, gravedigger	pink tunic	black pants	
	2-5	beaded dress	blue beaded dress		
Mary Pierce					
	1-2	very NYC - all in black, sexy and suggestive without her being aware of it.	striped dress	black character shoes	
	1-3	summer, first day of rehearsal		shorts, T-shirts	
	1-6	Kitty in Charley's Aunt rehearsal		shorts, T-shirts	
	1-8	Mina in Dracula rehearsal	vintage gown/shawl		
	2-2	Mina in Dracula performance	vintage gown/shawl		
	2-4	Ophelia in Hamlet performance	yellow tunic	black pants	
	2-5	closing night attire	taupe sparkle gown		
Tyler Taylor					
	1-2	Typical "NYC actor" wanna be, jeans, loafers, no socks, jacket with scarf		jeans, shirt, jacket, scarf	
	1-3	summer, first day of rehearsal		jean shorts, gray T-shirt	
	1-4	Dracula in Dracula rehearsal		jean shorts, gray T-shirt	
	1-6	Jack in Charley's Aunt rehearsal		khaki shorts, blue T-shirt	
	1-8	black pants, white shirt	cape	khaki shorts, blue T-shirt	
	2-1	summer casual		khaki shorts, colored T-shirt	
	2-2	black pants, white shirt	cape	black pants, white shirt	
	2-4	Laertes in Hamlet performance	yellow tabard	black pants, black shirt	
	2-5	closing night attire		dark suit, white shirt, tie	
Vernon Volker					
	1-2	pants, blazer, Steve Press's T-shirt	Steve's T-Shirt	jeans, blazer	
	1-3	jeans, button shirt	green ss shirt	khaki pants	
	1-6	jeans, button shirt		khaki pants, button shirt	
	1-8	Dr. Seward in Dracula rehearsal		khaki pants, button shirt	
	2-2	Dr. Seward in Dracula performance		sweater, black pants	
	2-3	jeans, button shirt		khaki pants, button shirt	
	2-4	black pants, Claudius	black/red costume	black pants	
	2-5	tuxedo		tuxedo	

■ **Figure 19.15** Sample costume breakdown.

going on in rehearsal unless the SM tells them. The daily reports are critical, but so is a comprehensive, coordinated list. A specific prop might require "fitting" to an actor— for example, a pair of glasses. Depending on the prop, the SM needs to coordinate with the scenic or costume designer and schedule a meeting between the designer and the actor for required customization of prop pieces.

The costume breakdown is similar, in theory, to the prop breakdown (Figure 19.15). Often, the costume designer will make a list and compare theirs to one made by the SM to ensure nothing is missed. Costume notes should include a description of the costume, the character name, accessories, what scene(s) it is worn in, and any special notations if a fast change is needed or if it needs a special effect to be rigged. Accessories can include jewelry, hats, undergarments, handbags, briefcases, canes, and the like. Special effects can include distressing, blood

packs, tearaways, and so on. The individual notes are somewhat different from the props, although they can include related props, as listed in Figure 19.15. Keep in mind that part of creating the breakdown includes making actors available for all costume fittings as required by the costume designer.

Production meetings are often referred to as a necessary evil. During pre-production they occur monthly, and once rehearsals begin you should schedule them weekly. One "good" thing that came out of COVID-19 is the use of Zoom and other video-conferencing options. It has made for easier scheduling of the entire team for meetings! During technical rehearsals they should happen daily. These meetings are a time for all concerned departments to get together and discuss progress and problems, so that everyone is in the loop, and any problems can be solved as a team.

CALLING SCRIPT

As rehearsals progress, the SM starts to accumulate even more information. Designers often begin coming to run-throughs to see how the show is shaping up. They make notes on what is needed within their designs to complete the director's vision and needs based on the movement of the actors. It is also the SM's job to keep the designers informed of any changes that happen during late stage rehearsals, so that the designers are working with the most up-to-date information. The designers then go away to do their work and eventually begin to provide the SM with cue sheets and other paperwork that will be needed for technical rehearsals. All of this compiled information transforms the SM's three-ring binder into the **SM Bible**. This then becomes *the* definitive authority for information about the show. The calling script is sometimes a completely different copy of the script than what you have been using so far for rehearsals, but often it is the same with more information added.

As technical rehearsals approach, the lighting designer gives information regarding when the lighting cues happen. They should also give the SM an idea of how long the lighting cue takes to happen and a brief idea of what the change does (Figure 19.16). This is the only way they will know what to expect and how to anticipate other cues, both for lighting and other departments, that the SM will need to call. The sound and video designers

Lost in Yonkers
Lighting Cue Synopsis

Cue	Time	Purpose	Placement	Page
97	5	Preset	1/2 Hour	5
98	5	Rita's Speech	Places	5
99	8	End Rita's Speech	FTB	5
ACT 1 SCENE 1				
100	3	Sunlight	Actors in Place	5
100.1	6	Hot August Early Evening	AUTO FOLLOW	
101	6	Front Door	Knock on Door	10
102	12	Front Door out	Bella hugs boys	10
103	6	Momma Chair	"*Her back is killing her"	26
103.5	30	Momma Sits	Walls toward red	27
104	3	Fade to Momma Chair	"Won't that be fun Momma*"	34
104.1	2	FTB	AUTO FOLLOW	
ACT 1 SCENE 2				
105	4	Moonlight	End of Voice Over	35
105.1	8	Late at Night	AUTO FOLLOW	
106	0	Light Switch	Jay turns off Table Lamp	37
107	3	Fade to Couch	"fingers chopped off*"	37
107.1	2	FTB	AUTO FOLLOW	
ACT 1 SCENE 3				
108	3	Sunlight	End of Voice Over	38
108.1	6	Sunday Afternoon	AUTO FOLLOW	
109	2	Fade to Couch	"Jew in Alabama*"	43
109.1	1	FTB	AUTO FOLLOW	
ACT 1 SCENE 4				
110	3	Moonlight	End of Voice Over	44
110.1	6	Midnight	AUTO FOLLOW	
111	0	Table Lamp On	Louie turns on lamp	45
111.1	15	Walls up	AUTO FOLLOW	
112	0	Table Lamp Off	Jay turns off Table Lamp	53
113	3	Fade to Couch	"Save it*"	53
113.1	2	FTB	AUTO FOLLOW	53
INTERMISSION				
197	5	Preset	Actors Clear	53
198	5	House to Half	Places	53
199	8	House Out	When Ready	53
ACT 2 SCENE 1				
200	3	Sunlight	End of Voice Over	55
200.1	6	Weekday Daytime	AUTO FOLLOW	55
200.5	30		Bella Enter	63
201	8	Reinforce Jay's speech	"*Don't do it"	71
202	12	Restore	"What's moxie*"	72

■ **Figure 19.16** Sample light cue synopsis.

do the same. If there are a lot of scenery movements, motorized or not, the technical director may give you a similar list. All of these various cues need to be noted in the calling script along with warnings and standbys for the cues.

The final thing that may happen in the rehearsal space is blocking the **curtain calls**. This may not happen until tech in the theater. Either way, the SM needs to discuss it with the director and notate it so that the technical designers have that information for their use. The order in which the actors appear, where they come from, and whether they appear by themselves or in groups need to be determined. A great deal of political craziness goes on with the curtain call order. Stay out of that part of it and let the director work it out. Simply document what is supposed to happen from entrances and groupings to exits.

TECHNICAL REHEARSALS

Oh goody! You finally made it into the theater. Now, what? Well, frankly, the only guarantee is that craziness will ensue. The actors have finally begun to feel at home in the rehearsal studio and now they have to get used to the stage. The long-awaited crew has finally shown up and has to get to know one another and the actors. The director, and everyone else, has suddenly realized that the show is *actually* going to happen. OK! The SM needs to be the one person who keeps calm, no matter what.

As SM, you have now become the "captain" of the ship. You set the **call times** for crew and cast. You also establish the schedule for what should happen in the rehearsal. Of course, you don't do all this by yourself. You consult with the director, designers, and union representatives, if they exist. There are many details to deal with in the theater. Your assistants and crew should help with all of this.

The actors need to be assigned dressing rooms. The SM team, which can consist of one to six people, makes a chart that shows the location of the dressing rooms and the names of the actors who are assigned to each one. Each dressing room should also be labeled so there is no confusion, and it's a good idea to assign a space within each dressing room for each performer. A green room needs to be established, where everyone can relax

between rehearsal scenes and before shows. Even small details such as which restaurants in the area deliver and where the closest coffee shop is are pieces of information that make life easier.

> ### Theatre Traditions: The Final Word
>
> Some theatre folks believe it is bad luck to speak the last line of the play before opening night, because the play isn't "finished" until performed. Well, given the number of tech cues associated with that last line—lights, sound, curtain—plus somewhat frenzied blocking to get everyone off stage and in position for the curtain call, isn't it awfully risky not to rehearse it?
>
> Somewhat connected, I've always postponed blocking the curtain call until the very last moment, mostly because doing it says "we're finished" when we aren't. Also, the way a curtain call is blocked necessarily indicates the relative importance of various roles, and I dislike making that statement to the cast, because it violates the idea of an *ensemble*, the creation of which is always one of my directorial goals.

The sound department is responsible for getting and setting up the headsets SMs need to talk to the technical crew. However, you must let them know where you want headset stations, as well as whether the stations can be wired or must be wireless. Headset systems can also have multiple channels. This is critical for communication in two ways. People must be able to talk to those with whom they need to communicate and, more important, not to talk to those they don't need access to. If everyone is on one channel, the chatter can become overwhelming. If one channel is all you can get, then you have to be very strict about who talks and when.

The sound department can also provide a paging microphone that can be heard in the backstage areas, the audience areas, and in both combined. There should be speakers in the dressing rooms, green room, backstage, control booth, and so forth. This microphone is used during technical rehearsals, so that those not on headsets can hear any special information or announcement that must be made to the whole company. It's also used if there is an emergency or you need to stop the show. We used to just yell, but the microphone saves us a sore throat or even worse, laryngitis! It's also more polite … There are times when you are in a space where no possibility of paging exists. This is where having a production assistant or one of your assistant SMs being the person relaying calls to dressing rooms or green room becomes paramount.

The lighting department can provide **cue lights** if needed. Usually, those will have been requested on a rehearsal report weeks ago. Visual cues work great, but only if you can actually see one another. Headset cues work great, but only if you have enough headsets for everyone. Cue lights can be placed in locations around the set and the theater where visual or headset cues are not an option. Cue lights are small lights that can be different colors. You establish with your cast and crew what the cue light colors mean, as well as whether the light is on, off, or blinking—and then all should go smoothly. Generally, a light turns on for a "stand by," and the "*go*" is when it turns off.

Cue light products now are available that make this idea much easier to set up. The NuDelta LogiCue system has six color options (Figure 19.17). All connections are with standard microphone cable. You can link up to 12 in a series. The lights are LED-based and can also be controlled from DMX to operate through your show's lighting board.

The first rehearsal scheduled in the theater is often a spacing rehearsal. This means the actors work through the entire show getting used to the actual, real spacing on the set. They now have real doors and stairs, which means their spacing may change as they deal with these elements. The actual furniture is here now too. That may require some adjustments, as very often the real furniture is a slightly different size than your rehearsal furniture. All of these minor adjustments can radically adjust the timing of the show. That is the entire purpose of the spacing rehearsal: To work out how these differences affect the show. In opera and musical theatre productions, you will also encounter two special rehearsals that do not exist in theater: A Sitzprobe and a Wandelprobe. Taken

■ **Figure 19.17** NuDelta LogiCue, the cue light solution.

from German, they literally mean "sitting rehearsal" and "walking rehearsal" and indicate the first time the performers rehearse with an orchestra/band and the first time the orchestra/band rehearses with the singers *on stage*.

The calling script that we already talked about becomes the most important binder of paperwork at this point in the process (Figure 19.18). A copy should always be left at the theater, and a copy should be taken home, just in case. The calling script should be viewed as the show's blueprint. All cues, warnings, standbys, and gos should be clearly labeled for all departments. This can include color coding the different departments' cues. Remember those highlighters and post-it notes? Well, now is the time they really come in handy. Let me explain.

For the technicians to be able to execute their technical movements, the SM has to let them know that the cue is coming up soon. This is called a **warning**. A **standby** means the cue is imminent. The **go** should be obvious, but just in case it's not, *go* means do the cue! *Never* joke around or say "go" or anything that sounds like it, such as "no, foe, beau, toe," etc., when you don't mean it, or things will happen that you didn't intend.

Most SMs go so far as to spell it, g-o, if they have to use the word for another meaning. In schools or if there has been a significant time since the last "go," the SM may ask the operators to give a verbal confirmation of the warning. Otherwise, the stage manager won't know if they are paying attention.

If the placement for the SM to call the show does not provide adequate visibility of the stage, they can request a mirror or video monitor, depending on which works best. This works well if a camera with a full-screen view is out in the house on a balcony. A monitor is then placed at the calling desk. This becomes critical if you have lots of moving scenery, as the video camera can be set up to get the image even in very low-light situations. Other possible camera locations that can be useful are in the orchestra pit, pointing toward the conductor, overhead, and possibly in the green room. These cameras can be particularly useful if there are large scenic elements moving during the show that prevent areas of the stage from being seen.

It is important for the SM to have visual as well as physical access to all areas backstage in case of emergencies. Therefore, the positioning of the SM is sometimes downstage left or right, depending on the

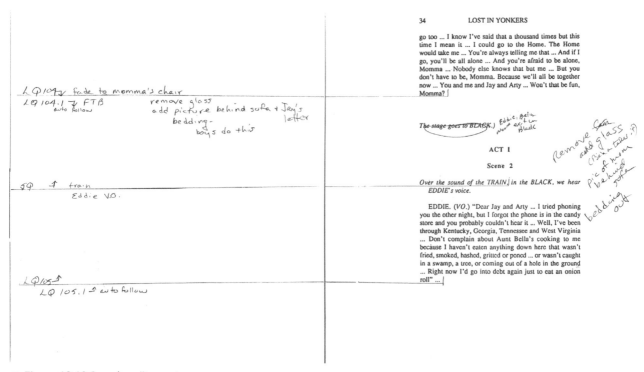

■ **Figure 19.18** Sample calling script.

■ **Figure 19.19** Global Design Systems SM Console.

layout of the theater. If there is no room backstage on the deck, a SM may be positioned in the booth or even the fly loft! It is a complicated position to set up, as the SM needs plenty of room for the SM Bible, headset station, video monitors, and so forth. A few companies now make customized desks with everything built in.

PERFORMANCES

The next thing to formulate is the preshow checklist. This list includes *everything* that must be set up before you start the show. It would include checking props, placing furniture, setting any scenery that moves to the starting position, making any food or drinks, setting any effects, and confirming with the department heads that they are ready. Keep in mind that the SM doesn't personally do all these things, but they have to check to make sure they've been done.

The call time for the actors is set based on how much time they need to get ready. This is usually an hour to an hour and a half prior to curtain time. This is the prep time for actors to get into hair, makeup, and costume. They also warm up during this time and do whatever preparatory work they need to get into character. If there are fight scenes in the show, there might be time needed for a **fight rehearsal**. Half hour is then called using the paging mic and any radios the crew may be using. This lets everyone know that the house is being opened for the audience, and that the performers need to stay backstage. Places is called a few minutes before the show begins, and all actors and technicians should go immediately to the positions where they will be needed to start the show. The assistant SMs will confirm to the SM calling the show that everyone is ready.

During each performance, the SM continues to keep notes for each department. These performance notes include any problems that may have arisen during the performance, such as a broken prop or ripped costume. The SM continues to be responsible for disseminating all of this information to the appropriate people. These reports are added to the files, and follow-up must be done to make sure problems have been dealt with in a timely fashion, usually before the next performance.

EXERCISES

EXERCISE 1

Create a daily report form for use at your school.

EXERCISE 2

Using Shakespeare's *The Tempest*, Act 1, Scene 1, create a calling script.

CHECK YOUR KNOWLEDGE

1. List items it is important to have in the SM kit. List items it is important to have in the SM's first aid kit.
2. Identify the different forms a SM creates and manages, explaining their importance.

- Accident report
- Audition form
- Blocking
- Call time
- Contact sheet
- Costume breakdown
- Cue lights
- Curtain calls
- Daily rehearsal report
- French scene breakdown
- Go
- Half hour
- Places
- Preshow checklist
- Prop breakdown
- Rehearsal schedule
- Sign-in sheet
- SM Bible
- SM kit
- Standby
- Warning

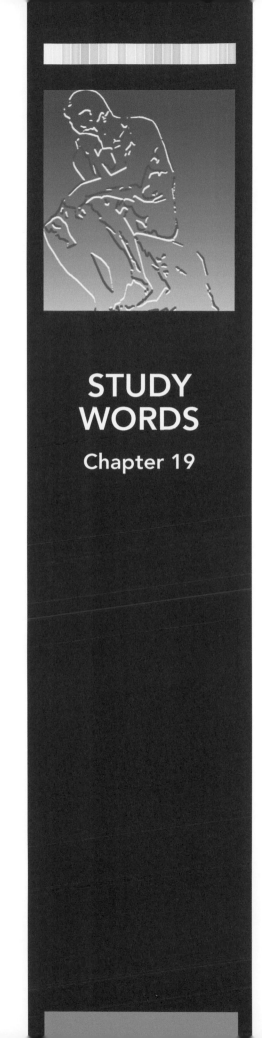

STUDY WORDS

Chapter 19

Taking the Show on the Road

Touring

CHAPTER TWENTY

Student Learning Outcomes

Students will acquire:

- An overview understanding of the major aspects, techniques, and styles in the area of touring.

- Fundamental, conceptual understanding of the expressive possibilities of theatre.

- A working knowledge of concepts applicable to the area of touring.

As this book is geared toward all areas of stagecraft, it seemed only logical to add a chapter dedicated to touring. The opportunities for employment on tours, both domestically and internationally, are constantly growing. We won't discuss cruise ships, but they are also a huge entertainment employer. Beyond simple employment, tours offer a variety of jobs available at all levels of experience and training. The possibilities continue to grow with each year.

Keep in mind that some shows establish themselves as a hit in a major city and then make the decision to tour to extend the run, sometimes indefinitely. Some shows start out as a tour, hoping to garner enough press that they can land in a major city. It can work in either direction. Let's start our discussion by examining the different kinds of tours that are fairly common. This information will establish our framework for all decisions to be made in setting up a tour.

TYPES OF TOURS

First class tours are usually the first tour that happens when a show is looking to extend its life after a successful run. Most often, first class tours will go to major cities and stay at a single theater

■ **Figure 20.1** Keith Urban Graffiti U Tour 2018. Two LED screens were automated to create a cage, a diamond, a header, etc., by FragmentNine.

for at least a week. The theaters are usually performing arts centers or larger theaters. Transportation is almost exclusively by plane.

Bus and truck tours are often a secondary tour that follows the first class one. These tours focus on smaller venues than the first class tours. The schedule happens really fast. Load-in is at 8 a.m., with a sound check at 5 p.m. and curtain going up at 8 p.m. As soon as the show ends, stagehands start the strike and load the trucks. Buses carrying personnel and trucks carrying equipment drive through the night to get to the next town and do it all over again. It is a grueling schedule.

Arena or stadium tours are most often the largest tours going to the largest venues. These buildings have multiple uses. Often, they double as the home of sporting teams or convention centers. Attendance can range from 10,000 and up.

Festivals usually happen during the summer, as all venues tend to be outdoors, with tents or other temporary roofed structures. Festivals are a little different in that there is usually a theme for the festival that brings together many different musicians. They often last for several days or weeks. The festival format is also popular with opera companies, symphonies, and established summer theaters.

Different size venues obviously require different setups. For example, festivals where multiple acts will perform rely heavily on floor packages owing to the ease of setup. Adding extra equipment in the air is a given for arena venues based solely on their size. Of course, scaling the rig up or down has to be done with the style of concept of the original design. Sound curfews in certain towns can mean a show might have to be shorter in order to end on time.

International versus domestic tours have many substantial differences, mostly owing to the history of the theater in a given country. For example, Asia tends to have very wide stages and large aprons. Everything

in England, for the most part, is more than 100 years old. Big performing arts centers are most often built for opera not theatre, giving them a very different feel. Copenhagen stages are narrow, at 26´ wide, as opposed to the American standard of 36´ wide. Not to mention that *everyone* outside of the US uses the metric system, which makes transfer of gear a very meticulous process.

Remember the history chapter? Think about the different kinds of theatrical performances that developed in different areas of the world. The styles of theatre drove the design of the theater building. Many of those buildings remain today and are the primary vehicles for tours. Taking a show from America to Denmark means most likely losing almost a third of the width from your stage! That's a major change to every aspect of a production, from blocking and choreography to scenery and lighting—just for starters.

DESIGN MODIFICATIONS

So, you might be thinking, where do you begin? Well. You start at the beginning. Sounds obvious, but it is. The key here is that the producer wants the same production that they've been watching for months or even years. So, how do you accomplish that?

Concept first. You have to boil the design down to its essence. According to Ken Billington, a lighting designer, ask yourself, "Do we need this? Does this tell the story? Is it just fluff?" A lot of time and money are spent analyzing what is needed to give the same emotional feeling as the original. Remember, you are not thinking technically regarding implementation yet. You are thinking concept and ideas. Once you have short-listed the important ideas, you move on to implementation.

As a designer, you *always* want a full set of specs for each and every venue so you can compare each space and check over your list of needs versus their list of haves. It is important to know that everything important can work in each venue.

> Do not tour a *Nutcracker* if the tree won't fit on the stage!
>
> —Campbell Baird,
> **American scenic and costume designer**

The show must look the same to every audience, regardless of the venue. How do you convey that in so many different places? The show must be efficient as

GEAR LIST
Summer 2017 Festival Tour
Rev D - For Bid

alt-J

FR∧GMEИT
NINE

PREP	See Schedule
REHEARSALS	See Schedule
START	See Schedule
END	See Schedule

This list is an overview. Shop is responsible for providing a complete and working system.
Spares are not included in these totals.
Please refer to tour schedule for routing/dates,

LOCAL SYSTEM - Picks up for each "tour"

QTY	WHAT	NOTES
LX CONTROL		
1	MA2 Lite	SW: 3.2.2.16
1	NPU Rack	
4	MA2 NPU	SW: 3.2.2.16 — this is a guess at QTY
2	Gigabit Un-Managed Network Switch	
VX CONTROL		
1	Switching System/Rack	
1	BlackMagic ATEM 1 M/E Studio	
1	BlackMagic ATEM 1 M/E Broadcast Panel	
2	BlackMagic HyperDeck Studio	
1	BlackMagic MultiDock	
4	SSD's for Recording	256 gb or bigger
4	Folsom	
VX CAMERAS / SWITCHING / PJs		
4	Lipstick or Stage Front Robo Cam	

alt-J | Gear List

■ **Figure 20.3** Alt-J summer festival 2017 gear list.

well as artistically satisfying to the audience. That can be a tall order under difficult circumstances. Consider the tight time frame of the bus and truck tours. If a truck gets lost or has a flat tire, how can you get the show ready on time? All these issues and so many more need to be considered at this point in the process.

Scenic designers often have to decide if a particular set can be effective with less scenery, different scenery, or a painted curtain substituted for hard scenery. Lighting designers most often have to cut the number of hanging positions both over the stage and front of house. Most often, you will have more control over what happens on the stage than what happens over the audience. Front of house hanging positions vary greatly from theater to theater. Generally speaking, there are never enough pipes in a **road house**, and the fly loft is never high enough. It's a given; accept it and move on.

Most designers who work internationally, whether it be touring or otherwise, will usually have an associate who is an extension of themselves with the same aesthetic. They will also have domestic assistants and international assistants. To have someone you trust is key. But, if they are also familiar with the city, the local labor, the power situation, and the language—that goes a long way toward a smooth production experience.

DEALING WITH RENTAL SHOPS

Always work directly with your shop and the tech director of the tour to make sure that the production elements can travel well and pack down as easily as possible. A good tip for early on in the process, from scenic designer Campbell Baird, is for ballet companies—but I think it works well for most productions. He has the scene shop

48	ROE Vanish 25 High Brightness	no substitution
1	LED processor system	
1	Power Distro System	
1	Cable Package	
1	Adapter Package	
1	Spares Package	

LX FIXTURES		
9	Robe BMFL Blade	or Viper Performance, or Scenius Unico — w/ shutters - No VL
96	GLP X4 Bar 20	no substitution
20	Clay Paky Mythos	or Robe Pointe
24	Chauvet Nexus 5x5 Aq	or similar
14	SGM P-5	or similar - no Clay Paky Stormy CC
44	Laser Blade Parallel	
6	base*haze*pro	or similar - no DF50
6	DMX Fan	

STRUCTURE		
1	System by others	see drawing

DISTRO AND DIMMING		
1	Full Distro/Data System	

mix a specific color for the back paint of all scenery so that, when the show is loading out, you can look around backstage and quickly spot elements that need to get on the truck. The color acts like a flashing sign that points towards a forgotten piece of the show.

An important part of the process that is seldom talked about is your touring crew. You need to have a voice in getting the best carpenter, props people, electricians, wardrobe staff, etc. Make sure their needs are addressed in terms of how trucks are packed and unloaded. A really good tour manager will be on top of that from the beginning.

MUSIC

One type of tour that crosses all venues while breaking many of the rules is music. I spoke in depth with Jeremy Lechterman of FragmentNine, based in North America, who is the product designer for Alt-J. His design process is a little different from what we've discussed in earlier chapters, as is his implementation, for many reasons. In order to give you a "feel" for how Lechterman works, below is a major part of my interview with him. I'll let him speak for himself!

Briefly describe your design process.

The process generally starts with a short creative brief from the artist/the artist management, and then quickly goes to the music. Often the artists don't have a good sense of what they want, but maybe a kernel or a very rough sketch of something that interests them. We pore over the music and any other visual branding/identity already associated with the artists and then usually present 1–3 rough concepts. If for a tour/album cycle, it's a bit more

■ **Figure 20.4** Production photo of Alt-J, designed by FragmentNine.

broad, showing options for festival, theater, arena, etc., depending where the artist is playing. Then it's budgeting/ drawing until we land the design within an appropriate budget the band can stomach (it's always more than they wanted initially).

Do you find it more challenging to work on new productions, revivals? Why? How do differing venues create differing challenges for a design?

I find working with established artists looking to "reinvent" the most difficult—so sort of a revival. They already have entrenched ideas or already have a vocabulary about design. This can be a blessing and a curse. Having someone who is experienced means they already understand the process, in part.

Does the audience's expectation change or influence how you design? This can include the venue, the current

entertainment offerings, in any medium, that may compete for our audience's focus.

I think a concert goer's desire to be "lost in the moment" can affect the design. You try to design for greater impact to more people, sometimes losing subtlety, which is a shame. Also, younger music audiences seem to expect sensationalism instead of depth of concept, so sometimes we compromise our original endeavor. I think this is true of all mass consumption art.

How do you incorporate new materials, equipment, and/or techniques into the implementation of your designs? How do you research and keep up with these new technological developments?

I use the right tool for the job, be it a console/light/etc. Sometimes new technology comes at a high price point. Sometimes you chose it specifically because it will achieve a "look no one has seen before." I think all too often, and I've definitely been the victim of this, we go for what's new and shiny instead of being inventive with the tools we already have at our disposal. That doesn't mean we need to be "retro" but there's a lot of waste in our industry with the turnover of gear as manufacturers come out with new shiny bits all the time. The touring music side of things is really at fault for this.

I stay current by going to trade shows and staying active with trade publications. I also have relationships with manufacturers who are always happy to demo a new kit *in the hopes you'll convince someone to buy their new light.*

Do you get support from your production team regarding using emerging technologies and breaking new ground?

Sometimes it's hard to convince rental shops to buy brand new kit unless they see a longevity in it, or unless you can guarantee a long-term rental on it. Either way, new kit will always be more expensive so you then have to convince whoever is holding the purse strings it's worth the extra money. If you're convincing enough with your argument, I usually find the support BUT the design still has to warrant the expenditure.

For instance, I had a tour recently where the "focus" of the design was an array of Magic Panels. At the time, they were quite new. I convinced production management to go for it by using much more "standard" kit everywhere else in the rig that we could get affordably and sourced everywhere. Which meant I freed up the money to ship Magic Panels around the world where we needed them.

Are there emerging trends that you have wanted to use, but have not had the opportunity? What are these technologies, and what has held you back? Are there new products in development that intrigue you?

I think there's a trend towards un-complicating stage design, towards design that makes large broad strokes and does away with making beamy shapes in the air that move in concert to the music, which I'm a fan of.

Technology wise, I personally haven't had the need to use software such as BlackTrack, which tracks a musician's

movement and has other visual elements react to it. It would be a nice technical and design challenge to integrate.

If you could design one new product without any constraints, what would it be?

I would figure out a way to telekinetically tell the lighting console what I want the look on stage to be. I find the process of explaining the look or movement to a programmer a difficult one at times, and I also find the limitations of the console's language frustrating. I wish that process from mental image or ideal to stage output was more fluid.

Briefly describe a recent design of yours. Why were you attracted to the project? Were any new and/or emerging technologies used? If not, do you feel the design suffered in any way because of this? If so, why did you feel these technologies were the right choice for your design?

The most recent album cycle for Alt-J was attractive because of the breadth of designs that would need to be accomplished over a stretch of multiple tours, creating continuity, and because the music created such evocative emotions and synesthesia. I was also a fan of how inventive and original the music is, while still remaining accessible to a large fan base allowing the project to have some latitude and scale.

Over the course of the almost 2 years, lots of technology was employed including new Ayrton lighting products, pixel mapping, automated LED screen content tracking, etc. They were all, in their own right, the right tool for the job to achieve a dynamic but simple and effective artistic interpretation to the music.

Theatre Traditions: Tripping

If an actress trips on the hem of her dress, she should pick it up and kiss the hem for good luck.

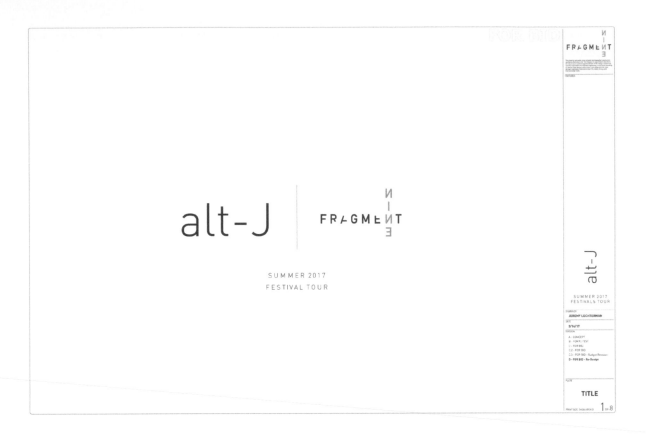

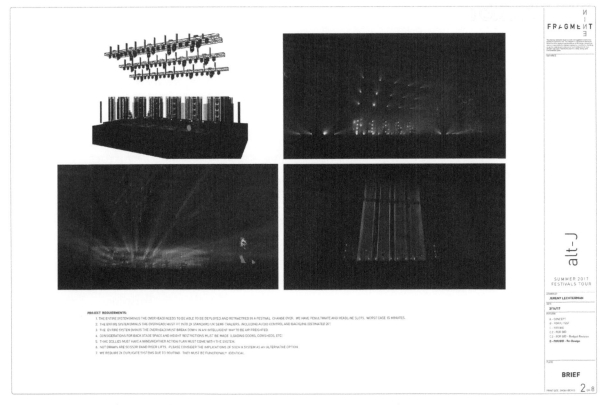

■ **Figure 20.5** Complete pack of drafting (eight pages) for an Alt-J tour. Design by FragmentNine.

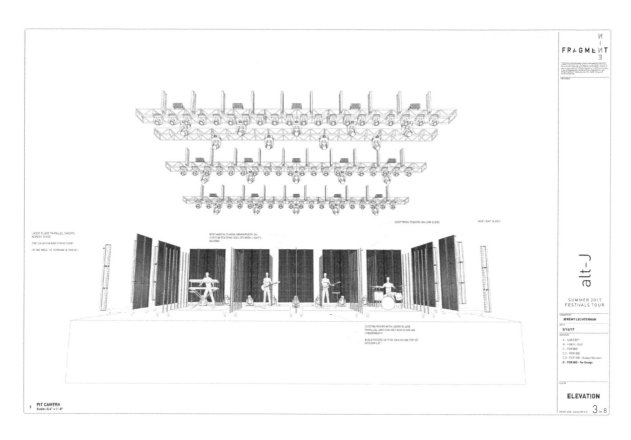

alt-J

SUMMER 2017
FESTIVALS TOUR

DRAWN BY
JEREMY LECHTERMAN

DATE
3/14/17

REVISION
A - CONCEPT
B - FOR FYI TEST
C - FOR BID
C.1 - FOR BID
C.3 - FOR BID - Budget Revision
D - FOR BID - Re-Design

PLATE
ELEVATION

3 OF 8

1 **PIT CAMERA**
Scale: 3/4" = 1'-0"

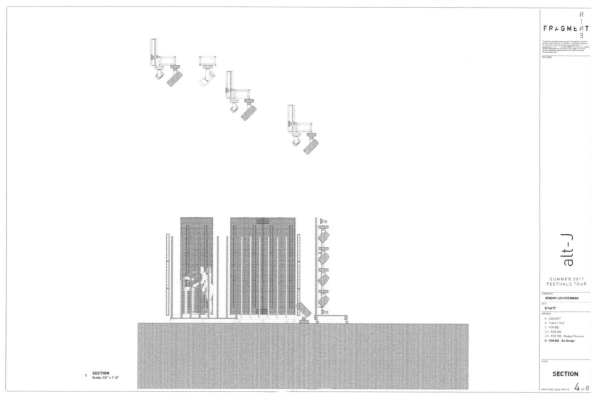

alt-J

SUMMER 2017
FESTIVALS TOUR

DRAWN BY
JEREMY LECHTERMAN

DATE
3/14/17

REVISION
A - CONCEPT
B - FOR FYI TEST
C - FOR BID
C.1 - FOR BID
C.3 - FOR BID - Budget Revision
D - FOR BID - Re-Design

PLATE
SECTION

4 OF 8

1 **SECTION**
Scale: 1/2" = 1'-0"

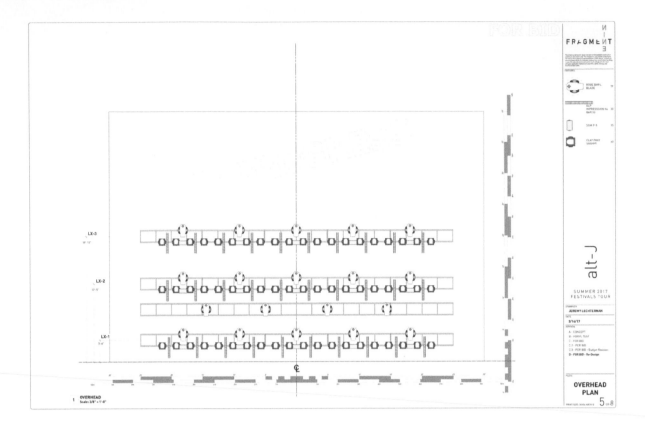

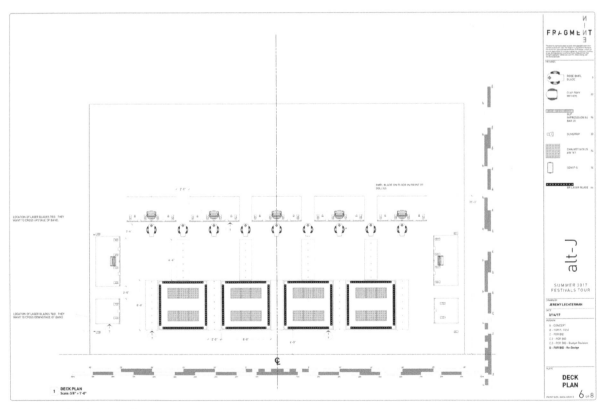

Figure 20.5 Continued

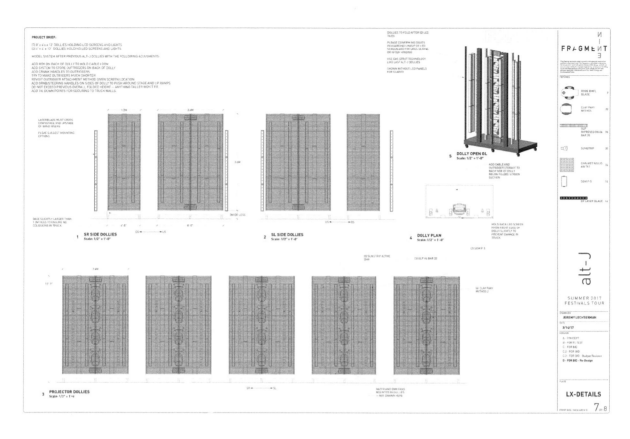

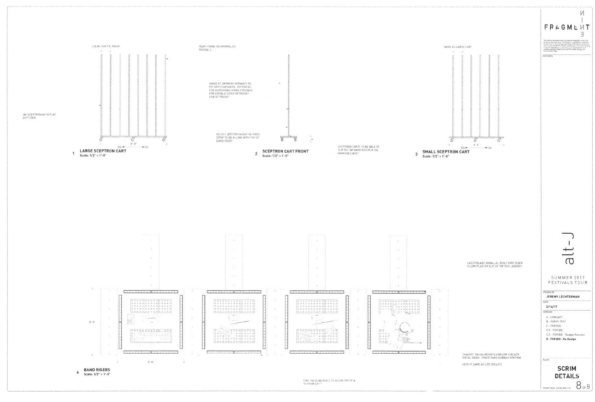

PROJECT BRIEF:

(1) 8' x 6 x 12' DOLLIES HOLDING LED SCREENS AND LIGHTS
(3) 4' x 6' x 17' DOLLIES HOLDING LED SCREENS AND LIGHTS

MODEL SYSTEM AFTER PREVIOUS ALT-J DOLLIES WITH THE FOLLOWING ADJUSTMENTS.

ADD BOX ON BACK OF DOLLY TO HOLD CABLE LOOM
ADD SYSTEM TO STORE OUTRIGGERS ON BACK OF DOLLY
ADD CRANK HANDLES TO OUTRIGGERS
TRY TO MAKE OUTRIGGERS MUCH SHORTER
REVISIT OUTRIGGER ATTACHMENT METHOD GIVEN SCREEN LOCATION
ADD GRAB/STEERING HANDLES ON SIDES OF DOLLY TO PUSH AROUND STAGE AND UP RAMPS
DO NOT EXCEED PREVIOUS OVERALL FOLDED HEIGHT — ANYTHING TALLER WON'T FIT
ADD TIE DOWN POINTS FOR SECURING TO TRUCK WALLS.

DOLLIES TO FOLD AFTER (2) LED TILES

PLEASE CONFIRM NO ISSUES REGARDING LINEUP OF LED SCREEN AND FIXTURES DURING OR AFTER HINGING

USE GAS STRUT TECHNOLOGY LIKE LAST ALT-J DOLLIES

SHOWN WITHOUT LED PANELS FOR CLARITY

5 DOLLY OPEN SL — Scale: 1/2" = 1'-0"

1 SR SIDE DOLLIES — Scale: 1/2" = 1'-0"

2 SL SIDE DOLLIES — Scale: 1/2" = 1'-0"

4 DOLLY PLAN — Scale: 1/2" = 1'-0"

3 PROJECTOR DOLLIES — Scale: 1/2" = 1'-0"

FRAGMENT NINE

alt-J
SUMMER 2017
FESTIVALS TOUR

DESIGNER: JEREMY LECHTERMAN
DATE: 3/14/17

VERSION
A - CONCEPT
B - FOR PLT TENT
C - FOR BID
C.2 - FOR BID
C.3 - FOR BID - Budget Revision
D - FOR BID - Re-Design

LX-DETAILS
7 OF 8

---

1 LARGE SCEPTRON CART — Scale: 1/2" = 1'-0"

2 SCEPTRON CART FRONT — Scale: 1/2" = 1'-0"

3 SMALL SCEPTRON CART — Scale: 1/2" = 1'-0"

4 BAND RISERS — Scale: 1/2" = 1'-0"

FRAGMENT NINE

alt-J
SUMMER 2017
FESTIVALS TOUR

DESIGNER: JEREMY LECHTERMAN
DATE: 3/14/17

VERSION
A - CONCEPT
B - FOR PLT TENT
C - FOR BID
C.2 - FOR BID
C.3 - FOR BID - Budget Revision
D - FOR BID - Re-Design

SCRIM DETAILS
8 OF 8

EXERCISE

Choose a type of venue that you think would be your favorite to work at. Describe why you chose it.

CHECK YOUR KNOWLEDGE

1. What is the first thing to consider when you find out a show you are working on is about to tour?
2. How important is advance prep for a tour? Why?
3. How do you approach a tour that will have outdoor venues as well as indoor arenas?

- Arena
- Bus and truck
- Festival
- First class
- Kit
- Road house

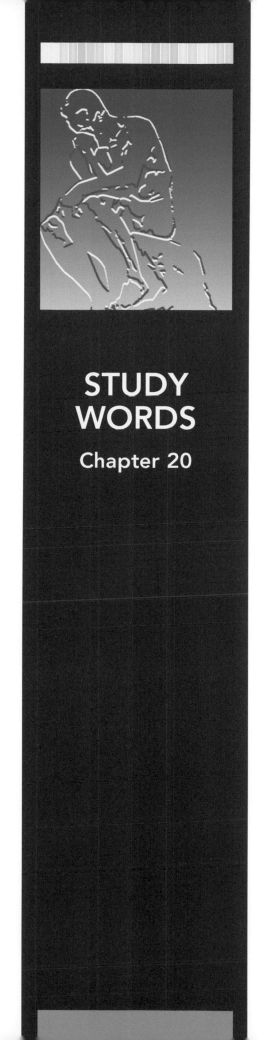

STUDY WORDS

Chapter 20

What's Next?

Career Choices

CHAPTER TWENTY ONE

Student Learning Outcomes

Students will acquire:

- An overview understanding of the major aspects, techniques, and directions in the area of careers.

- Fundamental, conceptual understanding of the expressive possibilities of theatre.

- A working knowledge of technologies, safety, and equipment applicable to the area of careers.

OK. Great! You learned all this stuff. We're almost at the end of the book. Ideally, you had fun learning and are now wondering, "What's next?" Everybody always tells you that you can't make a living in the theatre, right? Wrong! The first thing you need to think about before you look for a job is this: Do I really want to work in the theatre? Huh? What am I talking about? You are at the end of this book and *now* I ask that question? OK, now pay attention, this is important.

Being successful isn't about getting a prestigious job, having your name in lights, or making a boatload of money. Note I didn't say prosperous, I said successful. So, if it isn't about those things, you might ask, then what the heck is it about? Well, it's about *passion*. Your passion. What do you love to do? What would you miss the most if you could no longer do it? For some people, the answer is theatre. The job itself doesn't matter; just being a part of the theatre is enough. For others, it is very specific—say, makeup. They can do makeup in any situation and be happy; it isn't limited to theatre makeup. Only once you identify your passion will you be able to truly find a position, a job, a vocation, your life!

Sounds great, right? Well the theater is known for paying poorly and having a fairly abusive schedule. Not to mention more and more younger practitioners (especially after the pandemic shutdown) are leaving an industry that has been blind to any semblance of life–work balance. So, what should we do? Advocating for fair work practices is hard to do when you are first starting out. Luckily, this fight has begun, and it's now up to all of us to support it when and where we can!

This chapter works through how to take all the new knowledge and excitement from this course in order to find all the different places you might find employment. There are tons of job opportunities out there, some of which are actually related to the theatre. Many of the other possibilities are in related fields, and some employment is in what seem at first to be totally unrelated fields. We explore all these options to make sure your training gets put to good use and in an area where you will ultimately be happy.

> There's a lot of different kinds of jobs out there, and not everyone ends up being a designer or stagehand.
>
> —Anne Johnston,
> projection innovator

THEATRE CAREERS

Theatre jobs. OK, we discussed these, and most of you have now had experience with some of them, or at the very least have worked with people who do these jobs. Let's make a list based on when in the process of putting on a show the job is needed, although some start early on and continue until closing night. So, keep that in mind.

PRE-PRODUCTION

- Actor
- Choreographer
- Costume designer
- Director
- General manager
- House manager
- Lighting designer
- Makeup designer

- Playwright
- Producer
- Production manager
- Projection designer
- Property master
- Publicist
- Scenic designer
- Sound designer
- Stage manager
- Technical director

PRODUCTION

- Box office manager
- Carpenter
- Company manager
- Electrician
- Engineer
- Flyman
- Follow spot operator
- House manager
- Lightboard operator
- Makeup artist
- Master carpenter
- Master electrician
- Rigger
- Scenic artist
- Sound operator
- Special effects technician
- Stagehand
- Stage supervisor
- Wardrobe supervisor

Keep in mind that every one of these jobs has the potential for associates, assistants, and entire staffs within the varying departments. There are also specialties within each department that aren't listed, as these specialties are endless. Every time a new technology is introduced to the theatre, it causes new jobs to be created to keep up with the demand. Think about all the emerging trends we've discussed at the end of each chapter in this book. Those create new jobs and new job classifications!

A quick word about unions. Various unions, in certain situations, can represent many of the jobs just listed. Some of the same jobs are nonunion positions in other situations. If union jurisdiction applies to a job you want to do, contact the union. Many have apprenticeship programs that help you to gain admission. There are different unions for each job, depending on whether you want to work in theatre, television, or film: IATSE, AEA, AGMA, AFM, and SAG AFTRA. All of this can seem overwhelming at first. Don't panic. Just take it one step at a time.

Let's take a look at a few job descriptions that we haven't already discussed in detail. You might be surprised at what each position does. I won't go into each job from the list, but the following should give you a pretty good idea of what the business of show business is really like.

BOX OFFICE MANAGER

The box office manager's responsibilities include overseeing all ticketing and accounting, including daily receipts, deposits, and cash handling; supervising, instructing, and training all box office personnel; and maintaining and monitoring the electronic ticketing system. Other possible duties include partnering with event promoters and appropriate facility personnel to establish ticket pricing and seating configurations, updating management and promoters with ticket sales information, preparing final box office reports, completing event settlements, and establishing files on each event that consist of seats on hold for the building and promoter, complementary ticket vouchers, event audits, and ticket inventory schedules.

COMPANY MANAGER

The company manager's responsibilities include traveling, accommodations, and day-to-day needs of the acting, design, and technical company members. Often included are renting apartments and hotel rooms, booking plane tickets, dealing with furnishing and cleaning for rented apartments, and dealing with special needs and requests.

DIRECTOR

Directors oversee and orchestrate the mounting of a theatre production (a play, an opera, a musical, or a devised piece of work) by unifying various endeavors and aspects of production. The director's function is to ensure the quality and completeness of theatre production and lead the members of the creative team to realizing their artistic vision for it. The director, therefore, collaborates with a team of creative individuals and other staff, coordinating research, stagecraft, costume design, props, lighting design, acting, set design, and sound design for the production. If the production he or she is mounting is a new piece of writing or a (new) translation of a play, the director may also work with the playwright or translator. Directors also preside over the auditioning process as well as all rehearsals, guiding actors, designers, and all other staff toward their vision.

HOUSE MANAGER

The house manager's responsibilities include the ushering of patrons in front-of-house areas and the maintenance and management of the theater building itself. House management staff usually work for the theater, under the supervision of the house manager, and not for the theatrical company that is currently occupying it. Often, in regional or smaller theaters, the responsibility falls under the aegis of the production manager. In any case, house management works closely with the production management team for the presentation of the theatrical production.

MAKEUP ARTIST

The makeup artist applies makeup to the performer based on designs from the makeup designer. This can include makeup that reflects a specific period, setting, or situation. Special effect makeup can include applying prosthesis pieces or creating injuries. The makeup artist is sometimes also responsible for removing the makeup that has been applied and maintaining healthy skin under the makeup for the performers.

PRODUCER

The producer is the person ultimately responsible for overseeing all aspects of mounting a theatre production. The producer finds the script and the director, then begins the primary goal, which is to balance and coordinate the business and financial aspects of mounting the show in the service of the creative realization of the production's vision. This may or may not include casting, but often includes casting approval. The producer is responsible for securing funds for the production, either through his or her own company or by taking on investors. The producer will have optioned the play from the playwright, which would include all rights including film and television rights, if the production will enhance their value, and

may include the royalty agreement. Then comes the time to work with theatrical agents, negotiate with the unions, find other staff, secure the theater and rehearsal hall, obtain liability and workers' compensation insurance, and post bonds with the unions.

> Why didn't I listen to my mother and become a lawyer so I could be producing this and taking home real money.
> —Michael A. Fink,
> American environmental designer

The producer also hires the production team, including the general manager, production manager, house manager, stage manager, and the like, at his or her own discretion. In many cases, the producer is required to use front-of-house people (such as the house manager, box office manager, and ushers) and backstage personnel (stagehands, electricians, carpenters, etc.) supplied by the theater owner. The owner sets ticket prices and performance dates and times and develops a marketing and advertising strategy for the production. The hiring of a publicist and marketing team is one of the most important responsibilities of the producer. Last, the producer hires accountants and perhaps already has legal representation.

PRODUCTION MANAGER

The production manager's responsibilities include coordinating the operations of various production departments including scenic, wardrobe, lighting, sound, projection, automation, video, pyrotechnics, and stage management. In addition to management and financial skills, a production manager must have detailed knowledge of all production disciplines including a thorough understanding of the interaction of these disciplines during the production process. This may involve dealing with matters ranging from the procurement of staff, materials, and services to freight, customs coordination, telecommunications, labor relations, logistics, information technology, government liaison, venue booking, scheduling, operations management, and workplace safety.

RIGGER

Riggers specialize in the lifting and moving of extremely large or heavy objects. Riggers tend to be highly specialized in moving elements that cannot be accomplished by ordinary means and use equipment expressly designed for moving and lifting objects weighing hundreds of thousands or even millions of pounds in places where ordinary material-handling equipment cannot go. There are two main divisions of riggers in entertainment—theatrical and arena. The main difference is that arena riggers need to be trained in high steel work. Because of the highly specialized nature of the work riggers do, it is one of the few remaining occupations that can be learned only by apprenticeship. Riggers must work together as a cohesive team, and there must be an environment of trust among riggers because of the potentially dangerous nature of rigging.

SCENIC ARTIST

The scenic artist's responsibilities include reproducing color, texture, and aging of all building surfaces, whether they be two-dimensional or three-dimensional. They also interpret the scenic designer's sketches, models, and paint elevations to establish the best supplies and techniques to achieve the design. Similar to rigging, owing to the highly specialized nature of the work, it is one of the few remaining occupations that has an extensive apprenticeship program.

TECHNICAL DIRECTOR

It is a technical director's job to make sure the technical equipment in the theater is cleaned and safe, although these duties may be delegated to a shop or house manager. For a specific production, the technical director is responsible for working closely with the scenic designer and director. It is his or her responsibility to determine how the scenery will be built, out of what materials, and to oversee the implementation of all elements.

WARDROBE SUPERVISOR

At load-in, the wardrobe supervisor officially takes physical custody of all wardrobe pieces. Determining if a quick change is needed and supervising/assigning dressers if they exist are two of the main functions. They also ensure proper labeling, hanging, storage, and presetting of all costume pieces. Overseeing proper care and cleaning of all pieces is a major responsibility, especially since many costumes will need to be spot cleaned in between dry cleaning. Minor repairs will also be needed in a prolonged run.

NON-THEATRE CAREERS

Maybe you enjoy working in the theatre but you don't want to do it full time. Now that you have all these great skills—what can you do with them, you ask? Well, the sky is truly the limit. I've compiled a very small list of careers outside of the theatre; keep in mind this is only the tip of the proverbial iceberg.

- Advertising
- Architect
- Artist
- Construction
- Customer service
- Dramaturge
- Electrician
- Fundraiser
- Handyman
- Historian
- Lawyer
- Marketing director
- Newscaster
- Office manager
- Party planner
- Photographer
- Plumber
- Politician
- Principal
- Project management
- Research
- Restaurant host
- Sales
- Social worker
- Spatial reasoning
- Standardized patient testing
- Teacher
- Writer

Now you may ask, how? Well, it is easy to make a list, that's for sure. Let's go into a bit of depth about the qualities, traits, and skills you now have that will help in transferring to some of the above jobs.

When you work in customer service, you "put on" a persona so that you don't tell people what you really think or let things phase you, so you can deal with irate customers when they appear. That applies in any position dealing with the public. If you are trained in design, directing, or acting, you should be a good researcher. If your degree is in stage management, you would be good in any job dealing with organizational skills. The question really should be, why doesn't everyone get a theatre degree?

It teaches you to work with others, and realistically we all know that not everyone is a picnic to work for. Theatre training gives you people skills, the ability to improvise, thinking on your feet, spatial reasoning, problem-solving, and especially time management. All good qualities. But the list continues. As an office manager, it can help with all the organizational things that have to happen to keep things running smoothly.

Let's continue. Preparation. Punctuality. Problem-solving in time-sensitive situations. Everyone in theatre understands the curtain goes up at 8, and there's an audience that hasn't seen this show. That performance, that moment, needs to be at its best for them. The ability to pay attention to something you have seen a hundred times, making sure it is consistent and always appearing fresh to new people. Training also helps to find a way to fight off your own boredom!

Learning how to react quickly to changing circumstances, tactical planning, scheduling, managing others' schedules, and mostly being a people person. Being present, caring, and understanding. Discovery, mining the depths, making things fresh, creativity. Attention to detail, organizational and multitasking skills, being observant, time management, editing, memorization retention, organization, and prioritization! All good qualities that come from training in theatre.

You learn best by doing something hands-on. Doing a show, you learn determination, oral communication skills, creative problem-solving, motivation and commitment, cooperation skills. You learn interdependent relationships and budgeting skills; the ability to learn quickly and to work under pressure cannot be overrated. Flexibility and adaptability to any type of change. Thinking and moving quickly. Improvising materials to substitute other materials. Being especially aware of the surroundings by reading a room or group of people. Timing, punctuality, and teamwork are all fabulous skills.

Parenting. You have a script and you think you know a defined role in it, but it all becomes performance art! Being a train conductor—nothing makes the trip better than an animated conductor. That goes for flight attendants, tour guides, and the like. Painting murals for the townships. Parade organizer, summer camp counselor, and town park recreation manager. Nursing home activity organizer. Working for a business that offers a haunted house, Easter trail, or any holiday events. Even a sports mascot can benefit from theatre training.

Lastly, problem-solving—basic trouble-shooting. Thinking a problem through from the beginning in order to better find the proper solution. I truly believe in life there are really no actual problems, just opportunities to excel.

INTERVIEWS

OK, so that should give you an idea of the theatre jobs and what they entail. There are many other theatre jobs, but here is the key: What common traits do you need to land a job? Well, you need to be a responsible person, follow through on tasks, take initiative, and have a love of the *theatre* that inspires you to learn what you need so that you can stay in the business.

> Keep up the good work ... whoever you are!
> —Noel Coward,
> English playwright and composer

OK, great, you say. So what can I do other than theatre work with all these fabulous skills? Well, have I got answers for you: Television, film, architecture, advertising, internet design, gaming, military, to name just a few. Or maybe you'll find some combination that works for you. Perhaps, you'll get a job in a related field working full-time with benefits and vacations, and you'll use your vacation time to do shows. Oh, yeah, and how do you get that all-important job so you can show yourself off? I interviewed many people who all have one thing in common—theatre training. Here are a few stories from their travels.

PRUDENCE JONES INTERVIEW

Prudence Jones is currently the Assistant Department Head for Fine Arts and Associate Professor of Theatre at Tarleton State University, Stephenville, TX. She has also taught at University of Scranton in Scranton, PA, and Stephens College in Columbia, MO. Prudence earned a BA in Theatre from Cedar Crest College and an MFA in Theatre from California Institute of the Arts (Cal ARTS). Prudence has been a theatre artist for more than 25 years and has worked in various areas, including as actor, director, designer, stage manager, production manager, and technical director. Some of her favorite credits include lighting/set designer for Dallas African American Repertory Theater, lighting designer for New London Barn Theater in New Hampshire, actor for Sister Stage Theater in Allentown, PA, assistant technical director (ATD) for ACT in Seattle, WA, production stage manager for Long Beach Opera, TD for Reprise in Los Angeles, CA, ATD for Richard Foreman's *Bad Boy Nietzsche* NYC/European/Asian Tour, ATD for Travis Preston's *King Lear* in Los Angeles, and TD for Michael Counts' *Listen to Me* in Los Angeles.

What did I not learn as an undergraduate?

1. How to budget shows.
2. Structural engineering.
3. How to choose the right hardware.
4. The differences in paints and which one to pick for your show.
5. How to weld.

What did I not learn in graduate school?

1. Pedagogy.

I believe the biggest challenge I have faced after grad school is keeping up with technology such as projectors, hydraulics, computer boards (sound and lights), and the ever-changing software available for design. These have become a large part of theatrical design, but I did not learn about them in school, so I have had to learn them on my own. With that, I would say in undergrad and grad school I did learn the importance of continuous education.

KRISTI ROSS-CLAUSEN INTERVIEW

Unlike those who train for a theatre career through high-school participation and completion of a college major, I studied vocal music performance, education, and computer science at Lawrence University, a liberal arts college with a music conservatory. After using my computer knowledge in the business world, I went back to school for K–12 teaching certification and discovered my music teaching position also included teaching theatre skills. Having performed in 4-H and school shows, worked on the recording crew in college, and spent a summer at a performing arts camp on the recording crew, I knew the fundamentals, but still lacked knowledge in many areas of theatre production and direction. So I read every book I could get from the local public library, took summer classes at the University of Wisconsin–Madison's Summer Theater Institute that lead to a master's degree, joined the International Alliance of Theatrical Stage Employees (IATSE) by completing an apprenticeship, and began a lifetime of ongoing training to keep up with the advances in technology.

There is no one "right" way to a career in technical theater! More than one successful stagehand career started when a friend or family member invited them to help out, or they volunteered for school or community theatre productions.

JENNIFER NEWBOLD INTERVIEW

I'm going to try to speak for the re-enactor community as much as I can. As in any discipline, there are trends that some people follow, and there are others who do their own thing. No-one approaches clothing in the same way. We refer to our garments as clothing. To most of the country, we are wearing costumes, but we try to recreate the garments of the period as faithfully as we know how, using fabric that closely approximates the fabric and notions that would have been available in the mid to late

18th century and techniques that we can determine were used at the time from examining extant clothing. So, when someone says, "I love your costume," we frequently reply, "These are my clothes." It's a little pedantic, but it's become something of a custom.

Among Revolutionary War re-enactors, there are people who make garments which are practically museum reproductions. One such person is Henry Cooke, IV, who did make many of the clothes displayed on the mannequins at the new Museum of the American Revolution. Stephanie Smith and Hallie Larkin are also in that category. They do meticulous research on existing garments in various collections and then teach what they have learned. They use period-appropriate techniques and document everything. Members of this school of re-enactors are sometimes called "progressives." (It goes beyond clothing. These are people who will sleep in a field in the rain in a lean-to and fry eggs on their trenching shovel. As opposed to me; I keep a battery-operated fan hidden behind my trunk in my tent.) The rationale behind this method is sound: The objective is to portray our ancestors with as much dignity and respect and as faithfully as possible. Life was hard for a Revolutionary War soldier or a camp follower. Hygiene wasn't anything close to what it is today. And, since sewing machines didn't become available until the 19th century, everything was sewn by hand, with varying levels of skill. Most of the re-enactors I know acknowledge this, but they do bathe regularly and they eat far better than the soldiers did. (And have been known to "cheat" and sew seams that don't show with a machine, although usually the garments are hand-finished.)

Of course, this being a hobby for most re-enactors (and it is referred to as "The Hobby"), there are degrees of authenticity. I suspect that the majority of re-enactors, and most of the people I know, present as authentic an experience as possible to the public, but have modern coolers, plastic containers, and iPhones stowed away where they can't be seen. Part of our goal is to educate people about the American War for Independence. The other part is just having fun.

In designing and constructing a reproduction 18th-century garment, I usually start with photographs of extant period garments or paintings and a pattern that has been drawn from an existing garment. Janet Arnold, in her book *Patterns of Fashion* (1972), drew a lot of these patterns to scale. There are also patterns available developed by Henry Cooke and Hallie Larkin and Stephanie Smith, as well as other companies that specialize in period patterns. From the basic garment or pattern piece, I make a muslin of the fitted part of the garment and test it for fit on a dressmakers' form. Working with the muslin, I make stylistic changes based upon the garment I'm creating. The dressmakers' form is very important to the way I construct a garment. In the 18th century, tailors and mantua-makers fitted clothing to their wealthy clients by draping the garment specifically for the customer's body. When you get down to the level of a soldier or camp follower, the clothes were probably bought second-hand or taken off the back of a dead soldier and passed on to the next one. But they may or may not have been altered by the wearer to fit better.

Eighteenth-century clothing moved with the wearer, rather than the wearer moving within the clothes. Most garments were fitted, particularly for men. So, there wasn't extra fabric around the armscye of a coat, in the breadth of the waistcoat and coat, or in the bodice of a woman's gown. There weren't the tolerances we have with modern clothes. And women (and sometimes upper-class men) wore stays, which gave the wearer the straight, upright silhouette of the 18th century. If you're going to go to the trouble of putting on stays, you don't want baggy clothing to obscure your shape. Undergarments were constructed with gussets underneath the arm, but outer clothes were not. That's what makes the dressmakers' form important.

I try to use appropriate fabrics and finishes. Fabrics today are more loosely woven overall than 18th-century fabrics, which is going to affect the drape and movement of the clothes, as well as how much the fabric frays. Many women's silk taffeta gowns had pinked edges on the sleeve flounces and ruching. These unfinished edges didn't fray as easily in 18th-century gowns, but, because we can't usually find a silk as densely woven as, say, Spitalfields silk was in the 18th century, pinked edging is a time-consuming proposition. I have known re-enactors who brushed each scallop of the pinked edge with fray-check. I'm more likely to let it fray …

There are examples of period fabric designs, finishes, weaves, and colors that you can pull up online to get a general idea of what might be an appropriate facsimile.

Pinterest is an amazing resource if you are willing to sift through the random stuff that always comes up in a search and can document the image. Anna Maria Garthwaite was a famous Spitalfields silk designer in the first half of the 18th century, but, because such fabric was reused and garments were refashioned, her fabric designs persisted through the century. There are even instances when a gown fabric was used to reupholster a sofa or settee; I think there is one in the Winterthur Museum in Pennsylvania. You can see a lot of period fabrics in the Victoria and Albert Museum's textile collection, and there are a series of books published by the Trustees of the V&A that showcase many of the fabrics in the collection. Colonial Williamsburg has also done extensive research and has an admirable collection of period garments. The Metropolitan Museum, the Boston Museum of Fine Arts, LACMA, and the Kyoto Costume Institute are all excellent sources as well.

There are a number of specialty fabric merchants who stock period-appropriate fabrics, threads, and fasteners. I have found antique stores to be a useful source for thread, buttons, and bobbin lace. Hooks and eyes and buttons were used on men's garments, but women's garments usually tied and were pinned with straight pins. This is generally thought to be because women got pregnant, and their clothing had to expand and then shrink again; men didn't have that particular problem!

FERNANDO BERMUDEZ INTERVIEW

Theatrical design training gives you the basic knowledge you need to design for all of the performing arts. The method you use in theatre design can be applied to all the different forms of design for the performing arts. You need a concept, research, a design and production process, as well as evaluation of the product with directors and producers. I see this going on not only in my professional career as a television costume designer, but as a teacher as well. I teach students how to design for the theatre, and, at the end, they choose a variety of professions. Some of them do theatre, others movies or television, or even advertising. They choose what interests them the most. At the end, the method fits every shoe! By understanding the way a theatre designer works, you are able to be in touch with literary analysis; understand characters through light, sets, or costumes;

learn how to communicate atmospheres or personalities; manage budgets; and understand production. All of these are essential parts in the craft of designing for the performing arts. My job as a costume designer for television is not much different than that of a theatre designer. Only the timing changes—television is an ongoing process, it never ends, or at least it feels that way, as some projects can last for a year or more. You work on a show or series for maybe 10–12 months and then you might move to another one. Theatre and film don't usually take this long. Television is more immediate. You need to change design choices according to ratings *or* because no story is ever fully developed. Things change, and you must be ready for this.

GRACE BRANDT INTERVIEW

In high school, I painted backdrops for the school plays. I have a very heavy art background. Both my mother and grandmother were artists. In college, I became an art major, then found the theatre department, which led me to set design. I loved scenic painting immediately and moved to NYC as soon as I could. I knocked on Joe Papp's door, and he answered. I was very naïve. I was new and nonunion. I ended up meeting a scenic artist and took the apprentice exam at United Scenic Artists— and passed! I made it my mission to know all the scenic artists and know their stories. I spent a lot of time cutting paper for all painters just to learn from them. You have to want it really, really bad!

HEATHER CARSON INTERVIEW

After 32 years of lighting shows, I find myself focused solely on being a visual artist these days. Without realizing it at the time, my theatre work functioned as an artistic practice—meaning that each piece built on the last. When I was 28, my dad gave me the book *Seeing Is Forgetting the Name of the Thing One Sees* (2009), the seminal book by Lawrence Wechsler. It's a meditation on the work of artist Robert Irwin, one of the key members of the Light and Space art movement birthed in Los Angeles, California. Up to that point, it had never occurred to me that you could make "art" with light.

In 1995, I did my first lighting installation as part of Elizabeth Streb's *Action Occupation* performance that reopened the temporary Contemporary Museum (MOCA) in Los Angeles. My work for Streb was static—for each piece she created, I did a response to the structure she was interacting with and a response to the architecture of the movement. The structure was lit; when the movement started, the lights changed, and, when it finished, the lights went out. Or, as it evolved, the piece would end in a whiteout instead of a blackout—with a quick flash of light flooding the audience as the lights simultaneously went out on the performers before going to total black.

Somehow, it came about that I proposed making a piece that was just about light. I wanted it to be "before" the performance—both spatially and temporally. It was called *up/Down*. A grid of fluorescents facing up mirrored the lines in the wooden-beamed ceiling, and a grid of sodiums facing down echoed the number of panels in the skylights above. The lights facing up went on, the lights facing down were added, and then just the lights facing down were left on. That was the sequence—up/down—and it kept repeating from the time the audience entered until the performance began.

Little did I know that I would continue exploring the grid for the next 15 years, using the language of sodium vapor and fluorescent light to explore interior and exterior volumes of light. At that time, my lighting career had just taken off, and I was primarily lighting opera in Europe. Shortly after that, I read about a place called the Skowhegan School of Painting and Sculpture, a nine-week summer residency. You are given room and board and your own studio. You can do whatever you like and are heavily mentored by visiting and in-residence guest artists as well as weekly lectures. It was transformative for me to spend that kind of time with young artists—most were in their 20s, and I was in my late 30s. While there, I made three pieces.

I began to realize that what I was doing was installation, sculpture, emerging art, etc. and realized there were many opportunities for this. I received a NY Foundation for the Arts (NYFA) artists' grant in Architecture/Experimental forms. A few years after that I received the Rome Prize in Design Arts. I was the first lighting designer to receive it, and now it is listed as one of the categories. During my six months in Rome I made two pieces. A few years after that, I got another NYFA grant to make another piece. And so I continued,

lighting shows and doing my own work when I had the time or the funds, or the opportunity arose.

In 2004, I moved back to LA to head the lighting program at CalArts. I took advantage of that shift to get an artist's studio for the first time and commit to a studio practice. In 2006, I was invited by the same curator who had curated the Streb piece all those years ago, Julie Lazar, to be in my first "real" gallery exhibition. Shortly after that, I was asked to do an exhibition by Liza Simone of Phantom Galleries LA, which presents work in empty storefronts. That piece was seen by Doug Christmas of Ace Gallery, and he signed me immediately on seeing it.

And so, all these years later, I find myself back where I started out, but having come full circle to creating my own work. The theatre was the place where I developed all my ideas. It's where I sat in the dark, hour after hour, looking and thinking, making small adjustments, looking again. There is absolutely no way I would be making the work I'm making now without having spent all those years in the theatre and specifically in New York.

ANNE JOHNSTON INTERVIEW

I have a BFA in dance; I started at Production Arts in 1985, working in the office. It was supposed to be my day job while I stage-managed at night. Madonna's *Who's That Girl?* tour wanted to use the projectors, but no one knew how to pack projections for touring. They needed good road boxes, needed spares, needed tech, etc. I learned a lot quickly. We got the call about the Steel Wheels Tour right after the Madonna tour. By 1988, I was working full-time doing projection stuff. It was so different from lighting and 3D scenery; I really liked it. A couple of years ago, video started to approach the brightness and contrast to be usable in the theatre. When new technology starts in theatre, there is a big growth curve. Now, with media servers, you can make instant changes to the projections. Video has decreased the desire for still projections. The technology creates lots of new positions for the creative and technical team. You have to be willing to make the leap.

> I can't make you a great dancer ... or even a good dancer. But, if you keep trying and don't quit, I know I can make you a better dancer.
>
> —Joe Gideon,
> character from *All That Jazz*

MICHAEL RIZZO INTERVIEW

I left NYC in 1987 because the theatre industry was a dead end for me. How could I have decided this having just graduated from NYU Tisch School of the Arts just two years earlier? Once graduated and out in the world, it was obvious that New York theatre supported a finite and highly coveted population of professionals. Although passion and longevity would have been essential to maintain even a basic foothold, the payoff was not assured and unlikely at best. At the same time, a friend was headed toward Los Angeles with extra room for some basic essentials, so I closed up my life and copiloted the self-drive van to the West Coast. Granted, this was a cavalier thing for someone with no connections or hope for readymade work, but I saw the same opportunity available to me, an eager newcomer, on both coasts. The only difference was LA, city of reinvention, held the promise of Hollywood and a more tangible kind of immortality. My hunch turned out to be dead-on for two reasons: A larger industry base and my theatre training. Broadway is a tiny creative community tucked securely into the bustling northeast corner of the country. It is insular and self-driven—a complete ecosystem. Hollywood was and still is no longer in a centralized, studio-driven location; its expansion into Canada, Europe, and right-to-work states in America allowed me to work in locations I would've only imagined had I stayed put and carved a niche onstage. On top of that, my new employers on independent film projects were welcoming, and the work was dependably steady. I had little difficulty adjusting myself to the fast and furious pace. The social nature of the business was familiar enough, as were the large egos I had previously encountered. My transition was relatively easy. Mind you, none of this would've been possible without my comprehensive and practical theatre training born from firsthand experience in regional theatre and off-Broadway. I unwittingly drove away from the richness of my creative development fully prepared to perform as a "can-do" lighting tech, costumer, scenic painter, or draftsman/designer in any situation I encountered. Without the depth of such a technical/creative foundation, my emergence as a successful art director would've had little chance of happening.

Although there are noticeable differences in each of these media, the basis of design for a play manuscript or TV/film screenplay is the same: The translation of the literature into an appropriate visual concept. I simply transferred my knowledge of theatre craft directly into the other media.

EXERCISE

Write your résumé.

CHECK YOUR KNOWLEDGE

1. Illustrate one theatrical career you might be interested in and what specific skills you have learned that are appropriate to it.
2. Illustrate one non-theatrical career you might be interested in and what specific skills you have learned that are appropriate to it.
3. Name the interview that most affected you and describe why.

APPENDICES

Still Confused?

APPENDIX A: Glossary of Terms

APPENDIX B: Story Time—Theatre Traditions

A

Accessory slot
Also known as the drop-in slot, this is an opening, or aperture, in an ellipsoidal near the shutters made to hold specialized accessories.

Accident report
This form is to be filled out *every* time there is some sort of accident, so the incident is documented.

Acetate
Thin plastic, low in cost, and has good draping qualities.

Acoustics
The inherent sound qualities of a room in regard to the overall audio quality when no reinforcement is in use.

Actual size
Referring to lumber, the real dimensions.

Additive
A term used in color mixing—when all three primary colors of light are mixed together in equal parts, they make white light.

Adhesives
Products used to make items stick to the actor. They are used for things such as glitter, sparkles, and hair pieces.

Adjustable wrench
Often called a *crescent wrench*, it is an open-ended wrench with one fixed jaw and one adjustable jaw. The adjustment works by a screw positioned within the handle.

Ager/Dyer
Job title in the film and TV industry. An ager/dyer's work is distressing, painting, and dyeing costume.

Alginate
A compound made from algae. When mixed with water, it can be used as a casting material. It has many medical and dental applications.

Allen keys
Tools with a hexagonal head for adjusting screws or bolts with a recessed six-sided opening.

Alternating current
AC is electric current whose direction reverses cyclically.

Ambient noise
The sound in a room when there is no planned audio source.

Ampere
Amp (A) is a unit of electric current, or amount of electric charge per second.

Amplifier
A device that boosts the output to a level that drives the loudspeaker.

AMX
Analog multiplex is a control signal used to control SCR dimmers.

Analogous
This describes multiple hues that come from within the same area of the color wheel.

Angle brush
A brush with a tip that has an angle to it, used for very precise work, such as applying eye shadow, eyeliner, brow coloring, and lipstick.

Apron
This is the area of the stage that extends downstage of the proscenium arch.

Arbor
A carriage or rack that contains weights, usually of cast iron, called *pig iron*.

Arc dimensions
Used when measuring some kind of angle or radius.

Arc welding

Involves two large metal alligator clips that carry a strong electrical current. One clip is attached to any conductive part of the project being welded. The second clip is connected to a thin welding rod. When the rod touches the project, a powerful electrical circuit is created. The massive heat created by the electrical current causes both the project and the steel core of the rod to melt together, cooling quickly to form a solid bond.

Arch

Simply put, it is a large hole in a wall. There are many different styles of arches: Roman, Tudor, and Gothic, to name a few. Make sure to follow the designer's drawings to create the correct shape for the arch.

Archetype

A typical example of a "thing." Often a recurrent symbol in art or mythology, but also used for character types.

Area mic'ing

An array of floor microphones is used, and the sound operator rises and lowers the gain as needed.

Arena

Stages that are truly theatre in the round. The stage is in the center of the space, and the audience is seated on all sides. Or, the largest venues available, as these buildings have multiple uses.

Audition form

Actors fill out this form on arriving for an audition; it contains all pertinent information about the actor.

Auditorium

The area that the audience sits in is called the *auditorium*.

Autotransformer

This is a mechanical device used to dim lights. It works by moving a handle that physically moves a brush against a coil to change the voltage going to a lamp.

AutoYoke®

This motorized device allows the user to pan and tilt a number of lighting fixtures from the control console. Newer models can also control color scrollers and irises.

AWG

The abbreviation for American wire gauge.

B

Backdrop

This is a painted piece of scenery used to help create the environment for the play. This backdrop serves two purposes. It helps the audience to better understand where the play is taking place, and it provides a space for the actors to change their costumes and masks out of sight of the audience.

Balance

This is the contrast between all the different visual characteristics of a scene.

Ball peen hammer

A hammer, often called a "machinist's hammer," that has a rounded head used to bend, flatten, or shape metal.

Ballast

A device placed in line with the load to limit the amount of current in an electrical circuit, it can be used to start and properly control the flow of power going to a lamp.

Bamboo

A hollow stick used on the end of a paintbrush or stick of charcoal to extend an artist's reach.

Banana plug

A single-wire (one conductor) electrical connector used for joining wires to equipment. Although it can come in various sizes, the 4-mm size is the most common. They are often color-coded red and black.

Band saw

A stationary motorized tool used for cutting wood or metal into nonlinear shapes. The blade is one continuous loop, or band, stretched over two pulleys, with serrated edges.

Bar clamp

Has a fixed jaw and a sliding jaw, which makes it easily adjustable to different lengths. The determining factor of its usage is the bar to which it is attached. The longer the bar, the bigger an object to be clamped.

Barn door

This accessory fits on the front of a lighting fixture with movable blades used to cut light off from curtains or scenery projected from a soft-edge fixture.

Barrier cream

Often used during face casting for mask making, a barrier cream is a product applied to the skin to protect it from casting materials. Vaseline is sometimes used as a barrier.

Base

The color that is put on first. Other colors are applied over it to create textures.

Beam angle

The part of the light beam that puts out the best light. It is measured to be at a level of 50 percent of the maximum intensity of the beam.

Beam projector

An open-face fixture that produces a narrow beam of light. The result is an intense shaft of light.

Beam spread

When light comes out of a fixture, it's called a beam. The beam spread is the less-bright extra light that is around the more intense "beam angle."

Belaying

To secure a rope by winding it in a figure-eight pattern around a cleat. To secure the belay, the final figure-eight wrap gets a 180-degree twist, turning the end of the rope to the inside, before being put on the cleat.

Bevel gauge

The bevel gauge is used to check or copy the angle of an existing unit or drawing. It consists of a handle or stock and a blade or tongue, connected by a wing nut. This tool *does not* measure an angle. It simply copies the angle from something that already exists.

Black box

A big black room with absolutely nothing in it. Very simple, very plain. It's a space in need of a production! The production brings in chairs and maybe risers for the audience. It also brings in a stage, raised or not. This allows for infinite possibilities within one space.

Block and fall

A piece of equipment that simulates standard blocks, allowing multiple ropes to come in through the top. The difference is in the "fall" side, as it reduces the number of ropes coming back out to one.

Blocking

The director tells, or helps the actors find, where they should move for the proper dramatic effect to ensure sight lines for the audience and to work within the lighting design of the scene.

BNC

A coaxial connector, BNC has a miniature bayonet-locking connector.

Booms

Vertical pipes for mounting lighting equipment.

Borders

Hung overhead, originally painted to simulate the heavens, borders were added to complete the visual effect, complementing the backdrop. They also became known as *masking*, which had the added benefit that they blocked the audience's view of rigging and lights hung over the stage.

Bowline

One of the most important knots to know. If properly tied, it does not slip and can be used to secure things or lift people.

Box set

A set usually containing three walls and perhaps a ceiling. It was, and still is, used to represent interiors.

Box wrench

This closed-end wrench fits only one size of hardware. Typically, it has from 6 to 12 points of contact to the hardware.

Brazing

This uses molten metal to join two pieces of metal. The metal added during the process has a melting point lower than that of the material, so only the added metal is melted, not the material. Brazing uses metals with a higher melting point. Brazing produces a stronger joint than does soldering and often is used to join metals other than steel, such as brass.

Breakdown artists

Another name for an *ager/dyer*. Someone who distresses costumes.

Buckram

A coarsely woven fabric from cotton fibers made very stiff with starchy glue. It is also known as English blocking canvas

Burlap

A course, heavy fabric that is loosely woven of jute or hemp fibers.

Burping

A term used by dyers referring to pushing the fabric under the water surface in order to release the air bubbles to the surface.

Bus and truck

A tour utilizing buses for personnel transportation and trucks for production elements.

C

CAD

An acronym meaning computer-aided drawing.

Calling script

This is *the* authority for information about the show. This script contains all of the information needed to call the show once you are in the theatre.

Call time

This is the time when people are to arrive and be ready to work. On any given call, there may be several call times for different groups of people.

Carpenter clamp

A brace, band, or clasp used for strengthening or holding things together. Carpenter clamps are the basic clamps found in a scene shop. They are shaped like a C, with a screw that tightens and loosens. They can leave marks on wood, so they are usually used when that is not a factor.

Carpenter pencil

A pencil made in a flattened octagon shape that prevents it from rolling. The "lead" is thicker and stronger than in a regular pencil, which comes in handy when writing on wood instead of paper. You cannot sharpen this in a standard pencil sharpener; most people just use their pocketknife or a utility knife.

Cartoon

A simplified drawing of the basic design at full scale using vine charcoal.

Casing the leather

Casing is the process of adding moisture, such as water or casing solution, to the surface of vegetable tanned leather in order to soften the surface for tooling.

Cast

Noun: Usually made of plaster or another molding material, a face cast is an impression made from a face or head in order to mold a mask over it. *Verb*: Using a molding material to make a replica of a face or object.

Center line

Our only reference for left and right measurements in the theatre is the center line.

Center punch

Used primarily on metal to mark a starting point for drilling into the material. Once you have used the center punch, it is much easier to begin drilling into metal without the drill slipping.

Chain hoist

A mechanical device used for lifting heavy loads of objects and equipment.

Chainmail

Mesh fabric made of rings of metal that is fashioned into protective clothing and worn as armor. It was meant to deflect sword strikes.

Chalk line

An almost diamond-shaped container containing a very long string and powdered chalk, a chalk line is used to mark a straight line between two points.

Chicago screws

A type of fastener composed of two parts (a threaded barrel tube with a head and a threaded bolt with a head). They are used in place of rivets when the fastening may need to come apart.

Chip

A very inexpensive alternative to the standard paintbrush, a chip is less durable and considered to be disposable.

Chisel

A tool with a cutting edge on its end, it is used primarily for carving and cutting hard materials such as wood, stone, or metal and is specifically designed for each type of use. The sharp edge of the chisel is forced into the material, usually with a hammer or mallet.

Chop saw/Compound miter saw

A cutting tool with a circular saw blade similar to a circular saw but usually larger in diameter. They work by having a pivoting arm containing the blade, which is brought down to cut the material.

Chroma

A hue in its purest form.

Chrome tanning

A process of tanning leather using a chromium sulphate solution. Chrome tanning produces a softer leather often used in making garments.

Circular saw

One of the more popular portable tools in the shop, it gets its name from the circular saw blade it uses. It is designed to make long, straight cuts. This saw can crosscut or rip wood. The bottom foot can be angled to allow for a consistent angled cut.

Classicism

A style of architecture based on idealistic models or established conservative standards. This style embraces a high level of taste, sobriety, and proportion. Conventional formality is another way to think of classicism.

Claw hammer

The hammer you see the most in the scene shop. It has a metal head for striking a nail, or whatever else you need to hit, and a curved claw for ripping nails back out of the wood.

Cleansers

These products are made to clean a variety of things, such as skin or brushes.

Clove hitch

This knot is important to almost every rigging job in the theatre. Used as a traditional hitch, securing only one end, the clove hitch is liable to slip. It requires a load attached in each direction to be effective. The clove hitch is almost always a load-bearing knot.

Cluster

This is similar to a speaker array; however, it is almost always hung on center right above the edge of the stage.

Coaxial cable

This cable is made up of a single copper core, surrounded by a layer of insulation and covered by a copper shield, then a flexible plastic jacket.

Cobbler

Person who fixes your broken heels and worn-out soles of shoes, as well as broken zippers on your winter boots.

Coiling

One of the few ways you can safely store rope without putting any bends, kinks, or knots in it.

Collaboration

To work as a team. Collectively, you create a production where there once was none.

Combination square

Can handle 90-degree angles and it can also help you draw 45-degree angles. You can loosen a knob and slide the square's head along the ruler, then tighten it down at a different location on the ruler. This allows you to transfer measurements from one place to another. The sliding head of the square contains a level. This can be very useful for certain types of measuring.

Complementary

Colors that are opposite each other on the full color wheel.

Composite

An order of architecture devised by the Romans, the composite first appeared on the arch of Titus in Rome in 82 BCE.

Concealer

Used to blend away temporary and permanent imperfections, which can include birthmarks, blemishes, and tattoos, concealers are highly pigmented makeup. This is what helps them to cover up and is the inherent difference between a foundation and a concealer.

Concept

A unique way of looking at the show. Directors and designers use concepts to create an individualized approach to their production.

Condenser microphone

More versatile, more costly, and less durable than dynamic microphones, the condenser microphone is the choice for the theatre, given its range in quality for many purposes.

Construction drawings

Technically detailed drawings created by the scenic shop, usually by an assistant technical director, draftsperson, or technical director from which to build.

Contact pickup

Like microphones, contact pickups are attached to musical instruments and pick up sound through vibrations instead of from the air.

Contact sheet

This form shows everyone involved with the production, including directors, actors, producers, technicians, shops, and so on. The contact sheet is the phone book for the show. Any contact information you might need should be there. It should also include rehearsal and performance spaces.

Content creator

The person who finds and invents images and text as required by the design.

Contrast

Variations in line weight, direction, shape, texture, balance, proportion, pattern, and scale add interest to a composition. Contrast can help focus the viewer's eye. The better and more varied your contrast, the less you need other factors to define your shape.

Conventional lighting

A category of lighting fixtures that do not move or change colors.

Coping saw

Has a handle with a U-shaped steel frame. The very thin blade is held between the arms of the U. Turning the handle tightens or loosens the tension on the blade. Holders at either end of the blade can also be pivoted so that you can adjust the angle of the cut.

Corinthian

An order of architecture, the Corinthian was little used until the Romans adopted it. This order included leaves on the capitals in a more natural replica and dates from the end of the 5th century BCE.

Corner block

Triangular pieces of ¼-inch plywood used to hold together corners of a soft flat frame.

Costume breakdown

All the information about each of the costumes used in the production. It should include a description of the costume, complete with any accessories, what scene(s) it is worn in, how it gets on and off stage, the character name, and any special notations if a fast change is needed or if it is used with a special effect such as blood.

Costume prop

An object that may be worn by the actor.

Cotton

Often thought of as cool, soft, and comfortable, the fiber is from the cotton plant's seedpod. The filament is hollow in the center and under a microscope looks like a twisted ribbon. This thread absorbs and releases perspiration quickly, thus allowing the fabric to "breathe."

Counterweight

A technique for lifting heavy items where sandbags or pig iron are used to offset the weight of what you are trying to lift.

Creative director

The person responsible for the design of the content.

Crosscut blade

Saw blades for cutting wood; the teeth are designed to cut across the grain.

Cue lights

Placed in locations around the set and the theater where direct visual or headset cues are not an option. Establish with your cast and crew what the cue lights mean.

Curtain calls

The presentation of the actors in front of the audience at the end of the performance. The order in which the actors appear, where they come from, and whether they appear by themselves or in groups and any other information about the curtain call.

Cutter

Originally, a person who used patterns, or created patterns, and cut the pattern from the fabric.

Cyc

Shorthand for cyclorama, now used almost interchangeably with *backdrop*.

Cyclorama

Traditionally, this was a white, gray, or light blue seamless backdrop placed upstage, wide enough that the sides wrapped around and came downstage toward the audience.

D

Daily rehearsal report

This report is given to all departments concerning any changes, cuts, or additions that affect them as a result of the daily rehearsal.

Dead-blow hammer

A hammer whose head is filled with loose steel particles. This gives the hammer extra force on impact and very little recoil or bounce back

Dead lift

Used to lift the full weight of something with no rigging advantages.

Deck

A complete replacement for the existing stage floor *or* a term for the stage floor itself.

Deck plan

This is a drawing of the floor.

Deconstructivism

This style followed on the heels of the postmodern movement. It was characterized primarily by the fragmentation of buildings and ideas within the whole. In addition, the overall surface of the form could be distorted and dislocated into non-rectilinear shapes.

Deluge

Similar to a sprinkler system, except the sprinkler heads are open, and the pipe is not pressurized with air.

Depth of shade

In dyeing, *depth of shade* refers to an amount of dye to a given weight of fiber. It is notated as a percentage, such as 2 percent on weight of goods (OWG), meaning, if the fiber weighs 100 grams, the amount of dye would be 2 grams.

Designer drawings

These convey the artistic vision of the designer. They are critical to informing the shop what the designer's ideas and goals are.

Detail brush

Comes in a variety of shapes to help add or remove just the right amount of makeup.

Detail drawing

Used when parts of the set require a much closer look, these are drawn in full or close to full scale. They make dimensioning easier. Detail drawings also include practicals, scenic elements, or props that plug in to some form of electricity or require finer work that cannot be drawn in a smaller scale. These items must be planned out in great detail to make sure that they work properly and are safe.

Deus ex machina

Literally, "God from machine," this usually involves moving scenery.

Digital projection

Any image manipulated by computer in creation or displayed on the stage.

Dimmer

Simply put, its job is to make lights go up and down. A variety of technologies have been utilized over the history of dimming, from mechanical, manual devices to electronic, digitally controlled dimmers.

Direct current

DC is an electric charge that flows in one direction.

Direction

Creates visual movement.

Distressing

The craft and art of making items look older or dirtier than they really are.

Ditty bag

An accessory bag.

DMX

Digital multiplex has become a standard control signal for dimming and many other devices.

Dome brush

Made with rounded corners for soft edges, these are ideal for under-eye concealer as well as eye shadow.

Donut

A square piece of metal, with a circle cut out in the middle, that fits in the gel holder of the lighting instrument. It helps reduce lighting flare when using a template.

Doric

An order of architecture, it was the earliest order to develop and was used for the Parthenon and most early Greek temples. Its columns have no base; it was developed in about the 5th century BCE.

Double purchase

A system of rigging that puts the loading floor halfway between the stage floor and the loft blocks. Extra pulleys are both above and below the arbor to double the wire rope length. This is necessary to make this system work properly. The pipe travels 1 foot for every 2 feet the rope has to travel. You need to use twice the amount of weight of what is hung on the pipe. The advantage is that you lose no floor space. This is often the major deciding factor in which type of system to use.

Downstage

This is the stage area closest to the audience.

Drafting

Usually done shortly after the drawing and rendering are completed, drafting is meant to convey information not an emotion.

Drafting stool

This is a stool (or chair) that goes up and down to adjust to the height of your drafting or computer table. It should be comfortable and support your back.

Drafting table

Often used for sketching and layout as well as for drafting, the table height and angle can be adjusted to whatever is the most comfortable.

Drafting tape

Looks like regular masking tape, but it is less sticky. That means you can pull it up without leaving residue or tearing your paper.

Draper

Originally, the person who, instead of using a pattern, created a design by draping the fabric onto the actor.

Drawing

Often used interchangeably with *sketching*. Drawing pulls our ideas together, allows them to form on the outside of our head, and puts them on paper.

Drill

A tool for making holes of various sizes.

Drill press

A stationary tool that does the same job as a regular drill. It has the added advantage of being mounted over a tabletop.

Dry brush

Keeping the paintbrush as dry as possible, using only a minor amount of water and paint. Or, you use a brush with no paint to move around or remove paint that has already been applied to the surface.

Dry ice

Solid carbon dioxide that exists at a temperature of $-109.3°F$ or $-78.5°C$. Those are *negative* temperatures! It must be handled with extreme care.

Dump casting

The type of plaster casting where the plaster powder is mixed with water and poured into a mold, then left to set.

Dust mask

Helps protect you from inhaling many types of small particles.

Dyeing

The use of pigments, made from animals, vegetables, or minerals, to change the color of fabric or fiber. This process uses chemical bonding, unlike painting, which uses a medium to hold pigment to the surface.

Dynamic microphone

A good all-around microphone that is both durable and affordable.

E

Earmuffs

A full ear covering used to protect the ears from loud noise.

Earplugs

Go into the ear to provide some protection from loud noise.

Elevation

Takes a designer's ground plan and stands it up in three dimensions, one element at a time. This allows the scene shop and carpenters to see an individual piece as it is intended to be built.

Ellipsoidal

Also known as ERS, this is a focusable fixture with one or more lenses. The defining part is the ellipsoidal-shaped reflector.

Emphasis

To place particular importance on an area or item in the scene.

Environmental

This type of theatre came about during the 1960s with the help of many avant-garde groups. The basic idea is to provide integration between the audience and the actors. The audience was expected to participate in the performance at some greater level than usual. There are multiple areas of focus in the performance simultaneously. The chaos created by dividing the audience's focus is the whole point of the style. The actual spaces for these performances range from converted garages, to parks, to castles, to monuments. Scenery is used at a minimum, as the whole point is to go to a "realistic" setting. As the name suggests, environmental theatre brought the audience to the environment instead of creating a manufactured environment through traditional theatrical conventions.

Equalization

In the processing of the output of a sound system, this term applies to making sure the levels are proportional. This is achieved by using equalizers, which are the most common piece of equipment used for a basic signal processor. Think of the equalizer as a filter.

Erasing shield

This is one of the coolest things ever invented. A small, thin piece of polished steel has different shapes cut out of it. You lay the shield over your drawing, specifically the part you want to erase. Then, while holding it in place, you erase the offending line without the possibility of your eraser touching anything else on the paper. It's like magic, only better!

Expressionism

A style in which the artist seeks to express an emotional experience placed onto the subject matter. This style allows the artist and the art to combine and form an altered reality.

Eyecup

This is ergonomically designed to be used for washing a single eye.

Eyewash station

Provides an effective means of washing your eyes quickly to minimize the time an irritant comes in contact with them.

F

Fabric modification

The use of techniques, such as dyeing, painting, or pleating to change the look of fabric.

Face shield

Worn over the entire face to prevent flying items from hitting the face.

Facial shape

There are six shapes—oval, heart, pear, square, round, and long—and each has its own needs when applying makeup.

Fence

A guide for safely cutting straight lines with a power saw.

Festival

A themed event that brings together many different musical acts *or* a summer performance format, popular in opera and theatre, where multiple different productions can be attended in a short period of time (a weekend, a week).

Filament

The element of glowing wire carrying the current within a light bulb.

File

Similar to a rasp but with much finer teeth. It is used for fine shaping in wood or metal.

Finish

The surface of an object. Finish can refer to the coatings used to protect a surface or give it a particular look, such as matte or gloss.

Fire curtain

A fireproof curtain is hung between the audience and the stage, usually just upstage of the proscenium arch. Its main purpose is to keep the audience safe from a fire on stage.

Fireproof

An item that will not burn, smoke, or flame.

Fire retardant

An item that will burn, smoke, and flame, although it will do all of these slower than anticipated.

First class

Usually the first tour after a Broadway run. Personnel travel on planes and stay in first-class hotels. Production elements are trucked domestically or shipped internationally.

Fitch

A type of lining brush with a defined shape, seamless ferrule, and natural bristles. It comes in a wide variety of sizes.

Flat brush

Great for blending. The shape gives you great control when moving makeup around.

Flogger

A paintbrush with really, really long bristles, the flogger can be used for creating textures in wet paint or removing cartooned chalk and charcoal from the material's surface.

Floretta

A small, handheld version of the compression sprayer.

Fluorescent

A gas-discharge lamp that uses electricity to excite mercury vapor.

Flush cut saw

Has a handle with the blade coming straight out of one end. The blade is very flexible. It cuts flush with the bottom surface and has a very fine set of teeth that cut in one direction.

Fly loft

The space in a theater between the stage floor and the roof of the building containing all the ropes, pulleys, and blocks required to enable the stage crew to hoist scenery, lighting, and other items safely out of view and back again.

Foam

Brushes and pads come in a variety of sizes and are mostly rectangular or round. Instead of bristles, these brushes have a foam block that comes to a wedge at the tip. These are great for cutting in and keeping a straight line.

Foam sponge

These come in different shapes and sizes. They are ideal for applying creme makeup.

Focus

The process of aiming the lights to the place the designer wants the light to be.

Fog

When heated vapor mixes with cooler air outside a fog machine, it instantly forms an opaque aerosol—the effect we call *fog* or *smoke*.

FOH

Acronym for front of house.

Folding rule

This is a combination of a regular ruler and a yardstick. It is made up of small sections in 6-inch increments connected by pivot points.

Food prop

An object that can be eaten onstage or, at the very least, appears to be edible.

Footlights

Traditionally located on the downstage edge of the stage and/or apron, they focus upstage toward the back wall, pointing up into the actors' faces from below. Used primarily in the commercial theater.

Foreshortening

An optical illusion created by changing one's view of the vanishing point to one side rather than directly in front of the viewer.

Forstner bit

A drill bit with an upside-down letter T-shaped structure, a shaft on the top and a boring section on the bottom. It is perfect for drilling large-diameter holes.

Foundation

Usually the first layer of makeup to be applied, foundations glide on easily when using a foam sponge. They are long-lasting and provide a flawless finish. They come in a wide range of colors to match any skin tone. If, by chance, you can't find the exact color, you can mix them to create a new hue. Creme foundations need to be set with powder.

Foundation brush

The brushes made for applying foundation.

Fourth wall

The proscenium acts as a frame through which the audience views the play. This frame is often referred to as the *fourth wall*. The actors treat the "fourth wall" as if it is a real wall and ignore the audience. Some plays call for the actors to look right at the audience and deliver their lines. This is called "breaking the fourth wall."

Framing hammer

This is heavier and meant for larger nails and harder woods than the standard claw hammer. The claw is not as curved as on a standard claw hammer.

Framing square

Looks like a big L with the long side 24 inches long and the shorter side 16 inches long. It is made out of metal. It is the most accurate of the squares because it has a fixed angle; there are no adjustments you can make.

French curve

A template for drawing curves. It has rounded edges and several scroll-shaped cutouts in the middle. The device is used by placing it on a surface, and tracing along its edges.

French scene breakdown

A spreadsheet of all the acts and scenes in the play with a list of all the characters laid out in table form to show which characters are in which scenes.

Fresnel

A soft-edge light that can focus as a spot or flood. The defining part is the shaped lens.

Fresnel lens

Divided into a series of concentric circles that step in toward one another. Designed in such a way that light output is not sacrificed.

Frisket

A plastic sheet with an adhesive back. It is used when you need to mask a specific part of a design. You lay it down and cut a design out to reveal the portion you need to work on, leaving everything else masked.

Front of house

This refers to any part of a theater's infrastructure that is *not* over the stage. This can include the areas of the audience, lobby, and box office, to name a few.

Furniture prop

An object, such as a table or chair, that does not directly involve the actors or the blocking but appears primarily as a part of the composition.

Futuristic

Looking like something from the future.

G

Gain

What we usually think of as volume. However, it is a little different than volume. Gain is the amount of amplification available within the sound system.

Gel

Originally made of gelatin, which could melt or catch fire, gel is now made of a polyester film. The process to make gel involves adding color to the actual production process of the polyester sheeting. In this way, color is actually incorporated into the polyester.

Genre

A category of artistic composition characterized by similarities in form, style, or subject matter.

Glazes

Thinner than paint and transparent instead of opaque. Used for a variety of effects.

Glover's needle

A sewing needle with sharp triangular points for sewing through leather, also known as a *leather needle*.

Go

The word used to mean, do the cue!

Gobo

A *templat*e or sometimes called a *cookie*, a gobo is placed within an ERS or other focusable fixture to project patterns.

Goggles

The first line of defense for your eyes. Many styles can be worn over eyeglasses.

Gorgets

An article of clothing that covers or protects the neck and throat, such as in armor.

Graining

Uses specially textured brushes and tools to create wood grain pattern and texture.

Grand border

Usually hangs downstage of the house curtain. A border is a short curtain that hangs in the air and goes all the way across the stage. It helps mask the workings of the theater from the audience's view. In this case, the grand border is the one closest to the audience. It is often made of fabric to match the house curtain, rather than the plainer fabric traditional for other borders.

Grayscale

The chart of tones and tints from black to white with no actual hue.

Grid

Horizontal and vertical lines, creating equal-size squares, drawn on a drop to help enlarge an image to full size. Also a network of steel beams above the stage that supports the flying battens and other rigging.

Grid iron

A frame of parallel bars or I-beams in the ceiling of the fly loft.

Grinder

A tool that drives an abrasive disc mounted to a geared head.

Grommets

A type of two-part fastener, usually made of metal, that is hammered in place to protect a hole in fabric, such as for a lacing in a corset.

Ground

The wire that is there as a safety measure in case there is some sort of short circuit.

Ground plan

A drawing of the stage or set as seen from above.

H

Hacksaw

This has a metal handle shaped as an arch with two places to attach the blade. The blade is both narrow and rigid and the teeth are angled.

Half hitch

A knot that forms the basis for a multitude of other knots.

Half hour

A call is given to everyone backstage 30 minutes prior to the curtain going up that lets everyone know that the house is being opened up to the audience and they can no longer walk into the house.

Halogen light lamp

An incandescent lamp with a tungsten filament.

Hammer drill

This looks similar to an electric drill. It works in a similar way, with a drill bit that does the cutting. The added feature in a hammer drill is that the chuck creates a short, rapid hammer-type action to break through hard or brittle material. Hammer drills are used mostly when working with masonry or stone.

Hand

Refers to the feeling of the fabric, or hide, such as: stiff, smooth, crisp, or spongy.

Hand prop

An object that an actor holds in their hand.

Hand-screw clamp

An older style of clamp that is still used today, this is great when you need to be careful not to destroy your surface. This clamp is easy to recognize by its two heavy, broad, wooden jaws. Passing through the jaws are screws with reverse threads at the ends, so that the jaws come together rapidly and can clamp at many different angles.

Hard flat

A flat covered with ¼-inch plywood forming a hard surface.

Haze

Reveals light beams as it stays in the air. The machines use a water-soluble liquid that, when heated, turns to haze.

Head block

A pulley mounted to an overhead steel above the fly loft that changes the direction of multiple ropes.

Hemp house

A theater where the lift lines from the battens are rope, either organic or synthetic.

Hide

The skin of an animal, especially when it has been processed or tanned.

Hole saw

Used to cut larger holes, it is a piece of thin metal wrapped in a circle with teeth added on one side. Usually, a small twist bit in the center allows you to get the hole started in the exact place you want it.

Horizon line

The line that separates the earth from the sky. In the theater, it is the horizontal line that comes closest to the height of your eye.

Hot-glue gun

Used for heating and dispensing hot melted glue.

House curtain

A curtain is placed directly upstage of the proscenium and acts as a house curtain. The house curtain is used to mask the stage from the audience's view prior to the performance. The house curtain is not always used in this manner today, as some less-traditional productions choose to expose the stage and the scenery rather than hide them.

Hudson sprayer

A type of compression sprayer that is known by its brand name, Hudson.

Hue

Another word for color.

I

Impedance

The amount of resistance a microphone has to an audio signal. The lower the resistance, the fewer problems the microphone may have using longer cables and dealing with noise interference. Generally, low impedance means a better-quality microphone and therefore becomes a perfect choice for the theater.

Impressionism

A combination of realism and romanticism that seeks to allow the artist to define the personality of the subject matter. Through the use of color and light, the subject matter's personality is revealed.

Incandescent light lamp

A carbon filament electrified within a vacuum in a glass envelope. Frequently filled with argon or another inert gas instead of vacuum.

Input

Can be microphones, contact pickups, magnetic pickups, laser pickups, and optical pickups.

Insight

Observing the world around you and forming opinions.

Intelligent lighting

Any lighting fixture that requires DMX in addition to power to function.

Intensity

The brightness or dullness of a color. This helps describe our perception of a color.

Ionic

An order of architecture. Ionic columns with scroll-like capitals followed soon after Doric.

J

Jig
A guide used with cutting or joining tools to produce multiple cuts of the same size.

Jigsaw
Also known as a *saber saw*, it has a small straight blade that cuts with an up and down motion. Because of its small blade, it is great for cutting curves but not as good for cutting straight lines.

K

Kelvin
A color temperature scale for lighting sources; lower numbers are warm, higher numbers are cool.

Kerf
Refers to allowance made for the thickness of the materials.

Key to symbols
A box with different symbols to represent various items, such as different lighting units.

Keyhole saw
Also known as a *drywall saw*, it is a long, narrow saw used for cutting small, awkward holes into a variety of building materials.

Keystone
Originally shaped like a keystone, these rectangular pieces of ¼-inch plywood are used to hold the rails to the stiles in a soft, flat frame.

Kick-off meeting
The first major meeting once a job is awarded to a shop. It involves all of the pertinent people. Schedules and many other details are laid out.

Kit
British slang for lighting equipment.

Kraft paper
Produced by the Kraft process from wood pulp. It is strong and relatively coarse. Usually a brown color, but can be bleached to produce white paper. It is used for paper grocery bags, multiwall sacks, envelopes, and other packaging.

L

Lamellar
A type of armor made of pieces of hardened leather, hides, and fur sewn to a backing. This is the oldest type of armor.

Lamp
A light bulb.

Lamp housing
The part of the fixture into which the lamp is installed.

Laser level
The laser level is a tool consisting of a laser-generated beam mounted on a tripod. The laser projector continually emits a fixed beam along the horizontal and/or vertical axis allowing referencing of the level line throughout an ongoing project.

Laser measure
Typically more accurate than a traditional tape measure. Human error is all but eliminated. In most cases, you just press a button, the laser emits its beam until it hits a solid surface, and then a digital display shows the distance measured.

Lavalier
A very small microphone designed to be clipped to clothing or hung around the neck. As the need for sound design in the theatre has grown, lavaliers can now be attached in the hair or wigs, behind the ear, and even sewn into costumes, all to try to hide them.

Lay-in
Specialty brush used specifically for painting large areas, such as a drop or a large expanse of scenery. It is larger than most other brush types, with typical sizes of 5 and 6 inches.

Leather
An animal hide that has been preserved for use. Some hide types are: cowhide, elk, water buffalo, deerskin, goatskin, pigskin, lambskin, and sheepskin.

Leather needles
see *Glover's needles*.

Leather shears
Leather shears are a type of scissors manufactured to allow for the *kerf* of the materials.

LED

Light-emitting diode technology has been around for a long time. This high-output, low-wattage light source has only recently been integrated into theatrical lighting fixtures. When using color mixing of red, green, and blue, you can create virtually any color.

Leg

A rectangular shaped curtain that is tall but narrow, used for masking the wings. Opposite of border, which is a short but wide rectangle and is used for masking the space above the stage.

Leg greaves

Plate armor that is worn on the leg.

Lens

On a fixture, the lens is a piece of glass or other transparent substance with curved sides for concentrating or dispersing light rays.

Lettering guide

A template designed to make you letter perfectly.

Light plot

A drawing to show the lighting equipment for the show, in relation to the scenery and masking.

Lighting controller

An electrical device that sends a low-voltage or digital signal to the dimmers and other devices to control them.

Lighting prop

An object that is being electrified. See also: practical.

Limelight

An intensely bright light created when a gas flame is directed at a cylinder of calcium oxide.

Line

The mathematical definition of a *line* is the shortest distance between two points. A line has direction. The designer or artist often uses this to infer what that direction is as part of the composition.

Line array

This comprises multiple speakers hung together, either vertically or horizontally, so that they can act as one huge speaker.

Line weight

The thickness of a line. Varying the line weight within a composition creates contrast.

Linear dimensions

Used when measuring in a straight line.

Linen

This material is made from flax or, more specifically, a fiber taken from the stalk of the plant. It has a natural luster from the inherent wax content.

Line set

A combination of the individual rigging points, rope, and pipe used together for hanging pipes and scenery in the air.

Line set inventory

This tells everyone where the pipes are located in relation to the plaster line. Frequently called line set schedule.

Linesman's pliers

An all-around great pair of very strong pliers, they are terrific for holding, bending, and forming. The jaw surfaces are slightly toothed for better gripping. The jaws also have a built-in side-cutter tool.

Lining

Also known as a *fitch brush*.

Lining stick

A beveled straight edge that allows you to run a brush along the side, using it as a guide for creating precise lines. The stick usually has a handle to make holding it easier when working from a distance.

Linnebach projector

Early large-format image projector. The size and focus of the projected image were determined by the size of the glass slide installed and by moving the projector.

Liquid latex

A form of makeup used for special effects such as wrinkles, for filling in pock marks, and for building up wounds. *Always* check for allergy possibilities.

Live Foley

Live sounds produced during the performance.

Loading floor

In a fly system, this is where the technicians add and remove counterweights from the arbors.

Lobsterscope

Motorized disk with slits in it placed in front of a focusable light fixture, used to project a strobe-like light.

Locking rail

Where the fly operator adds and removes counterweights from the arbors.

Loft block

A pulley mounted to the gridiron or support steel that supports and changes the direction of a lift-line rope between the load and the head block.

Looper

A sewing machine that creates a thread loop that passes from the needle thread to the edges of the fabric so that the edges of the fabric are contained within the seam.

M

Magic sheet

Sometimes called a *cheat sheet*, it is a quick reference for the design team to be able to find the channel number quickly and easily. A magic sheet is a visual reference.

Mallet

A type of hammer with a soft rubberized head that helps avoid damaging delicate surfaces. The head is also substantially larger than a regular hammer, which helps to spread out the force of the hit.

Masking

A term used for the legs, borders, or flats utilized to block the audience's view of the backstage area or anything you don't want the audience to see.

Master clock

A master clock is a precision clock that provides timing signals to synchronize slave clocks as part of a clock network.

Measuring tape

Used for the creation of soft goods. This is a soft, flexible tape measure, usually about 60 inches long, that can conform to the curves of a body well. It is used for taking measurements of people and fabric.

Media server

A fancy name for a computer with a massive hard drive and a great graphics card.

Midrange

A speaker designed specifically for the midrange frequencies.

MIG

The abbreviation for metal inert gas. MIG uses a spool of continuously fed wire that allows the welder to join longer stretches of metal without stopping to replace rods.

Millinery

The design, manufacturing and sale of hats and other headwear.

Miter box

Used to create angled edges. The box has precut slots and/or a movable guide in it to fix a saw at a certain angle.

Miter saw

Having fine crosscut teeth, miter saws are often used in conjunction with a miter box.

Mixing console

This provides pre-amplification, which boosts the microphone-level signals to line level.

Mold

A hollow form or matrix for giving shape to something in a molten or plastic state.

Monkey's fist

A knot adds a substantial amount of weight to the end of the rope.

Monochromatic

Refers to an entire composition made up of tints, tones, and shades of the same hue.

Morgue

A morgue is an organized collection of images or sounds.

Mr. Puffy

A device created to make a chalk line for costume design. Tailor's chalk, ground to a powder, is put into a small container with a very focused spout. A hose is attached to the container, controlled by a squeeze ball. The whole thing is mounted on a stand that is measured and marked so you know how high it is off the ground. Squeeze the ball, and, *poof*, your hemline is marked.

Multipair cable

A single outer jacket and insulation with many internal balanced or twisted-pair lines.

Multiple dimensions

Used when measuring several things in a row from the same starting point.

N

Nail set

A small metal guide that is used with a hammer for driving the head of a nail either flush or just below the finished surface.

Naturalism

Describes a style of production. Naturalism is quite specific. There are no stereotypes per se, but specific characters in specific environments. The purpose of this very detailed world is to show how a person's character and life choices are determined in part by the environmental or social forces.

Needle-nose pliers

Similar to basic pliers, but the gripping end is not flat but comes to a small narrow point. This makes them great for holding much smaller items with more precision.

Nominal size

Referring to lumber, the dimensions used to create a name, i.e., 2 × 4.

Nut driver

A hand tool with a socket created to fit specific sized nut or bolt heads. This tool does not ratchet.

Nylon

A fiber that has the ability to be very lustrous, semi-lustrous, or dull.

O

On weight of goods (OWG)

The formula that calculates how much dye is required to dye a certain amount of fiber to a specific *depth of shade*.

Open-ended wrench

This nonadjustable type of wrench fits a specific size of hardware and has an open end.

Operating line

A big, thick, synthetic rope that attaches to the bottom of the arbor and goes around to the head block.

Orchestra pit

The area between the stage and the auditorium. The orchestra occupies this space if there is an orchestra for the show. If there is no orchestra in the show, the pit may be covered to provide extra acting area. The name *pit* comes from the fact that most often this area is lower than the auditorium floor, creating a "pit," similar to the standing-room area in Shakespeare's time.

Orthographic projection

A way of representing a 3D object in two dimensions using multiple views.

OSHA

The Occupational Safety and Health Administration is an agency of the US Government's Department of Labor. OSHA's mission is to "assure the safety and health of America's workers by setting and enforcing standards; providing training, outreach, and education; establishing partnerships; and encouraging continual improvement in workplace safety and health."

Output

A term used in sound design that describes the different pieces of equipment that allow us to hear sound. Examples are loudspeakers (woofers, midrange, and tweeters) and headphones.

Outrigger

These are stabilizing legs that attach to the base of a lift or other potentially unstable item.

Overhand knot

This is the simplest knot of them all.

Overlocking

A stitch that sews over the edge of one or two pieces of fabric for edging, hemming, or seaming.

Oxyacetylene

Commonly referred to as gas welding, it is a process that relies on the proper combination of oxygen and acetylene.

P

Paint elevation
A 2D, full-color, to-scale representation of exact paint details.

Palette
Typically made from plastic or wood to hold a variety of colors or types of makeup, it is also used for custom mixing.

Pan
When focusing a light, to move it from left to right.

Panel saw
A circular saw with a big bracket on it to allow for movement across a large-scale predetermined grid. The saw can be either horizontal or vertical, although most scene shops prefer the vertical type to save space. Cutting sheets of plywood into smaller pieces is this tool's specialty.

Pani
A German company that created the initial large-scale projectors.

Papier-mâché
A composite material consisting of paper pieces or pulp, sometimes reinforced with textiles, bound with an adhesive, such as glue, starch, or wallpaper paste.

PAR
This term is used for a light fixture that holds a parabolic aluminum reflector (PAR) lamp.

Parallel rule
A straight edge that travels up and down the drafting table on two cables. It allows you to draw horizontal lines that are consistently parallel to each other.

Passion play
A dramatic presentation representing the "Passion of Jesus Christ," his trial, suffering, and death. Generally performed as part of the Lenten season in several Christian denominations.

Pattern
An element or shape within a composition that repeats. See also: gobo.

Patterning template
A tool to help ease the transitions between pieces in a custom pattern.

Patterns
The diagrams of the pieces and parts of a garment that act as a guide for its construction.

Pepper's ghost
A stage illusion developed by chemist John Pepper to make a ghost appear and disappear or turn the reflection of one actor into another.

Performance prop
The final object as designed and approved.

Periaktoi
Triangular columns that revolve to reveal other sides and other sets.

Perspective
This type of drawing uses a 2D technique to approximate a 3D object.

Phillips screws
An inclined plane wrapped helically around an axis with an X slot indented into the top.

Physiognomy
The assessment we all tend to make about people's character, personality, and even emotions based on their outer appearance.

PIGI
A French company that created the next major breakthrough in projectors after Pani.

Pin rail
A locking device to hold ropes attached to things to be lifted, the ropes get belayed onto the pins.

Pipe clamp
Hardware used to attach a fixture to a pipe.

Pipe cutter
Shaped like a C with a handle coming out the bottom, the handle is tightened, which tightens the pressure on the pipe. This forces the sharp blade into the pipe while wheels around the clamp continuously rotate the pipe.

Pipe reamer
Used whenever a pipe or tube is cut to remove burrs.

Pipe threader

Used to cut threads into pipe.

Pipe wrench

Meant for gripping round objects, primarily it is used for metal pipes, hence its name. It has an adjustable jaw similar to the adjustable wrench. It closes and opens by screwing itself tighter as the wrench clamps down on the pipe.

Pixel

Minute area of illumination on a display screen, one of many from which an image is composed.

Pixel density

Number of pixels per inch.

Places

The word called out a few minutes before the show begins; this means that all actors and technicians should go immediately to the places where they are needed to start the show.

Plan view

An overhead view of the architecture of the theater or scenic or lighting elements.

Plane

A tool used to flatten, reduce the thickness of, and smooth the surface of a generally rough piece of lumber; planes usually have a cutting edge on the bottom attached to the solid body of the plane. They can also be used to cut specific shapes, depending on what cutting edge is installed.

Plaster bandage

Preshrunk cotton gauze impregnated with plaster. You can buy them premade in rolls or make your own.

Plaster line

Imaginary line that is drawn in line with the upstage side of the proscenium. It is indeed the zero point for all measurements, upstage and downstage.

Platform

A small section of flooring that adds height to the existing stage.

Plumb bob

A device used when trying to determine a level line from one point only. That means you can attach a string to the top of a wall. Let the string drop down with a plumb bob attached to the bottom. The plumb bob is a weight and stops swinging at the point of making the string level; also useful for determining a point directly below something hung over the stage.

Pneumatic

This refers to any tool that requires a compressor to generate air pressure.

Polyester

The most widely used human-made fiber in the world.

Postmodernism

This style rejects the preoccupation with purity of form and technique. Mixtures of style elements from the past are applied to spare modern forms. The observer is asked to bring his or her opinions of this combined form, as there is no real standard or unity.

Pounce

The abbreviation used for a process where the pounce wheel (a small tool with sharp teeth around it) is used to punch holes in Kraft paper while tracing an image. A pounce bag, filled with chalk or charcoal, is then used to transfer the design.

Powder brush

This is a full and luxurious brush for adding powder or removing excess powder without disturbing makeup.

Powder puff

Usually round, they are always soft, and some are washable. They are great for applying powder very specifically, and for blotting.

Practicals

Scenic elements or props that plug into some form of electricity.

Preshow checklist

A list of everything that needs to be in place for the show and where, or with whom, it should be. This includes props, costumes, scenery, lighting practicals and effects machines.

Preshrink

Most fabrics should be washed before you cut and assemble them into a garment. This allows them to be more their final size before fabrication, so that the sizing of the completed garment will be, and remain, more accurate.

Presentational

This offers a performance where everyone is fully aware that the actors are at work on a stage, speaking and acting out a script, under lights, and in costumes. There is no attempt to disguise the fact that a theatrical performance is taking place to entertain the audience.

Pressure-response microphone

Usually mounted to a flat surface with the attached plate, which increases gain.

Previsualization

Often referred to as *pre-vis*, it means just what you think. It's a way to "see" what the show will look like before you get to the theatre.

Previsualize

The use of 3D virtual space to approximate the way something will look in real life.

Primary

Used when referring to a color that cannot be created by mixing any other colors together.

Primer

The liquid or spray used to prepare a surface so it's ready to accept your design. Raw wood or fabric soaks in a great deal of the first layer of paint. This is the basis for priming.

Prop breakdown

This contains all information about each prop used in the production. It includes which actor(s) uses it, where they enter from, when they need it, which scene it is in, and where it comes back off stage. Also, and very important, how does the prop get off stage? It should also include descriptions of each prop and anything about the prop that may need to be preset.

Properties

Anything movable or portable onstage that performers touch, handle, brandish, and use. Props for short.

Proportion

In math, it defines the relationship between objects or parts of the same object.

Proscenium

The proscenium arch is what formally separates the audience from the acting area. It creates a frame around the stage just like a picture frame for a painting. It lets you know where to look and, more important, where not to look!

Pry bar

This is made of metal, and both ends are designed to be used for different purposes. They are used as leverage for separating objects. Some pry bars are meant to remove nails and do minor lifting. Some are bulky enough to be able to perform demolition.

Q

Quartz envelope

The clear covering over the filament of a lamp is the quartz envelope.

R

Radial arm saw

Works similarly to a circular saw. A crosscut saw blade is usually installed. The blade head is suspended from a long arm, hence the name, in a yoke that allows for selectable degrees of rotation. There is a handle for moving the blade head forward and back while cutting the wood.

Rag rolling

Used to create texture and can be done in two ways. You can use a roller and paint a surface, then take a cotton rag that has been bunched into a loose ball and roll the rag ball across the paint to remove paint while also making a texture. You can also do the reverse, by applying paint to the rag and rolling it onto the surface to add paint and texture at the same time.

Rail

The horizontal pieces of a frame for a flat.

Rake

An angled stage is called a *raked stage*. The rake also serves as the basis for our modern stage directions. Any part of the stage or house that is on an angle is considered to be on a rake.

Rasp

A woodworking tool for shaping the wood. It is made up of a long, narrow steel bar. A handle is on one end, while the rest of the rasp has triangular teeth cut into it. When drawn across a piece of wood, it shaves away parts of the wood, very coarsely.

Raster

A pixel-based technology *or* an image defined by the number of pixels wide by pixels high that becomes the boundary of a single or multiple screens.

Rayon

A very versatile man-made fiber made from cellulose, it has many of the same comfort properties as natural fibers.

Realism

A style of production where nature is represented without idealizing (as in classicism) or being emotional or extravagant (as in romanticism).

Reciprocating saw

A straight blade mounted at one end of the body. The blade moves back and forth (that is where it gets its name), much like the action of a jigsaw, but it is much more powerful and versatile than jigsaws. A variety of blade options means it can cut through almost anything. Frequently referred by a common brand name, Sawz-All.

Reference map

A render of the design, highlighting the names of each screen that will be used.

Reference white

The standard by which you judge all other colors; in actuality, white may not exist in the work. The reference established can be any color that you want the audience to perceive as white.

Reflector

This bounces light from the lamp, gaining brightness until the light comes out the front of the fixture.

Rehearsal prop

A temporary stand-in item used during the early part of the staging process while the final item is being created or found.

Rehearsal schedule

The master calendar. It should list dates, times, places, and which members of the cast and crew are required.

Release agent

A substance used in a mold that keeps the casting material from sticking to the mold.

Removers

Various products are made to dissolve and remove other products.

Rendering

A full-color, finished sketch.

Repeatable results

The outcome of using a scientific method to achieve the same results repeatedly.

Representational

The representational style shows naked truths about ordinary existence within specific situations. This style can be broken into two sub-styles, realism and naturalism.

Research

Any visual reference that helps inform your choices is considered research.

Respirator

Air-purifying and atmosphere-supplying devices are used when the face mask is inadequate to protect the worker.

Rip blade

A saw blade for cutting wood. The teeth are designed to cut with, or parallel to, the grain.

Rivets

Two-part metal hardware used to join pieces, instead or in addition to stitching.

Road box

A theatrical toolbox or storage box for equipment. It is built to withstand the rigors of touring, having castors and individual compartments customized for its intended use.

Road house
Theater for rent to touring companies.

Romanticism
Romanticism is the imaginative emphasizing individualism in thought and expression, in direct opposition to the restrictive formality of classicism. Other traits of this period are freedom of fancy in conception and treatment, picturesque strangeness, or suggestions of drama and adventure.

Round brush
Good for lining eyes, etching brows, and applying fine details to special effects makeup.

Router
Motorized tool that typically cuts grooves or decorative trims along the edge of a piece of wood.

Ruff
A starched frill worn around the neck and protruding outward. An important part of Elizabethan and Jacobean costume.

Rule of thirds
The basic rule of composition. An image can be broken into thirds both vertically and horizontally. Each piece of the main image, while having the ability to stand on its own, is an integral part of the whole and directs the viewer's focus.

S

Safety data sheet
Also known as SDS, a one-page guide that provides detailed hazard and precautionary information for hazardous materials.

Sandbag
Used as counterweight ballast in a hemp house.

Saturation
Describes the level of pure color a hue contains.

Scale
A term that relates to how big or small the object is. This is used in determining relationships and the surrounding proportions of a composition.

Scale rule
A scale rule is normally triangular-shaped with six sides containing 11 scales.

Scar wax
Pliable, yet firm, shaded makeup used to mold simulated injuries and moles.

Scene machine
Image projector with a highly efficient light source and lenses that focus the image.

Scenic ground row
Used to ease the stage floor into the backdrop, this is two-dimensional and usually has a cutout design on the top to help the transition to the drop.

Scoop
A very soft and gentle quality of light is produced, creating an even wash covering a large area.

SCR
A type of dimmer, introduced in 1958, the silicon-controlled rectifier is still used today. These were the first dimmers to be controlled electronically.

Screens engineering team
Technicians who are talented in the hardware required to project digital images based on a design.

Scroll saw
A bench-top tool used for freehand cutting of intricate shapes in fairly thin wood, the scroll saw uses thin blades, similar to a jigsaw, to allow for the small radius needed to complete these designs.

Scumble
Putting a small amount of paint on your brush and lightly dragging it across a dry surface, often used as an overlay to a background image, such as creating sunbeams coming out of clouds.

Seam ripper
The best tool for opening seams when changes in a constructed garment need to be made, since it is specifically designed for it.

Secondary
Referring to a color that combines any two primary colors.

Section

A visual cut through the middle of important details so that we can see how other parts of the show will relate.

Serger

An overlock sewing machine, or serger, cuts the edges of the cloth as they are fed through, though some are made without cutters.

Set prop

An object, formally called set dressing, that appears as part of the scenery for the purpose of completing the visual element.

Shackle

A U-shaped device with holes at each end to accommodate a pin or bolt.

Shade

A hue that has been mixed with black.

Shape

The definition of any 2D or 3D object.

Sheave

Basically a pulley, it has a groove around its circumference to support and contain a rope and a bearing at its center to permit rotation.

Shellac

A coating made of the resin from the lac beetle, harvested from the trees after the offspring has hatched. This can be brushed onto the finished cast to seal it.

Shield

A kind of insulation that is conductive to protect against electromagnetic and electrostatic fields, this helps keep the buzz and hum away from your audio system.

Show deck

The floor of the theatre is often covered completely with platforms, called a *show deck*.

Shutters

Shaped pieces of metal inside the ERS with a handle on the outside used to shape the beam.

Side view

A drawing showing the side view of a design.

Sight lines

The imaginary lines between the audience's eyes and the stage, also called *lines of sight*.

Sign-in sheet

This chart keeps track of who is at rehearsals and if the person arrived on time or not. It should be posted in the same place at every rehearsal. This is your best and only way to keep track of missing actors and crew.

Signal processor

This can include mixing console, equalizers, reverberation, delay, and amplifiers.

Silk

A natural protein fiber taken from the cocoon of the silkworm.

Single phase

This line comprises two hot wires (typically one black and one red), a neutral wire (the white one), and a ground wire (the green one).

Single purchase

A setup where the loading floor is on the stage floor. This means a lot of stage space is lost in wings to accommodate the arbors. The advantage of the single-purchase system is that the counterweight required is 1:1; that is, 1 pound of counterweight is added to the arbor for each pound on the pipe.

Sketch

The initial drawing of design concepts in black and white or color.

Slip-joint pliers

Similar to linesman's pliers with one major difference: The joint that holds the two sides together is keyed so that the jaws can be opened wider as needed for certain jobs.

Sloper

A basic pattern shape in a variety of sizes. Slopers come in different pattern shapes. They help you to get started with a custom pattern by letting you more easily fit the pattern pieces together as you are making adjustments.

Slotted screw

An inclined plane wrapped helically around an axis with a single straight indent in the top.

Slush casting

A type of casting that deposits small amounts of plaster in layers in the mold by swirling it around. This type of casting creates a hollow-backed cast that is lighter in weight than a dump cast.

SM Bible
Promptbook for the show inclusive of all schedules, contact lists, and notes.

SM kit
Stage manager's personal grouping of stationery supplies and other tools.

Smoke pocket
The guide on either side of the stage that the fire curtain travels within is the smoke pocket.

Snake
Several complete audio cables held together in a common jacket form a snake.

Socket set
Has a handle and a series of replaceable heads. Each head has an opening on one side; each opening is a different size to correspond to different sizes of bolt heads and nuts. Sockets work with a ratcheting technology that allows you to loosen or tighten the bolt or nut quickly.

Soft flat
The traditional theatre type of flat. It has a soft covering made of muslin.

Soft goods
All fabric items found in the theatre are considered soft goods.

Soldering
Uses molten metal to join two pieces of metal. The metal added during the process has a melting point lower than that of the material, so only the added metal is melted, not the material. Soldering uses metals with a melting point below 800°F. Soldering commonly is used to join electrical, electronic, and other small metal parts.

Spade bit
A drill bit with a straight shaft with a rectangular bottom that comes to a point, it is used for boring holes, typically of a larger size or depth, in wood.

Span set
Generically known as *round slings*, this has continuous loops of mono-filament or steel-galvanized aircraft cable in a canvas-like (polyester) sheath.

Spatter
Loading a brush with a small amount of paint and basically shaking the brush at the surface without allowing it to touch, thus creating a loose pattern of dots for texture.

Spatula
A tool used for mixing makeup and applying thicker products such as nose or scar wax and gel effects.

Special effects prop
An object that has a specific purpose with regard to creating the appearance of something other than what it actually is.

Speed square
A metal triangle containing both 90-degree and 45-degree angles. Measurement markings are along the sides. The important difference between the speed square and other types of squares is that the speed square has a flange on one side that you can use to hold it square against the edge of your material. It is sometimes referred to as a *roofer's square*.

Speed wrench
Similar to a box wrench with one major exception, it contains a ratchet on both ends.

Spirit level
Named because the little vial containing liquid is actually partially filled with ethanol (alcohol).

Sponging
Used to create a paint texture by dabbing paint onto, or off, a surface with a sponge.

Spot block
A pulley designed for temporary, and easily movable, connection to a gridiron or other theater structure.

Spring clamp
Often called a *squeeze clamp* and identified by the size the jaws can open, they are clamps that are strong and lightweight. They differ from other clamps in that they tighten and loosen based on a spring's tension.

Sprinkler system
A network of piping and sprinkler heads with water under pressure placed throughout the space.

Square knot

The basis for so much, it is used for binding together two ropes of the same size. Also known as a *reef knot*, the square knot is secure and easy to untie.

Stage

The performance area.

Stage blood

Commercial stage blood has many realistic qualities including color and viscosity. It can come in liquid or powder form for specific effects. It can also come in a peppermint flavor so that, if the blood must be put in the mouth, it is at least palatable. Staining can occur on skin and fabrics, so be careful of this.

Stage left

When an actor is facing the audience, to her left is considered stage left.

Stage manager kit

The kit should include a range of items such as pencils, erasers, highlighters, pads of paper, post-it notes, paper clips, stapler, and so forth—everything you need to do your job, plus spares.

Stage right

When an actor is facing the audience, to his right is considered stage right.

Standby

A standby call means the cue is imminent.

Stapler

A device that binds things together by forcing thin metal staples into the material with pressure.

Stile

The side or vertical pieces of a frame for a flat.

Stipple sponge

Very coarse, open sponge, it is great for adding texture, such as beards, bruising, and road rash.

Storyboard

A sequence of drawings or images representing the progression of projections.

String level

A small spirit level with hooks that are mounted on a string. The string is pulled fairly taut between two points in the area you are trying to measure.

Strip lights

Several fixtures built into one, it is used for washing cycs and other large areas, typically made with multiple circuits.

Strobe

Machine capable of producing bright flashes of light. Newer models can vary the speed and intensity of the flashes.

Style

The manner of presentation of the production.

Subtractive

In a color system, when all three primary colors are mixed together in equal parts, they "theoretically" make black.

Subwoofer

Speaker designed specifically to reproduce very low-frequency sounds.

Swatches

Small cuttings of fabric or other materials used as samples.

Symbol

A picture, object, or color that stands for something else.

T

Tab

A masking leg turned 90 degrees so that is it oriented upstage and downstage.

Table saw

This works similarly to the circular saw. It is mounted on a table, which gives it more stability and allows for a more powerful engine. A rip saw blade is usually installed. The tabletop gives stability to the material you are cutting, allowing you to cut bigger pieces of wood more easily.

Tack hammer

A small hammer usually used for the detail work on finishing projects.

Tailor's chalk

Perfect for marking where you will need to adjust the fit of a garment to an actor, use chalk to make markings before you cut and assemble. The reason tailor's chalk is so good for this purpose is that, when you no longer need the markings, the chalk can be brushed away without leaving any residue. During fittings, it is much faster to mark a garment with chalk than to have an actor stand there while you insert pin after pin.

Tanning

The process of converting animal skin into leather by soaking it in a liquid containing tannic acid, or by the use of other chemicals.

Tape measure

The tape measure we are most used to seeing these days is the self-retracting pocket tape measure. Its flexibility allows you to measure long lengths while still being easily carried in your pocket. A tape measure blade is usually marked in both inches and feet.

Tertiary

In color mixing, it is the result of two secondary colors mixed together.

Texture

A tactile or raised 3D finish on a project.

Thermal barrier

Some type of item is placed between a heat source and a combustible material to prevent the material from burning.

Thermoplastics

Thermoplastics are materials that can be manipulated by heating them gently and molding them.

Thimble

A thimble is a grooved fitting around which a wire rope is bent to form an eye. Also, a small metal cup protecting fingers when sewing by hand.

Three phase

This has three hot wires (black, red, and blue) along with the neutral and ground.

Thrust stage

Usually considered to be a hybrid of the proscenium, a thrust stage most often has a proscenium of some kind. The apron becomes much larger and "thrusts" into the auditorium. Many people compare it to a tongue or a fashion runway. There is no rule about its shape or size, just that it extends substantially into the audience area.

TIG

During tungsten inert gas (TIG) welding, the welder holds the welding rod in one hand and an electric torch in the other hand. The torch is used to simultaneously melt the rod and a portion of the project's material.

Tilt

When focusing a light, to move it up and down.

Tin snips

A scissor-like tool used to cut thin sheets of metal.

Tint

A hue that has been mixed with white.

Title block

Contains all important information regarding the production and, specifically, the drawing.

TNC

Threaded version of the BNC connector. The threads replace the bayonet.

Tone

A hue mixed with gray.

Top hat

Shaped like a man's top hat, this is used to cut down light spill and help in focusing a light.

Torx

A brand name for a type of screw or wrench with a six-pointed star on the end; it is not the same as an Allen key.

Trap

A hole in the floor with a replaceable plug.

Traveler

A curtain attached to wheels in a track suspended above the stage, usually operated by a pulley.

Traverse

The audience members sit on two opposing sides of the stage, looking at each other, with the stage between them. It is often used for period plays or fashion shows.

Triangle

A template used to draw vertical and angled lines.

Trunnion

Mounting hardware for placing a fixture, usually a strip light, on the floor.

Truss

Two or more pieces of pipe fabricated together with cross bracing, this is used in place of standard pipes when you have extremely heavy loads to lift or there are extended distances between lift lines.

T square

Shaped like a T, the short part of the T leans against the side of your table. By sliding it up and down the length of your table, the long part of the T becomes an edge you can use to draw a horizontal line. It is a replacement for the parallel rule.

Tuscan

An order of architecture, the Romans devised Tuscan for use in their temples and other public buildings. Although no Tuscan columns survived, it was thought to originate in Etruscan times.

Tweeter

Type of speaker designed specifically to reproduce high frequencies.

Twist bit

A straight drill bit with spiral twists down its length, it is typically used for metal but can also be used on wood, plastics, and many other materials. The front edge of each spiral is a cutting edge. The spiral design helps to remove the debris from the hole as you drill. These bits are usually made from high-speed steel, carbon steel, or tungsten carbide.

Twisted-pair cable

Two center conductors are twisted together. Many twisted pairs can share one insulation and jacket. All balanced audio cables are twisted-pair cables with a shield, which further protects the signal being transmitted from introduced noise.

U

Upstage

The area of the stage furthest from the audience.

Utility knife

Also known as a mat knife, this type of knife comes in a metal or plastic handle. The blade is retractable, meaning it stores completely in the handle. It uses a two-sided blade. This means, when the blade gets dull, you can open the handle, pull out the blade, turn it around, and put it back in.

V

Value

The lightness or darkness of a color. This helps describe our perception of a color.

Vanishing point

Refers to the point in space where two parallel lines "seem" to converge.

Vector

Images created using mathematical formulas to locate each point. Lines are then drawn to connect the dots.

Vise grips

Pliers with an adjustable locking mechanism. They come in a variety of sizes and shapes, which makes them applicable for many jobs.

Vises

Made from metal and usually attached to a shop bench for stability. Two jaws on the top are usually fairly wide and smooth, and, by turning a screw, the jaws are brought together, thereby holding whatever has been caught inside.

Voltage

The difference of electrical potential between two points of a circuit.

Vomitorium

A hallway where the actors can enter unseen from the middle of the audience. The area usually leads directly underneath the audience risers. The Roman theatre had at least two, one on each side. Not only do actors use these for entrances and exits, but also the audience is often ushered in and out of the theatre using them.

W

Walking foot

A type of sewing machine with a mechanism that raises and lowers the presser foot and the feed dog in order to move heavy materials, such as leather, through the machine.

Warning

A verbal signal that a cue is coming up soon.

Wattage

The rate at which electrical energy is transferred by an electric circuit.

West Virginia

A mnemonic device to remember the mathematical formula to find the watts, volts, or amps if you know two of the three values.

Wet blend

Applying one layer of paint and, while it is still wet, applying a second coat that blends partially or completely with the first.

Wet/Dry vacuum

A cleaner with a substantial tank for collecting whatever you're cleaning up. With the flick of a switch, depending on the brand, you can go from vacuuming sawdust to water!

White balance

This phrase often is used when shooting video or film, but it is equally important in the theatre. You "teach" your camera or your eyes what white really looks like, then all other colors are seen in relation, or in perspective, to this newly defined "white."

Winch

Geared mechanisms that can be either hand operated or motorized. They are used to raise, lower, or move heavy equipment. The gearing produces a mechanical advantage in both speed and load capacity.

Wing and drop

Legs and borders, often painted to complement the backdrop.

Wings

The areas just off stage, left and right of the acting area, are the wings.

Wire rope

This consists of a number of strands of steel wire twisted on the diagonal around a core. Each strand consists of a number of wires also twisted on the diagonal around a core.

Wire rope clip

A U-shaped bolt and a pad with two holes for sliding up the bolt; two small nuts are used for holding the pad in place. It is used for securing wire rope.

Woofer

Speaker designed to reproduce low frequencies.

Wool

A fiber that comes from a variety of different animal coats, some fine and soft, and some scratchy. Some are even extremely soft.

Workflow

The sequence of steps through which a design passes from design to completion.

X

XLR

With three pins or more, this connector is one of the most commonly used connectors in the sound world. Originally called the *X series* when it first came out, the L represents the added latch, and the R is for the rubber surrounding the internal contacts.

Y

Yankee screwdriver

Also referred to as the *push screwdriver* and an older style, this screwdriver has a spiral center so that, when you press down on the handle, the head turns the spiral center so you can drive in or back out a screw by just pushing down on the handle.

Yoke

Mounting hardware for hanging a fixture that is usually integral to the fixture.

Z

Zetex

A material that replaced asbestos as a thermal barrier.

INTRODUCTION: OPENING NIGHT AND PAYING CUSTOMERS

There is a superstition in theatre about the opening-night customers. As we all know, some tickets are given away through various connections with the production. These are called *comps*, or complimentary tickets. Supposedly, the first customer to be admitted into the auditorium must be a paying customer. This is said to ensure the financial success of the production. House managers have been known to refuse admittance to someone with a comp ticket prior to seating a paying customer.

THE ORIGINS OF THESPIANS

In the 6th century BCE, a priest of Dionysus named Thespis first engaged in direct dialogue with the traditional chorus of actors. This is widely considered to be the birth of theatre, and subsequently Thespis is considered to be the first true actor. Thus, actors ever since have been referred to as thespians.

THE SCOTTISH PLAY

Perhaps the most prevalent superstition in all of theatre is about *Macbeth*. We are never supposed to mention the name when we are in a theater building. It is said that, if you say the name, terrible things will happen. Apparently, this is based on the lustful greed for power that takes place in the plot of that play. Everyone calls it the *Scottish play* instead, and we all know what they mean.

Theatre veterans can tell many tales about bad luck happening when the name is said aloud. It is often thought that the supernatural forces of evil are behind this. But you are in luck, because there is a way to break the curse. If you say the name, you must spin around and spit on the floor. They say the spin turns back time, and the spit expels the poisonous word from your system.

BREAK A LEG

One possible explanation for this expression is its relation to "taking a knee," which itself has roots in chivalry. Meeting royalty, one would "take a knee"—in other words, bend down on one knee. That breaks the line of the leg, hence "break a leg," a wish that the performer will do so well that he or she will need to take bows.

GREEN IS A BAD COLOR

Don't wear green onstage. Actors used to perform outdoors on the green grass, so actors wearing green weren't seen very well. Also, a green light was often used to illuminate characters, and this limelight would make anyone wearing green appear practically invisible.

UMBRELLA PROBLEMS

For more than a century, opening umbrellas on stage has been perceived as bad luck. This belief actually started in 1868, when an orchestra leader named Bob Williams said goodbye to his theatre company before going away for the weekend. He opened his umbrella while standing on the stage, then walked out into a very rainy day. An hour later, he was standing on the stern of a boat, waving good-bye to a group of friends. As the boat sailed away from the dock, one of the engines exploded, and Williams was instantly killed. The publicity seemed to say that the accident and the opening of the umbrella were connected. A theatre superstition was born and lives to this day. As with many of the other superstitions, there is a "counterspell." This was especially needed with this belief, because occasionally an actor must open an umbrella as a stage direction in a play. If an actor opens the umbrella facing the ground, good luck is restored.

"STARS AND STRIPES FOREVER"

In show business, particularly theatre and the circus, this hymn is called the "Disaster March." It is a traditional code signaling a life-threatening emergency. This helps theatre personnel handle things and organize the audience's exit without panic. One example of its use was at the Hartford Circus Fire in July 1944.

MONKEY WRENCH

The monkey wrench is an adjustable wrench that is rarely used today. Its use has generally been replaced by the adjustable-end wrench, which has a compact head and so is more easily used in confined places.

EVIL CURTAINS

Even the drop curtain contributes its share of stage superstitions, as nearly every actor and manager believe it is bad luck to look out at the audience from the wrong side of it when it is down. Some say it is the prompt side that casts the evil spell, while others contend it is the opposite side. The management, not being sure from which side the bad luck is likely to accrue, places a peephole directly in the center.

PROPS—FLOWERS

It is bad luck for an actor to receive flowers before the play begins, though flowers given after the play has ended are considered good luck.

PAINT—THE GREEN ROOM

The green room in a theatre is known for being the one room where you can just go and hang out. You can meet with people to talk before or after a performance. Actors sometimes even meet the fans in the green room. But it is very rare that I've ever seen a green room that is actually green! So, how did it get its name?

One story says that the Gaelic word *grian* means sunlit, which is where we get the word *greenhouse*. Since the green room is often one of the few rooms in the theatre with windows, it was labeled the *green room*.

RIGGING—WHISTLING

Whistling backstage is a taboo, because it supposedly brings dire results. This superstition quite likely has its roots in the past, when managers hired sailors to run the fly loft, on the premise that the sailors' expertise with knots and raising and lowering sails made them ideal workers. A signal system of whistles cued the sailors. Someone whistling for personal enjoyment could sound like a cue, resulting in a dire event, such as a heavy batten falling on actors' heads. Therefore, whistling can be bad luck.

LIGHTING—GHOST LIGHT

Many theaters have ghosts, according to resident theatre personnel who will tell you they've seen or heard uncanny visitors, and some insist that to ward off bad-luck spirits there must always be a "ghost light" illuminating the stage when it is not in use. It is turned on as the actors and crews leave and burns all night. If the stage is dark, the superstition has it, ghosties can run free. Or, perhaps, we leave a light on so they can perform.

To me, the reason is less ghostly and more a statement of intense belief: We must be sure that concrete light always is on so that the metaphorical light of the theatre never will disappear. *Dark*, let us recall, refers to a time when there is no show (i.e., "We perform Tuesday through Sunday, but Monday is dark"). We want our art never to become "dark," but instead to remain brightly alive. Or, the stage should never be left dark. A light should always be on to keep the ghost company and happy. The light left on the stage is referred to as the ghost light.

Or, a burglar fell off the stage, broke his or her leg, and sued the theatre.

SOUND—CATS

Cats, on the other hand, are thought to be lucky in the theatre, that is, as long as they are content to watch plays from the wings. A black cat is supposed to be an even more infallible source of good luck. It is said that, all around the theatre world, dark felines are treated with the greatest care and consideration. If a cat crosses the stage though, it is thought to be a terrible omen.

COSTUMES—BABY DOLL

When baby dolls are off stage during a performance, set them face down on the props table instead of face up. This superstition comes from China. It is believed that, if a baby doll is left face up, its spirit (kind of like a poltergeist) will emerge from its eyes and do poltergeist-like things in the theatre.

LIPSTICK

When making up, an actress regards it as a sign that she will receive a good contract if she accidentally smears some lipstick onto her teeth.

PROJECTIONS—CHURCH KEY

Church key—the monks made their own ale. To keep the recipes secret, the monasteries were locked. Since the new bottle opener looked a bit like a skeleton key, it was referred to as a *church key*.

IN THE LIMELIGHT

This is not a superstition but instead illustrates the way some theatrical terms enter everyday conversation. You've heard of this or that athlete, politician, or rock star having his or her day "in the limelight"? The phrase dates back to 1808, when Sir Humphrey Davy, a British chemist, discovered that a brilliant white light resulted from heating calcium oxide ("lime") to an extreme temperature. This "limelight" became popular to illuminate the important actors on stage. Think *followspot*. It follows, then, that *in the limelight* came to mean "in the center of attention," and vice versa.

THE FINAL WORD

Some theatre folks believe it is bad luck to speak the last line of the play before opening night, because the play isn't "finished" until performed. Well, given the number of tech cues associated with that last line—lights, sound, curtain—plus somewhat frenzied blocking to get everyone off stage and in position for the curtain call, isn't it awfully risky not to rehearse it?

Somewhat connected, I've always postponed blocking the curtain call until the very last moment, mostly because doing it says "we're finished," when we aren't. Also, the way a curtain call is blocked necessarily indicates the relative importance of various roles, and I dislike making that statement to the cast, because it violates the idea of an *ensemble*, the creation of which is always one of my directorial goals.

TOURING—TRIPPING

If an actress trips on the hem of her dress, she should pick it up and kiss the hem for good luck.

BAD DRESS REHEARSAL—GOOD OPENING

There is a saying that "a bad dress rehearsal will equal a good opening night." It might have started with a producer who had a show underway that had an absolutely disastrous dress rehearsal. Not knowing how else to build morale, the producer glibly invented a quick excuse: "Well, you know the old saying that a bad dress rehearsal guarantees a great show!" And that propaganda is hauled out by its hind legs every time a dress rehearsal goes down the tubes. Plah! Most times, a cruddy dress rehearsal means a cruddy opening; a potent dress rehearsal, on the other hand, builds confidence and morale and it is a marvelous high leaping off place for the growth that will follow.

CHAPTER 1

Chapter Opening Photograph courtesy of John Carver Photography.

1.1 Image courtesy of Wikipedia as part of Creative Commons License.

1.2 Image courtesy of Wendy Herron.

1.3 Image courtesy of the author.

1.4 Image courtesy of Wikipedia as part of Creative Commons License.

1.5 Image courtesy of Wikipedia as part of Creative Commons License.

1.6 Image courtesy of Wikipedia as part of Creative Commons License.

1.7 Image courtesy of Wikipedia as part of Creative Commons License.

1.8 Image courtesy of Wikipedia as part of Creative Commons License.

1.9 Image courtesy of Wikipedia as part of Creative Commons License.

1.10 Image courtesy of Wikipedia as part of Creative Commons License.

1.11 Image courtesy of Wendy Herron.

1.12 Photo courtesy of cowardlion/Shutterstock.com.

1.13 Image courtesy of Wikipedia as part of Creative Commons License.

1.14 Image courtesy of Wikipedia as part of Creative Commons License.

1.15 Image courtesy of Wikipedia as part of Creative Commons License.

1.16 Image courtesy of Wendy Herron.

1.17 Image courtesy of the author.

1.18 Image courtesy of Wendy Herron.

1.19 Image courtesy of the author.

1.20 Image courtesy of the author.

CHAPTER 2

Chapter Opening Photograph courtesy of John Carver Photography.

2.1 Image courtesy of the author.

2.2 Image courtesy of the author.

2.3 Image courtesy of the author.

2.4 Image courtesy of the author.

2.5 Image courtesy of Wikipedia as part of Creative Commons License.

2.6 Image courtesy of Wikipedia as part of Creative Commons License.

2.7 Image courtesy of Wikipedia as part of Creative Commons License.

2.8 Image courtesy of Wikipedia as part of Creative Commons License.

2.9 Image courtesy of Wikipedia as part of Creative Commons License.

2.10 Image courtesy of Wikipedia as part of Creative Commons License.

2.11 © Rosaria Sinisi.

2.12 © Rosaria Sinisi.

2.13 © 2005 George Mott.

2.14 © Carol Rosegg.

2.15 Photo courtesy of Joan Marcus.

2.16 © Carol Rosegg.

2.17 © Carol Rosegg.

CHAPTER 3

Chapter Opening Photograph courtesy of John Carver Photography.

3.1 Photo courtesy of Wendy Herron.

3.2 © John Carver.

3.3 © John Carver.

3.4   Artwork courtesy of Isabella Rupp.

3.5   © John Carver.

3.6   Photo courtesy of Ken Billington.

3.7   Image courtesy of the author.

3.8   Image courtesy of the author.

3.9   Image courtesy of Wikipedia as part of Creative Commons License.

3.10 Image courtesy of the author.

3.11 Image courtesy of the author.

3.12 Image courtesy of Wikipedia as part of Creative Commons License.

3.13 Image courtesy of the author.

3.14 Image courtesy of the author.

CHAPTER 4

Chapter Opening Photograph courtesy of John Carver Photography.

4.1   © John Carver.

4.2   © John Carver.

4.3   Image courtesy of the author.

4.4   Image courtesy of Wendy Herron.

4.5   Image courtesy of Wendy Herron.

4.6   Image courtesy of Wendy Herron.

4.7   Image courtesy of Wendy Herron.

4.8   Image courtesy of Wendy Herron.

4.9   Image courtesy of Wendy Herron.

4.10 Image courtesy of the author.

4.11 Image courtesy of the author.

4.12 Artwork courtesy of Michael A. Fink.

4.13 Image courtesy of the author.

4.14 Image courtesy of the author.

4.15 Image courtesy of Wendy Herron.

4.16 Image courtesy of Wendy Herron.

4.17 Image courtesy of the author.

4.18 Images courtesy of the author.

4.19 Artwork courtesy of Michael A. Fink.

CHAPTER 5

Chapter Opening Photograph courtesy of John Carver Photography.

5.1   Image courtesy of the author.

5.2   Image courtesy of the author.

5.3   Image courtesy of Wikipedia as part of Creative Commons License.

5.4   © John Carver.

5.5   © John Carver.

5.6   © John Carver.

5.7   © John Carver.

5.8   © John Carver.

5.9   © John Carver.

5.10 © John Carver.

5.11 © John Carver.

5.12 Image courtesy of the author.

5.13 Image courtesy of the author.

5.14 © John Carver.

5.15 Image courtesy of the author.

5.16 © John Carver.

5.17 © John Carver.

5.18 © John Carver.

5.19 Image courtesy of the author.

5.20 © John Carver.

5.21 Image courtesy of the author.

5.22 Image courtesy of John Lee Beatty.

5.23 Image courtesy of John Lee Beatty.

5.24 Photo courtesy by Richard Finkelstein.

5.25 © John Carver.

5.26 © John Carver.

5.27 © John Carver.

5.28 Image courtesy of Wikipedia as part of Creative Commons License.

5.29 Image courtesy of the author.

5.30 Image courtesy of the author.

5.31 Image courtesy of the author.

5.32 © Rosaria Sinisi.

5.33 Image courtesy of the author.

5.34 Image courtesy of John Lee Beatty.

5.35 Image courtesy of the author.

5.36 Image courtesy of John Lee Beatty.

5.37 Image courtesy of Campbell Baird.

5.38 Image courtesy of Scott Pask.

5.39 Image courtesy of Roger Bardwell.

5.40 Image courtesy of the author.

5.41 Image courtesy of the author.

5.42 Image courtesy of Roger Bardwell.

5.43 Image courtesy of the author.

5.44 Image courtesy of John McKernon.

5.45 Image courtesy of the author.

5.46 Image courtesy of the author.

5.47 Image courtesy of John Lee Beatty.

5.48 Image courtesy of John Lee Beatty.

5.49 Image courtesy of John Lee Beatty.

CHAPTER 6

Chapter Opening Photograph courtesy of the author.

6.1 Image courtesy of the author.

6.2 Image courtesy of the author.

6.3 Image courtesy of the author.

6.4 Image courtesy of the author.

6.5 © John Carver.

6.6 Image courtesy of the author.

6.7 Image courtesy of the author.

6.8 Image courtesy of Wikipedia as part of Creative Commons License.

6.9 Image courtesy of Wikipedia as part of Creative Commons License.

6.10 Image courtesy of Wikipedia as part of Creative Commons License.

6.11 © John Carver.

6.12 Image courtesy of the author.

6.13 Image courtesy of the author.

6.14 Image courtesy of the author.

6.15 Image courtesy of the author.

6.16 Image courtesy of the author.

6.17 Image courtesy of the author.

6.18 Image courtesy of the author.

6.19 Image courtesy of Wikipedia as part of Creative Commons License.

6.20 Image courtesy of Wikipedia as part of Creative Commons License.

6.21 Image courtesy of William Domack.

6.22 Image courtesy of William Domack.

6.23 Image courtesy of Rosco.

CHAPTER 7

Chapter Opening Photograph courtesy of John Carver Photography.

7.1 © John Carver.

7.2 © John Carver.

7.3 © John Carver.

7.4 © John Carver.

7.5 © John Carver.

7.6 © John Carver.

7.7 Image courtesy of the author.

7.8 © John Carver.

7.9 © John Carver.

7.10 © John Carver.

7.11 © John Carver.

7.12 Images courtesy of the author.

7.13 © John Carver.

7.14 © John Carver.

7.15 © John Carver.

7.16 © John Carver.

7.17 © John Carver.

7.18 © John Carver.

7.19 © John Carver.

7.20 © John Carver.

7.21 © John Carver.

7.22 © John Carver.

7.23 © John Carver.

7.24 © John Carver.

7.25 © John Carver.

7.26 © John Carver.

7.27 Image courtesy of the author.

7.28 Image courtesy of the author.

7.29 Image courtesy of the author.

7.30 Photo courtesy of John McKernon.

7.31 Image courtesy of the author.

7.32 Image courtesy of the author.

7.33 © Beth Bergman.

7.34 Image courtesy of the author.

7.35 © Beth Bergman.

7.36 Photo courtesy of Ken Billington.

7.37 Image courtesy of the author.

7.38 Image courtesy of the author.

7.39 © John Carver.

7.40 © John Carver.

7.41 © John Carver.

7.42 Image courtesy of Wikipedia as part of Creative Commons License.

7.43 Image courtesy of Wikipedia as part of Creative Commons License.

7.44 © John Carver.

7.45 © John Carver.

7.46 Photo courtesy of Mutual Hardware.

CHAPTER 8

Chapter Opening Photograph courtesy of John Carver Photography.

8.1 Photo courtesy of Ella Bromblin.

8.2 Image courtesy of John Lee Beatty.

8.3 Image courtesy of John Lee Beatty.

8.4 Image courtesy of Scott Pask.

8.5 Image courtesy of Roger Bardwell.

8.6 Image courtesy of Roger Bardwell.

8.7 Image courtesy of Roger Bardwell.

8.8 Image courtesy of Carrie Silverstein.

8.9 Image courtesy of John Lee Beatty.

8.10 Photo courtesy of Richard Finkelstein.

8.11 Image courtesy of the author.

8.12 Image courtesy of the author.

8.13 Image courtesy of the author.

8.14 Image courtesy of John Lee Beatty.

8.15 Image courtesy of Roger Bardwell.

8.16 Image courtesy of Roger Bardwell.

8.17 Image courtesy of Phil Grayson.

8.18 Image courtesy of William Domack.

8.19 Image courtesy of Roger Bardwell.

8.20 Image courtesy of Roger Bardwell.

8.21 Image courtesy of Roger Bardwell.

8.22 Image courtesy of Roger Bardwell.

8.23 Image courtesy of John Lee Beatty.

8.24 Image courtesy of John Lee Beatty.

8.25 Image courtesy of Roger Bardwell.

CHAPTER 9

Chapter Opening Photograph courtesy of John Carver Photography.

9.1 Photo courtesy of Lawrence Heyman.

9.2 Photo courtesy of Lawrence Heyman.

9.3 Image courtesy of Lawrence Heyman.

9.4 Photos courtesy of Lawrence Heyman.

9.5 Photo courtesy of Lawrence Heyman.

9.6 Photo courtesy of Lawrence Heyman.

9.7 Photo courtesy of Lawrence Heyman.

9.8 Image courtesy of the author.

9.9 Photos courtesy of Lawrence Heyman.

9.10 Image courtesy of Campbell Baird.

9.11 Photo courtesy of Campbell Baird.

9.12 Image courtesy of the author.

9.13 Image courtesy of the author.

9.14 Image courtesy of Campbell Baird.

9.15 Image courtesy of Campbell Baird.

9.16 Photo courtesy of Campbell Baird.

9.17 Photo courtesy of Campbell Baird.

9.18 Photo courtesy of Campbell Baird.

9.19 Photo courtesy of Richard Finkelstein ©2021.

9.20 © John Carver.

9.21 © John Carver.

9.22 © John Carver.

9.23 © John Carver.

9.24 © John Carver.

9.25 © John Carver.

9.26 © John Carver.

9.27 © John Carver.

9.28 © John Carver.

9.29 © John Carver.

9.30 © John Carver.

9.31 © John Carver.

9.32 © John Carver.

9.33 © John Carver.

9.34 © John Carver.

9.35 © John Carver.

9.36 © John Carver.

CHAPTER 10

Chapter Opening Photograph courtesy of John Carver Photography.

10.1 Image courtesy of the author.

10.2 Photo courtesy of Grace Brandt.

10.3 Image courtesy of the author.

10.4. Image courtesy of Scott Pask.

10.5 Image courtesy of Scott Pask.

10.6 Photo courtesy of Grace Brandt.

10.7 Photo courtesy of Grace Brandt.

10.8 Photo courtesy of Grace Brandt.

10.9 Image courtesy of William Domack.

10.10 Image courtesy of the author.

10.11 Image courtesy of the author.

10.12 Image courtesy of the author.

10.13 Photo courtesy of Grace Brandt.

10.14 Photo courtesy of Grace Brandt.

10.15 Photo courtesy of Grace Brandt.

10.16 Photo courtesy of FragmentNine.

10.17 Image courtesy of the author.

10.18 Image courtesy of the author.

10.19 Image courtesy of the author.

10.20 Image courtesy of the author.

10.21 © Beth Bergman.

10.22 Image courtesy of the author.

10.23 Image courtesy of the author.

10.24 Photo courtesy of Michal Daniel.

10.25 Image courtesy of the author.

10.26 © Rosario Sinisi.

10.27 © Rosario Sinisi.

10.28 Photo courtesy of Jenny Knott.

10.29 Photo courtesy of Jenny Knott.

10.30 Photo courtesy of Jenny Knott.

10.31 Photo courtesy of Jenny Knott.

10.32 Photo courtesy of Jenny Knott.

10.33 Photo courtesy of Jenny Knott.

10.34 Photo courtesy of Jenny Knott.

10.35 Photo courtesy of Jenny Knott.

CHAPTER 11

Chapter Opening Photograph courtesy of John Carver Photography.

11.1 Photo courtesy of EA Kafkalas.

11.2 Image courtesy of the author.

11.3 Image courtesy of Wikipedia as part of Creative Commons License.

11.4 Image courtesy of Wikipedia as part of Creative Commons License.

11.5 © John Carver.

11.6 © John Carver.

11.7 © John Carver.

11.8 © John Carver.

11.9 © John Carver.

11.10 © John Carver.

11.11 Photo courtesy of Jason Adams.

11.12 Photo courtesy of Richard Finkelstein.

11.13 Image courtesy of Wikipedia as part of Creative Commons License.

11.14 Image courtesy of the author.

11.15 Image courtesy of William Domack.

11.16 © John Carver.

11.17 Image courtesy of William Domack.

11.18 Image courtesy of William Domack.

11.19 Image courtesy of the author.

11.20 Photo courtesy of Jason Adams.

11.21 Photo courtesy of Jason Adams.

11.22 Image courtesy of the author.

11.23 Courtesy of James Thomas Engineering.

11.24 Courtesy of James Thomas Engineering.

11.25 Courtesy of James Thomas Engineering.

11.26 Courtesy of James Thomas Engineering.

11.27 Image courtesy of Wikipedia as part of Creative Commons License.

11.28 Courtesy of James Thomas Engineering.

11.29 Courtesy of Sapsis Rigging.

11.30 Photo courtesy of Jason Adams.

CHAPTER 12

Chapter Opening Photograph courtesy of John Carver Photography.

12.1 Image courtesy of the author.

12.2 Photo courtesy of Ella Bromblin.

12.3 Image courtesy of Wikipedia as part of Creative Commons License.

12.4 Photo courtesy of Ella Bromblin.

12.5 Image courtesy of Wikipedia as part of Creative Commons License.

12.6 Image courtesy of Wikipedia as part of Creative Commons License.

12.7 Image courtesy of Wikipedia as part of Creative Commons License.

12.8 Image courtesy of Wikipedia as part of Creative Commons License.

12.9 Photo courtesy of Ken Billington.

12.10 © 2005   George Mott.

12.11 Image courtesy of Wikipedia as part of Creative Commons License.

12.12 Image courtesy of Wikipedia as part of Creative Commons License.

12.13 Image courtesy of Wikipedia as part of Creative Commons License.

12.14 Photo courtesy of Jason Adams.

12.15 Image courtesy of the author.

12.16 © Altman Lighting, Inc.

12.17 © Altman Lighting, Inc.

12.18 © Arri Group.

12.19 Image courtesy of Wikipedia as part of Creative Commons License.

12.20 © Altman Lighting, Inc.

12.21 © Altman Lighting, Inc.

12.22 © Altman Lighting, Inc.

12.23 © Robert Juliat.

12.24 © Altman Lighting, Inc.

12.25 © Robert Juliat.

12.26 © Robert Juliat.

12.27 © Robert Juliat.

12.28 © ETC.

12.29 Photo courtesy of Richard Finkelstein.

12.30 © Altman Lighting, Inc.

12.31 © Strong, Inc.

12.32 © Lycian.

12.33 © Lycian.

12.34 © Robert Juliat.

12.35 © Martin Professional.

12.36 © Robe.

12.37 © Martin Professional.

12.38 © City Theatrical, Inc.

12.39 © John Carver.

12.40 © ETC.

12.41 © ETC.

12.42 © Avolites.

12.43 © Avolites.

12.44 © ETC.

12.45 © City Theatrical, Inc.

12.46 Image courtesy of the author.

12.47 Image courtesy of Ken Billington.

12.48 Image courtesy of Ken Billington.

12.49 Image courtesy of Ken Billington.

12.50 Image courtesy of Ken Billington.

12.51 Image courtesy of Ken Billington.

12.52 Images courtesy of D. M. Wood.

CHAPTER 13

Chapter Opening Photograph courtesy of John Carver Photography.

13.1   Image courtesy of the author.

13.2   Image courtesy of Wikipedia as part of Creative Commons License.

13.3   © Sennheiser.

13.4   Image courtesy of Wikipedia as part of Creative Commons License.

13.5   Image courtesy of Justin Walsh.

13.6   Photo courtesy of Justin Walsh.

13.7   Image courtesy of the author.

13.8   © Yamaha Pro Audio.

13.9   © Avid.

13.10 Image courtesy of Wikipedia as part of Creative Commons License.

13.11 Photo courtesy of Jason Adams.

13.12 Photo courtesy of Jason Adams.

13.13 Image courtesy of the author.

13.14 Image courtesy of Wikipedia as part of Creative Commons License.

13.15 Image courtesy of Wikipedia as part of Creative Commons License.

13.16 © Clear-Com Communication Systems.

13.17 © Clear-Com Communication Systems.

13.18 Photos courtesy of Sound Associates, Inc.

CHAPTER 14

Chapter Opening Photograph courtesy of John Carver Photography.

14.1   Image courtesy of Campbell Baird.

14.2   Image courtesy of Campbell Baird.

14.3   © Carol Rosegg.

14.4   © Carol Rosegg.

14.5   Image courtesy of the author.

14.6   Image courtesy of the author.

14.7   Image courtesy of the author.

14.8   Image courtesy of the author.

14.9   Image courtesy of the author.

14.10 Image courtesy of the author.

14.11 Image courtesy of the author.

14.12 Image courtesy of the author.

14.13 Image courtesy of the author.

14.14 Image courtesy of the author.

14.15 Image courtesy of the author.

14.16 Image courtesy of the author.

14.17 Image courtesy of the author.

14.18 Image courtesy of the author.

14.19 Image courtesy of the author.

14.20 Image courtesy of the author.

14.21 Image courtesy of Wikipedia as part of Creative Commons License.

14.22 Image courtesy of Wikipedia as part of Creative Commons License.

14.23 Image courtesy of Campbell Baird.

14.24 Image courtesy of Campbell Baird.

14.25 Image courtesy of the author.

14.26 Image courtesy of the author.

14.27 Image courtesy of the author.

14.28 Image courtesy of the author.

14.29 Image courtesy of the author.

14.30 Photo courtesy of Richard Finkelstein.

14.31 Image courtesy of the author.

14.32 Image courtesy of the author.

14.33 Image courtesy of the author.

14.34 Image courtesy of the author.

14.35 Image courtesy of the author.

14.36 Image courtesy of the author.

14.37 Image courtesy of the author.

14.38 Image courtesy of the author.

14.39 Image courtesy of the author.

14.40 Image courtesy of the author.

14.41 Image courtesy of the author.

14.42 Image courtesy of the author.

14.43 Image courtesy of the author.

14.44 Image courtesy of the author.

14.45 Photo courtesy of Richard Finkelstein.

14.46 Photo courtesy of Ella Bromblin.

14.47 Photo courtesy of Richard Finkelstein.

14.48 Photo courtesy of Ella Bromblin.

14.49 © Patternmaker Software.

14.50 © Patternmaker Software.

CHAPTER 15

Chapter Opening Photograph courtesy of John Carver Photography.

15.1 Photos courtesy of Denise Wallace-Spriggs.

15.2 Photos courtesy of Denise Wallace-Spriggs.

15.3 Photo courtesy of Sandra Leko of Hats by Leko.

15.4 Photos courtesy of Denise Wallace-Spriggs.

15.5 Photo courtesy of Denise Wallace-Spriggs.

15.6 Photo courtesy of Denise Wallace-Spriggs.

15.7 Photo courtesy of Denise Wallace-Spriggs.

15.8 Photos courtesy of Denise Wallace-Spriggs.

15.9 Photos courtesy of Denise Wallace-Spriggs.

15.10 Photos courtesy of Denise Wallace-Spriggs.

15.11 Photo courtesy of Denise Wallace-Spriggs.

15.12 Photo courtesy of Denise Wallace-Spriggs.

15.13 Photos courtesy of Denise Wallace-Spriggs.

15.14 Photo courtesy of Denise Wallace-Spriggs.

15.15 Photos courtesy of Denise Wallace-Spriggs.

15.16 Photos courtesy of Denise Wallace-Spriggs.

15.17 Photo courtesy of Denise Wallace-Spriggs.

15.18 Photo courtesy of Denise Wallace-Spriggs.

15.19 Photos courtesy of Denise Wallace-Spriggs.

15.20 Photos courtesy of Denise Wallace-Spriggs.

15.21 Photo courtesy of Denise Wallace-Spriggs.

15.22 Photo courtesy of Denise Wallace-Spriggs.

15.23 Photo courtesy of Denise Wallace-Spriggs.

15.24 Photo courtesy of Denise Wallace-Spriggs.

15.25 Photo courtesy of Denise Wallace-Spriggs.

15.26 Photos courtesy of Denise Wallace-Spriggs.

15.27 Photo courtesy of Denise Wallace-Spriggs.

15.28 Photos courtesy of Denise Wallace-Spriggs.

15.29 Photos courtesy of Denise Wallace-Spriggs.

15.30 Photo courtesy of Denise Wallace-Spriggs.

15.31 Photos courtesy of Denise Wallace-Spriggs.

15.32 Photos courtesy of Denise Wallace-Spriggs.

15.33 Photos courtesy of Denise Wallace-Spriggs.

15.34 Photo courtesy of Denise Wallace-Spriggs.

15.35 Photos courtesy of Denise Wallace-Spriggs.

15.36 Photos courtesy of Denise Wallace-Spriggs.

15.37 Photos courtesy of Denise Wallace-Spriggs.

15.38 Photo courtesy of Denise Wallace-Spriggs.

15.39 Photos courtesy of Denise Wallace-Spriggs.

15.40 Photos courtesy of Denise Wallace-Spriggs.

CHAPTER 16

Chapter Opening Photograph courtesy of Natalie Taveras.

16.1 Photo courtesy of Richard Finkelstein.

16.2 Image courtesy of Wikipedia as part of Creative Commons License.

16.3 © Ben Nye Company, Inc.

16.4 © Ben Nye Company, Inc.

16.5 © Ben Nye Company, Inc.

16.6 © Ben Nye Company, Inc.

16.7 © Ben Nye Company, Inc.

16.8 © Ben Nye Company, Inc.

16.9 © Ben Nye Company, Inc.

16.10 © Ben Nye Company, Inc.

16.11 © Ben Nye Company, Inc.

16.12 © Ben Nye Company, Inc.

16.13 © Ben Nye Company, Inc.

16.14 © Ben Nye Company, Inc.

16.15 © Ben Nye Company, Inc.

16.17 © Ben Nye Company, Inc.

16.18 © Ben Nye Company, Inc.

16.19 © Ben Nye Company, Inc.

16.20 © Ben Nye Company, Inc.

16.21 © Ben Nye Company, Inc.

16.22 © Ben Nye Company, Inc.

16.23 © Ben Nye Company, Inc.

16.24 © Ben Nye Company, Inc.

16.25 © Ben Nye Company, Inc.

16.26 Image courtesy of Linda Mensching.

16.27 © Ben Nye Company, Inc.

16.28 © Ben Nye Company, Inc.

16.29 Photos courtesy of Paul Hadobas.

CHAPTER 17

Chapter Opening Photograph courtesy of John Carver Photography.

17.1 Image courtesy of Wikipedia as part of Creative Commons License.

17.2 © GAM Products, Inc.

17.3 Image courtesy of the author.

17.4 © Beth Bergman.

17.5 Image courtesy of the author.

17.6 Image courtesy of Wikipedia as part of Creative Commons License.

17.7 Image courtesy of Geoff Dunbar.

17.8 Image courtesy of Production Resource Group.

17.9 Image courtesy of Production Resource Group.

17.10 Image courtesy of Production Resource Group.

17.11 Photograph by Richard Finkelstein.

17.12 Images courtesy of FragmentNine.

17.13 Image courtesy of FragmentNine.

17.14 Image courtesy of FragmentNine.

17.15 Image courtesy of FragmentNine.

17.16 Image courtesy of FragmentNine.

17.17 Image courtesy of FragmentNine.

17.18 Image courtesy of FragmentNine.

17.19 Image courtesy of FragmentNine.

17.20 Image courtesy of FragmentNine.

17.21 Image courtesy of FragmentNine.

17.22 Image courtesy of FragmentNine.

17.23 Image courtesy of FragmentNine.

17.24 Image courtesy of FragmentNine.

17.25 Image courtesy of FragmentNine.

17.26 Image courtesy of FragmentNine.

CHAPTER 18

Chapter Opening Photograph courtesy of John Carver Photography.

18.1 © John Carver.

18.2 Image courtesy of FragmentNine.

18.3 © Beth Bergman.

18.4 Image courtesy of Wikipedia as part of Creative Commons License.

18.5 Image courtesy of Wikipedia as part of Creative Commons License.

18.6 Image courtesy of Wikipedia as part of Creative Commons License.

18.7 Image courtesy of Wikipedia as part of Creative Commons License.

18.8 Photo courtesy of Richard Finkelstein.

18.9 © Little Blizzard.

18.10 © Beth Bergman.

18.11 © Rosco.

18.12 Image courtesy of the author.

18.13 © Rosco.

18.14 Image courtesy of the author.

18.15 Image courtesy of the author.

18.16 Photo courtesy of Jason Adams.

CHAPTER 19

Chapter Opening Photograph courtesy of John Carver Photography.

19.1 Image courtesy of the author.

19.2 Image courtesy of the author.

19.3 Image courtesy of the author.

19.4 Image courtesy of the author.

19.5 Image courtesy of the author.

19.6 Image courtesy of the author.

19.7   Image courtesy of the author.

19.8   Image courtesy of the author.

19.9   Image courtesy of the author.

19.10   Image courtesy of the author.

19.11   © OSHA.

19.12   Image courtesy of the author.

19.13   Image courtesy of the author.

19.14   Image courtesy of the author.

19.15   Image courtesy of the author.

19.16   Image courtesy of the author.

19.17   © NuDelta.

19.18   Image courtesy of Andrea Newman-Winston.

19.19   © Global Design Systems.

CHAPTER 20

Chapter Opening Photograph courtesy of the author.

20.1   Photo courtesy of FragmentNine.

20.2   Image courtesy of FragmentNine.

20.3   Image courtesy of FragmentNine.

20.4   Photo courtesy of FragmentNine.

CHAPTER 21

Chapter Opening Photograph courtesy of the author.

Page numbers in italics refer to figures.
Page number in bold refers to table.

3D models 101, 194
3D texturing 255, *255*
12″ × 12″ truss 281
18″ × 12″ truss 281–282
20.5″ × 20.5″ truss 282
35-mm film 444
42nd Street tour (2016) *49*, *178*, *299*, *319–323*
55-gallon dry ice fogger *487*

A

absurd, theatre of 23
accessories 408–409, *410–411*, 411; lighting 316–317, *317*;
    sewing 367, *370*
accessory (ditty) bags 360, *364*, 551
accessory holder (lighting fixtures) 303
accessory slots (lighting) 316, 545
accident reports 504; definition of 545; OSHA sample *505*
accidents, managing 504–505
Ace Gallery 540
acetate 353, 545
acoustics 333; definition of 545; Greek theatre 5–6
acrylic paints 82
Action Occupation (Streb) 539–540
Actor's Equity Association (AEA) 496
actual size (lumber) 173, 545
Adams, Jason 275, 277, 289
Adams, Scott 255
additive color mixing 61, 545
adhesives 183–184, *184*; definition of 545; hair 433
adjustable triangles 86
adjustable wrenches (crescent wrenches) 163, *163*, 545
Adobe: Illustrator® 93; Photoshop® 92–93, 488
AEG 300
Aereographer 490
Aeschylus 4
age, and character analysis 421
ageing makeup 432
agers 393, 545
Ain't Misbehavin (Long Wharf Theatre), computer-generated
    drawings (Beatty) of 90–*91*

air conditioner foam 405
air pockets in garments 392–393
air-purifying respirators 134
alcohol-based markers 82
Aldredge, Theoni, *Tote Stadt* (New York City Opera, 1971) *481*
alginate casting 394–395, 545
Ali, Saheem, *Henry V* (Shakespeare) *294*
Allen keys 164, *164*, 545
allergies 137–138, 139–140
alley *see* traverse stage
Allison, George, sketch for *The Rape of Lucretia 100*
All that Jazz 541
alternative current (AC) 299, 545
Alt-J tour: Anthem, The (2022) *480*; Glastonbury Festival *250*;
    Glastonbury Festival previsualization *469–470*; London O2
    Arena *472*; production photo *522*; rough concept sketch
    519; Summer Festival 2017 *453–465*; Summer Festival
    2017 complete drafting pack *524–527*; Summer Festival
    2017 Gear List *520*, *521*; video system schematic *475*
Altman Lighting, 20-degree Shakespeare® 304
Altman Spectra: AltSpot follow spot *311*; cyc (LED) *310*;
    PAR (LED) *309*
ambient noise 333, 334, 545
Amelia Danehy, *PACK* (2022) *372*
American wire gauge (AWG) 302, 546
amp (ampere; A) 300, 545
amphitheaters (Greek) 4, *5*
amplification 333, 334; *see also* gain (sound systems)
amplifiers 330, 545
analog mixing consoles 336, *336*
analog multiplex (AMX) 314, 545
analogous colors *62*, *63*, 545
Ancient Voice of Children, lighting sketch *76*
angle brushes 423, 545
angled stage (rake) 6, *6*, 565
Animal Farm (Orwell/Hall) *372*
animators 452, 468
Apple Office 89
appliqués 356
apron 18–19, 545
aqua face paints 429, *429*
arbors 278, 545

Arcadia (Stoppard) 224, *224*

arc dimensions 104, 545

arches 546; building 205, *210–211*; types of 205

archetypes: definition of 546; and theatre of the absurd 23

architecture: orders of *36*, 37; styles of 35, 37

arc welding 170, 546

area mic'ing 333, 546

Arecchi, Kate, *Head over Heels* (2021) *373*

arena rigging 281, 535

arena/stadium tours 518

arena stage 20–21; definition of 546; layout of *20*

Aristophanes 4

Aristotle 63

armor 397, *415*; examples of *398–399*; leather buckle tabs *414*; making 400–402, *400*, *402*; materials 397, 400, 401; mock-up 397–398, *398*; pattern *397*; riveted *414*; surface finishes 403, *403*; types of 400; vacuum-formed 397, *397*, *398*; working with thermoplastics 401, *401*

Arnold, Janet 538

arrays, speaker 338, *339*, 559

Arsenic and Old Lace: hand drafting (Baird) *106*; set props (Baird) *227*

articulated ladders 135

assembly tools (hand tools): Allen keys 164, *164*, 545; chisels 166, *166*, 548; clamps 165, *165*; files 166, *166*, 553; hammers 161–162, *161*; nut drivers 163, *164*, 561; planes 166, *166*, 563; pliers 164–165, *165*; pry bars 162–163, *162*, 564; rasps 166, *166*, 565; screwdrivers 164, *164*; socket sets/wrenches 163, *164*, 568; staplers 162, *162*, 569; Torx® screws 164, 570; vise grips 571; vises 166; wrenches 163, *163*

assembly tools (pneumatic tools): compressors 169, *169*; grinders *169*; nailers 169–170, *169*; staplers 170

assembly tools (powered hand tools): drill bits 168, *168*; drill presses 167, 552; drills 166–167, *167*, 552; hammer drills 167, *167*, 556; hot-glue guns 168, *168*, 557; screw bits 168

assembly tools (welding tools): arc welding 170, 546; brazing 171–172, 547; gas tanks, gauges, and hoses *170*; MIG welding 170, 560; soldering 171–172, 568; TIG welding 170, 570

assistant prop manager 228

assisted-hearing devices 342–343, *343*

atmosphere-supplying respirators 134

audience 6; arena stage 20; and composition 46; and design 34, 42; expectations of 34, 522; and fire curtains 141, *141*; and fourth wall 18, 20, 191–192, 555; Kabuki 15–16; participation, in Roman theatre 6; proscenium theatre 17, 18, 19; sight line (line of sight) 6, 19; thrust stage 19–20; traverse stage 21; viewing, and Globe Theater 13

audio snakes 340, *341*, 568

audition(s): forms 497, *498*, 546; role of stage managers in 497

auditorium 19, 546

auger bits *168*

authority having jurisdiction (AHJ) 249

AutoCAD® 89, 92

Autodesk: AutoCAD® 89, 92; Maya® 93; SoftImage® 93

automated external defibrillator (AED) 496

automated/moving lights 308, *312*, *313*, *323*

automation department (scene shop) 198–199

autotransformer dimmers 313, 546

AutoYoke® 308, *313*, 546

Avalon, Zarah *394*

Avid, S6L digital console *337*

Avolites: Pearl 2010 moving light controller *315*; Sapphire Touch moving light controller *315*

B

baby dolls 358, 575

backdrops 6, 20, 190, 242–243, *244–245*, 248, 546; *see also* cycloramas; cycs

back-flap hinges 184–185

backup server 467

back walls 190

Bacon, Francis 12

bags (prop) 409

Baines, Leah, *PACK* (2022) *372*

Baird, Campbell 519, *520–521*; *Arsenic and Old Lace* hand drafting *106*; *Arsenic and Old Lace* set props *227*; *Crazy For You* car *229*; *Glass Menagerie, The 230–231*, 231; *Gypsy* costume sketches *350*; *Hello, Dolly!* (Muhlenberg Summer Music Festival) *174*; *Hello, Dolly!* candy box *232*

balance 546; and composition 51–52, 53; occult 53; symmetrical 53

ballast 297, 546

ballet shoes 390

ball peen hammers *161*, 162, 546

bamboo sticks 247, *248*, 546

banana plugs 340, *340*, 546

band saws *159*, 160, 546

bar clamps 165, *165*, 546

Bardavon 1869 Opera House: backstage *268*; hemp house 275, 277; rigger and chain hoist box *281*; safety issues 289; side boxes *18*; speaker array *339*; super title projections *489*

barn doors (lighting) 316, *317*, 546

barrier creams *394*, 547

base color, paint 253

base paint 547

baskets (span sets and shackles) 287–288

Bass, Steve, *People's Choice Awards* (2017) *473–474*

batting *see* body modification padding

beaded necklace *410*, 411

bead foam 179, *180*

beads 356

beam angle 304, *547*

Beam Bender® 316, *317*

beam projectors 304, *304*, 547

beam spread (field angle) 304, 547

Beatty, John Lee: backing wall drafting for *The Odd Couple* 192; computer-generated drawings for *Ain't Misbehavin* 90–91; deck plan for *The Odd Couple* 118–119; floor layout drafting for *The Odd Couple* 198; full-scale details for *The Odd Couple* 122–123; hand draftings for *The Odd Couple* 102–103; kitchen walls draftings for *The Odd Couple* 193; stair and railing details drawing for *The Odd Couple* 202; wall arches drafting for *The Odd Couple* 210; wall details for *The Odd Couple* 120–121

Becher-McKeever, Emily: *Head over Heels* (2021) *373*; *Sweet Charity* (2015) *199*

Beck, Dennis, *Everybody* (Jacobs-Jenkins, 2019) *275*

Beckett, Samuel 18

before & after plot 423

belaying 272, *273*, 276, 547

belt sander *168*

Benjamin Moore 251

Ben Nye 420, 437; brushes *423*, *425*; cheek colors *426*; clown colors *430*; combs and other tools *425*; concealer and neutralizer crayons *425*; creme colors *429*; creme foundations *425*; effects wheels *430*; eyebrow pencils and mascara *428*; eyeliners *427*, *428*; eye shadows *427*; face powders *427*; Fresh Scab 431; Grime FX 431; lipsticks and lip pencils *428*; liquid aqua face paints *429*; liquid hair color and tooth colors *432*; nose and scar wax *433*; removers and cleansers *433*; stage blood *432*; and sustainability 430

Berkshire Opera, *The Rape of Lucretia* sketch (Allison) *100*

Bermudez, Fernando (interview) 539

bevel gauges 151, 547

Bible 8

Billington, Ken 318, 519; *42nd Street* tour (2016) *49*, *178*, *299*, *319–323*; studio with drafting table *85*

binders, paint 250, 251, 252

bit depths 333

Bjornson, Maria, *Les Troyens* (Metropolitan Opera) *177*

black: and grayscale 64, *65*, 66; subtractive color mixing 59, 569

black box theaters 21, 547

black comedy 22

block and fall 277, 547

blocking 502, 505, 507; definition of 547; notations *506*, 507

blocking (hat) 381–382, *381*, 383–384, *383*

blood, stage 430–432, *432*, 487–488, 569

blue foam 179, *180*

Blue Man Group, The© 307

Bluetooth 332

BNC connectors 340, *340*, 547

body modification padding 404; mounted on wicking undergarments *404*; with outer garment *405*; polyester batting *407*; pregnancy pads *406–407*; reticulated *vs.* polyurethane foams 405–406, *406–407*; smoothing layers and coverings *407*; stitching *405*; on T-shirt base 408, *408*, *409*; weighted stuffing pouch *406*

Bolenbaugh, James *295*

bolts and screws 181, *182*

bonnet *389*

booms (lighting) 293, 317, 547

borders: drafting 107–108; wing and drop scenery 190, 547

Boritt, Beowulf, *42nd Street* tour (2016) *49*, *178*, *299*

Boston Museum of Fine Arts 539

bowlines 269–270, *271*, 547

box cutter *154*

box office managers 533

box sets 191, 547

box wrenches 163, *163*, 547

Boyd, Elise, *Medea* (2003) *484*

Brahic, Anne, CMT Music Awards (2017) *474*

braids/switches 431

Brandt, Grace 242, 256, 539

brazing 171–172, 547

"break a leg" expression 53, 573

breakdown artists 392–393, 547

breaking the fourth wall 18

breastplates (chest plates) 397, *398–399*, *403*

Bright Room Called Day, A (Kushner) 223–224, *224*

brim block *381*

broad butt hinges 185

Broadway (New York) 21, 541

Broadway flats (soft flats) 202, 204–205, *205*

Brokaw, Mark 225

Brooks, Avery *351*, *352*

brown butcher paper (kraft paper) 243, 558

Brunk, Jenner, *Medea* (2003) *484*

brushes: brush cleaners 252; caring for 252; chip 247, 548; drafting 83; floggers 554; foam 247, 554; graining 247, 556; lay-in 247, 558; lining (fitch) 247, 554, 559; pads 247; parts of 246, *246*; storage *247*; *see also* makeup brushes

brush markers 82

BTS, Citi Field (2018) *473*

buckle tabs, leather *414*

buckram (hat fabric) 383–384, *384*, 387, *388–389*

building techniques: ceilings 205; doors, arches, and windows 205, *207*, *210–211*; floors and stairs *198*, 200, *201*, 202, *202*; walls 202, *203*, 204, *204*, 205, *205*, *208–209*

Bunraku 13–14, *13*

buntal 384

burlap *178*, 395, 548

burping the bath 393, 548

Burton, Kate *385*

bus and truck tours 518, 520, 548

buttons *356*

C

cables (sound systems): audio snakes 340, *341*, 568; coaxial 340, *341*, 549; multi-pair 340, *341*, 561; shielded multi-pair 340, *341*, 567; twisted-pair 340, 571

calligraphy pens 81

calling scripts 509–510, 512, *518*, 548

call times 510, 513, 548

Camelot, watercolor rendering (Smith) *38*

candles 293, *294*, 314

Cantonese puppets 17

canvas blocks *381*, 382

cape net 384

caps *393*

carbide blades 155

carbon monoxide detectors 139

cardboard, armor mock-up with *398*

career choices 531–532; box office manager 533; company manager 533; director 533–534; house manager 534; interviews 536–541; makeup artist 534; non-theatre careers 535–536; and passion 531; pre-production 532; producer 534; production 532–533; production manager 534; rigger 535; scenic artist 535; technical director 535; theatre careers 532–535; wardrobe supervisor 535; *see also* interviews

Caroline Christie, *PACK* (2022) *372*

carpenter (carriage) clamps 165, *165*, 548

carpenter pencils 150, 548

carpentry shop 198

carpet knife *154*

carriage (carpenter) clamps 165, *165*, 548

Carrington, Sarah, *PACK* (2022) *372*

Carson, Heather (interview) 539–540

cartooning 242–243, 548

casing the leather 412, 548

casters 185–186, *186*; revolving stage 191; rolling platforms 191

casting (face) 394–395, 548; alginate 394–395, 545; plaster 394, *394–395*, 395, *396*; protective plastic layer *394*; types of 395

casting, male casting of female roles 8, 9, 11

cats, and good/bad luck 331, 575

Cat's Paw 389

catwalk *see* traverse stage

Caucasian Chalk Circle, The (Brecht) *373*

ceilings 205

cements 183–184, *184*

censorship in Middle Ages 9

center lines 109, 112, 318, 548

center punches 162, *162*, 548

Chagall, Marc 53, 61

chain hoist *281*, *282*, 289, 548

chain mail 400, 548

chalk, tailor's 357, *357*, 570

chalk lines 153, *153*, 548

character analysis: age 421; environment 421; evolution 422; heredity 421; temperament 421–422

character makeup 421

character powder 431

charcoal 80, 242

charcoal powder 431

Chase, Ronald, *Tote Stadt* (New York City Opera, 1971) *481*

cheat (magic) sheets 318, *322–323*, 560

cheek colors 426, *426*, 434

Chesterton, Gilbert K. 67

Chestnut Street Theater (Philadelphia) 293

chest plates *see* breastplates (chest plates)

Chicago screws 413, 548

chicken net 384

chicken wire 177

Chikamatsu, Monzaemon 13

China silk *178*

Chinese theatre 17

chip brushes 247, 548

chisels 166, *166*, 548

chop saws (compound miters) *159*, 160, 549

chorus 4, 333

Chrismas, Doug 540

chroma (saturation) 62, 549, 566

chrome tanning 411, 549

Churchill, Winston 61

church keys 467, 575

Cinema 4D® 93, *474*

circuit panel *314*

circular saws 157–158, *157*, *167*, 549

City Theatrical 316; AutoYoke® 308, *313*, 546; Beam Bender® 316, *317*; EFX Plus *317*; Image Multiplexer® 316, *317*; VSFX3 effects projector *316*

clamps: bar 165, *165*, 546; carpenter (carriage) 165, *165*, 548; hand-screw 165, *165*, 556; pipe 304, 562; spring (squeeze) 165, *165*, 568

Clarke, Michael 467

classical orders of columns *36*, 37

classicism (architecture) 35, 549

Claude, Georges 297

claw hammers 161, *161*, 549

cleaning tools 172, 252

cleansers 433, *433*, 549

Clear-Com wireless communication system 342, *342*

clip-in extensions 431

clothing, and safety 130, 131, *131*

clove hitches 271–273, *272*, 277, 549

clown white 429, *430*

clusters (speakers) 338, 549

CMT Music Awards (Brahic, 2017) *474*

coaxial cables 340, *341*, 549

cobalt steel blades 155

cobblers 390, 549

codecs (video) 467

coiling, rope 272, 549

collaboration 549; and design 31, 32, 37; production team, and design 28–29

Colonial Williamsburg 539

colored ribbons (symbol) *34*

color pencils 80, *80*

colors 57; additive mixing 61, 545; analogous *62*, 63, 545; black and white 64, *65*, 66; blood color 487, 488; Chinese shadow puppetry 17; complementary 61, *61*, 549; importance of 57–58, *58*; intensity 62, 571; meanings of 64; monochromatic composition 62–63, 560; pastel 61; perception of 64; pigment and light 58–61, *59–61*; primary 59, *59*, *60*, 61, 62, 564; reference white 66–68, *66–67*, 565; saturation (chroma) 62, 549, 566; secondary 59, *59*, *60*, 61, 566; subtractive mixing 59, 61, 569; tertiary 59, 570; tints, shades, and tones 61–63, 64; *Turtle, The* (Fink) *69*; value 62, 571; warm and cool 63–64, *63*; white balance 64, *65*, 66, 572

color wheel 58–59; for light 59, *60*, 61; for pigment 59, *59*, *60*

Colosseum 7, *7*

columns, classical orders of *36*, 37

combination squares 151, *151*, 549

comedy 22

commando cloth 179

commedia dell'arte 7–8, 10–11, 22; basic stories/topics 10; masks 11; Pierrot character *11*; stock characters 7, 11; troupe *10*, 11

community theaters 21

company contact sheets 497–498, *499–500*

company managers 533

compasses 151–152, *152*

complementary colors 61, *61*, 549

complimentary tickets (comps) xvii, 573

composite order *36*, 37, 549

composition 45; balance and proportion 51–52, 53, 546, 567; contrast 550, 559; definition of 45–46; lines and direction 49–50, *50*, 551; line weights 51, *51*, 550, 559; patterns 52, *53*, 562; rule of thirds 46–48, *46–49*, 566; scale 53, 566; shapes 50, *50*, 567; texture 50–51, *50–51*

compound miters (chop saws) *159*, 160, 542

compression sprayers 248

compressors (pneumatic tools) 169, *169*

computer-aided drawing and drafting (CAD) software 73, 89, 92, 104, 109, 160, 198, 548

computerized mixing 336

computer numerical control (CNC) routers 160, 198

computers, and drawing/drafting 89; *Ain't Misbehavin* (Beatty) 90–*91*; hardware 89; rendering 100; software 89, 92–93

concealers 425–426, *425*, 434, 549

concept, and design 32, *519*, 521, 549

condenser microphones 331, 549

conduit cutters *156*

Conery, Kathleen, *Midsummer Night's Dream* (James Madison University) *367*

cones (hat body) 384–385, *385*

confetti 488

confetti blowers 488

confetti canons 488

conformateur *381*

Conklin, John: *Ghosts of Versailles* (Metropolitan Opera, 1991) *486*; *Pelléas et Mélisande* (Metropolitan Opera) *175*

connectors (sound systems): banana plugs 340, *340*, 546; BNC 340, *340*, 547; TNC 340, *340*, 570; XLR 340, *340*, 572

Connick, Harry, Jr. 129

construction drawings 194, *194–195*, 196, 550

contact adhesives 183–184

contact pickups 330, 331, 332, 550

contact sheets 550; company 497–498, *499–500*; production 497, *499*

content creators 452, 468, 550

content/media manager 452, 467

continuous education 537

contour brushes 424

contour shader 424

contrast in line weights 51, *51*, 550

conventional lighting 293, 550

conversion table from US linear measurement to metric system *84*

Cooke, Henry, IV 538

cookie *see* gobos (templates)

cool colors 63–64, *63*

coping saws 155, *155*, 550

Corazzola, Alexandre, *The Crucible* production (2005) *39*

Corel, Painter® 93

Corinthian order *36*, 37, 550

Coriolanus (Shakespeare Theatre Company): Gaskill, William (1991) 39, *40*; Kahn, Michael (2000) 39, *40*

corner blocks 204, 550

Corn in Green, The (Huntington Theatre Company) *384*

correction fluids/tapes 83

corridor stage *see* traverse stage

Corriston, Ryan, *PACK* (2022) *372*

Corsaro, Frank, *Tote Stadt* (New York City Opera, 1971) *481*

costume breakdown 508, *508*, 550

costume crafts 379–380; accessories/jewelry 408–409, *410–411*, 411; body modification padding 404–*405*, 404–408, *406*, *407*, *408*, *409*; crafts person/dyer 379; dyeing and fabric modification 392–393, *392–393*; leather work 411–413, *412*, *413–415*; mask making 393–396, *394–395*, *396*; millinery 380–387, *380*, *381–384*, *385*, *386*, *387*, *388–389*; shoes 389–390, *389–390*, *391*; stage armor 397–403, *397*, *398–399*, *400*, *401*, *402*, *403*

costume props 550

costumes 349; and accessories 408–409, 411; affordability issue 349; and balance 53; colors and lighting 364; cutters and drapers 360, 550, 552; ditty (accessory) bags 360, *364*, 551; fabrics 351–353; fantasy 371; Kabuki *15*; measurements 358, *359*, 360, *361–364*; re-enacting 537–539; renting 367, 371; sewing 364–367, 371; shop walls 349, *349*; sketches 349, *349*; software 92, 93, 374–375; wardrobe supervisors 535; *see also* fabrics (costumes); measurements (costume-making); sewing

costume shop tools and accessories: appliqués 356; beads 356; buttons 356, *356*; lace 356; measuring tapes 354, *354*, 560; Mr. Puffy 357, *358*, 560; notions 356; patterning templates 355, *355*, 562; patterns 354, 360; pins and pincushions 355, *355*; scissors 355–356, *355*; seam rippers 357, *357*, 566; slopers 354–355, *355*, 567; storage *356*; tailor's chalk 357, *357*, 570; threads 356, *356*; zippers 356

cotton 351, 550

counterweight 275, *276*, 550

Counts, Michael 537

Covent Garden Theater (London) 21, *295*

coverings 407

Coward, Noel 20, 536

crayons 80

Crazy For You: car (Baird) *229*; vacuum cleaner 223, *223*

creative directors 452, 550

creme (wet) brushes 423

creme cheek colors 426

creme colors 429, *429*

creme foundations 425

creme shades 429

crescent wrenches (adjustable wrenches) 163, *163*, 545

crimping tool 278

crinoline (tarlatan) 384

Cross, Dustin, *Hello, Dolly!* (Muhlenberg Summer Music Festival) *174*

cross and crown (symbol) *35*

crosscut blades 154, *154*, 505

crown block *381*

Crucible, The, NYU Department of Graduate Acting/Department of Design for Stage and Film production (2005) *39*

cue lights 511, *511*, 550

Cunningham, Michael, *Animal Farm* (Orwell/Hall) *372*

Cunningham, Peter, *Romeo et Juliette* (Metropolitan Opera, 2005) *253*

Curtain (theater) 12

curtain calls 510, 550

curtains: backdrops 6, 20, 242–243, *244–245*, 248, 546; cycloramas 20, 551; cycs 20, 550, 551; drafting 107; evil 191, 574; fire 141, *141*, 554; grand borders 18, 556; house 18, *19*, 557; tab 192, 569; traveler tracks 190, 570

curved box truss *282*

curves, French 87, *87*, 555

cut and sewn hats 387, *387*

cutters (people) 360, 550

cutters (tools): conduit *156*; pipe 156, *156*, 562; PVC *156*; tube 156

cutting/shaping tools (hand tools) 153–154; metal-cutting saws 156, *156*; pocketknives 150, 154, *154*; powered hand tools 156–158, *157*; powered stationary tools 158–160, *158*, *159*; scissors 154, *154*; shears 154; utility (mat) knives 154, *154*, 571; wood-cutting saws 154–155, *154*, *155*

cutting/shaping tools (powered hand tools) 156–158; circular saws 157–158, *157*, *167*, 549; grinders 158, *167*, 556; jigsaws (saber saws) 157, *157*, 558; reciprocating saws 157, *167*, 565; routers *157*, 158, *167*, 566; spiral saws *157*

cutting/shaping tools (powered stationary tools): band saws *159*, 160, 546; CNC routers 160; compound miters (chop saws) *159*, 160, 549; drill presses *159*, 167, 552; oxyacetylene (gas) welding 160, 561; panel saws *158*, 160, 562; radial-arm saws 159, *159*, 564; scroll saws *158*, 160, 566; table saws 158–159, *158*, 569

cycle plays 9

cycloramas 20, 551

cycs 20, 550; far 306; lights 308, *310*

D

daily rehearsal reports 503–504, *503*, 551
Da Vinci, Leonardo: drawings of 51, 75; self-portrait of *50*; *Vitruvian Man* 52, *52*, 78
Davy, Humphrey 487, 575
dead-blow hammers *161*, 162
dead lift 278, 551
Dearborn, Karen, *Hello, Dolly!* (Muhlenberg Summer Music Festival) *174*
decks: building 202; definition of 551; plans 113, *118–119*, 551; show 113, 567
deconstructivism (architecture) 37, 551
Degas, Edgar 51
Delany, Colleen *352*
delays (sound) 330, 336
deluge systems 142, *142*, 551
depth of shade 392, 551
design 27; and audience 34, 42; and concept 32; drawing, rendering, and drafting 39–42; first reading of script 30–31; meetings 37; meeting with director 31–32; morgues (collections of images/sounds) 39, 560; orders of architecture *36*, 37; process 29–30; production styles 31–32; production team collaboration 28–29, 31, 32, 37; production team flow chart *28*; rehearsals 37; research 33–35, 37; script breakdown 32–33; script page with designer notes *30*; sketching 37; styles of architecture 35, 37; symbols 34; *see also* composition; drawing, rendering, and drafting; makeup; scenic design process
designer drawings 192, *192–193*, 194, 551
design plot (makeup design) 422–423
detail brushes 424, 551
detail drawings 113, 551; Beatty's full-scale details for *The Odd Couple 122–123*; Beatty's wall details for *The Odd Couple 120–121*; *Julius Caesar 324–325*
detail sander *168*
deus ex machina 190, 551
digital audio 340
digital mixing consoles 336, *337*
digital multiplex (DMX) 314, 316, 450, 484, 511, 551
digital projection 451, 490, 551
digital signal processor (DSP) 333
dimensional lumber 172–173, *173*
dimensions/dimensioning *105*, 113; arc 104, 545; linear 104, 559; multiple 104, 561
dimmers 313–314, *314*, 551
dinner theatre 21–22
Dior net (Paris net) 384
Dircks, Henry 447
direct current (DC) 299, 551

direction (composition) 49–50, *50*, 551
directors: creative directors 550; job description 533–534; meeting of designers with 31–32
"Disaster March" ("Stars and Stripes Forever") 145, 574
distressing 255, 551; fabric *393*; shoes 390, *391*
ditty (accessory) bags 360, *364*, 551
Dr. Faust (Metropolitan Opera, 2001) *446*
docudrama 22
dome brushes 423, *423*, 551
domestic tours 518–519, 520
Dominguez, Jorge, 3D renderings of sets (*Premios Juventud*, 2016) *471*
donut (lighting) 316, 551
doors, building 205
Doric order *36*, 37, 552
double-acting hinges 185
double purchase 279, *280*, 552
downstage 6, *6*, 552
drafting 101; Beatty's hand draftings for *The Odd Couple 102–103*; borders 107–108; conventions 104–105; curtains 107; definition of 75, 552; detail drawings 113, *120–123*, 551; dimensioning 104, 113; elevation 113, 553; flats 105; flooring 113, *118–119*; floors 105, *106*; ground plans 109, *110–111*, 112–113; hand *79*, 83, 89, 101, *102–103*, 104, *106*, 109; key to symbols 108–109; liability disclaimer 108; light plots 109, 113, *114–115*; lines and line weights 101; notes 109, 112; orthographic projection 101, *104*, 561; scenery pack 109, *109*, 192; section drawings 113, *116–117*; sketch 109; title blocks 107, *107*, 570; tools 84–89
drafting brushes 83
drafting chairs/stools 85
drafting machines 85
drafting stools 552
drafting tables 84–85, *85*, 552
drafting tape/dots 89, 552
drafting templates 87, *87*
draperies *see* curtains
drapers 360, 552
drapery steamer 382, *382*
drawing, rendering, and drafting 39–42, 73–74; computers 89, 90–*91*, 92–93; definitions of 74–75, 552; drafting 101, *102–103*, 104–105, *106*, 107–109, *110–111*, 112–113; erasers 82–83, *82*; hand drawing/drafting tools 84–89; information 75; insight 75; paint 82; paper 83, *83*; pastels and crayons 80, *81*; pencils 79–80, *79–80*; pens and markers 81–82, *81*; perspective drawing 93–98; proportions and *Vitruvian Man* 78; rendering *98–99*, 99–101, *100*; Sal's drawing test 76–77, 78, 124, *124*; supplies and tools 78–93; *see also* drafting; perspective drawing; rendering

drawing paper 83

drawings: construction 194, *194–195*, 196, 550; designer 192, *192–193*, 194, 551; detail 113, *120–123, 324–325*, 551; section 113, *116–117*

dressing rooms 510

dress rehearsals, bad dress rehearsals and good opening 533, 575

Dress Shop® 92

drilling: drill bits 168, *168*; drill presses *159*, 167, 552; drills 166–167, *167*, 552; hammer drills 167, *167*, 556; hole saws 168, *168*, 557; hot-glue guns *168*, 557

drill presses *159*, 167, 552

drop-in slots (lighting) 316

Drowsy Chaperone, The, Hudson Scenic's production flowchart *197*

dry brushing 254, 552

dry cleaning pad (eraser) 82–83

Dryfast™ foam 405, *406*

dry ice 487, *487*, 552

drying adhesives 183

drywall (keyhole) saws 155, *155*, 558

D-Scriptive (Sound Associates) 342–343

Duco® cement *184*

dump casting 395, 552

Dunbar, Geoff 29; on research 33; *Spirit Lodge* 448, *448*

Durer, Albrecht, *Hare* 77, *77*

dust masks 134, *134*, 552

duvetyn *178*, 179

dyers 392–393, 545

dyes/dyeing: definition of 552; fabric 392–393, *392*; hair 431, *432*; leather 413

Dykes Lumber 176

dynamic host communication protocol (DHCP) 343

dynamic microphones 331, 552

E

earmuffs 133–134, 552

earplugs 133–134, *133*, 552

Ebsen, Buddy 144

Edison, Thomas Alva 295, 296–297, *296*, 299

effects processors 336

effects projector *316*

effects wheels 430, *430*

EFX Plus *317*

Egypt, passion plays in 4

electrical department (scene shop) 199

electric erasers 83

electricity: alternative current (AC) 299, 545; amps (ampere; A) 45, 300; AWG 302, 546; DC 299, 551; electrical power 300–301; ground wires 301, 556; plug types 301, *302*; single-phase power 301, 567; three-phase power 301, 570; voltage 300, 301, *301*, 571; wattage 300, 572; West Virginia formulas 301, 572; *see also* light bulbs

Electrolux canister vacuum 223, *233*

Electronic Pounce Machine 243, *243*

elevation, drafting 113, 553

ellipsoidal reflector spotlights (ERS) 305–306, *306*, 307, 316, 553

Elmer's glue *184*

emphasis, and composition 53, 553

end stage 17

engineering department (scene shop) 196, 198

England, male casting for female parts in 9

environment, and character analysis 421

environmental theatre 22, 553

epic 22

Epidaurus Theater *5*

epoxy 184, *184*

equalization/equalizers 330, 336–337, 553

Equus (James Madison University, 2017) *233*

Erace 420

erasers 82–83, *82*

erasing shields 87–88, *87*, 553

esparterie (sparto cloth/sparterie/willow) 384

ETC: ×7 LED strip light *310*; Eos® lighting consoles *315*; Sensor® installation dimmer rack *314*

ethafoam rods 179, *180*

Ethernet 314

Euripides 4

EVA foam 400, *401*

Everybody (Jacobs-Jenkins, 2019) *275*

evil curtains 191, 574

evolution, and character analysis 422

exits, and fire safety 138

exit sign (symbol) *34*

expendables (lighting) 315

expressionism (architecture) 37, 553

extension ladders 135

eyecups 132, 553

eye makeup 419; eyebrow pencils 426, *428*, 429, 434; eyeliners 426, *427*, *428*, 434; eye shadows 426, *427*, 434

eyewash stations 132–133, *133*, 553

F

fabric masks 393

fabrics (costumes): acetate 353, 545; cotton 351, 550; hand of 392, 556; hat-making 383–384; linen 352, 559; modification 392–393, *393*, 553; nylon 353, 561; period

538–539; polyesters 353, 563; preshrink 353, 564; rayon 353, 565; silk 351–352, 567; swatch books *354*; wool 351, 572

fabrics (scenic materials) 177–179; burlap *178*, 395, 548; China silk *178*; crushed velvet *178*; duvetyn *178, 179*; felt *178*; muslin *178, 179*, 204–205, 364; scrim 179; tulle *178*; velour 178

face: casting 394–395, *394–395*; shapes 422, *422*, 553

face powders 426, *427*, 434

face shields 132, *132*, 553

Fails, Gary 316

falls (hair pieces) 431

fans 482; DMX controlled fans 484; floor fans *256*

fantasy 22

fantasy costumes 371

farce 22

far cycs 306

fasteners 180–185

feather duster (schlepitchka) 258, *258–259*

felt *178*, 402

felt bodies (hat) 385, *385*

felt capelines *383*

female Kabuki 14, 15

feminist theatre 22

fence (cutting guide) 157, 553

fence pliers *165*

Ferre, Veronica, *Hedda Gabler* (2005) *300*

festivals: fringe 22; touring 518, 553

field angle (beam spread) 304, 547

fight rehearsal 513

filaments 294–296, 553

files 166, *166*, 553

final word, and bad luck 510, 575

finishers, leather work 413

Fink, Michael A. 31, 32, 534; *Sorcerer, The 62*, 63, 64; *Turtle, The 69*

Finkelstein, Richard: *Equus* (2017) *233*; *Head over Heels* (2021) *373*; *Medea* (2003) *484*; *Midsummer Night's Dream* (James Madison University) *367*; *Sweet Charity* (2015) *199*

firearms 409, 411

fire curtains 141, *141*, 553

fire extinguishers 140, *140*

fireproof 138, 554

fire retardants 138, 554

fire safety 138–142, 248–249; AHJ 249; deluge systems 142, *142*, 551; examples of panic 145; exits 138; fire curtains 141, *141*, 553; fire extinguishers 140, *140*; fireproof material 138; fire retardants 138; flameproofing products *139*; prevention measures 138; protection techniques 139–142,

142; smoke detectors/alarms 139, *139*; sprinkler systems 141–142, 142, 569; thermal barrier (Zetex®) 138, *138*, 141, 570

fire special effects: modern 485; vintage 483, *483*; *see also* special effects

first aid kits 137, *137*, 496, 504

first class tours 517–518, 554

"Fish Tank, The" 480

fitch (lining) brushes 247, 554, 559

fittings (costume) 365–367, *368–369*

fixed casters 185, *186*

fixed-pin hinges 184

flameproofing products *139*

flame retardancy: paint 249; scenery 138; Supervision of Flame Retardancy certificate 138

flat brushes 423, *423*, 554

flats 202; building hard (Hollywood) flats 206, 556; detailed construction drawings for *204*; drafting 105; hard flats 205; hybrid style 205; soft flats 202, 204–205, *205*, 568

floggers 554

floor fans *256*

floors: drafting 105, *106*, 113, *118–119*; platforms 200, *201, 202, 202*; ramps 200; stairs 200, *202*; taping the floor 502

Floretta® sprayers 248, 554

flowcharts 196; Hudson Scenic's *The Drowsy Chaperone* production flowchart *197*; production team flow chart *28*

flowers, and bad/good luck 233, 574

fluff brushes 423

fluorescent lamps 85, 297, 307–308, 554

flush cut saws 155, 554

Flying by Foy 490

flying effects 190, 490

fly lofts 274, 554

foam brushes 247, 554

foam rollers 248

foams 179, *180*

foam sponges 424, *424*, 554

focus 46, 53, 99; *see also* composition

focus (lighting) 303, 554

fog fluids 485–486

fog special effects 554; 55-gallon dry ice fogger *487*; modern 485–487; Rosco V-Hazer *486*; *see also* special effects

folding rules 150–151, *150*, 554

Foley, Jack 334

Foley door *335*

Foley table *335*

fonts: computer *88*; CAD software 104

food props (consumables) 554

footlights 294–295, 554

forehead, lavalier microphones on 333

Foreman, Richard 22, 537

foreshortening 95, *95*, 554

Forstner bits 168, *168*

Fosshape 382

foundation brushes 424, *424*, 555

foundations 425, *425*, 434, 555

fountain pens 81

fourth wall 555; and arena stage 20; and box sets 191–192; breaking the fourth wall 18; proscenium theatre 18

Foy, Peter 490

FragmentNine 521; Alt-J tour *250, 453–465, 469–470, 472, 475, 480, 519, 522, 524–527*; BTS (Citi Field, 2018) *473*; *see also* Alt-J tour

frame rate (video) 467

framing hammers 161, *161*, 555

framing squares 151, *151*, 555

Franklin, Benjamin 135

Freeman, Morgan 232

French curves 87, *87*, 555

French scene breakdown 504, *504*, 555

Fresh Scab (Nye) 431

Fresnel, Augustin-Jean 305

Fresnel lenses 305, *305*, 555

Fresnel lights 304–305, *305*, 307, *309*, 555

Fringe (London) 21

fringe festivals 22

frisket 249–250, *250*, 555

front of house (FOH) 318, *319*, 554

full sketched design plot 423

furniture props 555

futuristic armor 400

G

gain (sound systems) 332, 555

galleries 13

Gallo, David 179

GAM Products: Film/FX® 316, *317*; scene machine *445*

Garment Designer 374

Garthwaite, Anna Maria 539

Gaskill, William, *Coriolanus* (1991) 39, *40*

gaslight 295

gas (oxyacetylene) welding 160, 561

Geiger, M. L. 29

gel 315, 555

genre 4, 17, 555; *see also* theatre, history of; theatre styles

geometric shapes 50, *50*

ghost effects 447–448, *447*, 562

ghost light 296, 574

Ghosts of Versailles (Metropolitan Opera, 1991) *486*

Gideon, Joe (*All that Jazz* character) 541

Glass Menagerie, The: Baird's design *230–231*, 231; glass unicorn prop 234–235, *234–237*

glazes/glazing 251, 255, 555; *see also* painting techniques

glitter (makeup) 429

glitter glue 433

Global Design Systems SM Console *513*

Globe Theater 12–13, *12*

glover's needle 413

gloves: costume 367; latex 246; work 134–135, *135*, 137, 156, 269

glues *see* adhesives

go (cues) 512, 555

gobos (templates) 306, 308, 316, 556

goggles (safety glasses) 132, *132*, 156, 556

Goldoni, Carlo 11

Google Office 89

Google Sheets 220, *221*

gore 431

gorgets 397, 556

Gorilla® glue 183, 184, *184*

gouache 82

Graffiti U tour (Urban, 2018) *518*

Graftobian Makeup Company, F/X Powdered Blood *432*

Graham, Colin, *Ghosts of Versailles* (Metropolitan Opera, 1991) *486*

graining brushes 247, 556

grand borders 18, 556

graphic arts artisans 230

graphics software 92

Graphic Standards Board (USITT) 101

grayscale chart 64, *65*, 556

Greek orders of columns 37

Greek theatre 3, 4–6; amphitheater 4, *5*; chorus 4; deus ex machina 190, 551; Epidaurus Theater *5*; masks 11, 393; playwrights and plays 4; proscenium arch 6, 17, 564; scenic techniques 190; sound and acoustics 5–6; special effects 479; stage and seating 6, *6*; sun as lighting 293

green: as a bad color 63, *573*; different, paint samples of *62*

Greene, Sarah, *Hedda Gabler* (2005) *300*

green room 250, 510, 574

Greenwood, Jane 75

grid iron 276, 556

grids 242, 556

Grime FX (Nye) 431

grinders 158, *167*; definition of 556; pneumatic *169*

grommets 413, *413*, 556

ground plans 105; definition of 556; drafting 109, *110–111*, 112–113

ground wires 301, 556
gum erasers 82
gun belt 409
Guthrie Theatre, *Pride and Prejudice* (2003) *256*
Gypsy, costume sketches of (Baird) *350*

H
hacksaws 156, *156*
Hadobas, Paul 437
haiku 9
hair: actor's own 431; adhesives 433, 545; clip-in extensions 431; dye 431, *432*; falls 431; removers and cleansers 433, *433*; and safety 131, *131*; switches/braids 431; wiglets 431; wigs 367, *370*, 431
hair pieces 431
hair smudge brushes 424
half-face after/half-face chartered plot 423
half-face sketched/half-face chartered plot 423
half hitches 272, 556
half hour calling 513, 556
Hall, Peter, *Animal Farm 372*
halogen light bulbs 297, 556
hammer drills 167, *167*, 556
hammers 161; ball peen *161*, 162, 546; center punches 162, *162*, 548; claw 161, *161*, 549; dead-blow *161*, 162; framing 161, *161*, 555; mallets *161*, 162, 560; nail sets 162, *162*, 561; sledge *161*; tack 161–162, *161*, 162, 569
hand drafting 79, 83, 89, 101, *102–103*, 104, *106*, 109
hand-held clothing steamer 382, *382*
hand-held hole punch *415*
handheld microphones 331, 332
hand props 218, 556
hand pull 279
hand saws 155, *155*
hand-screw clamps 165, *165*, 556
hand sewing 364
hand-tied wigs 431
Hansbury, Lorraine 218
Harada, Kai 330, 333, 338
hardboard (Masonite) *174*, 175–176
hard flats (Hollywood flats) 205, *206*, 556; *see also* flats
hard-front wigs 431
hard pastels 80
hardware: computer 89; leather work 413
hardware (projections) 466; LED 466; media server 467; projectors 466; screens 466
hardware (scenery): adhesives 183–184, *184*; casters 185–186, *186*; fasteners 180–185; hinges 184–185, *185*; nails 180–181, *181*; screws and bolts 181, *182*; staples 183, *183*; washers and nuts 182–183, *182*

hardwoods 172
Hare (Durer) 77, *77*
Hartford Circus Fire (1944) 144, 145, 574
hat blocks 381–382, *381*, *383*
hat bodies 384–385, *385*
hatchets *161*
hats 367, *371*, 380; hat stretchers *382*; millinery 380–387
hazardous materials 142, 144; *see also* safety data sheets (SDSs)
haze special effects 487, 557; *see also* special effects
Head, Edith 360, 367
head blocks 276–277, *381*, 557
head circumference 386
headdress *410*
Head over Heels (2021), James Madison University *373*
headphones 330
headsets 342, *342*, 510, 511
hearing impairment: assisted-hearing devices 342–343, *343*; infrared hearing assist devices 330
heart face 422, *422*
Hedda Gabler, NYU Department of Graduate Acting/ Department of Design for Stage and Film production (2005) *300*
Hello, Dolly!: candy box (Baird) *232*; Muhlenberg Summer Music Festival *174*; watercolor rendering (Smith) *257*
helmets 397
hemlines 357, *358*
hemp (rope) house *269*, 275–278, *277*, 557
Henry Box Brown (Kushner) *295*
Henry V (Shakespeare) *294*
heredity, and character analysis 421
Hewlett Packard 466
Heyman, Lawrence *223*
hide (animal skin) 400, 412, 557
Higgins, Kyle *243*, *254*
high (top) hats (lighting) 316, *317*, 570
high-speed steel blades 155
high volume low pressure (HVLP) sprayers 248
Hill, Jennifer, *The Caucasian Chalk Circle 373*
hinges 184–185, *185*
Hockney, David 50, 53
Holcomb, Catherine, *Midsummer Night's Dream* (James Madison University) *367*
hole saws 168, *168*, 557
Hollywood, *vs.* Broadway 541
Hollywood flats (hard flats) 205, *206*, 556; *see also* flats
Hollywood makeup 419
homasote 175
horizon lines 94–95, *94*, 97, 557
hot-glue guns 168, *168*, 557

house curtains 18, *19*, 557

house managers xvii, 534

Hudson Scenic Studio, Inc.: 3D texture project *255*; backdrop painting for *Nine 244–245*; bamboo sticks *248*; club wall hanger shop drawing of *The Wedding Singer 194*; drawings for *The Odd Couple 212–213*; flameproofing products *139*; floor fans *256*; ground plan for *The Odd Couple 110–111*; paint bay *242–243*; painter Kyle Higgins applying texture *254*; painter Kyle Higgins using electronic pouncer *243*; painting with frisket *250*; paint storage *252*; production flowchart for *The Drowsy Chaperone 197*; rentals 199; Rosie's porch framing shop drawings of *The Wedding Singer 195*; Rosie's porch receivers and trap door drawings *The Wedding Singer 203*; scenic brush storage *247*; scenic tools in storage *250*; services provided 196, *197*; shop drawing of flat for *The Odd Couple 203*; shop drawing of hard flats for *The Odd Couple 206*; shop drawing of wall for *The Odd Couple 208–209*; shop drawing of window for *The Odd Couple 207*; shop drawings for *The Odd Couple 195*; title block for *The Odd Couple 107*; tool storage *252, 253*

Hudson® sprayers 248, 254, 557

hue 61, 557

Hultgren, Kacie, *42nd Street* tour (2016) *49*, *178*, *299*

human hair in wigs 431

Hurricane Diane (Huntington Theatre Company) *403*

I

I-Caption system (Sound Associates) 343

Illingworth, Scott, *Animal Farm* (Orwell/Hall) *372*

illustration boards 83

Illustrator® 93

Image Multiplexer® 316, *317*

impedance (microphone) 331, 557

impressionism (architecture) 35, 37, 557

improvisation (commedia dell'arte) 11

improvisational theatre 22

incandescent light bulbs 295–297, 557

infrared hearing assist devices 330

Ingalls, James, *Les Troyens* (Metropolitan Opera) *177*

injuries makeup 432

inner above/inner below 13

inputs (sound systems) 330, 557

insight, and design 75, 557

intelligent lighting 293, 557

intensity, color 62, 557

international tours 518–519, 520

internet reference images for design plot 422–423

inter-related pendulum 490

interviews 536–537; Bermudez, Fernando 539; Brandt, Grace 539; Carson, Heather 539–540; Johnston, Anne 540; Jones, Prudence 537; Lechterman, Jeremy 521–523; Newbold, Jennifer 537–539; Rizzo, Michael 451; Ross-clausen, Kristi 537

Ionic order 36, 37, 557

IP addresses (sound systems) 343

iron department (scene shop) 198

Irwin, Robert 539

Isadora 467

J

Jacobs-Jenkins, Branden 275

James, Skyler, *Midsummer Night's Dream* (James Madison University) *367*

James Madison University (JMU) 233; *Equus* (2017) *233*; *Everybody* (2019) *275*; *Head over Heels* (2021) *373*; *Machinal* (2014) *310*; *Medea* (2003) *484*; *Midsummer Night's Dream 367*; *PACK* (2022) *372*; *Sweet Charity* (2015) *199*

James Thomas Engineering: 18″ × 12″ truss 281–282, *283*; pre-rig truss 282, *285*, 286; SuperTruss 287, *288*; tower systems 287; triangular truss *284*

Jang, Hahnji *403*

Japanese theatre: Bunraku 13–14, *13*; Kabuki 14–16, *14*, *15*, *16*; Noh 9, *9–10*

Jara, Jorge, *Romeo et Juliette* (Metropolitan Opera, 2005) *253*

jewelry 131–132, *132*, 367, *370*, *410–411*, 411

jig (cutting guide) 159, 557

jigsaws (saber saws) 157, *157*, 558

Johnson, Pam, *Equus* (James Madison University, 2017) *233*

Johnston, Anne 448, 484, 532; interview 540; *Who's That Girl* tour (Madonna) 450

Jones, Prudence (interview) 537

Jonson, Ben 12

Joosten, Guy, *Romeo et Juliette* (Metropolitan Opera, 2005) *253*

jugglers 8

Julius Caesar, detail drawings of *324–325*

K

Kabuki 14–16, *14*, *15*, *16*

Kahn, Michael: *Coriolanus* (2000) 39, *40*; *Othello* (2005) *41*, 42, *351*, *352*

Kelly, Jude, *Othello* (1997) *41*, 42

Kelvin temperature scale 297, 298, 558

kerf 412, 558

keyhole (drywall) saws 155, *155*, 558

keystones 204, 558

key to symbols (drafting) 108–109, *108*, 558

kick-off meetings 196, 558

King, Ashleigh, *Head over Heels* (2021) *373*

King, Tom, *Medea* (2003) *484*

Kirk, Roger, *42nd Street* tour (2016) *49*, *178*, *299*

kits (lighting equipment) 523, 558

kneaded erasers 83

knives: pocketknives 150, 154, *154*; utility (mat) 154, *154*, 571

knots 269–274; belaying 272, *273*, 276, 547; bowlines 269–270, *271*, 547; clove hitches 271–272, *272*, 277, 549; coiling 272, 549; half hitches 272, 556; monkey's fist 272–274, *273*, 560; overhand 269, *270*, 561; square (reef) 269, *270*, 569

Knott, Jenny 251

Kodak Carousel 445, *445*

Kogler, Al 150

kohl 419

kraft paper (brown butcher paper) 243, 558

Kushner, Tony 223, *295*

Kyoto Costume Institute 539

L

labeling 101; *see also* lettering

lace 356

lace-front wigs 431

LACMA 539

ladders 135–136, *136*

Lambert, Ben, *Equus* (James Madison University, 2017) *233*

lamellar armor 400, 558

lamp housing 304, 558

lamps 558; drafting table 85; standard theater lamp types 298, *298*; *see also* light bulbs; lighting fixtures

LAN 343

Larkin, Hallie 538

laser levels *152*, 153, 558

laser measures 151, 558

laser pickups 330

laser projectors 466

latex: allergy to 137–138; and flame retardancy 138; gloves 246; liquid 432, 559

lauan 175, 204

Laughing Stock: audition forms *498*; costume breakdown *508*; explosion special effect *480*; French scene breakdown *504*; prop breakdown *507*; rehearsal schedule *501*

lavalier microphones 331, 332–333, 558; mounting options 332, *332*, 333; Sennheiser MKE-2 332

lay-in brushes 247, 558

layout markers 82

layout men 196, 198

Lazar, Julie 540

lead, pencil 79–80, *79*

leather: armor *399*, *402*; definition of 558; masks 393, 396; shears 412, 558

leather work 411; casing the leather 412, 548; finishing details 413; hardware 413, *413*, *415*; pattern pieces 412; stitching techniques 413; surface design and tooling 412, *412*; tools 412; types and weights of leather 411–412

Lechterman, Jeremy (interview) 521–523

LED screens 466, *518*

LED tech 452

LED walls 466

Lee, Eugene 160

leg greaves 397, 559

legs: extension of backdrop 190, 559; platforms 200

Leiacker, Johannes, *Romeo et Juliette* (Metropolitan Opera, 2005) *253*

lenses (lighting fixtures) 303, 305, *305*, 555, 559

Les Troyens (Metropolitan Opera) *177*

lettering 88; Ames Lettering Guide 88–89, *88*, 104; drafting 101, 104; guide 559; styles *88*

levels 152; laser *152*, 153, 558; spirit 152, *152*, 568; string 152, *152*, 569

liability disclaimer 108

lifts, personnel 136–137, *136*

light: additive color mixing 61, 545; color wheel 59, *60*, 61, *65*

Light and Space art movement 539

light bulbs: components of *297*; Edison's original patent *296*; envelope shapes 298, *298*; fluorescent lamps 297, 307–308, 554; halogen 297, 556; incandescent 295–297, 557; standard theater lamp types 298, *298*; *see also* electricity

light cue synopsis 509, *509*

light-emitting diode (LED) fixtures 308, 559; Altman's Spectra LED cyclorama *310*; cue lights 511; ETC x 7 LED strip light *310*; Robe Robin 1200 LED wash moving light *312*; Robert Juliat LED Fresnel *309*

lighting *93*; accessories 316–317, *317*; arena stage 20–21; and balance 53; candles 293, *294*, 314; controllers 314–315, *315*, 559; conventional 293, 550; and costume colors 364; dimmers 313–314, *314*, 551; electricity 299–302; and fire effects 483; fluorescent lamps 297, 307–308, 554; focus 303; footlights 294–295, 554; gaslight 295; ghost light 296, 574; instruments, and fire safety measures 138; intelligent 293, 557; Kelvin temperature scale 297, 298, 558; light bulbs 295–298, *296*, *297*, *298*; limelight 295, *295*, 559; paperwork 318, *319–325*; and scenery sketch 98; software 89, 93; sun as 293; traverse stage 21; and wind special effects 484; *see also* electricity; light bulbs; light plots

lighting controllers 559

lighting fixtures 318; automated/moving lights 308, *312*, *313*, *323*; beam projectors 304, *304*, 547; ellipsoidal reflector spotlights 305–306, *306*, 307, 316, 553; fluorescent lights 297, 307–308, 554; Fresnel lights and lenses 304–305, *305*, 307, *309*, 555; hanging on pipes 316–317; LED fixtures 308, *310*, *312*; lighting load-in *303*; moving light trusses 286–287, *286*; PAR lamps 306, *307*, *309*, 562; parts of 303–304, *303*; scoops 304, *305*, 566; spot fixtures 308; spot lights *311*, *311–312*; strip lights 306–307, *307*, *310*, 569; UV lights 307; wash fixtures 308, *309*, *312*

lighting props 553

lightning special effects 485; *see also* special effects

light plots 559; *42nd Street* tour (Billington) *321*; centerline 318; drafting 109, 113; front of house (FOH) 318, *319*, 554; *Julius Caesar* detail drawings *324–325*; key to symbols 318; lighting notes 109; magic (cheat) sheets 318, *322–323*, 560; *Nutcracker, The* (McKernon) *114–115*; symbols for fixtures 318; symbols/key to symbols 108–109, *108*, 558

Light Shop® 89

LightWave® 93

Lightwright® 89

limelight 295, *295*; definition of 559; "in the limelight" 487, 575

Lindenberg, Konrad, *Dr. Faust* (Metropolitan Opera, 2001) *446*

linear dimensions 104, 559

linear measurements, conversion table from US to metric system *84*

line arrays (speakers) 338, *339*, 559

linen 352, 559

lines 49–50, *50*; centerlines 109, 112, 318, 548; chalk lines 153, *153*, 548; definition of 559; and direction 551; horizon lines 94–95, *94*, 97, 557; line weights 86, *86*, 101, 550, 559; plaster lines 112, 113, 563; sight lines 6, 19, 20, 567; types of 86, *86*, 101

line set inventory 112–113, *112*, 274, *274*, 559

line set schedule *see* line set inventory

line shaft winches 280

linesman's pliers 164, *165*, 559

line weights 51, *51*, 86, *86*, 101, 550, 559

lining (fitch) brushes 247, 554, 559

lining sticks 247, 559

Linnebach, Adolf 444

Linnebach projectors 444, *444*, 559

linoleum knife *154*

lip balm 429, 434

lip brush 424

lip glosses 419, 429, 434

lip pencils *428*, 429

lipsticks 429, 434; Ben Nye *428*; lipstick smear and good luck 429, 575

liquid eyeliners 426

liquid face paints 429, *429*

liquid hair color 431, *432*

liquid latex 432, 559

Little Blizzard snow machine *485*

Little Night Music, A 411

Little Shop of Horrors 224

Little Women 218, *221*

liturgical drama 8

live Foley 334; Foley door *335*; Foley table *335*

live radio plays 334

live sounds 334

loading floor 559

lobsterscopes 445, 447, *447*, 560

locking rail 278, 279

loft blocks 276–277, 278, 560

Logan, John 250

London: Fringe 21; West End 21

Long, William Ivey 92, 351, 364

Long Beach (Rupp) *33*

long face 422, *422*

Long Wharf Theatre, computer-generated drawings for *Ain't Misbehavin* (Beatty) 90–*91*

loopers 365, 560

loose-pin hinges 184

Lost in Yonkers: blocking notes *506*; calling scripts *518*; light clue synopsis *509*

loudspeakers *see* speakers

luggage 409

Luminys, LightningStrikes® 485

Lunt-Fontanne Theatre, assisted-hearing devices 342

Lustig, Rebecca, *Sweet Charity* (2015) *199*

Lycian: 1275 follow spot *311*; M2 follow spot *311*

M

Macbeth 31, *32*, 575

Macbeth (Verdi), Salvatore Tagliarino's sketch *32*

Machinal, James Madison University (2014) *310*

Madonna, *Who's That Girl* tour 450, 540

magic (cheat) sheets 318, *322–323*, 560

magnetic pickups 330

magnetic pincushions 355, *355*

makeup 419; application 434, 437; brief history 419–420; character analysis 421–422; chart 434, *434*; design 420–421; design plot 422–423; facial shapes 422, *422*, 553; hair 431–433; injury/ageing makeup (scar wax) 432, *433*, 566; Kabuki 16; kits *435*; process 422–423; removers and cleansers 433, *433*, 565; and sustainability 430; tattoos 426; techniques, examples *436–437*; *see also* hair; makeup categories; makeup styles; makeup tools makeup artists 534

makeup brushes: angle brushes 423, 545; creme (wet) brushes 423; detail brushes 424, 551; dome brushes 423, *423*, 551; flat brushes 423, *423*, 554; fluff brushes 423; foundation brushes 424, *424*, 555; powder brushes 424, 563; round brushes 423, *423*, 566; sponge brushes *424*

makeup categories: cheek colors 426, *426*, 434; clown white 429, *430*; concealers 425–426, *425*, 434, 549; creme colors 429, *429*; effects wheels 430, *430*; eyebrow pencils 426, *428*, 429, 434; eyeliners 426, *427*, *428*, 434; eye shadows 426, *427*, 434; face powders 426, *427*, 434; lip balm 429, 434; lip glosses 419, 429, 434; lip pencils *428*, 429; lipsticks *428*, 429, 434, 575; liquid face paints 429, *429*; mascara 426, *428*, 429; neutralizers *425*, 426; Special FX 430–431; UV makeup 307

makeup styles: character makeup 421; natural makeup 421; stylized makeup 421

makeup tools: brushes 424–424, *424*; palettes 424, *435*, 562; powder puffs 424, *424*, 563; spatulas 424, *425*, 568; sponge applicators 424–425, *424*; see also makeup brushes

mallets *161*, 162, 560

Manhatco *383*

man-made dyes 392

mannequins 360, 367, *369*, 397

markers 81–82, *81*

marking tools see measuring/marking tools

Marlowe, Christopher 12

Martin: Atomic strobes 485; MAC 2000® profile moving light *312*; MAC 2000® wash *312*

mascara 426, *428*, 429

masking (borders) 190, 547, 560

mask making 393; casting 394–395, *394–395*, *396*, 548; comfort of the model 395; fitting of mask 396; sculpting/manipulating of face shape 396, *396*; types of casting 395

masks: commedia dell'arte 11; Greek theatre 11; Noh 9, *10*; see also dust masks

Masonite (hardboard) *174*, 175–176

masques 11

master (world) clock 331, 560

materials (scenic): fabric 177–179; foams and plastics 179–180; hardware 180–186; metal 176–177; wood 172–176; see also specific materials

mat (utility) knives 154, *154*, 571

Matsuo, Basho 14

Max Factor 419

Maxon, Cinema 4D® 93, *474*

May, Melanie, *Henry V* (Shakespeare) *294*

Maya® 93

Mazur, Tim 337

McGann-Bartleman, Daniel, *Everybody* (Jacobs-Jenkins, 2019) *275*

McGovern, Taylor, *PACK* (2022) *372*

McGowan, Samantha, *PACK* (2022) *372*

McKernon, John 89; *Hello, Dolly!* (Muhlenberg Summer Music Festival) *174*; *Nutcracker, The* light plot *114–115*

McLane, Derek 27, 308

measurements (costume-making) 358, 360; men's costume pieces forms 360, *363*; men's measurement instructions/chart 360, *361*; women's costume pieces forms 360, *362*; women's measurement instructions/chart 358, *359*

measurements (hat-making) 386, *386*

measuring/marking tools 150–153; bevel gauges 151, 547; carpenter pencils 150, 548; chalk lines 153, *153*, 548; combination squares 151, *151*, 549; compasses 151–152, *152*; folding rules 150–151, *150*, 554; framing squares 151, *151*, 555; laser measures 151, 558; levels 152–153, *152*; protractors *151*; speed squares 151, *151*, 568; tape measures 150, *150*, 570; tri-squares *151*

measuring tapes (costume-making) 354, *354*, 560

mechanical pencils 79–80, *79*

Medea (King, 2003) *484*

media server programmers 468

media servers 452, 467, 560

media server tech 452

medium-density fiberboard (MDF) 176

meetings: design 31–32, 37; kick-off 196, 558; production 508

melodrama 22–23

Mensching, Linda, makeup chart *434*

mesh-backed necklace 411, *411*

metal-cutting saws 156; conduit cutters *156*; hacksaws 156, *156*; pipe cutters 156, *156*, 562; pipe reamers 156, *156*, 562; pipe threaders 156, *156*, 563; PVC cutters *156*; tin snips 156, *156*, 570; tube cutters 156; see also wood-cutting saws

metal flake 246

metal inert gas (MIG) welding 170, 560

metallic paints and powders 251–252

metals 176–177, *177*

Metropolitan Museum 539

Metropolitan Opera: *Dr. Faust* (2001) *446*; *Ghosts of Versailles* (1991) *486*; *Les Troyens* *177*; *Pelléas et Mélisande* *175*; *Romeo et Juliette* (2005) *253*

Metropolitan Opera (New York) 21

Meyes, Oliver, *Midsummer Night's Dream* (James Madison University) *367*

Michelangelo, drawings of 75

microphones 330, 331–333, 510–511; area mic'ing 333, 546; condenser 331, 549; dynamic 331, 552; gain 332, 555; handheld 331, 332; impedance of 331, 557; inputs 557;

lavalier 331, 332–333, *332*, 558; outputs 561; pressure-response 331, 564; styles and types of *331*; wireless 332, *332*; *see also* contact pickups

Microsoft Office 89

Middle Ages 8–9; mobile theatre 8; plays 8–9; sponsorship and censorship 9

Mid-Hudson Bridge (Poughkeepsie, NY) *94*

midrange speakers 337, *338*, 560

Midsummer Night's Dream (James Madison University) *367*

Mill, Olga *295*

Miller, Arthur 21

Miller, Jonathan, *Pelléas et Mélisande* (Metropolitan Opera) *175*

millinery 380; blocking 381–382, *381*, 383–384, *383*; conformateur *381*; covered buckram frame hats 387, *388–389*; cut and sewn hats 387, *387*; fabrics 383–384, *383*, *384*; felt capelines *383*; hat bodies 384–385, *385*; hat-making supplies *380*; materials 383–385; measurements 386, *386*; milliners 380, 381; mock-up 386, *387*, *388*; needles *380*; pattern 386; steaming 382, *382*; tools *381*; wire *380*

Milwaukee Tool, Sawzall® 157

mimes 8

mineral-oil-based fog fluids 485–486

minstrels 8

Mr. Puffy 357, *358*, 560

Mitchell, Clare, *Pelléas et Mélisande* (Metropolitan Opera) *175*

miter boxes 155, 560

miter saws 155, *155*, 560

mixing consoles 330, 334, 335, 560; analog 336, *336*; computerized mixing 336; digital 336, *337*; relative mixing 336

mobile theatre 8

mock-up: armor 397–398, *398*; hats 386, *387*, *388*; masks 396

modern theatre 17; arena stage 20–21, 547; black box theaters 547; environmental theatre 553; proscenium theatre 17–19, *18*; theatre styles 22–23; thrust stage 19–20, 570; traverse stage 21; *see also* proscenium theatre; theatre styles

molding 176, *176*, 560

monkey's fists 272–274, *273*, 560

monkey wrenches 153, 574

monochromatic composition 62–63, 560

Moore, Daniel 297

More, Thomas 12

Moreira, Emily, *PACK* (2022) *372*

Morgan, Robert: *Corn in Green, The 384*; *Seagull, The 385*

morgues (collections of images/sounds) 39, 560

Moser, Katerina, *Everybody* (Jacobs-Jenkins, 2019) *275*

moving/automated lights 308, *312*, *313*, *323*

moving light truss 286–287

Moyer, Allen 225

Muhlenberg College, turkey hat *371*

Muhlenberg Summer Music Festival, *Hello, Dolly! 174*

multi-pair cables 340, *341*, 561

multiple dimensions 104, 561

Munoz, Rodrigo, *Animal Farm* (Orwell/Hall) *372*

Murphy's Oil Soap 252

Museum of the American Revolution 538

music tours 521–523; *see also* Alt-J tour

muslin *178*, 179, 204–205, 364

Mussbach, Peter, *Dr. Faust* (Metropolitan Opera, 2001) *446*

Musser, Tharon 313, 315, 318

My Fair Lady, watercolor rendering (Smith) *98–99*

My Pattern Designer® 92

mysteries 8

N

nailers, pneumatic 169–170, *169*

nails 180–181, *181*

nail sets 162, *162*, 561

natural dyes 392

natural fabrics 351–352

naturalism 23, 31–32, 561

natural makeup 421

natural ropes 268, 269, *269*

natural sponge roller sleeves 248

nature (vintage effects) 481–483

necklaces 410, 411, *411*

needle-nose pliers 164, *165*, 561

needles: leather work 412, 413, 558; millinery *380*

Nemetschek 92, 93, 109, *471*

neon lighting 297

networks (sound systems) 343

neutralizers *425*, 426

Newbold, Jennifer (interview) 537–539

newsprint paper 83

NewTek, LightWave® 93

New Voices in Dance (Contemporary Dance Ensemble), *PACK* (2022) *372*

New York: Broadway 21; Off-Broadway 21; Off-Off-Broadway 21

New York City Opera, *Tote Stadt* (1971) *481*

Nihill, Kelsey, *PACK* (2022) *372*

Nine: elevation (Pask) *244*; full-color model (Pask) *244*; Hudson Scenic backdrop panting *244–245*

Noh 9, *9–10*

noise hazards 133–134

Nomathemba (Huntington Theatre Company) *410*

nominal size (lumber) 173, 561

non-tactile textures 51

nose and scar wax 424, 432, *433*, 566

notes, drafting 109, 112

notions (sewing) 356

NuDelta LogiCue 511, *511*

Nutcracker, The, John McKernon's light plot *114–115*

nut drivers 163, *164*, 561

nuts 182–183, *182*

Nye, Ben 420

Nye, Eric 425, 430

nylon 353, 561

NYU Department of Graduate Acting/Department of Design for Stage and Film: *Crucible, The* (2005) *39*; *Hedda Gabler* (2005) *300*

O

Oberammergau (Bavaria, Germany) 3

"obstructed view" seats 19

occult balance 53

Occupational Safety and Health Administration (OSHA) 130, 246, 561; accident report *505*; requirements for safe use of ladders/lifts 136; safety data sheets 144

Odd Couple, The (Simon): Beatty's backing wall drafting *192*; Beatty's deck plan *118–119*; Beatty's drafting for kitchen walls *193*; Beatty's drafting of floor layout *198*; Beatty's drawing of stair and railing details *202*; Beatty's full-scale details *122–123*; Beatty's hand draftings *102–103*; Beatty's wall arches drafting *210*; Beatty's wall details *120–121*; Hudson Scenic's drawings of *212–213*; Hudson Scenic's ground plan *110–111*; Hudson Scenic's shop drawing of a flat *203*; Hudson Scenic's shop drawing of hard flats *206*; Hudson Scenic's shop drawing of wall *208–209*; Hudson Scenic's shop drawing of window *207*; Hudson Scenic's title block *107*; Hudson Scenic's Wall A. shop drawings *195*; title block *107*

Odeum (Pompeii, Italy) *8*

Off-Broadway (New York) 21

Off-Off-Broadway (New York) 21

O'Hara, Shane, *PACK* (2022) *372*

oil color pencil 80

oil paints 82

oil pastels 80

O'Keefe, Georgia 255

Oklahoma City University School of Theatre *219*

Oliver perspective 96

Olson, Gordon, *PACK* (2022) *372*

Onat, Cigdem, *Hedda Gabler* (2005) *300*

one-point perspective *94*, 95

on weight of goods (OWG) 392, 561

open-ended wrenches 163, *163*, 561

opening night, and paying customers xvii, 575

opera 21, 218

operating line 278–279, 561

optical pickups 330

orchestral reinforcement 333

orchestra pit 19, 561

organic shapes 50, *50*

orthographic projection 101, *104*, 561

Orwell, George, *Animal Farm 372*

Osiris 4

Ostermann, Curt 156, 160, 488

Othello (Shakespeare Theatre Company): Kahn, Michael (2005) *41*, 42, *351*, *352*; Kelly, Jude (1997) *41*, 42

outputs (sound systems) 330, 561

outriggers 136–137, 561

oval face 422, *422*

overhand knots 269, *270*, 561

overlocking stitch 364, 365, 561

overlock sewing machines (sergers) 364–365, *366*, 567

oxyacetylene (gas) welding 160, 561

P

PACK (2022) *372*

paddle bits *see* spade bits

pads 247

paging microphones 510

paint 82, 241–243; backdrops 242; caring for paints and tools 252; cartooning 242–243, 548; chemistry 251–253; elevation for *Nine* (Pask) *244*; full-color model for *Nine* (Pask) *244*; *vs.* glazes 251; green practices 262; Hudson Scenic' paint storage 252; Hudson Scenic's paint bay *242–243*; Hudson Scenic's tool storage *252*, *253*; leather 413; metallic paints and powders 251–252; painting techniques 255; paint manufacturers 251; priming 255; removing 253; safety 246, 248–249, 252; samples 242; scenic artists 241–242; shoe *389*, 390; surface textures 248; texturing 254–255, *254–255*; tools and supplies 246–250; types of 251; ultraviolet 251, 252; *see also* painting techniques; paint tools and supplies; texturing

paintbrushes *see* brushes

paint elevations 255–256, *257*, 562

Painter® 93

painter's tape 249

painting techniques: drying time 255; floor fans at Hudson Scenic *256*; glazing 255; researching 255–256; schlepitchka (feather duster) 258, *258–259*; wood 260–261, *260–261*

paint markers 82

paint rollers 248, 252

paint tools and supplies: bamboo sticks 247, *248*, 546; brushes 246–247, *247*, 252; caring for 252; frisket 249–250, *250*, 555; lining sticks 247, 559; painter's tape 249; rollers 248, 252; sponges, plastic wrap, and rags 249; sprayers 248, 254; *see also* brushes

palettes 424, *435*, 562

palm sander *168*

pan (light movement) 304, 562

pancake makeup 419

panel saws *158*, 160, 562

panic, examples of 144–145

Pani projectors 448, *449–450*, 450, 562

Pan Stick makeup 419–420

paper 83, *83*; hats, mock-up *387*; kraft paper (brown butcher paper) 243, 558; masks 393

papier-mâché 562; armor *397*, *398–399*; masks 393, 396

parabolic aluminized reflector (PAR) lamps 306, *307*, *309*, 562

parallel rules 85, 104, 562

parasols 408–409

Paris net (Dior net) 384

Pask, Scott: club wall hanger drawing of *The Wedding Singer* *193*; *Nine* elevation *244*; *Nine* full-color model *244*; title block of *The Wedding Singer* *107*

passion plays 3–4, 9, 562

pastel colors 61

pastels 80, *81*

patterning templates 322, *355*, 562

Patternmaker® 92, 374, 375; costume options *374*; step-by-step corset instruction *375*

patterns: armor *397*; body padding *406*; and composition 52, *53*, 562; costume-making 354, 562; hats 386; leather work 412; period 538; software 374

Patterns of Fashion (Arnold) 538

pear face 422, *422*

Pegasus® 490

Pekingese puppets 17

Pelléas et Mélisande (Metropolitan Opera) *175*

pencils 79–80, *79–80*, 150, 548

pens 81

People's Choice Awards (Bass, 2017) *473–474*

Pepper, John 447

Pepper's ghost 447–448, *447*, 562

performance props 220, 562

performances: call times 510, 513, 548; half hour calling 513, 556; note taking 513; places calling 513, 563; preshow checklists 513, 563

periaktoi 190, 562

personal protective equipment (PPE) 132

Personals, video projection slides 488, *489*

personal safety: allergies 137–138, 139–140; clothing 130, 131, *131*; dust masks 134, *134*, 552; earmuffs 133–134, 552; earplugs 133–134, *133*, 552; examples of panic 144–145; eyecups and eyewash station 132–133, *133*, 553; face shields 132, *132*, 553; first aid kits 137, *137*, 496, 504; goggles 132, *132*, 156, 556; hair 131, *131*; jewelry 131–132, *131*; ladders 135–136, *136*; personnel lifts 136–137, *136*; respirators 134, *134*, 565; *see also* Occupational Safety and Health Administration (OSHA); safety data sheets (SDSs)

personnel lifts 136–137, *136*

perspective drawing 93–98, 562; foreshortening 95, *95*, 554; horizon lines 94–95, *94*, 97, 557; Oliver perspective 96; one-point perspective *94*, 95; perspective projection 93; three-point perspective 96; two-point perspective 95, 96–97, *96*, *97*; vanishing points 94, 96, 97, 571; zero-point perspective 94

Pesta, Desira, *Henry V* (Shakespeare) *294*

Phantom Galleries LA 540

Phillips screwdrivers/screws 164, *164*, 181, 562

photo manipulation software 73

Photoshop® 92–93, 488

physiognomy 421, 562

piano hinges 185

Picasso, Pablo 247

pickups (sound inputs) 330, 331, 332

Pierrot (commedia dell'arte character) *11*

PIGI projectors 450–451, 562

pig iron 278

pigment color wheel 59; full *60*; and grayscale 64, *65*; primary colors 59; secondary colors 59

pigskin 402

pinak pok 384

pincushions 355, *355*

pink erasers 82

pink foam 179, *180*

pin rails 276, 277, 562

pins 355

Pinterest 539

pipe clamps 304, 562

pipe cutters 156, *156*, 562

pipe reamers 156, *156*, 562

pipe threaders 156, *156*, 563

pipe wrenches 163, *163*, 563

pits: for audience 13; orchestra 19, 561

pixels 467; definition of 563; density *473*, 563

places calling 513, 563

plaids 52

plain dust 431

planes 166, *166*, 563

plan views 101, 563

plastalina clay 396, *396*

plaster bandage *394*, 395, 563

plaster casting 394, *394–395*, 395

plaster lines 112, 113, 563

plastic masks 393

plastics 180

plate armor 400, *415*

platforms 191, 200, *201*, *202*, 563

Plautus 6, 7

pliers: fence *165*; linesman's 164, *165*, 559; needle-nose 164, *165*, 561; slip-joint 164, *165*, 567; tongue and groove *165*; vise grips 165, *165*

plugs, electrical 301, *302*

plumb bobs *152*, 153, 563

plywood 174–175, *174*

pneumatic tools 563; compressors 169, *169*; grinders *169*; nailers 169–170, *169*; staplers 170

pocketknives 150, 154, *154*

Pollock, Jackson 75

polyester batting 407

polyesters 353, 563

polyurethane foams (body padding) 405–406

Ponselle, Rosa 218

posing, Kabuki 16, *16*

Posteraro, Jessica, *The Caucasian Chalk Circle 373*

postmodernism (architecture) 37, 563

pounce wheels 243, 563

powder (face makeup) 426, *427*, 434

powder brushes 424, 563

powder cheek colors 426

powder puffs 424, *424*, 563

power, electrical 300–301

PowerPoint slide shows 488

practicals 113, 563

pregnancy pads *406–407*

Premios Juventud: 3D renderings of sets (Dominguez, 2016) *471*; raster *473*

pre-rig truss 282, *285*, 286

presentational production style 31, 564

preshow checklists 513, 563

preshrink (fabric) 353, 564

pressure-response microphones 331, 564

Preston, Travis 537

Preval sprayers 248

previsualization (pre-vis) 92; Alt-J Glastonbury Festival (FragmentNine) *469–470*; definition of 564

Pride and Prejudice (Guthrie Theatre, 2003) *256*

primary colors 59, *59*, *60*, 61, 62, 564

primer/priming 255; definition of 564; PVC primer *184*

ProCreate 92–93

producers 534

Production Arts (PA) 448, 450

production: contact sheets 497, *499*; meetings 508; presentational style 31, 564; representational style 31–32, 565

production managers 495, 534

Production Resource Group, curved box truss *282*

production team: collaboration 28–29, 31, 32, 37; flow chart *28*

projection designers 452

projectionist/projector tech 452

projection mapping 466

projections 443–444; Alt-J 2017 tour video system schematic *475*; Alt-J Glastonbury Festival previsualization *469–470*; Alt-J Summer 2017 tour *453–465*; CMT Music Awards (Brahic, 2017) *474*; digital 451, 490, 551; hardware 466–467; history of 444–451; orthographic projection 101, *104*, 561; Pani projectors 448, *449–450*, 450, 562; *People's Choice Awards* (Bass, 2017) *473–474*; PIGI projectors 450–451, 562; *Premios Juventud* 3D renderings of sets (Dominguez, 2016) *471*; *Premios Juventud* raster *473*; simpler 488; software 467; video projection 451, 488, *489*, 490, 540; *see also* special effects; video

projectors 443–444, 466; beam 304, *304*, 547; lenses 466; Linnebach 444, *444*, 559; Pani 448, *449–450*, 450, 562; PIGI 450–451, 562; projection surface 466; rigging of 466; Rosco X-Effects LED 488, *488*; slide 445, *445*

prop artisans 225, 228

prop breakdown 507–508, *507*, 564; *see also* props (properties)

prop buyer 228

prop carpenter 229–230

ProPlus rescue system™ 287, *289*

proportion: and balance 51–52; and composition 50; definition of 564; and drawing 78; and textures 51

props (properties) 217–218, 564; and accessories 408–409, 411; breakdown 507–508, *507*, 564; costume props 550; *Crazy For You* car (Baird) *229*; *Crazy For You* vacuum cleaner 223, *223*; defining 218–220; department 199; furniture props 555; *Glass Menagerie, The*, father's portrait *230–231*, 231; *Glass Menagerie, The*, glass unicorn 234–235, *234–237*; hand props 218, 556; *Hello, Dolly!* candy box (Baird) *232*; jobs related to 225, 228–230; lighting props 559; list **218**, 220, *221*; list, breaking down 221; performance props 220, 562; rehearsal props 220, 565; set decoration props 218–219, *219*; set props (set dressing) 218, *227*, 567; shopped *vs.* built 224–225, *225*, *226*; special 223–224, *224*; special effects props 568; storage *222–223*

prop supervisors 218, 220, 221, 228

proscenium arch 6, 17, 564

proscenium theatre 17–19; apron 18–19, 545; auditorium 19, 546; backdrop 546; Bardavon Opera side boxes *18*; cyclorama 551; end stage 17; fire curtains 141, *141*, 554; fourth wall 18, 555; grand borders 18, 556; house curtains 18, *19*, 557; layout of *18*; orchestra pit 19, 561; sight line (line of sight) 19, 567; *see also* backdrops

protractors *151*

pry bars 162–163, *162*, 564

Pterodactyls (Silver) 225, *226*

"Pull, Build, Find, Buy" system 221

pulleys 276–277

puppets: Bunraku 13–14, *13*; Chinese theatre 17

purses 409

push screwdrivers (Yankee screwdrivers) 164, *164*, 572

PVC: cement *184*; cutters *156*; primer *184*

Q

QLab 467

quartz envelope 297, 564

quilt padding 407

R

radial-arm saws 159, *159*, 564

raffia 384

rag rolling 254, 564

rails 202, *202*, 564

rain special effects: modern 485; vintage 482–483, *482*; *see also* special effects

Raisin in the Sun, A (Hansbury) 218, 220

rake (angled stage) 6, *6*, 565

ramps 200

Rape of Lucretia, The (Berkshire Opera), sketch by Allison *100*

Raphael, drawings of 51, 75

rasps 166, *166*, 565

raster 92–93, 468, *473*, 565

rayon 353, 565

razor scraper *154*

reactive adhesives 184

realism 23, 31, 191; and architecture 35; definition of 565

reamers 156, *156*

reciprocating saws 157, *167*, 565

recorded sounds 334

Red (Logan) 250

red (color), paint samples of *63*

reef (square) knots 269, *270*, 569

re-enactors 537–539

reference white 66–68, *66–67*, 565

reflectors 304, 565

regional theaters 21

Rehberger, Gustav *74*

rehearsal props 220, 565

rehearsals: accident reports 504, *505*, 545; blocking 502, 505, *506*, 507, 547; company contact sheets 497–498, *499–500*; contact sheets 497–498, *499–500*, 550; costume breakdown 508, *508*, 550; curtain calls 510, 550; daily reports 503–504, *503*, 551; and designers 37; dress, and good opening 533, 575; fight 513; first 502; French scene breakdown 504, *504*, 555; items required for 502–503; light cue synopsis 509, *509*; managing accidents 504–505; production contact sheets 497, *499*; production meetings 508; prop breakdown 507–508, *507*, 564; schedules 498, *501*, 502, 565; sign-in sheets *502*, 503, 567; space 502; spacing 511–512; taping the floor 502; *see also* technical rehearsals

reinforcement (sound) 333, 334

relative mixing 336

release agent 394, 565

religious theatre: cycle plays 9; liturgical drama 8; passion plays 3–4, 9, 562

removers 433, *433*, 565

Renaissance 11–13; Globe Theater 12–13, *12*; masques 11; playwrights 11–12; theaters 12

rendering 99–101; definition of 74–75, 565; hand *vs.* computer 100; *vs.* model 101; *My Fair Lady* watercolor rendering (Smith) *98–99*; *Rape of Lucretia, The* (Allison) *100*; *see also* drawing, rendering, and drafting

rental department (scene shop) 199

rental houses 371

rental shops 451, 520–521, 523

repertory theaters 21

representational production style 31–32, 565

research: definition of 565; and design 33–35, 37; *see also* morgues (collections of images/sounds)

resin, molding 176

resistance dimmers 313

resolution (video) 466, 467

respirators 134, *134*, 565

reticulated foams (body padding) 405, *406*

reverberation 330, 337

Revolutionary War re-enactors 538

revolving stages 191

Rhode Island, nightclub fire (2003) 144–145

Richter, Charles, *Hello, Dolly!* (Muhlenberg Summer Music Festival) *174*

riggers: job description 535; at rest *290*

rigging 267–268; Bardavon 1869 Opera House *268*, 275, 277, *281*; knots 269–274, *270*, *271*, *272*, *273*; of projectors 466; rigged boat *268*; ropes 268–269, *269*; sample conversation 278; *see also* arena rigging; knots; rigging systems rigging systems: chain hoist *281*, *282*, 289, 548; double purchase 279, *280*, 552; fly lofts 274, 554; hemp (rope) house *269*, 275–278, *277*, 557; line sets/line set inventory 274, *274*; safety issues 289–290; single purchase 278–279, *279*, 567; span sets 287–288; trusses 280–282, *281–286*, 286–287, *288*, 289–290, *289*, *469–470*; winches 279–280, 572; *see also* trusses

rip blades 154, *154*, 565

rivets 413, *414–415*, 565

Rizzo, Michael, interview 541

road boxes 450, 565

road houses 520, 566

Robbins, Ashley, *PACK* (2022) *372*

Robe Robin, 1200 LED wash moving light *312*

Robert Juliat: cyc light *310*; Fresnel lamps *309*; Plano-Convex wash fixture *309*; profile fixtures *309*; Super Korrigan follow spot *312*

Rocheleau, Patrick 352

rockers 247

rollers: foam 248; paint 248, 252; rubber 247

rolling platforms 191

Rolling Stones, Steel Wheels tour 450, 540

Roman orders of columns 37

Roman theatre 6–8; Colosseum 7, *7*; Odeum, Pompeii *8*; playwrights and plays 6, 7; special effects 479; sun as lighting 293; vomitorium 7

romantic comedy 23

romanticism (architecture) 35, 566

Romeo et Juliette (Metropolitan Opera, 2005) *253*

rope hand pull 279

rope (hemp) house *269*, 275–278, *277*, 557

rope line (hat block) 382

ropes: rigging 268–269, *269*; wire 278, *278*, 572; *see also* coiling, rope

Rosco: I-Cue *317*; iPro Image Projector® 316; paints *261*; products 251; V-Hazer *486*; X-Effects LED projector 488, *488*

Rose (theater) 12

Ross-Clausen, Kristi (interview) 537

Rothko, Mark 75, 250

rouge brushes 424

round brushes 423, *423*, 566

round face 422, *422*

routers *157*, 158, 160, *167*, 198, 566

rubber cement 183, *184*

rubber rollers 247

rubber soles, shoe 389–390, *390*, *391*

Rudolph, Kelly, *Equus* (James Madison University, 2017) *233*

ruff 408, 566

Ruggaber, Brian, *Everybody* (Jacobs-Jenkins, 2019) *275*

rule of thirds 46–48, *46–49*, 566

Rupp, Isabella: *Long Beach 33*; *Sunday 48*

S

saber saws (jigsaws) 157, *157*, 558

safety 129–130; dry ice 487; examples of panic 144–145; and firearms 409, 411; fire safety 138–142; foams 179; MDF 176; paint shops 246, 248–249, 252; personal 130–138; rigging systems 289–290; SDSs 134, 142, *143*, 144, 246, 252, 560; shoes 130–131, *131*; "Stars and Stripes Forever" ("Disaster March") 145, 574; tools 149, 156, 157, 158; work gloves 134–135, *135*, 137, 156; *see also* fire safety; Occupational Safety and Health Administration (OSHA); personal safety

safety data sheets (SDSs) 134, 142, *143*, 144, 246, 251, 560

safety goggles 132, *132*, 156, 556

saltwater dimmers 313

sample rates 333

sandbags 276, *276*, 278, 566

sanders *168*

Sapsis Rigging Inc., ProPlus rescue system™ 287, *289*

saturation (chroma) 62, 549, 566

saws *see* cutting/shaping tools (powered hand tools); cutting/shaping tools (powered stationary tools); metal-cutting saws; wood-cutting saws; *specific types*

SawStop 159

Sawzall® 157

Sayeg, Jared A. *93*

scabbard 409

scale, and composition 53, 566

scale rules 84, *84*, 566

scar wax 424, 432, *433*, 566

scene machines 444–445, *445*, 566

scenery drafting 107, 109; conventions *86*; scenery notes 109

scenery pack 109, *109*, 192

scenery techniques and practices 189; building techniques 200–205, *201–213*; scenic design process 192–200; scenic techniques 189–192; *see also* building techniques; scenic design process; scenic techniques

scene shops 196; departments 196, 198, 242; Hudson Scenic example 196; Hudson Scenic production flowchart *197*

scenic artists 199, 241–242; Brandt, Grace (interview) 539; job description 535

scenic design process: construction drawings 194, *194–195*, 196, 550; designer drawings 192, *192–193*, 194, 551; models 194; packs of draftings 192; scene shops 196, 198; services provided by Hudson Scenic 196, *197*

scenic ground rows 191, 566

scenic models 101, 194

scenic techniques: backdrops and back walls (Greek theatre) 190; box sets 191, 547; deus ex machina 190, 551; periaktoi 190, 562; scenic ground rows 191, 566; tab curtains 192, 569; traps 190–191, 570; traveler tracks 190, 570; wing and drop scenery 190, 191, 572

scenic tools and materials 149; cutting 153–160; measuring/ marking 150–153; supplies 172–186; tools 149–172; *see also* materials (scenic); tools

schlepitchka (feather duster) 258, *258–259*

Schmidt-Futterer, Andrea, *Dr. Faust* (Metropolitan Opera, 2001) *446*

Schuler, Duane, *Pelléas et Mélisande* (Metropolitan Opera) *175*

scissors 154, *154*, 355–356, *355*

scoops 304, *305*, 566

Scottish Play (*Macbeth*) 31, *32*, 575

screens (projection) 466; LED 466, *518*; naming *474*

screens producer 452

screw bits 168

screwdrivers 164; Phillips 164, *164*, 562; slotted 164, *164*, 567; star 164; Yankee (push) 164, *164*, 572

screws and bolts 181, *182*

scrim 179

script(s): breakdown 32–33; calling 509–510, 512, *518*, 548; first reading 30–31; page with designer notes *30*; stage management 505

scrolling blades 155

scroll saws *158*, 160, 566

scumbling 254, 566

Seagull, The (Huntington Theatre Company) *385*

seam rippers 357, *357*, 566

sea sponges 254

secondary colors 59, *59*, *60*, 61, 566

section(s): definition of 566; drawings 113, *116–117*

Sedaris, Amy 233

Seeing Is Forgetting the Name of the Thing One Sees (Wechsler) 539

seesaws 275, 276

Seneca 6

Sennheiser: MKE-2 lavalier 332; wireless microphones *332*

sergers (overlock sewing machines) 364–365, *366*, 567

set decoration props 218–219, *219*

set props (set dressing) 218, *227*, 567

Seurat, Georges 75

sewing: accessories 367, *370*; body modification padding *405*; fantasy costumes 371; fittings 365–367, *368–369*; hand 364; PatternMaker "costume" options *374*; PatternMaker step-by-step corset instruction *375*; shortcuts for period feel 371, *371*; trim work on mannequins 367, *369*

sewing machines 364, *365*, *366*; overlock sewing machines (sergers) 364–366, *366*, 567; walking foot 413, 572

sewing scissors 355–356, *355*

Shabalala, Joseph, *Nomathemba 410*

shackles 287, 567

shade 62, 64, 567

shadow puppetry, Chinese theatre 17

Shakespeare, William 18, 220, 293; *Henry V 294*; insight into human condition 75; *Julius Caesar* detail drawings *324–325*; *Macbeth* 31, *32*, 573; Renaissance theatre 11, 12; *Romeo et Juliette* (Metropolitan Opera, 2005) *253*

Shakespeare Festival prop shop 220

Shakespeare Theatre Company: *Coriolanus* (Gaskill, 1991) 39, *40*; *Coriolanus* (Kahn, 2000) 39, *40*; *Othello* (Kahn, 2005) *41*, 42, *351*, *352*; *Othello* (Kelly, 1997) *41*, 42

shapes: and composition 50, *50*, 567; facial 422, *422*, 553; light bulbs envelope 298, *298*

shears 154, 412, 558

sheaves 276–277, 567

Sheehan, Dans, *Hedda Gabler* (2005) *300*

sheet lumber 174–176; definition 173; hardboard (Masonite) *174*, 175–176; homasote 175; lauan 175, 204; MDF 176; plywood 174–175, *174*

shellac 413, 567

Shelton, Shelbi, *PACK* (2022) *372*

shielded multi-pair cables 340, *341*, 567

shoes 367, 389–390; paint *389*; rubber soles 389–390, *390*, *391*; and safety 130–131, *131*; woman's *370*

shop walls 349, *349*

show decks 113, 567

shutters 306, 567

sidearms 317

side views 101, 567

sight lines 6, 567; proscenium theatre 19; thrust stage 20

signal processors 330, 567

signal-to-noise ratio 333

sign-in sheets *502*, 503, 567

silicon controlled rectifiers (SCRs) 314, 566

silicones 179

silk *178*, 351–352, 567

Silver, Nicky 225

Silverstein, Carrie 200

Simmons, Sabrina, *Head over Heels* (2021) *373*

Simon, Neil *192–193*, *202*, *203*; *see also Odd Couple, The* (Simon)

Simone, Liza 540

sinamay hats 384, *384*, *385*

Singin' in the Rain 485

single drum winches 280

single-phase power 301, 567

single purchase 278–279, *279*, 567

sketch/sketching 37, *74*; definition of 74, 567; in scenery pack 109; *see also* rendering

Skowhegan School of Painting and Sculpture 540

skull and crossbones (symbol) 34, *34*

sledge hammers *161*

slide projectors 445, *445*

slip-joint pliers 164, *165*, 567

slopers 354–355, *355*, 567

slotted screwdrivers 164, *164*, 567

slotted screws 181

slush casting 395, 568

SM bible 509, 568

Smith, Dante *295*

Smith, Oliver 96; *Camelot* watercolor rendering *38*; *Hello, Dolly!* watercolor rendering *257*; *My Fair Lady* watercolor rendering *98–99*; *Sound of Music, The*, watercolor rendering *257*

Smith, Stephanie 538

smoke (or fog) 554; *see also* fog special effects

smoke (special effects) 486; *see also* special effects

smoke detectors/alarms 139, *139*

smoke pockets 141, 568

smoothing layers 407

snakes (audio) 340, *341*, 568

snow special effects 483; Little Blizzard snow machine *485*; modern 485; vintage 483; *see also* special effects

Sobo® glue 183, 184, *184*

social change, theatre for 23

socket sets/wrenches 163, *164*, 568

soft flats (Broadway flats) 202, 204–205, *205*, 568; *see also* flats

soft goods 107, 568

soft goods artisans 230

SoftImage®® 93

soft pastels 80

Soft Plot® 89

Soft Plot 3D® 89

software: CAD 73, 89, 92, 104, 109, 160, 198, 548; costume-making/patterns 92, 93, 374–375; drawing/drafting 89, 90–*91*, 92–*93*; graphics 92; lighting 89, 93; photo manipulation 73; projection 467; *see also* computers, and drawing/drafting

softwoods 172

soldering 171–172, 568

soles, shoe 389–390, *390*, *391*

solvents 246

Sons, Sophie, *Midsummer Night's Dream* (James Madison University) *367*

Sophocles 4

Sorcerer, The (Fink) *62*, *63*, 64

sound 329–330; basics of 333–334; Greek theatre 4–6; live sounds 334; recorded sounds 334; *see also* sound systems

Sound Associates: D-Scriptive 342–343; I-Caption system 343; infrared assistive devices 342, *343*; ShowTrans 342

Sound of Music, The, watercolor rendering (Smith) *257*

sound systems 330–331; assisted-hearing devices 342–343, *343*; basic sound design layout *330*; connectors and cables 340, *340–341*; equipment 330–331; headsets 342, *342*; inputs 330; IP addresses 343; microphones 331–333, *332*; mixing consoles 334, 335, *336*, *337*; networks 343; outputs 330; processing 330; signal processing 336–337, 567; speakers 337–338, *338–339*; world (master) clock 331; *see also* cables (sound systems); connectors (sound systems); microphones; speakers

spacing rehearsals 511–512

spade bits 168, *168*, 568

span sets 287–288, 568

sparkles (makeup) 429

sparterie (esparterie) 384

sparto cloth (esparterie) 384

spattering 254, 568

spatulas 424, *425*, 568

speakers 330, 510–511; clusters 338, 549; line arrays 338, *339*, 559; midrange 337, *338*, 560; subwoofers 337, *338*, 569; sweet spot 338; tweeters 337, *338*, 571; wedges 338, *339*; woofers 337, *338*, 572

special effects 479; Alt-J tour *480*; Bardavon 1869 Opera House super title projections *489*; blood (modern effects) 487–488; confetti 488; experts 479; fire (modern effects) 485; fire (vintage effects) 483, *483*; flying effects 190, 490; fog and haze (modern effects) 485–487, *486*, *487*, 554, 557; *Ghosts of Versailles* (1991) special effects *486*; *Laughing Stock* explosion effect *480*; lightning (modern effects) 485; nature (modern effects) 484–485; nature (vintage effects) 481–483; *Personals* video projection slides 488, *489*; projection segue 488, *489*, 490; props 568; rain (modern effects) 485; rain (vintage effects) 482–483, *482*; snow (modern effects) 485, *485*; snow (vintage effects) 483, *483*; special effects props 568; thunder (modern effects) 484–485; thunder (vintage effects) 482, *482*; *Tote Stadt* (1971) *481*; wind (modern effects) 484; wind (vintage effect) 482

Special FX (makeup) 430–431

specialty designers 31

speed squares 151, *151*, 568

speed wrenches 163, *163*, 568

spike tape 502

spiral saws *157*

spirit gum 433

spirit levels 152, *152*, 568

Spirit Lodge 448, *448*

sponge applicators 424, *424*; foam sponges 424, *424*, 554; stipple sponges 424–425, *424*, 569

sponge brushes *424*

sponging 254–255, 568

spot blocks 276–277, 568

spot fixtures 308

Spotlight® 92, 109

spot lights *311*, *311–312*

sprayers (for paint) 248, 254; *see also* Floretta® sprayers; Hudson® sprayers

spring (or squeeze) clamps 165, *165*, 568

sprinkler systems 141–142, *142*, 569

square face 422, *422*

square (reef) knots 269, *270*, 569

squares: combination 151, *151*, 549; framing 151, *151*, 555; speed 151, *151*, 568; tri- *151*; T 85–86, *85*, 104, 571

squeeze (or spring) clamps 165, *165*, 568

Staatsoper (Vienna) 21

stadium/arena tours 518

stage: definition of 569; downstage 6, *6*, 552; end stage 17; Greek theatre 6, *6*; inner above/inner below 13; rake (angled stage) 6, *6*, 565; revolving stages 191; Roman theatre 6; stage left 6, *6*, 569; stage right 6, *6*, 569; upstage 6, *6*, 571; *see also* arena stage; black box theaters; proscenium theatre; thrust stage

stage armor *see* armor

stage blood 430–432, *432*, 487–488, 569

stage management 495–496; auditions 497, *498*, 546; calling scripts 509–510, 512, *518*, 548; performances 513; production management 495; production meetings 508; rehearsals 497–498, 502–505, 507–508; scripts 505; technical rehearsals 510–513; *see also* performances; rehearsals; technical rehearsals

stage managers (SMs) 497; customized desks for 513; Global Design Systems SM Console *513*; kits 496–497, 568; positioning of 512–513; role of 495–496; visibility of stage 512

stained-glass art: *Long Beach* (Rupp) *33*; *Sunday* (Rupp) *48*

stairs 200, 202, *202*

standby (for cues) 512, 569

staplers 162, *162*; definition of 569; pneumatic 170

staples 183, *183*

"Stars and Stripes Forever" ("Disaster March") 145, 574

star screwdrivers 164

steaming, hat 382, *382*

steam jacketed kettles *392*

steel-toe work boots 130–131

Steel Wheels tour (Rolling Stones) 450

step ladders 135, 136

stiles 202, 204, 569

stipple sponges 424–425, *424*, 569

stitching: body modification padding *405*; techniques, leather work 413; *see also* sewing

Stoppard, Tom 224

strap hinges 184

straw bodies (hat) 385, *385*

Streb, Elizabeth 539–540

street theatre 22

string levels 152, *152*, 569

strip lights 306–307, *307*, *310*, 569

strobes 447, 485, 569

Strong, Super Trouper follow spot *311*

StudioMax 406

style 569; *see also* production styles; theatre styles

stylized makeup 421

Styrofoam® 179, *180*

subtractive color mixing 59, 61, 569

subwoofers 337, *338*, 569

summer stock 21

Sunday (Rupp) *48*

SuperTruss 287

Supervision of Flame Retardancy certificate 138

supplies *see* materials (scenic); paint tools and supplies

surface design, leather 412, *412*

surface finishes 403, *403*, 554

sustainability 430

Svoboda, Josef 74, 172

Swan, Joseph Wilson 295–297

swatches 392, *403*, 569

Sweeney Todd 224

sweet spot 338

Sweet Charity (James Madison University, 2015) *199*

switches/braids 431

swivel casters 185, *186*

Swope, G. Benjamin, *The Crucible* production (2005) *39*

sword 409

sword belt 409

symbols: blocking notations *506*, 507; and design 34–35, *34–35*, 569; for fixtures 318; key to (drafting) 108–109, *108*, 558

symmetrical balance 53

synthetic fabrics 352–353

synthetic hair in wigs 431

synthetic ropes 268–269, *269*

T

tab curtains 192, 569

table saws 158–159, *158*, 569

tack hammers 161–162, *161*, *162*, 569

tactile textures 51

Tagliarino, Salvatore: line and direction *50*; line weights *51*; patterns *53*; Sal's drawing test 76–77, *78*, 124, *124*; shapes *50*; sketch for Verdi's *Macbeth 32*; textures *51*

tailor's chalk 357, *357*, 570

tanning 411, 549, 570

tape: armor mock-up with *398*; drafting 89, 552; painter's 249

tape measures 150, *150*, 570

taping the floor 502

tarlatan (crinoline) 384

tattoos 426

Taylor, Clifton 313

technical directors 535

technical rehearsals: call times 510, 513, 548; cue lights 511, *511*, 550; customized desks for stage managers 513; dressing rooms and green room 510; headsets 510, 511; microphones and speakers 510–511; positioning of stage managers 512–513; spacing rehearsals 511–512; stage visibility of stage managers 512; warning, standby, go 512, 555, 569, 572

temperament, and character analysis 422

templates (gobos) 306, 308, 316, 556

templates, drafting 87, *87*

Temporary Contemporary Museum (MOCA) 540

tertiary colors 59, 570

Tesla, Nicolas 297, 299

texture 50–51, *50–51*, 248, 570

texturing: distressing 255, 551; dry brushing 254, 552; at Hudson Scenic *254*; priming 255, 564; rag rolling 254, 564; scumbling 254, 566; spattering 254, 568; sponging 254–255, 568; three-dimensional texture 255, *255*; wet blending 254, 572

Tharp, Twyla 533

theatre: careers 535–537; etymology of 4; venues 21–23

theatre, history of: Bunraku 13–14; Chinese theatre 17; commedia dell'arte 7–8, 10–11; Greek theatre 4–6; Kabuki 14–16; Middle Ages 8–9; modern theatre 17–21; Noh 9; passion plays 3–4, 9, 562; Renaissance 11–13; Roman theatre 6–8

theatre for social change 23

theatre in the round, arena stage 20–21

theatre of the absurd 23

theatre styles 22–23; black comedy 22; comedy 22; commedia dell'arte 7–8, 10–11, *10–11*, 22; docudrama 22; epic 22; fantasy 22; farce 22; feminist theatre 22; melodrama 22–23;

naturalism 23, 31–32, 561; realism 23, 31, 565; romantic comedy 23; theatre for social change 23; theatre of the absurd 23; total theatre 23; tragedy 23

theatre traditions 511; baby dolls 358, 575; bad dress rehearsals and good opening 533, 575; "break a leg" expression 53, 573; cats and good/bad luck 331, 575; church keys 467, 575; evil curtains 191, 574; final word and bad luck 510, 575; flowers and bad/good luck 233, 574; ghost light 296, 574; green as bad color 64, 573; green room 250, 574; "in the limelight" 487, 575; lipstick smear and good luck 429, 575; monkey wrench 153, 574; opening night and paying customers xvii, 575; Scottish Play 31, 573; "Stars and Stripes Forever" ("Disaster March") 145, 574; thespians, etymology of 4, 573; tripping and good luck 523, 575; umbrellas as bad luck 77, 573; whistling and bad luck 267, 574

themed entertainment 22

thermal barrier 138, *138*, 141, 570

thermoplastics: armor 400, 401, *401*; definition of 570; masks 393

thespians, etymology of 4, 573

Thespis 4, 573

thimbles (wire rope) 278, *278*, 570

T-hinges 184

Thompson, Tazewell: *Caucasian Chalk Circle, The 373*; *Crucible, The* production (2005) *39*

Thoreau, Henry David 49

threaders *see* pipe threaders

threads 356, *356*

three-phase power 301, 570

three-point perspective 96

thrust stage 19–20, 570; backdrop 20; cyclorama 20; layout of *19*; sight line (line of sight) 20

thunder special effects: modern 484–485; vintage 482; vintage thunder-making machine *482*; *see also* special effects

tiles (LED screens) 466

tilt (light movement) 304, 570

tin snips 156, *156*, 570

tint 61–62, 64, 570

Tisch School of the Arts Graduate Acting/Design for Stage and Film *294*, *295*, *372*, *373*

title blocks 107, *107*, 570

TNC connectors 340, *340*, 570

Tobins Lake Studios, vacuum-formed armor 397, *397*

tone (color) 62, 64, 570

tongue and groove pliers *165*

tooling, leather 412, *412*

tools *171*; assembly 160–172; cleaning 172, 252; cutting/shaping 154–160; hand drawing/drafting 84–89;

Hudson Scenic's tool storage *252, 253*; leather work 412; measuring/marking 150–153; paint 246–250; safety 149, 156, 157, 158; safety precautions 149; *see also* costume shop tools and accessories; makeup tools; *specific categories*

tooth colors *432*

top (high) hats (lighting) 316, *317*, 570

Torx® screws 164, 181, 570

total theatre 23

Tote Stadt (New York City Opera, 1971) *481*

touring: arena/stadium tours 518; bus and truck tours 518, 520, 548; design modifications 519–520; festivals 518, 553; first class tours 517–518, 554; international *vs.* domestic tours 518–519, 520; music tours 521–523; rental shops 520–521; *see also* Alt-J tour

tower systems 287

tracing paper 83

tracking decks 190

tragedy 23

trammel points 152

translucent paper 83

traps 190–191, 570

traveler tracks 190, 570

traverse stage 21

triangles 86–87, *86*, 570

triangular truss *248*

tripping, and good luck 523, 575

tri-squares *151*

trolleys (scenic technique) 190

trucking department (scene shop) 199–200

trunnions 303, 306, 571

trusses 266, 273, 571; 12″ × 12″ truss 281; 18″ × 12″ truss 281–282, *283*; 20.5″ × 20.5″ truss 282; box truss with chain hoist *282*; curved box *282*; moves, previsualization *469–470*; moving light 286–287, *286*; pre-rig 282, *285*, 286; ProPlus rescue system™ 287, *289*; styles and sizes of *281*; SuperTruss 287, *288*; triangular *248*

T-shirt base, body padding on 408, *408, 409*

T squares 85–86, *85*, 104, 571

tube cutters 156

tulle *178*

tungsten inert gas (TIG) welding 170

turkey hat *371*

Turtle, The (Fink) 69

Tuscan order *36*, 37, 571

tweeters 337, *338*, 571

twist bits 168, *168*, 571

twisted-pair cables 340, 571

two-point perspective 95, 96–97, *96, 97*

U

ultraviolet (UV) lights 307

ultraviolet (UV) makeup 307

ultraviolet (UV) paint 251, 252

umbrellas 77, 408–409, 573

Uncle Vanya 221, 223

unions 532–533

United Scenic Artists 539

Univision, *Premios Juventud* raster *473*

upholstery padding 407

upstage 6, *6*, 571

Urban, Keith *518*

urea formaldehyde 176

USA International Ballet Competition (2018) *93*

U.S. Institute for Theatre Technology (USITT): Graphic Standards Board 101; hand drafting symbol guidelines 109

utility (mat) knives 154, *154*, 571

V

vacuum cleaners, wet/dry 172, 572

vacuum-formed armor 397, *397, 398*

value, color 62, 571

vambraces *402, 413*

Van Gogh, Vincent 59

vanishing points 94, 96, 97, 571; *see also* perspective drawing

Van't Hoff, Tim, *Henry V* (Shakespeare) *294*

Vardalos, Nia 231

Vaseline 394

Vaudevillian, The 218, *219*

vector-based images 92, 93, 571

Vectorworks® 92, 93, 109, *471*

vegetable tanning 411–412

vellum 83

velour 178

velvet, crushed *178*

venues, theatre 21–23

Verdi, Giuseppe, Tagliarino's sketch for *Macbeth 32*

vice grips *165*

Victoria and Albert Museum 539

video 443–444; codecs 467; content 468; department, roles in 451–452; frame rate 467; hardware 466–467; pattern, color, and gradient test slide for *472*; resolution 466, 467; software 467

video crew chefs 452

video designers 452, 468

video engineers 452

video programmers 452

video projection 443–444, 451, 488, *489*, 490, 540

Vienna Opera House *141*

vine charcoal 80, 242

vinyl erasers 83

vise grips 165, 571

vises 166, 571

Vitruvian Man (Da Vinci) *52*, 78

Vitruvius 52, 53, 78

vocal reinforcement 333

voltage (V) 300, 301; definition of 571; world map *301*

vomitoriums 571; arena stage 20; Roman theatre 7; thrust stage 20

VSFX3 effects projector *316*

W

walking foot sewing machine 413, 572

Wallace-Spriggs, Denise 391

walls: back 190; building techniques *203*, 204, *205*, *208–209*; on set 105, *105*; *see also* flats

Wang, Xizhi 17

wardrobe supervisors 535

Warfel, Andy 34

Warhol, Andy 75

warm colors 63–64, *63*

warning (for cues) 512, 571

washers 182–183, *182*

wash fixtures 308, *309*, *312*

Wasserstein, Wendy 21

WatchOut 467

water-based markers 82

water-based paint 251

watercolor paints 82

watercolor paper 83

watercolor pencils 80

waterproof makeup 420

water-soluble foggers 485, 486

wattage (W) 300, 571

weaponry 409

Webster, John 12

Wechsler, Gil, *Ghosts of Versailles* (Metropolitan Opera, 1991) *486*

Wechsler, Lawrence 539

Wedding Singer, The: Hudson Scenic's club wall hanger shop drawing *194*; Hudson Scenic's Rosie's porch framing shop drawings *195*; Hudson Scenic's Rosie's porch receivers and trap door drawings *203*; Pask's title block *107*; Scott Pask's club wall hanger drawing *193*; title block *107*

wedges (speakers) 338, *339*

Weigh, Annie, *PACK* (2022) *372*

welding 170; arc 170, 546; brazing 171–172, 547; gas tanks, gauges, and hoses *170*; iron department (scene shop) 198; MIG 170, 560; oxyacetylene (gas) 160; soldering 171–172, 568; TIG 170, 570

West End (London) 21

West Virginia formulas 301, 572

wet blending 254, 572

wet (creme) brushes 423

wet/dry vacuums 172, 572

whistling, and bad luck 267, 574

white: balance 64, *65*, 66, 572; and grayscale 64, *65*; reference 66–68, *66–67*, 565

white glue 183, 184

white light 61, 68, 487, 575

Whole Hog II®, moving lighting console *315*

Who's That Girl tour (Madonna) 450, 540

WiFi networks 343

wiglets 431

wigs 367, *370*, 431; hair dye 431, *432*; hand-tied 431; hard-front 431; human *vs.* synthetic hair 431; lace-front 431

Wilde, Oscar 57

Wilder, Thornton 139

Williams, Bob 77, 573

willow (esparterie) 384

willow charcoal 80

Wilmore, David, *Sweet Charity* (2015) *199*

winches 279–280, 572

windows, building techniques 205, *207*

wind special effects: modern 484; vintage 482; *see also* special effects

wing and drop scenery 190, 191, 572

Wing-Davey, Mark *295*

wings 190, 572

Winterthur Museum 539

wireless microphones 332, *332*

wires: AWG 302; chicken 177; ground 301, 556; millinery *380*; rope 278, *278*, 572

Wislar, Elizabeth, *PACK* (2022) *372*

Wizard of Oz (1939) 144

women: female Kabuki 14, 15; feminist theatre 22; male casting of female roles 8, 9, 11

Wonder, Erich, *Dr. Faust* (Metropolitan Opera, 2001) *446*

wonderbars 162

wood: dimensional lumber 172–173, *173*; hardwoods *vs.* softwoods 172; molding 176, *176*; painting techniques 260–261, *260–261*; sheet lumber 173, 174–176, *174*; *see also* flats; platforms

wood-cutting saws: coping saws 155, *155*, 550; crosscut blades 154, *154*, 550; flush cut saws 155, 554; hand saws 155, *155*; keyhole (drywall) saws 155, *155*, 558; miter saws 155, *155*, 561; rip blades 154, *154*, 565; *see also* metal-cutting saws

wood glue 183, 184, *184*

wood masks 393

woofers 337, *338*, 572

wool (fabric) 351, 572

workflow 572

work gloves 134–135, *135*, 137, 246, 269

world (master) clock 331

wrenches: adjustable (crescent) 163, *163*, 545; box 163, *163*, 547; monkey 153, 574; open-ended 163, *163*, 561; pipe 163, *163*, 563; socket sets/wrenches 163, *164*, 568; speed 163, *163*, 568

Wyatt, Lizzy, *PACK* (2022) *372*

X

Xacto knife *154*

XLR connectors 340, *340*, 572

Y

Yamaha, CL5 digital console *337*

Yankee screwdrivers (push screwdrivers) 164, *164*, 572

Yavich, Anita, *Les Troyens* (Metropolitan Opera) *177*

yin-yang symbol *34*

yokes (lighting fixtures) 303, 572

Yu-Hsuan Chen, *The Caucasian Chalk Circle 373*

Yu-Ting Lin, *Animal Farm* (Orwell/Hall) *372*

Z

Zambello, Francisco, *Les Troyens* (Metropolitan Opera) *177*

Zeder, Meg, *The Crucible* production (2005) *39*

zero-point perspective 94

Zetex® 138, *138*, 141, 572

zipper-back padding *408*, *409*

zippers 356

Zulu style: headdress *410*; necklace *410*